Rick Mercer

COMPUTING FUNDAMENTALS WITH C++

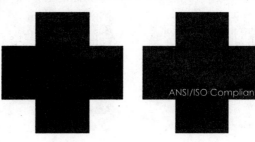

ANSI/ISO Compliant

object-oriented programming & design

2nd edition

Franklin, Beedle & Associates, Inc.
8536 SW St. Helens Drive, Suite D
Wilsonville, Oregon 97070
503/682-7668
www.fbeedle.com

President & Publisher	Jim Leisy (jimleisy@fbeedle.com)
Production	Stephanie Welch
	Susan Skarzynski
	Tom Sumner
Manuscript Editor	Sheryl Rose
Development Editor	Sue Page
Marketing Group	Cary Crossland
	Carrie Widman
	Jason Smith
	Marc Chambers
	Amy Kasner
Order Processing	Chris Alarid

Rights and Permissions
Franklin, Beedle & Associates, Incorporated
8536 SW St. Helens Drive, Suite D
Wilsonville, Oregon 97070
503/682-7668
www.fbeedle.com

Features

Traditional Topics. This textbook recognizes the relevance and validity of object-oriented programming and design while it emphasizes traditional computing fundamentals. The book's breadth of topics and flexibility allow for presentation of other traditional topics such as pointers and recursion. It also presents some C++ features that could well become traditional topics during the first two or three courses, such as templates for generic classes, operator overloading, and standard containers with iterators.

Standard C++. Because the International Standards Organization (ISO) has approved the C++ standard document, students can now study C++ as a language that has an internationally accepted standard. Many compilers now conform to the standard or soon will. This textbook, and I suspect most other new ones, will use the standard `string` and `vector` classes and the operations that work on any standard compiler. Your compiler may not yet be able to handle a few of these standards, but these can be easily fixed with one or two differences from the standard approach used in this text. At the time of this writing, you may have to slightly modify what you do with namespaces and the `#include` directives, but eventually the compilers will catch up. On older compilers, you might need to use the `string` and `vector` classes that come with this textbook.

Flexibility. This second edition maintains the objects-early approach of the first, but now C++ classes can optionally be introduced earlier (Chapter 6). Several programming projects and a few sections identified with a Chapter 6 prerequisite should be postponed until after presenting Chapter 6, "Class Definitions and Member Functions." You may select from a wide array of additional topics after Chapter 10, "Vectors." These include container classes and iterators (Chapter 11), indirection and dynamic memory allocation (Chapters 14 and 15), inheritance (Chapter 16), templates (Chapter 17), operator overloading (Chapter 18), doubly subscripted objects (Chapter 19), recursion (Chapter 20), and object-oriented analysis and design (Chapters 12 and 13).

Gentle Objects-Early Approach: Use, Modify, then Implement Classes. This second edition begins by placing the student in the role of a consumer—you begin by using existing objects while honing problem-solving and program-development skills. You will then modify, enhance, and ultimately design and implement your own classes of increasing complexity.

Carefully Chosen Subset of Analysis, Design, and C++. Because students using this textbook might have little or no programming or design experience, several C++ features and subtleties are not presented. Students concentrate on a solid subset of this feature-

Preface

This textbook is written for a first course in C++ programming and design. This book has been used extensively in the introductory computer science course (CS1) and introductory courses for engineering and business majors. It is appropriate for students with no programming or design experience, or for students with programming experience in another language.

This textbook emphasizes traditional computing fundamentals while recognizing the relevance and validity of object-oriented programming and design. Students completing the first 10 chapters will be comfortable with structured programming, vectors, and using standard C++ classes. They will also have the opportunity to implement some classes that have already been designed. After this, there are many options to choose for the first course.

I prefer to cover Chapters 1 through 13 during the introductory computer science course. This introduces problem solving, programming, and design using a team experience in object-oriented analysis and design (Chapters 12 and 13). I then use some of the remaining seven chapters to support my second course textbook (in CS2). The bonus chapters and built-in flexibility accommodate a range of preferences.

You have the option to cover classes early (before control structures) or later (after vectors). If presenting objects later, you may instead present matrix objects, recursion, and/or pointers with dynamic memory management.

This textbook is the result of 10 years of reasoning about how best to use the first year of the computer science curriculum and how best to integrate object technology into it. I believe that this process will continue for quite some time.

—Rick H. Mercer

http://www.cs.arizona.edu/people/mercer/_
email: **mercer@cs.arizona.edu**

Extensively Tested in the Classroom and Lab. This textbook was six years in the making. Students supplied many useful comments and suggestions concerning manuscript clarity, organization, projects, and examples. The tremendous personal contact and testability was made possible with closed lab sections for all students. This edition has been class tested over six consecutive terms, from summer 1996 to spring 1998 in four slightly different courses at Pennsylvania State University. The first edition also was extensively class tested over a three-year period.

Pedagogy

This textbook has many pedagogical features that make this introduction to programming, design, and object technology accessible to students.

Self-Check Questions. These short questions and answers allow students to evaluate whether they understand the details and terms presented in the reading. The answers to all self-check questions are included in the appendix at the back of this book.

Exercises. These transitional problems examine the major concepts presented in the chapter. Answers are in the instructor's manual and at this textbook's Web site in order to encourage students to write down the answers with paper and pencil, as if it were a practice test.

Programming Tips. Each set of weekly programming projects is preceded by a set of programming tips intended to help students complete programs, warn of potential pitfalls, and promote good programming habits.

Programming Projects. Many relatively small-scale problems have been extensively lab tested to ensure that projects can be assigned and completed with little or no instructor intervention. The programming projects are strategically positioned to occur every week of lecture to reinforce the concepts just presented. Chapter 7, "Selection," Chapter 8, "Repetition," and Chapter 10, "Vectors," all have two sets of exercises, programming tips, and programming projects.

Analysis and Design Projects. Chapters 1, 12, and 13 have analysis and design projects that allow students to participate in other aspects of program and software development. Chapter 1 projects allow students to begin by doing something in the lab without the computer. The projects in Chapters 12 and 13 allow students to participate in team projects at the analysis and design phases rather than implementation.

rich language. Some of C++'s trickier topics are delayed until the later chapters; for example, using the standard `string` class avoids early coverage of pointers.

Not Tied to a Specific System. There is little bias toward a particular operating system or compiler. However, this textbook presents `#includes` and namespaces according to the C++ standard. All other material applies to any computer system using standard C++. All software has been tested on the following systems: Borland C++ version 5.02; Microsoft Visual C++ version 5.0; Metrowerks Codewarrior (for both Macintosh and Windows); and GNU g++ 2.90.27 in a Unix environment.

Object-Oriented Analysis and Design Case Studies. This textbook is unique among first course textbooks in that it contains two complete and accessible case studies featuring object-oriented analysis and design. The cashless jukebox of Chapters 12 and 13 allows students to experience more than just programming language features and typing at the computer. Students work in teams as they analyze and design object-oriented solutions. This allows progress as students make design decisions about their systems. End-of-chapter projects ask for specific analysis and design deliverables:

- Role playing to indicate an understanding of the system.
- A set of CRH cards to capture analysis and design decisions.
- The C++ class definitions that represent the design.

If teams are not possible, or for those reading this textbook on their own, Chapters 12, 13, and 16 are written in an interesting narrative form to capture real-life team analysis and design experiences.

Another object-oriented analysis and design case study—the college library system—introduces students to the concepts of inheritance and polymorphism. Additionally, object-oriented design heuristics provide insights into the proper object decomposition and classification of systems. This edition emphasizes design.

Algorithmic Patterns. Algorithmic patterns help beginning programmers design algorithms around a set of common algorithm generalities. The first algorithmic pattern, and perhaps one of the oldest—Input/Process/Output (IPO)—- is introduced in Chapter 1. It is reused in subsequent chapters. The IPO pattern is especially useful to students with no programming experience and to the lab assistants helping them. Other algorithmic patterns introduced in the appropriate places include Guarded Action and Determinate Loop.

Object-Oriented Design Heuristics. In his book *Object-Oriented Design Heuristics,* Arthur Riel catalogs about 60 guidelines to good design. This textbook integrates several of these guidelines in context. Students can make informed decisions that result in better designs.

Scaffolding. Scaffolding is a teaching and learning technique that provides support for new concepts. The scaffolding is slowly removed as more is asked from students. Scaffolding is used in these ways:

- Applications presented in the chapters solve problems similar to some of the programming projects—this allows students to generalize on specific examples before implementing solutions to problems from different domains.
- Example dialogues allow for easier identification of input and output requirements—especially in the early chapters. This prepares students for designing their own input and output requirements later in the book.
- Students are initially given function headings and test drivers so they need to complete only the function body; later on, projects ask students to create all three items.
- Test drivers are provided (many on disk) for testing functions; later in the book, students must write their own test drivers.
- In the early chapters, students are given a class definition and some member functions, and are then asked to add other member functions to a class. Later on, students implement all member functions given the class definition.
- Students are first asked to implement member functions specified in the design (the C++ class definition). In Chapters 12 and 13, students analyze a problem and design class definitions before implementing member functions.
- Students begin by analyzing small problems; by Chapter 13 students analyze small systems.

What's New in the Second Edition

This improved and expanded second edition has taken almost as much time to complete as the first. The major changes deal with integrating design and introducing students to object-oriented software development. For example, to help with algorithm design, this edition presents algorithmic patterns such as Input/Process/Output and Guarded Action. These are particularly helpful to students with no experience as they reason about algorithm design. Object-oriented design heuristics such as 6.1, "All data should be hidden within a class," and 12.1, "Model the real world whenever possible," help students think about the many design decisions to make during software development. Several object-oriented design heuristics and two design patterns, State Object and Iterator, guide students through algorithmic patterns.

These new chapters have been added:

12: Object-Oriented Software Development: Analysis and Design

13: Object-Oriented Software Development: Design and Implementation

16: Object-Oriented Software Development: Inheritance and Polymorphism

18: Operator Overloading (from a first edition appendix)

20: Recursion

Additional changes include, but are not limited to the following:

* The standard `vector` class is presented before primitive C arrays.
* The `grid` class (inspired by Rich Pattis's "Karel the Robot") replaces the `ATM` and `bank` classes as an author-supplied class that presents new concepts over several chapters.
* New programming projects have been added.
* The standard list and iterator objects are presented as examples of a container object and the means to iterate over the elements.
* Classes are covered earlier (Chapter 6), or could be postponed until after control structures, functions/parameters, and vectors.
* A linked list class has been added.
* Chapter size has been reduced to allow coverage at the rate of one chapter per week.

Instructor's Manual

The instructor's manual is available on a disk obtained from the publisher, Franklin, Beedle & Associates. It contains the following:

* Solutions to all programming projects.
* Several sample tests for each chapter.
* Chapter-by-chapter suggestions.
* Answers to all exercises (also at this textbook's Web site).
* The directory of files (also at this textbook's Web site).
* Slide shows for every chapter (also at this textbook's Web site).

World Wide Web Site

http://www.cs.arizona.edu/people/mercer/_
email: **mercer@cs.arizona.edu**

Acknowledgments

Critical feedback from students and other instructors is essential to creating a solid textbook. I have been fortunate enough to have small lecture sizes (10 to 35 students) and to be in all labs with all of my students for the past 10 years. This has enabled me to keep track of their progress and of their problems, which has dramatically helped produce a textbook that is accessible to the intended audience. I acknowledge and thank the students at Penn State Berks in past years and those students in the following courses that class tested this second edition: CSE 103 (fall '96 and fall '97), CmpSc 201 (fall '96, spring '97, fall '97, and spring '98), CmpSc 101 (the summers of '96 and '97), and CmpSc 203 (the summers of '96 and '97).

I have been fortunate to encounter many excellent educators and industry people who care and think about the same issues. The debates and new ideas generated in discussions, both live and by email, have allowed me to make the plethora of informed decisions necessary for producing a high-quality textbook. I wish to acknowledge the following people (listed in reverse alphabetical order) with apologies to those whom I have unintentionally left out: Gene Wallingford, Doug Van Weiren, David Teague, Dave Richards, Stuart Reges, Margaret Reek, Ken Reek, Rich Pattis, Linda Northrop, Zung Nguyen, John McCormick, Carolina McCluskey, Mary Lynn Manns, Mike Lutz, David Levine, Jim Heliotis, Peter Grogono, Adele Goldberg, Michael Feldman, Ed Epp, Robert Duvall (not the actor, the guy from Duke), Ward Cunningham, Alistair Cockburn, Mike Clancy, Tim Budd, Barbara Boucher-Owens, Michael Berman, Joe Bergin, Owen Astrachan, and Erzebet Angster. In addition, my thanks go to the following individuals at Franklin, Beedle & Associates: Jim Leisy, Dan Stoops, Stephanie Welch, Susan Skarzynski, Tom Sumner, Sue Page, Cary Crossland, Carrie Widman, Jason Smith, Marc Chambers, Amy Kasner, and Chris Alarid.

Though too numerous to mention, I also acknowledge the many authors and presenters who have influenced me during my 17-year career in this field.

Reviewers spend countless hours poring over material with critical eyes and useful comments. Because of the high quality of their work, criticisms and recommendations were always considered seriously. I thank the reviewers of both the first edition and of this second edition:

Seth Bergman	*Rowan University*
Michael Berman	*Rowan University*

Tom Bricker	*University of Wisconsin, Madison*
David Teague	*Western Carolina University*
Ed Epp	*University of Portland*
James Murphy	*California State University, Chico*
Rich Pattis	*Carnegie Mellon University*
Jerry Weltman	*Louisiana State University, Baton Rouge*

Reviewers of the second edition:

John Miller	*St. John's University*
Stephen Leach	*Florida State University*
Alva Thompson	*University of South Florida*
Norman Jacobson	*University of California, Irvine*
David Levine	*Gettysburg College*
H. E. Dunsmore	*Purdue University*
Howard Pyron	*University of Missouri at Rolla*
Lee Cornell	*Mankato State University*
Eugene Wallingford	*University of Northern Iowa*
David Teague	*Western Carolina University*
Michael Berman	*Rowan University*
Clayton Lewis	*University of Colorado*
Tim Budd	*Oregon State University*
Jim Miller	*University of Kansas*
Art Farley	*University of Oregon*
Richard Enbody	*Michigan State University*
Van Howbert	*Colorado State University*
Joe Burgin	*Texas Tech University*
Robert Duvall	*Duke University*
Jim Coplien	*Bell Labs*
Dick Weide	*Ohio State University*
Gene Norris	*George Mason University*

Table of Contents

Chapter One

Analysis and Design

Coming Up

First there is a need for a computer-based solution to a problem. The need may be expressed in one or two paragraphs as a *problem statement.* The progression from understanding a problem statement to achieving a working computer-based implementation is known as *program development.* After studying this chapter, you will be able to

- understand one simple example of program development
- understand the characteristics of a good algorithm
- understand how algorithmic patterns help in program design
- provide a deliverable from the analysis phase of program development
- provide a deliverable from the design phase of program development
- understand the relationship between a class and its many objects
- understand objects as having a name, state, and set of operations

You can practice problem solving and program implementation in subsequent chapters by completing the many end-of-chapter programming projects. Chapters 12 and 13 present a case study in object-oriented software development. In Chapters 1 through 11 you will study many computing fundamentals that will prepare you for larger scale software development.

1.1 Program Development

There is a lot to program development—and there are a variety of methods for doing it. This chapter begins by examining a three-step methodology of analysis, design, and implementation.

Phase of Program Development	Activity
Analysis	Understand the problem
Design	Develop a solution
Implementation	Make the solution run on a computer

The progression from analysis of a problem to computer-based implementation is known as program development. Our study of computing fundamentals begins with an example of this particular methodology.

Each of the three phases is followed by an example of how it is applied to one particular problem. Emphasis is placed on the *deliverables*—the tangible results—of each phase. Here is a preview of the deliverables for each of the three stages:

Phase	Deliverable
Analysis	A document that lists the data objects that store relevant information
Design	An algorithm that outlines a solution
Implementation	An executable program ready to be used by the customer (or handed in to your instructor)

Self-Check

1-1 List two synonyms for *analysis* (feel free to use a dictionary or a thesaurus).

1-2 List two synonyms for *design*.

1-3 List two synonyms for *implementation*.

1-4 What is the deliverable at the end of a completed college career?

1.2 Analysis

Synonyms for analysis: *inquiry, examination, study*

Program development may begin with a study, or *analysis*, of a problem. To determine what a program is to do, we must first understand the problem. If the problem is written down, we begin the analysis phase by simply reading the problem.

While analyzing the problem, it proves helpful to name the pieces of the solution that store information. For example, to compute the distance between two points, the unknown that represents the result could be appropriately named `distance`. Other data named `x1`, `y1`, `x2`, and `y2` could represent the two points.

Here's another example. You might be asked to compute the maximum weight allowed for a successful liftoff of a particular airplane from a given runway under certain thrust-affecting weather conditions such as temperature and wind direction. While analyzing the actual problem statement, you could name the desired information `maximumWeight`. The data required to compute that information could be named `airplaneCode`, `runwayCode`, `temperature`, and `windDirection`.

Although such data names do not represent the entire solution, they do represent an important piece of the puzzle. The data names are symbols for what the program will need and what the program will compute. One set of values needed to compute `maximumWeight` might be `"BOEING777"` for `airplaneCode` and `19.0` for `temperature`. Such data values must often be manipulated—or processed—in a variety of ways to produce the desired result. Some values must be obtained from the keyboard, other values must be multiplied or added, and other values must be displayed on the computer screen. These processes are referred to as *operations*.

So there is more to these data things than just their names. They have values. They also have operations that manipulate those values in some meaningful way. These things are called *objects*.

DEFINITION: *Object*

> **Object:** An entity stored in computer memory that has a name, value(s), and set of operations to manipulate the value(s).

It also helps when the analyzer distinguishes the data that must be displayed—objects that will be *output*—from the objects that must be input to compute that information—the *input*. These objects summarize what the program must do.

DEFINITION: *Output and input*

Output: Information the computer must display after the processing has occurred.

Input: Information the user must supply to solve the problem.

A problem is better understood by answering this question: What is the output given certain input? So it is a good idea to provide an *instance,* or example, of the problem with pencil and paper. Here are three problems with object names selected to accurately describe the objects' values.

PROBLEM 1 ANALYSIS DELIVERABLE

Problem	Object Name	Input/Output	Sample Problem
Compute the roots of a quadratic	`a`	Input	`1.1`
equation ($ax^2 + bx + c$)	`b`	Input	`0.0`
	`c`	Input	`-1.0`
	`root1`	Output	`1.0`
	`root2`	Output	`-1.0`

PROBLEM 2 ANALYSIS DELIVERABLE

Problem	Object Name	Input/Output	Sample Problem
Compute a monthly loan payment	`amount`	Input	`12500.00`
	`rate`	Input	`0.08`
	`months`	Input	`48.00`
	`payment`	Output	`303.14`

PROBLEM 3 ANALYSIS DELIVERABLE

Problem	Object Name	Input/Output	Sample Problem
Count how often William Shakespeare	`aBardsWork`	Input	`All's Well That Ends Well`
wrote "thee"	`numberThees`	Output	`88`

In summary, problems are analyzed by doing these things:

1. Reading and understanding the problem statement.
2. Deciding what object(s) represent the answer—the output.

3. Deciding what object(s) the user must enter to get the answer—the input.
4. Creating a document (like one of those above) that summarizes the analysis. This document is input for the next phase of program development—design.

In textbook problems, the object names and values that must be input and output are either provided or they are relatively easy to recognize. In real-world problems of significant scale, a great deal of effort is expended during the analysis phase. In such cases, the documentation is much more extensive. The next subsection provides an analysis of a small problem.

Self-Check

1-5 Given the problem of converting British pounds to U.S. dollars, name an object whose value must be input by the user and name an object whose value must be output.

1-6 Given the problem of selecting one CD from a 200-compact-disc player, name an object that stores all the CDs. What name would be appropriate to bestow upon an object that represents the selected CD?

1.2.1 An Example of Analysis

Problem: Using the grade assessment scale to the right, compute a course grade as a weighted average for any combination of two tests and one final exam. The dialogue must look exactly like this for the given input of `74.0`, `79.0`, and `84.0`:

Grade Assessment Item	Percentage of Final Grade
Test 1 (0.0 to 100.0)	25%
Test 2 (0.0 to 100.0)	25%
Final exam (0.0 to 100.0)	50%

```
Test 1: 74.0
Test 2: 79.0
Final Exam: 84.0
Course Grade: 80.25%
```

Analysis begins by reading the problem statement and establishing the desired output and the required input to solve the problem. Determining and naming the output is a good place to start. This object stores the answer to the problem. The output provides insight into what the program must do. Once the need for an object is discovered and given a meaningful name, the focus can shift to what must be accomplished. For this particular problem, the desired output is the actual course grade (`80.25%` above). The name `courseGrade` can represent the requested information to be output to the user.

A complete analysis might answer other questions such as:

* What happens when the user enters non-numeric data?
* Is it okay to enter `74` instead of `74.0`?
* Is `74.5` okay as input? What about `74.6`?

However, for the purpose of illustrating analysis with a short example, this problem will be simplified by presuming these are not issues.

This problem becomes more generalized when the user enters values to produce the result. If the program asks the user for data, the program can be used later to compute course grades for many students with any set of grades. So let's decide the values that must be input and create names for those objects. To determine `courseGrade`, three values are required: `test1`, `test2`, and `finalExam`. The first three analysis activities are now complete.

1. Problem understood.
2. Objects to be output: `courseGrade`.
3. Objects to be input: `test1`, `test2`, and `finalExam`.

However, an example problem is still missing. Many problem statements in this textbook provide a sample dialogue that summarizes the input that must be supplied by the user and the output the user must see. This textbook sets user input in orange (`74.0`, for example). Everything else is program output.

Sample dialogues provide another important benefit. They show an answer (`80.25%`) for one particular set of inputs. Such dialogues are included in the early part of this textbook to help introduce new concepts. When you encounter a problem without a sample dialogue, you should supply extra example problems. If a dialogue is not given, you should write down something similar—a combination of input data and the output expected from those input data.

To create an instance of this `courseGrade` problem, the programmer must understand the difference between a simple average and a weighted average. Because the three input items comprise different portions of the final grade (either 25% or 50%), the problem involves computing a *weighted average.* The simple average of the set 74.0, 79.0, and 84.0 is 79.0. With equal weight, each test is measured equally. However, the weighted average computes differently for this problem. Recall that test 1 and test 2 are each worth 25%, and the final exam weighs in at 50% of the final grade. When test 1 is 74.0, test 2 is 79.0, and the final exam is 84.0, the weighted average computes to 80.25.

(0.25 * test 1)	+	(0.25 * test 2)	+	(0.50 * final exam)
(0.25 * 74.0)	+	(0.25 * 79.0)	+	(0.50 * 84.0)
18.50	+	19.75	+	42.00
80.25				

With the same exact grades, the weighted average of 80.25 is different from the simple average (79.0). Failure to follow the problem specification could result in students receiving grades lower, or higher, than actually deserved.

The problem has now been analyzed, the objects needed for input and output have been named, it is understood what the computer-based solution is to do, and one example problem has been given. The following deliverable from the analysis phase summarizes these activities:

COURSE-GRADE PROBLEM ANALYSIS DELIVERABLE

Problem	Object Name	Input/Output	Sample Problem
Compute a course grade	`test1`	Input	`74.0`
	`test2`	Input	`79.0`
	`finalExam`	Input	`84.0`
	`courseGrade`	Output	`80.25`

This is the first deliverable. It is now time to move from analysis to design. The next section presents a method for designing a solution. The emphasis during design focuses on placing the appropriate activities in the proper order to solve the problem.

Self-Check

1-7 Complete an analysis deliverable for the following problem:

Compute the distance traveled for any moving vehicle. Let the user choose the unit of measurement (meters per second, miles per hour, or kilometers per hour, for example).

1-8 Complete an analysis deliverable for the following problem. You will need a calculator to determine the output.

Show the future value of an investment given its present value, the number of periods (years, perhaps), and the interest rate. Be consistent with the interest rate and the number of periods; if the periods are in years, then the annual interest rate must be supplied (0.085 for 8.5%, for example). If the period is in months, the monthly interest rate must be supplied (0.0075 per month for 9% per year, for example). The formula to compute the future value of money is

future value = present value * (1 + rate)^{periods}

1.3 Design

Synonyms of design: *model, think, plan, devise, pattern, propose, outline*

Design refers to the set of activities including (1) defining an architecture for the program that satisfies the requirements and (2) specifying an algorithm for each program component in the architecture [Davis 95]. In later chapters you will see functions used as the basic building blocks of programs. Then you will see classes used as the basic building blocks of programs. A class is a collection of functions. In this chapter, the architecture is intentionally constrained to a component known as a *program*. Therefore the design activity that follows is limited to specifying an algorithm for this program.

An *algorithm* is a step-by-step procedure for solving a problem or accomplishing some end, especially by a computer [Merriam 97]. A good algorithm must

- list the activities that need to be carried out
- list those activities in the proper order

Consider an algorithm to bake a cake:

1. Preheat oven.
2. Grease pan.
3. Mix ingredients.
4. Place ingredients in cake pan.

5. Place cake pan in oven.

6. Remove cake pan from oven after 35 minutes.

If the order of the steps is changed, the cook might get a very hot cake pan with raw cake batter in it. If one of these steps is omitted, the cook probably won't get a baked cake—or there might be a fire. An experienced cook may not need such an algorithm. However, cake mix marketers cannot and do not presume that their customers have this experience. Good algorithms list the proper steps in the proper order and are detailed enough to accomplish the task at hand.

Self-Check

1-9 Cake recipes typically omit a very important activity. What activity is missing?

An algorithm often contains a step without much detail. For example, step 3, "Mix ingredients," isn't very specific. What are the ingredients? If the problem is to write a recipe algorithm that humans can understand, step 3 should be refined a bit to instruct the cook on how to mix the ingredients. The refinement to step 3 could be something like this:

3. Empty the cake mix in the bowl and mix in the water until smooth.

or for scratch bakers:

3a. Sift the dry ingredients.

3b. Place the liquid ingredients in the bowl.

3c. Add the dry ingredients ¼ cup at a time, whipping until smooth.

Algorithms may be expressed in *pseudocode*—instructions expressed in a noncomputer language. Pseudocode is written for humans, not for computers. However, pseudocode algorithms are an aid to program design.

Pseudocode is very expressive. One pseudocode instruction may represent many computer instructions. Pseudocode algorithms are not concerned about issues such as misplaced punctuation marks or the details of a particular computer system. Pseudocode solutions make design easier by allowing details to be deferred. Writing an algorithm can be viewed as planning ahead. A programmer can design with pencil and paper and sometimes in her or his head.

1.3.1 Algorithmic Patterns

Problems often require input from the user in order to compute and display the desired information. This particular flow of three activities—input/process/output—occurs so often, in fact, that it can be viewed as a pattern. It is one of several algorithmic patterns you will find helpful in the design of programs.

A *pattern* is anything shaped or designed to serve as a model or a guide in making something else [Funk/Wagnalls 68]. An *algorithmic pattern* serves as a guide to help solve problems. For instance, the following Input/Process/Output (IPO) algorithmic pattern can be used to help design our first problem. In fact, this pattern can be used to help design almost all of the programs in the first five chapters of this textbook.

ALGORITHMIC PATTERN 1.1

Pattern: Input/Process/Output (IPO)

Problem: The program requires input from the user in order to compute and display the desired information.

Outline:
1. Obtain the input data.
2. Process the data in some meaningful way.
3. Output the results.

Code Example:

```
// Input
cout << "Enter three numbers: ";
cin >> n1 >> n2 >> n3;

// Process
average = (n1 + n2 + n3) / 3.0;

// Output
cout << "Average = " << average;
```

This algorithmic pattern is the first of several. In subsequent chapters, you'll see other algorithmic patterns such as Guarded Action, Alternative Action, and Indeterminate Loop. To use an algorithmic pattern effectively, you should first become familiar with it. Register this Input/Process/Output algorithmic pattern and look for this pattern while developing programs. This allows you to design programs more easily. For example, if you discover you have no meaningful values for the input data, it may be because you have placed the process step *before* the input step. Or you may have skipped the input step altogether.

Patterns help solve other kinds of problems. Consider this quote from Christopher Alexander's book, *A Pattern Language* [Alexander 77]:

> Each pattern describes a problem which occurs over and over again in our environment, and then describes the core of the solution to that problem, in such a way that you can use this solution a million times over, without ever doing it the same way twice.

Alexander was describing patterns in the design of furniture, gardens, buildings, and towns, but his description of a pattern can also be applied to program development. The IPO pattern frequently pops up during program design. It guides the solution to many problems—especially in the first five chapters of this textbook.

1.3.2 An Example of Algorithm Design

The deliverable from the design phase is an algorithm that solves the problem. The Input/Process/Output pattern guides the design of the algorithm that relates to our `courseGrade` problem.

IPO Pattern	Pattern Applied to Specific Algorithm
1. Input	1. Obtain `test1`, `test2`, and `finalExam`
2. Process	2. Compute `courseGrade`
3. Output	3. Display `courseGrade`

Although algorithm development is usually an iterative process, the pattern helps to quickly provide an outline of the activities necessary to solve the `courseGrade` problem.

Self-Check

1-10 Read the three activities of the algorithm above. Do you detect a missing activity?

1-11 Read the three activities of the algorithm above. Do you detect any activity out of order?

1-12 Would this previous algorithm work if the first two activities were switched?

1-13 Is there enough detail in this algorithm to correctly compute `courseGrade`?

There currently is not enough detail in the process step of the `courseGrade` problem. The algorithm needs further refinement. Specifically, exactly how should the input data be processed to compute the course grade? The algorithm omits the weighted scale specified in the problem statement. The process step should be refined a bit more. Currently, this pseudocode algorithm does not describe how `courseGrade` must be computed.

GUIDELINE

If an algorithm does not include a required formula, it is not refined enough.

The refinement of this algorithm (below) shows a more detailed process step. The step "Compute `courseGrade`" is now replaced with a *refinement*—a more detailed, specific, clear activity. The input and output steps have also been refined. This is the design phase deliverable—an algorithm with enough detail to pass on as the input into the next phase, implementation.

REFINEMENT OF A SPECIFIC INPUT/PROCESS/OUTPUT (IPO) ALGORITHM

1. Obtain `test1`, `test2`, and `finalExam` from the user.
2. Compute `courseGrade` = (25% of `test1`) + (25% of `test2`) + (50% of `finalExam`).
3. Display the value of `courseGrade`.

Try to think of program development in terms of the deliverables. This provides a checklist. What deliverables exist so far? From the analysis phase there is

- ☑ a document with a list of objects and an example problem

From the design phase there is

- ☑ an algorithm

1.3.3 Algorithm Walkthrough

Recent studies indicate that programs can be developed more quickly and with fewer errors by reviewing algorithms before moving on to the implementation phase. Are the activities in the proper order? Are all the necessary activities present? This review is accomplished with an algorithm walkthrough. An *algorithm walkthrough* simulates what a computer would do by stepping through the instructions of the algorithm.

A *computer* is a programmable electronic device that can store, retrieve, and process data. Simulation of an electronic version of the algorithm is attained by humans who follow the algorithm and manually perform the activities of storing, retrieving, and processing data using pencil and paper. The following algorithm walkthrough is a human (nonelectronic) execution of the algorithm:

1. Retrieve some example values from the user and store them into the objects as shown:

`test1`	80
`test2`	90
`finalExam`	100

2. Retrieve the values and compute `courseGrade` as follows:

   ```
   courseGrade = (0.25 * test1) + (0.25 * test2) + (0.50 * finalExam)
                 (0.25 * 80.0)  + (0.25 * 90.0)  + (0.50 * 100.0)
                 20.0           + 22.5           + 50.0
   courseGrade = 92.5
   ```

3. Show the course grade to the user by retrieving the data stored in `courseGrade` to show `92.5%`.

It has been said that good artists know when to put down the brushes. Deciding when a painting is done is critical for its success. By analogy, the designer must decide when to stop designing. This is a good time to move on to the third phase of program development. In summary, here is what has been accomplished so far:

- The problem is understood.
- Objects are identified and named.
- Output for two sample problems is known (`80.25%` and now `92.5%`).
- An algorithm has been developed.
- Computer activities have been simulated by walking through the algorithm.

Now on to the implementation phase of program development.

Self-Check

1-14 Walk through the previous algorithm when `test1` is input as `0.0`, `test2` is input as `50.0`, and `finalExam` is input as `100.0`. What value is stored in `courseGrade`?

1.4 Implementation

Synonyms for implementation: *accomplishment, fulfilling, making good, execution*

Whereas the analysis and design of simple problems could be done with pencil and paper, the implementation phase of program development requires both software and hardware to achieve the deliverable of the implementation phase. The deliverable is a program that runs correctly on a computer. The *implementation phase* is the collection of activities required to complete the program so someone else can use it. Here are some implementation activities and their associated deliverables:

Activity	Deliverable
Translate an algorithm into a programming language.	Source code
Compile the source code into object code.	Machine language
Link together object-code files.	Running program
Verify that the program does what it is supposed to do.	Your grade

This is not the time or place to describe all the details of how a program actually runs on the computer. However, the gist of it can be understood by viewing the computer and its programs in a hierarchy of abstractions called *virtual machines* [Aho/Ullman 92]. Most computer users view the machine at its highest level—the application software. Examples of software at this level include word processors, games, Internet browsers, appointment calendars, and real-time applications to control electromechanical devices.

Level	Virtual Machine (abstraction)
6	Application software
5	High-level programming language
4	Assembly language
3	Operating system
2	Machine-level programming language
1	Microprogram
0	Digital logic

The top six levels (see the table to the left) are implemented by interpreting the instructions with the available operations of the level under it. For example, the implementation phase of program development is concerned with the high-level programming language at level 5. The programming language translates the needs of the user into a form that can be translated into lower level virtual machines.

So our view of the computer in the implementation phase begins with the level 5 abstraction—the programming language virtual machine. This implies that the computer is a virtual machine controlled by programming language instructions. There are hundreds of level 5 programming languages that could be used. This book uses the programming language named *C++*.

Whereas the design phase provided a solution in the form of a pseudocode algorithm, the implementation phase requires the nitty-gritty details. The programming language translation must be written in a precise manner according to the rules of that programming language. Attention must be paid to the placement of semicolons, commas, and periods. For example, an algorithmic statement like this:

3. Display the value of `courseGrade`.

translates into C++ source code that might look like this:

```
cout << "Course Grade: " << courseGrade << "%" << endl;
```

This output step generates output to the computer screen that might look like this (assuming the state of `courseGrade` is 92.5):

```
Course Grade: 92.5%
```

Once the programmer has translated the pseudocode into a programming language, software is utilized to translate level 5 instructions into the lower levels of the computer. Fortunately, there is a tool for performing these translations. Programmers use the *compiler* to translate the C++ code into its machine-level equivalent.

Once this is done, another program known as the *linker* collects all the necessary pieces of machine code to create one *executable program*.

Finally, to verify that the program works, the behavior of the executable program is observed. Input data may be entered and the corresponding output is observed. The output is compared to what was expected. If the two match, the program works for at least one particular set of input data.

Other sets of input data can be entered while the program is running to build confidence that the program works as specified by the problem statement. Program development is summarized in Figure 1.1.

FIGURE 1.1. *A review of program development*

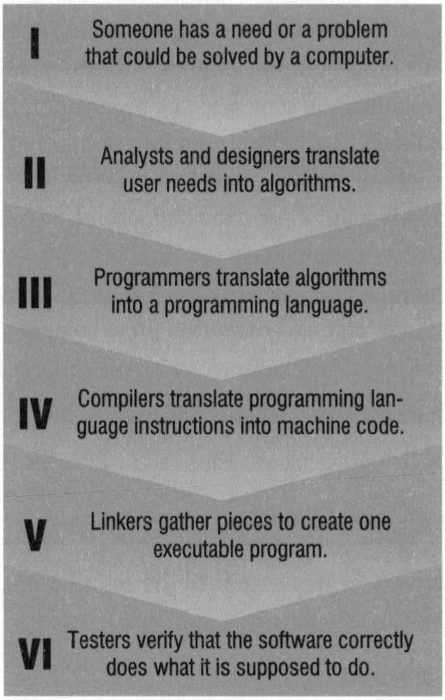

Although you will likely be using the same compilers and linkers as those used in industry, the roles of people will differ. In a large software organization, analysis, design, implementation, and testing are performed by many people, usually in teams. In many simple textbook problems, the user needs are what your instructor requires, usually for grade assessment. Also, you will often play the role of analyst, designer, programmer, *and* tester—perhaps as part of a team, but for a while by yourself.

It should be noted that the process of compile/link/run varies among different computer systems and compilers—and there is a wide variety of computers and compilers! The instructions for some popular systems and compilers are provided at the Web site listed in the preface of this textbook. If you do not have access to the Internet, you will have to ask your instructor and/or use the documentation for your particular system and compiler. Again, the steps for going from an algorithm to the running program vary from one system to another.

Self-Check

1-15 Review Figure 1.1 above and list the phases that are -a primarily performed by humans and -b primarily performed by software. Select your answers from the set of I, II, III, IV, V, and VI.

1-16 Must the level-6 user of software applications understand the level-5 programming language to use the computer?

1-17 Must the programmer implement the level-5 programming language that translates source code into lower levels?

1.4.1 An Example of Implementation

The following C++ program—a complete C++ translation of the algorithm—previews many programming language details. This program provides an opportunity to see the object names within the context of the virtual machine known as the high-level programming language. Do not try to understand the details of this C++ program (they are presented in Chapter 2). Instead, just peruse it. Observe that the highlighted object names `test1`, `test2`, and `finalExam` represent the user input; `courseGrade` represents the answer; `cin`, the keyboard; and `cout`, the computer screen.

```
// This program computes and displays a final course grade as a
// weighted average after the user enters the appropriate input

#include <iostream>   // For std::cin, std::cout, and std::endl

using namespace std;  // This allows programmers to write cin and cout
                      // instead of std::cin and std::cout
int main()
{
  // Declare and initialize the numeric objects
  double test1 = 0.0;
  double test2 = 0.0;
  double finalExam = 0.0;
  double courseGrade = 0.0;

  // 1. Obtain values for test1, test2, and finalExam from the user
  cout << "Enter first test: ";
  cin  >> test1;  // Modify test1's state with input

  cout << "Enter second test: ";
  cin  >> test2;
```

```
  cout << "Enter final exam: ";
  cin >> finalExam;

  // 2. Process (25% of test1) + (25% of test2) + (50% of finalExam)
  courseGrade = (0.25 * test1) + (0.25 * test2) + (0.50 * finalExam);

  // 3. Display the value of courseGrade
  cout << "Course Grade: " << courseGrade << "%" << endl;

  return 0;
}
```

DIALOGUE

```
Enter first test: 80.0
Enter second test: 90.0
Enter final exam: 100.0
Course Grade: 92.5%
```

At the end of most program examples in this textbook, you will find a section titled either "Dialogue" or "Output." A "Dialogue" section shows the program output and shows any user input in orange. If there is no user input, the section is simply titled "Output."

1.4.2 Testing

Although this "Testing" section appears at the end of our first example of program development, don't presume testing must be deferred until implementation. The important process of testing may, can, and should occur at any phase of program development. The actual work can be minimal, and it's worth the effort (although you may not feel that way until you have felt the pain of *not* testing).

TESTING DURING ALL PHASES OF PROGRAM DEVELOPMENT

- During analysis, establish an example problem to confirm your understanding of the problem.
- During design, walk through the algorithm to ensure that it represents the proper steps in the proper order.
- During testing, run the program several times with different sets of input data. Confirm that the results are correct.
- Review the problem statement. Does the running software do what was requested?

You should have an example of the problem before the program is coded—not after. However, if you do decide to wait, it's still better late than never. Work out an example now. If nothing else, at least look at the input and the result of one program run and convince yourself that it is correct in at least that one instance.

When the C++ implementation finally does generate output, the predicted results can then be compared to the output of the running program. Adjustments must be made any time the predicted output does not match the program output. Such a conflict indicates that the problem example, the program output, or perhaps both have been incorrectly calculated. Using problem examples helps avoid the misconception that a program is correct just because the program runs successfully and generates output. The output could be wrong! Simply executing a program doesn't make it right.

Even exhaustive testing—many sample problems—does not prove the program is correct. E. W. Dijkstra has argued that testing only reveals the presence of errors, not the absence of errors. Even with correct program output, the program is not proven to be correct. However, testing increases confidence that the algorithm, now implemented as a program, at least appears to be reliable.

Self-Check

1-18 If the user predicts `courseGrade` should be `100.0` when all three inputs are `100.0` and the program displays `courseGrade` as `75.0`, what is wrong: the prediction, the program, or both the prediction and the program?

1-19 If the user predicts `courseGrade` should be `90.0` when `test1` is `80`, `test2` is `90.0`, and `finalExam` is `100.0` and the program outputs `courseGrade` as `92.5`, what is wrong: the prediction, the program, or both the prediction and the program?

1-20 If the user predicts `courseGrade` should be `92.5` when `test1` is `80`, `test2` is `90.0`, and `finalExam` is `100.0` and the program outputs `courseGrade` as `90.0`, what is wrong: the prediction, the program, or both the prediction and the program?

1.5 Objects and Classes

This chapter began with an example of program development using the three-step methodology of analysis, design, and implementation. Although this was not the complete picture—the all-important maintenance phase was omitted—it is enough to keep us going for a while. This section discusses the data objects discovered during analysis in the context of examining operations performed on those objects. You will also discover that every object is associated with a type, or *class*. So let's begin by understanding the relationships between an object and the type of object—its class.[1]

1.5.1 Objects

Objects are entities stored in computer memory. An object is understood through the type of values the object stores—its *attributes*—and the operations that can be applied to that object—its *behavior* [Booch 92]. Every object has a

1. name
2. state—value(s) stored in computer memory[2]
3. set of operations such as multiplication (*), addition (+), input, and output

These three characteristics of objects—name, state, and operations—were all illustrated in the previous program. The `courseGrade` program used three numeric objects[3] named `test1`, `test2`, and `finalExam` to store numeric values that were input from the keyboard. Each of these objects is capable of storing the value of a number such as 79.0 or 90.0. These objects along with available operations—such as input, multiplication, and addition—computed the final `courseGrade`. The computed answer, also stored as the numeric object named `courseGrade`, was output so the user could see the results of the processing. In between, arithmetic operations helped process the result (see the table below).

1. *Type* and *class* are interchangeable terms.
2. *State* and *value(s)* are interchangeable terms.
3. *Object* and *variable* are interchangeable terms. However, your instructor may use *variable* as the more technically correct term to describe `test1`, `test2`, and `finalExam`.

CHARACTERISTICS OF OBJECTS

Name:	Each of the four numeric objects has its own identity because each has its own name. The first of four numeric objects was named `test1`: `double test1 = 0.0;`

State:	Although the initial state of `test1` was set to `0.0`, there are several operations that alter the state or value of an object. For example, the state of `test1` was set through this input operation:
	`cin >> test1; // Modify test1's state with input`
	The state of `courseGrade` was defined with an assignment operation (= is read as "becomes"):
	`courseGrade=(0.25*test1)+(0.25*test2)+(0.50*finalExam);`
	The state of `courseGrade` was examined with this output operation (the value of `courseGrade` is sent to `cout`—the screen):
	`cout << "Course Grade: " << courseGrade << "%" << endl;`

Operations:	Other operations available for numeric objects include addition (+) and multiplication (`*`): `(0.25 * test1) + (0.25 * test2) + (0.50 * finalExam);`

It should be noted that there are many classes of objects besides those that store numbers. Another class of objects named `string` stores a string of characters (`"Your name"`, for example). Another class of objects represents the movable, resizeable windows that appear on the computer screen. Other objects manipulate the data stored in a file on a disk. And there are objects that store a collection of objects. The kinds of values stored in an object and the operations that can be performed on those objects are both determined by the class. So far, `double` is the only class name that has been shown.

1.5.2 Classes

The class name used to bring objects into a program provides the following information:

1. the value(s) stored in an object
2. the operations that can be applied to an object

For example, any object of the `double` class can store a numeric value. If you know something about numbers, you know something about the kinds of values stored in objects of the `double` class. More specifically, an instance of the `double` class[4] stores a floating-point value—a number with a fractional component, such as -12.34 or 0.07. Many objects of the same class may exist in a program (see Figure 1.2).

FIGURE 1.2

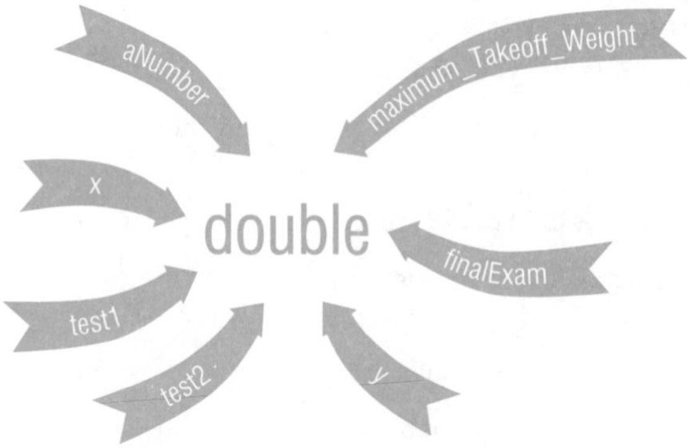

The programmer must also know about operations. For example, if you know something about the operations associated with numbers, you know something about the operations that are available to numeric objects of the `double` class. These operations include the basic arithmetic operations (addition with `+`, subtraction with `-`, division with `/`, and multiplication with `*`). Other available operations applicable to a numeric object include input, output, assignment, and mathematical and trigonometric functions such as square root and sine.

Analysis identifies and names the objects needed to solve a problem. However, how does a developer determine the kind or class of objects needed to solve a problem? Although a lot can be done with just one numeric class named `double`, you will soon discover other useful classes.

Objects and classes are so important to program development that objects are used in all programs. The `double` class stores a numeric value with a fractional part. The C++ `int` class stores and manipulates whole numbers (*int*egers). The C++ `string` class creates objects to store characters such as `"Firstname I. Lastname"`. The C++ `vector` class stores a collection of objects (see Chapter 10). The `istream` object named `cin` and the `ostream` object named `cout` perform keyboard input and screen output, respectively.

4. *Object* and *instance of a class* are interchangeable terms.

The following table summarizes some of the classes used during the early chapters. They are but a few of the many *standard*—must be part of—classes supplied with a C++ system.[5]

THE STANDARD C++ CLASSES DISCUSSED IN CHAPTERS 1 THROUGH 10

Class	Comment
`double`	Stores numbers with a decimal point, such as `99.5`.
`int`	One `int` object stores one whole (integer) number such as `100`.
`string`	One `string` object stores a collection of characters such as `"A name"`.
`ostream`	An instance of the `ostream` class is `cout`.
`istream`	An instance of the `istream` class is `cin`.
`bool`	Stores a `true` or `false` value.
`char`	Stores one character.
`vector`	One `vector` object stores a collection of objects, all of the same class.

Self-Check

1-21 What kind of values are stored in objects of the `double` class?

1-22 What kind of values are stored in objects of the `string` class?

1-23 What kind of values are stored in objects of the `int` class?

1-24 List three operations available to objects of the `double` class.

1-25 Which of the standard classes above store just one value?

1-26 Which of the standard classes above may store many values?

Chapter Summary

- This chapter presented a three-step program development strategy of analysis, design, and implementation. The table below shows some of the activities performed during each of these three phases. The maintenance phase has been added to show

5. Although `double` and `int` are not implemented in the same manner as other standard classes, at the programming language virtual machine, they are very similar (differences will be discussed wherever it is appropriate to do so).

how the three steps fit into the complete program life cycle. The maintenance phase requires the majority of the time, energy, and money of the program's life cycle.

Phase	Activities You Might Perform
Initiation	Specify the problem.
Analysis	Read and understand the problem statement. Determine the input and output objects. Solve a few sample problems.
Design	Look for patterns to guide algorithm development. Write an algorithm—steps needed to solve the problem. Refine the steps in the algorithm and walk through it.
Implementation	Translate the design into a programming language. Fix errors. Create an executable program. Test the program.
Maintenance	Update the program to keep up with a changing world. Enhance it. Correct bugs as they're found.

* Each phase can be viewed in terms of the deliverables:

PHASE	DELIVERABLE
Initiation	Problem statement
Analysis	Object names, input, output, and sample problems
Design	Refined pseudocode algorithm
Implementation	C++ source code and tested executable program

* Some useful analysis and design tools were introduced:
  * naming the objects that help solve a problem
  * developing algorithms
  * refining one or more steps of an algorithm
  * using the Input/Process/Output pattern

Exercises

Use this table for exercises 1, 3, and 5:

Problem (short description)	Object Name	Input/Output	Sample Problem

Problem: Compute a student's cumulative grade point average (GPA).

1. Complete an analysis deliverable for the GPA problem.
2. Write an algorithm that outlines a solution to the GPA problem.

Problem: Find the number of occurrences of any given word for any given work of William Shakespeare.

3. Complete an analysis deliverable for the Shakespeare problem.
4. Write an algorithm that outlines a solution for the Shakespeare problem.

Problem: Make up your own problem.

5. Complete an analysis deliverable for your own problem.
6. Write an algorithm that outlines a solution.
7. What is the difference between objects used to store output values and objects that store the values input by the user?
8. List the three characteristics of an object.
9. What activities are performed when you design programs?
10. Describe the deliverable of the design phase of program development.
11. What is the deliverable from the implementation phase of program development?

12. What are the characteristics of a good algorithm?

13. Does a program that runs work correctly? Justify your answer.

14. Describe the value(s) stored in numeric objects (`double`).

15. Write an algorithm that describes how to get to where you live.

16. Write an algorithm for finding any phone number in the phone book. Will the search always be successful?

17. Write an algorithm for tying your shoelaces.

Analysis/Design Projects

Note: The following projects do not require a computer.

1A Directions

Write an algorithm that instructs someone to arrive at your home by automobile.

1B From Source Code to Executable Program

Obtain the instructions necessary to create, compile, link, and execute a C++ program on your system. You may need to seek out a login procedure and/or basic editing commands and compiling commands. After this, write a complete algorithm that provides all necessary steps to successfully guide a novice to complete a program through testing. Your algorithm may contain steps such as "Compare example output to program output," "Create a new file," and "Compile the program."

1C Simple Arithmetic

For any two numeric inputs for `a` and `b`, compute the product (`a * b`) and the sum (`a + b`). Display the difference between the product and the sum.

1. Complete an analysis deliverable for this problem with at least one example problem.

2. Complete a design deliverable by writing an algorithm that solves the simple arithmetic problem.

1D Simple Average

Find the average of three tests of equal weight.

1. Complete an analysis deliverable for this problem with at least one example problem.

2. Complete a design deliverable by writing an algorithm that solves the simple average problem.

1E Weighted Average

Determine the course grade using this weighted scale:

1. Complete an analysis deliverable for this problem with at least two example problems.

2. Complete a design deliverable by writing an algorithm that solves the weighted average problem.

	Weight
Quiz average	20%
Midterm	20%
Lab grade	35%
Final exam	25%

1F Wholesale Cost

You happen to know that a store has a 25% markup on compact disc (CD) players. If the retail price (what you pay) of a CD player is $189.98, how much did the store pay for that item (the wholesale price)? In general, what is the wholesale price for any item given its retail price and markup? Analyze the problem and design an algorithm that computes the wholesale price for *any* given retail price and *any* given markup. *Clue:* If you can't determine the equation, use this formula and a little algebra to solve for wholesale price:
retail price = wholesale price * (1 + markup)

1. Complete an analysis deliverable for this problem with at least three example problems.

2. Complete a design deliverable by writing an algorithm (with formula) that solves the wholesale cost problem.

1G Combinations

Design an algorithm for a program that must ask the user to input three unique digits (0 through 9) to create and output six unique numbers. Also show the sum of those six new values. Each number is calculated as a unique combination of the three digits as summarized in the following dialogue:

```
Enter three unique digits [0 through 9]
Enter digit 1:  8
```

```
Enter digit 2:  0
Enter digit 3:  3

The six new numbers:
803
830
83
38
380
308
Sum of the six new numbers: 2442
```

Some background: The familiar base 10 number system uses the following scheme to symbolize numeric values:

digit * 10^4 + digit * 10^3 + digit * 10^2 + digit * 10^1 + digit * 10^0

For example, the number 25,678 is derived like this:

$2 * 10^4 + 5 * 10^3 + 6 * 10^2 + 7 * 10^1 + 8 * 10^0$
$2 * 10{,}000 + 5 * 1{,}000 + 6 * 100 + 7 * 10 + 8 * 1$

1. Using the sample problem represented in the dialogue above, name seven objects that store values that will eventually be output.

2. Using the sample problem represented in the dialogue above and the object names you choose, write the formula that computes the second number (830) and the fourth number (38).

1H Distance

Compute the distance between any two points (x_1, y_1) and (x_2, y_2). Use the Pythagorean theorem:

$$\text{distance} = \sqrt{(x_1 - x_2)^2 + (y_1 - y_2)^2}$$

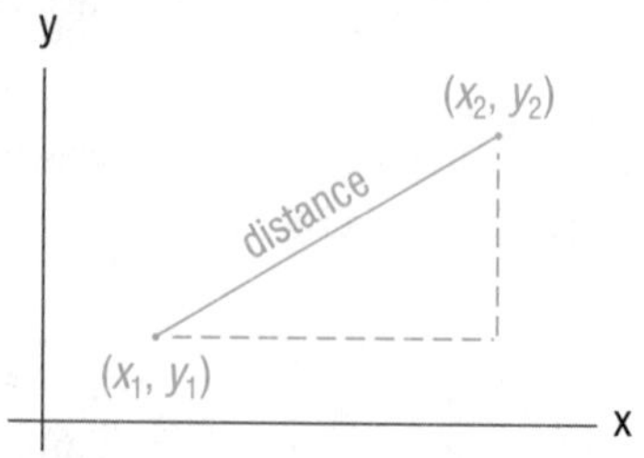

1. Complete an analysis deliverable for this problem with at least two example problems.

2. Complete a design deliverable by writing an algorithm (with formula) that solves the problem.

Chapter Two

Implementation

Summing Up

The first chapter introduced a real-world program development strategy of analysis, design, and implementation. You are encouraged to do some analysis and design before writing code. However, many problems encountered in the first five chapters of this book will not require much effort to produce analysis and design deliverables. Analysis may simply be "Read the problem." Design might end up as "I can picture the solution in my head." You were also introduced to objects—entities with a name, state, and set of operations.

Coming Up

In this chapter, the emphasis will be on translating algorithms into programs using the C++ programming language. The resulting source code you type is the input to the compiler. The compiler translates the source code into machine code that your particular computer understands. However, the compiler expects source code to follow the precise rules of the programming language. Understanding how to translate a pseudocode algorithm into its programming language equivalent requires understanding the smallest pieces of a program and how to correctly gather them together to create statements. This chapter also examines operations that can be performed on many objects. After studying this chapter, you will be able to

- understand how to include existing source code in your programs
- obtain data from the user and display information to the user
- evaluate and create arithmetic expressions
- understand that these common operations are available to many objects: initialization, output, assignment, input

  Exercises and programming projects to reinforce implementation

2.1 The C++ Programming Language: A Start

A C++ *program* is a sequence of characters stored as a file. The name of the file holding a C++ program typically ends with either `.cc`, `.C`, `.cp`, or `.CPP` (`first.cc`, `first.C`, or `FIRST.CPP`, for example). Some programming environments require or assume certain file-naming conventions. Therefore, when you create a file to translate an algorithm into its C++ programming language equivalent, create the file with the extension you should—or must—use.

The text contained in the file is introduced as the *general form* of a C++ program (below). A general form describes the *syntax*—the correct language—necessary to write legal programming language constructs. This general form, like all others in this textbook, follows these conventions:

1. Boldface elements must be written exactly as shown. This includes certain words such as `int main()`, `cout`, and `cin` and symbols such as <<, >>, and `;`.
2. The portions of a general form written in italic must be supplied by the programmer—for example, *expression* means you must supply a valid expression.
3. An item in italic is defined somewhere else.

GENERAL FORM 2.1. *Standard C++ program*

```
// comment: This general form assumes you have a standard compiler
#include-directives
using namespace std;
int main()
{
  object-constructions
  statements
  return 0;
}
```

The parts of a general form in boldface must be written exactly as shown. The *#include-directives* and *object-constructions* syntax are described shortly. The *statements* part refers to a collection of different statements. A few statements are described in this chapter. And although not necessary with standard C++, the last line of the C++ programs in this textbook will be `return 0;`.

Before getting into the details, here is a syntactically correct standard C++ program. (*Note:* `std` is an abbreviation for *standard.*)

```
// This C++ program gets a number from the user and displays its
// squared value
#include <iostream>    // For std::cout, std::cin, and std::endl
using namespace std;   // This allows programmers to write cin and
                       // cout instead of std::cin and std::cout
int main()
{
  // 0. Initialize objects
  double x = 0.0;
  double result = 0.0;

  // 1. Input
  cout << "Enter a number: ";
  cin >> x;

  // 2. Process
  result = x * x;  // The C++ symbol for multiplication is *

  // 3. Output
  cout << x << " squared = " << result << endl;

  return 0;
}
```

Dialogue

```
Enter a number: -1.2
-1.2 squared = 1.44
```

This source code represents input to the compiler. The compiler translates source code like this into machine code. Along the way, the compiler may generate error and warning messages. The errors are detected as the compiler scans the source code of the program and any `#include` files that represent additional source code. For example, the file named `iostream` precedes the code beginning at `int main()` and so the source code in the file becomes part of the program. The `#include` directive is conceptually replaced by the text contained in the `#included` file.

Web Release

Morristown, New Jersey, USA — Friday, November 14, 1997

International standard for the C++ programming language approved!

FOR IMMEDIATE RELEASE

This week, technical experts representing eight countries and about 40 companies involved with software technologies met in Morristown, New Jersey, and completed the content of an international standard for the C++ programming language.

At the time of this writing, the International Standards Organization and several national standard committees completed work that had begun in 1989. Their efforts make it easier to teach, learn, and develop C++ programs. While many compiler vendors have been following the changes and implement C++ close to the standard, at the time of this writing not all compilers accept the form of the program just shown. Even though they might be made standard by the time this textbook is released, you may still have an older C++ compiler. If you do not have a standard C++ compiler, the only differences you need to know for now occur at the top of the program.

1. Change `#include <iostream>` to `#include <iostream.h>`.
2. Do not write `using namespace std;`.

The following program will run on older compilers and most standard compilers:

```
// This C++ program gets a number and displays its squared value
#include <iostream.h>  // 1. Nonstandard compilers need .h
// 2. Do not write using namespace std;

int main()
{
  // a. Initialize objects
  double x = 0.0;
  double result = 0.0;

  // b. Input
  cout << "Enter a number: ";
```

```
    cin >> x;

    // c. Process
    result = x * x;  // The C++ symbol for multiplication is *

    // d. Output
    cout << x << " squared = " << result << endl;

    return 0;  // This avoids warnings on older compilers
}
```

Every C++ program uses more than one file to take advantage of the code produced by other programmers. In fact, C++ compilers are delivered with a large number of files. Below is the general form that adds other source code to a program.

General Form 2.2. *Include directive*

#include <*include-file*>

- or -

#include "*include-file*"

The `#include` and angle brackets (< >) or double quote marks (" ") must be written exactly as shown. The *include-file* is the name of an existing file. For example, the previous program contains the following `#include` directive in order to furnish `cout`, `cin`, and `endl`:

```
#include <iostream>
```

However, this `#include` directive actually provides `std::cout`, `std::cin`, and `std::endl`. The C++ standard library, of which `iostream` is a part, is defined in a namespace called `std`. So to avoid repetitiously writing `std::`, this line should accompany `#include <iostream>` and other `#includes` seen later:

```
using namespace std; // Allows the programmer to write cout and cin
```

Care should be taken to avoid any blank spaces between the < > or " ".

```
#include <iostream >   // ERROR
#include " cdplayer"   // ERROR
```

Any included file with angle brackets (< >) must be part of the system. Your system should be able to find those files automatically. However, the file names included within quotes (" ") may need to be stored in the same directory as the program that includes them.[1] It depends on your system.

2.1.1 Tokens: The Smallest Pieces of a Program

Before looking at the general forms for object initializations and statements, consider the smallest pieces of the programming language that make up the larger constructs. This should help you to

- more easily code syntactically correct statements
- better understand how to fix errors detected by the compiler
- understand general forms

As the C++ compiler reads the source code, it identifies individual *tokens,* which are the smallest recognizable components of a program. Tokens fall into four categories:

Category	Examples
Special symbols	`;` `( )` `<<` `>>`
Keywords	`return` `double` `int`
Identifiers	`main` `test2` `firstName`
Constants	`"Hello World!"` `507` `-2.1`

2.1.2 Special Symbols

A special symbol is a sequence of one or two characters with one or possibly many specific meanings. Some special symbols—such as `{`, `;`, and `,`—separate other tokens. Other special symbols—such as `+`, `-`, and `<<`—represent operators in expressions. Here is a partial list of single-character and double-character special symbols frequently seen in C++ programs.

```
( )   .   +   -   /   *   =<   >=   //   { }   ==   ;   <<   >>
```

2.1.3 Keywords

Keywords are words that have a specific purpose. They are words whose meaning is fixed by the standard language definition, such as the keywords `double` and `int`.

1. If your system cannot find the files, refer to the `readme.txt` file on the disk or check out this textbook's Web site (**http://www.cs.arizona.edu/people/mercer/_**) for the latest updates.

Here is a partial list of C++ keywords.

C++ KEYWORDS

break	do	for	operator	switch
case	double	if	return	typedef
char	else	int	sizeof	void
class	float	long	struct	while

The case sensitivity of C++ applies to keywords. For example, there is a difference between `double` (a keyword) and `Double` (not a keyword). C++ keywords are always in all lowercase letters.

2.1.4 Identifiers: Standard and Programmer-Defined

A C++ *identifier* is a word-like token that represents a variety of things. For example, `cout` is the program name for the computer screen. Another identifier, `cin`, is the program name for the computer keyboard. Here are some other standard C++ identifiers. (However, `string` and `queue` may not be available on older compilers. You can get the `string` class from this textbook's disk.)

```
endl  sqrt  fabs  pow  string  vector  width  precision  queue
```

Programmer-defined identifiers have meaning for the programmer who created the program, for others who might later use it, and for those who must maintain the program. For example, `test1`, `finalExam`, and `courseGrade` are programmer-defined. Here are the rules that govern the creation of C++ identifiers.

- Identifiers begin with upper- or lowercase letters a through `z` (or `A` through `Z`) or the underscore character (_).
- The first letter may be followed by a number of upper- and lowercase letters, digits (`0` through `9`), and underscore characters.
- Identifiers are case sensitive. For example, `Ident`, `ident`, and `iDENT` are three different identifiers.
- An identifier cannot be a keyword.

VALID IDENTIFIERS

main	cin	incomeTax	j	MAX_SIZE
Maine	cout	employeeName	x	all_4_one
miSpel	string	A1	n	world_in_motion

INVALID IDENTIFIERS

```
1A           // It begins with a digit
miles/Hour   // The / is unacceptable
first Name   // The blank space is unacceptable
pre-shrunk   // The operator - means subtraction
double       // It is a keyword
```

Remember the case sensitivity of C++. For example, every complete program must include the identifier `main`. `MAIN` or `Main` won't do. Also note that several conventions may be used for upper- and lowercase letters. Some programmers prefer avoiding uppercase letters, others prefer to use uppercase letters for each new word. The convention used in this textbook is the "camelBack" style where each word after the first has an uppercase letter. For example, you will see `letterGrade` rather than `lettergrade`, `LetterGrade`, or `letter_grade`. Other programmers use different styles.

2.1.5 Constants

The C++ compiler recognizes `string`, integer, and floating-point constants (also called *literals*). A `string` constant is zero or more characters enclosed within a pair of double-quote special symbols and finished on the same line:

```
"Double quotes are used to delimit string constants."
"Hello, World!"
```

Integer constants are numbers without decimal points. Floating-point constants are numbers with decimal points or written in exponential notation (5e3 = $5 * 10^3$ = 5000.0 and 1.23e-4 = $1.23 * 10^{-4}$ = 0.0001234). Here are some tokens that represent constants in C++.

Integer Constants	Floating-Point Constants	`string` Constants
-32768	-1.0	"A"
-1	0.0	"Hello World"
0	39.95	"\n is like endl"
1	1.234e02	"1.23"
32767	-1e6	"And the answer is "

2.1.6 Comments

Comments are portions of text that annotate a program. Comments fulfill any or all of the following expectations:

- Provide internal documentation to help one programmer read another's program—assuming those comments clarify the meaning of the program.
- Explain certain code fragments or the purpose of an object.
- Indicate the programmer's name and the goal of the program.
- Describe a wide variety of program elements and other considerations.

Comments may be added anywhere throughout a program, including to the right of any C++ statement, on a separate line, or over several lines. They may begin with the two-character special symbol `/*` when closed with the corresponding symbol `*/`:

```
/*
   A comment may
   extend over
   many lines
*/
```

An alternate form for comments is to use `//` before the text. Such a comment may appear on a line by itself or at the end of a line:

```
//  A complete C++ program
int main()
{
  // This program does nothing
  return 0;
}
```

Within the context of the programs in this textbook, comments are most often written as one-line comments like `//Comment` rather than `/*Comment*/`. All code after `/*` is a comment until `*/` is encountered, so a large portion of the program can accidentally be turned into a comment by forgetting `*/` at the end! The one-line comments make it more difficult to accidentally "comment out" large sections of code.

Comments are added to help clarify and document the purpose of the source code. The goal is to make the program more understandable, easier to debug (correct errors), and easier to maintain (change when necessary). Programmers need comments to understand programs that may have been written days, weeks, months, years, or even decades ago.

Self-Check

2-1 How many special symbols are there in the first program of section 2.1 on page 31 (the program that gets a number and displays a squared value)? (*Note:* Comments and `#include`s are *not* considered to be tokens.)

2-2 List each of the following as a valid identifier or explain why it is not valid.

-a	`abc`	-l	`H.P.`
-b	`123`	-m	`double`
-c	`ABC`	-n	`55_mph`
-d	`#include`	-o	`sales Tax`
-e	`my Age`	-p	`main`
-f	`#define`	-q	`a`
-g	`Abc!`	-r	`_`
-h	`identifier`	-s	`___1___`
-i	`(identifier)`	-t	`Mile/Hour`
-j	`Double`	-u	`os`
-k	`mispellted`		

2-3 List two special symbols that are one character long.

2-4 List two special symbols that are two characters long.

2-5 List two standard identifiers.

2-6 Create two programmer-defined identifiers.

2-7 Which of these tokens are valid

-a `string` constants?

-b integer constants?

-c floating-point constants?

```
234    1.0    'H'    "integer"    -123    1.0e+03    "H"
```

2-8 Which of the following are valid C++ comments:

-a `//  Is this a comment?`

-b `/ / Is this a comment?`

-c `/* Is this a comment?`

-d `/* Is this a comment? */`

2.2 Common Operations on Objects

A *statement* is composed of several components that have been legally grouped together to perform some operation. The tokens discussed in the previous section are used to build these statements. In particular, this section presents statements that allow for the following operations, which are available to many classes of objects:

- construction—bring an object into a program
- output—display the state of an object
- assignment—set an object's state with a new value
- input—define an object's state through keyboard input

2.2.1 Object Declarations and Initializations

A *declaration* introduces one or more object names into a program. An *initialization* also introduces object names into a program with the additional feature of setting the initial state to whatever the programmer wants. These object names are used later when the programmer is interested in the current value of the object or needs to change the state of that object. Here are the general forms for declaring and/or initializing objects:

GENERAL FORM 2.3. *Declaration (some classes have a default initial state)*

class-name identifier;

GENERAL FORM 2.4. *Initialization (declare an object and give it any state you want)*

class-name identifier = *initial-state* ;

- or -

class-name identifier(*initial-state*) ; // *For when you need more than one value*

The *class-name* may be `double`—to store numbers with a decimal point—or a class introduced here named `string` to store a collection of characters (many other classes exist).

The following C++ program declares one numeric object with an unknown initial state (`credits`) and two objects that can store floating-point numbers with an initial state of 0.0. Both `string` objects have an initial state of the null string, which is the default initial state for the `string` class.

```
// A program that declares and/or initializes objects only
#include <iostream>
#include <string>     // For std::string
using namespace std;  // Allow string instead of std::string

int main()
{
  double credits;
  // The state of credits is unknown!

  double points = 0.0;
  double GPA = 0.0;
  // Both points and GPA are completely initialized

  string firstName;
  string lastName = "Goldman";

  // . . . nothing visible happens
  return 0;
}
```

Some of the differences between `double` and `string` relate to the fact that `double` was implemented as a primitive data type long before the `string` class came along. Because objects of the `double` class have no default initial value, you will often find them initialized to 0.0. This is done to satisfy all three attributes of an object: (1) the name as specified by the identifier, (2) the operations as specified by the class name, and (3) the state as specified by the initial value between parentheses. On the other hand, `string` objects do have a default initial state. A `string` object declared without `(`*initial-state*`)` automatically has the value of a null string, which is a `string` with zero characters.

The table on the right summarizes the initial state of these objects (the question mark after `credits` indicates an unknown state—it was declared, but not initialized).

Object Name	Object State
`credits`	?
`points`	`0.0`
`GPA`	`0.0`
`firstName`	`""`
`lastName`	`"Goldman"`

2.2.2 Output with `cout`

Programs communicate with users. Such communication is provided through—but not limited to—keyboard input and screen output. This two-way communication is a critical component of many programs. Here is the general form of the C++ output statement (also know as the `cout` statement).

General Form 2.5. *The cout statement*

cout << *expression-1* << *expression-2* , . . . , << *expression-n* << **endl;**

The object named `cout` (pronounced "see-out") represents the computer screen and *expression-1* through *expression-n* may take the form of object names such as `GPA` and `firstName` or constants such as `"Credits: "` and `99.5`. The output operator `<<` indicates the direction in which data are flowing—toward the screen object named `cout`. Finally, a semicolon (`;`) terminates the statement. Here are some legal output statements:

```
cout << 99.5 << endl;
cout << "Show me literally too" << endl;
cout << "First Name: " << firstName << endl;
cout << "Credits: " << credits << endl;
```

When a `cout` statement is encountered, the expressions are inserted into a data stream going toward the computer screen. The expressions are output in the same order as they are encountered in the statement—in a left-to-right order. When the expression `endl` is encountered, a new line is generated, so any subsequent output starts at the beginning of a new line (`endl` is read as "end-ell" and means end of line).

The above object declarations and output statements are placed together in a new C++ program:

```
// This program only constructs some numeric and string objects
#include <iostream>    // This #include is in almost every program
#include <string>      // For std::string
using namespace std;   // Allow use of cout, cin, endl, and string

int main()
{
  // Initialize some numeric objects
  double credits, points, GPA = 0.0;
  // Initialize some string objects. lastName will be
  // set to "" (null string).
  string firstName = "Bob";
  string lastName;

  // Some output statements
  cout << 99.5 << endl;
  cout << "First name: " << firstName << endl;
  cout << "Last name: " << lastName << endl;
```

```
  cout << "Credits = " << credits << endl;

  return 0;
}
```

OUTPUT

```
99.5
First name: Bob
Last name:
Credits = 0
```

Self-Check

2-9 Initialize two objects that represent numbers with an initial value of -1.0.

2-10 Declare one object named `address` that could store a street address.

2-11 Write a complete C++ program that displays your name.

2.2.3 Assignment

Assignment statements set the state of an object. The value of the expression to the right of = replaces whatever value was in the object to the left of =.

GENERAL FORM 2.6. *The assignment statement*

object-name = *expression*;

The *expression* must be a value that can be stored by the object to the left of the assignment operator =. For example, an expression that results in a floating-point value can be stored in a numeric object, and a `string` expression (characters between " and ") can be stored in a `string` object. Here are some other example assignment operations:

```
// There is no I/O here, only examples of assignment operations
#include <string>      // For std::string
using namespace std;   // Allow string instead of std::string

int main()
{
  double x = 0.0;
  string s;
```

```
  x = 456.789;
  s = "A string";
  // x and s have had their states modified from the initial values

  return 0;
}
```

After the two assignment operations execute, the state of both objects is modified and the state of these objects can be shown like this:

Object	State
x	456.789
s	"A string"

There are some assignment compatibility rules. For example, a `string` constant cannot be stored in a numeric object.

```
x = "Noooooo, you can't do that";   // ERROR
```

A `double` cannot be stored in a `string` object.

```
s = 12.34;   // ERROR
```

The compiler will report errors at both attempted assignment statements.

Self-Check

2-12 Given these object initializations, which of the following are valid attempts at assignment?

```
string s;
double x = 0.0;
```

-a `s = 1.5;`

-b `s = "1.5";`

-c `x = 1.5;`

-d `x = "1.5";`

The following program uses the C++ assignment statement to give specific value to the five objects declared earlier. The initial state is replaced by one specific set of data to produce at least one specific result.

```
// This program uses assignment statements to produce a meaningful,
// although very specific, result
#include <iostream>  // For cout and endl
#include <string>    // For the string class
```

```
using namespace std;

int main()
{
  // Some object constructions
  double credits = 0.0;
  double points = 0.0;
  double GPA = 0.0;
  string firstName;
  string lastName;

  // Some assignment statements
  firstName = "Chris";
  lastName = "Goodsmith";

  credits = 16.0;
  points = 49.5;
  GPA = points / credits;  // The / operator causes division. GPA
                           // now stores a value for 16 credits.

  // Some output statements
  cout << "Name    : " << firstName << " " << lastName << endl;
  cout << "Credits : " << credits << endl;
  cout << "Points  : " << points  << endl;
  cout << "GPA     : " << GPA     << endl;

  return 0;
}
```

Output

```
Name    : Chris Goodsmith
Credits : 16
Points  : 49.5
GPA     : 3.09375
```

Be wary of a meaningless object state. It can cause unpredictable errors. Make sure you define all objects either through initialization, an assignment operation, or keyboard input (discussed in the next section). In summary, to properly use objects in a program, all three characteristics must be considered.

1. An object must be given a name in an object declaration or initialization.
2. An object must be declared as an instance of a specific class.
3. At some point, an object should be given a meaningful value.

2.2.4 Input with `cin`

To make programs more general—for example, to find the GPA for *any* student—the state of objects is often set through keyboard input. This allows the user to enter any data desired. Input happens with the istream object named `cin` (common *in*put) and the stream extraction operator `>>`. For example, the following statements modify the state of two objects with data supplied by the user:

```
cin >> firstName;   // User must input a string
cin >> credits;     // User must input a number
```

Here is the general form of the input statement with `cin`:

General Form 2.7. *The `cin` statement*

cin >> *object-name* **;**

- or -

cin >> *object-name-1* **>>** *object-name-2* **>>** *object-name-n* **;**

The *object-name* must be an instance of a class whose value can be typed in at the keyboard. This form of input operation is defined for many but not all objects in this textbook. Input with `cin` is defined for the `double` and `string` classes.

When a `cin` statement is encountered, the program pauses until the user types the proper input value and presses the Enter key. If everything goes okay, the value typed by the user is converted into the proper machine representation and stored in the object as the state of that object.

In addition to the Enter key, input data is also separated by one or more blank spaces. This makes it difficult to read in a `string` with blank spaces, such as a person's full name or address. Given the following code:

```
string name;
cout << "Enter your name: ";
cin >> name;
```

and this dialogue:

```
Enter your name: Kim McPhee
```

`Kim` is stored into `name`, not `Kim McPhee` as one would hope. The blank space after `Kim` terminates the input value. Later on you'll see an operation named `getline` for reading `string`s with blank spaces. For now, you'll need separate `string` objects for the first name and the last name.

You may write the `cin` statement with more than one object for input. If you do, you must assume that the user knows to separate each input from the preceding one with a blank space (press the Spacebar), a new line (press Enter or Return), or a tab (press the Tab key). If you cannot assume this, then you should supply the appropriate messages to properly instruct the user on how to input data. A simple alternative that avoids this mess is to use only one object per `cin`. This will be done in the majority of input statements in this textbook.

2.3 Arithmetic Expressions

Many of the problems in this chapter require you to write arithmetic expressions. Arithmetic expressions are made up of two components: operators and operands. An arithmetic *operator* is one of the C++ special symbols `+`, `-`, `/`, or `*`. The *operands* of an arithmetic expression may be a numeric object name such as `test1` or a numeric constant such as `0.25`. Assuming `x` is an instance of the `double` class, the following expression has operands `x` and `4.5`. The operator is `+`.

```
x + 4.5
```

Together, the operator and operands determine the value of the arithmetic expression.

The simplest arithmetic expression is a numeric constant or numeric object name. Arithmetic expressions may also have two operands with one operator (see the table below).

An Arithmetic Expression May Be	Example
Numeric object	`x`
Numeric constant	`100` or `99.5`
Expression + expression	`x + 2.0`
Expression - expression	`x - 2.0`
Expression * expression	`x * 2.0`
Expression / expression	`x / 2.0`
(Expression)	`(x + 2.0)`

The previous definition of expression also suggests that more complex arithmetic expressions are possible, such as this:

```
1.5 * ((x - 99.5) * 1.0 / x)
```

Since arithmetic expressions may be written with many constants, numeric object names, and operators, rules are put into force to allow a consistent evaluation of expressions. The following table lists four C++ arithmetic operators and the order in which they are applied to numeric objects.

```
double x = 1.0;
double y = 2.0;
double z = 3.0;
double answer = 0.0;
answer = x + y * z / 4.0;
```

The following simulation evaluates this arithmetic expression by first substituting the value for all objects and then evaluating each subexpression using the C++ precedence rules:

```
answer = x + y * z / 4.0;
answer = 1.0 + 2.0 * 3.0 / 4.0   // Substitute values of all objects
answer = 1.0 + 6.0 / 4.0         // * has precedence over +
answer = 1.0 + 1.5               // / has precedence over +
answer = 2.5
```

The preceding discussion of arithmetic expressions is all you'll need to complete the programming projects at the end of this chapter. However, other arithmetic expressions involving integers complete the entirety of numeric operations in C++. These will be considered in the next chapter as part of looking at an integer class named `int`. One `int` object stores a whole number—an integer—like 1, 100, -32,000, or 99. Discussion of `int` objects is delayed until the subtleties of the `double` class have become more familiar.

Self-Check

2-13 Evaluate the following arithmetic expressions:

```
double x = 2.5;
double y = 3.0;
```

-a `x * y + 3.0`

-b `0.5 + x / 2.0`

-c `1 + x * 3.0 / y`

-d `1.5 * (x - y)`

-e `y + -x`

-f `(x - 2) * (y - 1)`

2.4 Constant Objects

The state of any object can be, and usually is, altered during program execution. However, it is sometimes convenient to have data with values that cannot be altered during program execution. C++ provides the keyword `const` for this purpose. Constant objects are created by specifying and associating an identifier with a value

SOME BINARY ARITHMETIC OPERATORS

Operators	Precedence Rule
* /	In the absence of parentheses, multiplication and division evaluate before addition and subtraction. In other words, * and / have precedence over + and -. If more than one of these operators appear in an expression, the leftmost operator evaluates first.
+ -	In the absence of parentheses, + and - evaluate after all * and / operators, with the leftmost evaluating first. Parentheses may override these precedence rules.

The operators of the following expression are applied to the operands in this order: /, +, and lastly -.

```
2.0 + 5.0 - 8.0 / 4.0  // Evaluates to 5.0
```

Parentheses may alter the order in which arithmetic operators are applied to their operands.[2]

```
(2.0 + 5.0 - 8.0) / 4.0  // Evaluates to -0.25
```

With the parentheses, the / operator evaluated last, rather than first. The same set of operators and operands with parentheses results in a different value (-0.25 rather than 5.0).

These precedence rules apply to binary operators only. A *binary operator* is one that requires one operand to the left and one operand to the right. A unary operator only requires one operand on the right. Consider this expression, which has the binary operator * and the unary minus operator -.

```
3.5 * -2.0  // Evaluates to -7.0
```

The unary operator evaluates before the binary * operator: 3.5 times negative 2.0 results in negative 7.0.

Arithmetic expressions usually have object names as operands. When C++ evaluates an expression with double objects, the object name is replaced with its state. Consider the following code:

2. You will see later, in Chapter 3, that the division operator / behaves differently when both operands are integers. The result is always an integer (5/2 is 2, not 2.5, for example).

preceded by the keyword `const`. In essence, this is an object whose state cannot be changed through assignment or stream extraction operations. The general form used to initialize a constant object is a combination of an initialization preceded by the keyword `const`.

General Form 2.8. *Initializing a constant object*

`const` *class-name identifier* = *expression* ;

For example, the value stored in the constant object `PI` is the floating-point number `3.1415926`, and `TAX_RATE` is 7.51%.

```
const double PI = 3.1415926;
const double TAX_RATE = 0.0751;
const string PAUSE_MESSAGE = "Press any key to continue . . .";
```

These constant objects represent values that cannot be changed while the program is executing; therefore a statement such as `PI=PI*r*r;` generates an error because `PI` is declared as constant. The value cannot be destroyed with an input statement such as `cin >> PI;`.

Objects represent values that change while the program is executing. If the state of an object is not changed at least once in a program, it should be declared as a constant object.

2.5 Another Algorithmic Pattern: Prompt then Input

The output and input operations are often used together to obtain values from the user of the program. The program informs the user what must be entered with an output statement and then performs an input operation to set the state of the object. This happens so often that this activity can be considered to be a pattern. The Prompt then Input algorithmic pattern has two activities:

1. Ask the user to enter a value (prompt).
2. Obtain the value for the object (input).

ALGORITHMIC PATTERN 2.1

Pattern:	Prompt then Input
Problem:	The user must enter something.
Outline:	1. Prompt the user for input. 2. Obtain the input.
Code Example:	`cout << "Enter your first name: ";` `cin >> firstName;`

Strange things can happen if the prompt is left out. The user will not know what must be entered. So whenever you require user input, make sure you prompt for it first. Write the code that tells the user precisely what you want. First output the prompt, then obtain the user input. Here is one instance of the Prompt then Input pattern:

```
cout << "Enter test #1: ";
cin >> test1;
```

and another:

```
cout << "Enter credits: ";
cin >> credits;
```

In general, tell the user what value is needed, then input a value into that object with `cin`.

```
cout << "the prompt for the_object: ";
cin >> the_object;
```

The following program uses the Prompt then Input pattern four times. It also reviews operations such as object initialization, assignment, input, and output. This program illustrates a more general approach to computing *any* grade point average. By requesting input data from the user, it can be used over and over again with *different* sets of input to produce *different* results. Also notice the presence of the IPO pattern in the implementation.

```
// This program uses input statements to produce a meaningful
// result that can be used in a variety of examples

#include <iostream>  // For input and output
#include <string>    // For the string class
```

```
using namespace std;

int main()
{
  // 0. Initialize some objects
  double credits = 0.0;
  double points = 0.0;
  double GPA = 0.0;
  string firstName;
  string lastName;

  // 1. Input
  cout << "Enter first name: ";
  cin >> firstName;
  cout << "Enter last name: ";
  cin >> lastName;
  cout << "Enter credits: ";
  cin >> credits;
  cout << "Enter points: ";
  cin >> points;

  // 2. Process
  GPA = points / credits;

  // 3. Output
  cout << "Name    : " << firstName << " " << lastName << endl;
  cout << "Credits : " << credits << endl;
  cout << "Points  : " << points  << endl;
  cout << "GPA     : " << GPA     << endl;

  return 0;
}
```

DIALOGUE

```
Enter first name: Pat
Enter last name: McCormick
Enter credits: 97.5
Enter points: 323.75
Name    : Pat McCormick
Credits : 97.5
Points  : 323.75
GPA     : 3.32051
```

Care must be taken when entering numeric data. If you—the user—enter a nondigit instead of valid numeric input, the input object `cin` may no longer be in a "good" state and all subsequent `cin` statements will be ignored. Some systems may simply terminate the program with a message indicating the error. On other systems, incorrect input results in even worse problems requiring system administrator intervention.

Self-Check

2-14 Write the value for GPA given each of the dialogues shown below.

```
// This program uses input statements to produce a
// meaningful result that can be used for a variety of
// examples
#include <iostream>  // For cin, cout, and endl
#include <string>    // For the string class
using namespace std;

int main()
{
  // 0. Initialize some numeric objects
  double c1 = 0.0;
  double c2 = 0.0;
  double g1 = 0.0;
  double g2 = 0.0;
  double GPA = 0.0;
  // 1. Input
  cout << "Credits for course 1: ";
  cin >> c1;
  cout << "  Grade for course 1: ";
  cin >> g1;
  cout << "Credits for course 2: ";
  cin >> c2;
  cout << "  Grade for course 2: ";
  cin >> g2;
  // 2. Process
  GPA = ( (g1*c1) + (g2*c2) ) / (c1 + c2);
  // 3. Output
  cout << "GPA: " << GPA << endl;
  return 0;
}
```

Dialogue 1:

```
Credits for course 1: 2.0
  Grade for course 1: 2.0
Credits for course 2: 3.0
  Grade for course 2: 4.0
```

-a ________ GPA

Dialogue 2:

```
Credits for course 1: 4.0
  Grade for course 1: 1.5
Credits for course 2: 1.0
  Grade for course 2: 3.5
```

-b ________ GPA

Dialogue 3:

```
Credits for course 1: 1.0
  Grade for course 1: 2.0
Credits for course 2: 4.0
  Grade for course 2: 3.0
```

-c ________ GPA

2-15 Given the following program and dialogues, what values are stored in `aNumber` and `aString`?

```
// String input is separated by one or more spaces or a
// new line
#include <iostream>  // For the cin and cout objects
#include <string>    // For the string class
using namespace std;

int main()
{
  // Initialize objects
  double aNumber = 0.0;
  string aString;
  // Prompt then Input
  cout << "Enter number: ";
  cin >> aNumber;
  // Prompt then Input
  cout << "Enter string: ";
  cin >> aString;
  return 0;
}
```

Dialogue 1:

```
Enter number: 99.9
Enter string: Canada
```

-a _______ aNumber   -b _______ aString

Dialogue 2:

```
Enter number: 1.5
Enter string: Two Strings
```

-c _______ aNumber   -d _______ aString

Dialogue 3:

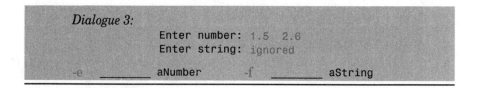

```
Enter number: 1.5  2.6
Enter string: ignored
```

-e ________ aNumber -f ________ aString

Chapter Summary

- The smallest pieces of a program (tokens) were shown to help you understand general forms and fix errors:
  - special symbols
  - identifiers
  - keywords
  - constants
- Objects are entities that have a name, state (value), and operations. Output (`cout <<`) and input (`cin >>`) operations are used in concert with `double` and `string` objects to set their states. There are at least these three techniques for modifying the state of an object:
  1. initialization with `double x = 0.0;`
  2. input with `cin >>`
  3. assignment with `=`
- Knowledge of existing objects aids the program development process. For example, knowing about `cin`, `cout`, `string`, and numeric objects (`double`) precludes the necessity of implementing many intricate operations such as input, output, addition, and multiplication. Fortunately, other programmers have already built them.
- The objects named `cout` and `cin` are so frequently used that they are automatically made available for easy screen output and keyboard input with `#include <iostream>`.
- Arithmetic expressions are made up of operators such as `+`, `-`, `*` (multiplication), and `/` (division). A binary arithmetic operator requires two operands, which may be numeric constants (1 or 2.3), numeric objects, or other arithmetic expressions.
- Declare an object as const if you do not want to accidentally alter the state of that object. Objects representing constants like π should be const objects.
- Instances of the Prompt then Input pattern will occur in many programming projects. Use it whenever a program needs to get some input from the user.

Exercises

1. List three operations that may be applied to numeric objects (`double`).

2. Describe the value(s) stored in `string` objects.

3. List three operations that may be applied to any `string` object.

4. Describe three different ways to set the state of an object.

5. List four types of C++ tokens and give two examples of each.

6. Which of the following are valid identifiers?

   a. `a-one`
   b. `R2D2`
   c. `registered_voter`
   d. `BEGIN`
   e. `1Header`
   f. `$money`
   g. `1_2_3`
   h. `A_B_C`
   i. `all right`
   j. `'doubleObject'`
   k. `{Right}`
   l. `Mispelt`

7. Declare `totalPoints` as an object capable of storing a number.

8. Write a statement that sets the state of `totalPoints` to 100.0.

9. Write the entire dialogue generated by the following program when `5.2` and `6.3` are entered at the prompt. Make sure you write the user-supplied input as well as all program output including the prompt.

```
#include <iostream>
using namespace std;
int main()
{
  double x = 0.0;
  double y = 0.0;
  double answer = 0.0;
  cout << "Enter a number: ";
  cin >> x;
  cout << "Enter another number: ";
  cin >> y;
  answer = x * (1.0 + y);
  cout << "Answer: " << answer << endl;
```

```
  return 0;
}
```

10. Write C++ code that declares `tolerance` as a numeric object set to 0.001 that cannot be changed while the program is running.

11. Write a statement that displays the value of a numeric object named `total`.

12. Given these two object initializations, either write the value that is stored in each object or report the attempt as an error.

```
string aString;
double aNumber = 0.0;
```

a. `aString = "4.5";`

b. `aNumber = "4.5";`

c. `aString = 8.9;`

d. `aNumber = 8.9;`

13. With paper and pencil, write a C++ program that prompts for a number from 0.0 to 1.0 and stores this input value into the numeric object named `relativeError`. Echo the input (output the input). The dialogue generated by your program should look like this:

```
Enter relativeError [0.0 through 1.0]: 0.341
You entered: 0.341
```

14. Assuming `x` is 5.0 and `y` is 7.0, evaluate the following expressions:

a. `x / y`

b. `y / y`

c. `2.0 - x * y`

d. `(x * y) / (x + y)`

15. Predict the output generated by the following programs:

a.
```
#include <iostream>
using namespace std;
int main()
{
  double x = 1.2;
  double y = 3.4;
  cout << (x + y) << endl;
  cout << (x - y) << endl;
  cout << (x * y) << endl;
  cout << (x / y) << endl;
  return 0;
}
```

b.
```
#include <iostream>
using namespace std;
int main()
{
  double x = 0.5;
  double y = 2.3;
  double answer = 0.0;
  answer = x * (1 + y);
  cout << answer << endl;
  answer = x / (1 + y);
  cout << answer << endl;
  return 0;
}
```

16. Write the complete dialogue (program output and user input) generated by the following program when the user enters:

    a. `10.00`

    b. `12.34`

    c. `100.00`

    d. `0`

```
#include <iostream>
using namespace std;

const double TAX_RATE = 0.05;

int main()
{
  double sale, tax, total;
  // Input
  cout << "Enter sale: ";
  cin >> sale;  // User enters 10.00, 12.34, 100.00, and 0
  // Process
  tax = sale * TAX_RATE;
  total = sale + tax;
  // Output
  cout << "Sale: " << sale << endl;
  cout << "Tax: " << tax << endl;
  cout << "Total: " << total << endl;
  return 0;
}
```

17. When used in an output statement, the expression `endl` generates a new line on the computer screen. If you omit `endl`, the output appears "scrunched up" on the same line. Write the output generated by the following programs:

    a.
```
#include <iostream>
using namespace std;
int main()
{
  cout << "+--+"
       << "+  +"
       << "+--+" << endl;
  return 0;
}
```

    b.
```
#include <iostream>
using namespace std;
int main()
{
  cout << "+--+" << endl
       << "+  +" << endl
       << "+--+" << endl;
  return 0;
}
```

c.
```
#include <iostream>
using namespace std;
int main()
{
  cout << 1;
  cout << 2 << endl;
  return 0;
}
```

d.
```
#include <iostream>
using namespace std;
int main()
{
  cout << 1 << endl;
  cout << 2 << endl;
  return 0;
}
```

Programming Tips

1. First determine if you have a standard compiler.

Perhaps the most important thing to determine now is whether or not you have a standard compiler. If you have an older compiler, you are likely to get many errors by following the examples in this textbook. Here is a simple test. Retype the following program and compile it.

```
// This program sends a greeting if you type in your name

#include <iostream>  // For std::cout, std::cin, std::endl
#include <string>    // For std::string

using namespace std;  // Allow cout, cin, endl, string instead of
                      // std::cout, std::cin, std::endl, std::string

int main()
{
  string name;

  cout << "Enter your name: ";
  cin >> name;
  cout << "Hello " << name << endl;

  return 0;
}
```

DIALOGUE

```
Enter your name: Shelly
Hello Shelly
```

If you get no errors and the program runs with a dialogue as shown, you are okay. You will need to use a different `#include`.

```
iostream: no such file or directory
```

If you have a standard compiler, skip to programming tip 2. If you do not have a standard compiler, do the following:

* Always use the alternative `#include <iostream.h>`.

```
#include <iostream.h>  // Add .h to iostream

// Do not write using namespace std;
// although you may need it later

int main()
{
  string name;

  cout << "Enter your name: ";
  cin >> name;
  cout << "Hello " << name << endl;

  return 0;
}
```

2. Semicolons terminate statements.

Make sure you terminate statements with `;`. However, do *not* place semicolons after `#includes` and `int main()`.

```
#include <iostream> ;   // Error found on this line
int main() ;            // Error found on this line
{
```

3. Fix the first error first.

When you compile, you may get dozens of errors. Don't panic. Try to fix the very first error first. That may fix several others. Sometimes fixing one error causes others. Don't be too surprised to find out that after fixing an error, the compiler generates errors that went undetected before.

4. Do more than is required.

Consider doing more of the programming projects than assigned. Experience makes you a better programmer. You'll do better on tests.

5. Omitting a class may result in the default of `int`.

Don't forget to write the class name in a const object initialization. Unfortunately, in the absence of a data type, C++ assumes an integer was intended. For example, to get a constant object with a fractional component, `double` must be supplied. Forgetting `double` results in an `int`. A conversion from `double` to `int` can cause great lost value. For example, `TAX_RATE` becomes 0.00% here when 7.51% was really intended:

```
const TAX_RATE = 0.0751;   // Without double, int is assumed and
                           // TAX_RATE is 0 rather than 0.0751
```

Best wishes.

Programming Projects

2A The Classic "Hello World!" Program

While designing the C language at AT&T, Dennis Ritchie suggested that a first program in any language be one that displays `Hello World!` Many first programs have continued this "Hello World!" tradition. Create a new file called `hello.cc` in the Unix environment (or `hello.cpp` in Windows, NT, or MacOS). Then, carefully retype the following program exactly as shown. Save this file, then compile and run the program.

```
// Programmer: Firstname Lastname
// This programs displays a simple message
#include <iostream>    // For std::cout
using namespace std;   // Allow cout instead of std::cout

int main()
{
  cout << "Hello World!" << endl;
  return 0;
}
```

2B Experience Errors Generated by the Compiler (must have a standard compiler)

One small coding error may cause the report of many errors at compiletime—this can be misleading. For example, a missing semicolon may result in dozens of errors throughout a program. Remember to fix the first error first. Start by fixing the earliest discovered error in the source code. You are now asked to observe what happens when a left curly brace is left out of a program. Carefully retype the following program exactly as shown.

```
// Observe how many errors occur when { is missing
#include <iostream>   // For cout
using namespace std;  // To make cout known

int main()
// <- Leave off {
   double x = 2.4;
   double y = 4.5;
   cout << "x: " << x << endl;
   cout << "y: " << y << endl;
   return 0;
}
```

1. Compile your source code and write the number of errors that occur.
2. Add `{` after `int main()` and compile again. Make corrections until you have no errors.
3. Now remove the `#include` directive `#include <iostream>` and compile the program. How many errors do you get?
4. Replace `#include <iostream>` and remove the `()` after `main`. How many errors do you get?
5. Comment out `using namespace std;`. How many errors do you get now?
6. If necessary, edit and compile this program until there are no compiletime errors. Execute it. What is the output?

2C Big Initials

Write a C++ program that displays your initials on the screen in large letters. There are no input or process steps, only output. For example, if your initials are E. T. M., the output should look like this (generated by six `cout` statements—no object construction required):

```
EEEEE   TTTTTTT      M     M
E          T         M M M M
EEEEE      T         M  M  M
E          T         M     M
EEEEE o    T    o    M     M o
```

2D Yoda

Write a C++ program that obtains any three `strings` from the user and outputs them in reverse order with one space between them. (*Hint:* There is no process step; only input followed by output.)

```
Enter string one: happy
Enter string two: am
Enter string three: I
I am happy
```

2E Simple Arithmetic

Implement and test a C++ program that solves the problem specified in analysis/design project 1C, "Simple Arithmetic." *The problem:* For any two numeric inputs for `a` and `b`, compute the product (`a * b`) and the sum (`a + b`). Then display the difference between the product and the sum. Your dialogue must look exactly like this:

```
Enter a number: 5.0
Enter a number: 10.0
Product = 50
Sum = 15
Difference = 35
```

Note: A `Difference` of `-35` would be okay. See the `fabs` function in Chapter 3 to fix.

2F Simple Average

Implement and test a C++ program that solves the problem specified in analysis/design project 1D, "Simple Average." *The problem:* Find the average of three tests of equal weight. One dialogue must look exactly like this:

```
Enter three tests: 70.0  90.0  80.0
Average =  80
```

2G Weighted Average

Implement and test a C++ program that solves the problem specified in analysis/design project 1E, "Weighted Average." *The problem:* Determine the course grade using the weighted scale shown below. One dialogue must look exactly like this:

	Weight
Quiz average	20%
Midterm	20%
Lab grade	35%
Final exam	25%

```
Enter Quiz Average: 90.0
Enter Midterm: 90.0
Enter Lab Grade: 90.0
Enter Final Exam: 90.0
Course Average = 90
```

2H Wholesale Cost

Implement and test a C++ program that solves the problem specified in analysis/design project 1F, "Wholesale Cost." *The problem:* You happen to know that a store has a 25% markup on compact disc (CD) players. If the retail price (what you pay) of a CD player is $189.98, how much did the store pay for that item (the wholesale price)? In general, what is the wholesale price for any item given its retail price and markup? Analyze the problem and design an algorithm that computes the wholesale price for *any* given retail price and *any* given markup. *Clue:* If you can't determine the equation, use this formula and some algebra to solve for wholesale price:

retail price = wholesale price * (1 + markup)

One dialogue must look exactly like this:

```
Enter the retail price: 200
Enter markup [e.g. 0.50 for 50%]: 0.50
Wholesale price = 133.33
```

Here is another dialogue to try out:

```
Enter the retail price: 200
Enter markup [e.g. 0.50 for 50%]: 1
Wholesale price = 100.0
```

2I Combinations

Implement and test a C++ program that solves the problem specified in analysis/design project 1G, "Combinations." Write a program that asks the user to input three unique digits (0 through 9) to create and output six unique numbers. Also show the sum of those six new values. Each number is calculated as a unique combination of the three digits as summarized in the following dialogue:

```
Enter three unique digits [0 through 9]
Enter digit 1:  8
Enter digit 2:  0
Enter digit 3:  3
The six new numbers:
803
830
83
38
380
308
Sum of the six new numbers: 2442
```

Chapter Three

Function Calls and Headings

Summing Up

You should have now gained valuable hands-on experience with your system, the syntax of the language, error messages, and program development—from beginning to end. Most programming projects in the early chapters of this textbook are instances of the IPO algorithmic pattern. You should now be able to put these three steps in the proper order and understand the ramifications of omitting one or mixing up the order.

Coming Up

Software developers often use *existing* software—a practice that saves time and money. This chapter introduces one way to reuse existing software. Programmers begin with a substantial base of tested software. You will learn how to use existing functions by reading function headings and to determine what the functions do by reading their pre- and postconditions—the contracts for using those functions. The chapter ends with a review of the categories of errors you will probably have encountered. After studying this chapter, you will be able to

- evaluate a few mathematical and trigonometric functions
- use arguments in function calls
- appreciate why programmers divide software into functions
- read function headings so you can use existing functions
- use integer objects
- use quotient remainder integer division
- understand the categories of errors that occur during the implementation phase of software development

Exercises and programming projects to reinforce use of existing functions

3.1 cmath Functions

C++ defines a large collection of mathematical and trigonometric functions that may be used with `double`s. Here are two:

```
sqrt(x)   // Return the square root of x
pow(x,y)  // Return x to the yth power
```

These functions are *called* by specifying the name of the function, followed by the appropriate number and class of *arguments* within the parentheses. Here is one general form to call certain functions.

GENERAL FORM 3.1. *Function call*

function-name **(** *arguments* **)**

The *function-name* is a previously declared identifier representing a function name. The *arguments* represent a set of zero or more expressions separated by commas. In the following function call, the function name is `sqrt` (*sq*uare *r*oo*t*) and the argument is `81.0`:

```
sqrt(81.0)   // An example of a function call
```

Functions may have zero, one, or even more arguments. Although most math functions require exactly one argument, one—the `pow` function—requires exactly two arguments. In the following function call, the function name is `pow` (for *pow*er), the arguments are `base` and `power`, and the function call `pow(base, power)` is replaced with $base^{power}$, which returns `8.0`:

```
double base = 2.0;
double power = 3.0;
cout << pow(base, power);   // Output: 8.0
```

Any argument used in a function call must be an expression from an acceptable class. For example, the function call `sqrt("Bobbie")` results in an error because the argument is not one of the numeric classes.

The function must also be supplied with reasonable arguments. For example, the function call `sqrt(-4.0)` could be a problem because `-4.0` is not in the domain of `sqrt`. The square root function is not defined for negative numeric values. The `sqrt` function operates correctly only if certain conditions are met, i.e., the argument $\geq$ 0.0.

Here are some mathematical and trigonometric functions available when you `#include <cmath>`. This is followed by a program that calls several of these functions.

A Partial List of `cmath` Functions

Function	Class of Argument	Class of Result	Value Returned	Example Call	Return Result
`ceil(x)`	`double`	`double`	Smallest integer ≥ x	`ceil(2.1)`	`3.0`
`cos(x)`	`double`	`double`	Cosine of x radians	`cos(1.0)`	`0.5403`
`fabs(x)`	`double`	`double`	Absolute value of x	`fabs(-1.5)`	`1.5`
`floor(x)`	`double`	`double`	Largest integer ≤ x	`floor(2.9)`	`2.0`
`pow(x, y)`	`double`	`double`	x to the yth: x^y	`pow(2, 4)`	`16.0`
`sin(x)`	`double`	`double`	Sine of x radians	`sin(1.0)`	`0.84147`
`sqrt(x)`	`double`	`double`	Square root of x	`sqrt(4.0)`	`2.0`

With `#include <cmath>` at the "top" of the program near `#include <iostream>`, the programmer can successfully compile a program with calls to the functions declared in `cmath`.[1] This means that the following program compiles successfully:

```
// Show some mathematical functions available from cmath

#include <iostream>  // For cout
#include <cmath>     // For fabs, ceil, floor, and pow

using namespace std;

int main()
{
  double x = -2.1;

  cout << "fabs(x)      :   " << fabs(x)      << endl
       << "ceil(x)      :   " << ceil(x)      << endl
       << "floor(x)     :   " << floor(x)     << endl
       << "pow(x, 2.0)  :   " << pow(x, 2.0)  << endl;
  return 0;
}
```

1. If you do not have a standard compiler, `#include <math.h>`.

OUTPUT

```
fabs(x)      :  2.1
ceil(x)      :  -2
floor(x)     :  -3
pow(x, 2.0)  :  4.41
```

It should be noted that integer expressions may also be used as arguments to `cmath` functions. As with assignment, the integer value will be promoted to a `double`. So `sqrt(4)` returns the same result as `sqrt(4.0)` without error.

Self-Check

3-1 Evaluate `pow(4.0, 3.0)`.

3-2 Evaluate `pow(3.0, 4.0)`.

3-3 Evaluate `floor(1.6 + 0.5)`.

3-4 Evaluate `ceil(1.6 - 0.5)`.

3.2 Using `cmath` to Round x to n Decimals

Problem: Write a program that rounds a number to a specific number of decimal places. For example, 3.4589 rounded to two decimal places should be 3.46 and -3.4589 rounded to one decimal place should be -3.5.

3.2.1 Analysis

The analysis/design/implementation software development strategy begins with these analysis activities:

1. Read and understand the problem.
2. Decide what object(s) represent the answer—the output.
3. Decide what object(s) the user must enter to get the answer—the input.
4. Create a document that summarizes the analysis and can be used as input to the design phase.

Self-Check

3-5 Complete the analysis deliverable:

Problem	Object Name	Input/Output	Sample Problem
Round x to n decimals			

3.2.2 Design

The deliverable from this design phase is the algorithm. A pseudocode algorithm can be developed with the help of the Input/Process/Output pattern. That pattern is repeated here for your convenience:

Pattern:	Input/Process/Output (IPO)
Problem:	The program requires input from the user in order to compute and display the desired information.
Outline:	1. Obtain the input data. 2. Process the data in some meaningful way. 3. Output the results.
Example:	See the problem of rounding x to n decimals that follows.

Self-Check

3-6 Write an algorithm that solves this problem.

The Input/Process/Output pattern helps guide placement of the appropriate activities in the proper order. The algorithm represents the general design—an outline of the solution. Add two instances of the Prompt then Input pattern and a more detailed algorithm might now look like this:

1. Prompt for the number to round (call it x).
2. Input x.
3. Prompt for the number of decimals places (call it n).

4. Input n.
5. Round x to n decimals.
6. Display the modified state of x.

Steps 1, 2, 3, 4, and 6 are easy. They can be implemented as input and/or output statements. However, the details of step 5, "Round x to n decimals," are not present. Step 5 needs refinement. With the rest of the problem out of the way, you can focus on the more difficult process of rounding x to n decimals. A solution is a bit tricky, so one method is provided.

To round a number x to n decimal places, first multiply x by 10^n. Then add 0.5 to the new state of x. Then store `floor(x)` in x. Finally, divide x by 10^n. The refined algorithm now becomes

1. Prompt for x, the number to round.
2. Input x.
3. Prompt for n, which is the number of decimal places.
4. Input n.
5. a. Let x become x * 10^n.
   b. Add 0.5 to x.
   c. Let x become `floor(x)`.
   d. Let x become x divided by 10^n.
6. Display the modified state of x.

3.2.3 Walkthrough

Recall from Chapter 1 that algorithm walkthroughs can save time and money. The following walkthrough simulates what will happen to x when it starts at 3.4567 and is rounded to two decimal places.

Round 3.4567 to Two Decimal Places

x = x * 10^n	= 3.4567 * 10^2	= 345.67
x = x + 0.5	= 345.67 + 0.5	= 346.17
x = `floor(x)`	= `floor(346.17)`	= 346
x = x / 10^n	= 346.17 / 100.0	= **3.46**

Self-Check

3-7 Walk through the same algorithm with the different example problem of rounding 9.99 to one decimal place. What is the result? Write the new value for x in the white boxes (x changes state four times after being input).

Algorithm	x	n
1. Prompt for the number to round (call it x).	?	?
2. Input x.	9.99	?
3. Prompt for the number of decimals places (call it n).	9.99	?
4. Input n.	9.99	1
5. Let x become x * 10^n.		1
6. Add 0.5 to x.		1
7. Let x become floor(x).		1
8. Let x become x divided by 10^n.		1
9. Display the modified state of x.		1

3.2.4 Implementation

The complete C++ source code version is a translation of the previous algorithm. Notice that the algorithm steps are embedded as comments in the source code to show how each was translated into C++.

```
// Round a given number to a specific number of decimal places

#include <iostream>  // For cin and cout
#include <cmath>     // For pow(10, n) and floor(x)

using namespace std;

int main()
{
  // Declare objects identified during analysis
  double x = 0.0;
  double n = 0.0;
                                      // Algorithm step number:
  // Input
  cout << "Enter number to round : ";             // 1.
  cin >> x;                                        // 2.
```

```
    cout << "Enter number of decimal places : " ;          // 3.
    cin >> n;                                               // 4.

    // Process (Round x to n decimals)
    x = x * pow(10, n);                                     // 5a.
    x = x + 0.5;                                            //  b.
    x = floor(x);                                           //  c.
    x = x / pow(10, n);                                     //  d.

    // Output (Display the modified state of x)
    cout << "Rounded number : " << x << endl;               // 6.
    return 0;

}
```

DIALOGUE

```
Enter number to round : 3.4567
Enter number of decimal places : 2
Rounded number : 3.46
```

Self-Check

3-8 List at least three sample problems that test the rounding program above.

3-9 What is the final state of `x` after the user enters `3.15` for `x` and `1` for `n`?

3-10 Given the table on page 67, "A Partial List of `cmath` Functions," find a slightly different algorithm that accomplishes the same task where 3.15 rounded to one decimal place would be 3.1 instead of 3.2. (*Hint:* Consider subtracting 0.5 rather than adding it.)

3-11 What values are returned with these function calls?

-a `pow(2.0, 4.0)`

-b `sqrt(16.0)`

-c `ceil(-1.7)`

-d `floor(1.0)`

-e `fabs(-23.4)`

-f `pow(4.0, 2.0)`

3.3 Calls to Documented Functions

All functions must first be declared with a function heading so the compiler can determine whether the function calls are correct. These function headings also help the programmer properly call those functions. If you peruse the file `cmath`, you will see many such function headings.[2]

This section concentrates on how to read these function headings and how to use other documentation describing what a particular function expects and what that function will do. These are called the function's preconditions and postconditions, respectively.

3.3.1 Preconditions and Postconditions

For a function to behave properly, certain conditions are presumed. Consider the `sqrt` function, which presumes that the argument is greater than or equal to 0.0. The *preconditions* of a function state assumptions made about arguments to the function. If the preconditions are not met, all bets are off—the function's behavior is undefined. Some systems cause program termination with an arithmetic overflow error. Other systems may return values such as `-1.#IND` or `NaN`, which represents the value "*N*ot *a* *N*umber." The function call must satisfy the preconditions in order to have predictable results.

The other part of the contract is the *postconditions*—the statements that describe what the function does if the preconditions were met. The pre- and postconditions are often written as part of the function documentation. For example, here is the `sqrt` function documented with preconditions and postconditions:

```
double sqrt(double x)
// precondition:  x is not negative (x >= 0)
// postcondition: Square root of x replaces the function call
```

The comments indicate the argument must be greater than or equal to 0.0. If this precondition is met, the square root of that argument is returned to the *client*—the code that called the function. If the precondition is not met, the result is undefined.

2. Or you might find that `cmath` `#includes` `math.h`, in which case, you should look at the file named `math.h`.

Function Call	Return Result
`sqrt(4.0)`	The precondition was met: `2.0` is returned.
`sqrt(-1.0)`	The precondition was *not* met: result is undefined.[3]

Another implied precondition to calling a function and getting predictable results is this: the client code must supply a proper class of argument. For example, the `ceil` function takes one `double` argument. This implies the argument must be convertible to a `double`. For example, `ceil` will not accept a `string` argument. This could be stated as an obvious precondition like this:

```
double ceil(double x)
// preconditions:  The argument must be convertible to a double
// postconditions: Return the smallest integer >= x
```

However, this information is implied in the parameter declaration. Since failure to provide a proper argument is usually detected by the compiler, from now on such function preconditions will not be written.

It should be noted that most preconditions are not checked by the compiler. For example, it is syntactically correct to have a program with this:

```
cout << sqrt(-1.0);  // Error occurs at runtime, not compiletime
```

From now on, the label for preconditions will be abbreviated as `pre:` and for postconditions as `post:`. The same function (`ceil`) may now be documented as follows:

```
double ceil(double x)
// post: Return the smallest integer >= x
```

3.3.2 Function Headings

Pre- and postconditions help programmers determine the proper use of functions. If provided as documentation, they are usually listed after the function heading. The function heading also provides very important usage information such as the type of value returned and the number of arguments required by the function. Here is the general form of a function heading:

3. This situation is changing because more and more compilers define the square root of a negative number as not a number—appearances vary (`NaN` or `-1.#IND`).

GENERAL FORM 3.2. *Function heading*

return-type function-name **(** *parameter-1, parameter-2, parameter-n* **)**

The *return-type* may be any valid C++ class or the keyword `void`. A `void` function does not return anything. The *parameters* between `(` and `)` may either be value parameters, reference parameters (see Chapter 5), or const reference parameters (see Chapters 5 and 10). Value parameters are first up.

A function may require one or more arguments. Values are passed to functions by adding value parameters of this form:

GENERAL FORM 3.3. *Value parameter*

class-name identifier

EXAMPLES OF FUNCTION HEADINGS

```
double differentParms (double x, string s)
int lesser(int n1, int n2)
string toUpper(string s)
void clearScreen()  // A function with no arguments
```

Function headings specify the type of value returned by the function, the function name, and the number of arguments the programmer must supply. The class of arguments required is specified as the *class-name* of each parameter between the parentheses. For example, because the parameters in `pow` below, `x` and `y`, are declared as `double`, one can ascertain that the class of each argument in calls to `pow` must be `double`, or at least convertible to `double`—an integer constant in line 4, for example.

```
double pow(double x, double y)
// pre:  When y has a fractional part, x must be positive
//       When y is an integer, x may be negative
// post: Returns x to the yth power
```

Also note that the function name is `pow` and its return type is `double`.

Although the complete implementation of the `pow` function is not present, the information supplied by the preconditions, the postconditions, and these function headings is enough to utilize most functions effectively.

To summarize, a function heading with pre- and postconditions provides the following information:

1. the *return-type* that provides the type of value returned by the function
2. the *function-name* that begins a valid function call
3. the *parameter-list* that provides the number and class of arguments required in the function call
4. `pre:`, which describes what must be true before calling this function
5. `post:`, which describes what the function does if the preconditions are met

In addition to revealing information to programmers, function headings supply information to the compiler to verify the validity of every attempt to call that function. The compiler informs you if a function is not called properly.

Consider the `floor` function heading:

```
double floor(double x)
// post: Returns the largest integer <= x
```

The return type is `double`. This means that a `double` replaces any valid call to `floor`. Therefore, the function call can be used wherever a `double` value is legal—in an arithmetic expression, for instance. Also present is the function name `floor`—very important information for effectively calling this or any particular function. The parameter list shows one `double` parameter named `x`. So the client code must supply exactly one numeric argument to properly call `floor`. For example, the following is a valid call to `double` and it is used in a proper spot in the code:

```
double x;
x = floor(5.55555);  // This assignment is okay
```

However, these function calls are invalid:

```
string s;
s = floor(5.5555);  // Error: floor doesn't return a string
cout << floor(1.0, 2.0);       // Error: too many arguments
cout << floor("wrong type");  // Error: wrong class of argument
cout << floor();               // Error: too few arguments
```

3.3.3 The `void` Return Type

All functions shown so far have returned a value—either an `int` or a `double`. Calls to those functions typically exist as a part of another statement. More specifically, you have only seen functions that returned numbers, so the function calls were used as arithmetic expressions (or as part of arithmetic expressions). However, C++ also uses the `void` return type to indicate a function that does not return anything. You will see many `void` functions. Here are two author-supplied `void` functions made available with the file named `compfun`. Neither of these `void` functions requires any arguments. No `void` function can return a value.

```
void causeApause()
// post: The user presses Enter to resume program execution

void clearScreen()
// post: The screen is blank with cursor in upper-left corner
```

This author-supplied `causeApause` function asks the user to press the Enter key before continuing. On at least one system, this function comes in very handy. You can't see the program output without this (or something like `causeApause`). The `clearScreen()` function also does what it sounds like it does.

Here is the major difference between a `void` function and functions that return something:

`void` FUNCTIONS

Rather than being part of statements, `void` functions are statements unto themselves.

The following program illustrates two different function calls that are complete statements by themselves. They do not return anything (as it happens, neither accept any arguments either).

```
#include "compfun"    // For causeApause() and clearScreen()
#include <iostream>   // For cout
using namespace std;

int main()
{
  cout << "This program calls functions that don't return values." << endl;

  causeApause();

  cout << "You won't see me until you've pressed the Enter key." << endl;

  clearScreen();
  cout << "Now you'll see me on a screen that is emp-tee." << endl;
  causeApause();

  return 0;
}
```

OUTPUT: *Screen 1 (the last line was actually unreadable because of clearScreen())*

```
This program calls functions that don't return values.

. . . Press Enter to continue . . .
You won't see me until you've pressed the Enter key.
```

OUTPUT: *Screen 2*

```
Now you'll see me on a screen that is emp-tee.

. . . Press Enter to continue . . .
```

The function call

```
causeApause();  // A statement by itself
```

does not return anything so it would be an error to attempt to display it

```
cout << causeApause() << endl;  // ERROR
```

or to attempt to assign something to it

```
double x = causeApause();       // ERROR
```

It should be noted that, for better or worse, a programmer may ignore the return value for nonvoid functions. The following program executes:

```
#include <cmath>       // For sqrt, ceil, floor
#include <iostream>    // For cout
using namespace std;

int main()
{
  sqrt(4.0);           // Ignore all three return values
  ceil(1.001);
  floor(0.999);

  return 0;
}
```

However, there must be some sort of intent error. The three values returned from the three function calls were ignored. This is the "worse" part. The "better" part of ignoring return values can be summarized by another author-supplied function named `decimals` that does in fact return something:

```
long int decimals(ostream & os, int n)
// pre:  n >= 0
// post: All floating-point output shows n decimal places and the
//       current state of os is returned
```

However, this function return value of `long int` often gets ignored. Instead, the `decimals` function is most often used as if it were a `void` function. The `decimals` function call used as a stand-alone statement formats floating-point output like this (see Chapter 5):

```
#include "compfun"    // For decimals(cout, 2)
#include <iostream>   // For cout
using namespace std;

int main()
{
  double money = 100.00;

  cout << money << endl;

  decimals(cout, 2);

  cout << "Just called decimals(cout, 2)" << endl;

  cout << money << endl;

  return 0;
}
```

OUTPUT

```
100
Just called decimals(cout, 2)
100.00
```

Notice the second output of `money` has a decimal point and trailing zeros.

Self-Check

3-12 Given the following function heading, write "valid" for each correct function call or explain why it is not valid.

`double ceil(double x)`

-a `ceil(1.1)`

-b `floor(2.9)`

-c `ceil(1.2, 3.0)`

-d `ceil("Ceila")`

-e `ceil -0.1`

-f `ceil(-3)`

3-13 Describe the error in each of the following attempts at function headings:

-a `double f ( x )`

-b `int smaller(int n1 int n2)`

-c `toUpper(string s)`

-d `myClass g()`

-e `int foo(string s1, string s2,)`

-f `grid initialize("filename.dat")`

For 3-14 and 3-15, given the following function heading with pre- and postconditions:

```
double floor(double x)
// post: The floor function returns a floating-point value
//       representing the largest integer that is less than or
//       equal to x
```

3-14 Write four function calls (with different arguments) that would help explain how `floor` works to someone who has never seen it before.

3-15 Write the values returned from each of the four function calls in your answer to the preceding question.

3.3.4 Argument / Parameter Associations

A function heading may list zero, one, two, and sometimes more parameters. If there is more than one, the parameters must be separated by commas. The next function heading has two parameters—`str` and `x`.

```
double twoParms(string str, double x)
```

Exactly one argument of an acceptable class is required for each parameter listed in a function heading. Therefore, precisely two arguments must be present in every call to `twoParms`. The compiler will report an error if you call this particular function (`twoParms`) with any other number of arguments than two. Additionally, the class of the arguments must match the class of the parameter. For example, a `double` argument cannot be associated with a `string` parameter. Here are some examples of correct calls of `twoParms`:

Valid Calls to the `twoParms` Function

```
twoParms("abc", 1.2);
twoParms("another string", 15);
twoParms("$", 3.4);
```

The following attempts to call `twoParms` result in compiletime errors:

Error	Reason for Error
`twoParms("a");`	Needs two arguments.
`twoParms("1.1", "2.2");`	The `string` `"2.2"` can't be assigned to a `double`.
`twoParms(1.1, 1.1);`	The number `1.1` can't be assigned to a `string`.
`twoParms("a", 2.2, 3.3);`	One too many arguments.
`twoParms;`	This may only be a warning. Nothing happens—the line of code is ignored.

Arguments associate with parameters by position—first argument to the first parameter, second argument to the second parameter, and so on. For example, when `twoParms` is called, the first parameter is assigned the value of the first argument and the second argument to the function is copied into the second parameter `x`. When `twoParms` is called with arguments `"abc"` and `1.2`, like this:

```
int twoParms (string str, double x)
                           ↑         ↑
result4 = twoParms ("abc",     1.2);
```

it's as if these two assignment operations occur:

```
str = "abc";
x = 1.2;
```

Whatever happens inside `twoParms` now depends on the values of these two parameters. The parameters are used inside the function to produce the return result.

Self-Check

3-16 What value is sent to parameter `str` with `twoParms("1st", 1.2)`?

3-17 What value is sent to parameter `x` with `twoParms("2nd", 3.4)`?

Much can be deduced from a function heading when it is accompanied with the function pre- and postconditions. As review, here is the `sin` function heading complete with pre- and postconditions:

```
double sin(double x)
// post: Returns the sine of x radians
```

The following information is ascertained:

- What happens: returns the sine of x radians
- Return type: `double`
- Function name: `sin`
- Number of arguments: one
- Class of argument: `double` (or an expression convertible to `double`)

The return results can now be determined (with the help of a scientific calculator in radian mode).

Function Call	Return Result
`sin(3.1415926/2.0)`	`1.0`
`sin(1.0)`	`0.8421 // Approximately`
`sin(3.1415926)`	`0.0`

Self-Check

3-18 Given the following `cmath` `pow` function complete with precondition and postcondition documentation, determine the information below:

```
double pow(double x, double y)
// pre:  When y has a fractional part, x must be positive.
//       When y is an integer, x may be negative.
// post: Returns x to the yth power
```

-a return type
-b function name
-c number of arguments
-d class of first argument
-e class of second argument
-f class of third argument

3-19 Write one proper function call to `pow`.

3-20 Is `pow(-81.0, 0.5)` a valid function call? What is the return value?

3-21 Is `pow(-10.0, 2)` a valid function call? What is the return value?

3-22 Is `pow(2, 5)` a valid function call? What is the return value?

3-23 Is `pow(4.0, 0.5)` a valid function call? What is the return value?

3-24 Is `pow(5.0)` a valid function call? What is the return value?

3-25 Write a function heading that returns the fractional component of the first number divided by the second number. Write appropriate pre- and postconditions. For example, `remainder(5.0, 2.0)` must return `0.5` and `remainder(1, 3)` must return `0.3333333`.

3.4 `int` Arithmetic

The C++ language provides several numeric classes. Perhaps the two most often used are `double` and `int`. Discussion of the `int` class was intentionally postponed until now so you had a chance to become comfortable with the `double` class.

An `int` object represents a limited range of *whole numbers*—numbers with no fraction. There are times when `int` is the correct choice over `double`. An `int` object has operations similar to `double` (+, *, -, =, <<, >>), but some differences do exist. For example, a fractional part cannot be stored in an `int` object. The fractional part is lost during the assignment operation.

```
int anInt = 1.999;
// assert: The state of anInt is 1, not 1.999
```

The `/` operator has different meanings for `int` and `double` operands. Whereas the result of `3.0 / 4.0` is `0.75`, the result of `3 / 4` is `0`. Two integer operands with the `/` operator have an integer result—not a floating-point result. So what happens? An integer divided by an integer results in the integer quotient. For example, the quotient obtained from dividing 3 by 4 is 0. This implies that the same operator (`/` in this case) has a different meaning when it has two integer operands.

Another difference is that `int` objects have a remainder operation symbolized with the `%` operator. For example, the result of `18 % 4` is the integer remainder after dividing 18 by 4, which is 2. Here are three more examples (Figure 3.1).

Figure 3.1

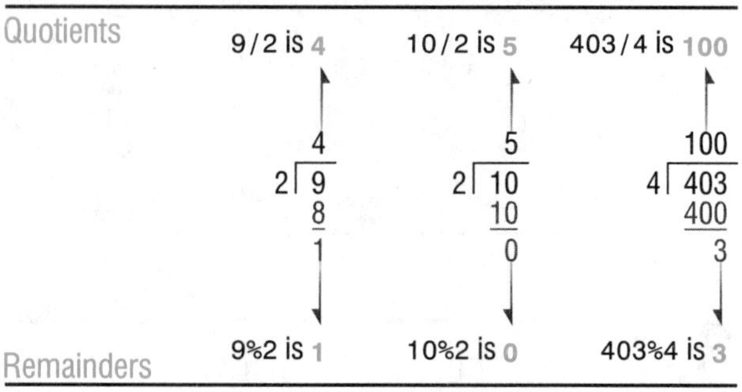

These differences are illustrated in the following program, which shows `%` and `/` operating on integer expressions and `/` operating on floating-point operands. In this example, the integer results describe whole hours and whole minutes rather than the fractional equivalent.

```
// This program provides an example of int division with '/' for
// the quotient and '%' for the remainder

#include <iostream>

using namespace std;

int main()
{
  // Declare objects that will be given meaningful values later
  int totalMinutes, minutes, hours,
  double fractionalHour;

  // Input
  cout << "Enter total minutes: ";
  cin >> totalMinutes;

  // Process
  fractionalHour = totalMinutes / 60.0;
  hours = totalMinutes  / 60;
  minutes = totalMinutes % 60;

  // Output
  cout <<  totalMinutes  << " minutes can be rewritten as "
       << fractionalHour << " hours " << endl;  // Shows a fraction
  cout << "or as "
       << hours   << " hours and "
       << minutes << " minutes"       << endl;
```

```
  return 0;
}
```

DIALOGUE (EXACT APPEARANCE OF FLOATING-POINT OUTPUT VARIES BETWEEN SYSTEMS)

```
Enter total minutes: 254
254 minutes can be rewritten as 4.23333 hours
or as 4 hours and 14 minutes
```

The preceding program indicates that even though `int`s and `double`s are similar, there are times when `double` is the more appropriate class than `int`, and vice versa. The `double` class should be specified when you need a numeric object with a decimal component. If you need whole numbers, select the `int` class. Also, once the class is chosen, you should consider the differences in some of the arithmetic operators. For example, although the `+`, `-`, `/`, and `*` operations can be applied to `double` operands, the `%` operator may only be used with two integer operands.

Self-Check

3-26 What value is stored in `nickel`?

```
int change = 97;
int nickel = 0;
nickel = change % 25 % 10 / 5;
```

3-27 What value is stored in `nickel` when `change` is initialized to:

-a 4
-b 5
-c 10
-d 15
-e 49
-f 0

3.4.1 Mixing Integer and Floating-Point Operands

Whenever integer and floating-point values are on opposite sides of an arithmetic operator, the integer operand is promoted to its floating-point equivalent (3 becomes 3.0, for example). The expression then results in a floating-point number. The same rule applies when one operand is an `int` object and the other a `double`.

```
// Display the value of an expression with a mix of operands
#include <iostream>
using namespace std;
```

```
int main()
{
  int n = 10;
  double sum = 567.9;

  cout << (sum / n) << endl;

  return 0;
}
```

OUTPUT

```
56.79
```

Self-Check

3-28 Evaluate the following expressions:

-a `5 / 9`

-b `5.0 / 9`

-c `5 / 9.0`

-d `2 + 4 * 6 / 3`

-e `(2 + 4) * 6 / 3`

-f `5 / 2`

3.5 Implementation Errors and Warnings

There are several types of errors and warnings that occur during the implementation phase of program development:

- *compiletime*—errors that occur during compilation
- *warnings*—there may be something wrong, but the compiler will accept what you have
- *linktime*—errors that occur when the linker cannot find what it needs
- *runtime*—errors that occur while the program is executing
- *intent*—the program does what was typed, not what was intended

The next figure illustrates that the compiler translates source code into machine code and that the linker puts together several pieces of machine code to create an executable program. Both the compiler and the linker detect and report certain errors and warnings.

FIGURE 3.2. *Compiling and linking to create an executable program*

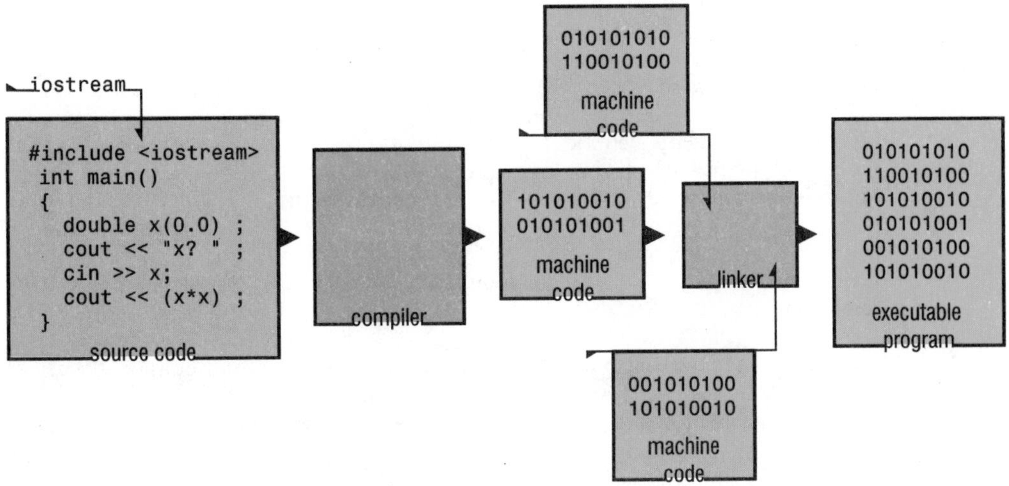

3.5.1 Errors Detected at Compiletime

A programming language requires strict adherence to its own set of formal syntax rules. Unfortunately, it is easy to violate these syntax rules while translating algorithms into their programming language equivalents. All it takes is a missing { or ; to really foul things up. As the C++ compiler translates source code into a program that can be run on the computer, it also

- locates and reports as many errors as possible
- warns of potential problems that are syntactically legal, but might cause errors later

A *compiletime error* occurs when the C++ compiler recognizes the violation of a syntax rule. The machine code cannot be created until all compiletime errors have been removed from the program. And if the machine code is not created, the linker cannot create an executable program. Many strange-looking error messages can be generated by the compiler as it reads the source code. Unfortunately, deciphering these compiletime error messages takes practice, patience, and prematurely, a fairly complete knowledge of the language. So in an effort to improve this situation, here are some examples of common compiletime errors and how they are corrected. *Note:* Your compiler will generate different error messages.[4]

4. Each compiler has its own way of telling the programmer that something is wrong. Your error messages will look nothing like those in the left column. The messages are likely to be much more cryptic such as `Parse error at line 23`.

Error Detected by a Compiler	Incorrect Code	Corrected Code
Splitting an identifier	int Total Weight = 0;	int total_Weight = 0; // Or totalWeight = 0;
Misspelling a keyword	integer sum = 0 ;	int sum;
Misspelling a standard identifier	out << "Hello";	cout << "Hello";

Misspelling an identifier	int studentNumber;
	studentNum = 1;
		// Missing 'ber'
		studentNumber = 1012;

Leaving off a required semicolon	double x = 0.0 x = 1.23;	double x = 0.0; x = 1.23;
Not closing a string constant	cout << "Hello;	cout << "Hello";
Failing to declare an object	cin >> testScore;	double testScore; cin >> testScore;
Ignoring case sensitivity	double x; X = 5.0;	double x; x = 5.0;
Forgetting the argument	cout << sqrt;	cout << sqrt(x);
Using wrong class of argument	cout << sqrt("12");	cout << sqrt(12.0);
Using too many arguments	cout << ceil(1.2, 3);	cout << ceil(1.2);

Forgetting namespace std; on standard compilers	#include <iostream>
	int main()
	{ // cout is unknown
	  cout << "Hello";
	}
		#include <iostream>
		using namespace std;
		int main()
		{
		  cout << "Hello";
		}

Adding using namespace std; on older nonstandard compilers	#include <iostream>
	using namespace std;
	int main()
	{
	  cout << "Hello";
	  return 0;
	}
		#include <iostream>
		int main()
		{
		  cout << "Hello";
		  return 0;
		}

Compilers generate many error messages. However, please realize that it is your source code that is the source of these errors. Whenever your compiler appears to be nagging you, remember that the compiler is trying to help you correct *your* errors as much as possible. The compiler is your friend—believe it or not.

The following program attempts to show several errors the compiler should eventually detect and report. Because error messages generated by compilers vary among systems, the comments indicate the reason for the error—they are not an attempt to match your compiletime error messages. Your system will certainly generate quite different error messages.

```
// This attempt at a program contains many errors--over a dozen.
// Add #include <iostream>, and there are only eight errors.
using namespace std;

int main   // 1. No () after main
{          // 2. All occurrences of cin and cout are errors because
           //    the directive #include <iostream> is missing
  int pounds = 0;

  cout << "Begin execution" << endl      // Missing ; after endl
  cout >> "Enter weight in pounds: ";    // >> should be <<
  cin << pounds;                         // << should be >>
  cout << "In the U.K., you";            // Extra ;
       << " weigh " << (Pounds / 14)     // Pounds is not declared
       << " stone, " (pounds % 14)    // Missing << after "stone, "
       << endl                        // Missing ; after endl
  return 0;                           // Missing right brace }
```

Compilers generate some rather cryptic messages. When the program shown above compiled with one particular compiler, six errors occurred, all reporting `Type name expected`. Other systems generate a different crop of errors. Another Unix compiler generated eight completely different errors. Compiletime error messages take some getting used to, so try to be patient and observe the location where the compiletime error occurred. The error is usually in the vicinity of the line where the error was detected, although you may have to fix preceding lines. Always remember to fix the first error first. The error not reported until line 23 may be the result of a forgotten semicolon on line 4.

The corrected source code, without error, is given next, followed by an interactive dialogue:

```
// There are no compiletime errors here
#include <iostream>
using namespace std;

int main()
{
  int pounds;
```

```
  cout << "Begin execution" << endl;
  cout << "Enter your weight in pounds: ";
  cin >> pounds;
  cout << "In the U.K., "
       << "you weigh "  << ( pounds / 14 )
       << " stone, "    << ( pounds % 14 )  << endl;

  return 0;
}
```

DIALOGUE

```
Begin execution
Enter your weight in pounds: 146
In the U.K., you weigh 10 stone, 6
```

It should also be noted that one small compiletime error can result in a cascade of errors. For example, omitting `{` after `int main()` in an otherwise error-free program caused the GNU g++ compiler to generate 12 compiletime errors!

```
#include <iostream>  // For the cout and cin objects
#include <string>    // For a string class
using namespace std;

int main()
{ // <- Without the left curly brace, there were 12 errors!
  double x;
  string str;

  cout << "Enter a double: ";
  cin >> x;

  cout << "Enter a string: ";
  cin >> str;

  return 0;
}
```

On the other hand, the SunOS C++ compiler only reported one error, and it was more decipherable: `"{" expected not double`. So it is possible that fixing the first error might correct many other errors. It is also true that fixing one error might let the compiler find new ones! Try to concentrate on the first error your compiler reports. The compiler usually, but not always, will be able to approximate the location of the error in your source code. The error may be on the line above, or many lines above. Also, realize that statements are terminated by a semicolon (`;`). Exclusion of this statement terminator or its presence where it does not belong are common syntax violations. Missing semicolon errors are not usually detected until the compiler has already gone past the line with the offense. So look at the statement above the location of the error.

3.5.2 Warnings Generated at Compiletime

Compilers also generate *warnings,* which are messages intended to help programmers avoid errors later on. Consider the following code:

```
#include <iostream>
using namespace std;
int main()
{
  double x, y;
  y = 2 * x;
  cout << y << endl;
  return 0;
}
```

Self-Check

3-29 What is the output of the preceding program?

The preceding program has an error, but none that the compiler will catch. The compiler happily translated the source code into machine code and the linker created an executable program. However, the output from one program was this rather inexplicable number: `1.09087e+82`. Fortunately, some compilers will generate a warning like this (`definition` here means "assigned a value"):

```
Warning: Possible use of 'x' before definition in function main()
```

The warning states that `x` has been used before it was defined (initialized, actually). This is a good warning that should not be ignored. The program does not initialize `x`. It has an unknown state sometimes referred to as *garbage.* Unfortunately, not all compilers will warn you of this potential error.

This is not a violation of any syntax rule. It is legal to *declare* objects without an initial value. However, this warning should not be ignored. You should read it and make sure `x` has an initialized state before using the object in an arithmetic expression.[5]

5. To get a full list of warnings in GNU g++ (if the program is in a file named `p91.C`), issue this command: `g++ -O -Wall p91.C`

This is but one example of a warning. You will see more. You will likely ignore many. However, warnings are hints that something is going to go wrong. Don't ignore them. If you are getting incorrect results, look to see if there are any warnings—they may be clues to the source of the error.

On the other hand, there are some warnings that can be ignored if you understand what they mean. For example, many compilers like to have the statement `return 0;` at the bottom of `main`, as shown here:

```
int main()
{
  return 0;
  // Some compilers issue a warning if return 0; is not present
}
```

Writing `return 0;`, a tradition for C and C++ programs, is no longer required by the new C++ standard. But your compiler may not yet recognize this recent change. So if you omit `return 0;`, you may get a warning that looks something like this:

```
main function should return a value
```

or

```
void return type assumed
```

You can eliminate this warning by adding `return 0;` immediately before the closing curly brace `}`. Or you can safely ignore the warning. However, if you get the same warning when implementing functions later on, do not ignore this warning. Then it will have significant meaning. In fact, your compiler might generate an error and the program will never run until you return something. In either case, you should read the warnings. Unfortunately, you might spend a good deal of time trying to decipher error messages such as `Invalid indirection` or `type mismatch in call to sqrt` and warnings such as `converted main function to int` or `possibly suspicious assignment`. With time and further study, these compiler messages will make more sense and become more beneficial.

3.5.3 Linktime Errors

Computer systems use a *linker* to combine pieces of machine code to create executable programs. Among other things, the linker must resolve details such as locating the identifier `main` in one of these files. If `main` is not found during the linking process, the linker generates an error that displays `Undefined symbol main`. If this takes place, verify that your program starts with `int main`.

```
int main()
{ // . . .
}
```

Make sure that `main` is not typed as `mane`, `Main`, or `MAIN`.

3.5.4 Runtime Errors

A program may execute after all compiletime errors have been removed and the linker has created an executable program. But errors may still occur while the program is running. A *runtime error* may cause the program to terminate before it should because some event occurs that the computer cannot handle. Examples of runtime errors include invalid numeric input and an attempt to pick up a cookie that is not there (see the `grid` class in the next chapter). First, consider the following program that runs without error:

```
// When this program is run and 0 is entered for n, a runtime error
// occurs (division by 0)
#include <iostream>
using namespace std;

int main()
{
  double sum = 0.0;
  double average = 0.0;
  int n = 0;

  // Input
  cout << "Enter sum : ";
  cin >> sum;
  cout << "Enter n   : ";
  cin >> n;

  // Process
  average =  sum / n;

  // Output
  cout << "Average   : " << average << endl;
  return 0;
}
```

When the input data is `291` followed by `3`, the program executes and terminates normally after showing the average.

```
Enter sum : 291
Enter n   : 3
Average   : 97
```

However, if 0 is used to define n, division by zero occurs. Since division by zero is not defined mathematically, the program may terminate abnormally. And it is preferable to have programs terminate normally—under the control of the user.

The dialogue shown next indicates that the output for average never occurred. The division by zero caused abnormal program termination before the output statement.

```
Enter sum : 291
Enter n   : 0      <ERROR>
```

The error message is system dependent. Two errors encountered on two particular compilers included: `Arithmetic exception (core dumped)` and `Floating point error: Divide by 0 Abnormal program termination`. However, with a standard C++ compiler, there is no runtime error. Instead a special value for infinity or "not a number" may be returned. These values might look something like `-1.#IND` or `NaN`. So the program may terminate normally with a dialogue like this:

```
Enter sum : 291
Enter n   : 0
Average   : -1.#IND
```

Using the same program with invalid numeric input results in a different type of runtime error. The input stream is corrupted with invalid numeric input, and subsequent input operations may be ignored. In at least two environments, this does occur and `cin >> n` is ignored. This results in an undefined value for the expression `sum / n`.

```
Enter sum : BadData
Enter n   :   Average : 6.56360e-20
```

Your environment may handle this situation differently. For example, another system generated the bogus runtime error `Square root of a negative number`. Hey, the compiler is a very complex program. It is not always perfect. Like any other product, some are better than others.

3.5.5 Intent Errors

Even when no compiletime errors are found and no runtime errors occur, the program still may not execute properly. A program may run and terminate normally, but it may not be correct. Let's make one small change to the previous program to get an incorrect program.

```
cout << "Average   : " << (n / sum);
```

The interactive dialogue may now look like this:

```
Enter sum : 291
Enter n   : 3
Average   : 0.010309
```

Such *intent errors* occur when the program does what was typed, not what was intended. Unfortunately, the compiler does not locate intent errors. The expression `n / sum` is syntactically correct—the compiler just has no way of knowing that this programmer intended to write `sum / n` instead.

Of these categories of errors, intent errors are the most insidious and usually the most difficult to correct. They may also be difficult to detect—the user, tester, or programmer may not know they even exist! Consider the program controlling the Therac 3 cancer radiation therapy machine. Patients received massive overdoses of radiation resulting in serious injury and death while the indicator displayed everything as normal. Another infamous intent error involved a program controlling a probe that was supposed to go to Venus. Because a period was used instead of a comma in the Fortran source code, an American Viking Venus probe burnt up in the sun. Both controlling programs had compiled successfully and were running at the time of the accidents. However, they did what the programmers had written—clearly not what was intended.

Self-Check

3-30 Assuming a program is supposed to find an average given the total sum and number of objects in a set, then the following dialogue is generated. What clue reveals the presence of an intent error?

```
Enter sum: 100
Number   : 4
Average  : 0.04
```

3-31 Assuming the following code was used to generate the dialogue above, how is the intent error to be corrected?

```
// Input
cout << "Enter sum: ";
cin >> n;
cout << "Number   : ";
cin >> sum;
```

```
// Process
average = sum / n;
// Output
cout << "Average  : " << average << endl;
```

3-32 List the type of error (compiletime, runtime, linktime, or intent) or warning that exists when the last statement in the preceding program is changed to:

-a `cout << "Average: " << "sum / n";`

-b `cout << "Average: " << sum / (n - n);`

-c `cout << "Average: ", sum / n;`

-d `cout << "Average: " << sum / n`

3.5.6 When the Software Doesn't Match the Specification

Even when a process has been automated and delivered to the customer in working order as per the perceptions of the developers, there may still be errors. There have been many instances of software working, but not doing what it was supposed to do. This could be from a failure to meet the problem statement, which occurs when the software developers don't understand the customer's problem statement. Something could have been missed. Something could have been misinterpreted.

A related error occurs when the customer specifies the problem incorrectly. This could be the case when the requester isn't sure what she or he wants. A trivial or critical omission in specification may occur, or the request may not be written clearly. Also, the requester may change her or his mind after program development has begun.

For the most part, the programming projects in this textbook simply ask you to fulfill the problem statement. If you think there is an omission or there is something you don't understand, don't hesitate to ask questions. It is better to understand the problem and know what it is that you are to trying to solve, before getting to the design and implementation phases of program development. Although not intended, the problem may be incorrectly or incompletely specified—this does actually happen in the real world!

Chapter Summary

You have now been confronted with a large variety of details concerning the C++ programming language, expressions, program development, function calls, and the types of errors that occur during program development. This can be somewhat overwhelming at first, especially if you have never programmed before. However, most of these details are necessary for implementation of even the simplest program:

- Including `cmath` provides access to many mathematical and trigonometric functions.
- Functions that have a return type of `double` can be used wherever a `double` (or floating-point expression) can be used. Many of the `cmath` functions return `double`.
- Most `cmath` functions require one numeric argument; `pow` requires two.
- Rounding `x` to `n` decimals is yet another instance of the IPO algorithmic pattern. The process step was more complex than others to date.
- Preconditions and postconditions represent a contract between the function and the client code that calls the function. This documentation or some other form of documentation helps someone understand what the function does.
- The function heading itself provides vital usage information such as the return type, the function name, and the number of parameters so the programmer knows how many arguments to include in the call.
- Arguments are associated with parameters by position. It doesn't matter what names are used. The first argument is associated with the first parameter, the second argument with the second parameter, and so on.
- Arguments passed to parameters are like assignment statements. The argument must be compatible with the parameter (the same class). Passing a `double` to an `int` results in loss of value.
- When `/` has two integer operands, the result is an integer, so `5 / 2` is `2`.
- When `/` has at least one floating-point operand, the result is a floating-point number, so `5 / 2.0` is `2.5`.
- The `%` operator returns the integer remainder of one integer operand divided by another, so `5 % 2` is `1`.
- The `%` operator cannot have a floating-point argument, so `5 / 2.0` is a compiletime error.
- Be careful in choosing `int` and `double`. Always use `double` to store numbers unless it makes sense that the object can only store integers. (*Note:* In Chapter 10, "Vectors,"

you will be required to use `int` instead of `double` to specify the number of elements in a collection.

- This chapter ended with a discussion of the variety of errors that occur during implementation. You will continue to encounter errors. It is part of the process.
- Errors may be present because the problem statement was incorrect or incomplete.
- Intent errors eventually prove to be the most difficult to fix—they are often difficult even to detect. Nothing is perfect, including the programs that you pay for that are often released with known errors (called *bugs* or *issues* in an effort to pretend they are not errors).
- Testing is important, but it does not prove the absence of errors. Testing can and does detect errors, but it can only build confidence that the program appears to work.

Exercises

1. Write the output generated by the following programs:

a.
```
#include <iostream>
using namespace std;
int main()
{
  const int MAX = 5;
  cout << (MAX / 2.0) << endl;
  cout << (2.0 / MAX) << endl;
  cout << (2 / MAX) << endl;
  cout << (MAX / 2) << endl;
  return 0;
}
```

b.
```
#include <iostream>
using namespace std;
int main()
{
  int j = 14;
  int k = 3;
  cout << "Quotient: "
       << (j / k) << endl;
  cout << "Remainder: "
       << (j % k) << endl;
  return 0;
}
```

c.
```
#include <iostream>
using namespace std;
int main()
{
   int j = 4;
   double x = 3.5;
   j = j + x;
   cout << j << endl;
   return 0;
}
```

d.
```
#include <iostream>
using namespace std;
int main()
{
  const double PI = 3.14159;
  int j = 150;
  j = j * 0.1;
  cout << j << endl ;
  cout << (2 * PI) << endl;
  return 0;
}
```

e.
```
#include <iostream>
using namespace std;
#include <string>
int main()
{
  const string pipe = " | ";
  cout << pipe << (1 + 5.5)
       << pipe << (3 + 3 / 3)
       << pipe << (1 + 2) / (3 + 4)
       << pipe << (1 + 2 * 3 / 4);
   return 0;
}
```

f.
```
#include <iostream>
using namespace std;
int main()
{
  int j = 11;
  cout << "  " << (j % 2)
       << "  " << (j / 2)
       << "  " << ((j - j) / 2);
   return 0;
}
```

2. Evaluate the following expressions. Use a decimal point to distinguish integer and floating-point values.

   a. `5 / 2`
   b. `5 / 2.0`
   c. `101 % 2`
   d. `5.0 / 2.0`
   e. `1.0 + 2.0 - 3.0 * 4.0`
   f. `100 % 2`

3. Write the return result for each function call or explain the error.

   a. `pow(3.0, 2.0)`
   b. `pow(-2, 5)`
   c. `ceil(1.001)`
   d. `ceil(-1.2)`
   e. `pow(16.0, 0.5)`
   f. `pow(-16.0, 2)`
   g. `fabs(-123.4)`
   h. `sqrt(-1.0)`
   i. `sqrt(sqrt(16.0))`
   j. `ceil 1.1`
   k. `floor()`
   l. `sqrt(0)`

4. Use these object initializations to evaluate the expressions that follow:

```
double x = 5.0;
double y = 7.5;
```

a. `sqrt(x - 1.0)`

b. `ceil(y - 0.5)`

c. `sqrt(y - x + 2.0)`

d. `pow(10, 2)`

e. `floor(y + 0.5)`

f. `pow(x, 3.0)`

g. `fabs(y - x)`

h. `pow(10, 3)`

5. What is the value of `pow(4, pow(2, 3))`?

6. Write an algorithm that shows the range of a projectile. The formula is range = sin(2 * *angle*) * *velocity*^{2} / *gravity*, where *angle* is the angle of the projectile's takeoff (in radians), *velocity* is the initial velocity of the projectile (in meters per second), and *gravity* is acceleration due to gravity at 9.8 meters per second.

7. What happens if the client program does not satisfy the preconditions of a called function?

8. What information do postconditions provide?

9. Which of the following represent valid function headings?

a. `int large(int a, int b)`

b. `double(double a, double b)`

c. `int f(int a; int b;)`

d. `int f(a, int b)`

e. `double f()`

f. `string c(string a)`

10. Name at least three possible return types from a C++ function.

11. What is the value of `quarter` when `change` is initialized as follows:

a. `0`

b. `74`

c. `49`

d. `549`

```
int change = 0, quarter = 0;
change = __?__;
quarter = change % 50 / 25;
```

12. Is this code legal?

```
const double EPSILON = 0.000001;
EPSILON = 999999.9;
```

13. Given the following function heading with pre- and postconditions,

```
double fmod( double x, double y )
// post: Calculates the floating-point remainder.
//       fmod returns the floating-point remainder of x / y.
//       If the value of y is 0.0, fmod returns Not a Number.
// Header required: <cmath>
```

write six function calls (with different arguments) that would adequately test `fmod` and would also help explain how `fmod` works to someone who has never seen it before.

14. Write the values returned from each of the six function calls in your answer to the preceding question.

15. Write C++ code that generates a runtime error and give the reason for the error.

16. At what time will the error in this code be detected?

```
#include <iostream>
using namespace std;
int Main()
{
  cout << "Hello world";
  return 0;
}
```

17. Explain how to fix the error in each of these lines:

a. `cout << "Hello world"`

b. `cout >> "Hello world";`

c. `cout "Hello World";`

d. `cout << "Hello World;`

18. Explain the error in this attempt at a program:

```
int main()
{
  cout << "Hello world";
}
```

19. Describe the phrase *intent error*.

20. Does the following code always correctly assign the average of the three `doubles` `x`, `y`, and `z` to `average`?

```
double average =  x + y + z / 3.0;
```

21. What value is stored in `average` after this expression executes?

```
double average = (81 + 90 + 83) / 3;
```

22. Given this assignment statement for the slope of a line,

```
slope = (y2 - y1) / (x2 - x1);
```

evaluate the value stored in `slope`:

x1	y1	x2	y2	slope
0.0	0.0	1.0	1.0	_____
0.0	0.0	-1.0	1.0	_____
6.0	5.2	6.0	-14.5	_____

Programming Tips

1. If you don't have a standard compiler, use the following program beginning to access the math functions:

```
// 1. Add .h after iostream
// 2. Change cmath to math.h
// 3. Don't write using namespace std;

#include <iostream.h>  // For cout
#include <math.h>      // For sqrt

int main()
{
   cout << sqrt(16.0) << endl;
   return 0;
}
```

2. Make sure you supply the correct number and class of arguments.

The function heading provides this information. Count the number of parameters between `(` and `)`. Make sure the arguments are of the same class.

3. Integer arithmetic behaves unexpectedly for some students.

Integer division results in an integer. Therefore `5 / 2` is `2`, not the `2.5` your brain and calculator feel are so right.

4. The `%` arithmetic operator causes confusion.

Experience shows some students never understand `%`, or at least they still get the wrong answers on the final exam. The expression `a % b` is the integer remainder after dividing `a` by `b`. Try these now:

```
99 % 50 = ___                    101 % 2 = ____
99 % 50 % 25 = ____              102 % 2 = ____
4 % 99 = ____                    103 % 2 = ____
```

5. The computer is more than a calculator.

You might have the impression that the computer is nothing more than a fancy calculator. Please wait until you get through Chapter 13 to decide. By that point you will have seen other classes besides numbers and strings. You will see `bankAccount`, `cardReader`, `CD`, and `jukeBox` objects and other objects for storing collections of anything (`vector`, `bag`, and `list`).

Programming Projects

3A `cmath` Functions

Write a program that allows the user to enter any number. After an appropriate label, show the return value from each of the following functions (assume `x` represents the number input by the user):

1. the square root of `x`
2. `x` to the 2.5 power
3. the ceiling of `x`
4. the floor of `x`
5. the absolute value of `x`

Your dialogue should look like this:

```
Enter a number for x: 2.5
sqrt(x)      : 1.5814
pow(x, 2.5)  : 6.25
ceil(x)      : 3
floor(x)     : 2
fabs(x)      : 2.5
```

3B Circle

Write a C++ program that inputs a value for the radius of a circle (`r`) from the keyboard and then outputs the diameter, circumference, and area of the circle. Use the `pow` function to compute the area.

- diameter = 2 * radius
- circumference = pi * diameter
- area = pi * radius^2

Initialize `PI` as a constant object with the value of 3.14159. Your dialogue should look like this (*Note:* Output of floating-point numbers varies among C++ compilers, so your output might be slightly different—especially in the number of decimal places shown for `Circumference` and `Area`):

```
Enter Radius   : 1.0
Diameter       : 2.0
Circumference  : 6.28318
Area           : 3.14159
```

Run your program with radius = `1.0`. Verify that your values for circumference and area match the preceding dialogue. After this, run your program with the input radii of `2.0` and `2.5` and verify that the output is what you expect.

3C More Rounding

Write a program that asks the user for a number and displays that number rounded to zero, one, two, and three decimal places. Your dialogue should look like this:

```
Enter the number to round:    3.4567
3.4567 rounded to 0 decimals = 3
3.4567 rounded to 1 decimal  = 3.5
3.4567 rounded to 2 decimals = 3.46
3.4567 rounded to 3 decimals = 3.457
```

3D Range

Write a program that determines the range of a projectile using this formula:

range = sin(2 * *angle*) * $velocity^2$ / *gravity*

where *angle* is the angle of the projectile's path (in radians), *velocity* is the initial velocity of the projectile (in meters per second), and *gravity* is acceleration at 9.8 meters per second (a constant).

The takeoff angle must be input in degrees, therefore you must convert this angle to its radian equivalent. This is necessary because the trigonometric function `sin(x)` assumes the argument (`x`) is an angle expressed in radians. An angle in degrees can be converted to radians by multiplying the number of degrees by $\pi/180$ where $\pi \approx 3.14159$. For example, 45° = 45 * 3.14159/180, or 0.7853975 radians. The velocity is presumed to be input in meters per second. Make your interactive dialogue look like this:

```
Takeoff Angle (in degrees): 45.0
Initial Velocity (meters per second): 100.0
Range = 1020.41 meters
```

3E F to C

Use the following formula that converts Fahrenheit (F) temperatures to Celsius (C):

C = $^5/_9$(F - 32)

Write a C++ program that inputs a Fahrenheit temperature and outputs the Celsius equivalent. Your dialogue must look like these two dialogues when `212` and `98.6` are entered for `F`:

```
Enter F: 212
212 F is 100 C
```

```
Enter F: 98.6
98.6 F is 37 C
```

3F C to F

Use algebra and the formula of the preceding programming project to convert degrees Celsius (C) to degrees Fahrenheit (F). Write a C++ program that inputs any Celsius temperature and displays the Fahrenheit equivalent of any degrees Celsius. Your dialogue must look like this when the user enters `-40` and `37` for `C`:

```
Enter C: -40
-40 C is -40 F
```

```
Enter C: 37
37 C is 98.6 F
```

3G Seconds

Write a program that reads a value in seconds and displays the number of hours, minutes, and seconds represented by the input. Here are two sample dialogues:

```
Enter seconds: 32123
8:55:23
```

```
Enter seconds: 61
0:1:1
```

3H U.S. Change

Write a C++ program that prompts for an integer that represents the amount of change (in cents) to be handed back to a customer in the United States. First, display the minimum number of half dollars, quarters, dimes, nickels, and pennies that will make the correct change. (*Hint:* With increasingly longer expressions, you could use `/` and `%` to evaluate the number of each coin. Or you could calculate the total number of coins with `/` and the remaining change with `%`.) Verify that your program works correctly by running it with a variety of input. Here are two sample dialogues:

```
Enter change [0...99] : 83
Half(ves)  : 1
Quarter(s) : 1
Dime(s)    : 0
Nickel(s)  : 1
Penny(ies) : 3
```

```
Enter change [0...99] : 14
Half(ves)  : 0
Quarter(s) : 0
Dime(s)    : 1
Nickel(s)  : 0
Penny(ies) : 4
```

3I U.K. Change

Write a C++ program that prompts for an integer that represents the amount of change in pence to be handed back to a customer in the United Kingdom. Display the minimum number of coins that will make the correct change. The available coins are (p represents pence) 1p, 2p, 5p, 10p, 20p, 50p, and 100p (the one-pound coin). Verify that your program works correctly by running it with a variety of input. Here are two sample dialogues:

```
Enter change: 298
100p : 2
 50p : 1
 20p : 2
 10p : 0
  5p : 1
  2p : 1
  1p : 1
```

```
Enter change: 93
100p : 0
 50p : 1
 20p : 2
 10p : 0
  5p : 0
  2p : 1
  1p : 1
```

Chapter Four

Messages and Member Functions

Summing Up

Chapter 3 presented calls to functions that performed arithmetic and trigonometric operations with numbers. These functions represent only a small portion of available nonmember functions. Nonmember functions—those that are not part of a specific class—continue to play a role in the C++ language. You can use new functions by reading the function headings and associated documentation. By now you should have completed enough programs to appreciate the variety of errors discussed at the end of the previous chapter.

Coming Up

Chapter 4 introduces messages to existing objects, which have a calling syntax different from the nonmember function calls discussed in Chapter 3. This chapter explores some of the standard member functions of the classes `string`, `ostream`, and `istream`. Other author-supplied classes (`bankAccount` and `grid`) will also help you develop problem-solving skills while encouraging you to contemplate the increasing importance of objects during analysis, design, and implementation. After studying this chapter, you will be able to

* send messages to objects
* send a few `string` and `ostream` messages and understand their effects
* problem solve with `grid` and `bankAccount` objects
* appreciate why programmers partition software into classes, which are collections of member functions combined with related data

Exercises and programming projects to reinforce sending messages

4.1 Modeling the Real World

Consider the following problem statement from the realm of banking:

Implement a bank teller application to allow bank customers to access bank accounts through an identification number. The customer, with the help of the teller, may complete any of the following transactions: withdraw money, deposit money, query account balances, and view transactions between any two given dates. The system must maintain the correct balances for all accounts and produce monthly statements.

You are not expected to develop a solution at this point. However, you should be able to pick out some objects relevant to the banking industry. This is the first step in the analysis phase of object-oriented software development (see Chapter 12). One simple tool for finding objects to model a solution is to write down all the reasonable nouns and noun phrases in the problem statement. Consider each as a potential class for representing part of a solution. The major classes during analysis come from sources such as these:

- the problem statement
- an understanding of the problem domain (knowledge of the system that the problem statement may have missed or taken for granted)
- the words floating around in the air during analysis of the problem

The classes should model the real world whenever possible. Here are some possible classes that may need to be either bought or built.

POTENTIAL CLASSES TO MODEL A SOLUTION (SIMPLIFIED BY AVOIDING REDUNDANCIES)

```
teller                      transaction
customer                    list of transactions
bank account                date
identification number       monthly statement
```

After studying this textbook through Chapter 13, you will be able to implement this bank teller application and others like it: a jukebox for the student union, a voice-mail system, and a video-rental system. For the time being, let's consider one of the classes identified as a potential partial solution to this problem: the bank account.

4.1.1 The bankAccount Class

The bankAccount class has become a canonical first example in the study of object-oriented programming. It is easy to relate to. For example, it is probably easier to understand withdrawing money from a bankAccount than finding the floor of a number.

The bankAccount class allows for many objects, each representing a checking or savings account at a bank. Using your knowledge of bank accounts, you might recognize that each bankAccount object should at least know its own account number and its own account balance. Many other elements could be part of the state of every bankAccount object—transaction list, personal identification number (PIN), and mother's maiden name, for example. You might visualize other banking operations such as creating a new account, making deposits and withdrawals, and being able to access the current balance. There could also be many other banking operations—applying interest and printing statements, for example. However, this particular bankAccount class that is about to be presented has been intentionally kept simple for ease of study.

The bankAccount objects shown in this text are initialized with two arguments in this order:

1. a string to represent the account ID
2. a number to represent the initial account balance

Whereas ints, doubles, and strings could be initialized with only one argument, like this:

```
                                  // Equivalent initializations
int n = 0;                        // int n(0);
double x = 0.000001;              // double x(0.0);
string name = "Initial string";  // string name("Initial string");
```

bankAccount objects require two. Initialization with = is not an option. Some object constructions require more than one value to set the initial state. This is accomplished as a function call to the class constructor. Wrap the arguments in parentheses like this:

```
// Initialize one bankAccount object with two arguments
bankAccount anAccount("Gosch", 100.00);
```

Later in this chapter you will see an object that requires five arguments in the call to the constructor.

4.1.2 Messages

True objects such as `cin`, `cout` and any `string` object have *class member functions* attached to them. Using them is a bit different from using the nonmember (free) functions such as those declared in `cmath`. A different syntax is required to call class member functions. This different type of function call is even distinguished with a different name—*message,* which is the object-oriented term for function call.

Some messages return the object's state. Other messages tell an object to do something:

- A message that asks the object to return its state:

```
cout << anAccount.balance() << endl;
```

- A message that tells the object to do something:

```
anAccount.withdraw(25.00);
```

The state of an object is made accessible through certain operations (class member functions such as `balance`) of the class. Other class member functions exist so programmers can modify the state of the object (`withdraw` and `deposit`, for example). Here is the general form used to send messages to objects:

GENERAL FORM 4.1. *Sending a message to an object*

object-name **.** *function-name* **(** *argument-list* **)**

Although this is an example of a valid message,

```
anAccount.deposit(237.42);
```

the following are not valid messages. (*Note:* Error messages differ dramatically between compilers—they won't look like the comments.)

BAD MESSAGES

```
anAccount.deposit();          // Needs an argument
deposit();                    // Missing the object name
anAccount.balance;            // Missing the parentheses
anAccount.withdraw("10");     // Wrong class of argument
anAccount;                    // Missing member function name
anAccount.withdrawl(10);      // bankAccount does not have a withdrawl
                              // function
```

Fortunately, failure to supply the object name, the dot, and the operation name in the proper order usually generates an error message or warning. Also, as with any other function, the compiler complains if the client code does not supply the proper arguments between parentheses.

The `bankAccount` class (and therefore all instances of `bankAccount`) has two member functions to access the state of the object: `name` and `balance`. The `bankAccount` class has two member functions that modify the state—`withdraw` and `deposit`. These operations are exemplified in the following program that constructs two `bankAccount` objects and sends messages to both of those objects. Those messages result in the following actions:

- Deposit $133.33 to the object named `anAcct`.
- Withdraw $250.00 from the object named `anotherAcct`.
- Display the names and modified balances of both objects.

```
// Initialize two bankAccount objects and send some messages
#include <iostream>  // For cout
using namespace std;
#include "baccount"  // For the bankAccount class[1]

int main()
{
  bankAccount anAcct("Hall", 100.00);  // Construct a bankAccount
  bankAccount anotherAcct("Fuller", 987.65);

  anAcct.deposit(133.33);  // Send a deposit message to anAcct
  anotherAcct.withdraw(250.00);

  cout << anAcct.name() << ": " << anAcct.balance() << endl;
  cout << anotherAcct.name() << ": " << anotherAcct.balance() << endl;

  return 0;
}
```

OUTPUT

```
Hall: 233.33
Fuller: 737.65
```

1. This textbook distinguishes author-supplied `#include` files with double quotes " " rather than the angle brackets < >. This means that you will need these files in your working directory (or folder) or in a folder (directory) that your compiler will search.

Objects store varying amounts of data depending on the class to which they belong. The state of an object may require many values—and these values also may be of different classes. For example, a `bankAccount` object stores a `string` object to represent the account ID, and at the same time stores a number to represent the balance. A `weeklyEmp` object might store several `string`s such as name, address, and social security number and several numbers such as pay rate and hours worked. A `robot` object may store a current position, a map, and the state of its arm mechanism.

This `bankAccount` class will be used again in Chapter 6 to present the first example of reading class definitions and implementing class member functions. The simplified `bankAccount` class definition is presented here as a preview.

CLASS DEFINITION: *bankAccount (see Chapter 6)*

```
class bankAccount {
public:
  bankAccount(string initName, double initBalance);
  void deposit(double depositAmount);
  void withdraw(double withdrawalAmount);
  double balance() const;
  string name() const;
private:
  string my_name;
  double my_balance;
};
```

4.1.3 Class and Object Diagrams

Another way to represent the relationship between a class and its objects can be found in the Unified Modeling Language (UML), which is currently being proposed as standard documentation for managing large-scale software systems throughout their life cycles. Part of the UML uses a simple box diagram to capture the essence of a class. It lists the class name, the names of the data representing the state, and the public *interface*—the list of messages any instance of the class can understand. A class can be used to construct many objects, each with its own state. The state of individual objects can be written inside object diagrams. Figure 4.1 captures the effect of the messages in the following self-check question:

FIGURE 4.1

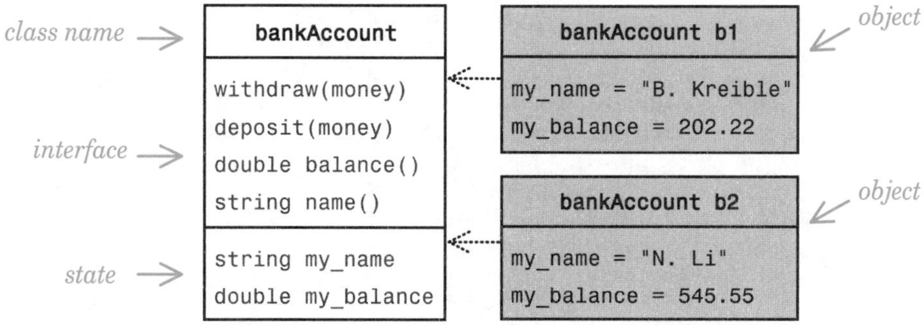

Class diagrams summarize the messages that can be sent to instances of the class—the interface. They also reveal details about the data being stored for each instance of the class—the state.

Self-Check

4-1 Each of the lettered lines has an error. Explain why.

```
#include <iostream>  // For cout
using namespace std;
#include "baccount"  // For the bankAccount class
int main()
{
  bankAccount b1("B. Kreible");         // -a
  bankAccount b2(500.00);               // -b
  BankAccount b3("N. Li", 200.00);      // -c
  b1.deposit();                         // -d
  b1.deposit;                           // -e
  b1.deposit("100.00");                 // -f
  B1.deposit(100.00);                   // -g
  b1.Deposit(100.00);                   // -h
  withdraw(100);                        // -i
  cout << b4.name() << endl;            // -j
  cout << b1.name << endl;              // -k
  cout << b1.name(100.00) << endl;      // -l
  return 0;
}
```

4-2 Write the output generated by the following program:

```
#include <iostream>  // For cout
using namespace std;
#include "baccount"  // For the bankAccount class
int main()
{
  bankAccount b1("B. Kreible", 0.00);
  bankAccount b2("N. Li", 500.00);
  b1.deposit(222.22);
  b1.withdraw(20.00);
  b2.deposit(55.55);
  b2.withdraw(10.00);
  cout << b1.name() << ": " << b1.balance()  << endl;
  cout << b2.name() << ": " << b2.balance()  << endl;
  return 0;
}
```

4.2 Standard Messages and Member Functions

Consider the common operations of the three classes of objects under study—`double`, `int`, and `string`:

1. initialization of objects
2. modification of object state through assignment and input operations
3. inspection of the state of an object with output operations
4. accessibility to the state of objects through use of the object name

The `double` and `int` classes store just one value per object. One object of the `double` class stores exactly one floating-point number. One `int` object stores exactly one integer. However, most objects store *many* values. And they may be different classes of values—a `double`, an `int`, and a `string`, perhaps. For example, the simple `bankAccount` class just presented constructs objects that have a `string` to store the account name and a `double` to store the account balance. A class may also store many values of the same type. For example, every `string` object stores a collection of characters.

4.2.1 `string` Messages and Member Functions

Because each `string` object stores a collection of characters, a programmer is sometimes interested in one single character. At other times the programmer may require several characters or the current length of a `string` (number of characters stored). It is sometimes necessary to discover if a certain substring exists in a `string`. For example, is `the` in `Mother`, and if so, where does this substring `the` begin?

Programmers sometimes make one `string` out of two with the + operator, which instead of adding two integers or two `doubles`, concatenates (connects) two or more `strings` into one.

The `[ ]` operator is presented along with some named functions that require the dot notation. The first character in a `string` object is referenced as `aString[0]`, the second character is referenced as `aString[1]`, and the last character is referenced as `aString[aString.length()-1]`.

```
// Show a few string operations

#include <iostream>  // For the cout object and endl
#include <string>    // For the string class
using namespace std;

int main()
{
  string a("Any old");
  string b(" string");
  string aString(a + b);  // Concatenate a and b to create a string
  // assert: aString is "Any old string"2

  cout << aString[0] << endl;
  // assert: aString[0] returned A (C++ begins to count at 0)

  cout << aString[1] << endl;
  // assert: aString[1] returned n (the second letter in aString)

  cout << aString.length() << endl;
  // assert: aString.length returned 14

  cout << aString.find("ring") << endl;
  // assert: aString.find("ring") returned 10

  cout << aString.substr(4, 7) << endl;
  // assert: aString.substr(4, 7) returns the string "old str",
  //         which is the seven characters starting at aString[4]
  return 0;
}
```

2. Comments beginning with `// assert:` are a textbook convention for explaining the effect of executing the previous statement or statements in an efficient and positive fashion.

Output

```
A
n
14
10
old str
```

There simply aren't enough operators like + and << to handle the large number of operations for the large number of objects required by standard C++. Names are used instead. There is a side benefit. Descriptive names such as `length` make for more easily understood programs (try thinking of a symbol for the number of characters in a `string`).

Actually, by design, objects are attached to a collection of named functions that implement their operations. For example, the standard `string` class has other named functions such as `insert` and `replace`. The functions differ from the nonmember functions of Chapter 3 in that `length`, `insert`, and `find` are class member functions.

One of the differences between class member functions and nonmember functions shows up in the previous program. Some member functions are called differently. Instead of passing `string` objects *to* a function, for example with `length(aString)`, the object name is written first, then a dot (period), and then the parentheses.

```
cout << aString.length() << endl;
```

Self-Check

4-3 What is the value of `positionOfG`?

```
string s("abcdefghi");
int positionOfG = s.find("g");
```

4-4 What is the value of `s2`?

```
string s1("abcdefghi");
string s2(s1.substr(4, 3));
```

4-5 What is the value of `len`?

```
string s3("abcdefghi");
int last = s3.length()-1;
```

4-6 Write the value of the expression `"Wheatley" + ", " + Kay;`.

4-7 Write expressions that will store the three middle characters of a `string` into a `string` named `mid`. Assume the `string` always has a length of five or more.

4-8 For each of the following messages, if there is something wrong, write "error"; otherwise write the value of the expression.

```
string s("Any string");
```

-a	`length(s)`	-d	`s.find(" ")`
-b	`s.length`	-e	`s.substr(2, 5)`
-c	`s(length)`	-f	`s.substr("tri")`

4.2.2 `ostream` and `istream` Member Functions

Some `ostream` and `istream` operations also require the dot notation. To demonstrate, here is a member function of the `ostream` class named `width` that modifies the state of the `ostream` object named `cout`.

```
#include <iostream>  // For the ostream class (and cout)
using namespace std;
int main()
{
  cout << 1;
  cout.width(5);
  cout << 2;
  // assert: 2 appears right-justified in five columns following 1
  return 0;
}
```

OUTPUT

```
1    2
```

The `width` member function is an example of a message that *modifies* the state of the object. Normally, the state of `cout` is set to display the next output in the minimum number of columns—with no leading spaces—the default state of `cout`. The following message modifies the state of `cout`:

```
cout.width(5);
```

This `width` message temporarily alters the state of `cout` such that the very next output will be output in a minimum of five columns. After the next output on the screen, the default situation is back in force.

4.2.2.1 The `ostream` Member Function Named `precision`

If you'd like to gain some control over the appearance of floating-point output, consider using the `ostream` member function named `precision`. A `precision` message tells the `ostream` object (usually `cout`) to show a specific number of digits.

```
// Send two precision messages to the ostream object named cout
#include <iostream>
using namespace std;

int main()
{
   double x = 1.23456;

   cout << x << endl;   // Default (1.23456)
   cout.precision(1);   // Modify the state of cout
   cout << x << endl;   // Show only one significant digit (1)
   cout.precision(4);   // Modify the state of cout
   cout << x << endl;   // Show four digits rounded (1.235)

   return 0;
}
```

OUTPUT

```
1.23456
1
1.235
```

In a later section, you will see how the `ostream` member function named `setf` (*set f*ormat) guarantees the decimal point always shows, trailing zeros always appear, and the rightmost significant digit is rounded.

4.2.3 The `istream` Member Function `good`

The member function `good` of the `istream` class returns the state of an input object (usually `cin`). The `good` member function is an example of a message that accesses the state of an object. Normally, `cin.good()` returns `1` (which means true) if `cin` is still capable of reading from the input device. However, if someone enters an improper value (such as input of `BAD` instead of a number as shown below), the `good` message returns `0` (which means false).

```
cout << cin.good();  // Returns 1 for good, 0 for bad
```

Whenever `cin.good()` is false, no more input is allowed from `cin` (the keyboard) unless other steps are taken. So if you enter a `string` instead of a number—an easy input mistake to make—strange things may occur.

```
// Demonstrate what happens with bad input
#include <iostream>  // For the cout and cin objects
using namespace std;

int main()
{
  int x(0.0);

  cout << "Is cin good? " << cin.good() << endl;
  cout << "Enter either a good or bad int: ";
  cin >> x;
  cout << "Is cin still good? " << cin.good() << endl;
  return 0;
}
```

DIALOGUE 1

```
Is cin good? 1
Enter either a good or bad int: 123
Is cin still good? 1
```

DIALOGUE 2

```
Is cin good? 1
Enter either a good or bad int: BAD
Is cin still good? 0
```

4.2.4 Class Member Function Headings

When a function is a member of a class, the function heading is qualified with the class name followed by the symbol `::`. Not only is this necessary to successfully build a class (see Chapter 6), it also helps the reader determine when the dot notation is required to send a message. Any function heading of the following form identifies the function as a class member function:

GENERAL FORM 4.2. *Class member function headings*

class-name `::` *function-name* `(` *parameters* `)`

So for example, `int string::length()` indicates that `length` is a member of the `string` class. It is different from the nonmember functions `sqrt` and `pow`.

Here is the complete list of class member function headings that have been revealed so far (there are many others):

Examples of Class Member Function Headings

Class	Code

`string`	`int string::length()`
	`// post: Return the current length of the string`
	
	`int string::find(string subString)`
	`// post: Return position of first subString or -1 if not found`
	
	`string string::substr(int pos, int n)`
	`// pre:  pos < this string's length`
	`// post: Return the n character to the right of and including this`
	`//       string[pos] or up to this string's length`

`ostream`[3]	`int ostream::width(int nCols)`
	`// post: Next output to this ostream object (cout, e.g.) will be`
	`//       displayed in nCols columns or minimum of columns required.`
	`//       Also returns the previous width (but it can be ignored).`
	
	`int ostream::precision(int nDigits)`
	`// post: Show floating-point output with nDigits of digits. Also`
	`//       returns the current precision.`

`istream`	`int istream::good()` `// post: Return 1 if istream object can read input or 0 if corrupt`

`bankAccount`	`bankAccount::bankAccount(string initName, double initBalance)`
	`// post: Construct a bankAccount with two arguments when called like`
	`//       this: bankAccount anAcct("Hall", 100.00);`
	
	`void bankAccount::deposit(double depositAmount)`
	`// pre:  depositAmount >= 0`
	`// post: depositAmount is credited to this object's balance`
	
	`void bankAccount::withdraw(double withdrawalAmount)`
	`// pre:  withdrawalAmount >= 0 and <= this object's balance`
	`// post: withdrawalAmount is debited from this object's balance`
	
	`double bankAccount::balance() const`
	`// post: Return this object's current balance`
	
	`string bankAccount::name() const`
	`// post: Return this object's name`

3. `width` and `precision` are member functions of the `ios` class, but `ostream` inherits these two member functions. This heading could also be written as `int ios::width`.

The class name and : : should help you determine whether you must call a nonmember (free) function without the function name first or send a message with the object name followed by a dot.

Nonmember Function Heading	Function Call

`double pow(double base, double power)`
`// post: Return base to the power power`
	`double answer = 0.0;`
	`double x = 1.023102;`
	`answer = pow(x, 360.0);`

Member Function Heading	**Message**

`string string::substr(int pos, int n)`
`// post: Return n characters of this`
`//       string beginning at position`
`//       pos`
	`string name, last;`
	`int n;`
	`cin >> name;`
	`n = name.find(",");`
	`last = name.substr(0, n);`

Additionally, to document a function name as a class member function requiring the dot notation, you will often see member functions referred to without the parameter list and return type like this: `string::length`, `bankAccount:withdraw`. This is true in the context of this textbook and with most compiler documentation.

Self-Check

4-9 Write the output generated by the following program. Make sure you line up all output in the exact column.

```
#include <iostream>  // For cout
using namespace std;
int main()
{
  cout << "123456789012345" << endl;
  cout.width(3);
  cout << 1;
  cout.width(5);
  cout << 2.3;
  cout.width(6);
  cout << "who" << endl;
  return 0;
}
```

4-10 Write the exact output generated by the following program:

```
#include <iostream>  // For cout
using namespace std;
```

```
int main()
{
  cout.precision(3);
  cout << 9.876543 << endl;
  cout.precision(1);
  cout << 1.2 << endl;
  cout.precision(8);
  cout << 1.2 << endl;
  return 0;
}
```

4-11 Write the complete dialogue generated by the following program when:

-a the user enters `123`

-b the user enters `XYZ`

```
#include <iostream>
using namespace std;
int main()
{
  int anInt(0);
  cout << "Enter an integer: ";
  cin >> anInt;
  cout << "Good? " << cin.good() << endl;
  return 0;
}
```

4-12 What class does each class member function belong to?

-a `istream::clear`

-b `grid::move`

-c `ostream.width`

-d `string::replace`

-e `bankAccount::withdraw`

-f `istream::good`

4-13 Using the following member function heading,

```
string::replace(int pos, int n, string s)
// post: Replace n characters in this string with s
//       beginning at position pos
```

write code that sends a `string::replace` message (you supply any valid arguments) and then describe the changes made to the `string` object.

```
string changeMe("abcdefghklmnopqrstuvwxyz");
```

4.3 Another Nonstandard Class: grid

This section presents another nonstandard class that will be used occasionally over the next several chapters to help you think in terms of objects while providing opportunities to improve problem-solving skills.

This section presents a `grid` class—one of the dozen or so nonstandard classes of this textbook. Before you study this section, please realize that the `grid` class is meant to be used for teaching and learning purposes only. It will be used occasionally in later chapters to demonstrate new concepts in a visual manner. However, the `grid` class is not meant to predominate any of those new concepts. The graphical state of `grid` is meant to help you more readily grasp the access and modification of object state through messages. You will be able to complete a few programming projects comprised only of messages to this object.

The `grid` class presented here is based on the work of Rich Pattis' "Karel the Robot" [Pattis 81] and a game seen at Disney World's Epcot Center. The game asked the question, Could you be a programmer? The player was invited to guide a pirate ship to a treasure while avoiding obstacles.

A `grid` object stores a little rectangular map of rows and columns with an object to move. A `grid` object is initialized with five arguments:

`grid` *grid-name* `(` *rows* `,` *cols* `,` *mover-row* `,` *mover-col* `,` *direction* `);`

where the first two arguments represent the size of the grid in rows and columns; the next two arguments are the mover's starting row and column; and the last argument is the mover's starting direction. The direction must be listed either as `north`, `south`, `east`, or `west`.

The following program provides an example initialization with an output message (`grid::display`) that allows the programmer to inspect the state of the `grid`. (*Note:* To maintain consistency with C++, which begins counting at 0, 0 refers to the first row. The first column is also referenced as 0.)

```
// Initialize and display a grid object
#include "grid"   // For the grid class
// <iostream> not needed--there is no cout, cin, or endl

int main()
{
  // Arguments used to initialize a grid object go like this:
  // #rows, #columns, StartRow, StartColumn, StartDirection
```

```
  grid aGrid(8, 10, 6, 0, east);  // 6 is the seventh row, 0 is the
                                  // first column
  aGrid.display();
  return 0;
}
```

Output

```
The grid:
. . . . . . . . . .
. . . . . . . . . .
. . . . . . . . . .
. . . . . . . . . .
. . . . . . . . . .
. . . . . . . . . .
> . . . . . . . . .
. . . . . . . . . .
```

A `grid` object's state is accessed with class member functions such as (*Note:* This is not a complete list):

1. `grid::row`
2. `grid::nRows`
3. `grid::nColumns`
4. `grid::display()`
5. `grid::frontIsClear`

Although you may not see the need for these operations at this point, they will come in handy if you do any problem solving associated with `grid` objects.

```
// Access the state of a grid object with messages
#include <iostream>  // For the cout object
using namespace std;
#include "grid"      // For the grid class

int main()
{
  grid aGrid(7, 14, 5, 8, east);  // Column 8 is the ninth column
  cout << "Current row      : " << aGrid.row()          << endl;
  cout << "Current column   : " << aGrid.column()       << endl;
  cout << "Number of rows   : " << aGrid.nRows()        << endl;
  cout << "Number of columns: " << aGrid.nColumns()     << endl;
  cout << "Front is clear?  : " << aGrid.frontIsClear() << endl;
  return 0;
}
```

Output

```
Current row       : 5
Current column    : 8
Number of rows    : 7
Number of columns: 14
Front is clear?   : 1
```

The state of any `grid` object is modified with the messages `grid::move` and `grid::turnLeft`. Whereas the `move` message requires exactly one argument, the `turnLeft` message does not require an argument.

```
#include "grid"  // For the grid class

int main()
{
  grid aGrid(9, 7, 4, 2, east);

  aGrid.move(3);
  aGrid.turnLeft();
  aGrid.move(3);
  aGrid.turnLeft();
  aGrid.move(4);
  aGrid.turnLeft();
  aGrid.move(7);
  aGrid.display();
  return 0;
}
```

Output

```
The grid:
. . . . . . .
.           .
.   . . .   .
.   . . .   .
.           .
.   . . . . .
.   . . . . .
.   . . . . .
. V . . . . .
```

Self-Check

4-14 Write the output of the following program:

```
#include <iostream>  // For cout
using namespace std;
#include "grid"      // For the grid class

int main()
{
  grid aGrid(6, 6, 4, 2, east);
  aGrid.move(2);
  aGrid.turnLeft();
  aGrid.move(3);
  aGrid.turnLeft();
```

```
    aGrid.move(2);
    aGrid.display();
    cout << "row: " << aGrid.row() << endl;
    cout << "col: " << aGrid.column() << endl;
    return 0;
}
```

4.3.1 Other `grid` Operations

There are several other `grid` operations, some of which will be needed in this chapter's programming projects. Completing those projects provides practice at sending messages to objects—calling member functions—and developing algorithms resulting in a more graphical result.

The class diagram to the right lists all `grid` member functions. It is not necessary to know the data members to use objects, so the state is omitted here.

Although this class diagram provides a summary of legal messages, it does not explain the number and class of arguments to use when sending messages to a `grid` object. For that, the following subset of the member function headings is provided (all the ones you need to do the programming projects in this chapter) with pre- and postconditions.

grid
move(nSpaces) turnLeft() putDown(row, column) toggleShowPath() pickUp() block(row, column) bool frontIsClear() bool rightIsClear() int row() int column() int nRows() int nColumns() display()

SUBSET OF `grid` MEMBER FUNCTIONS

```
grid::grid(int Rows, int Cols, int startRow, int startCol, int direction)
// post: Construct a 10-by-10 grid object with five arguments like this:
//       grid aGrid(10, 10, 0, 0, east);

void grid::move(int nSpaces)
// pre:  The mover has no obstructions in the next nSpaces
// post: The mover is nSpaces forward

void grid::putDown(int putDownRow, int putDownCol)
// pre:  The intersection (putDownRow, putDownCol) has nothing at it except,
//       perhaps, the mover
// post: There is one thing at the intersection (putDownRow, putDownCol)
```

```
void grid::pickUp()
// pre:  There is something to pick up at the mover's location
// post: There is nothing to pick up from the current intersection

void grid::turnLeft()
// post: The mover is facing 90 degrees counterclockwise

void grid::block(int blockRow, int blockCol)
// pre:  There is nothing at all at the intersection (blockRow, blockCol)
// post: The intersection can no longer be visited

void grid::display() const
// post: The current state of the grid is displayed on the screen
```

For example, a few `grid::putDown` messages can be used to place a few "cookies" (or whatever you want to call the things) on the table (or whatever you want to call the grid). Then the challenge is sending the proper messages to move the kid (or whatever you want to call the mover) to eat (or whatever you want to call the `grid::pickUp` operation) the cookies. Here is a program that instructs a kid to eat two cookies:

```
// This program sets two cookies on the table and instructs a kid
// on how to locate them, "eat" them, and return home
#include "grid"  // For the grid class

int main()
{
  grid kid(8, 12, 0, 0, south);
  kid.putDown(4, 0);
  kid.putDown(4, 3);
  kid.block(3, 2);
  kid.block(4, 2);
  kid.block(5, 2);
  // Show the state of kid
  kid.display();

  // "Eat" two cookies
  kid.move(4);
  kid.pickUp();
  kid.move(2);
  kid.turnLeft();
  kid.move(3);
  kid.turnLeft();
  kid.move(2);
  kid.pickUp();
```

OUTPUT

```
The grid
v . . . . . . . . . . .
. . . . . . . . . . . .
. . . . . . . . . . . .
. . # . . . . . . . . .
O . # O . . . . . . . .
. . # . . . . . . . . .
. . . . . . . . . . . .
. . . . . . . . . . . .
The grid
<       . . . . . . . .
  . .   . . . . . . . .
  . .   . . . . . . . .
  . #   . . . . . . . .
  . #   . . . . . . . .
  . #   . . . . . . . .
        . . . . . . . .
. . . . . . . . . . . .
```

```
    // Get the kid back home
    kid.move(4);
    kid.turnLeft();
    kid.move(3);

    // Show the ending state
    kid.display();
    return 0;
}
```

4.3.2 Failure to Meet the Preconditions

There are many "illegal" messages you can send to a `grid` object. For example, you could try sending a `move` message that asks the mover to move through a block (#) or off the edge of the grid. All it takes is one incorrect message—moving four rows instead of three, for example.

Self-Check

4-15 If you were designing the operations for a `grid` object, what would you want to prevent from occurring?

So what should a `grid` object do when sent an illegal message? Quite frankly, it's a bit awkward. The object could respond by doing nothing. In this case, the state of the object would remain unaltered. Or the object could travel off the end of the grid or move through blocks—but this sounds more like a Superman object. Here's yet another snippy answer: The behavior is *undefined.*

For a function to behave properly, certain conditions are presumed. For example, the `sqrt` function of `cmath` presumes the argument is greater than or equal to 0.0. But what happens when this condition is not upheld in the client program? The behavior is undefined. Even though `sqrt` is a standard function that must be part of the C++ math library, its behavior when an illegal argument is sent is determined by the implementers of the compiler. Different compilers do different things.

This awkwardness is circumvented by the notion of preconditions presented in the previous chapter. A function's precondition is what the function presumes to be true when a function is called or the message is sent. For example, the `move` operation has the precondition that there is no block or grid edge in the path of the mover. Also, the `grid::pickUp()` message presumes there is something to pick up.

```
void grid::move(int nSpaces)
// pre:  The mover has no obstructions in the next nSpaces
// post: The mover is nSpaces forward
```

```
void grid::pickUp()
// pre:  There is something to pick up at the mover's location
// post: There is nothing to pick up from the current intersection
```

So what does happen when you violate one of these preconditions? You'll likely find out if you work on certain `grid`-related programming projects.

4.3.3 Functions with No Arguments Still Need ( )

You have now seen several messages that require no arguments. If a function has no parameters, it requires no arguments. Here are two examples:

```
cout << aString.length() << endl;
cout << aGrid.row() << endl;
```

It should be noted, before you do any of this chapter's programming projects, that even though no values need to be passed as arguments to either `string::length` or `grid::row`, the parentheses must still be included in the message. The following code will not do what you might expect:

```
cout << aString.length << endl;  // ERROR: Missing () after length
cout << aGrid.row << endl;       // ERROR: Missing () after row
```

The parentheses represent the function call operator. Without `(` and `)`, there is no function call—even when zero arguments are needed by the function.

4.4 Why Functions and Classes?

Abstraction is the process of pulling out and highlighting the relevant features of a complex system. One aspect of abstraction is understanding the computer from the programming-language level without full knowledge of the details at the lower levels. Abstraction is our weapon against complexity.

You can use operations such as `sqrt`, `pow`, `grid::move`, and any other new function without knowing the implementation details coded by other programmers. Abstraction allows programmers to quickly and easily use `int`, `double`, `string`, `bankAccount`, and `grid` objects. The characteristics of `int` data (a specific range of integer values) and `int` operations (such as addition, multiplication, assignment, input, and output) can be understood without knowing the details of those operations, or even how those values are stored, or how these operations are implemented in the hardware and software. Abstraction is friendly. Abstraction makes life easier. Abstraction helps keep us sane.

A class is also understood through the abstraction outlined by its interface. The interface of a class is the collection of operations that may be applied to the objects of the class. For example, the interface for the `double` class includes operations such as `sqrt`, `pow`, `+`, `-`, `*`, and `=`. The interface for the `string` class includes operations such as `=`, `[]`, `string::find`, `string::length`, and `string::replace`. The interface for the `bankAccount` class includes `bankAccount::withdraw`, `bankAccount.deposit`, and `bankAccount::balance`. The interface for the `grid` class includes `grid::display`, `grid::turnLeft`, and `grid::move`. The essential usage details are understood by concentrating on the interface.

Even though C++ is delivered with a large set of abstractions known as functions and classes, additional functions and classes will still be required. New abstractions are built from existing objects, operations, and algorithms. As you begin to create function and class abstractions, set a goal to build these abstractions so they are easy to use and perform a well-defined operation. When the details of implementation are long forgotten, you will still be able to use the abstraction because you know *what* it does. You won't have to remember *how* it does it.

You have now used existing functions. By the end of Chapter 5, you will be able to implement your own nonmember functions. In this chapter you also used objects. By the end of Chapter 6, "Class Definitions and Member Functions," you will observe how the C++ class mechanism encapsulates state with behavior. You will be able to at least read C++ class definitions and use instances of new classes. Additionally, if you do read Chapter 6 in order, you will also be able to implement class member functions and understand how messages modify and/or access the state of objects.

As you continue to study computing fundamentals, you will see a persistent use of these two major software components—functions and classes. Let's now consider the abstraction provided by some of the `grid` class member functions.

Instead of representing one operation as a function, all of the code could have been written in place of one function call. However, as the table below shows, the detailed way is quite extensive in the number of lines required. It should also be noted that the hidden details are pretty much incomprehensible until most of this textbook has been mastered.

The Actions Represented by One Message

Operation	The Object-Oriented Way	The Detailed Way
Construct one `grid` object	`grid g(15,15,9,4,east);`	35 lines
Move in current direction	`g.move(2);`	112 lines
Output the `grid`	`g.display();`	6 lines
Change direction	`g.turnLeft();`	10 lines

The four messages in the middle column represent the abstract equivalent of coding the 163 lines the nonobject way in the right column. Now imagine a six-message program that moves and turns three times. The equivalent nonobject way would require approximately 366 detailed lines of code rather than the six messages!

By placing the many lines of detailed code into a function, the programmer may execute the operation with one message. The same message may be sent over and over again. So whenever you have code that can be used more than once in a program, it is preferable to implement that behavior within the confines of a free (nonmember) function or as one of many messages available to the instances of a class. Function calls and messages represent many hidden instructions and details. The programmer need not see, nor understand, that implementation.

Self-Check

4-16 Using the previous table, how many lines of code are required to initialize the state of one `grid` object using a `grid` object?

4-17 Using the previous table, how many lines of code are required to initialize the state of one `grid` object when the detailed way is used (right column)?

4-18 Write a paper and pencil program that constructs a `grid` object and moves in every direction.

4-19 Using the previous table, determine how many lines of code would be necessary to write the program of 4-18 using the detailed lines of code.

By partitioning low-level details into one function, the implementation need only be written once. Another advantage of functions is that the same operation can be used over and over again with a one-line message. Rather than one huge `int` `main() { }`, programs are comprised of more manageable calls to nonmember (free) functions (`sqrt` and `pow`) and messages to class member functions (`string::substr` and `grid::move`). Here are some reasons why C++ programmers use existing functions and objects to better manage the complexity of software development:

- to reuse existing code rather than write it from scratch
- to concentrate on the bigger issues at hand
- to reduce errors by writing the function only once and testing it thoroughly

In the early days of programming, programs were written as one big `main` program. As programs became bigger, *structured programming* techniques became popular. One major feature of structured programming was to partition programs into functions for more manageable modules. Programmers found this helped people understand the program better. It is easier to maintain programs that place related processing details in an independent function. It is easier to fix a 20-line function in a program with 100 functions than it is to fix a 2,000-line program.

Other reasons for dividing a program into smaller functions include:

- there is enough to do that putting the details into a function or class makes the client code easier to comprehend
- the same actions need to be achieved more than once in a program
- the function or class can be reused in other applications

With free functions, the data are passed around from one nonmember function to another. When the data are available everywhere throughout a large program, they become dangerously susceptible to accidental changes.

Now as software has become even more complex, object technology encapsulates collections of functions with the data manipulated by those functions. Developers don't throw the data around between disparate groups of nonmember functions or leave them open for accidental attack. As you will see in Chapter 6, with object-oriented programming, data are encapsulated with the functions—nice and safe.

FIGURE 4.2. *Historical progression of how programs are organized into modules*

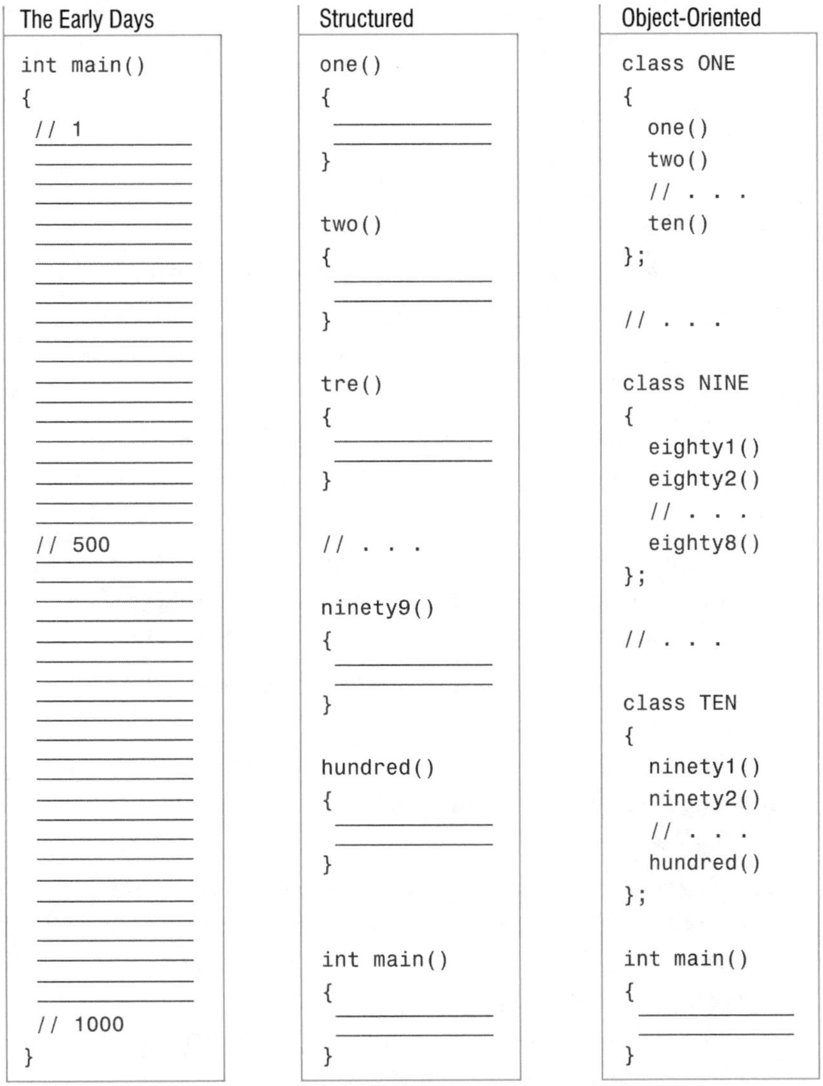
The Early Days
int main()
{
// 1
// 500
// 1000
}
Structured
one()
{
}
two()
{
}
tre()
{
}
// . . .
ninety9()
{
}
hundred()
{
}
int main()
{
}
Object-Oriented
class ONE
{
one()
two()
// . . .
ten()
};
// . . .
class NINE
{
eighty1()
eighty2()
// . . .
eighty8()
};
// . . .
class TEN
{
ninety1()
ninety2()
// . . .
hundred()
};
int main()
{
}

Self-Check

4-20 What reason for using functions makes the most sense to you right now?

4-21 Describe one example of how abstraction helps you get through the day.

Chapter Summary

- The `string` class has a number of operations for manipulating all or part of a `string`. These include `substr`, `find`, `replace`, and `length`.
- Some messages require the object name and a dot (.) before the member function name and arguments. Use `aString.substr(2, 5)` rather than `substr(aString, 2, 5)`.
- Consider using `cout.width(10)` to right justify numeric output in 10 columns (or `cout.width(8)` for 8 columns, and so on).
- Class member functions are often written with the class name and the scope resolution operator `::` to indicate the class of objects that would understand the message, so you'll see `ostream::width` rather than simply `width`.
- Class member function headings supply the same usage information as their non-member cousins (`sqrt`, `pow`, `fmod`). The return type is given, as is the function name and the number and class of arguments that must be used.
- Class member functions additionally are qualified with their class names, for example, `void grid::move()`.
- Most classes in this textbook are part of the C++ standard. The `bankAccount` and `grid` classes are supplied on the disk that comes with this textbook and at this textbook's Web site.
- A class diagram summarizes the names of the messages understood by any instance of a class (object). The programmer needs more information to correctly send a message such as number and class of arguments. That is why some of the class member functions were shown with pre- and postconditions.
- In the 1960s, programs were written as collections of statements. By the 1970s programs were usually collections of free functions. In the 1990s, more and more programs are collections of interacting objects, where each object is an instance of a class containing a collection of member functions. Each improvement allows more complex software to be built.

- Abstraction means the programmer can call a function or send a message without knowing the implementation details. The programmer does need to know the function name, the return type, or the number and class of arguments.

Exercises

1. Write the output generated by the following program:

```
#include <iostream>  // For cout
using namespace std;
#include "baccount"  // For the grid class

int main()
{
  bankAccount b1("One", 100.00);
  bankAccount b2("Two", 200.00);
  b1.deposit(50.00);
  b2.deposit(30.00);
  b1.withdraw(20.00);
  cout << b1.balance() << endl;
  cout << b2.balance() << endl;

  return 0;
}
```

2. Write the complete dialogue of this program when the user enters this input in the order requested: `MyName    100    22.22    44.44`

```
#include <iostream>  // For cout and endl
using namespace std;
#include "baccount"  // For the bankAccount class
int main()
{
  string name;
  double start, amount;
                                 // Input:
  cout << "name: ";              // MyName
  cin >> name;
  cout << "initial balance: ";  // 100
  cin >> start;

  // Construct a bankAccount
  bankAccount one(name, start);

  cout << "deposit? ";           // 22.22
  cin >> amount;
```

```
  one.deposit(amount);

  cout << "withdraw? ";          // 44.44
  cin >> amount;
  one.withdraw(amount);

  cout << "balance for " << one.name() << " is " << one.balance()
       << endl;

  return 0;
}
```

3. Write the output generated by the following program:

```
#include <iostream>  // For the object cout
using namespace std;
#include "grid"      // For the grid class
int main()
{
  grid aGrid(6, 6, 1, 1, south);
  aGrid.putDown(2, 3);  // Place an object even if mover is not there
  aGrid.block(0, 0);
  aGrid.block(5, 5);
  aGrid.move(2);
  aGrid.turnLeft();
  aGrid.putDown();      // Place object where the mover is located
  aGrid.move(3);
  aGrid.turnLeft();
  aGrid.putDown();      // Place object where the mover is located
  aGrid.move(1);
  aGrid.turnLeft();
  aGrid.move(1);
  aGrid.display();
  cout << "Mover: row#" << aGrid.row() << " col#" << aGrid.column()
       << endl;
  return 0;
}
```

4. What is the value of `position`?

```
string s("012345678");
// Initialize position to the first occurrence of "3" in s
int position = s.find("3");
```

5. What is the value of s2?

```
string s1("012345678");
string s2(s1.substr(3, 2));
// assert: s2 is a substring of s1
```

6. What is the value of `lengthOfString`?

```
string s3("012345678");
int lengthOfString = s3.length();
// assert: lengthOfString stores the number of characters in s3
```

7. Choose the most appropriate classes for each of the following from this set of classes: `double`, `int`, `ostream`, `istream`, `string`, `bankAccount`, or `grid`.

   a. Represent the number of students in a section.

   b. Represent a student's grade point average.

   c. Represent a student's name.

   d. Represent the number of questions on a test.

   e. Represent a person's savings account.

   f. Simulate a very limited version of the arcade game PacMan.

   g. Get input.

   h. Display output.

8. Name two reasons why programmers use or implement functions.

9. What is meant by the *interface* of a class?

10. Must a programmer understand the implementation of `grid::move` to use it?

11. Answer the following questions given the member function heading:

```
void grid::block(int blockRow, int blockCol)
// pre:  The intersection at (blockRow, blockCol) has nothing at all
//       on it, not even the mover
// post: The intersection at (blockRow, blockCol) is blocked. The
//       mover cannot move into this intersection.
```

   a. What is the member function name?

   b. What type does it return?

   c. What class does it belong to?

   d. Write a valid message assuming a `grid` object named `aGrid` exists.

Programming Tips

1. You will need author-supplied files to complete some programming projects.

Some programming projects require author-supplied files. These are the files included with `"` and `"` rather than `<` and `>` (`grid` and `bankAccount`, for example). If you are using a personal computer (PC or Mac), simply use the disk that comes with this textbook. Store your programming projects on that disk in the same folder as the proper files such as `baccount`, `baccount.h`, and `baccount.cpp`. If you have your own personal computer, you can work from the hard drive. If you are working on a system with no disk drive, you can download the proper files from this textbook's Web site into your personal directory where you store your program files.

2. If you don't have a standard compiler, you might not be able to `#include <string>`.

At the time of this writing, not all C++ systems provided a file named `string`. You may need to include a different file name appropriate to your system. If you don't have a `string` class, you could use the one provided on this textbook's disk.

3. Distinguish standard `#include` files from nonstandard files.

`#include` standard libraries (classes and objects) with `< >` and nonstandard classes with `" "`. Here are some examples:

```
#include <string>    // For the standard string class
#include <iostream>  // For cout, cin, ostream, istream
using namespace std; // Required to avoid writing std::cout all the time
#include "string"    // For a subset of the standard string on this disk
#include "baccount"  // For the bankAccount class of this chapter
```

4. Even if no arguments are required, end the message with `()`.

Do not forget parentheses in messages that do not require arguments.

```
cout << myAcct.balance;    // Error: This references a memory location
cout << myAcct.balance();  // Good
```

5. C++ begins counting at 0, not 1.

The first character in a `string` is referenced with subscript 0, not 1.

```
cout << aString[0];  // Return the first character
cout << aString[1];  // Return the second character
```

6. Don't reference `aString[aString.length()]`.

This is an attempt to reference a single value that is not in the range of `0` to `aString.length()-1`. In general, do not reference characters in a `string` that do not exist.

```
string aString;
aString = "This string has 29 characters";
cout << aString[-1];  // ERROR: -1 is out of range, only use 0...28
cout << aString[aString.length()];  // ERROR: 29 is also out of range
```

7. There are two ways to initialize an object when it is declared.

Standard compilers allow two different kinds of constructions when only one argument is required. This causes an error on some compilers.

```
string last("Feng, ");
string first = "Sue-Chen";
int n1(0);                // May not work on really old compilers
int n2 = 0;
double x1(0.0);           // May not work on really old compilers
double x2 = 0.0;
```

However, when two or more values are needed to initialize an object, you *must* use parentheses like this:

```
bankAccount myAcct("Rick", 23.41);
grid myGrid(12, 12, 0, 0, east);
```

This textbook typically uses `=` to initialize `int` and `double` objects and `()` for most `strings` and constructors that need two or more arguments. You may use whatever you feel more comfortable with.

8. The :: operator indicates the class to which a function belongs.

The class name followed by the :: operator documents a function as a member function. Any instance of that class will understand the message. Therefore, `string::length` documents that any `string` object will understand the `length` message. However, the class name and :: are not to be used in the message.

```
bankAccount anAcct("Jerry", 345.67);
cout << balance();  // bankAccount:: not needed
cout << anAcct.balance();  // A valid message
```

Programming Projects

4A string::find

Write a program that obtains two `strings` from the user and shows the position of the first `string` as a substring in the second. The `string::find` message returns -1 if the second `string` is not found in the first.[4] The last line of output must include the actual `strings` just input by the user.

DIALOGUE 1

```
Enter string 1: another
Enter string 2: the
'the' is in 'another' at position 3
```

DIALOGUE 2

```
Enter string 1: one
Enter string 2: huh
'huh' is in 'one' at position -1
```

4B string::substr

Write a C++ program that inputs a name in the form last name, comma, first name, an initial, and a period (as your name may be stored in a file somewhere). Display the names

4. The standard specifies `-1`; however, some compilers do not obey this. For example, one compiler returned `4,294,967,295`, the maximum `unsigned long int`.

as `firstName` first, `lastName` last with the initial and the period in between. Match the following dialogue using this exact input, making sure the comma is after `Jones` on input but not in the rearranged name.

DIALOGUE

```
Enter name as Last, First I. Jones, Kim R.
Rearranged name: Kim R. Jones
```

4C A Little Cryptography

Write a C++ program that hides a message in five words. Use one of the characters in the five input `strings` to spell out one new word. Make up at least one other message besides this one:

```
Enter five words: cheap energy can cause problems
Enter five integers: 4 2 1 0 5
Secret message: peace
```

4D Two Bank Accounts

Write a complete C++ program that will

* initialize two different `bankAccount` objects, both with an initial balance of $500.00
* make a deposit of $123.45 to one and a deposit of $50.00 to the other
* make a withdrawal of $20.00 from one and a withdrawal of $60.00 from the other
* show the names and balances of both objects
* show the combined balances of both objects after the four transactions (*Hint:* the combined balance that you must output should be $1,093.45)

If your `bankAccounts` are initialized like this:

```
bankAccount one("Mellisa", 500.00);
bankAccount theOther("Miguel", 500.00);
```

Your output should look like exactly like this:

```
Mellisa: 603.45
Miquel: 490
Combined: 1093.45
```

4E Final Balance

Write a C++ program that initializes a `bankAccount` with user-supplied input. Ask the user for an amount to deposit and another to withdraw. Then show the final balance. Make sure you show the balance of the `bankAccount`. Do not maintain the balance separately as a `double`. (*Hint:* Do not construct the `bankAccount` until you have the initial values first. You can declare a `bankAccount` anywhere in the program.) Your dialogue must look like this:

```
Enter bank account holder's name: Samir
Enter starting balance: 100
Enter amount to deposit: 20
Enter amount to withdraw: 30
Samir's balance: 90
```

4F Pick Up

Write a complete C++ program that constructs a reasonably-sized `grid` object, places at least four things at four different locations, and directs the mover to "pick them up." Show the grid before the mover starts moving and after the mover has "picked up" the four things. Your output might look like this:

```
The grid:
. . . . . . . . . . . . .
. . O . . . . < . . . . .
. . . . . . . . . . . . .
. . O . . . . . . . . . .
. . . . . . . . . . . . .
. . . . . . . . . . . . .
. . . O . . . . . . O . .
. . . . . . . . . . . . .

The grid:
. . . . . . . . . . . . .
. .             . . . . .
. .   . . . . . . . . . .
. .   . . . . . . . . . .
. .   . . . . . . . . . .
. .   . . . . . . . . . .
. .                   > .
. . . . . . . . . . . . .
```

4G Letter

Write a C++ program that constructs a 13-by-7 grid and then instructs the mover to "draw" the letter I exactly as shown (the mover could be left anywhere next to the I). (*Hint:* You can turn around by turning left twice. You can turn right by turning left three times.)

```
. . . . . . .
. . . . . . .
. .       . .
. . .   . . .
. . .   . . .
. . .   . . .
. . .   . . .
. . .   . . .
. . .   . . .
. . .   . . .
. .       > .
. . . . . . .
. . . . . . .
```

4H Bread Trail

Write a C++ program that constructs a 3-by-24 grid with the mover in row 1, column 0. Then instruct the mover to leave this pattern:

```
. . . . . . . . . . . . . . . . . . . . . . . .
  O   O   O   O   O   O   O   O   O   O   O   >
. . . . . . . . . . . . . . . . . . . . . . . .
```

4I Find Cookie

Write a C++ program that constructs an obstacle course and places a O as shown below. Instruct the mover to pick up the O after maneuvering the miniature obstacle course. Show the grid before and after the moves.

```
The grid:
. . . . . # . . . . . . .
. . . . . # . # . . . . .
. . . . . . . # . . . . .
. . . . . # . # . . . . .
. . . O . # . # ^ . . . .
. . . . . . . # . . . . .

The grid:
. . . . . #       . . . .
. . . . . #   #   . . . .
. . .         #   . . . .
. . .   . # . #   . . . .
. . .   . # . #   . . . .
. . . V . . . # . . . . .
```

4J Hurdles

Write a program that constructs a hurdle course as shown below and instructs the runner to jump the hurdles. The runner must touch the ground between each hurdle. Show the grid before and after the course is run. Your output should look like this:

```
The grid:
. . . . . . . . . . . . . . . . . . . . . . .
. . . . . . . . . . . . . . . . . . . . . . .
> . . # . . . # . . . # . . . # . . . # . . .
. . . . . . . . . . . . . . . . . . . . . . .

The grid:
. . . . . . . . . . . . . . . . . . . . . . .
. .       .       .       .       .       . .
      #       #       #       #       #     >
. . . . . . . . . . . . . . . . . . . . . . .
```

Chapter Five

Functions and Parameters

Summing Up

You have now been exposed to the hybrid nature of C++. The class construct was added to the C language to provide object-oriented capabilities. This provides flexibility in the way programs can be built—around functions, objects, or both. However, this flexibility comes at the cost of managing the differences between nonmember functions and member functions. Part of the cost was revealed in the previous two chapters. Chapter 3 dealt with calling nonmember functions. Chapter 4 dealt with sending messages using class member functions.

Coming Up

The next two chapters once again meet the hybrid nature of C++ head on. The first part of Chapter 5 introduces implementation of nonmember functions. Then, at your choice, you can use Chapter 6 to learn more about classes and class member function implementations—they aren't much different from their nonmember cousins of this chapter. In subsequent chapters you can choose programming projects that reinforce functions, classes, or both. After studying this chapter, you will be able to

* implement nonmember functions
* pass values to your functions as input
* return values from your functions as output

  Exercises and projects to reinforce nonmember function implementations
* begin to see the differences between the three types of parameters
* begin to understand the scope of objects and functions

  Exercises and projects to reinforce parameter modes

5.1 Implementation of Nonmember (Free) Functions

Nonmember functions—such as `pow` and `sqrt`—are defined as a function heading followed by a block.

GENERAL FORM 5.1. *Nonmember function*

function-heading // Described in Chapter 3
block // Described next

A block begins with `{` and ends with `}`. It contains components such as object initializations and executable statements. One of those statements is often the C++ `return` statement.

GENERAL FORM 5.2. *Block*

{
  object-initializations
  statements
}

The following function named `f` implements the function $f(x) = 2x^2 - 1$. Notice that the function must be coded before it can be called—the entire function `f` is located before the call to it from `main`.

```
#include <iostream>  // For cout
#include <cmath>     // For pow
using namespace std;

double f(double x)
{ // post: Return 2 * x * x - 1
  double result;

  result = 2 * pow(x, 2) - 1.0;
  return result;
}

int main()
{
  // 0. Declare objects
  double x, y;
```

```
    // 1. Input
    cout << "Input x: ";
    cin >> x;

    // 2. Process (occurs in function f)
    y = f(x);

    // 3. Output
    cout << "f(" << x << ") = " << y << endl;

    return 0;
}
```

DIALOGUE

```
Input x: 1.01
f(1.01) = 1.0402
```

Self-Check

5-1 What is the return type for each of the following functions?

-a `sqrt` -c `string::length`

-b `pow` -d `string::substr`

5-2 What value is returned for each of these function calls? If there is an error, explain it (use $f(x) = 2x^2 - 1$ of the previous example).

-a `f(0.0)` -d `f(1, 2)`

-b `f(-2.0)` -e `f()`

-c `f(3)` -f `f(5.8)`

5.1.1 The Return Statement

Functions get their input via the arguments in the function call. The function uses these input values to compute a result, which is then returned to the caller. You have now seen how arguments are associated with parameters to get input into the function. This section discusses the means for sending the result back to the caller.

Functions communicate values to the calling code through the *return statement*. Here is the general form.

GENERAL FORM 5.3. *Return statement*

```
return expression ;
```

EXAMPLE OF RETURNING A VALUE BACK TO THE CLIENT CODE

```
double f(double x)
{ // post: Return f(x) = 2x - 1
  double result;
  result = 2 * x - 1;
  return result;
}
```

When the return statement is encountered, the *expression* that follows `return` replaces the function call in the client code. Then program control returns to that client code—to the place where the function was called. In the next example, the function `serviceCharge` is declared with the `double` return type. The call to `serviceCharge` is replaced by a `double` value that depends on the values of the arguments.

```
// Call serviceCharge to determine a bank debit
#include <iostream>
using namespace std;

const double MONTHLY_FEE = 5.00;

double serviceCharge(int checks, int ATMs)
{ // pre:  checks >= 0 and ATM >= 0
  // post: Return a banking fee based on local rules
  double result;

  result = 0.25 * checks + 0.10 * ATMs + MONTHLY_FEE;
  return result;
}

int main()
{ // 0. Initialize objects
  int checks;
  int ATMs;
  double fee;  // Stores the function return result

  // 1. Input
  cout << "Checks this month? ";
  cin >> checks;
  cout << "ATMs this month? ";
  cin >> ATMs;
```

```
    // 2. Process
    fee = serviceCharge(checks, ATMs);

    // 3. Output
    cout << "Fee = " << fee << endl;

    return 0;
}
```

DIALOGUE

```
Checks this month? 17
ATMs this month? 9
Fee = 10.15
```

Here is what happens in the preceding program:

1. The user is asked to supply input for the number of checks and ATM transactions.
2. The values of the arguments (`17` and `9`) are passed on to the parameters of `serviceCharge` (`checks = 17` and `ATMs = 9`). These particular values will be used by the function to return the proper monthly bank fee.
3. The statements in `serviceCharge` begin to execute.
4. The return is encountered in `serviceCharge`.
5. The function call in `main` is replaced by 10.15.
6. The function's return value is assigned to `fee`.
7. The fee is displayed.

5.1.2 Test Drivers

When a function requires arguments, it is not unusual to have the same object names declared in two different places. Consider the previous program that declares `checks` and `ATMs` in `main` and also as parameters within the function `serviceCharge`. The objects declared in `main` are used to obtain user input. The parameters declared as parameters in `serviceCharge` obtain input from `main`. Although they have the same names, they are different objects. This extra work is necessary to communicate values between functions and will seem more appropriate in complex functions rather than in this small example.

Sometimes the duplication of parameter names in `main` is not required. In the next program, you'll see there is no user input, so the duplicated objects are not necessary. Instead, the arguments used to test the function are constants. Rather than being assigned to another object, the program simply displays the return results. The only purpose of this program is to test the function—to verify that the return values are what was expected. This is a good thing to do before the function becomes incorporated into a larger program. In fact, many of the programming problems ask you to carry out this form of testing.

```
// The main function makes several calls to test a new function

#include <iostream>
using namespace std;

const double MONTHLY_FEE = 5.00;

double serviceCharge(int checks, int ATMs)
{ // pre:  checks >= 0 and ATM >= 0
  // post: Return a banking fee based on local rules
  double result;

  result = 0.25 * checks + 0.10 * ATMs + MONTHLY_FEE;
  return result;
}

int main()
{ // Test drive serviceCharge                // Sample problems:
  cout << serviceCharge(0, 0) << endl;    //  5.00
  cout << serviceCharge(1, 0) << endl;    //  5.25
  cout << serviceCharge(0, 1) << endl;    //  5.10
  cout << serviceCharge(1, 1) << endl;    //  5.35
  return 0;
}
```

OUTPUT

```
5
5.25
5.1
5.35
```

This version of `main` is called a test driver. A *test driver* is a `main` function with the sole purpose of testing a new function. Functions like `serviceCharge`, `sqrt`, and `pow` are intended to be small parts of much bigger programs. Therefore all functions should be thoroughly tested before they are used by larger programs. The four sample problems shown above were predicted and documented in the comments of `main`. The output does match (except for the decimal points and trailing zeros). This has been a successful test of the `serviceCharge` function.

5.1.3 Functions with Only a Return Statement

Some functions are so simple, they may contain only a return statement.

```
double serviceCharge(int checks, int ATMs)
{ // pre:  checks >= 0 and ATM >= 0
  // post: Return a banking fee based on local rules
  return (0.25 * checks + 0.10 * ATMs + MONTHLY_FEE);
}
```

However, this textbook will often use the following convention in addition to the above shortcut (one return statement):

1. Declare a local object named `result`.
2. Store the desired value in `result`.
3. Return `result`.

This is extra work for simple functions. This convention only really helps when the processing gets more complex, beginning in Chapter 7, "Selection."

Also, the extra two lines of code are likely to prevent you from making a very common mistake. Perhaps because other languages use this technique to return values or perhaps because it simply appears to be the right thing to do, students often attempt to assign the expression to the function name. This is a compiletime error. You can only assign values to objects.

```
double serviceCharge(int checks, int ATMs)
{ You cannot assign a number to a function name
  serviceCharge = 0.25 * checks + 0.10 * ATMs + 5.00;   // ERROR
  return 0.25 * checks + 0.10 * ATMs + MONTHLY_FEE;     // OKAY
}
```

If you do make this common mistake, the compiler will tell you. Fix the error by placing the expression after the keyword `return`.

Self-Check

5-3 Given the following function `f1`, what value is returned with `f1(9.0)`?

```
double f1(double x)
{ // pre:  x is zero or positive, but not 1.0
  // post: Return f(x) = (square root of x) / ( x - 1.0 )
  return sqrt(x)/(x - 1.0);
}
```

5-4 Does the function call `f1(-1.5)` satisfy the previous function's precondition? What happens during a call to `f1` with a negative number for an argument?

5-5 Given the following function `f2` (assuming `#include <cmath>`), what value is returned with the function call `f2(1.5, 1.6)`?

```
double f2(double n1, double n2)
{ // post: Return the difference between any two numbers
  return fabs(n1 - n2);
}
```

5-6 Describe how to fix the error in each function.

-a
```
double f1(int j);
{
  return 2.5 * j;
}
```

-b
```
double f2(int)
{
  return 2.5 * j;
}
```

-c
```
double f3(int x)
{
  return 2.5 * j;
}
```

-d
```
double f4(double x)
{
  f4 = 2.5 * x;
}
```

-e
```
double f5(double x)
{
  return double;
}
```

-f
```
int f6(string s)
{
  return s;
}
```

5-7 Write a function `times3` that returns a value that is three times greater than the argument (`times3(2.0)` should return `6.0`).

5.2 Analysis, Design, and Implementation of Functions

Let's talk a little about designing functions before reviewing function implementation. Rather than writing a program, consider a problem that implements a function that may be a very small part of a large program. It may represent just one step of an algorithm, but it is frequently called.

Problem: Compute the distance between two points.

5.2.1 Analysis

Recall that the analysis phase of program development involves determining input and output. Also recall that while developing computer-based solutions to problems involving the IPO algorithmic pattern, the developer determines the output that must be sent to the user and also determines the input required from the user. Replace the word *user* with *client* in the preceding sentence, and the IPO pattern can be applied again to assist the design of functions. Except now the output from the function is expressed in the return statement. And the input is expressed in terms of the argument/parameter associations. Here is a generalized IPO algorithm as it relates to functions instead of programs.

IPO ALGORITHM APPLIED TO FUNCTIONS

Input:	Input values to the function via argument/parameter associations.
Process:	Compute the result to be returned.
Output:	Return the result.

Sample problems are a good way to confirm understanding of a problem. Sample problems also provide expected results that can be compared to program output during program testing. It is a good idea to develop sample problems for new functions. This will help you decide what the function needs as input and, therefore, the number and class of parameters to write in the function heading. The sample problems also provide the expected output of the test driver.

Four `doubles` are required to compute the distance between two points (x_1, y_1) and (x_2, y_2) using the formula distance = $\sqrt{(x_1 - x_2)^2 + (y_1 - y_2)^2}$. The standard `complex` class simplifies this to two complex arguments; however, four `doubles` are used here to avoid introducing the `complex` class. Here are some predicted outputs for a few sets of values for x_1, y_1, x_2, and y_2.

SAMPLE PROBLEMS

x_1	y_1	x_2	y_2	Distance
1.0	1.0	2.0	2.0	1.414
0.0	0.0	3.0	4.0	5
-5.7	2.5	3.3	-4.7	11.5256
0.0	0.0	0.0	0.0	0.0

The IPO pattern is now applied to this function as follows:

- Input: Input two points from the client, (x_1, y_1) and (x_2, y_2).
- Process: Evaluate $\sqrt{(x_1 - x_2)^2 + (y_1 - y_2)^2}$.
- Output: Return the result.

5.2.2 Design

The designer must decide how many and what class of parameters are required for a function. In this example, four values are needed to represent the two input points (`x1`, `y1`, `x2`, and `y2`). The best class of parameters is `double` to allow points such as 5.62 and -9.864. The best return type is `double`. With the square root function involved, `double` helps return precise answers. A good function name is `distance`—it describes what the function does. This leads to a function heading with a return type of `double`, a function name of `distance`, and four descriptively named `double` parameters.

```
double distance(double x1, double y1, double x2, double y2)
// post: Return distance between two points (x1, y1) and (x2, y2)
```

Now, within the body of the function (the block), the parameters `x1`, `y1`, `x2`, and `y2` can be used in the distance formula to compute the result.

```
result = sqrt(pow((x1 - x2), 2) + pow((y1 - y2), 2));
```

5.2.3 Implementation

The following program puts this all together with a `main` function written exclusively to test the function (a test driver):

```
// Call distance four times

#include <iostream>  // For cout
#include <cmath>     // For sqrt and pow
```

```
using namespace std;

double distance(double x1, double y1, double x2, double y2)
{ // post: Return the distance between any two points
  double result;

  result = sqrt(pow((x1 - x2), 2) + pow((y1 - y2), 2));

  return result;
}

int main()
{ // Test drives the distance function
  cout << "(1.0, 1.0) (2.0, 2.0): " << distance(1.0, 1.0, 2.0, 2.0) << endl;
  cout << "(0.0, 0.0) (3.0, 4.0): " << distance(0.0, 0.0, 3.0, 4.0) << endl;
  cout << "(-5.7,2.5) (3.3,-4.7): " << distance(-5.7,2.5, 3.3,-4.7) << endl;
  cout << "(0.0, 0.0) (0.0, 0.0): " << distance(0.0, 0.0, 0.0, 0.0) << endl;
  return 0;
}
```

OUTPUT

```
(1.0, 1.0) (2.0, 2.0): 1.41421
(0.0, 0.0) (3.0, 4.0): 5
(-5.7,2.5) (3.3,-4.7): 11.5256
(0.0, 0.0) (0.0, 0.0): 0
```

Argument/parameter associations are analogous to program input. For example, in the second call to `distance`, the four values are first copied as input to the function `distance`.

```
double distance(x1,  y1,  x2,  y2)
                 ↑    ↑    ↑    ↑
        distance(0.0, 0.0, 3.0, 4.0)
```

Control then transfers to the function where the parameters are used to compute the distance between the two points represented by those arguments. Here is the step-by-step computation:

```
sqrt(pow((x1 - x2), 2) + pow((y1 - y2), 2))
sqrt(pow((0.0 - 3.0), 2) + pow((0.0 - 4.0), 2))
sqrt(pow((-3.0), 2) + pow((-4.0), 2))
sqrt(9.0 + 16.0)
sqrt(25.0)
5.0
```

The four arguments become input to the function as the system copies the value of each argument to its associated parameter. This particular mode of argument/parameter association is named *pass by value* because the values are passed to the function. When a function requires input of small objects such as `double` or `int`, write the function heading with value parameters of this form:

class-name identifier

5.2.4 Testing

It is often desirable to test functions individually. The previous program did just that. It didn't do anything else. The only purpose for this particular `main` function is to call the function `distance` with different sets of arguments and display the return results. Notice the similarity of the four calls to `distance` and the sample problems. The arguments are the input to the function. The return result should match the expected results.

It is recommended that you test new functions with a test driver. The `main` function written for the sole purpose of testing a new function may consist only of calls to a function in a `cout` statement. Many of the programming projects suggest this approach:

Code a little, test a lot!

5.3 Scope of Identifiers

The *scope* of an identifier is the part of a program from which an identifier can be referenced. The scope of an identifier extends from the point of the identifier's declaration to the end of the block in which it is declared (recall that a block is delimited by the left and right braces, `{` and `}`). For example, the scope of `j` in the following program is the function `one`. This `j`, declared in `one`, cannot be referenced from `main`.

```
// Illustrate the scope of an object
#include <iostream>
using namespace std;

const int currentYear = 2000;

void one()
{
```

```
  int j = 0;                                  // The scope of j is
  j = j + 1;                                  // limited to this
  // currentYear is a global identifier      // block, i.e., function
  cout << currentYear;                        // one()
}

int main()
{
  j = 5;  // <- This is an error; j is an unknown identifier
  cout << currentYear << endl;
  return 0;
}
```

When an object is declared outside of a block—as in the case of `currentYear`—its scope begins at the point of declaration and extends to the end of the file. Objects declared in a block can be referenced only from within that block. These are *local objects.* Identifiers declared outside of a block (such as `currentYear`) are said to be global. *Global objects* may be referenced from any subsequent part of the program, unless that identifier is declared again (redeclared) within another block. In this case, the object that was declared first becomes hidden from the block in which it is redeclared. Since many blocks often exist within one program, determining the scope of an object can be somewhat complicated. For example, try to predict the output of the following program, which includes four different declarations of the `int` object `j`:

```
// This program is a tedious test of your ability to determine
// which of the four int objects identified as j is being
// referenced at any given point

#include <iostream>
using namespace std;

const int j = 0;  // Global object j

void one()
{
  cout << j;       // This is a reference to the global j
}

void two()
{
  int j = 1;       // This j is local to two()
  cout << j;
}

int main()
{
```

```
    int j = 2;      // This j is local to main()
    one();
    two();
    cout << j;
    return 0;
}
```

When the function one is called, the global const object j initialized as 0 is referenced. This global j can be referenced from within any function that does not declare another identifier named j. Therefore, the j that was declared first and initialized to 0 is known (can be referenced) from the one function even though it was not declared inside one. But when a reference is made to j in function two, the global j is hidden because of the local j. To this point in program execution, the function one has caused the output 0, and the function two has caused 1 to be displayed. The final statement in main references the j local to main—this j is initialized as 2. Therefore the output would be 0, 1, and 2.

Typically, a function will have one or more objects declared at the beginning of the block. These objects are said to be local to the function because they may be referenced only from within the function. The same protection applies to the parameters of a function. Parameters are local to the function in which they are declared. The restriction on access provides safekeeping for the local objects so they are not accidentally altered from some other portion of a program.

```
void f1(double x)
{
  int j = 0;
  str = "A";  // Error attempting to reference main's local
              // object str
  // . . .
}

int main()
{
  string str;  // str is local to main

  x = 5.0;  // Error attempting to reference f1's parameter x
  j = 1;    // Error attempting to reference f1's local object j
  // . . .
  return 0;
}
```

Self-Check

5-8 Use the partial program shown below to determine the functions from which each of the following identifiers may be referenced. (*Hint:* `cin` and `cout` are initialized in `iostream` and made global with `using namespace std;`.)

```
// cout   b   cin   MAX   c   f1   a   d  f2  main   e

#include <iostream>
using namespace std;

const int MAX = 999;

void f1(int a)
{
  int b;
}

void f2(float c)
{
  double d;
}

int main()
{
  char e;
  return 0;
}
```

5-9 Name two things that may be declared local to a function.

5-10 If an object is declared outside of a function, from where may it be referenced?

5.3.1 Scope of Function Names

Now what about function names? After all, they too are identifiers. What is their scope? Like `cin` and `cout`, the scope of functions in an included file like `cmath` also extends to the end of their own file and any file that includes `cmath`. So global functions such as `sqrt`, `pow`, `ceil`, and `fabs` may be called from within any block unless the function name is redeclared to be something else.

In the programs you write, the function names you place in a function heading can be used anywhere after the heading. You can even call a function from within its own block! However, this is recursive problem solving that becomes useful in a second course. It is not recommended that you do this—you'll probably crash the system.

5.3.2 Global Identifiers

The problems presented so far are not relatively complex. They are certainly not large. You have probably been working pretty much on your own. However, when programs get large and a programming team becomes involved, practice caution with scope.

Global identifiers are known everywhere after they are declared. This opens them up for accidental alteration from *anywhere* in a very large program. It is difficult to ensure that no one will accidentally modify an object at the wrong time. So try to get in the habit of using local objects everywhere possible. This means you use parameters between `(` and `)` and objects between `{` and `}`. For example, `main` declares `localX` and `localY` locally.

```
int main()
{
 double localX, localY;
  // . . .
}
```

If you need to move data between functions, pass them as arguments. This means you must declare parameters rather than having some global `x`.

```
double f(double x)  // x is local to f
{
  double result;     // Result is local to f
  // Do something with x . . .
}
```

If you need a value in many places throughout a program, make it const.

```
#include <iostream>
using namespace std;

const int MAXIMUM_ENTRIES = 100;

// . . . a large program with many functions may follow
```

On the other hand, C++ often uses global identifiers. Consider the fact that after including `<iostream>`, `cout` is known everywhere, assuming `using namespace` `std;` is written before `cout` is referenced (left column below) or `cout` is qualified with `std::` (right column).

```
#include <iostream>
using namespace std;
void f()
{
  cout << "In f";
}

void g()
{
  cout << "In g";
}

int main()
{
  f();
  g();
  cout << "In main";
  return 0;
}
```

```
#include <iostream>
// Equivalent code with std::
void f()
{
  std::cout << "In f ";
}

void g()
{
  std::cout << "In g ";
}

int main()
{
  f();
  g();
  std::cout << "In main ";
  return 0;
}
```

In effect, `using namespace std;` makes `cout` a global identifier. Is this okay? Well, a lot of computer scientists believe so. There is usually only one screen, so any output to `cout` will go to the same screen, no matter which function sends output to it. `cout` and other global identifiers are unknown until you add the line `using namespace std;` or precede the identifiers with `std::`. The use of `std` is relatively new to C++. It was added to help programmers avoid the problems with global identifiers.

Self-Check

5-11 What other identifiers are global after these three lines of code?

```
#include <iostream>  // For cin, cout, endl
#include <string>    // For the string class
using namespace std;
```

Exercises

1. Write the general form of nonmember functions.
2. Where can a function with a return type of `double` be called from?
3. How many statements may be written in a block delimited by `{ }`?
4. Which function is called first when a C++ program executes?
5. May a function be called more than once?
6. Write a function `f` that returns 2.0 * `x` - 1.0 where `x` is a floating-point number.
7. Is `f(1.0)` a proper call to your answer for exercise 6?
8. Is `f("1.0")` a proper call to your answer for exercise 6?
9. Write the output generated by the following program:

```
#include <iostream>
using namespace std;

double f2(double x, double y)
{
  return 2 * x - y;
}

int main()
{
  cout << f2(1, 2.5) << endl;
  cout << f2(-4.5, -3) << endl;
  cout << f2(5, -2) << endl;
  return 0;
}
```

10. Write the output generated by the following function:

```
#include <iostream>
#include <cmath>
using namespace std;

double mystery(double p)
{
  return pow(p, 3) - 1;
}
int main()
```

```
{
  double a = 3.0;
  cout << mystery(  a) << endl;
  cout << mystery(4.0) << endl;
  cout << mystery( -2) << endl;
  return 0;
}
```

11. Write a function `returnSum` that returns the sum of any three numbers.

12. Write a valid call to the `returnSum` function.

13. Write the output generated by the following program:

```
#include <iostream>
#include <string>  // For the string class
using namespace std;

string ends(string s)
{ // pre:  s must have length > 1
  // post: Return the first and last characters of s
  string result;
  string first(s[0]);
  // assert: first is the first character in s
  string last(s[s.length()-1]);
  // assert: last is the last character in s
  result = first + last;  // Combines first and last into one string
  // assert: result is precisely two characters in length
  return result;
}

int main()
{
  cout << ends("Till now ");
  cout << ends("it's ");
  cout << ends("too easy ");
  cout << ends("as we gain ");
  cout << ends("dependence on ");
  cout << ends("software like the functions from cmath ");
  cout << ends("offered for you ");
  cout << ends("to use at no cost to you!");
  return 0;
}
```

14. Complete the output generated by the following program:

```
#include "grid"      // For the grid class
#include <iostream>  // For cout and cin
using namespace std;
```

```
grid initializedGrid()
{ // post: Return a grid object with user-supplied initial values
  int rows, columns, startRow, startCol;
  cout << "Enter grid size in rows and columns: ";
  cin >> rows >> columns;
  cout << "Enter the mover's start row and start column: ";
  cin >> startRow >> startCol;
  grid g(rows, columns, startRow, startCol, south);
  return g;
}
int main()
{
  grid g;
  g = initializedGrid();
  g.display();
  return 0;
}
```

INCOMPLETE DIALOGUE (YOU WRITE THE REMAINING OUTPUT)

```
Enter grid size in rows and columns: 4  4
Enter the mover's start row and start column: 2  2
```

15. Use the partial program shown below to determine the functions from which each of the following identifiers may be referenced. (*Hint:* `cin` and `cout` are initialized in `<iostream>` and made global with `using namespace std;`.)

a. `cout`

b. `cin`

c. `MAX`

d. `string`

e. `length`

f. `functionOne`

g. `aaa`

h. `bbb`

i. `ccc`

j. `s`

```
#include <iostream>
#include <cmath>
using namespace std;

const int MAX = 999;

void functionOne(int aaa)
{
  int bbb;
}

int main()
```

```
{
  string s("a string");
  cout << s.length();
  char ccc;
  return 0;
}
```

Programming Tips

1. Use `decimals` to easily format floating-point output.

Many of these programming projects ask for floating-point output with a specific number of decimal places. To accomplish this, use the following `decimals` function that modifies the `ostream` object (`cout`, most likely) to always show `n` decimal places in floating-point output. You will need to `#include "compfun"` to get `decimals`.

```
void decimals(ostream & os, int n)
// pre:  n >= 0
// post: All floating-point output shows n decimal places
```

2. Here are some common mistakes made when writing functions:

* Placing the semicolon at the end of a function heading:

```
grid moveThree(grid g) ;  // ERROR
{  // Many errors flagged here. Remove ; from the line above.
}
```

* Assigning a value to the function name:

```
double f(double x)
{
  f = 2 * x;   // ERROR: Cannot assign value to function
  return f;    // ERROR: Cannot return a function name
}
```

The solution: Declare a local object, assign it the value, and return it. Or, in the case of simple functions, simply return the expression:

```
double f(double x)
{
  return 2 * x;
}
```

or do this when there is more going on inside the function (see Chapters 7 and 8):

```
double f(double x)
{
  double result;
  result = 2 * x;
  return result;
}
```

- Failing to return a value from a nonvoid function:

```
double f2(double x);
{
  double result;
  result = 2 * x;
  // ERROR: f2 must return a number
}
```

- Returning a value from a void function:

```
void foo(double x)
{
  return 2 * x;  // ERROR
}
```

Programming Projects

5A Practice Typing Functions

Retype and run the following program that has two programmer-defined functions named f and g:

```
#include "compfun"    // For decimals(cout, 2);
#include <iostream>   // For cout and width
#include <cmath>      // For pow(x, y)
using namespace std;

double f(double x)
{
  double result;
  result = sqrt(fabs(x - 0.3));
  return result;
}
```

```
double g(double x)
{
  double result;
  result = 2 * pow(x, 2.0);
  return result;
}

int main()
{ // Test drive f and g
  decimals(cout, 5);  // Described in first programming tip
  // assert: All floating-point output will show five decimal places
  cout.width(12);                          // Output:
  cout << f(3.0) << endl;                  //     1.64317
  cout.width(12);                          //   512.00000
  cout << g(16.0) << endl;                 // 20009.98499
  cout.width(12);                          //     4.20714
  cout << f(100.0) + g(100.0) << endl;     //     5.40000
  cout.width(12);
  cout << f(g(3.0)) << endl;
  cout.width(12);
  cout << g(f(3.0)) << endl;
  return 0;
}
```

5B Sum Three

Write the function `returnSum` that returns the sum of any three numbers.

```
#include "compfun"    // For decimals(cout, 1);
#include <iostream>   // For cout
using namespace std;

double returnSum(double n1, double n2, double n3)
{
  // Complete this function block (remember to return the result)
}

int main()
{ // Test drive returnSum                         Output:
  decimals(cout, 1);                              // 6.6
                                                  // 0.0
  cout << returnSum(1.1, 2.2, 3.3) << endl;
  cout << returnSum(-1, -2, 3) << endl;
  return 0;
}
```

5C Middle Three

Implement a function `middleThree` so it returns the middle three characters of any `string` that has three or more characters. (*Hint:* Consider using these useful member functions: `string::length` and `string::substr`.)

```
#include <iostream>  // For cout
#include <string>    // For string objects
using namespace std;

string middleThree(string s1)
{ // pre: s1.length() > 2
  // Complete this function block (remember to return the result)
}

int main()
{ // Test drive middleThree                      Output:
  cout << middleThree("Rob") << endl;            // Rob
  cout << middleThree("Roby") << endl;           // oby
  cout << middleThree("Robie") << endl;          // obi
  cout << middleThree("Robbie") << endl;         // bbi
  cout << middleThree("Roberto") << endl;        // ber

  return 0;
}
```

5D Move Three

Write a function that directs the mover on a `grid` object three spaces. (*Hint:* Modify the `grid` parameter and return this modified object. A more efficient way to do this using reference parameters (`grid & g`) is presented in the second part of this chapter.)

```
#include "grid"       // For the grid class
#include <iostream>  // For cout
using namespace std;

grid moveThree(grid g)
{  // pre: The mover can move three spaces in its current direction
   // Complete this function block (remember to return the result)
}

int main()
{ // Test drive moveThree              Output:
  grid tarpit(4, 10, 1, 1, east);     // . . . . . . . . . .
  tarpit = moveThree(tarpit);         // .       > . . . . .
  tarpit.display();                   // . . . . . . . . . .
  return 0;                           // . . . . . . . . . .
}
```

5E Block Three

Write a function that blocks all the edges of a 3-by-3 grid. (*Hint:* Modify the `grid` parameter and return this modified object. A more efficient way to do this using reference parameters (`grid & g`) is presented in the second part of this chapter.)

```
#include "grid"       // For the grid class
#include <iostream>  // For cout
using namespace std;

grid blockThree(grid g)
{ // pre:  g is a 3-by-3 grid
  // post: The associated argument has the entire outer edge blocked with #

  // Complete this function block
}

int main()
{ // Test drive blockThree
  grid tarpit(3, 3, 1, 1, east);  // Output:
                                  // # # #
  tarpit = blockThree(tarpit);    // # > #
  tarpit.display();               // # # #

  return 0;
}
```

5F Rounding to n Decimal Places

Write a function named `round` that returns the value of its `double` argument rounded to the number of decimal places specified as the second argument. The algorithm was first discussed in section 3.2. (*Note:* The function must *return* a new value, not just *show* a rounded value!)

```
#include <iostream>  // For the cout object
#include <cmath>     // For the ceil, floor, and pow functions
using namespace std;

// Completely implement double round(double x, int n) here

int main()
{ // Test drive round                        Output:
  cout << round(-2.9, 0)      << endl;  // -3
  cout << round(-2.59, 1)     << endl;  // -2.6
  cout << round(0.0059, 2)    << endl;  // 0.01
  cout << round(1.23467, 3)   << endl;  // 1.235
  cout << round(9.999999, 4)  << endl;  // 10.0000
```

```
  return 0;
}
```

5G Payment (you need compfun)

The payment on a loan is a function of the interest rate, the number of payments (periods), and the amount borrowed. Pass these three values as arguments to a function `payment` that returns the loan payment. The function heading is provided for you along with a test driver and predicted output that illustrates the differences in 30-year mortgages at 11.5, 9.5, and 7.5 annual percentage interest rates. Observe that the return results are rounded to two decimal places with trailing zeros. Therefore, you must `#include "compfun"` for the `decimals` function.

```
#include <iostream>  // For the cout object
#include <cmath>     // For pow, which you definitely need here
using namespace std;
#include "compfun"   // For decimals(cout, 2)


double payment(double amtBorrowed, double interestRate, int numPeriods)
{
  // Complete this function block (remember to return the result)
}

int main()
{ // Test drive payment
  decimals(cout, 2);  // Show loan payments with two decimals

  // 11.5 needs to be divided by 100 to become an annual percentage 0.115
  // but it also needs to be divided by 12 to get the monthly rate. The
  // number of years (30) also needs to multiplied by 12. So the payment in
  // this case is a monthly payment.
  cout << payment(95000.00, 11.5/12/100.0, 30*12) << endl;  // 940.78
  cout << payment(95000.00,  9.5/12/100.0, 30*12) << endl;  // 798.81
  cout << payment(95000.00,  7.5/12/100.0, 30*12) << endl;  // 664.25

  return 0;
}
```

The formula used to calculate monthly payments on a loan given the amount borrowed, interest rate, and the total payments is written as:

$$\texttt{amtBorrowed} * \texttt{intRate} * \frac{(\texttt{intRate} + 1)^{\texttt{numPeriods}}}{((\texttt{intRate} + 1)^{\texttt{numPeriods}} - 1)}$$

5H Future Value

Write a function `futureValue` that returns the future value of an investment at the end of `n` periods. The formula is `futureValue = presentValue * (1 + rate)`^{n} where `presentValue` is the amount invested today, `rate` is the interest rate the investment is to earn for each period, and `n` is the number of periods the investment earns interest.

Use the following function heading:

```
double futureValue(double presentValue, double rate, int n)
```

to allow function calls like this:

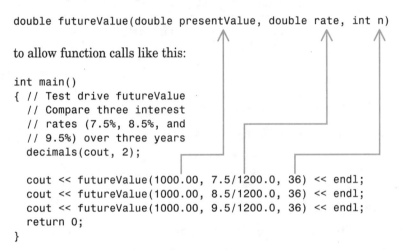

```
int main()
{ // Test drive futureValue
  // Compare three interest
  // rates (7.5%, 8.5%, and
  // 9.5%) over three years
  decimals(cout, 2);

  cout << futureValue(1000.00, 7.5/1200.0, 36) << endl;
  cout << futureValue(1000.00, 8.5/1200.0, 36) << endl;
  cout << futureValue(1000.00, 9.5/1200.0, 36) << endl;
  return 0;
}
```

5.4 void Functions and Reference Parameters &

The keyword `void` is used as the return type of functions that do not return anything. Instead of returning values back to the client, `void` functions are often employed to modify the state of the object(s) passed to them. For example, `grid::turnLeft`, `grid::move`, and `grid::putDown` all have `void` return types. These `grid` class member functions return nothing. Instead they modify the state of the `grid` object.

Nonmember functions might also return nothing. For example, `void clearScreen()` clears the screen without returning anything. Also, `void causeApause()` asks the user to press the Enter key before continuing with the program. Both perform well-defined functions, but neither need to return anything. Both `clearScreen` and `causeApause` are `void` functions.

Other `void` functions are often used to modify the state of one or more objects. This section shows a `void` function called `swap`, which modifies two arguments. Later, the `decimals` function is shown to modify one object—`cout`. A function must employ the reference parameter to modify the state of the object(s) in the function call or message. Here is the general form.

GENERAL FORM 5.4. *Reference parameter*

class-name **&** *identifier*

EXAMPLES OF REFERENCE PARAMETERS IN FUNCTION HEADINGS

```
void swap(double & parameterOne, double & parameterTwo)
void moveMoverToExit(grid & g)
void decimals(ostream & os, int n)
```

MEANING

A change to a reference parameter (with &) also modifies the associated argument. The parameter name is a reference to the associated argument.

5.4.1 Changes to More than One Object

Although parameters typically obtain input from the caller, they can sometimes establish a stronger connection between argument and parameter. In this first example of reference parameter usage, the swap function must modify two objects. Since only one value can be returned through a return statement, the function requires something besides the return statement to communicate more than one value back to the caller. This is accomplished when the special symbol & is placed before the parameter name in the function heading. Instead of receiving a copy of the argument, the function receives the memory location of the argument (a reference to the argument).

When a change is made to a reference parameter, the argument is also changed. For example, in the following program, when the swap function alters the parameters parmOne and parmTwo, the arguments argOne and argTwo also change state:

```
// Notice the reference symbol & is in front of parmOne and
// parmTwo. Now a change to parmOne or parmTwo alters the
// associated object argument.
#include <iostream>
using namespace std;
```

```
// & means that any change to the parameter also alters argument
void swap(int & parmOne, int & parmTwo)

{
  int temp = parmOne;
  parmOne = parmTwo;   // Change argument argOne in main
  parmTwo = temp;      // Change argument argTwo in main
}

int main()                                    // argOne:  argTwo:
{
  int argOne = 89, argTwo = 76;               // 89       76
  cout << argOne << "  " << argTwo << endl;

  swap(argOne, argTwo);                       // 76       89

  cout << argOne << "       " << argTwo << endl;

  return 0;
}
```

OUTPUT

```
89  76
76  89
```

If the &s are removed from the program above, no change is made to the arguments. In this case, the values of `argOne` and `argTwo` would be passed by value, not by reference. Without the reference symbol `&`, the values of `parmOne` and `parmTwo` are changed locally (within the function only) and the values of the associated arguments are unaffected.

Here is another example of reference parameter usage. The function named `getData` obtains input from the keyboard and then makes changes to both parameters. This has the effect of setting the state of two arguments in the call from `main`.

```
// Use references to return more than one value
#include <iostream>
#include <string>
using namespace std;

void getData(string & name, int & age)  // Reference parameters
{ // post: Returns a person's name and age
  string first, middle, last;

  cout << "Enter your first name: ";  cin >> first;
  cout << "  your middle initial: ";  cin >> middle;
  cout << "   and your last name: ";  cin >> last;
```

```
  name = last + ", " + first + " " + middle + ".";
  cout << "        Enter your age: ";  cin >> age;
}

int main()
{
  string name;
  int age = 0;

  getData(name, age);
  // assert: name and age have been modified

  cout << name << " will be " << age + 1 << " next year" << endl;
  return 0;
}
```

DIALOGUE

```
Enter your first name: Jody
  your middle initial: M
   and your last name: Manwiller
        Enter your age: 19
Manwiller, Jody M. will be 20 next year
```

The following figures illustrate the difference between reference and value parameters.

FIGURE 5.1. *Reference parameters*

With & the argument references the same memory as the parameter

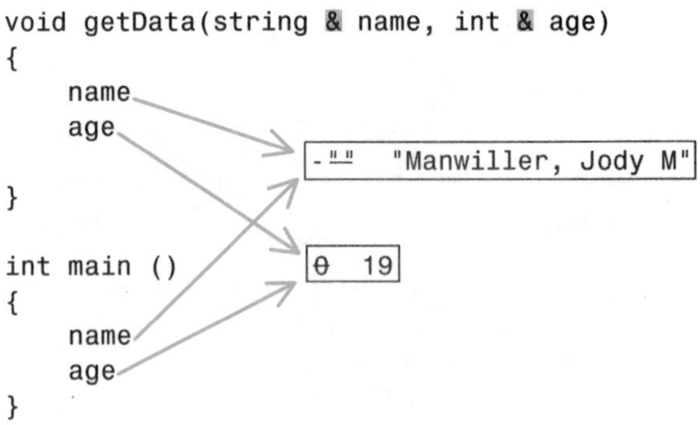

FIGURE 5.2. *Value parameters*

Without & the argument and parameter are different objects

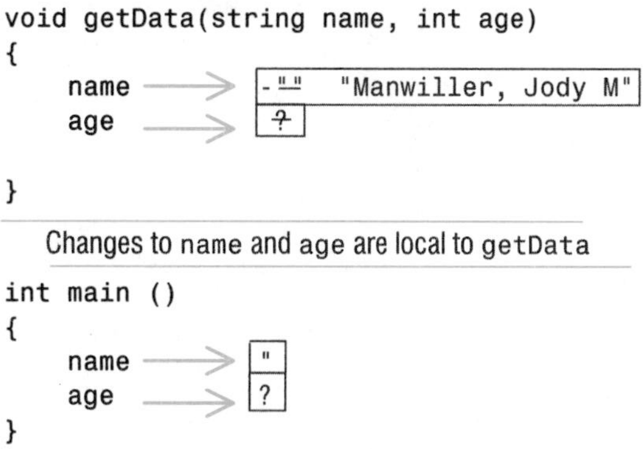

DIALOGUE (WITH & REMOVED FROM BOTH PARAMETERS)

```
Enter your first name: Jody
  your middle initial: M
    and your last name: Manwiller
        Enter your age: 19
 will be 0 next year
```

Self-Check

5-12 What are the values for arg1 after each program runs? Assume the user enters 77 at the prompt Enter an int:.

-a

```
#include <iostream>
using namespace std;
void getData(int anInt)
{
  cout << "Enter an int: ";
  cin >> anInt;
}

int main()
{
  int arg1 = 0;
  getData(arg1);
  return 0;
}
// arg1 ____
```

-b
```
#include <iostream>
using namespace std;
void getData(int & anInt)
{
  cout << "Enter an int: ";
  cin >> anInt;
}

int main()
{
  int arg1 = 0;
  getData(arg1);
  return 0;
}
// arg1 ____
```

5-13 Write the values of arg1 and arg2 at the moment when `return 0;` executes.

-a
```
#include <iostream>
using namespace std;
void changeOr(int a, int b)
{
  a = a * 2 + 1;
  b = 123;
}
int main()
{
  int arg1 = 5;
  int arg2 = 5;
  changeOr(arg1, arg2);
  return 0;
}
// arg1 ____    arg2 _____
```

-b
```
#include <iostream>
using namespace std;
void changeOr(int & a, int & b)
{
  a = a * 2 + 1;
  b = 123;
}
int main()
{
  int arg1 = 5;
  int arg2 = 5;
  changeOr(arg1, arg2);
```

```
    return 0;
  }
  // arg1 ____   arg2 ____
```

5.5 void decimals(ostream & os, int n)

Programmers must often control the number of decimals shown in floating-point output. The *default* situation—what happens unless something additional is done about it—is to show the minimum digits. This often produces bad-looking output. For example, the actual output below does not look like the preferred currency amounts.

```
// Show the default appearance of floating-point numbers
#include <iostream>  // For cout
using namespace std;

int main()
{
  double money = 112.50;
                           // Preferred output (two decimals):
  cout << money << endl;   // 112.50
  money = 123.00;          // 123.00
  cout << money << endl;   // 1234567890.00
  money = 1234567890.00;
  cout << money << endl;

  return 0;
}
```

OUTPUT

```
112.5
123
1.23457e+009
```

The appearance of floating-point output can be controlled with `ostream` class member functions. The `ostream::setf` (*set f*ormat flags) member function is used to modify the state-formatting characteristics of `cout` to control the appearance of floating-point values. The class member function `ostream::precision` controls the number of decimal places that show. For example, the following three messages modify the state of `cout` to ensure that floating-point values will always show with exactly two decimal places:

```
cout.setf(ios::fixed, ios::floatfield);
cout.setf(ios::showpoint);
cout.precision(2);
```

By placing these messages in a `void` function named `decimals`, any `ostream` object can be changed—such as the output that goes to a file on a disk (see Chapter 9, "File Streams"). Additionally, the precision can be set to any number of decimals. Notice that `void` represents the return type of `decimals`. This `void` function does not return any value. Instead, `decimals` is responsible for modifying the state of the first argument—`cout`. This function is so useful that it becomes available by including the file `compfun` that comes with this book. (*Note:* `decimals` is not a standard function; nor is the file `compfun`.) Here is a simplified implementation of `void decimals`:

```
void decimals(ostream & os, int n)  // void means no return allowed
{ // pre:  n >= 0
  // post: All subsequent floating-point output to the first
  //       argument, associated with os, is shown with a decimal
  //       point and n decimals
  os.setf(ios::fixed, ios::floatfield);
  os.setf(ios::showpoint);
  os.precision(n);
}
```

This `decimals` function changes the state of the first argument in the function call, so all subsequent floating-point output is shown with `n` decimal places specified as the second argument. Therefore, the function call

```
decimals(cout, 2);
```

ensures that all floating-point output to `cout` (the screen) will show the decimal point and two decimal places with rounding or trailing zeros as appropriate. This is in effect until the function is called again with a different second argument or until the program terminates.

The following program demonstrates the effect of calling `decimals` several times. (*Note:* Since `void` functions return nothing, `void` function calls are written as complete statements, rather than just as parts of statements. For example, you can't use the `decimals` function as part of another statement or as part of an expression with `*`, `+`, `<<`, or `=`.)

```
// Test drive the new decimals function

#include "compfun"    // For decimals(cout, 2)
#include <iostream>   // For cout
using namespace std;
```

```
int main()
{
  double x = 234.57;

  cout << "Default appearance: " << x << endl;

  decimals(cout, 1);
  cout << x << endl;

  decimals(cout, 2);
  cout << x << endl;

  decimals(cout, 3);
  cout << x << endl;

  return 0;
}
```

OUTPUT

```
Default appearance: 234.57
234.6
234.57
234.570
```

In the previous program, `cout` was *not* passed by value. If it had been, the formatting characteristics of `cout` would not have been altered and the output from `main` would have continued to show the value of `x` in the default state (minimum number of columns and always all five digits, 234.57). The presence of the `&` symbol ensures that any change made to the parameter named `os` also modifies the state of the associated argument `cout`. The presence of `&` makes the parameter `os` a reference to the argument `cout`.

In summary, the presence of `&` ensures that the identifiers `os` and `cout` are the same object. This is different from passing the value to a function. The `&` means the function call passes a *reference* to the function. The parameter `os` in this case is known as a reference parameter. The argument `cout` is *passed by reference.*

Although the parameters of functions are usually used for input, reference parameters with the `&` symbol are used to either

1. modify the state of an object, or
2. return more than one value from a function by modifying two or more arguments passed by reference.

The `decimals` function requires the reference parameter to alter the state of the associated argument—`cout`. Because object-oriented programming languages like C++ normally modify the state of objects through member functions, you will rarely see reference parameters (with `&`) in the member functions. Reference parameters are more typical in free (nonmember) functions such as `decimals`.

Self-Check

5-14 Write the output generated by the following four programs, which illustrate the difference between passing by value and passing by reference:

-a
```
#include <iostream>
using namespace std;
void addTwo(int & n1)
{ // Pass by reference
  n1 = n1 + 2;
}

int main()
{
  int anInt = 0;
  addTwo(anInt);
  addTwo(anInt);
  cout << anInt << endl;
  return 0;
}
```

-b
```
#include <iostream>
using namespace std;
void decimals(ostream & os, int n)
{
  os.setf(ios::fixed, ios::floatfield);
  os.setf(ios::showpoint);
  os.precision(n);
}

int main()
{
  decimals(cout, 5);
  cout << 0.0 << endl;
  cout << 1.23456789 << endl;
  return 0;
}
```

-c
```
#include <iostream>
using namespace std;
void addTwo(int n1)
{ // Pass by value
  n1 = n1 + 2;
```

```
}

int main()
{
  int anInt = 0;
  addTwo(anInt);
  addTwo(anInt);
  cout << anInt << endl;
  return 0;
}
```

-d
```
#include <iostream>
using namespace std;
void decimals(ostream os, int n)
{
  os.setf(ios::fixed, ios::floatfield);
  os.setf(ios::showpoint);
  os.precision(n);
}

int main()
{
  decimals(cout, 5);
  cout << 0.0 << endl;
  cout << 1.23456789 << endl;
  return 0;
}
```

5.6 Const Reference Parameters

You have now seen two of the parameter passing modes in C++. There are three:

1. value parameters—for passing the values of small objects such as `int`
2. reference parameters—to allow a function to modify the state of one or more arguments
3. const reference parameters—for safety and efficiency

The third parameter category is typically used for "big" objects (although any object could be passed by const reference rather than by value). A big object is one that requires a lot of memory. For example, `grid` represents a big object. The sizes of several objects are shown in the following program that compares the number of bytes required to store objects of five different classes. It uses the C++ `sizeof` operator, which returns the number of bytes required to store one default object of that class.

```
// This program shows the sizes of several classes
#include "baccount"   // For the bankAccount class
#include "grid"       // For the grid class
#include <iostream>
using namespace std;

int main()
{
  cout << "One int is " << sizeof(int) <<  " bytes" << endl;
  cout << "One double is " << sizeof(double) <<  " bytes" << endl;
  cout << "One bankAccount is " << sizeof(bankAccount) <<  " bytes" << endl;
  cout << "One ostream object is " << sizeof(ostream) <<  " bytes" << endl;
  cout << "One grid object is " << sizeof(grid) <<  " bytes" << endl;
  return 0;
}
```

OUTPUT (THE SIZE OF A CLASS VARIES BETWEEN COMPILERS; YOUR OUTPUT IS LIKELY DIFFERENT)

```
One int is 4 bytes
One double is 8 bytes
One bankAccount is 16 bytes
One ostream object is 72 bytes
One grid object is 820 bytes
```

To understand why programmers pass large objects by const reference, consider what happens to get an argument to the function. In general, a function call requires extra memory from the computer to copy the arguments into the function. For value parameters, the state of the object is copied to the function. For reference parameters, the object's address is copied so the function can modify the argument. Arguments associated with value parameters cannot be modified by the function. Arguments associated with reference parameters can be modified by the function. Arguments associated with const reference parameters cannot be modified by the function. The following table summarizes these points:

Pass by Value `int f1(int j)`	Pass by Reference `int f2(bankAccount & b)`	Pass by Const Reference `void f3(const grid & g)`
Grab enough memory to store the entire object and copy the value to the function. A change to the parameter has no effect on the argument.	Grab about four bytes of memory to store the address of the object and copy that address to the function. Use this when you need to modify the argument. It's efficient too.	Like pass by reference, except the `const` means the argument cannot be changed. Attempting a change results in a compiletime error. This is the efficient and safe parameter passing mode.
`f1` *cannot* modify the argument's state.	`f2` *can* modify the argument's state.	`f3` function *cannot* modify the argument's state. This is efficient.

There are two reasons to use const reference parameters. The first is efficiency—the program executes more quickly. The other consideration is better memory utilization—less memory is required to store the large object in the function. For example, passing a small object such as `int` by value only requires the function to allocate and then copy four bytes of memory. By contrast, one `grid` object passed by value requires 820 bytes. The program might exhaust available memory.

Additionally, every single byte of an argument passed by value will be copied to the function. The computer has to do a lot of unnecessary work. The program might run noticeably slower.

Here are two alternatives to make any program more efficient in terms of space (saves memory) and time (runs faster):

1. Pass big objects by reference—efficient but somewhat dangerous.
2. Pass big objects by const reference—efficient and safe.

The second option is highly recommended. The program now has much less work to do. For example, passing one `grid` object by value requires consuming 820 additional bytes of memory. The program must then wait until every single byte is copied from the caller to the function. If passed by const reference, only four bytes are required while the safety of value parameters (cannot change the state of the argument) remains intact.

Of course, if you are passing an argument to a function in order to modify the state, you must pass it by reference. Attempts to modify objects passed by const reference result in compiletime errors.

Using const is also an antibugging technique that will let the compiler catch attempts to modify the const objects. Any member function that does not modify the object may still be called—`grid::row`, for example. However, the compiler will flag any attempt to call functions such as `grid::move` that is clearly intended to modify the state of the object.

```
void foo(const grid & g)
{
  cout << g.row() << endl;  // OKAY
  g.move();  // ERROR: Attempt to modify a const object
}
```

However, when using value parameters only, you get no such error message. You might just sit there scratching your head wondering why, when your code modifies the parameter, the argument does not change.

Changing `x` in `f` Does Not Change `x` in `main`	Results in Compiletime Error Such as `cannot modify a const object`

`#include <iostream>`
`using namespace std;`
 	
`double f(double x)`
`{`
`  double result;`
`  // This does not modify`
`  // main's x`
`  x = x - 1;`
`  result = 2 * x;`
`  return result;`
`}`
 	
`int main()          // Output:`
`{                   // 8`
`  double x = 5.0; // x is 5`
`  cout << f(x) << endl;`
`  cout << "x is " << x << endl;`
`  return 0;`
`}`
	`#include <iostream>`
	`using namespace std;`
	
	`double f(const double & x)`
	`{`
	`  double result;`
	`  // This generates an error.`
	`  // Good!`
	`  x = x - 1;`
	`  result = 2 * x;`
	`  return result;`
	`}`
	
	`int main()`
	`{`
	`  double x = 5.0;`
	`  cout << f(x) << endl;`
	`  cout << "x is " << x << endl;`
	`  return 0;`
	`}`

It should be noted that only a few objects will be passed by const reference until Chapter 10—just the "big" `grid` objects. So you will only occasionally see a `grid` or another big object passed by const reference in the next several chapters. Also, value parameters will be more common than reference parameters.

Chapter Summary

- Chapter 5 began by showing how to implement C++ nonmember functions. Functions perform some well-defined services and can have two-way communication through argument/parameter associations and the return statement. The client code supplies input values to the function as arguments. The result is returned via the return statement.
- There are several new implementation issues related to functions such as the scope of identifiers:
  - All identifiers must be declared before they can be referenced.
  - The scope of an object is limited to the block where it is declared.
  - Some identifiers are not declared within a block. In this case, they are global identifiers. Examples of global identifiers include the `sqrt` function after `#include <cmath>`, the global object `cout` after `#include <iostream>`, and the const `int` objects `north`, `south`, `east`, and `west` after `#include "grid"`. This assumes `using namespace std;` has been written after the `#includes`.
  - The scope of a parameter is limited to its function.
  - The scope of a function begins at the function heading and continues to the end of its file, or the end of the file that included the function.
- There are many details to remember when using argument/parameter associations. Here are a few that apply to both nonmember and class member functions:
  - The number of arguments used in a function call must match the number of parameters declared in the function heading.
  - The `void` return type precedes the function name when no value is to be returned. You cannot return anything from a `void` function.[1]
  - When one value is to be returned from a function, a non`void` return type must begin the function heading. The return statement must also be included in the function block. The expression in the return statement should be the same class as the return type.
  - Sometimes a function needs input—that's what parameters are for. Sometimes a function must return something—that's what the return statement is for. Sometimes a function needs to modify objects in the client code—that's what reference parameters are for.

---

1. However, `return` can be used in a `void` function by itself to terminate the function. In this case it looks like this: `return;`

- The argument used in a function call should usually be the same class as its associated parameter. There are exceptions; for example, an `int` argument may be associated with a `double` parameter.
- Parameters intended only to receive copies of the argument values (input parameters) should be declared as value parameters without `&`.
- Reference parameters (with `&`) must be used if the intention is to modify the associated argument—a change to a reference parameter alters the argument (a change to a value parameter does not).
- Const reference parameters are used to pass large objects. Instead of consuming extra bytes of memory, the address is copied—because of `&`. However, the safety of value parameters is ensured by making the parameters const.

Exercises

16. Will a change to a value parameter modify the associated argument?

17. Will a change to a reference parameter modify the associated argument?

18. Will a change to a const reference parameter modify the associated argument?

19. Write the output generated by the following program:

```
#include <iostream>  // For the object cout
using namespace std;
int main()
{
  double x = 9.87654321;
  cout.setf(ios::fixed, ios::floatfield);
  cout.setf(ios::showpoint);
  cout.precision(4);
  cout << x << endl;
  return 0;
}
```

20. Write the output generated by the following program:

```
#include "grid"  // For the grid class
#include <iostream>
using namespace std;

void setBlocks(grid & g)
{ // pre:  The argument associated with g is a 4-by-4 grid object
  // post: The upper-left edge of the argument is blocked
```

```
  g.block(0,0); g.block(0,1); g.block(0,2); g.block(0,3);
  g.block(1,0); g.block(2,0); g.block(3,0);
}

int main()
{
  grid tarpit(4, 4, 1, 1, east);
  setBlocks(tarpit);
  tarpit.display();
  return 0;
}
```

21. Explain why no blocks would be set in `tarpit` if `&` is removed from before `g`.

Programming Tips

3. There are several ways that functions communicate with each other.

- The caller can send values and objects to a function by value.
- The caller sends objects as arguments to a function by reference when the function is designed to change the arguments.
- The caller sends objects as arguments to a function by const reference to save time and memory when the function is not supposed to change the arguments.
- The caller gets values back from a function via the return statement.
- The caller gets values back from a function by having the function change arguments associated with reference parameters changed in the function.

4. If you want two or more values back from a function, use reference parameters.

The return statement returns only one thing. If you need more than one thing back from a function, use one or more reference parameters in addition to a return statement.

5. If the object is big and you don't want to change it, pass it by const reference.

You will probably not notice any difference in the programs you write. But it can make a big difference in certain circumstances so get in the habit now.

Programming Projects

5I Move Three

Complete the `moveThree` function that directs the mover on a `grid` object three spaces. This version uses the efficient reference parameter (`grid & g`). Use the following test driver:

```
#include <iostream>  // For cout
#include "grid"      // For the grid class

void moveThree(grid & g)  // Reference parameter
{  // pre: The mover can move three spaces in its current direction
   // Complete this function block (remember to return the result)
}

int main()
{ // Test drive moveThree                Output:
  grid tarpit(4, 10, 1, 1, east);        // . . . . . . . . . .
  moveThree(tarpit);                     // .       > . . . . .
  tarpit.display();                      // . . . . . . . . . .
  return 0;                              // . . . . . . . . . .
}
```

5J Block Three

Complete a function `blockThree` that blocks all the edges of a 3-by-3 grid. This version uses the efficient reference parameter (`grid & g`). When you have finished, change the parameter from a reference parameter to a value parameter by deleting the `&`. What is the consequence? Next change `g` to a const reference parameter. What is the consequence?

```
#include <iostream>  // For cout
#include "grid"      // For the grid class

void blockThree(grid & g)  // Pass by reference
{ // pre:  g is a 3-by-3 grid
  // post: The associated argument has the entire outer edge blocked with #
  // Complete this function block
}

int main()
{ // Test drive blockThree               Output:
  grid tarpit(3, 3, 1, 1, east);        // # # #
                                        // # > #
  blockThree(tarpit);                   // # # #
```

```
  tarpit.display();
  return 0;
}
```

5K modifyGrid: A void Function with Reference Parameters

Complete a function `modifyGrid` that places blocks on all outer edges of a 5-by-5 grid and things on all inner intersections except where the mover is (in row 2, column 2). When you have finished, change the parameter from a reference parameter to a value parameter by deleting the `&`. What is the consequence? Next change `g` to a const reference parameter. What is the consequence?

```
#include <iostream>  // For cout
#include "grid"      // For the grid class

void modifyGrid(grid & g)  // Pass by reference
{ // pre:  g is a 5-by-5 grid with the mover in row 2, column 2
  // post: The associated argument has the entire outer edge blocked with #
  //       and there is a cookie on the other rows and columns
  // Complete this function block
}
int main()
{ // Test drive blockThree             Output:
  grid tarpit(5, 5, 2, 2, north);    // # # # # #
                                     // # O O O #
  modifyGrid(tarpit);                // # O ^ O #
  tarpit.display();                  // # O O O #
                                     // # # # # #
  return 0;
}
```

5L Display bankAccounts

Complete a function `display` that shows one bank account in the format shown:

```
#include <iostream>   // For cout
#include "baccount"   // For the bankAccount class

void display(const bankAccount & anAcct)  // Pass by reference
{
  // You implement the function. Make sure your output matches exactly.
}

int main()
{
  bankAccount a("Annie Hill", 123.00);
```

```
  bankAccount b("Bob Becker", 45.60);
  display(a);
  display(b);
  return 0;
}
```

OUTPUT

```
{ bankAccount: Hill, Annie, $123.00 }
{ bankAccount: Becker, Bob, $45.60 }
```

5M Hurdles

Write a program that constructs a hurdle course as shown below and instructs the runner to jump the hurdles. The runner must touch the ground between each hurdle. Show the grid before and after the course is run. First retype the following test driver and then implement the functions `initializedGrid` and `jumpHurdle`.

```
#include "grid"  // For the grid class

void jumpHurdle(grid & g)
{ // post: The mover has jumped one hurdle
  // You complete this
}

grid initializedGrid()
{ // post: Return a 4-by-22 grid ready to run a 4x hurdle race
  // You complete this
}

int main()
{ // Test drive initializedGrid and jumpHurdle
  grid jumper = initializedGrid();

  jumper.display();
  jumpHurdle(jumper);
  jumpHurdle(jumper);
  jumpHurdle(jumper);
  jumpHurdle(jumper);
  jumpHurdle(jumper);
  jumper.display();
  return 0;
}
```

OUTPUT

```
The grid:
. . . . . . . . . . . . . . . . . . . . . .
. . . . . . . . . . . . . . . . . . . . . .
> . . # . . . # . . . # . . . # . . . # . .
. . . . . . . . . . . . . . . . . . . . . .

The grid:
. . . . . . . . . . . . . . . . . . . . . .
. .       .       .       .       .       .
      #       #       #       #       # > .
. . . . . . . . . . . . . . . . . . . . . .
```

Chapter Six

Class Definitions and Member Functions

Summing Up

Functions hide details, can be called many times, can be reused in other programs, and help in the design of larger programs. Each function performs a well-defined service.

Coming Up

When a function belongs to a class, it becomes a class member function. Class member functions have a lot in common with their nonmember cousins. Chapter 6 presents an introduction to C++ class definition and member function implementations. You will learn to read and understand classes by their definitions—the collection of member function headings (the interface) and data members (the state). In the second part of this chapter, you will learn to implement class member functions. You will also see a few appropriate object-oriented design heuristics that help explain why classes are designed the way they are. After studying this chapter, you will be able to

- read and understand class definitions (interface and state)
  Exercises and projects to reinforce reading new class interfaces
- implement class member functions using existing class definitions
- apply some object-oriented design heuristics
  Exercises and projects to reinforce member function implementation

---

This chapter could be studied after Chapter 10, "Vectors." Some projects and a few subsections marked with a Chapter 6 prerequisite would have to be skipped. This provides the flexibility to learn classes early, late, or not at all. This textbook is designed to accommodate all three approaches.

6.1 The Interface

Abstraction refers to the practice of using and understanding something without full knowledge of its implementation. Abstraction allows the programmer using a class to concentrate on the data characteristics and the messages that manipulate state. For example, a programmer using the `string` class need not know the details of the internal data representation nor how those operations are implemented in the hardware and software. The programmer can concentrate on the set of allowable messages—the *interface.*

This chapter presents some implementation issues that so far have been hidden. In the first part of this chapter, the `bankAccount` class will be studied at the implementation-detail level. However, before examining the physical side of class design let's consider some of the design decisions that were made for this textbook's `bankAccount` class.

6.1.1 Design Decisions with the `bankAccount` Class

All `bankAccount` objects have four allowable operations: `deposit`, `withdraw`, `balance`, and `name`. There could have been more, or there could have been less. The member functions for `bankAccount` were chosen to keep the class simple and to provide a collection of operations that are relatively easy to relate to. A compromise was made. The design decisions were influenced by the context—a first example of a C++ class used in a particular domain—the area of banking.

The `bankAccount` member functions that make up the interface are only a subset of the operations named by students who were asked this question: What should we be able to do with bank accounts? The data members are also a subset of the operations named by students who were asked this question: What should bank accounts know about themselves?

Many additional operations that were recognized by students—`transfer`, `applyInterest`, `printMonthlyStatement`—and many additional data members—type of account, record of transactions, address, social security number, and mother's maiden name—were not included. The design of these classes was affected by the intention of keeping these objects as simple as possible while retaining some realism. However, a group of object-oriented designers developing large-scale applications in the banking domain would likely retain many of the operations and attributes recognized by students. There is rarely one single design that is correct for all circumstances.

Designing anything requires making decisions in an effort to make the thing "good." Good might mean having a software component that is easily maintainable; it might mean classes that can be reused in other applications; or it might mean a system that is very robust—one that can recover from almost any disastrous event. Good might mean a design that results in something that is easier to use, prettier, etc. There is rarely ever a single perfect design. There are usually trade-offs. Design is an iterative process that evolves with time. Design is influenced by personal opinion, evolving research, the domain (banking, information systems, process control, engineering, for example), and a variety of other influences. Fortunately, there are design heuristics (guidelines) to show the way, a few of which are presented later.

Let's now turn to the construct that captures many of these design decisions in object-oriented software development—the class definition.

6.2 Class Definitions

The classes of objects under study—`ostream (cout)`, `istream (cin)`, `string`, `int`, and `double`—are building blocks of larger programs. However, programs typically require many other classes. They may be standard classes, classes that are bought off the shelf, or other classes that must be designed and implemented by the programming team.

Because it is difficult to have mastery of all classes in a large project, this section provides some general techniques for understanding unfamiliar classes. The knowledge attained here also provides experience with the major component of object-oriented software development—the class.

This process begins with learning to read class definitions. You will also implement member functions and add new operations to existing classes. This approach has the added benefit of making it easier to design and implement new classes of your own. You will not be asked to design new classes until Chapters 12 and 13, when you design classes after discovering the need for them during analysis.

A *class definition* lists member functions after the keyword `public:`. This set of operations represents the class interface. The class definition also lists the *data members*—the object declarations after `private:`. This set of data members represents the state of the objects.

A class definition provides a lot of information. A class definition stresses the *what,* not the *how.* It lists the messages understood by the objects. It specifies the number and type of arguments required when sending a message to one of the objects. When documented with preconditions, postconditions, and example messages, a class definition also explains how to use instances of the class. The documentation may provide other pertinent information. All of these things allow the programmer to use objects of the class without knowing the details of the implementation.

General Form 6.1. *Class definition*

```
class class-name {
public:   // MEMBER FUNCTIONS (the interface)
//--constructors
  class-name() ;                        // Default constructor
  class-name(parameter-list) ;          // Another constructor
//--modifiers
  function-heading ;                    // Member function that modifies the state
  function-heading ;                    // Member function that modifies the state
//--accessors
  function-heading const;               // Member function that accesses the state
  function-heading const;               // Member function that accesses the state
  ...
private:   // STATE
  object-declaration                    // Data member
  object-declaration                    // Data member
  ...
} ;
```

6.2.1 An Example Definition: The `bankAccount` Class

Now, let's get down to a concrete, familiar example. You are probably familiar with your own bank account. Recall that a `bankAccount` object stores the data necessary to manipulate one account at a bank. Each `bankAccount` object stores some unique identification (`string my_name;` below) and an account balance (`double my_balance;` below). Operations in `bankAccount` include making deposits, making withdrawals, and accessing the current balance.

The data members in the private section represent the state. The data members maintained by every `bankAccount` object include `my_name` (a string) and `my_balance` (a double). Every instance of this `bankAccount` class stores its own private name and balance data (the object's state). In other words, every `bankAccount` object knows its own name and current balance.

Class Definition: *bankAccount*

File baccount.h

Class Diagram

```
class bankAccount {
public:  // OPERATIONS

//--constructors

  bankAccount();
  // post: Construct a default bankAccount object

  bankAccount(string initName, double initBalance);
  // post: Construct with two arguments:
  //       bankAccount anAcct("Hall", 100.00);

//--modifiers

  void deposit(double depositAmount);
  // post: Credit depositAmount to the balance

  void withdraw(double withdrawalAmount);
  // post: Debit withdrawalAmount from the balance

//--accessors

  double balance() const;
  // post: Return this account's current balance

  string name() const;
  // post: Return this account's name

private:  // STATE
  string my_name;
  double my_balance;
};
```

Example messages in the context of a program provide a valuable resource for understanding the behavior of unfamiliar objects written by other programmers. The messages could be gathered together within the context of a program that uses every operation (class member function) listed in the class definition. Such a test driver acts as a summary of the entire interface.

The following program sends every possible message to `anAcct`. Additionally, a default object is constructed to illustrate the default state of `bankAccount` objects. Now there are two different classes of objects that represent the state of a `bankAccount`—a `string` name and a numeric balance.

```
// Send every possible message to one bankAccount object and show
// the default bankAccount state

#include <iostream>
using namespace std;
#include "baccount"  // For the bankAccount class

int main()
{
  bankAccount anAcct("Moss", 500.00);  // Construct an object
  bankAccount defaultAccount;  // Default name is "?name?".
                               // Default balance is 0.00.

  anAcct.withdraw(100.00);                          // Modify state
  anAcct.deposit(40.00);                            // Modify state
  cout << "Name: " << anAcct.name() << endl;        // Access state
  cout << "Balance: " << anAcct.balance() << endl;  // Access state

  cout << "Default Name: " << defaultAccount.name() << endl;
  cout << "Default Balance: " << defaultAccount.balance() << endl;

  return 0;
}
```

To test the success of the documentation, your ability to read class definitions, and the use of descriptive identifiers to properly represent the operations, you will be asked questions similar to these later on but with new classes. In fact, the first three programming projects require you to read new class definitions.

Self-Check

6-1 Write the output generated by the preceding program.

6-2 List the operations that make up the interface of the `bankAccount` class.

6-3 List the data members of this `bankAccount` class.

6-4 Use the class definition to answer the questions that follow:

-a What happens during a withdraw message when an argument of `-20.00` is passed to `withdrawalAmount`?

-b What happens during a withdraw message when an argument of `100.00` is passed to `withdrawalAmount` and the balance is `50.00`?

-c What happens during a withdraw message when an argument of `100.00` is passed to `withdrawalAmount` and the balance is `300.00`?

-d What happens during a deposit message when an argument of `-20.00` is passed to `deposit`?

-e What happens during a deposit message when an argument of `20.00` is passed to `deposit`?

6.2.2 Constructors

Most `bankAccount` function headings are similar to the nonmember function headings discussed earlier—they usually have return types and parameters. However, two member functions do not fall into this category. Did you notice something different about the two function headings named `bankAccount`?

First of all, the two `bankAccount::bankAccount` member functions have no return type. They also have the same name as the class! These special member functions are dubbed *constructors* because they are used to "build" objects. Constructors associate the object name with a portion of memory and initialize the data members of the object. Here are some examples of messages that result in execution of a class constructor:

```
grid aGrid(10, 10, 5, 4, east);
string name;
string aString("The initial value of this object");
bankAccount a;
bankAccount b("Katey Jo Delong", 10.00);
```

Object construction is different from other messages, both in semantics and in syntax. There is no "dotting" and you don't need parentheses for the default constructor.

GENERAL FORM 6.2. *Calling a constructor (initializing objects)*

class-name *object-name* ;

- or -

class-name *object-name* (*initial-state*) ;

The *class-name* is the name of its class. The *object-name* is any valid identifier and *initial-state* is represented by the arguments supplied in the client code. When a constructor is encountered with arguments, the *initial-state* is passed to the object's data members. The state of the object is initialized. For example, the following code constructs a `bankAccount` object with an initial name of `"Patricia Patterson"` and an initial balance of `507.34`:

```
bankAccount one("Patricia Patterson", 507.34);
```

When another object is constructed like this:

```
bankAccount another("Bob Zimmerman", 437.05);
```

there exists a separate `bankAccount` object with its own name of `"Bob Zimmerman"` and its own initial balance of `437.05`. So the return values of these two messages would be `507.34` followed by `437.05`.

```
cout << one.balance() << " " << another.balance() << endl;
```

When the default constructor is used—as in the following two lines of code—the object is initialized to the default state appropriate for that class of objects:

```
bankAccount aDefaultAccount;
string name;
```

For example, the default `string` state is the null string, and for `bankAccount` the default name is `"?name?"` and the default initial balance is `0.00`—guaranteed, every time.

Self-Check

Use this class definition to answer the self-check questions that follow:

```
class libraryBook {
public:
//--constructors
  libraryBook();
  // post: Create a default libraryBook object
  // ex: libraryBook aBook;

  libraryBook(string initTitle, string initAuthor);
  // post: Initialize a libraryBook object
  // ex: libraryBook aBook("Patriot", "Clancy");

//--modifiers
  void borrowBook(string borrowersName);
  // post: Records the borrower's name
```

libraryBook
borrowBook (borrower) returnBook() string borrower
string my_author string my_title string my_borrower

```
  // ex:   aBook.borrowBook("Wilma Riveria");

  void returnBook();
  // post: The book becomes available
  // ex:   aBook.returnBook();

//--accessor
  string borrower() const;
  // post: Returns "not currently borrowed" if the book is
  //       available or the borrower's name if the book is out
  // ex:   aBook.returnBook();

private:
  string my_author;
  string my_title;
  string my_borrower;
};
```

6-5 What is the name of the class shown above?

6-6 Except for constructors, name all the operations.

6-7 What type of value is returned by `libraryBook::borrower`?

6-8 What type of value is returned by `libraryBook::borrowBook`?

6-9 What class of argument must be part of all `libraryBook::borrowBook` messages?

6-10 How many arguments are required to initialize one `libraryBook` object?

6-11 Initialize one `libraryBook` object using your favorite book and author.

6-12 Send the message that borrows your favorite book. Use your own name as the argument.

6-13 Write the message that reveals the borrower's name of your favorite book.

6-14 Without knowing the implementation of the class member functions, write the output generated by the following program. Assume the class is defined by including the file named `libbook`.

```
// Send every possible message to a libraryBook object
#include <iostream>   // For cout
using namespace std;
#include "libbook"    // For the libraryBook class
```

```
int main()
{
  libraryBook aBook("Little Drummer Girl", "John LeCarre");

  cout << aBook.borrower() << endl;
  aBook.borrowBook("Chris Miller");
  cout << aBook.borrower() << endl;
  aBook.returnBook();
  cout << aBook.borrower() << endl;

  return 0;
}
```

6.3 The State Object Pattern

Even though quite different in specific operations and state, `string`, `bankAccount`, and `libraryBook` objects have the following common characteristics:

- private data members store the state of the object
- constructors initialize the state
- some messages modify the state
- other messages allow access to the current state of the object

These commonalities guide the effective use of these and similar classes of objects. Later on, these commonalities will also help guide effective implementation of C++ classes. These common traits are a pattern, or more specifically they represent an object pattern as described by Eugene Wallingford [Wallingford 96]. An *object pattern* is a guide for designing and implementing new classes. In his paper, Wallingford describes several object patterns, the first of which is State Object, a pattern that describes objects that "maintain a body of data and provide suitable access to it by other objects and human users."

6.3.1 Using Constructors, Modifiers, and Accessors

Object patterns also help programmers understand how to use new objects. The constructors, modifiers, and accessors in the `public:` section of a class definition are the operations available to all instances of the class.

6.3.1.1 Constructors

Constructors are present for many reasons, including initializing the state of any instance of the class. As shown earlier, objects are initialized like this:

```
string aString("initial string");
// assert: State of aString is "initial string", length of 14

string aDefaultString;
// assert: State of aDefaultString is ""

bankAccount anAcct("Early Grey", 2150.67);
// assert: Early Grey has a starting balance of 2,150.67

bankAccount aDefaultAccount;
// assert: aDefaultAccount.name() would return "?name?" and
//         aDefaultAccount.balance() would return 0.0

libraryBook aBook("Pride and Prejudice", "Jane Austen");
// assert: aBook represents a classic book written by Jane Austen
```

6.3.1.2 Modifiers

Modifiers[1] modify the state of an object. Modifiers are part of the State Object pattern for a variety of reasons. Perhaps it's best to simply show some example messages that modify the state of an object.

```
aString.replace(1, 3, "NEW");
// assert: s2 is "iNEWial string"

g.move(5);
// assert: The mover is five spaces forward

anAcct.withdraw(50.00);
// assert: The balance of anAcct is 50.00 less

aBook.borrowBook("Fred Featherstone");
// assert: aBook's borrower has become Fred Featherstone
```

Sending a modifier message results in a change of state. Modifiers are not declared with const after the function heading—accessors are.

6.3.1.3 Accessors

Accessors are part of a state object simply because programmers often need to access the state of an object. An accessor message returns information related to the state of an object. An accessor may simply return the value of a data member as with `libraryBook::borrower` and `bankAccount::balance`. Accessors may also need to do some internal processing using the state of an object to return the information

1. Some computer scientists and software engineers use the word *mutator* rather than *modifier.*

(`employee::incomeTax`, for instance). Here are some example messages that access the state of objects:

```
s2.length()         // Return the number of characters in s2
g.row()             // Return the mover's current row
anEmployee.incomeTax() // Return income tax based on IRS tax tables
anAcct.balance()    // Return the current balance of anAcct
aBook.borrower()    // Return the borrower's name of aBook
```

6.3.2 Naming Conventions

Modifying operations are typically given a name that indicates the message will change the state of the object. This is easily accomplished if the designer of the class simply gives a descriptive name to the operation. The name should describe—as best as possible—what the operation actually does. Another way to help programmers who use a class to distinguish modifiers from accessors is to give the modifiers names that can be used as verbs:[2] `withdraw`, `deposit`, `borrowBook`, and `returnBook`, for example. The accessors are given names that can be used as nouns: `borrower` and `balance`. Considering that the constructor has the same name as the class, some guidelines are now established (as a pattern) for designing and reading class definitions. These three categories of operations—typical of state objects—can be distinguished by following these naming conventions:

Operation	Name
Constructor	Same name as the class
Modifier	Identifier name that could be used as a verb
Accessor	Identifier name that could be used as a noun

Above all, always try to use identifiers that describe what the object is. For example, don't use `x` as the name of the operation to withdraw money from a `bankAccount` (or `turnRight` to make the mover `turnLeft`).

Self-Check

6-15 What is meant when the `const` keyword is part of the function heading in a class definition?

2. Because many words can be used as verbs and nouns (*balance,* for instance), some programmers precede modifiers with `set` and accessors with `get`.

6-16	Which member functions have the same name as the class?
6-17	What do accessors do?
6-18	What do modifiers do?
6-19	What do constructors do?
6-20	What are the data members for?

6.4 public: or private:

One of the considerations in the design of a class is the placement of member functions and data members under the most appropriate access mode, either `public:` or `private:`. Whereas public members of a class can be called by a client (outside of the class), the scope of private members is limited to the class member functions. For example, the `bankAccount` data member named `my_balance` is only known to the member functions of the class. On the other hand, any member declared in the `public:` section of a class is known everywhere in the class and also in the block of source code where the object is declared (or globally, if constructed outside of a block).

Access Mode	Where Is the Member Known?
`public:`	In all class member functions and in the block of the client code where the object has been declared (in `main`, for instance)
`private:`	Only in class member functions

Although the data members representing state could have been declared under `public:`, it is highly recommended that all data members be declared under the `private:` access mode. There are several reasons for this.

The consistency helps simplify some design decisions. More importantly, when data members are made `private:`, the state can be modified only through a member function. This prevents client code from indiscriminately changing the state of objects. For example, it's impossible to accidentally make a credit like this:

```
bankAccount myAcct("Mine", 100.00);

// An error occurs: attempting to modify private data
myAcct.my_balance = myAcct.my_balance + 100000.00;  // <- ERROR
```

or a debit like this:

```
// An error occurs: attempting to modify private data
myAcct.my_balance = myAcct.my_balance - 100.00;
```

6.4.1 Separating Interface from Implementation

The practice of studying a class through its interface represents a principle in software engineering. It allows one to separate the interface from the implementation (the details of how the operations actually work). In C++, the completed member function implementations are often separated from the interface (the class definition) by placing them in separate files. Historically, class definitions have been kept in `.h` files with member function implementations in `.cpp` files (or `.cc` files in Unix). However, this is changing. Some programmers implement the member functions directly in the same file as the class definitions.

The convention used for the programming projects in this textbook is to separate the definition from the implementation by storing the class definition in a `.h` file and the member function implementation in a `.cpp` file. To simplify things, this textbook's disk contains additional `#include` files that `#include` the class definition from the proper `.h` file and the member function implementations from the proper `.cpp` file. For example, when a program includes a file like this,

```
#include "baccount"  // For the bankAccount class
```

additional *preprocessor directives* come into effect:

```
// File name: baccount
#ifndef _BACCOUNT_  // The first two lines mean the two #includes
#define _BACCOUNT_  // that follow will only be performed once
#include "baccount.h"     // For the bankAccount class definition
#include "baccount.cpp"   // For the member function implementations
#endif
```

Therefore, one `#include` actually `#includes` both parts of a class—the class definition and the member function implementations (discussed in the second part of this chapter). The first two lines, `#ifndef _BACCOUNT_` and `#define _BACCOUNT_`, ensure that the files are included only once. It reads like this: If the identifier `_BACCOUNT_` is not defined, define it. Then, at an attempt to `#include baccount` a second or third time, everything is skipped down to `#endif`. This prevents errors such as "class/function already defined."

Exercises

Use the `room` class definition from the domain of a home heating system to answer exercises 1–11.

Class Definition
(not implemented anywhere)

```
class room {
public:
//--constructors
  room();
  room(string initName);
//--modifiers
  void set_desiredTemp(int newTemp);
//--accessors
  int desiredTemp() const;
  // post: Return des. temp. setting
  int actualTemp() const;
  // post: Return current room temp.
  int isOccupied() const;
  // post: Return 1 if someone is in
           the room and 0 if no one
           is present
private:
  string my_roomName;
  int desiredTempSetting;
  actualTempDevice my_actDev;
  desiredTempDevice my_desDev;
  occupancySensorDevice my_occDev;
};
```

Class Diagram

room
set_desiredTemp(int) int desiredTemp() int actualTemp() int isOccupied()
string my_roomName int my_desiredTempSetting actualTempDevice my_actDev desiredTempDevice my_desDev occupancySensorDevice my_occDev

1. What is the name of the class?
2. Name all the operations besides the constructors.
3. How many data members are there?
4. `room::desiredTemp` returns what type of value?
5. Which operations can modify any `room` object?
6. Which operations do not modify `room` objects?
7. Construct an object named `kitchen` that has a `room` name of `kitchen`.

8. Set the desired temperature to 70 degrees Fahrenheit.

9. Write a statement that displays the `room`'s desired temperature.

10. Write a statement that displays the `room`'s actual temperature.

11. Write a message that returns the integer 1 if someone is in the `room`.

Use this class definition to answer exercises 12–19:

Class Definition (not implemented anywhere)

```
class ATM {
public:
//--constructors
  ATM();
  ATM(int dollars);
//--modifiers
  void startUp();
  void getEnvelope();
  void dispenseCash();
//--accessor
  int dollarLevel() const;
private:
  cardReader my_cardReader;
  keyPad my_keyPad;
  cashDispenser my_cashDispenser;
  receiptPrinter my_receiptPrinter;
  transactionList my_transactionList;
};
```

Class Diagram

ATM
startUp() getEnvelope() dispenseCash() int dollarLevel()
cardReader my_cardReader keyPad my_keyPad cashDispenser my_cashDispenser receiptPrinter my_receiptPrinter transactionList my_transactionList

12. What is the name of the class?

13. How may constructors are there?

14. Name all operations other than the constructors named `ATM`.

15. How many data members does this class have?

16. What type of value is returned by `ATM::dollarLevel`?

17. Which operations modify any `ATM` object?

18. Which operations only access the state of any `ATM` object?

19. Write a test driver that sends every possible message to one `ATM` object. Assume the class becomes available with `#include "ATM"`.

Programming Tips

1. Be sure to `#include "weekemp"` for the first three programming projects.

The first three programming projects (6A, 6B, and 6C) require the definition of the `weeklyEmp` class from the file `weekemp.h`. They also require the member functions from `weekemp.cpp`. If these two files are in your working folder (directory), simply place this at the beginning of your program:

```
#include "weekemp"  // #include weekemp.h and weekemp.cpp
```

2. Here is your chance to read a new class definition.

The first three programming projects (6A, 6B, and 6C) require the `weeklyEmp` class. It is repeated here for your convenience, followed by a summary class diagram.

```
// You can include this class definition in your program with
// #include "weekemp" which includes the class definition of weekemp.h
// and member function implementations of weekemp.cpp
class weeklyEmp {
public:

//--constructors
  weeklyEmp();

  weeklyEmp(string initName,
            double initHours,
            double initRate,
            int initExemptions,
            string initFilingStatus);
  // post: A weeklyEmp object is initialized with five arguments:
  //       weeklyEmp anEmp("Hall, Rob", 40.0, 9.75, 3, "M");
  //       The fourth argument must be in the range of 0 to 99. The
  //       last argument is either "M" for married or "S" for single.

//--modifiers

  void set_hours(double thisWeeksHours);
  // post: Set the hours worked for a given week

  void set_rate(double thisWeeksRate);
  // post: Change the employee's hourly rate of pay
```

```
//--accessors

  double grossPay() const;
  // post: Return gross pay with overtime

  double incomeTax() const;
  // post: Return the federal income tax

  double FICATax() const;
  // post: Return the social security tax

  string name() const;
  // post: Return the employee's name

 private:
  string my_name;
  double my_hours;
  double my_rate;
  int my_exemptions;
  string my_filingStatus;
};
```

weeklyEmp
set_hours(newHours) set_rate(newRate) double grossPay() double incomeTax() double FICATax() string name()
string my_name double my_hours double my_rate int my_exemptions string my_filingStatus

Programming Projects

6A weeklyEmp

Write a complete C++ program that will

* initialize one `weeklyEmp` object (see the `weeklyEmp` class definition above)
* display the `weeklyEmp` object's gross pay
* display the `weeklyEmp` object's income tax

6B Payroll for One

Write a payroll program that produces a simple paycheck for one weeklyEmp object. The program must input the employee's name, filing status (S or M), number of exemptions, hourly rate of pay, and hours worked. The paycheck should be formatted to always show currency amounts rounded to the nearest hundredth. The output must include the employee's name, the gross pay, all taxes, and the net pay. Here is one sample dialogue and an example paycheck with headings:

```
Name: Lucas
Hourly Rate: 10.00
Hours Worked: 40
```

```
Exemptions: 2
S)ingle M)arried: M

Employee: Lucas
  Gross  Income     FICA      Net
    Pay     Tax      Tax      Pay
 ======  ======   ======  =======
 400.00   ??.??    ??.??  ????.??
```

6C Raise and Overtime

Write a C++ program that will:

- initialize a `weeklyEmp` object who is married (use `"M"` as the fifth argument in the constructor), has three exemptions (the fourth argument), and worked 40.0 hours at $10.00 per hour
- display the gross pay and income tax
- give the employee a raise to $11.50 per hour
- display the gross pay and income tax
- change hours worked to 42.0 (overtime)
- display the gross pay and income tax

Your output must look *exactly* like this (consider using a `void` function named `show` that displays the output. Use `cout.width(9)` and the `decimals` function from `"compfun"`):

```
Gross Pay  Income Tax
=========  ==========
   400.00       32.51
   460.00       41.51
   494.50       46.69
```

6.5 Implementing Class Member Functions

Class member function implementations are similar to those of their nonmember relatives—with these differences:

- Class member functions implemented outside of the class definition must be qualified with the class name and the scope resolution operator `::`. This tells the compiler they are member functions of a particular class and as such they are allowed to directly reference the private data members.
- The constructors are class member functions with the same name as the class and they do not have a return type.

The relatively familiar `bankAccount` class will be used to demonstrate member function implementations.

6.5.1 Implementing Constructors

A constructor is a special member function that always has the same name as the class. It never has a return type. Although member functions can be defined within a class definition, this textbook uses the software engineering principle of separating interface from implementation by implementing the member functions in a separate file. In this case, the member functions must begin with *class-name* `::`.

6.5.1.1 Default Constructor

The programmer can specify whatever default state seems appropriate in the default constructor. The following code implements the default constructor—a constructor with zero parameters:

```
// Member function implementations are in the separate file named
// baccount.cpp

bankAccount::bankAccount()
{ // post: This object has the default state
  my_name = "?name?";
  my_balance = 0.0;
}
```

Why have default constructors like this? There are several reasons.

- They are required to have collections of objects (see Chapter 10, "Vectors").
- They guarantee initialization to a specific state. Programmers always know what to expect (more vivid examples are yet to come).

This default constructor is the class member function that is executed whenever a bankAccount is declared and initialized like this:

```
bankAccount anAcct;
                                   // Output:
cout << anAcct.name() << endl;     // ?name?
cout << anAcct.balance() << endl;  // 0
```

6.5.1.2 A Constructor with Parameters

The following code implements the two-parameter constructor:

```
bankAccount::bankAccount(string initName,  double initBalance)
{
  my_name = initName;
  my_balance = initBalance;
}
```

This is the function that executes whenever a bankAccount is initialized with two arguments (a string followed by a number).

In the following code, the account name `"Stein"` is passed to the parameter `initName`, which in turn is assigned to the private data member `my_name`. The starting balance of `250.55` is also passed to the parameter named `initBalance`, which in turn is assigned to the private data member `my_balance`.

```
// Call the two-parameter constructor to initialize
// anInitializedAccount

bankAccount anInitializedAccount("Stein", 250.55);
                                                   // Output:
cout << anInitializedAccount.name() << endl;       // Stein
cout << anInitializedAccount.balance() << endl;    // 250.55
```

After an object is constructed, the object knows how to respond to its accessor messages. That's because every object is responsible for knowing its own name and its own balance.

The major difference between implementing class member functions and their nonmember cousins is this: Class member functions must be preceded with the class name and the `::` operator. For example, the bankAccount constructor is preceded with `bankAccount::` to inform the compiler that it is a member function and as such, has access to the object's private data members. Failure to add `bankAccount::` results in a nonmember function that can reference neither `my_balance` nor `my_name`. For example, the compiler will generate error messages at both attempts to use the private data members (`my_name` and `my_balance`) because `bankAccount::` is missing:

```
bankAccount(string initName, double initBalance)  // <-- WHOOPS
{
  my_name = initName;          // ERROR: my_name is not known
  my_balance = initBalance;    // ERROR: my_balance is not known
}
```

This scope error is due to the following fact:

SCOPE RULE FOR C++ CLASSES

The scope of private members is limited to the class member functions.

So remember to precede a class member function implementation with the class to which it belongs and `::`. This defines the function as a class member function that can access the private data members. A member function can do whatever it has to do with the state.

6.5.1.3 Function Overloading

You may be wondering how there could be two constructors with the same name. Through a technique known as *function overloading,* more than one function with the same name is allowed to exist. However, there has to be something that distinguishes two functions with the same name. One of these distinguishing characteristics is having a different number of parameters. Function overloading allows the programmer to have a default constructor with zero parameters at the same time as constructors with one or more parameters. This is allowed if the second function of the same name has a different number of arguments. In other words C++ can distinguish between these two constructor function headings inside the class definition:

```
class bankAccount {
public:
  bankAccount();  // Zero parameters
  bankAccount(string initName, double initBalance);   // Two
                                                      // parameters
  // . . .
private:
  // . . .
};
```

Both constructors (named `bankAccount`) are used in the following code:

```
bankAccount a;  // Initialize object with the default constructor
bankAccount b("Bob", 678.99);  // Initialize two parameters
```

6.5.2 Implementing Modifiers

A member function may either modify the state or access the state of an instance of the class. For example, consider `bankAccount::deposit`, which modifies the private data member named `my_balance`.

```
void bankAccount::deposit(double depositAmount)
{
```

```
    my_balance = my_balance + depositAmount;
  }
```

When the following `deposit` message is sent, the argument (`157.42`) is copied by value to the parameter `depositAmount`, which is then added to this object's balance:

```
anAcct.deposit(157.42);
```

Notice that the function heading matches the heading in the class definition.[3] Specifically, the return type of `bankAccount::deposit` is `void` and there is one double argument.

```
class bankAccount {
public:
// . . .
//--modifiers
  void deposit(double depositAmount);
  void withdraw(double withdrawalAmount);
private:
// . . .
};
```

The `bankAccount::withdraw` function is another modifying member function that changes the state of a bankAccount object. Specifically, a withdraw message deducts `withdrawalAmount` from `my_balance`:

```
void bankAccount::withdraw(double withdrawalAmount)
{
  my_balance = my_balance - withdrawalAmount;
}
```

When the following `withdraw` message is sent, the argument (`50.00`) is copied by value to the parameter `withdrawalAmount`, which would then be subtracted from `anAcct`'s balance:

```
anAcct.withdraw(50.00);
```

As you are implementing class member functions, make sure all function headings match the appropriate function heading in the class definition. Your implemen-

3. Once again, semicolon placement can create havoc. Remember that the class definition (in `.h` files) terminates function headings with the semicolon. However, the member function implementations (in `.cpp` files) do not. Also, the qualifications of *class-name*`::` must be added to implement the class member function.

tations, usually stored in a different file, must have the same exact return type, function name, and number and class of parameters as shown in the class definition. And don't forget to eliminate the semicolon and to add *class-name*`::` to the implementation.

It should be noted here that there could be much more processing within a class member function. For example, programming project 7N, "Maintain `weeklyEmp`," asks you to update `weeklyEmp::incomeTax`. This class member function does not return any of the values stored in the `private:` access section. Instead, some of the state is used to help compute the U.S. income tax based on the Internal Revenue Service tax tables. Incidentally, the code is approximately 38 lines long and fairly complex. The member function implementations in this chapter have been kept intentionally simple during this introduction to class definitions and member function implementations.

6.5.3 Implementing Accessors

The state pattern indicates that functions are provided to allow access to the state of the objects. Some accessor functions simply return the value of individual data members.

```
string bankAccount::name() const
{
  return my_name;
}

double bankAccount::balance() const
{
  return my_balance;
}
```

Because these accessing functions in the class definition have the keyword `const`, the implementation must also include `const` after the function heading and before the block beginning with `{`. The keyword `const` denotes a member function that does not modify state. If you examine the accessor implementations above, you'll notice nothing is changed in the block. `name` and `balance` simply return values. On the other hand, go back to the modifiers `withdraw` and `deposit` to observe that both modifiers modify the balance.

Also remember to make sure all member function headings exactly match the headings in the class definitions (without `;`). And remember to type the class name and `::` before the class member function name in the `.cpp` files.

To summarize, here is the implementation of all of the `bankAccount` member functions:

```
// File name: baccount.cpp
#include "baccount.h"       // Allows for separate compilation

//--constructors
bankAccount::bankAccount()  // Default constructor
{
  my_name = "?name?";
  my_balance = 0.0;
}

bankAccount::bankAccount(string initName, double initBalance)
{
  my_name = initName;
  my_balance = initBalance;
}

//--modifiers
void bankAccount::deposit(double depositAmount)
{
  my_balance = my_balance + depositAmount;
}

void bankAccount::withdraw(double withdrawalAmount)
{
  my_balance = my_balance - withdrawalAmount;
}

//--accessors
double bankAccount::balance() const
{
  return my_balance;
}

string bankAccount::name() const
{
  return my_name;
}
```

Self-Check

6-21 How does a function implementation become a member of a class?

6-22 Can class member functions reference the private data members?

6-23 Can nonmember functions reference private data members?

6.6 Object-Oriented Design Heuristics

One particular object-oriented design decision involves determining where to place the data members that store object state. More specifically, since this text uses C++ as the implementation language, the designer has to decide if data member functions go in the `public:` or the `private:` section of a C++ class. The following design heuristic[4] states that a good design protects object state from the outside world:

OBJECT-ORIENTED DESIGN HEURISTIC 6.1

All data should be hidden within its class.

Although data members could be `public:`, the convention used in this text—and in any well-designed class—is this: Hide the data members. C++ data members are easily hidden when declared in the `private:` section of the class definition. This simplifies some design decisions that must be made in any new classes that you develop.

A `private:` data member can only be modified or accessed through messages. This prevents users of the class from indiscriminately changing certain data such as an account balance. The state of an object can be protected from accidental or improper alteration. With data members declared in the `private:` section, the state of any object can only be altered through a message. It becomes impossible to accidentally make a false debit like this:

```
// Compiletime error: attempt to modify private data
// If my_balance is public:, what is the new balance?

myAcct.my_balance = myAcct.my_balance - myAcct.my_balance;
```

However, if `my_balance` had been declared in the `public:` section, the compiler would not protest. The resulting program would allow you to destroy the state of any object. The hidden balance is more properly modified only when the transaction is allowed according to some policy. What happens, for instance, if a withdrawal amount exceeds the account balance in a withdraw message? Some accounts allow this by transferring money from a savings account. Other bank accounts may generate loans in increments of $100.00.

4. A design heuristic is a guideline intended to help produce good object-oriented programs. Some design heuristics (including this one) are from the book *Object-Oriented Design Heuristics*, by Arthur J. Riel [Riel 96], who catalogued and/or developed 60 design heuristics in all.

With `my_balance` declared in the `private:` access section, users of the class must instead send a withdraw message. The client code relies on the `bankAccount` to determine if the withdrawal is to be allowed. Perhaps the `bankAccount` object will ask some other object if the withdrawal is to be allowed. Perhaps it delegates authority to some unseen `bankManager` object. Perhaps the `bankAccount` object itself can decide what to do. Although this text's implementation of `bankAccount` doesn't do much, real-world withdrawals do.

By hiding data and other details, all credits and debits must "go through the proper channels." This might be quite complex. For example, each withdrawal or deposit may be recorded in a transaction file to help prepare monthly statements for each `bankAccount`. The withdraw and deposit operations may have additional processing to prevent unauthorized credits and debits. Part of the hidden red tape might include manual verification of a deposit or a check-clearing operation at the host bank; there may be some sort of human or computer intervention before any credit is actually made. Such additional processing and protection within the deposit and withdraw operations help give `bankAccount` a "safer" design. Because all hidden processing and protection is easily circumvented when data members are exposed in the `public:` section, the object designer must enforce proper object use and protection by hiding the data members.

6.6.1 Cohesion within a Class

This set of messages described in the class interface should be strongly related. A class stores data. The data should be strongly related. In fact, all elements of a class should have a persuasive affiliation with each other. These ideas relate to the preference for tight cohesion (solidarity, hanging together, adherence, unity) within a class. For example, don't expect a `bankAccount` object to understand the message `areYouPreheated`? This may be an appropriate message for an oven object, but certainly not for a `bankAccount` object. Here is one heuristic related to the desirable attribute of cohesion.

Object-Oriented Design Heuristic 6.2

> Keep related data and behavior in one place.

The `bankAccount` class should hide certain policies such as handling withdrawal requests greater than the balance. The system's design improves when behavior and data combine to accomplish the withdrawal algorithm. This makes for nice clean messages from the client code, like this:

```
anAccount.withdraw(withdrawalAmount);
```

This client code relies on the `bankAccount` object to determine what should happen. The behavior should be built into the object that has the necessary data. Perhaps the algorithm allows a withdrawal amount greater than the balance—with the extra cash coming as a loan or as a transfer from a savings account. Even though the `bankAccount` class of this textbook does very little, a real bank account class might have eight different actions that are triggered for every withdrawal—all behind the scenes.

6.6.2 Why Are Accessors Const and Modifiers Not?

You may be wondering why `const` is added to function headings intended to access, rather than modify, the object's state. The answer has to do with the three different parameter modes.

When an object is passed by value or by reference to a function, that function can send any and all possible messages to that object. However, when the const reference parameter mode is utilized, the function promises not to change that object. In fact, it cannot.[5] To illustrate, consider the following function that will not compile—there is a compiletime error at the attempt to withdraw from the const object `b`. This is actually a good thing. The reason for using const parameters is to avoid accidental modification of the associated argument.

```
// Illustrate connection between member functions tagged as const
// functions and passing an object of that class as const parameter

#include <iostream>  // For cout and endl
using namespace std;
#include "baccount"  // For the bankAccount class

void display(const bankAccount & b)
{
// OKAY to send name and balance messages--they are declared const
   cout << "{ bankAccount: " << b.name()
        << ", $" << b.balance() << " }" << endl;

  // This modifying message to a nonconst member function was not
  // tagged as a const member, so this should be an error:
  b.withdraw(234.56);  // ERROR
```

5. This is true for most compilers; however, Turbo/Borland compilers allow const objects to be modified! Here is what Borland says: "This is an error, but was reduced to a warning to give existing programs a chance to work." Be careful with Borland compilers; const does not work as it should.

```
}

int main()
{
  bankAccount anAcct("Rita Jupe", 1234.56);

  display(anAcct);
  return 0;
}
```

This protection works fine for standard classes such as `string`. The same protection will only work with your new classes if care is taken to tag the accessors as const and leave the modifiers as nonconst.

A consistent use of const accessors allows the accessing messages to be sent to the const parameters. At the same time, by not using const with modifiers, a const parameter disallows modifying messages.

Only const messages are allowed on const parameters.

On the other hand, it is okay to send messages that do not modify the object. This safety net is possible only when the programmer diligently tags accessing class member functions with const and always remembers not to tag a modifier that way.

```
class bankAccount {
public:
//--modifiers
  void deposit(double depositAmount);  // No const for modifiers
  void withdraw(double withdrawalAmount);
//--accessors
  double balance() const;  // Use const on accessors
  string name() const;
// . . .
```

This leads to another design heuristic.

OBJECT-ORIENTED DESIGN HEURISTIC 6.3

Always declare accessor member functions as const.

Perhaps the biggest problem with this guideline is in remembering the heuristic. It is easily violated. You'll never know the ramifications until an instance of your class is passed as a const reference parameter. As another example, consider the `grid` class modifiers, which are nonconst, and some accessors, which are declared as const functions.

```
class grid {
public:
. . .
//--modifiers
  void move(int nMoves);
 . . .
//--accessors
  int row() const;
  int column() const;
  . . .
};
```

The presence of const tells the compiler to allow the message to be sent even for objects passed by const reference (g here):

```
void foo(const grid & g);
{
  cout << g.row() << endl;        // OKAY
  cout << g.nColumns() << endl;   // OKAY
  g.display();                    // OKAY
  g.move(1);                      // Compiletime ERROR
  g.pickUp();                     // Compiletime ERROR
}
```

On the other hand, the attempt to send nonconst function messages such as grid::move results in a compiletime error like these (more cryptic errors exist):

```
nonconst member function 'grid::move()' called for const object
```

- or -

```
attempt to modify a const object
```

Declaring accessors as const functions allows existing objects to be safely passed to a const parameter. However, it takes diligence to maintain the same safety net for the new classes that you write. Remember these two class design guidelines.

1. Modifiers should *not* be declared const so the compiler can catch attempts to modify const objects.
2. Accessors should be declared const so objects can be safely passed to const parameters and still allow nonmodifying messages.

It would be easier to completely ignore these rules, but the only way to get away with it would be to never pass objects to const parameters. This textbook uses const in a member function because it says something about whether or not a function modifies the state of an object. And this is something object-oriented programmers must know about. The designer of the class must still decide if the message will modify an instance of the class or not.

Self-Check

6-24 Using the class definition of the `bankAccount` class, list the lines that cause errors in a standard C++ compiler (1, 2, 3, and/or 4).

```
#include <iostream>
using namespace std;
#include "baccount"  // For the bankAccount class

void check(const bankAccount & b, double amount)
{
  cout << b.name() << endl;     // 1
  b.deposit(45.00);             // 2
  b.withdraw(12344.00);         // 3
  cout << b.balance() << endl   // 4
}

int main()
{
  bankAccount myAcct("Me", 12345.00);
  check(myAcct, 50.00);
  return 0;
}
```

6-25 Does the interface of a class refer to its member functions or its data members?

6-26 Does the client code need to know the names of data members to use objects of the class?

6-27 Does client code need to know the names of member functions to use objects?

6-28 Describe the scope of the public members of a class.

6-29 Describe the scope of the private members of a class.

6-30 Give one justification for making the data members of a class private.

6-31 If the designer of a class changed the name `my_balance` to `myBalance`, would programs using `bankAccount` need to be changed?

6-32 If a designer changed the name of the `withdraw` message to `withdrawThisAmount` after the class was already in use by dozens of programs, would these dozens of programs need to be changed?

6-33 Who is responsible for knowing if a particular `libraryBook` is available for lending, the `libraryBook` or the program using `libraryBook`?

6-34 Should a `bankAccount` object understand the message `isThisBrakeLockingUp`?

6-35 Should a thermostat object know the current room temperature?

6-36 If an object is passed by value, which set of messages can be sent—modifiers, accessors, or both?

6-37 If an object is passed by reference (with `&`), which set of messages can be sent—modifiers, accessors, or both?

6-38 If an object is passed by const reference (`const grid & aGrid`), which set of messages can be sent—modifiers, accessors, or both?

6-39 Can a function change the state of an argument passed by value?

Chapter Summary

- Chapter 6 showed class definitions with a collection of function headings that represent the class interface. These are the message names that any object of the class will understand.
- A class definition lists
  - the class member functions with parameters and return types, collectively known as the interface
  - the data members, known collectively as the state
- Each object of a class may store many values, which may be of different classes. For example, each `bankAccount` object stores string data for the name and numeric data for the balance.
- The state pattern guides class design when the primary need for the object is to store state and provide adequate access to it. The state pattern in C++ recommends that the following items be included in a class definition:
  - a default constructor
  - a constructor to initialize objects with programmer-supplied state

    - modifying functions
    - accessor functions
    - private data members to store the state of every object
- Class constructors declare and initialize objects like this:

```
bankAccount anotherAccount("Calissario", 4320.10);
```

- Modifying class member functions changes the state of the object.
- Accessor functions provide access to the state of an object.
- Accessors have the keyword `const` attached at the end of the function heading.
- Ramifications of adhering to Object-Oriented Design Heuristic 6.1, "All data should be hidden within its class," include:
    - Good: Can't mess up the state (compiler complains).
    - Bad: Need to implement additional accessors (`balance`, for example).
- The ramifications of adhering to Design Heuristic 6.2, "Keep related data and behavior in one place," include:
    - Good: Results in a more intuitive design.
    - Good: Easier to maintain.
- The ramifications of adhering to Design Heuristic 6.3, "Always declare accessor member functions as const," include:
    - Good: Helps the user distinguish between modifiers and accessors.
    - Good: Adheres to the principle that objects passed as const reference parameters cannot be accidentally modified by the function while allowing the function to send const messages.
    - Bad: It is easy to forget to use `const` and the error will not show up until the object is passed in the three different modes—the result is more extensive testing to ensure the safety of const and the efficiency of const reference parameters.
- Class member functions are implemented in a manner similar to nonmember functions. However, class member functions must be qualified with the class name and `::` (the scope resolution operator). This gives the function access to the private data members.
- The class definitions have historically been stored in `.h` files.
- The member function implementations have historically been stored in `.cpp` files.
- A class should be designed to exhibit high cohesion.
    - The data should be related to the operations.
    - The messages should be related to each other.

Exercises

20. Use the one class and the two class definitions that follow to list:
    a. the data members of class one
    b. the member functions of class one
    c. the data members of class two
    d. the member functions of class two

```
class one {
public:
//--constructors
  one();
  // post: Set both operands to 0
  one(double initOp1, double initOp2);
  // post: Initialize object
//--accessor
  double sum() const;
  // Return the sum of the data
private:
  double op1;
  double op2;
};
```

```
class two {
public:
//--constructors
  two();
  // post: Data members are set to 0
  two(double initOp1, double initOp2);
  // post: Initialize object
//--accessor
  double product() const;
  // post: Return product of operands
private:
  double op1;
  double op2;
};
```

21. Using the class definitions and documentation for the one class and the two class above, write the output generated by the following program, assuming both classes are completely included by one_two:

```
#include <iostream>
using namespace std;
#include "one_two"  // Includes one.h, two.h, one.cpp, and two.cpp
int main()
{
  one a(1.9, 2.8);
  one b(5.0, -7.0);
  two c(4.5, 6.0);
  two d(1.4, 2.1);
  cout << a.sum() << "  " << b.sum() << endl;
  cout << c.product() << "  " << d.product() << endl;
  return 0;
}
```

22. With pencil and paper, implement the default constructor for class `one` such that both `op1` and `op2` are set to 0.0.

23. With pencil and paper, implement the other constructor for class `one` such that both `op1` and `op2` can be initialized to client-supplied arguments.

24. With pencil and paper, implement `one::sum` that returns the sum of the private data `op1 + op2`. Do not forget to place `const` after the parentheses and before the left curly brace `{`. Don't forget to add `one::`.

25. With pencil and paper, implement all three member functions for class `two` including both constructors.

26. Given this definition for a `counter` class, predict the output generated by the test driver below:

Definition

```
class counter {
public:
  counter(int startingValue, int maxValue);
  // post: Initialize counter to startingValue
  //       and set the maximum count

  void click();
  // post: If count is at maximum, set count
  //       to 0, otherwise add 1 to the count

  void reset();
  // post: Resets the counter to 0

  int count() const;
  // post: Return the current count

private:
  int my_count;
  int my_maxValue;
};
```

Diagram

counter
`click()`
`int count()`
`int my_count`
`int my_maxValue`

TEST DRIVER

```
#include <iostream>
using namespace std;
#include "counter"   // For the counter class definition and member
                     // functions
```

```
int main()
{ // Test drive counter class
  counter aCounter(0, 2);
  aCounter.click();
  cout << aCounter.count() << endl;
  aCounter.reset();
  cout << aCounter.count() << endl;
  aCounter.click();
  cout << aCounter.count() << endl;
  aCounter.click();
  cout << aCounter.count() << endl;
  aCounter.click();
  cout << aCounter.count() << endl;
  return 0;
}
```

27. With paper and pencil, write the implementation for the constructor of the `counter` class. Make sure all postconditions will be met.

28. With paper and pencil, write the implementation of `counter::click`. Make sure all postconditions will be met, assuming the client satisfies all preconditions. You will need the `%` operator.

29. With paper and pencil, implement the `counter::reset` member function with zero parameters.

30. With paper and pencil, send an `add` message to the object named `aCounter`.

Programming Tips

3. The following programming projects require some author-supplied files.

These files are available on the disk and also at this textbook's Web site. The convention used in these programming projects is to have your program `#include` a file that `#includes` the correct class definition from the proper `.h` file and also the correct member function implementations from the correct `.cpp` file. For example, `#include "libbook"`, that is required in project 6D, should be placed before `int main()` like this:

```
#include "libbook"  // Includes the class definition (libbook.h) and
                    // member function implementations (libbook.cpp)
```

```
int main()
{
  libraryBook aBook( "The Old Man and the Sea", "Ernest Hemingway" );
  // . . .
  return 0;
}
```

4. Here is what happens when you `#include libbook` and other files.

This file named `libbook` `#includes` the file with the class definition (`libbook.h`). It also includes the file that has the member function implementations (`libbook.cpp`). It looks something like this:

```
// File name: "libbook"
#ifndef _LIBBOOK_       // Avoid duplicate compilation
#define _LIBBOOK_       // This will be defined the next time
#include "libbook.h"    // For the libraryBook class definition
#include "libbook.cpp"  // For the member function implementations
#endif
```

5. Working with three files is more difficult than working with one.

Some programming projects will now require that you work with three files, not just one. This takes a little patience as you grow accustomed to working with multiple files. Remember, the `.h` file contains the class definition; the `.cpp` file contains the member function implementations. The third file has the `main` function.

6. There is a variety of ways to make classes available.

Even though the convention of having one file include the `.h` and `.cpp` files is atypical, it makes things easier and matches the standard (many `#include` files do not have `.h` anymore). However, someday you may be asked to create object files or project files to compile and link programs using author-supplied classes. Then your program may just include the `.h` file so it can compile. Linking comes later.

```
#include "baccount.h"  // Other steps required to link
int main()
{ // . . .
```

7. The nonmember function syntax applies to member function headings also.

The function heading in the implementation must match the function heading in the class definition in terms of

- return type (none for constructors)
- function name
- number of parameters
- class of parameters
- use of `const` in both places

8. Be aware of these differences.

The function heading in the implementation differs in the following ways:

- add the class name and `::`
- do not write the semicolon after the member function heading; instead, replace it with the function body: `{ }`

```
// Part of a CD class definition file in cd.h
class CD {
public:
  // . . .
  CD(string initArtist, string initTitle, int initCdNumber);
  // Initialize a CD with zero tracks

  string artist() const;
  // . . .
private:
  // . . .
};

// Member function implementations in cd.cpp
CD::CD(string initArtist, string initTitle, int initCdNumber)
{
}

string CD::artist() const
{
  // . . .
}
```

Programming Projects

6D Author/Title

Add two accessor member functions to the libraryBook class named author and title so they return the book's author and title, respectively. You may use the following activities to complete this project:

* Add both function headings for author and title to the class definition in the file libbook.h. Since these are accessor functions, remember to write const after both function headings. Remember to add the semicolon.
* Save libbook.h.
* Implement both member functions inside the file libbook.cpp. Remember to include const in the implementation. Do not add the semicolon.
* Save libbook.cpp.
* Test your changes with this test driver (file name: test6d.cpp):

```
// File name: test6d.cpp
#include <iostream>
using namespace std;
#include "libbook"   // For libraryBook class definition (libbook.h) and
                     // member function implementations (libbook.cpp)

int main()
{ // Test drive libraryBook
  libraryBook aBook("The Mythical Man Month", "Fred Brooks");
  cout << "borrower at initialization: " << aBook.borrower() << endl;
  cout << "Author: " << aBook.author() << endl;
  cout << "Title: " << aBook.title() << endl;
  return 0;
}
```

OUTPUT

```
borrower at initialization: not currently borrowed
Author: Fred Brooks
Title: The Mythical Man Month
```

6E Transaction Count

Allow bankAccount objects to keep track of and report the number of transactions—number of deposits and withdrawals—made since initialization for any bankAccount object.

- Open the file baccount.h. Add a private data member named my_transactionCount.
- Save baccount.h.
- Open the file baccount.cpp and modify both constructors (the default with zero parameters and the single parameter constructor) so my_transactionCount always begins at 0, no matter which constructor is used to initialize the object.
- Save baccount.cpp.
- Use this test driver and ensure your output matches (file name: test6e.cpp):

```
// File name: test6e.cpp
#include <iostream>
using namespace std;
#include "baccount"

int main()
{
  bankAccount anAcct;
  // assert: Transaction count should start at 0

  cout << "transaction count = " << anAcct.transactionCount() << endl;
  anAcct.deposit(10.00);
  anAcct.deposit(20.00);
  anAcct.deposit(30.00);
  cout << "after three transactions: " << anAcct.transactionCount() << endl;

  bankAccount another("Bob", 100.00);
  // assert: Transaction count should be 0

  another.deposit(25.00);
  cout << "Should be 1: " << another.transactionCount() << endl;

  return 0;
}
```

Output

```
transaction count = 0
after three transactions: 3
Should be 1: 1
```

6F The counter Class

Using the definition for the counter class in exercise 26, completely implement and test the class by performing four major activities:

- Define the class in counter.h by retyping the counter class definition exactly as shown in exercise 26.

```
class counter {
public:
```

```
  // . . .
private
  // . . .
} ;  // Do NOT forget this semicolon!
```

- Implement the `counter` class member functions in a new file named `counter.cpp`. The postconditions of `counter::click` indicate the number will turn over (like the odometer on a car or a 100,000 mile click counter). To simulate this, use the `%` operator to make sure the counter resets to 0 when a click operation occurs and the counter is at the maximum value (see output that follows).
- Make sure you include `const` after the accessors.

```
int counter::count() const  // Keep the const, get rid of the ;
{
  // You fill this in
}
```

- Test your member functions with the following test driver (file name: `test6f.cpp`):

```
// File name: test6f.cpp
#include <iostream>
using namespace std;
// The file named "counter" is included on the disk
#include "counter"   // For the counter class definition and member
                     // functions. You have to create both files.

int main()
{ // Test drive counter class
  counter aCounter(0, 3);

  cout << aCounter.count() << endl;  // 0
  aCounter.click();

  cout << aCounter.count() << endl;  // 1
  aCounter.click();

  cout << aCounter.count() << endl;  // 2
  aCounter.click();

  cout << aCounter.count() << endl;  // 3
  aCounter.click();

  cout << aCounter.count() << endl;  // 0
  aCounter.click();

  cout << aCounter.count() << endl;  // 1
  aCounter.reset();
```

```
    cout << aCounter.count() << endl;  // 0

    return 0;
  }
```

6G turnAround/turnRight

Add the following operations to the definition of the `grid` class in the file named `grid.h`:

```
// You add turnAround and turnRight to the class definition

void turnAround();
// post: The mover is facing the opposite direction

void turnRight();
// post: The mover is facing 90 degrees clockwise
```

Also add both class member functions at the top of the file named `grid.cpp`. Please try to ignore all the other stuff in that rather long file. You will find it easier to use the existing member function `grid::turnLeft` to implement these new ones. Feel free to retype this implementation for `grid::turnAround`:

```
void grid::turnAround()
{ // post: The mover is facing the opposite direction
  turnLeft();  // Note: The object name and dot are not needed before
  turnLeft();  //       turnLeft because turnLeft is a member of grid
               //       and the message is sent from a member of grid
}
```

Test these new functions with `test6g.cpp`:

```
// File name: test6g.cpp
#include "grid"

int main()
{
  grid g(10, 10, 8, 8, north);

  g.display();
  g.move(5);
  g.turnAround();
  g.move(3);
  g.turnRight();
  g.move(6);
  g.display();

  return 0;
}
```

Chapter Seven

Selection

Summing Up

Until this point, all programs in this textbook executed all statements in a sequential fashion—in order, from the first statement of each block to the last. The function calls and messages executed unseen code that involved other forms of statement control.

Coming Up

Chapter 7 examines statements that select which actions execute. Depending on the current circumstances, an action may execute one time but not the next. The alternatives are made possible with the C++ `if`, `if...else`, and `switch` statements. After studying this chapter you will be able to

- recognize when to use the Guarded Action pattern (do something only under certain conditions)
- implement the Guarded Action pattern with the C++ `if` statement
- use relational operators such as < and >
- create and evaluate expressions with the logical operators "not," "and," and "or"
- use `bool` objects
- understand the Alternative Action pattern
- implement the Alternative Action pattern with the C++ `if...else` statement

  Exercises and programming projects to reinforce selective control
- implement the Multiple Selection pattern with `if...else` and `switch`
- solve problems using the Multiple Selection pattern

  Exercises and programming projects to reinforce multiple selection and testing

7.1 Selective Control

Programs must often anticipate a variety of situations. For example, an automated teller machine (ATM) must serve valid bank customers—but it must also reject invalid access. Once validated, a customer may wish to perform a balance query, a cash withdrawal, or a deposit transaction. The code that controls an ATM must permit these different requests. Without selective forms of control—the new statements of this chapter—all bank customers could only perform one particular transaction. Worse yet, invalid PINs could not be rejected!

Before any ATM becomes operational, programmers must implement code that anticipates all possible transactions. The code must turn away customers with invalid PINs. The code must prevent invalid transactions such as cash withdrawal amounts that are not in the proper increment (of $5.00, $10.00, or $20.00, for instance). The code must be able to deal with customers who attempt to withdraw more than they have. To accomplish these tasks, a new form of control is needed—a statement to permit or prevent execution of certain statements depending on certain inputs.

7.1.1 The Guarded Action Pattern

Programs often need actions that do not always execute. At one moment, a particular action must occur. At some other time—the next day or the next millisecond perhaps—the same action must be skipped. For example, one student may have made the dean's list because the student's grade point average (GPA) was 3.5 or higher. That student becomes part of the dean's list. The next student may have a GPA lower than 3.5 and should not become part of the dean's list. The action—adding a student to the dean's list—is guarded. The Guarded Action pattern and the C++ means of implementing it are shown next.

ALGORITHMIC PATTERN 7.1

Pattern: Guarded Action

Problem: Do something only if certain conditions are true.

Outline:

```
if (true-or-false condition is true)
   execute this action
```

Code Example:

```
if(GPA >= 3.5)
  cout << "Made the dean's list" << endl;
```

7.1.2 The `if` Statement

This Guarded Action pattern is often implemented with the C++ `if` statement.

GENERAL FORM 7.1. *`if` statement*

if(*logical-expression* **)**
    true-part **;**

The *logical-expression* is any expression that evaluates to either true or false. The *true-part* may be any valid C++ statement, including a block `{ }`.

EXAMPLE `if` STATEMENTS

```
cin >> hoursStudied;
if(hoursStudied > 4.5)
  cout << "You are ready for the test" << endl;

if(hours > 40.0)
{
  regularHours = 40.0;
  overtimeHours = hours - 40.0;
}
```

When an `if` statement is encountered, the logical expression is evaluated to a false (zero) or true (nonzero) value. The true part executes only if the logical expression is true. So in the first example above, the output `"You are ready for the test"` appears only when the user enters something greater than 4.5 hours. When the input is 4.5 or less, the true part is skipped—the action is guarded. Here is a flowchart view of the Guarded Action pattern:

FIGURE 7.1. *Flowchart view of the `if` statement*

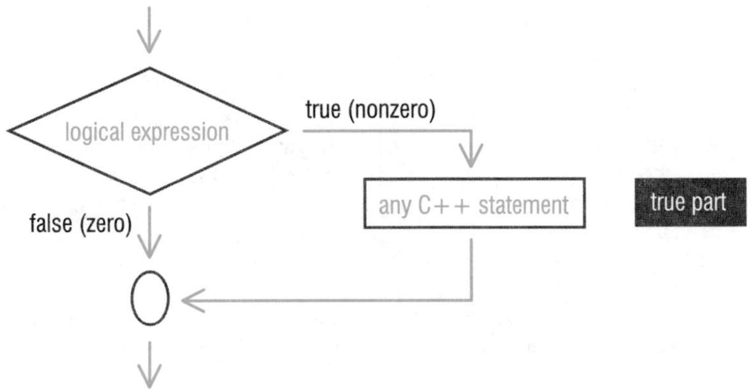

The next program illustrates how selection alters the flow of control. Each of the sample dialogues below illustrates that the code performs different actions due to the variety of conditions. More specifically, the `musicAward` function returns a different `string` due to the different arguments in the three function calls from `main`.

```
// Show that the same code can return three different results.
// showAward has three instances of the Guarded Action pattern.

#include <iostream>  // For cout and endl
#include <string>    // For the string class
using namespace std;

string musicAward(long int¹ recordSales)
{ // pre:  Argument < maximum long int (usually 2,147,483,647)
  // post: Return a message appropriate to record sales
  string result;

  if(recordSales < 500000)
    result = "--Sorry, no certification yet. Try more concerts.";

  if(recordSales >= 500000)
    result = "--Congrats, your music is certified gold.";

  if(recordSales >= 1000000)
     result = result + " It's also gone platinum!";

  return result;
}

int main()
{ // Test drive showAwards three times with different results
  cout <<  123456 << musicAward( 123456) << endl;
  cout <<  504123 << musicAward( 504123) << endl;
  cout << 3402394 << musicAward(3402394) << endl;
  return 0;
}
```

OUTPUT

```
123456--Sorry, no certification yet. Try more concerts.
504123--Congrats, your music is certified gold.
3402394--Congrats, your music is certified gold. It's also gone
platinum!
```

1. `long int` is like the `int` class except it can store more than two billion integers. The `int` class on some older systems has a maximum integer size of 32,767—too small for platinum records.

Through the power of the `if` statement, the same exact code results in three different versions of statement execution. The `if` statement controls execution because the true part executes only when the logical expression is true. The `if` statement also controls statement execution by disregarding statements when the logical expression is false. For example, the platinum message is disregarded when `recordSales` is less than one million.

7.2 Logical Expressions with Relational Operators

Two new operators, < and >=, test the relationship between the value of `recordSales` and the numeric values 500,000 and 1,000,000. They are part of the set of relational operators that create logical expressions—an important part of `if` statements (see table below):

Relational Operator	Meaning
`<`	Less than
`>`	Greater than
`<=`	Less than or equal to
`>=`	Greater than or equal to
`==`	Equal to
`!=`	Not equal to

When a relational operator is applied to two operands that can be compared, the result is one of two values: `true` or `false`. The next table shows some examples of simple logical expressions and their resulting values. Notice that objects such as `double` and `string` can be compared to other objects of the same class. `string` objects are related alphabetically—`"A"` is less than `"B"` and `"D"` is greater than `"C"`, for example.

Logical Expression	Result	Logical Expression	Result
`double x = 4.0;`		`string name = "Bill";`	
`x < 5.0`	`true`	`name == "Sue"`	`false`
`x > 5.0`	`false`	`name != "Sue"`	`true`
`x <= 5.0`	`true`	`name < "Chris"`	`true`
`5.0 == x`	`false`	`"Bobbie" > "Bobby"`	`false`
`x != 5.0`	`true`	`"Bob" < "Bobbie"`	`true`

This is a good time to point out an all-too-common and difficult-to-track-down error that can create havoc. All math courses you have ever taken use = for algebraic equality. When you try to do that in C++, you will actually be using the assignment operator = rather than ==, the C++ equality operator. The problem is, the compiler does not detect an error. Consider this `if` statement:

```
int x = 0;
if(x = 3)
  cout << x << " equals 3" << endl;
```

OUTPUT

```
3 equals 3
```

First `x` was 0, then it became 3 while testing the logical expression `x = 3`, which is an assignment.

It turns out that C++ assignment operations evaluate to the value being stored. The expression `x = 3` not only assigns `3` to `x`, it also evaluates to the value actually assigned, which in this case is 3, or nonzero, or true. If you want to compare `x` to `3`, use == like this:

```
int x = 0;
if(x == 3)
  cout << x << " equals 3" << endl;
```

OUTPUT

There is no output.

Self-Check

7-1 Determine which expressions evaluate to true, assuming `j` and `k` are initialized like this:

```
int j = 4;
int k = 8;
```

-a `(j + 4) == k`

-b `0 == j`

-c `j >= k`

-d `j != k`

-e `j < k`

-f `4 == j`

-g `j = 0` (careful)

-h `j = 165` (careful)

7-2 Write the output generated by the following code:

-a
```
string option = "A";
if(option == "A")
  cout << "addRecord";
if(option == "D")
  cout << "deleteRecord";
```

-b
```
string option = "D";
if(option == "A")
  cout << "addRecord";
if(option == "D")
  cout << "deleteRecord";
```

-c
```
string option = "a";
if(option == "A")
  cout << "addRecord";
if(option == "D")
  cout << "deleteRecord";
```

-d
```
int grade = 45;
if(grade >= 70)
  cout << "passing" << endl;
if(grade < 70)
  cout << "dubious" << endl;
if(grade < 60)
  cout << "failing" << endl;
```

-e
```
int grade = 65;
if(grade >= 70)
  cout << "passing" << endl;
if(grade < 70)
  cout << "dubious" << endl;
if(grade < 60)
  cout << "failing" << endl;
```

-f
```
int g = 45;
// Careful!
cout << "g: " << g << endl;
if(g = 70)
  cout << "at cutoff" << endl;
cout << "g: " << g << endl;
if(g = 1)
  cout << "you get one" << endl;
cout << "g: " << g << endl;
```

7.3 The Alternative Action Pattern

Programs must often select from a variety of actions. For example, one student passes with a final grade of >= 60.0 and the next student fails with a final grade of < 60.0. This is an example of the Alternative Action algorithmic pattern. The program must choose one course of action or an alternative.

ALGORITHMIC PATTERN 7.2

Pattern:	Alternative Action
Problem:	Need to choose one action from two alternatives.

Outline:	if (true-or-false condition is true)
	  execute action-1
	else
	  execute action-2

Code Example:	`if(finalGrade >= 60.0)`
	  `cout << "passing" << endl;`
	`else`
	  `cout << "failing" << endl;`

7.3.1 The `if...else` Statement

The Alternative Action pattern is implemented in C++ with the `if...else` statement. This control structure can be used to choose between two different courses of action (and as shown later, to choose between more than two alternatives).

GENERAL FORM 7.2. *`if...else` statement*

if (*logical-expression*)
    true-part ;
else
    false-part ;

The `if...else` statement is an `if` statement followed by the alternate path after an `else`. The *true-part* and the *false-part* may be any valid C++ statement including a block.

EXAMPLES OF `if...else` STATEMENTS

```
if( sales <= 20000.00 )
  cout << "No bonus this month" << endl;
```

```
else
  cout << "Bonus coming" << endl;

cout << "Enter amount to withdraw: ";
cin >> withdrawalAmount;
if( withdrawalAmount <= myAcct.balance() )
{
  myAcct.withdraw(withdrawalAmount);
  cout << "Current balance: " << myAcct.balance() << endl;
}
else
{
  cout << "Insufficient funds" << endl;
  double thisMuch = withdrawalAmount - myAcct.balance();
  cout << "You lack "<< thisMuch << endl;
}
```

When an `if...else` statement is encountered, the *logical-expression* evaluates to either false or true. When true, the true part executes—the false part does not. When the logical expression is false, only the false part executes.

The next example illustrates how `if...else` works. When `x` has a value less than or equal to zero, the output is `FALSE`. When `x` is positive, the true part executes and `TRUE` is output.

```
double x;
cout << "Enter x: ";
cin >> x;
if(x > 0.0)
  cout << "TRUE" << endl;
else
  cout << "FALSE" << endl;
```

Figure 7.2. *Flowchart view of the Alternative Action pattern*

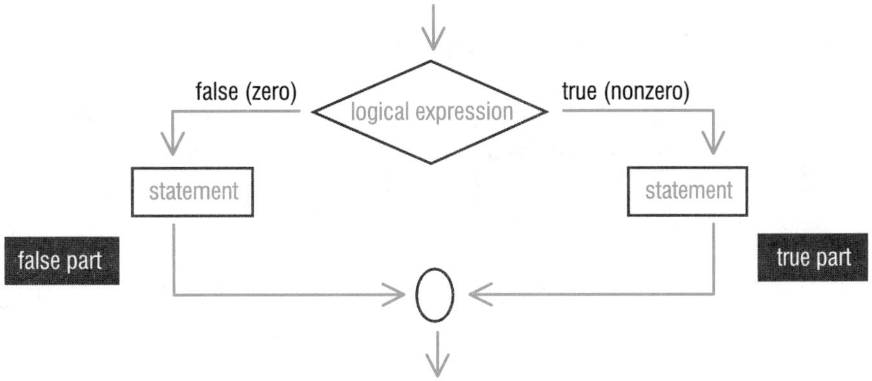

Here is another example of `if...else` that also demonstrates alternative action that depends on the value of the logical expression `(miles > 24000.0)`. Sometimes the true part executes—when `miles` is greater than 24,000; otherwise, the false part executes—when `miles` is not greater than 24,000.[2]

```
double miles;
cout << "Enter miles: ";
cin >> miles;
if(miles > 24000.0)
{
  cout << "Tune-up " << (miles-24000) << " miles overdue" << endl;
}
else
{
  cout << "Tune-up due in " << (24000-miles) << " miles" << endl;
}
```

When `miles` is input as `30123.0`, the output is `Tune-up 6123 miles overdue`, but when `miles` is input as `23500.0`, the false part executes; the output is `Tune-up due in 500 miles`.

Self-Check

7-3 What output is generated when `miles` is `24000.0`?

The ability to choose is a powerful feature of any programming language. The `if...else` statement provides the means to make a program general enough to generate useful information appropriate to a variety of data. For example, an employee's gross pay may be calculated as hours times the rate when hours is less than or equal to 40. However, certain employers must pay time-and-a-half to employees who work more than 40 hours per week. Gross pay with overtime can be computed as follows:

```
pay = (40 * rate) + (hours - 40) * 1.5 * rate;
```

With alternative actions, a program can correctly compute gross pay for a variety of values including those less than 40, equal to 40, and more than 40. This instance of the Alternative Action pattern is now placed in the context of a complete program.

2. Blocks are not necessary if there is only one statement in the true part and one statement in the false part, but they are included in this tune-up example to show they can be.

```
// Illustrate the flexibility offered by Alternative Action

#include <iostream>
using namespace std;
#include "compfun"  // For round(x, n)

int main()
{
  double pay = 0.0;
  double rate = 0.0;
  double hours = 0.0;

  cout << "Enter hours worked and rate of pay: ";
  cin >> hours >> rate;

  if(hours <= 40.0)
    pay = hours * rate;  // True part
  else
    pay = (40 * rate) + (hours - 40) * 1.5 * rate;  // False part

  pay = round(pay, 2);
  cout << "pay " << pay << endl;

  return 0;
}
```

Dialogue 1

```
Enter hours worked and rate of pay: 38.0  10.0
pay 380.00
```

Dialogue 2

```
Enter hours worked and rate of pay: 42.0  10.0
pay 430.00
```

It should be noted that semicolon placement in `if...else` statements is somewhat confusing at first. If you observe a compiletime error near an `if...else` statement, look closely at the placement or lack of semicolons. Also be careful that you don't place a semicolon immediately after the logical expression. This is a common mistake. In this case, the true part is the null statement and what follows the `;` is *not* part of the `if` statement.

Self-Check

7-4 What is the final value of `hours` when `hours` starts as:

-a 38 -c 42

-b 40 -d 43.5

```
if(hours >= 40.0);
   hours = 40 + 1.5 * (hours - 40);
```

7-5 Write the output generated by each of the following programs given these initializations of `j` and `x`:

```
int j = 8;
double x = -1.5;
```

-a
```
if(x < -1.0)
  cout << "true" << endl;
else
  cout << "false" << endl;
  cout << "after if...else";
```

-b
```
if(j >= 0)
  cout << "zero or pos";
else
  cout << "neg";
```

-c
```
if(x >= j)
  cout << "x is high";
else
  cout << "x is low";
```

-d
```
// True part is another if...else
if(x <= 0.0)
  if(x < 0.0)
    cout << "neg";
  else
    cout << "zero";
else
  cout << "pos";
```

7-6 Write an `if...else` statement that displays your name if `option` has the value 1, and displays your school if `option` has the value 0.

7.4 The Block with Selection Structures

The special symbols `{` and `}` have been used to gather a set of statements that are treated as one inside the body of a function. These two special symbols delimit—mark the boundaries of—a block. The block groups together many actions, which can then be treated as one. The block is also useful for combining more than one action as the true or false part of an `if...else` statement.

```
// This program uses blocks for both the true and false parts. The
// block makes it possible to treat many statements as one.
#include <iostream>
using namespace std;

int main()
{
  double GPA = 0.0;
  double margin = 0.0;  // How far from dean's list cut-off

  cout << "Enter GPA: ";
  cin >> GPA;
  if(GPA >= 3.5)
  {
    // True part contains more than one statement in this block
    cout << "Congratulations, you are on the dean's list." << endl;
    margin = GPA - 3.5;
    cout << "You made it by " << margin << " points." << endl;
  }
  else
  {
    // False part contains more than one statement in this block
    cout << "Sorry, you are not on the dean's list." << endl;
    margin = 3.5 - GPA;
    cout << "You missed it by " << margin << " points." << endl;
  }
  return 0;
}
```

The block makes it possible to treat several statements as one. When `GPA` is input as `3.7`, `onDeansList` becomes true and the following output is generated:

Dialogue

```
Enter GPA: 3.7
Congratulations, you are on the dean's list.
You made it by 0.2 points.
```

When GPA is 2.9, deansList becomes false and this output occurs:

DIALOGUE

```
Enter GPA: 2.9
Sorry, you are not on the dean's list.
You missed it by 0.6 points.
```

This alternative execution is provided by the two possible evaluations of the logical expression GPA >= 3.5. If true, the true part executes; if false, the false part executes.

7.4.1 The Trouble in Forgetting { and }

Neglecting to use the block can cause a variety of errors. Modifying the previous example illustrates what can go wrong if the block is not used when attempting to execute both cout statements.

```
if(GPA >= 3.5)
  margin = GPA - 3.5;
  cout << "Congratulations, you are on the dean's list." << endl;
  cout << "You made it by " << margin << " points." << endl;
else  // <- ERROR: Unexpected else
```

With { and } removed there is no block; the two highlighted statements no longer belong to the preceding if...else—even though the indentation might make it appear as such. This previous code represents an if statement followed by two cout statements followed by the reserved word else. When else is encountered, the C++ compiler complains because there is no statement that begins with an else.

Here is another example of what can go wrong when a block is omitted. This time, { and } are omitted after else.

```
else
  margin = 3.5 - GPA;
  cout << "Sorry, you are not on the dean's list." << endl;
  cout << "You missed it by " << margin << " points." << endl;
```

There are no compiletime errors here, but the code does contain an intent error. The final two statements always execute! They do not belong to if...else. If GPA >= 3.5 is false, the code does execute as one would expect, but when this logical expression is true, the output is not what is intended. Instead, this rather confusing output shows up:

```
Congratulations, you are on the dean's list.
You made it by 0.152 points.
Sorry, you are not on the dean's list.
You missed it by -0.152 points.
```

Although not necessary, it could help if you always use blocks as the true and false part of `if` and `if...else` statements. The practice can make for more readable code and at the same time prevent intent errors such as the one above. One of the drawbacks is that there are more lines of code and more sets of curly braces to line up. Also, as you'll see in the second part of this chapter with the Multiple Selection pattern, the action is most often only one statement. The block is not required.

7.5 bool Objects

C++ has `bool` objects to store either one of these constants: `true` or `false`. Named after the mathematician George Boole, `bool` objects simplify logical expressions as demonstrated in the following program:

```
// Demonstrates bool initialization and assignment. A standard C++
// compiler has bool, true, and false built in.
#include <iostream>
using namespace std;

int main()
{
  // Initialize three bool objects to false
  bool ready, willing, able;
  double credits = 28.5;
  double hours = 9.5;
  // Assign true or false to all three bool objects
  ready = hours >= 8.0;
  willing = credits > 20.0;
  able = credits <= 32.0;

  // If all three bools are true, the logical expression is true
  if(ready && willing && able)
    cout << "YES";
  else
    cout << "NO";

  return 0;
}
```

OUTPUT

```
YES
```

Like other objects, `bool` objects can be declared, initialized, and assigned a value. The assigned expression should be a logical expression—one that evaluates to true or false. Two new constants are also added: `true` and `false`. This is shown in the initializations of the three `bool` objects in the previous program.

The `bool` class is often used as the return type in both nonmember and class member functions. For example, a `libraryBook` class might have a member function that returns `true` when a book is available or `false` if the book is checked out.

```
bool libraryBook::isAvailable()
// post: Return true if this book is available, or false if not
```

Here is an example nonmember function that returns true if the integer argument is odd:

```
// Demonstrate a simple bool function

#include <iostream>
using namespace std;

bool odd(int n)
{ // post: Return true if n is an odd integer
  return (n % 2) != 0;
}

int main()
{
  int j = 3;

  // Ensure j is an even number
  if(odd(j))
  {
    j = j + 1;
  }
  cout << j << endl;

  return 0;
}
```

OUTPUT

```
4
```

7.5.1 Boolean Operators

C++ has three Boolean operators, `!` (not), `||` (or), and `&&` (and), to create more complex logical expressions. For example, this logical expression:

```
(test >= 0) && (test <= 100)
```

shows the logical "and" operator (&&) applied to two logical operands. Since there are only two logical values, true and false, the following table shows every possible combination of logical values and the logical operators !, ||, and &&:

! (not)		|| (or)		&& (and)	
Expression	Result	Expression	Result	Expression	Result
! false	true	true || true	true	true && true	true
! true	false	true || false	true	true && false	false
		false || true	true	false && true	false
		false || false	false	false && false	false

The next example logical expression uses the Boolean operator && (logical "and") to ensure a test is in the range of 0 through 100 inclusive. The logical expression is true when `test` has a value greater than or equal to 0 `(test >= 0)` and at the same time is less than or equal to 100 `(test <= 100)`.

```
if((test >= 0) && (test <= 100))
  cout << "Test is in range";
else
  cout << "**Warning--Test is out of range";
```

Here is how the `if` statement evaluates its logical expressions when `test` has the value 9 and then 977 (to simulate an attempt to enter 97 when the user accidentally presses 7 twice):

When test Is 97	When test Is 977
`(test >= 0) && (test <= 100)`	`(test >= 0) && (test <= 100)`
`( 97 >= 0) && ( 97 <= 100)`	`(977 >= 0) && (977 <= 100)`
`true && true`	`true && false`
`true`	`false`

7.5.2 Operator Precedence Rules

Programming languages have precedence rules governing the order in which operators are applied to the operand(s). For example, in the absence of parentheses, the relational operators >= and <= are evaluated before the && operator. Most operators are grouped (evaluated) in a left-to-right order: `a / b / c / d` is equivalent to `(((a / b) / c) / d)`.

However, there is one notable exception. The assignment operator groups in a right-to-left order to allow multiple assignments such as this: `x = y = z = 0.0` is equivalent to `(x = (y = (z = 0.0)))`. The expression `z = 0.0` returns 0.0, which is then transferred to `y`, which is transferred to `x`.

The following table lists some (though not all) of the C++ operators in order of precedence. The `::` and `()` operators are evaluated first (have the highest precedence), and the assignment operator `=` is evaluated last. Although there are more operators in C++, this table represents all the operators used in this textbook, and they have all been discussed already.

PRECEDENCE RULES OF C++ OPERATORS (PARTIAL LIST)

Category	Operators	Descriptions	Grouping
Highest	`::` , `()`	Scope resolution, Function call	Left to right
Unary	`!` , `+` , `-`	Not, Unary plus, Unary minus	*Right to left*
Multiplicative	`*` , `/` , `%`	Multiplication, Division, Remainder	Left to right
Additive	`+` , `-`	Binary plus, Binary minus	Left to right
Input/Output	`>>` , `<<`	Stream extraction, Insertion	Left to right
Relational	`<` , `>`	Less than, Greater than	Left to right
	`<=` , `>=`	Less or equal, Greater or equal	
Equality	`==` , `!=`	Equal, Not equal	Left to right
And	`&&`	Logical and	Left to right
Or	¦¦	Logical or	Left to right
Assignment	`=`	Assign left value to right value	*Right to left*

One of the problems with these elaborate precedence rules is simply trying to remember them. So when unsure, use parentheses to clarify these precedence rules. Using parentheses makes the code more readable and therefore more understandable.

Self-Check

7-7 Evaluate the following expressions to true or false:

-a `(false || true)`

-b `(true && false)`

-c `(1 * 3 == 4 - 1)`

-d `(false || (true && false))`

-e `(3 < 4 && 3 != 4)`

-f `(! false && ! true)`

-g `(((5 + 2) > 3) * 4) && (11 < 12)`

-h `! ((false && true) || false)`

7-8 Write an expression that is true only when the `int` object named `score` is in the range of 1 through 10 inclusive.

7-9 Write an expression that is true if `test` is outside the range of 0 through 100 inclusive.

7-10 Write the output generated by the following code (be careful):

```
double GPA = 1.03;
if(GPA = 4.0)
  cout << "President's list";
```

7.5.3 The Boolean "or" `||` with a `grid` Object

The next sample logical expression uses the operator `||` (logical "or") to determine if the mover in a `grid` object is on one of the four edges. The logical expression is true when the mover is in row number 0, column number 0, the last row `(g.row()==g.nRows()-1)`, or the last column, which is computed as `(g.column()==g.nColumns()-1)`.

```
   (g.row()==0)
|| (g.row()==g.nRows()-1)
|| (g.column()==0)
|| (g.column()==g.nColumns()-1)
```

This logical expression evaluates like this when the mover is in row 1, column 5 of a 6-by-6 grid object (the `||` operator evaluates in a left-to-right order):

```
The grid:
. . . . . .
. . . . . >
. . . . . .
. . . . . .
. . . . . .
. . . . . .
g.row()==0 || g.row()==g.nRows()-1 || g.column()==0 || g.column()==g.nColumns()-1
      1==0 ||         1==5          ||          5==0 ||               5==5
     false ||        false          ||          5==0 ||               5==5
         false                      ||         false ||               5==5
                                  false              ||               true
                                                   true
```

The only time this expression is false is when all four subexpressions are false. If any one of them is true, the expression evaluates to true, in fact, more quickly than you might think (see short circuit Boolean evaluation below). Now here is the same expression put into the context of a function that determines if the mover is on the edge of *any* `grid` object:

```
// Show a more complex logical expression inside a bool function

#include <iostream>  // For cout
using namespace std;
#include "grid"  // For the grid class

bool moverOnEdge(const grid & g)
{ // post: Return true if the mover is on an edge or false otherwise
  bool result = false;

  result =     (g.row() == 0)                         // On north edge?
            || (g.row() == g.nRows()-1)               // On south edge?
            || (g.column() == 0)                      // On west edge?
            || (g.column() == g.nColumns()-1);        // On east edge?

  return result;
}

int main()
{ // Test drive moverOnEdge
  grid tarpit(6, 6, 2, 5, east);

  if(moverOnEdge(tarpit))
  {
     cout << "On edge" << endl;
  }
  else
  {
     cout << "Not" << endl;
  }

  return 0;
}
```

OUTPUT

```
On edge
```

Self-Check

7-11 Many tests are necessary for the `moverOnEdge` function. Write the output generated by the preceding program when the mover is at each of the following intersections:

Row	Column	Output
3	4	
4	3	
2	2	
0	2	
2	0	

7.5.4 Short Circuit Boolean Evaluation

In the logical expression `(E1 && E2)`, `E1` is evaluated first and if it is false, `E2` is not evaluated. This is called *short circuit evaluation.* It is satisfactory because `false && false` is `false`. So is `false && true`. Evaluating the second expression `E2` is not necessary. This is the way C++ evaluates logical expressions—stopping as soon as possible. Short circuit evaluation is also possible with the "or" operator `||`. In the expression `(E1 || E2)`, `E1` is evaluated first and if `E1` is true, `E2` is not evaluated. A programmer can actually get away with code like this:

```
if((x >= 0.0) && (sqrt(x) <= 4.0))
```

When `x` is negative, the second expression with `sqrt(x)` is never evaluated. By checking for `x >= 0.0` first, the square root of a negative number never occurs. Switch the order of statements and a runtime error occurs when `x < 0.0`.

Also consider the previous example of Boolean evaluation in the `bool` function `moverOnEdge`. When the mover was in row 2 and column 5, the first three Boolean subexpressions were false. Therefore, the evaluation had to carry on until the fourth (and final) subexpression. This entire expression would also be evaluated whenever the mover was not on an edge—all four subexpressions would be false. However, consider the same expression if the mover had been in row 0:

```
The grid:
. . . . . >
. . . . . .
. . . . . .
. . . . . .
. . . . . .
. . . . . .

g.row()==0 || g.row()==g.nRows()-1 || g.column()==0 || g.column()==g.nColumns()-1
      true ||           ?           ||       ?       ||              ?
```

This expression could be shortened to `E1 || E2 || E3 || E4`. However, as soon as `E1` (actually `g.row()==0`) is true, the subexpressions `E2`, `E3`, and `E4` need not be evaluated. Short circuit Boolean evaluation is part of C++ because it improves the runtime efficiency. Imagine evaluating one or two fewer subexpressions millions of times.

Self-Check

7-12 Evaluate the following expressions after each set of assignments to `x` and `y`:

```
((fabs(x - y) >= 0.001) && (x >= 0.0) && (sqrt(x) < 6.5))
```

-a `x = 1.0`
`y = 2.0`

-b `x = 56.77779`
`y = 56.77777`

-c `x = -1.0`
`y = 2.0`

-d `x = -1.0`
`y = 1.0`

7-13 How many subexpressions evaluate when the mover is in row 5, column 3, assuming a 6-by-6 grid?

```
g.row()==0 || g.row()==g.nRows()-1 || g.column()==0 || g.column()==g.nColumns()-1
```

7-14 Predict the output from this program. (*Hint:* `cout << 1` returns true.)

```
#include <iostream>
using namespace std;  // To allow cout instead of std::cout
int main()
{
  bool a = ((cout << 1) || (cout << 2) || (cout << 3) || (cout << 4));
  return 0;
}
```

7-15 Predict the output from this program when:

-a the user enters `1 2 3 4`

-b the user enters `1 2 3 Bad`

-c the user enters `Bad 2 3 4`

```
#include <iostream>
using namespace std;
int main()
{
  int a, b, c, d;

  cout << "Enter four integers: ";
```

```
  bool inputOkay( (cin >> a) && (cin >> b) && (cin >> c) && (cin >> d) );

  if(inputOkay)
    cout << "Success!" << endl;
  else
    cout << "Failure!" << endl;

  cout << "The four ints: " << a << " " << b << " " << c << " " << d << endl;

  return 0;
}
```

7.6 A bool Member Function (prerequisite: Chapter 6)

The class definition of bankAccount has a void withdraw member function with the precondition that the withdrawal amount must not be greater than the balance. This implementation currently allows the balance to go negative when the preconditions are not met by the client code (the following member function is from baccount.cpp).

```
void bankAccount::withdraw(double withdrawalAmount);
{ // pre: withdrawalAmount <= my_balance
  my_balance = my_balance - withdrawalAmount;
}
```

A better design would be to disallow negative balances. Then the client code wouldn't have to worry about satisfying the precondition. The withdraw message could avoid negative balances. The return type could also become bool so the client code has the chance to determine if the withdraw message was successful or not. First, the class definition would have to be changed. void is changed to bool in the file baccount.h:

```
bool withdraw(double withdrawalAmount);
// post: If withdrawalAmount <= my_balance && withdrawalAmount > 0.0,
//       debit withdrawalAmount from this balance and return true.
//       Otherwise don't change anything--just return false.
```

Then the implementation is changed in baccount. The Alternative Action pattern chooses between debiting the account and returning true or returning false when the balance is not large enough.

```
bool bankAccount::withdraw(double withdrawalAmount)
{
  bool result = true;

  if((withdrawalAmount > my_balance) || (withdrawalAmount <= 0.00))
    result = false;
  else
    my_balance = my_balance - withdrawalAmount;

  return result;
}
```

The following program test drives this new behavior. Because withdraw returns either true or false, the message can be used as a test expression.

```
#include <iostream>
using namespace std;
#include "compfun"   // For decimals(cout, 2);
#include "baccount"  // Pretend it is a modified "safe" bankAccount

int main()
{ // Test drive the "safe" bankAccount::withdraw
  bankAccount aSafeAccount("Krista Guido," 50.00);
  double withdrawalAmount;

  decimals(cout, 2);
  cout << "Enter amount to withdraw: ";
  cin >> withdrawalAmount;
  if(aSafeAccount.withdraw(withdrawalAmount))
  {
    cout << "Success. Balance = $" << aSafeAccount.balance() << endl;
  }
  else
  {
    double over = withdrawalAmount - aSafeAccount.balance();
    cout << "could not withdraw " << withdrawalAmount << endl;
    cout << "You need $" << over << endl;
  }

  aSafeAccount.withdraw(1000.00);  // Ignore the return value

  return 0;
}
```

DIALOGUE 1

```
Enter amount to withdraw: 75.00
could not withdraw 75.00
You need $25.00
```

DIALOGUE 2

```
Enter amount to withdraw: 20.00
Success. Balance = $30.00
```

Recall that in C and C++, any function return result can be ignored. This means that `bankAccount::withdraw` could be used as it was before—as a stand-alone statement rather than as part of an `if` statement. This is done at the attempt to withdraw $1,000.00 (just before `return`).

Self-Check

7-16 Using this new safe version of the `bankAccount::withdraw` function, write the output generated by the program given below for each value of `wAmount`:

-a `double wAmount = 100.00;`

-b `double wAmount = -100.00;`

-c `double wAmount = 112.50;`

-d `double wAmount = 200.00;`

```
#include <iostream>  // For cout
using namespace std;
#include "baccount"  // For the bankAccount class

int main()
{
  bankAccount b("Kilroy," 112.50);
  double wAmount = -100.00;  // Substitute new values here
  if(b.withdraw(wAmount))
  {
    cout << "okay" << endl;
  }
  else
  {
    cout << "failed" << endl;
  }
  return 0;
}
```

Exercises

1. *True or False:* When an `if` statement is encountered, the true part always executes.

2. *True or False:* When an `if` or `if...else` statement is encountered, valid logical expressions are evaluated to either true, false, or maybe.

3. Proper indentation and spacing improves readability. The next code segment is an example of poor indentation; try to predict the output.

```
int j=123;if(j>=0)if(0==j)cout<<"one";else cout<<"two";else cout<<"three";
```

4. Write the output from the following code fragments:

a.
```
double x = 4.0;
if(10.0 == x)
  cout << "is 10";
else
  cout << "not 10";
```

b.
```
string s1 = "Ab";
string s2 = "Bc";
if(s1 == s2)
  cout << "equal";
if(s1 != s2)
  cout << "not";
```

c.
```
int j = 0, k = 1;
if(j != k) cout << "abc";
if(j == k) cout << "def";
if(j <= k) cout << "ghi";
if(j >= k) cout << "klm";
```

d.
```
double x = -123.4, y = 999.9;
if(x < y)  cout << "less ";
if(x > y)  cout << "greater ";
if(x == y) cout << "equal ";
if(x != y) cout << "not eq. ";
```

5. Write the output from the following code fragments:

a.
```
string name = "PEREZ";
if(name >= "A" && name <= "F")
  cout << "A...F";
if(name >= "G" && name <= "N")
  cout << "G...N";
if(name >= "O" && name <= "T")
  cout << "O...T";
if(name >= "U" && name <= "Z")
  cout << "U...Z";
```

b.
```
int t1 = 87, t2 = 76, larger = 0;
if(t1 > t2)
  larger = t1;
else
  larger = t2;
cout << "larger: " << larger;
```

c.
```
double x1 = 2.89), x2 = 3.12;
if(fabs(x1 - x2) < 1)
  cout << "true";
else
  cout << "false";
```

6. Write the output generated from the following program fragments, assuming `j` and `k` are `int` objects with the values 25 and 50, respectively.

```
int j = 25;
int k = 50;
```

a.
```
if(j == k)
  cout << j;
cout << k;
```

b.
```
if(j <= k && j >= 0)
  cout << "ONE" << endl;
else
  cout << "TWO"
```

c.
```
if(j > k || k < 100)
  cout << "THREE";
else
  cout << "FOUR";
```

d.
```
if(j >= 0 && j <=100)
  cout << "FIVE";
else
  cout << "SIX";
```

7. Write a statement that displays `YES` if `intObject` is positive, `NO` if `intObject` is negative, or `NEUTRAL` if `intObject` is zero.

8. Write a statement that will add 1 to the `int` object `j` only when the `int` object `counter` has a value less than the `int` object `n`.

9. Write a statement that displays `Hello` if the `int` object hours has a value less than 8, or `Goodbye` if `hours` has any other value.

10. Write a program fragment that guarantees that the `int` object `amount` is even. If `amount` is odd, increment `amount` by 1.

11. Write a program segment that adds 1 to the `int` object `amount` if `amount` is less than 10. In this case, also display `Less than 10`. If `amount` is greater than 10, subtract 1 from `amount` and display `Greater than 10`. If `amount` is 10, just display `Equal to 10`.

12. Write an expression that is true if and only if the mover in the `grid` object `myGrid` is on one of the four corners of the grid.

13. Write a function that returns the largest of any three numbers. The function call `largest(1.2, 3.4, 1.2)` must be legal and return 3.4.

14. To test the preceding function `largest`, walk through your code for each call:

```
largest(1, 2, 3)  largest(1, 3, 2)  largest(2, 1, 3)  largest(3, 3, 2)
largest(2, 3, 1)  largest(3, 2, 1)  largest(3, 1, 2)  largest(2, 2, 3)
largest(3, 3, 1)  largest(3, 1, 3)  largest(1, 3, 3)  largest(3, 3, 3)
```

15. Write a function inc3 that increments by 1.0 all three arguments associated with the parameters. The following function call must change the objects as shown:

```
double x = 0.0, y = 0.0, z = 0.0;
inc3(x, y, z);
// assert: x, y, and z all equal 1.0
```

Programming Tips

1. Beware this "gotcha": using = instead of ==.

Take notice of the difference between = and ==. = assigns and == compares. It is very easy, even natural, to write = instead of ==. The following code will always execute the true part because `grade = 100` returns `100`, which is nonzero, which is true.

```
if(grade = 100)
  cout << "another perfect score" << endl;
else
  cout << "this never ever executes" << endl;
```

2. The compound statement may be used even if it is not required.

Consider always using curly braces to mark the beginning and end of the true part and the false part of an `if...else`. You *must* use the block to treat several statements as one. You *may* use the block for readability and to help avoid bugs.

3. The way a mathematician writes an expression does not always work in C++.

It is easy, even natural, to write the following code that checks to see if a value is in a certain range:

```
int x = 2222;
if( 0 <= x <= 100 )
{
   cout << x << " is in the range of 0 through 100" << endl;
}
```

If you're lucky, you will get a warning on a compiler. However, in either case, the code compiles. Then when `x` is `2222`, you get this output indicating an intent error:

```
2222 is in the range of 0 through 100   // Wrong
```

That's because the logical expression evaluates like this:

```
if( 0 <=  x  <= 100 )
    0 <= 222 <= 100
     true    <= 100   // True is like 1 and 1 <= 100
           true
```

4. Short circuit evaluation makes programs more efficient and comes in handy sometimes.

Short circuit Boolean evaluation is always in effect to make programs run more quickly, especially when millions of comparisons are made. You might find that fact useful occasionally. One particular algorithm (sequential search) in Chapter 10 employs short circuit evaluation to avoid runtime errors.

Programming Projects

7A Gross Pay with Overtime

Implement a nonmember function pay that determines an employee's pay based on hours worked and hourly rate of pay. Overtime hours (over 40) are calculated at 1.5 times the hourly rate. Test your function with the following code after writing down the expected output. The first argument to pay represents the hours worked; the second argument is the hourly rate of pay. Use this test driver to test your pay function:

```
#include <iostream>  // For cout
using namespace std;
#include "compfun"   // For decimals(cout, 2)

// Complete the pay function here

int main()
{
  decimals(cout, 2);                 // Output:
  cout << pay(38, 10.00) << endl;   // 380.00
  cout << pay(40, 10.00) << endl;   // 400.00
  cout << pay(42, 10.00) << endl;   // 430.00
  cout << pay(43, 10.00) << endl;   // 445.00
  return 0;
}
```

7B Salary with Bonus

Implement a nonmember function `salary` that returns a salesperson's salary for the month based on this table:

Sales Over	But Not Over	Monthly Salary
0	10,000	Base salary
10,000	—	Base salary plus 5% of sales over 10,000

The base salary is $1,500.00, which means `salary` must return a value that is never less than `1500.00`. When sales are over $10,000, commission is added to the base salary. For example, when sales equals `10001`, the monthly salary is $1,500.00 + 5% of 1.00 for a total of $1,500.05. Use this test driver to test your `salary` function:

```
#include <iostream>  // For cout
using namespace std;
#include "compfun"   // For decimals(cout, 2)

// Complete the salary function here

int main()
{
  decimals(cout, 2);                    // Output:
  cout << salary(9999.99)  << endl;     // 1500.00
  cout << salary(10001.00) << endl;     // 1500.05
  cout << salary(10202.00) << endl;     // 1510.10
  cout << salary(15000.00) << endl;     // 1750.00
  return 0;
}
```

7C Quadratic Equation

Implement and test a nonmember function `roots` that returns true if the three coefficients of a quadratic equation represent a function with either one nondistinct root or two distinct roots. If this is the case, also modify the fourth and fifth arguments (`root1` and `root2`) by using reference parameters (the following file is on your disk). Use the quadratic formula to determine the real roots of any polynomial of degree 2 that has real roots.

$$\frac{-b \pm \sqrt{b^2 - 4ac}}{2a}$$

If there are no real roots, that is, $b^2 - 4ac < 0.0$, don't change the state of the arguments. Instead, simply let the function return false.

```
// File name: test7c.cpp
#include <iostream>
using namespace std;

bool roots(double a, double b, double c, double & root1, double & root2)
{ // Implement roots here. Remember to return true or false in addition to
  // altering the last two arguments via reference (&) parameters.
  // . . .
  // Complete the statements of the roots function
  // . . .
}

int main()
{
  double a, b, c, root1, root2;

  cout << "Enter a, b, and c like this:  1.0  0.0  -1.0";
  cin >> a >> b >> c;

  if(roots(a, b, c, root1, root2))
    cout << "roots: " << root1 << " and " << root2 << endl;
  else
    cout << "no real roots for the given coefficients" << endl;

  return 0;
}
```

7D The quadraticEquation Class (prerequisite: Chapter 6)

Given the definition of the quadraticEquation class in the file quad.h, implement all member functions in a new file that must be named quad.cpp. Make sure all of your member functions satisfy the postconditions shown in the following class definition of quad stored in the file named quad.h:

```
// File name: quad.h

class quadraticEquation {
public:
//--constructor (no default constructor here)
  quadraticEquation(double initA, double initB, double initC);
  // post: Initialize coefficients of quadratic equation:
  //       initA * x^2 + initB * x + c

//--accessors
  double root1() const;
  // pre:  There is at least one real root: b * b - 4 * a * c >= 0.0
  // post: Returns one real root as (-b + sqrt(b * b - 4 * a * c)) / (2 * a)
```

```
  double root2() const;
  // pre:  There is at least one real root: b * b - 4 * a * c >= 0.0
  // post: Returns one real root as (-b - sqrt(b * b - 4 * a * c)) / (2 * a)

  bool hasRealRoots() const;
  // post: Returns true if b * b - 4 * a * c >= 0.0, otherwise returns false

  void display() const;
  // post: Shows the quadratic equation like this: -1x^2 + 3x - 9.7 when
  //       -1 == my_a, 3 == my_b, and -9.7 == my_c

private:
  double my_a, my_b, my_c;  // Coefficients of the quadratic equation
};
```

Test your class with the test driver stored in `test7d.cpp` and make sure your dialogues match the dialogues shown below.

```
// File name: test7d.cpp
#include <iostream>
using namespace std;
#include "quad"  // Includes quad.h and quad.cpp

int main()
{
  double a, b, c;
  cout << "enter three coefficients for equation ax^2 + bx + c: 1.0 0.0 -1.0";
  cin >> a >> b >> c;
  quadraticEquation qe(a, b, c);
  qe.display();
  if( qe.hasRealRoots() )
  {
    cout << "roots for equation ";
    qe.display();
    cout << " are " << qe.root1() << " and " << qe.root2() << endl;
  }
  else
  {
    cout << "The equation ";
    qe.display();
    cout << " has no real roots for the coefficients given." << endl;
  }

  return 0;
}
```

DIALOGUE 1

```
enter three coefficients for equation ax^2 + bx + c: 1.0 0.0 -1.0
roots for equation 1x^2 + 0x - 1 are -1 and 1
```

DIALOGUE 2 (YOUR ROOTS MAY BE FORMATTED DIFFERENTLY)

```
enter three coefficients for equation ax^2 + bx + c: -2.5 4 -3
roots for equation -2.5x^2 + 4x - 3 are -0.556466 and 2.15647
```

DIALOGUE 3

```
enter three coefficients for equation ax^2 + bx + c: 3 4 5
The equation -3x^2 + 4x + 5 has no real roots for the coefficients
given.
```

7E moverOnCorner

Write a `bool` function named `moverOnCorner` that returns true if and only if the mover in the `grid` object argument is on one of the four corners of the grid. Completely test your function with this test driver stored in `test7e.cpp`. The file is not included here to save space (it's 70 lines long).

7F Leap Year: A `bool` Function

A leap year is a year that is evenly divisible (no remainder after division) by 4 unless it is the end of a century. In this case—where the year is also evenly divisible by 100—year must also be divisible by 400. For example, 1996 and 2000 are leap years but 1900, 1999, and 2100 are not. Write `bool leapYear` to return `true` if the argument represents a leap year or `false` if it does not. Test your function with the following test driver (`test7f.cpp` is on your disk):

```
// File name: test7f.cpp
#include <iostream>
using namespace std;

bool leapYear(int year)
{ // post: Return true if year will be/is/was a leap year and
  //       return false if year will be/is/was not a leap year
```

```
  // Complete leapYear here
}

int main()
{ // Test drive leapYear                          Expected output:
  cout << "1900: " << leapYear(1900) << endl;  // 1900: 0
  cout << "1998: " << leapYear(1998) << endl;  // 1998: 0
  cout << "2000: " << leapYear(2000) << endl;  // 2000: 1
  cout << "2004: " << leapYear(2004) << endl;  // 2004: 1
  cout << "2100: " << leapYear(2100) << endl;  // 2100: 0
  return 0;
}
```

7G libraryBook::isAvailable (prerequisite: Chapter 6)

Modify the `libraryBook` class by adding a `bool` data member named `my_availability` that is always true upon initialization (both constructors) and also true whenever the book is available. It must be set to false whenever the book is borrowed.

Also add member function `bool libraryBook::isAvailable()` that returns `true` if the book is not borrowed and `false` if it is checked out. Since this is an accessor function, declare it with `const`. Test your changes with the following test driver (it's on your disk). Your output must exactly match the output below.

```
// File name: test7g.cpp
#include <iostream>  // For cout
using namespace std;
#include "libbook"   // For the libraryBook class in libbook.h and the
                     // member function implementations in libbook.cpp

int main()
{
  libraryBook aBook("The Mythical Man Month," "Fred Brooks");

  if(aBook.isAvailable())
    cout << "Book is available" << endl;

  aBook.borrowBook("Chris Miller");

  if(aBook.isAvailable())
    cout << "ERROR: Something is wrong!" << endl;
  else
    cout << "Not available, " << aBook.borrower() << " has it" << endl;

  aBook.returnBook();
```

```
  if(aBook.isAvailable())
    cout << "Available again" << endl;
  else
    cout << "ERROR: Something is wrong!" << endl;

  return 0;
}
```

OUTPUT

```
Book is available
Not available, Chris Miller has it
Available again
```

7H Safe Accounts (prerequisite: Chapter 6)

Modify the `bankAccount` class in the following three ways:

1. Do not let any `bankAccount` object complete a negative withdrawal. This message must result in no changes to `anAcct`.

```
bankAccount anAcct("Larry," 200.00);
anAcct.withdraw(-20.0);  // anAcct is not modified
```

2. Do not allow negative deposits. If the deposit amount is less than 0.0, the state of the object should not change.

```
anAcct.deposit(-20.0));  // anAcct is not modified
```

3. Allow withdrawals that are greater than the balance. When an attempt is made to withdraw more money than the customer has, add the excess to a separate loan amount indicating the customer owes money to the bank. Maintain a loan amount data member that is incremented by the amount the customer does not have in the account. Add a member function that provides access to how much the customer owes the bank. For example, if Larry has a balance of $200.00, an attempt to withdraw $201.01 results in a loan amount of $1.01 and a balance of $0.00.

```
anAcct.withdraw(201.01);            // anAcct is modified
cout << anAcct.balance() << endl;   // Output: 0.00
cout << anAcct.overdrawn() << endl; // Output: 1.01
```

4. Use the following test driver stored in `test7h.cpp` to test your changes:

```
// File name: test7h.cpp
#include <iostream>
using namespace std;
#include "compfun"
#include "baccount"

int main()
{ // Test drive the modified bankAccount class
  decimals(cout, 2);
  bankAccount anAcct("Larry," 200.00);

  anAcct.withdraw(-20.0);    // anAcct is not modified
  anAcct.deposit(-20.0);     // anAcct is not modified
  cout << anAcct.balance() << endl;     // Output: 200.00
  anAcct.withdraw(201.01);   // anAcct is modified
  cout << anAcct.balance() << endl;     // Output: 0.00
  cout << anAcct.overdrawn() << endl;   // Output: 1.01
  anAcct.withdraw(300.00);
  cout << anAcct.balance() << endl;     // Output: 0.00
  cout << anAcct.overdrawn() << endl;   // Output: 301.01

  return 0;
}
```

7.7 Multiple Selection

Multiple selection refers to the times when the programmer needs to select one action from many possible actions. And this occurs often. The pattern that solves this problem can be implemented as an `if...else` statement that has other `if...else`s nested inside its false part. The more actions there are to choose from, the more nesting occurs. This pattern is summarized as follows:

Algorithmic Pattern 7.3

Pattern:	Multiple Selection
Problem:	Must execute one set of actions from three or more alternatives.

Outline:	if(condition 1 is true)
	   execute action 1
	else if(condition 2 is true)
	  execute action 2

//...
else if(condition n-1 is true)
  execute action n-1
else
  execute action n

Code Example:

```
if(grade < 60.0)
  result = "F";
else if(grade < 70)
  result = "D";
else if(grade < 80)
  result = "C";
else if(grade < 90)
  result = "B";
else
  result = "A";
```

The following program contains an instance of the Multiple Selection pattern to select from one of the three possible actions:

```
// Multiple selection where exactly one cout statement executes.
// The output is dependent on the input value for GPA.

#include <iostream>
using namespace std;

int main()
{
  double GPA;
  cout << "Enter your GPA: ";
  cin >> GPA;

  if(GPA < 3.5)
  {
    cout << "Try harder" << endl;
  }
  else
  { // Execute this multiple selection statement
    if(GPA < 4.0)
      cout << "You made the dean's list" << endl;
    else
      cout << "You made the president's list" << endl;
  }
}
```

Notice that the false part of the first `if...else` statement is another `if...else` statement. If `GPA` is less than 3.5, `Try harder` is output and the program skips over the nested `if...else`. However, if the logical expression is false (when `GPA` is greater than or equal to 3.5), the second `if...else` statement determines if `GPA` is high enough to qualify for either the dean's list or the president's list. Here one alternative selection is nested inside another alternative selection.

When implementing the Multiple Selection pattern, it is important to use proper indentation so the code will execute as its written appearance suggests. The readability realized by good indentation habits can save you time during program implementation, which includes testing. To illustrate the flexibility in formatting, the previous multiple selection may be rewritten in the following preferred manner to line up the three paths through this control structure:

```
if(GPA < 3.5)
  cout << "Try harder" << endl;
else if(GPA < 4.0)
  cout << "You made the dean's list" << endl;
else
  cout << "You made the president's list" << endl;
```

The previous formatting represents the preferred method of this textbook. However, you could also use blocks to make multiple selection look like this:

```
if(GPA < 3.5)
{
  cout << "Try harder" << endl;
}
else if(GPA < 4.0)
{
  cout << "You made the dean's list" << endl;
}
else
{
  cout << "You made the president's list" << endl;
}
```

7.7.1 Another Example: Determining Letter Grades

Some instructors use a scale like the following to determine the proper letter grade to assign to a student. The letter grade is based on a percentage representing a weighted average of all work for the term.

Value of Percentage (should be in the range [0...100])	Assigned Grade
90.0 ≤ percentage	A
80.0 ≤ percentage < 90.0	B
70.0 ≤ percentage < 80.0	C
60.0 ≤ percentage < 70.0	D
percentage < 60.0	F

A function could be implemented with five separate `if` statements that start like this:

```
if( percentage >= 90.0)
  result = "A";

if( percentage >= 80.0 && percentage < 90 )   // Not necessary
  result = "B";

if( percentage >= 70.0 && percentage < 80 )   // Not necessary
// . . .
```

However, when given the problem of choosing from among five different actions, try to remember that the choice is multiple selection, not guarded action. The preferred multiple selection implementation is also more efficient at runtime.[3] The Multiple Selection pattern is also less prone to intent errors.

```
string letterGrade(double percentage)
{ // pre:  percentage >= 0.0 && percentage <= 100.0
  // post: Return letter grade according to external documentation
  string result;
  // Determine the proper result . . .

  if(percentage >= 90.0)
    result = "A";
  else if(percentage >= 80.0)
    result = "B";
  else if(percentage >= 70.0)
    result = "C";
```

3. It is more runtime efficient because the logical expressions are shorter (no &&) and it is not likely that all logical expressions need to be evaluated. In fact, it is only as likely as everyone receiving an F. Short circuit Boolean evaluation was made part of the language for the reasons of runtime efficiency.

```
  else if(percentage >= 60.0)
    result = "D";
  else
    result = "F";

  // . . . and return it
  return result;
}
```

Here, the output depends on the value of `percentage`. If `percentage` is greater than or equal to 90.0, then the statement `result = "A";` executes. The program skips over all other statements after the first `else`. If `percentage == 50.0`, then all logical expressions are false and the program executes the action after the final `else`: `result = "F";`.

When `percentage` has a value between 60.0 and 90.0, logical expressions evaluate until the first one that is true. When `percentage >= 90.0` is false, the opposite logical expression, `percentage < 90.0`, must be true. The second logical expression, `percentage >= 80.0`, evaluates when the first expression is false. When the first true logical expression is finally encountered, the very next true part executes and the program skips over the remaining alternative(s).

This function could be improved by ensuring that letter grades are returned only when `percentage` is within the range of 0.0 through 100.0 inclusive. There is a possibility, for example, that an argument will be passed as 777 instead of an intended input of 77. Since 777 >= 90.0 is true, the function improperly returns `"A"` when `"C"` would have been the correct result. `letterGrade` could be modified to contain a test for out-of-range input. This first logical expression now checks to see if `percentage` is either less than 0.0 or greater than 100.0.

```
if((percentage < 0.0) || (percentage > 100.0))
  result = "**Error--Percentage is not in range [0...100]";
else if(percentage >= 90)
  result = "A";
```

If `percentage` is out of range, the result becomes an error message and the program skips over the remainder of the nested `if...else` structure. Rather than returning an incorrect letter grade for percentages less than 0 or greater than 100, this string is returned instead:

```
777 = **Error--Percentage is not in range [0...100]
```

7.7.2 Multiple Returns

The previous implementation of `letterGrade` shows that the proper letter grade is first assigned to the local object named `result`. Another implementation option uses multiple return statements. The first time any return statement executes, the function terminates. Therefore, a function could be written with many return statements:

```
string letterGrade(double percentage)
{
  if(percentage >= 90)
    return "A"
  if(percentage >= 80)
    return "B";
  if(percentage >= 70)
    return "C";
  if(percentage >= 60)
    return "D";
  if(percentage >= 0)
    return "F";  // ERROR: runtime error when percentage < 0
}
```

If you do use the technique of multiple returns, ensure that something is always returned. For example, the previous code will not return anything for arguments that are less than 0.0. This code might cause a warning or a compiletime error. Worse, some systems will wait until it is too late and generate a runtime error. The problem goes away when the block ends like this instead:

```
  // . . .
  if(percentage >= 0)
    return "F";

  return "Error: argument to letterGrade < 0";
}
```

And while you're at it, consider returning an error message when percentage > 100 if that would in fact be an error.

7.8 Testing Multiple Selection

Consider how many function calls should be made to test the `letterGrade` function with multiple selection—or for that matter, any function or segment of code containing multiple selection. To test this particular example to ensure that multiple selection is correct for all possible percentage arguments, the function could be called with all numbers in the range from -1.0 through 101.0. However, this would require a virtually infinite number of function calls. This is unnecessary!

First consider a set of test data that executes every possible *branch* through the nested `if...else`. *Branch coverage testing* occurs by observing what happens when each and every statement (the true or false part) of a nested `if...else` executes once. These three things are necessary to correctly perform branch coverage testing:

- Establish a set of data that executes all branches of the multiple selection.
- Execute the portion of the program containing the multiple selection for all selected data values. This can be done with a test driver.
- Observe that the program segment behaves correctly for all data values.

For example, the following data set executes all branches of `letterGrade`:

```
-1.0  55.0  65.0  75.0  85.0  95.0  101.0
```

A test driver could start like this:

```
int main()
{
  cout << "-1.0 = " << letterGrade(-1.0) << endl;
  cout << "55.0 = " << letterGrade(55.0) << endl;
  cout << "65.0 = " << letterGrade(65.0) << endl;
  // . . .
```

and then the program output must be examined to indicate that every function call returned the proper value:

```
-1.0 = **Error--Percentage is not in range [0...100]
55.0 = F
65.0 = D
. . .
```

7.8.1 Boundary Testing

Boundary testing occurs by observing what happens for each cut-off (boundary) value. This extra effort could go a long way. For example, boundary testing avoids situations where students with 90 are accidentally shown to have a letter grade of B rather than A. This would occur when the logical expression `(percentage >= 90)` is accidentally coded as `(percentage > 90)`. The arguments of 60, 70, 80, and 90 complete boundary testing of the code above.

Perhaps the best testing strategy is to select test values that combine branch and boundary testing at the same time. For example, a percentage of 90.0 should return A. The value of 90 not only checks the path for all As, it also tests the boundary—90.0 is the cut-off. Counting down by tens to 60 checks all boundaries. But it misses one path: the one that sets result to F. Adding 59.9 completes the test driver.

```
int main()
{ // A test driver for string letterGrade(double percentage)
  cout << "90.0: " << letterGrade(90.0) << endl;  // 90.0: A
  cout << "80.0: " << letterGrade(80.0) << endl;  // 80.0: B
  cout << "70.0: " << letterGrade(70.0) << endl;  // 70.0: C
  cout << "60.0: " << letterGrade(60.0) << endl;  // 60.0: D
  cout << "59.9: " << letterGrade(59.9) << endl;  // 59.9: F
  return 0;
}
```

Self-Check

7-17 Which value of percentage would detect the intent error in the following code?

```
if(percentage >= 90)
  result = "A";
else if(percentage >= 80)
  result = "B";
else if(percentage > 70)
  result = "C";
else if(percentage >= 60)
  result = "D";
else
  result = "F";
```

7-18 What string is incorrectly assigned to letterGrade for the value of percentage you answered for 7-17?

7-19 Would you be happy with the result if your grade were computed with this argument?

7-20 Using the nested structure below, write the return value for each of these six different arguments for weather: -40 20 -1 42 15 31

```
string weather(int temp)
{
  if(temp <= -40)
    return "extremely frigid";
```

```
    else if(temp < 0)
      return "below freezing";
    else if(temp < 20)
      return "freezing to mild";
    else if(temp < 30)
      return "warm";
    else if(temp < 40)
      return "very hot";
    else
      return "toast";
  }
```

7-21 List the range of integers that would cause the previous program to display `warm`.

7-22 List the range of integers that would cause the previous program to display `below freezing`.

7-23 Establish a list of arguments that completely test the preceding multiple selection structure.

7.9 The `switch` Statement

The C++ `switch` statement also implements the Multiple Selection pattern. Although nested `if...else`s can do anything the `switch` statement does, it is included here because you will see it in other C++ programs and because some programmers prefer this implementation of multiple selection.

GENERAL FORM 7.3. *The C++ `switch` statement*

```
switch ( switch-expression )
{
  case constant-value-1 :
    statement(s)-1
    break ;
  case constant-value-2 :
    statement(s)-2
    break ;
  ...
```

```
    case constant-value-n :
      statement(s)-n
      break ;
    default :
      default-statement(s) ;
}
```

When a `switch` statement is encountered, the *switch-expression* is compared to *constant-value-1, constant-value-2,* through *constant-value-n* until a match is found. When the switch expression matches one of these values, the statements following the colon execute. If no match is made, *default-statement(s)* execute.

`default` needs to be present only if some processing is desired whenever the `switch` expression cannot match any of the case values. If absent, it is possible that no statements will execute inside the `switch` statement. Sometimes that is the appropriate design.

The following `switch` statement chooses one of three paths based on the input value of `option`. If the user enters `1`, the first case section of code is executed. The first `break` terminates the `switch` statement.

```
int option = 0;
cout << "Enter option 1, 2, or 3: ";
cin >> option;

switch(option)
{
  case 1:
     cout << "option 1 selected" << endl;
     break;
  case 2:
     cout << "option 2 selected" << endl;
     break;
  case 3:
     cout << "option 3 selected" << endl;
     break;
  default:
     cout << "option < 1 or option > 3" << endl;
} // End switch
```

If neither `1`, `2`, nor `3` are entered, default statement(s) execute.

The switch expression (`option` above) and each constant value (`1`, `2`, and `3` above) after `case` must be compatible. In fact, the constants must be one of the C++ *integral* types, which consists of the integer types (`int`, `long`, and so on) or `char`—the class discussed in the next section.

The `break` statement—a new reserved word—causes an exit from the control structure the program is executing. The `break` statement at the end of each `case` section causes a jump out of the `switch` statement. In fact, the `switch` statement typically requires many `break` statements. They avoid unintentional execution of the remaining portions of the `switch` statement.

7.9.1 char Objects

The `char` class of objects is an integral type often used as the constant value in `switch` statements. A `char` object stores one character constant—a character between single quotes (apostrophes):

```
'A'   'b'   '?'   '8'   ' '   ','
```

There are several special escape sequences—a backward slash (`\`) followed by one of a select few characters that have special meaning (see the following table).

Escape Sequence	Meaning
`'\n'`	New line
`'\"'`	Double quote in a `char`
`'\''`	Single quote in a `char`
`'\\'`	One backward slash
`'\t'`	Tab

`char` objects are declared, initialized, assigned values, and displayed in the same way as the other fundamental types like `int`.

```
// Use some char objects

#include <iostream>
using namespace std;

int main()
{ // Declare and initialize some char objects
  char one, two;
  char letterGrade = 'A';
  char newLine = '\n';

  // Assignment is possible with character expressions
```

```
  one = 'T';
  two = 'o';

  // Output some char objects, char constants, and escape sequences
  cout << "letterGrade is " << letterGrade << endl;
  cout << one << two << newLine << one << '\t' << two << endl;
  cout << '\"' << 'A' << ' ' << '\\' << ' ' << 'S' << 't'
       << 'r'  << 'i' << 'n' << 'g' << '?' << '\'' << endl;

  return 0;
}
```

OUTPUT (THE TAB WIDTH BETWEEN T AND o MAY VARY ON YOUR SYSTEM)

```
letterGrade is A
To
T       o
"A \ String?'
```

The char type has its own set of nonmember functions included in cctype.[4] For example, the toupper function returns the numeric code for the uppercase equivalent of its argument (typecast with char() to see the character equivalent of 68):

```
cout << toupper('d') << endl;        // Output: 68
cout << char(toupper('d')) << endl;  // Output: D
```

Here is a switch statement that uses characters as the constant expressions. It chooses one of five paths based on the value of the char object option:

```
// Illustrate another switch statement
#include <iostream>  // For cout <<
using namespace std;
#include <cctype>  // For toupper(char) returns uppercase char

int main()
{
  char option = ' ';

  cout << "B)alance  W)ithdraw  D)eposit  Q)uit: ";
  cin >> option;
  switch(toupper(option))
  {
    case 'B':
      cout << "Balance selected" << endl;
      break;
```

4. You can use ctype.h if your system cannot find <cctype>.

```
      case 'W':
        cout << "Withdraw selected" << endl;
        break;
      case 'D':
        cout << "Deposit selected" << endl;
        break;
      case 'Q':
        cout << "Quit selected" << endl;
        break;
      default:
        cout << "Invalid choice" << endl;
    } // End switch

    return 0;
  }
```

ONE POSSIBLE DIALOGUE

```
B)alance  W)ithdraw  D)eposit  Q)uit: D
Deposit selected
```

If the value extracted for option is `'B'`, the message `Balance selected` is output and `break` is executed to exit the `switch` control structure. If `Q` or `q` is input, `Quit selected` is output and another `break` is executed. In this example, each case is evaluated until `option` is matched to one of the four `char` values following `case`. If `option` is any other value, the message `Invalid choice` is displayed.

One final comment on the `switch` statement: Don't forget to include the optional `break` statements in the `case` portions of `switch`. Failure to break out of the `switch` causes all remaining statements to execute. Although this may be what you want in some unusual circumstance, it is usually not a good idea to forget the `break`s. For example, imagine the preceding `switch` with all `break` statements removed.

```
switch(toupper(option))
  {
    case 'B':
      cout << "Balance selected" << endl;
    case 'W':
      cout << "Withdraw selected" << endl;
    case 'D':
      cout << "Deposit selected" << endl;
    case 'Q':
      cout << "Quit selected" << endl;
    default:
      cout << "Invalid choice" << endl;
  } // End switch
```

Now, when `B` is input, every statement executes—including the default!

```
B)alance  W)ithdraw  D)eposit  Q)uit: B
Balance selected
Withdraw selected
Deposit selected
Quit selected
Invalid choice
```

Self-Check

7-24 Write the output produced by the following `switch` statements:

-a
```
char option = 'A';
switch(option)
{
  case 'A':
    cout << "AAA";
    break;
  case 'B':
    cout << "BBB";
    break;
  default:
    cout << "Invalid";
}
```

-b
```
double x = 0.65;
switch (ceil(x))
{
  case 0:
    cout << "zero";
    break;
  case 1:
    cout << "one";
    break;
  default:
    cout << "Neither";
}
```

7-25 What is the output from -a above when `option` is `B`?

7-26 What is the output from -a above when `option` is `C`?

7-27 What is the output from -a above when `option` is `D`?

7-28 Write a `switch` statement that displays your favorite music if the `int` object `choice` is `1`, your favorite food if `choice` is `2`, and your favorite instructor if `choice` is `3`. If the option is anything else, display `Error`. Don't forget the `break` statements.

Chapter Summary

- Selection requires logical expressions that evaluate to true or false. The logical expressions usually have one or more of the following relational, equality, or logical operators:

```
<   >   <=   >=   !=   ==   !   ||   &&
```

* The Guarded Action pattern is implemented with the `if` statement that either executes a collection of statements or skips them depending on the circumstances.
* The Alternative Action pattern, implemented with the C++ `if...else` statement, is used to choose one action or its alternative—two choices.
* Multiple selection can be implemented with nested `if...else` statements or with the `switch` statement. Multiple selection should be used whenever there are three or more actions to select from.
* Selection control allows the program to respond to a variety of situations in an appropriate manner.
* The `bool` class and the `bool` constants `true` and `false` are sometimes used as the return type of a function to conveniently return information about the state of an object. Is the book available? Was the withdraw message successful or not? Are there real roots to this equation?
* Several examples of multiple selection showed the need for thorough testing.
* When implementing the Multiple Selection pattern, be sure to thoroughly test the code with the multiple selection. Establish a set of data that executes all branches and tests all cut-off (boundary) values.
* Without thorough testing, a program may only appear to work when in fact there is perhaps one value among thousands that does not work.

Exercises

16. What is the output from the following program fragments, assuming `j` and `k` are `int` objects with the values `25` and `50`, respectively?

```
int j = 25;
int k = 50;
```

a.
```
if(j == k)
  cout << 1;
else if(j < k)
  cout << 2;
else
  cout << 3;
```

b.
```
if(j + 25 < k)
  cout << "aaa";
else if(j > k)
  cout << "bbb";
else
  cout << "ccc";
```

c.
```
if(j < 10)
  cout << j << " One";
else if(j < 20)
  cout << j << " Two";
else if(j < 30)
  cout << j << " Three";
else
  cout << j << " Four";
```

d.
```
if(k >= 100)
  cout << "Five";
else if(k >= 75)
  cout << "Six";
else if(k >= 50)
  cout << "Seven";
else
  cout << "Eight";
```

e.
```
if(j > 0)
{
  if(j < 50)
    cout << "Eight";
  else
    cout << "Nine";
}
```

f.
```
if(k <= 100)   // Careful
  cout << "Ten ";
if(k <= 50)
  cout << "Eleven ";
if(k <= 10)
  cout << "Twelve ";
else
  cout << "Hmmmm";
```

17. Show the output from the previous exercise when `j` is `30` and `k` is `10`.

18. Show the output from the previous exercise when `j` is `20` and `k` is `20`.

19. Write a function that returns the largest of three numbers. Develop a test plan to completely test your program.

20. Write a `string type` function named `stringDay` that returns `Monday` if the `int` argument named `day` is 0, `Tuesday` if `day` is 1, and so on up through `Sunday` if the value of `day` is passed to the function as 6.

21. Write the output from the following program when:

a. `option = 3`

b. `option = 1`

c. `option = 2`

d. `option = 0`

```
#include <iostream>
using namespace std;
int main()
{
  int choice = 3;  // Change 3 to 1, 2, and then 0
  switch(choice)
  {
    case 1:
      cout << "1 selected" << endl;
      break;
    case 2:
      cout << "2 selected" << endl;
      break;
```

```
      case 3:
        cout << "3 selected" << endl;
        break;
      default:
        cout << "Invalid choice" << endl;
    } // End switch
    return 0;
  }
```

22. Write a `switch` statement that displays `Monday` if `int day` is 0, `Tuesday` if `day` is 1, and so on up through `Sunday` if `day` is 6.

23. Write the output of the following program:

```
#include <iostream>  // For cout
using namespace std;
#include <cctype>    // For toupper

int main()
{ // Declare and initialize some char objects
  char a = 'a';
  char b = 'b';
  char line = '\n';
  char tab = '\t';

  cout << "one\n";  // \n generates also when in a string constant
  cout << "two: ";
  cout << a << b << tab;
  a = toupper(a);
  b = toupper(b);
  cout << a << b << line;
  return 0;
}
```

Programming Tips

5. Remember to use == for comparison.

Perhaps the most famous C++ "gotcha" is caused by using = instead of == in an `if` statement. If your program with logical expressions doesn't seem to be working, make sure you are comparing for equality with == rather than assigning with =. For example, if `result` in the following code is always 1, no matter what `romanChar` is, then replace `= 'I'` with `== 'I'`.

```
int result = 0;
char romanChar = 'C';
```

```
if(romanChar = 'I')  // romanChar becomes 'I', which is nonzero (true)
  result = 1;
else if(romanChar == 'V')
  result = 5;
else if(romanChar == 'X')
  result = 10;
else
  result = 100;
return result;
```

6. Test drivers help protect against errors.

Use test drivers with many calls to the function containing the multiple selection. Send arguments that check all boundary values. Send arguments that ensure that each branch executes at least once.

7. Don't forget to use `break`s in the `switch` statements.

Don't forget to use the `break` statement to terminate `switch` statements. C++ executes all code to the bottom of the `switch` or until the first `break` is encountered. The following code works correctly when `option == 'W'`. On the other hand, when `option == 'B'`, both options execute as shown in the accompanying output.

```
switch(option)
{
  case 'B':
     cout << "Balance selected" << endl;
  case 'W':
     cout << "Withdraw selected" << endl;
}
```

OUTPUT (WHEN `option == 'B'`)

```
Balance selected
Withdraw selected
```

8. Use `toupper` to simplify code.

Use `toupper` from `<cctype>` (or `<ctype.h>`) to convert an input character to its uppercase equivalent. Or you could write code like this that will check for lower- and uppercase characters (it's much longer, though):

```
cout << "B)alance  W)ithdraw  D)eposit  Q)uit: ";
cin >> option;
switch(option)
{
  case 'b':
    case 'B':
      cout << "Balance selected" << endl;
      break;
```

```
case 'w':
  case 'W':
     cout << "Withdraw selected" << endl;
     break;
case 'd':
  case 'D':
     cout << "Deposit selected" << endl;
     break;
case 'q':
  case 'Q':
     cout << "Quit selected" << endl;
     break;
default:
     cout << "Invalid choice" << endl;
}
```

9. You might find multiple cases useful.

Sometimes multiple cases work well. For example, if you want to perform the same actions for two or more values, use multiple cases.

```
switch(ch)
{
  case '*': case '/': case '%':
      cout << "higher precedence" << endl;
      break;
  case '+': case '-':
      cout << "lower precedence" << endl;
      break;
   default:
      cout << "not an arithmetic operator";
}
```

10. Make sure all nonvoid functions always return something.

If a function is undefined for certain values, check for those values and return something even if the function has an invalid argument.

```
string letterGrade(double ave)
{
  string result
  if( (ave < 0.0) || (ave > 100.0) )
     result = "Error, argument out of range";
  else if ( . . .
```

11. Avoid unnecessary comparisons. The following logical expression can be simplified by removing `&& ave < 90`. If `ave >= 90` is false, there is no need to check it again with `ave < 90`.

```
if(ave >= 90)
  return "A"
else if (ave >= 80 && ave < 90)
  return "I already know ave must be less than 90";
```

Programming Projects

7I Salary with Bonuses

Implement the `salary` function that returns a salesperson's salary for the month based on this table:

Sales Over	But Not Over	Monthly Salary
0	10,000	Base salary
10,000	20,000	Base salary plus 5% of sales over 10,000
20,000	30,000	Base salary plus 500.00 plus 8% of sales over 20,000
30,000	—	Base salary plus 1,300.00 plus 12% of sales over 30,000

The base salary is $1,500.00, which means `salary` returns a value that is never less than `1500.00`. When sales are over $10,000, commission is added to the base salary. For example, when sales equals `10001`, the monthly salary is $1,500.00 + 5% of $1.00 for a total of $1,500.05, and when sales is `20001`, the monthly salary is $1,500.00 + $500.00 + 8% of $1.00 for a total of $2,000.08. Test your function with the test driver shown below where the arguments represent sales.

```
int main()
{
  cout << salary(10000.00) << endl;
  cout << salary(10001.00) << endl;
  cout << salary(20000.00) << endl;
  cout << salary(20002.00) << endl;
  cout << salary(30000.00) << endl;
  cout << salary(30002.00) << endl;
  return 0;
}
```

7J Letter Grades

Implement the `grade` function that returns the proper letter grade as a `string` for a plus/minus system with the following scale:

Percentage	Grade
93.0 ≤ percentage	A
90.0 ≤ percentage < 93.0	A-
87.0 ≤ percentage < 90.0	B+
83.0 ≤ percentage < 87.0	B
80.0 ≤ percentage < 83.0	B-
77.0 ≤ percentage < 80.0	C+
70.0 ≤ percentage < 77.0	C
60.0 ≤ percentage < 70.0	D
percentage < 60.0	F

After implementing the function, perform branch and boundary testing. If the argument is a value outside the range of 0.0 through 100.0, return `??` as the `string` letter grade.

7K Roman Numerals

Write the `romanNumeral` function that returns the numeric equivalent of an upper- or lowercase Roman numeral (actually a `char`). If the input is not a valid Roman numeral, display an appropriate message. Write a program that tests for every possible upper- or lowercase Roman numeral. Roman numerals and their decimal equivalents are I = 1, V = 5, X = 10, L = 50, C = 100, D = 500, and M = 1,000. Perform branch coverage testing on the function.

- First, create a new file with a `main` function that begins and ends like this (you don't need to copy the output written as comments, but use the output to test the function later):

```
int main()
{                                             // Expected output:
  cout << romanNumeral('i') << endl;   // 1
  cout << romanNumeral('I') << endl;   // 1
  cout << romanNumeral('v') << endl;   // 5
  // . . .

  cout << romanNumeral('m') << endl;   // 1000
  cout << romanNumeral('M') << endl;   // 1000
  return 0;
}
```

7L turnTillClear

Implement a `turnTillClear` function that faces the mover in the first direction that has a clear front like the mover in the left column below. Make it a `bool` function that also returns `false` when the mover is surrounded as shown with the grid on the right.

OUTPUT 1

```
The grid:
. . . . . . . . . .
. . . # < . . . . .
. # # # # # # # # .
mover can move forward

The grid:
. . . . . . . . . .
. . . # > . . . . .
. # # # # # . . . .
```

OUTPUT 2

```
The grid:
. . . # # # . . . .
. . . # < # . . . .
. # # # # # # # # .
mover is trapped

. . . # # # . . . .
. . . # ^ # . . . .
. # # # # # # # # .
```

Hints:

- Use multiple returns in the function (you may end up with five returns).
- Use `bool grid::frontIsClear()` and `void grid::turnLeft()`.
- Use the test driver stored as `test7l.cpp` that looks something like this:

```
bool turnTillClear(grid & g)
{
  // Implement bool turnTillClear(grid & g) here
}

int main()
{ // Test drive turnTillClear
  grid aGrid(6, 6, 4, 4, north);

  // Run this five times
  // . . .

  if(! turnTillClear(aGrid))
  {
    cout << "mover is trapped" << endl;
  }
  else
  {
    cout << "mover can move forward" << endl;
  }
```

```
    aGrid.display();

    return 0 ;
  }
```

7M Student (prerequisite: Chapter 6)

Implement the member functions in a new file named `student.cpp` for the `student` class such that they satisfy all postconditions in the class definition (shown below). Use this table to satisfy the postconditions of `student::standing`:

Credits Completed	`string` Return Value
Less than 30 credits	"Freshman"
30 credits to less than 60 credits	"Sophomore"
60 credits to less than 90 credits	"Junior"
90 credits or more	"Senior"

```
class student {
public:
//--constructors
  student();
  // post: Initialize a student object with a name as "?name?," 0.0 credits,
  //       and 0.0 quality points

  student(string initName, double initCredits, double initQualityPoints);
  // post: Initialize a student object with this three-argument constructor
  //       student("Delaisio, Donna," 30.0, 120.0);
  //       A straight-A sophomore at one school

//--modifier
  void completedCourse(double credits, double numericGrade);
  // post: Record a completed course by adding credits to my_credits and
  //       incrementing qualityPoints by (credits * numericGrade)
  //       aStudent.recordCourse(4.0, 3.67)  // A 4 credit A-

//--accessors
  double GPA() const;
  // post: Return the current grade point average as the accumulated quality
  //       points divided by the total number of credits

  string standing() const;
  // post: Use selection to return the current standing as either Freshman,
  //       Sophomore, Junior, or Senior
```

```
  string name() const;
  // post: Return the student's name

private:
  string my_name;
  double my_credits;        // Total credits completed
  double my_qualityPoints;  // Sum of credits multiplied by grades
};
```

Hand in the file `student.cpp` along with your own test driver named `test7m.cpp` that test drives the `student` class. Construct at least four students at the cut-offs for the standings. Make sure you call every member function at least once.

7N Maintain `weeklyEmp`

In this project, you are asked to update the `weeklyEmp` class to reflect recent changes in tax laws. In particular, the `WEEKLY_ALLOWANCE` constant in `employee.h` needs updating. Also, `weeklyEmp::incomeTax` must be updated according to the following table:

WEEKLY PAYROLL PERIOD

```
(a) SINGLE Person (including head of household)

If the amount of wages
(after subtracting               The amount of income tax
withholding allowances) is:      to withhold is:

Not over $49 . . . . .           $0

Over-      But not over-                  Of excess over-
$49        $451  . . .           15%                  $49
$451       $942  . . .           $60.30  plus 28%     $451
$942. . . . . . . .              $197.78 plus 31%     $942
```

```
(a) MARRIED Person

If the amount of wages
(after subtracting               The amount of income tax
withholding allowances) is:      to withhold is:

Not over $119 . . . .            $0

Over-      But not over-                  Of excess over-
$119       $784  . . .           15%                  $119
$784       $1,563. . .           $99.75  plus 28%     $784
$1,563 . . . . . . .             $317.87 plus 31%     $1,563
```

1. First change the weekly allowance for each exemption from 39.42 to 45.19 in `weekemp.cpp` (near line 20).

```
const double WEEKLY_ALLOWANCE = 39.42;   // <- Update to 45.19
const int    MAX_EXEMPTIONS = 99;
```

2. Once you have changed the `WEEKLY_ALLOWANCE`, go to line 117 (approximately) and locate `double weeklyEmp::incomeTax()`.

3. Observe that the number of categories has been reduced from five to four (compare the code in `weeklyEmp::incomeTax` to the table above). Also notice that the cut-offs will have to be modified (the first cut-off of 23.00 must be changed to 49.00).

4. Use the table to modify the `weeklyEmp::incomeTax` member function. (*Note:* You will have to delete one of the branch categories from the `weekemp.cpp` file that you are modifying.)

Test the Maintenance for Single and Married Employees

You are now asked to perform branch and boundary testing for both the single and married filing status. This will require 12 different `weeklyEmp` objects—six single and six married. Start with six single filers. The table above was used to determine the income tax to be withheld for each of the following adjusted wages:

Taxable Income:	49.00	50.00	451.00	452.00	942.00	943.00
Income Tax:	0.00	0.15	60.30	60.58	197.78	198.09

Now, you compute the income tax for the married categories and these adjusted wages:

Taxable Income:	119.00	120.00	784.00	785.00	1563.00	1564.00
Income Tax:	______	______	______	______	______	______

Write your own test driver, or use the file `test7n.cpp` to test your maintenance. Does your output match your hand-calculated results? If your answer is no, recheck the hand-calculated results that do not match the program output. If they are correct, check your code for bugs. Do not continue until you have adequately tested the single filers.

Chapter Eight
Repetition

Summing Up

Two important control structures have now been discussed—sequence and selection. Sequential control refers to the time when every statement executes—one after another. One of those statements could be a selection statement; in that case, one or more statements may be skipped. Selection executes different actions under different circumstances. Of course, it is your responsibility as a programmer to ensure that the proper actions always occur under the proper circumstances.

Coming Up

Chapter 8 begins a study of repetitive control, the third major control structure. Repetition is discussed within the context of two major algorithmic patterns—the Determinate Loop pattern and the Indeterminate Loop pattern. These two patterns may be implemented with the C++ `for` and `while` statements, respectively. A repetitive control structure executes some actions a specified, predetermined number of times or until some event terminates the loop. After studying this chapter, you will be able to

- recognize and use the Determinate Loop pattern to execute a set of statements a predetermined number of times
- implement determinate loops with the C++ `for` statement
- recognize and use the Indeterminate Loop pattern to execute a set of statements until some event occurs to stop it (no more data, for example)
- implement indeterminate loops with the C++ `while` statement

Exercises and programming projects to reinforce repetition

8.1 Repetitive Control

Repetition refers to the repeated execution of a set of statements. Repetition occurs naturally in noncomputer algorithms such as these:

- For every name on the attendance roster, call the name. Mark 0 if absent or a checkmark if present.
- Practice the fundamentals of a sport.
- Add the flour ¼ cup at a time, whipping until smooth.

Repetition is also used to express algorithms intended for computer implementation. If something can be done once, it can be done repeatedly. These examples have computer-based applications:

- Process any number of customers at an automated teller machine (ATM).
- Continuously accept reservations.
- While there are more fast food items, sum each item.
- Compute the course grade for every student in a class.
- Microwave the food until either the timer reaches 0, the cancel button is pressed, or the oven door is opened.

This chapter examines repetitive algorithmic patterns and the C++ statements that implement them. It begins with a statement that executes a collection of actions a fixed, predetermined number of times.

8.1.1 Why Is Repetition Needed?

Many jobs once performed by hand are now accomplished by computers at a much faster rate. Think of a payroll department with the job of producing employee paychecks. With only a few employees, this task could certainly be done by hand. However, with several thousand employees, a very large payroll department would be necessary to hand compute and generate that many paychecks in a timely fashion. Other situations requiring repetition include, but are certainly not limited to: finding an average, searching through a collection of objects for a particular item, alphabetizing a list of names, and processing all the data in a file. Let's start with the following code that finds the average of exactly three numbers. No repetitive control is present yet.

```
double sum = 0, average, number;
cout << "Enter number: ";  // <- Repeat
cin >> number;             // <- these
sum = sum + number;        // <- statements
```

```
cout << "Enter number: ";
cin >> number;
sum = sum + number;

cout << "Enter number: ";
cin >> number;
sum = sum + number;

average = sum / 3.0;
cout << "average = " << average;
```

There is a drawback to this brute-force approach to repetition. Any time a larger or smaller set of numbers needs averaging, the program itself must be modified. It is not general enough to handle various-sized input sets. Using the previous approach, the three statements would need to be repeated for every number. This means averaging 100 numbers would require an additional 97 copies of these three statements. Also, the constant `3.0` in `average = sum / 3.0;` would have to be changed to `100.0`. A situation like this is improved with a structure that can execute these three statements over and over again.

8.1.2 Algorithmic Pattern: The Determinate Loop

Without the selection control structures of the preceding chapter, computers are little more than nonprogrammable calculators. Selection control makes computers more adaptable to varying situations. However, what makes computers even more powerful is their ability to repeat the same actions accurately and very quickly. Two algorithmic patterns emerge. The first involves performing some action a specific, predetermined (known in advance) number of times. For example, to find the average of 142 test grades, repeat some process exactly 142 times. To pay 89 employees, repeat some process 89 times. To produce grade reports for 32,675 students, repeat some process 32,675 times. There is a pattern here.

In each of these examples, the program requires that somehow, the exact number of repetitions be predetermined. In these situations, the number of times to repeat the process must be pre-established and constant. One too many or one too few repetitions results in an incorrect algorithm. This pattern of predetermining the number of repetitions and then executing a set of statements precisely that number of times is called the Determinate Loop pattern.

Algorithmic Pattern 8.1

Pattern: Determinate Loop

Problem: Do something exactly `n` times, where `n` is known in advance.

Algorithm:

determine `n`
repeat the following `n` times
{
  perform these actions
}

Code Example:

```
double sum = 0.0;
int j, n;

cout << "Enter n: ";
cin >> n;
// Do something n times
for(j = 1; j <= n; j = j + 1)
{
  cout << "Enter number: ";  // <- Repeat these
  cin >> number;             // <- statements
  sum = sum + number;        // <- n times
}
```

The Determinate Loop pattern uses some integer object—named `n` here—to represent the number of times the process must repeat. However, other appropriately named objects certainly are allowed, such as `numberOfEmployees`. So the first thing to do in the Determinate Loop pattern is to determine `n` somehow.

n = number of repetitions

The number of repetitions may come from keyboard input as in `cin >> n;`. Or `n` may be defined at compiletime, `int n = 124;`. Or `n` may be passed as an argument to a function as in `cout << average = 89`. Once `n` is defined, another object—named `j` here—controls the loop iterations. Other appropriately named objects could be used, `counter`, for example. The Determinate Loop pattern is shown next in the context of a small program. It is implemented with the C++ `for` statement.

```
// Determine the average of n inputs. The user must supply n.

#include <iostream>  // For cout, cin, and endl
using namespace std;

int main()
```

```
{
  int n = 0;            // The number of inputs--supplied by user
  double sum = 0.0;     // Keep running sum
  double number;        // Temporarily store each input
  double average;       // Holds the average for potential future use
  int j;                // The loop counter

  cout << "How many numbers do you need to average? ";
  cin >> n;
  for(j = 1; j <= n; j = j + 1)
  {
    cout << "Enter number: ";
    cin >> number;
    sum = sum + number;
  }

  average = sum / n;
  cout << "Average of " << n << " numbers is " << average;

  return 0;
}
```

DIALOGUE

```
How many numbers do you need to average? 4
Enter number: 70
Enter number: 80
Enter number: 90
Enter number: 100
Average of 4 numbers is 85
```

C++ has several structures for implementing the Determinate Loop pattern. The `for` statement is most frequently used because it combines everything needed after `n` is determined.

8.1.3 The `for` Statement

The following `for` statement shows the three components that maintain the Determinate Loop pattern with the C++ `for` statement.

```
int j;
int n = 5;  // Predetermined number of iterations
for(j = 1; j <= n; j = j + 1)
{
  // Execute this block n times
}
```

In the preceding `for` loop, `j` is first assigned the value of 1. Next, `j <= n` (1 <= 5) evaluates to true and so the block executes. When the statements inside the block are done, `j` increments by 1 (`j = j + 1`). These three components

```
j = 1       // Initialize counter
j <= n      // Loop test
j = j + 1   // Update counter
```

ensure that the block executes `n` times. Here is the general form of the C++ `for` loop:

General Form 8.1. *`for` statement*

for(*init-statement***;** *loop-test***;** *update-step* **)**
{
*repeated-part***;**
}

When a `for` loop is encountered, the *init-statement* is executed first—and only once. The *loop-test* is then checked before each execution of the *repeated-part*. The *update-step* executes after each iteration of the repeated part. This process continues until the loop test is false. This generalized behavior of a `for` loop is summarized in this flowchart view (Figure 8.1):

Figure 8.1

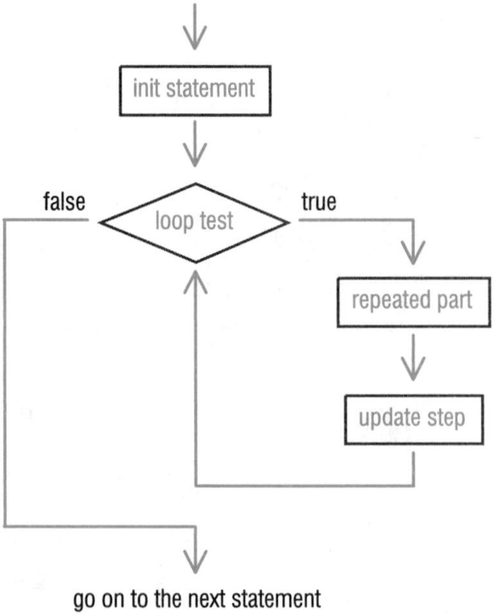

The following `for` statement simply displays the value of the loop counter named `j` as it ranges from 1 through 5 inclusive:

```
int j;
int n = 5;
for(j = 1; j <= n; j = j + 1)
{
  cout << j << " ";
}
```

OUTPUT

```
1 2 3 4 5
```

Although a block is not necessary to repeat one statement, consider always using a block (`{ }`) with the `for` loop. This practice helps avoid difficult-to-detect intent errors later if you get into the habit of using `{` and `}`.

8.1.4 Other Increment and Assignment Operators

Assignment operations alter computer memory even when the object on the left of = is also involved in the expression to the right of =. For example, the `int` object `j` is updated by +1 with this assignment operation:

```
j = j + 1;
```

This type of update—incrementing an object—is used so frequently that C++ offers other, additional incrementing operators. The ++ and -- operators increment and decrement an object by 1, respectively. For example, the expression `j++;` adds 1 to the value of `j`, and the expression `x--` reduces `x` by 1. The ++ and -- unary operators alter the numeric object that they follow (see the table below).

Statement	State of `j`
`int j(0);`	0
`j++;`	1
`j++;`	2
`j--;`	1

So, within the context of the counting `for` loop, the update step can be written as `j++` rather than `j = j + 1`. The `for` loop

```
for(j = 1; j <= n; j = j + 1)
  // . . .
```

may now be written as this equivalent loop with the ++ operator used in the update step:

```
for(j = 1; j <= n; j++)
  // . . .
```

These new assignment operators are shown because they provide a convenient method for accomplishing incrementing and decrementing operations in the `for` loop. Another reason has to do with the fact that most C and C++ programs[1] use the ++ operator in `for` loops.

C++ also has several assignment operators in addition to =. Two of them are used to add and subtract value from an object.

Operator	Equivalent Meaning
+=	Increment object on left by value on right.
-=	Decrement object on left by value on right.

These two new operators alter the numeric object that they follow (see the table below).

Statement	State of j
int j = 0;	0
j += 3;	3
j += 4;	7
j -= 2;	5

Whereas the operators ++ and -- increment and decrement the object by one, respectively, the operators += and -= increment and decrement the object by any amount. The += operator is most often used to accumulate values inside a loop. For example, the following code sums all input by the user:

```
// Demonstrate the summing pattern
#include <iostream>
using namespace std;

int main()
{
  int j, n;
  double aNum;
  double sum = 0.0;  // Maintains running sum, so start at 0.0

  cout << "How many numbers are there to sum? ";
  cin >> n;
  cout << "Enter " << n << " numbers now: ";
  for(j = 1; j <= n; j++)
  {
    cin >> aNum;
    sum += aNum;   // Equivalent to sum = sum + aNum;
  }
  cout << "Sum: "  << sum << endl;
```

1. An early version of the C++ programming language was called *C with classes*. In 1983, the name "C++" was coined to signify that the language was adding something to the popular C language. The name C++ states that something was added to C.

```
  return 0;
}
```

Dialogue

```
How many numbers are there to sum? 4
Enter 4 numbers now: 7.5  3.0  1.5  2.0
```

for Loop Iteration	State of j	State of aNum	State of sum
0	0	0.0	0.0
1	1	7.5	7.5
2	2	3.0	10.5
3	3	1.5	12.0
4	4	2.0	14.0

The += and -= operators also increment and decrement for the loop counters by values other than 1:

```
for(j = 0; j <= 10; j += 2)  // Count by twos
{
  cout << j << "  ";
}
// Output: 0  2  4  6  8  10
```

Self-Check

8-1 Does a `for` loop evaluate the loop test first?

8-2 Must a `for` loop update step increment the loop counter by + 1?

8-3 Do all `for` loops always execute the repeated part at least once?

8-4 Describe a situation when the loop test `j <= n` of a `for` loop never becomes false.

8-5 Write the output from the following program segments. Assume both `j` and `n` have been declared as `int` objects.

-a
```
for(j = 1; j < 5; j = j + 1)
{
  cout << j << " ";
}
```

-b
```
n = 5;
for(j = 1; j <= n; j++)
```

```
{
  cout << j << " ";
}
```

-c
```
n = 3;
for(j = -3; j <= n; j += 2)
{
  cout << j << " ";
}
```

-d
```
for(int j = 0; j < 5; j++)
{
  cout << j << " ";
}
```

-e
```
for(int j = 5; j >= 1; j--)
{
  cout << j << " ";
}
```

-f
```
cout << "before" << endl;
n = 0;
for(j = 1; j <= n; j++)
{
  cout << j << " ";
}
cout << "after" << endl;
```

8-6 Write a `for` loop that displays all the integers from 1 to 100 on separate lines.

8-7 Write a `for` loop that displays all the integers from 10 down to 1.

8.1.5 Determinate Loops with `grid` Objects

A `grid` object has row numbers that range from `0` to `aGrid.nRows()-1` inclusive. The column numbers range from `0` to `aGrid.nColumns()-1` inclusive. Using these facts and the Determinate Loop pattern allows us to manipulate `grid` objects more compactly. For example, the `blockBorder` function (below) has two `for` loops that block all intersections on all four edges of any `grid` object.

```
// Use for loops to set blocks around a grid of any size
#include "grid"  // For the grid class

void setBorder(grid & g)  // A change to g changes myGrid
{ // pre:  The mover is not on an edge
  // post: The entire outside border is blocked
  int r, c;

  // It is useful that objects know things about themselves--number
  // of rows and columns for example, which vary from grid to grid
  for(r = 0; r < g.nRows(); r++)
  {
    g.block(r, 0);               // Block west edge
    g.block(r, g.nColumns()-1);  // Block east edge
  }

  // The first and last columns are blocked already so block
  // column #1 up to 1 less than the last column
  for(c = 1; c < g.nColumns() - 1; c++)
  {
    g.block(0, c);            // Block most of the north edge
    g.block(g.nRows()-1, c);  // Block most of the south edge
  }
}

int main()
{
  grid myGrid(8, 10, 1, 1, east);
  grid anotherGrid(3, 30, 1, 28, west);

  setBorder(myGrid);
  myGrid.display();

  cout << endl;

  setBorder(anotherGrid);
  anotherGrid.display();
  return 0;
}
```

OUTPUT

```
The Grid
# # # # # # # # # #
# > . . . . . . . #
# . . . . . . . . #
# . . . . . . . . #
# . . . . . . . . #
# . . . . . . . . #
# . . . . . . . . #
# # # # # # # # # #

The grid
# # # # # # # # # # # # # # # # # # # # # # # # # # # # # #
# . . . . . . . . . . . . . . . . . . . . . . . . . . . < #
# # # # # # # # # # # # # # # # # # # # # # # # # # # # # #
```

The `for` loops—applied in yet another instance of the Determinate Loop pattern—reduce the number of instructions. For example, a 20-by-20 grid would require exactly 76 `block` messages. More importantly, such a brute-force approach would allow the function to work only on a 20-by-20 grid. The accessor functions `grid::nColumns` and `grid::nRows` and the determinate `for` loop pattern allow the function to work properly for any sized grid. This is because every `grid` object knows its own size.

Self-Check

8-8 What difference occurs when the first `for` loop in `setBorder` is changed to

```
for(r = 0; r <= g.nRows(); r++)
```

8-9 What difference occurs when the second `for` loop in `setBorder` is changed to

```
for(c = 1; c < g.nColumns(); c++)
```

8-10 What difference would occur when the function heading is changed to

```
void setBorder(grid g)
```

8.2 Application of the Determinate Loop Pattern

Problem: Write a program that determines a range of temperature readings. Range is defined as the difference between the highest and lowest. The user must supply the number of temperature readings first.

In this application, the user is required to enter the total number of temperature readings before entering the actual temperatures. The output must be labeled as `Range` followed by the range of temperatures (23–11 or 12 with this dialogue). The dialogue must look like this:

DIALOGUE

```
Enter number of temperature readings: 6

Enter temperatures:
11
15
19
23
20
16
Range: 12
```

8.2.1 Analysis

The number of temperature readings will first be obtained from the user. An integer named `n` will serve nicely. Another numeric object is required to hold the individual temperature readings as they are processed. This object could be appropriately named `aTemp`. The range of temperature readings is the difference between the highest and lowest temperature readings in the list. So two more objects are needed to store the highest and lowest.

To find the range without the aid of a computer (easier with a small number of temperature readings), one could glance at the list of numbers and simply keep track of the highest and lowest while scanning the list from top to bottom:

aTemp	highest	lowest
-5	-5	-5
8	8	-5
22	22	-5
-7	22	-7
15	22	-7

For this set of data, the range = highest - lowest = 22 - (-7) = 29. The analysis deliverable summarizes the problem:

ANALYSIS DELIVERABLE

Mini Problem Description	Object Name	Sample Values	Input/Output
Compute the range of	`n`	`5`	Input
temperature readings	`aTemp`	`-5, 8, 22, -7, 15`	Input
	`highest`	`22`	Process[2]
	`lowest`	`-7`	Process
	`range`	`29`	Output

8.2.2 Design

For a large list—an approach more suited to a computer—the algorithm mimics the repetition of the hand-operated version just suggested. It uses a determinate loop to compare every temperature reading in the list to the highest and lowest—updating them if necessary.

DETERMINING THE RANGE ALGORITHM

```
input the number of temperature readings (n)
for each temperature reading
{
  input aTemp from user
  if aTemp is greater than highest so far,
    store it as the highest
  if aTemp is less than lowest so far,
    store it as the lowest
}
range = highest - lowest
```

As usual, it is a good idea to walk through the algorithm to verify its soundness.

1. Input the number of temperature readings (`n == 5`)
2. Input `aTemp` from user (`aTemp == -5`)

2. Process objects are used to help compute answers—not to store input or output.

3. If `aTemp` > `highest` so far (`-5 > Whoops!`), store it as `highest`

There is no value for `highest`! There is no value for `lowest`. Let us now assume the program will initialize `highest` and `lowest` to 0:

0. `lowest = 0;`   `highest = 0;`
1. Input the number of temperature readings (`n == 5`)
2. Input `aTemp` from user (`aTemp == -5`)
3. If `aTemp` is greater than `highest` so far (`-5 > 0`), store it as `highest` (`highest` stays `0`)
4. If `aTemp` is less than `lowest` so far (`-5 < 0`), store it as `lowest` (`lowest` becomes `-5`)

Well, this seems to work. How about one more iteration?

2. Input `aTemp` from user (`aTemp == 8`)
3. If `aTemp` is greater than `highest` so far (`8 > 0`), store it as `highest` (`highest` becomes `8`)
4. If `aTemp` is less than `lowest` so far (`8 < 0`), store it as `lowest` (`lowest` stays `-5`)

Seems okay. Try three more inputs to verify that `highest` and `lowest` are correct. Finally, the last step in the algorithm (after the repetition) produces the range: range = highest - lowest.

Self-Check

8-11 Determine the range when `n` is `4` and the temperature readings are `1 2 3 4`.

If you did the previous self-check question correctly, you will notice that `lowest` stays 0. The initial value of `lowest` is less than all subsequent inputs. So what might have seemed to work does not. The first test set works only because a negative temperature was input. The same algorithm will not work on a warmer day when all temperatures are positive. So instead of initializing both `highest` and `lowest` to 0, consider setting `highest` to something ridiculously low, say `-9999`, so low that any input will have to be higher. Set `lowest` to something ridiculously high like `9999`, so high that any input will have to be lower. Now walk through the algorithm with a few test sets. As long as all valid temperature inputs fall into the range of `-9999` to `9999`, the algorithm should work.

8.2.3 Implementation

Since the problem stated that the user must first supply the number of inputs, the exact number of repetitions is determined. This is an instance of the Determinate Loop pattern.

```
for(j = 1; j <= n; j++)
{
  // Process one input
}
```

The following program implements a corrected algorithm (written now in C++ rather than pseudocode). Notice that the user need not input the same set of temperature readings twice—the checks are made for both the highest and the lowest within the same loop.

```
// Determine the range of temperatures in a set of known size

#include <iostream>
using namespace std;

int main()
{
  int aTemp;
  int highest = -9999;  // No temperature will be less than -9999
  int lowest = 9999;    // No temperature will be greater than 9999
  int j, n, range;

  cout << "Enter number of temperature readings: ";
  cin >> n;

  // Input first temperature to record it as highest and lowest
  cout << "Enter readings 1 per line" << endl;

  // Use a determinate loop to process n temperatures
    for(j = 1; j <= n; j++)
    {
      // Get the next input
      cin >> aTemp;

      // Update the highest so far, if necessary
      if(aTemp > highest)
        highest = aTemp;

      // Update the lowest so far, if necessary
      if(aTemp < lowest)
        lowest = aTemp;
    }
```

```
  range = highest - lowest;
  cout << "Range: " << range << endl;
  return 0;
}
```

DIALOGUE

```
Enter number of temperature readings: 5
Enter readings 1 per line
-5
8
22
-7
15
Range: 29
```

8.2.4 Test the Implementation

Testing could be performed by finding the range of many lists of temperature readings and comparing them with many hand-checked results. For example, one set of inputs could include values that are all the same—the range would be 0. With two temperatures to check, the range should be computed as the difference between those two values. Another test would be to have just one input to verify that the range is also 0. The testing should also include a set of values where the number of inputs is greater than 2. This leads to many possible test sets, especially when attempting to input all possible orderings. Three inputs have 6 orderings, four inputs have 24 orderings, and in general n inputs have $n!$ (n factorial orderings or ($n * (n - 1) * (n - 2) *, \ldots, * 3 * 2 * 1$). Such exhaustive testing is not only impractical, it is also unnecessary.

The tester begins to gain confidence in the algorithm by picking an arbitrary number of tests—for example, when n was 5 and the inputs were -5, 8, 22, -7, and 15. This set of inputs shows the difference between the highest and lowest is (22 - (-7)) or 29. Looking at the dialogue and seeing the range is 29 could lead us to believe that the algorithm and implementation are correct. However, the only thing that is sure is this: When those particular five temperatures were entered, the correct range was displayed. The data used in this previous test would indicate that everything is okay.

But testing only reveals the presence of errors, not the absence of errors. If the range were shown as an obviously incorrect answer (-11, for example), hopefully, you would detect the presence of the error. Now consider this slightly different implementation seen in programs around the world:

```
// assert: highest == -9999 and lowest == 9999
for(j = 1; j <= n; j++)
{
  cin >> aTemp;
  if(aTemp > highest)
    highest = aTemp;
  else if(aTemp < lowest)
    lowest = aTemp;
}
```

Self-Check

8-12 Trace the code above using the same input (assume `n` is 5):

```
-5  8  22  -7  15
```

and predict the value stored in `range`. Is it correct?

8-13 Trace through the same code with these inputs (assume `n` is 5):

```
5  4  3  2  1
```

Predict the value stored in `range`. Is it correct?

8-14 Trace through the same code with these inputs (assume `n` is 5):

```
1  2  3  4  5
```

Predict the value stored in `range`. Is it correct?

8-15 *Multiple Choice:* When is `range` incorrectly computed?

-a When the input is entered in descending order.

-b When the input is entered in ascending order.

-c When the input is entered in neither ascending or descending order.

8-16 What must be done to correct the error?

8.2.5 What to Do When an Intent Error Is Detected

When you detect an intent error and a loop is involved, it is recommended that you display important values, such as `highest` and `lowest`, for each iteration of the loop. This simple debugging tool reveals what is happening and in so doing helps the debugging process. A few well-placed output statements can be very revealing. For example, a debugging output statement could be included in the loop that contained the intent error.

```
for(j = 1; j <= n; j++)
{
  cin >> aTemp;
  // Add an output statement in the loop to aid debugging
  cout << highest << "   " << lowest << endl;
  . . .
```

Now the dialogue, while testing the incorrect algorithm just before the preceding self-checks, would look like this:

```
Enter number of temperature readings: 3
-9999  9999
5
5  9999
12
12  9999
7
12  9999
Range: -9987
```

The extra debugging output statement vividly shows the lowest value is not changing, even though 5, 12, and 7 are all less than 9999. On the other hand, no error would occur with an improved algorithm that reads the first input and assigns it to both `highest` and `lowest`. The loop would then execute `n` - 1 times.

8.3 Algorithmic Pattern: The Indeterminate Loop

Although the Determinate Loop pattern occurs frequently in many algorithms, it has a serious limitation—someone, somehow, must determine the number of repetitions in advance. Quite often this is impossible, or at least very inconvenient and difficult. For example, an instructor may have a different number of tests to average as attendance varies between terms. A company may not have a constant number of employees as there are hires, fires, layoffs, transfers, and retirements. The schools where the software is distributed may have a different number of students each day.

It is often necessary to execute a set of statements an undetermined number of times, for example, to process report cards for *every* student in a school—not precisely 310 every term. Programs cannot always depend on prior knowledge to determine the exact number of repetitions. It is often more convenient to think in terms of "process a report card for all students" rather than "process precisely 310 report cards." This leads to another recurring pattern in algorithm design that captures the essence of repeating a process an unknown number of times. It is a pattern to help design a process that iterates until some event occurs to indicate the looping is finished. Here are some events used in this textbook to terminate loops:

* The loop counter becomes greater than the desired number of iterations.
* The mover on a grid can no longer move forward.
* The user enters a special value to indicate there is no more input.
* The end of the file is reached (see Chapter 9, "File Streams").

Whereas the number of repetitions for determinate loops is known in advance, the Indeterminate Loop pattern uses other techniques to stop. With indeterminate loops, the number of repetitions need not be known in advance.

ALGORITHMIC PATTERN 8.2

Pattern:	Indeterminate Loop
Problem:	Some process must repeat an unknown number of times so some event is needed to terminate the loop.

Algorithm:	while (the termination event has not occurred)
	{
	  perform these actions
	  do something to bring loop closer to termination
	}

Code Example:	`// Place things until the mover is blocked`
	`while(myGrid.frontIsClear())`
	`{`
	`  myGrid.putDown();`
	`  myGrid.move();`
	`}`

The C++ `while` statement is often used to implement the Indeterminate Loop pattern:

GENERAL FORM 8.2. *`while` statement*

while (*loop-test*)
{
  repeated-part
}

The *loop-test* is a logical expression that evaluates to either true or false. The *repeated-part* may be any C++ statement, but it is usually a set of statements enclosed in `{` and `}`.

When a `while` loop is encountered, the loop test evaluates to either true or false. If true, the repeated part executes. This process continues while (as long as) the loop test is true.

Figure 8.2

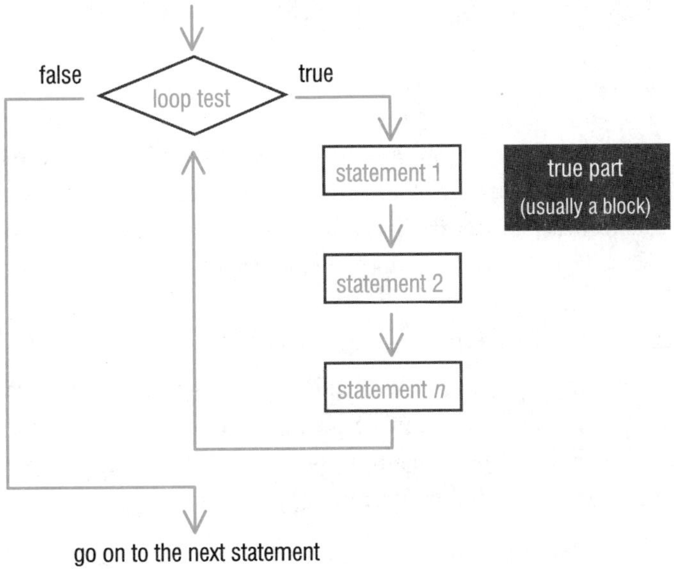

8.3.1 The Use of `while` to Implement the Determinate Loop Pattern

The `while` loop could also implement the Determinate Loop pattern. It is simply a matter of moving the initialization before the `while` loop and the update step to the bottom of the repeated part.

```
initialization
while( loop-test )
{
  // Activities to be repeated
  update-step
}
```

The following code represents an alternate implementation of the Determinate Loop pattern:

```
// Sum the first n integers
int accumulator = 0;
int j = 1;                             // Initialization
int n = 5;                             // Initialization
while(j <= n)                          // Loop test
{
  accumulator = accumulator + j;       // Action
  j++;                                 // Update step
}

cout << "Sum of the first " << n << " integers is " << accumulator;
```

Although the `while` loop can also implement the Determinate Loop pattern, the `for` loop is more concise and convenient. It is recommended that you use the `for` loop when the number of iterations is known in advance. When this cannot be determined, as with indeterminate loop problems, use the `while` statement instead.

8.3.2 Indeterminate Loop Pattern with `grid` Objects

There are many events used to terminate the loop in an Indeterminate Loop pattern. Consider moving the mover up until the edge of a grid or perhaps a block prevents the mover from continuing—a subproblem that will come in very handy for one of the grid-related programming projects.

```
// The event loop terminates when the front is no longer clear

#include "grid"        // For the grid class
#include <iostream>    // For cout
using namespace std;

void moveTillStopped(grid & g)
{ // post: The mover is facing a block or edge in front
  while(g.frontIsClear())
  {
    g.move();
  }
}

int main()
{
  // This grid constructor--with only two arguments--will place the
  // mover at some random location and in some random direction inside
  // an enclosed grid with exactly one random opening
  grid tarpit(5, 10);
```

```
  cout << "When initialized with only the number of rows\n"
       << "and columns, a grid object gets a random opening\n"
       << "with the mover at a random location and direction\n" << endl;
  moveTillStopped(tarpit);
  tarpit.display() << endl;

  return 0;
}
```

DIALOGUE

```
When initialized with only the number of rows
and columns, a grid object gets a random opening
with the mover at a random location and direction

The grid
# # # # # # # # # #
. . . . . . . . . #
# . . .         > #
# . . . . . . . . #
# # # # # # # # # #
```

Because of the randomness of the `grid` object `tarpit`, `moveTillStopped` uses an indeterminate loop to advance the mover. The `g.move()` message may repeat the move message once, twice, or as many times as are necessary to get the mover up against the "wall."

Self-Check

8-17 Why must `moveTillStopped` use an Indeterminate Loop rather than a Determinate Loop pattern?

8.3.3 The Indeterminate Loop Using a Sentinel

A *sentinel* is a specific input used to terminate an indeterminate loop. A sentinel value should be the same class of data as the other input. However, the sentinel is not meant to be processed as a valid part of the input. For example, the following set of inputs hints that the input of -1.0 is the event that terminates the loop and that -1.0 is not to be counted as a valid test score. Otherwise, the average would not be 80.0.

DIALOGUE

```
Enter tests scores [0.0 through 100.0] or -1.0 to quit
80.0
90.0
70.0
-1.0
Average of 3 tests = 80
```

This dialogue asks the user either to enter data in the range of 0.0 through 100.0 inclusive or to enter -1.0 to signal the end of data.

With sentinel indeterminate loops, a message is usually displayed to indicate how the user must end the input. It is important to inform the user that a sentinel is being used. The user must be told what that sentinel value is. It could have been -999 or any other negative number, for example.

8.3.4 The Use of `cin >>` as a Loop Test

Up to this point `cin >>` has often been used for input. What hasn't been revealed is this: A `cin` statement returns true when it is successful. If the input operation fails to get a number, `cin >>` is replaced with false. This means that a `cin >>` statement can be and often is used as the logical expression in an `if...else` or `while` statement:

```
if(cin >> intObject)      - or -      while(cin >> intObject)
```

Both of the above logical expressions return true when `cin` successfully extracts a valid integer from the input stream. However, the same logical expressions return false if an invalid integer is encountered in the input stream (or as shown later in Chapter 9, the end of file is encountered).

With this new information, implementation of sentinel loops are simplified when the `cin` extraction is part of the loop test.

```
// The priming extraction is now part of the loop test
while( (cin >> testScore) && (testScore != sentinel) )
{
  accumulator = accumulator + testScore;  // Update accumulator
  n++;                                     // Update total inputs
}
```

The actual return value of the input statement `cin >> testScore` isn't all that important. However, because `cin >> testScore` is guaranteed to execute first, `testScore` is guaranteed to have obtained a valid numeric value through keyboard input before it is compared to sentinel. The second part (`testScore != sentinel`) evaluates to true *only* if the input was the sentinel (-1.0 in this case). So for any valid data, this loop test is `true && true`, which evaluates to true. In this case, the loop executes the repeated part. This loop repeats the loop until the user enters the sentinel (-1.0 in this case). For example, the loop test is evaluated like this when 95.0 is entered:

LOOP TEST EVALUATION WHEN INPUT IS 95.0

```
while( (cin >> testScore) &&  (testScore != sentinel) )
     (      true            &&  (    95.0     !=     -1.0   ) )
     (      true            &&               true            )
                           true
```

The loop test is true only if a valid number is input and that number is not -1.0. With 95.0, the loop test is true (`true && true` is true). When the sentinel of -1.0 is entered, the loop test is false (`true && false` is false)—the termination condition is reached.

LOOP TEST EVALUATION WHEN INPUT IS -1.0 (OR -1)

```
while( (cin >> testScore) && (testScore != sentinel) )
             true           && (    -1.0     !=     -1.0 )
             true           &&             false
                          false
```

This loop test is now placed into the context of a program that computes the average of any number of inputs.

```
// Use a sentinel of -1 to terminate a loop
#include <iostream>
using namespace std;

int main()
{
  const double sentinel = -1.0;  // User enters this to terminate
  double accumulator = 0.0;      // Maintain running sum of inputs
  int n = 0;                     // Maintain total number of inputs
  double testScore, average;

  // Prompt
  cout << "Enter test scores [0.0 through 100.0] or " << sentinel
       << " to quit" << endl;

  // Input and process at the same time
```

```
  while( (cin >> testScore) && (testScore != sentinel) )
  {
    accumulator += testScore;  // Update accumulator
    n++;                       // Update total inputs
  }

  if(n > 0)
  {
    average = accumulator / n;
    cout << "Average of " << n << " tests = " << average << endl;
  }
  else
    cout << "Can't average 0 numbers" << endl;
}
```

Dialogue

```
Enter test scores [0.0 through 100.0] or -1.0 to quit
80.0
90.0
70.0
-1.0
Average of 3 tests = 80
```

The following table traces the changing state of the important objects to simulate execution of the previous program. In addition to keeping the running sum of the test scores in `accumulator`, `n` must also be incremented by 1 for each valid `testScore`.

Iteration Number	`testScore`	`accumulator`	`n`	`testScore != sentinel`
Before the loop	NA	0.0	0	NA
Loop 1	70.0	70.0	1	true
Loop 2	90.0	160.0	2	true
Loop 3	80.0	240.0	3	true
After the loop	NA	240.0	3	NA

Self-Check

8-18 Determine the average for each of the following code fragments by simulating execution when the user inputs 70.0, 90.0, 80.0, and -1.0.

-a
```
cin >> testScore;
while(testScore != sentinel)
{
  cin >> testScore;
  accumulator += testScore;  // Update accumulator
  n++;                       // Update total inputs
}
average = accumulator / n;   // Division by 0 possible
```

-b
```
cin >> testScore;
while(testScore != sentinel)
{
  accumulator += testScore;  // Update accumulator
  n++;                       // Update total inputs
  cin >> testScore;
}
average = accumulator / n;   // Division by 0 possible
```

8-19 If you answered 80.0 for both -a and -b above, redo both until you get different answers for -a and -b.

8-20 Which code (-a or -b) is equivalent to the previous complete program where the loop test is `while((cin >> testScore) && (testScore != sentinel))`?

8.3.5 Infinite Loops

It is possible that a loop may never execute, not even once. It is also possible that a `while` loop will never terminate. Consider the following `while` loop that potentially continues to execute until external forces are applied (turning off the computer or a hardware failure, for example). This is potentially an *infinite loop,* something that is usually undesirable.

```
cin >> testScore;
while(testScore != sentinel)
{
  accumulator += testScore;  // Update accumulator
  n++;                       // Update total inputs
}
```

The loop repeats virtually forever. The termination condition can never be reached. The loop test is always true because there is no statement in the repeated part that brings the loop closer to the termination condition of `testScore == sentinel`. When writing `while` loops, remember to ensure that the loop test will eventually become false.

When you do get a program that executes a loop over and over again—and you will—use the system-dependent method necessary to terminate the program that is executing the infinite loop (ask your instructor).

Self-Check

8-21 How many iterations of the previous loop occur when the user enters the sentinel (-1.0) as the very first input?

8-22 What activity should be added to the previous `while` statement so each loop iteration brings the loop one step closer to termination?

8-23 The following code represents another example of an infinite loop. What must be done to make this loop terminate as intended?

```
while(g.frontIsClear());
{
  g.move();
}
```

8-24 Write the output from the following C++ program fragments:

-a
```
int n = 3;
int counter = 1;
while(counter <= n)
{
  cout << counter << "  ";
  counter++;
}
```

-b
```
int last = 10;
int j = 2;
while(j <= last)
{
  cout << j << "  ";
  j += 2;
}
```

8-25 Write the number of times each `while` loop repeats its repeated part. Assume `j`, `counter`, `accumulator`, and `n` have been declared as `int` objects. "zero," "infinite," and "unknown" are perfectly valid answers.

-a
```
while(counter <= n)
{
  cout << counter << endl;
}
```

-b
```
counter = 1;
n = 0;
while(counter <= n)
  cout << " " << counter;
```

-c
```
counter = 1;
n = 5;
while(counter <= n)
{
  counter++;
}
```

-d
```
n = 5;
j = 1;
while(j <= n)
  cout << j << endl;
  j++;
```

-e
```
j = 1;
sum = 0;
while(j <= 5)
{
  sum += j;
  sum++;
}
```

-f
```
counter = 10;
while(counter >= 0);
{
  counter = counter - 2;
}
```

8-26 Write a code fragment that sums all integers until the user enters 999.

Exercises

1. How many times will the following loops execute `cout << "Hello ";`? "zero," "unknown," and "infinite" are perfectly legitimate answers. Assume `j` and `n` have been declared as `int` objects.

a.
```
n = 5;
for(j = 1; j <= n; j++)
{
  cout << "Hello ";
}
```

b.
```
n = 0;
for(j = 5; j >= n; j--)
{
  cout << "Hello ";
}
```

c.
```
n = 5;
for(j = 1; j <= n; j--)
{
  cout << "Hello ";
  j++;
}
```

d.
```
n = 0;
for(j = 1; j <= n; j++)
{
  cout << "Hello ";
}
```

2. Write the output produced by these `for` loops:

```
for(counter = 1; counter <= 5; counter++)
  cout << "   " << counter;
  cout << "Loop One";  // Incorrectly indented to confuse
for(counter = 10; counter >= 1; counter--)
  cout << "   " << counter;
cout << "Blast Off";  // Correctly indented to avoid confusion
```

3. Write loops to produce the outputs shown.

a. `10 9 8 7 6 5 4 3 2 1 0`

b. `0 5 10 15 20 25 30 35 40 45 50`

c. `-1000 -900 -800 -700 -600 -500 -400 -300 -200 -100 0`

4. Write the output generated by the following code:

```
int j = 0;
while(j < 5)
{
   cout << "   " << j;
   j = j + 1;
}
```

5. Write a loop that sums all the integers between `start` and `stop` inclusive that are input from the keyboard. You may assume `start` is always less than or equal to `stop`. If the input were 5 for `start` and 10 for `stop`, the sum would be 5 + 6 + 7 + 8 + 9 + 10 (45).

6. How many times will `Hello` be displayed using the following program segments? "zero," "undetermined," and "infinite" are perfectly legitimate answers.

   a.
   ```
   while(j <= 10)
     cout << "Hello";
   ```

   b.
   ```
   j = 1;
   while(j <= 7)
   {
     cout << "Hello";
   j++;
   }
   ```

   c.
   ```
   j = 7;
   while(j <= 1)
   {
     cout << "Hello";
   }
   ```

   d.
   ```
   j = 1;
   while(j <= 5)
     cout << "Hello";
     j++;
   ```

7. Write a loop that produces this output:

```
-4   -3   -2   -1    0    1    2    3    4    5    6
```

8. Write a loop that displays 100, 95, . . ., 5, 0 on separate lines.

9. Write a loop that counts how many perfect scores (the number 100) are entered from the keyboard.

10. Convert the following code to its `for` loop counterpart:

```
cout << "Enter number of ints to be summed: ";
cin >> n;
counter = 1;
sum = 0;
while(counter <= n)
{
```

```
  cin >> intObject;
  sum = sum + intObject;
  counter++;
}
cout << sum;
```

11. Write a loop that counts the number of words input by a user until the user enters the `string` `ENDOFDATA` (must be uppercase letters, no spaces).

12. Write the complete output generated by the following program when the user enters 1, 2, 3, 4, and -1 on separate lines.

```
#include <iostream>
using namespace std;

int main()
{
  double test;
  double sum = 0.0;
  cout << "Enter tests or a negative number to quit: " << endl;
  while( (cin >> test) && (test >= 0.0) )
  {
    sum = sum + test;
  }
  cout << "Sum: " << sum < endl;
}
```

13. Write the output generated by the following code:

```
string choice("BDWBQDW");
int j = 0;
while( choice[j] != 'Q' )
{
  cout << "Opt: " << choice[j] << endl;
  j++;
}
```

Programming Tips

1. Pick the type of loop you want to use.

After recognizing the need for repetition, decide if the number of repetitions can be determined in advance. If so, this is a determinate loop that is best implemented as a `for` loop. If the number of iterations cannot be determined in advance, first determine the event that will terminate the loop. Use its logical negation as the loop test.

For example, the loop will terminate when someone enters the word `STOP`. The termination condition is `(word == "STOP")`. The loop test is the logical negation `while (word != "STOP")`.

2. Beware of infinite loops.

Watch out for infinite loops. They are easy to create and sometimes very difficult to find. Can you spot why these are infinite loops?

```
int j = 1;  // Assume j and sum are present
int sum = 0;

while(j <= 100);
{ // Sum the first 100 integers
  sum += j;
  j++;
}

while(j <= 100)
{ // Sum the first 100 integers
  sum += j;
}

while(j <= 100)
  // Sum the first 100 integers
  sum += j;
  j++;

while(j <= 100)
{ // Sum the first 100 integers
  sum += j;
}
j++;

for(j = 0; j <= 100; j++);
{ // Sum the first 100 integers
  sum += j;
}

for(j = 0; j <= 100; j++)
{ // Sum the first 100 integers
  sum += j;
  j--;
}
```

3. Always write a compound statement for the iterative part of a `while` loop even if it is not necessary.

This provides a better chance of including any increment statement as part of the loop rather than accidentally leaving it outside the loop.

4. Use debugging `cout`s to find out what is going on in a loop.

When in doubt, place a debugging output statement inside the loop to display some important object that should be changing. This can be very revealing. Sometimes you'll spot an infinite loop. Other times you might spot that the loop test was never true.

```
while( . . . )
{
  // . . .
  mid = (lo + hi) / 2.0;
  cout << "In loop, mid == " << mid << endl;
}
```

5. Loops may not always execute the iterative part.

It is possible that a loop will execute zero times, or less than you might have thought.

```
int n = 3;
int j;
for(j = 1; j >= n; j++)  // 1 >= n is false
{
  cout << "You'll not see me!";
}

for(j = 1; j <= n; j++);  // Get rid of ;
{
  cout << "You see me only once, not thrice" << endl;
  cout << "for I'm not part of the for!" << endl;
}
```

6. Things become much simpler when the input statement is part of an indeterminate loop test.

If you are used to a priming read for sentinel loops—especially you Pascal programmers—try to forget it. C++ allows input as part of the loop test, so it is easier to write sentinel loop tests like this:

```
while((cin >> aNumber) && (aNumber != sentinel))
{
  // Process aNumber but not the sentinel
}
```

7. Sometimes a quasi "infinite loop" with a break is the easiest way to implement a loop.

If you are having trouble with loop tests, consider using a loop with a guarded break (this code is equivalent to the previous sentinel loop):

```
while( true )
{
```

```
        cin >> aNumber;
        if(aNumber == sentinel)  // The termination condition
           break;  // Exit the loop when termination condition occurs
        // Otherwise process aNumber
    }
```

Programming Projects

8A Wind Speed

Write a program that determines the lowest, highest, and average of a set of wind speed readings. Prompt the user for the number of wind speed readings in the set.

```
Enter number of wind speed readings: 4
5.0
6.0
2.0
8.0
   n: 4
High: 8
 Low: 2
 Ave: 5.25
```

8B Factorial

Write a function that returns $n!$ (n factorial) where $n!$ is the product of all the positive integers from 1 to n. For example, $5! = 1 * 2 * 3 * 4 * 5 = 120$; $4! = 1 * 2 * 3 * 4 = 24$; and $0! = 1$ (by definition). Test your function with these arguments: 0, 1, 2, and 7

8C Squaring Integers

The square of an integer value n can be found by adding the first n positive odd integers. For example, both 4 squared and -4 squared are the sum of the first four positive odd integers (1 + 3 + 5 + 7 = 16). Write a function that displays the square of an integer using your own function. Do not use the built-in function pow or the multiplication operator (*). Complete your function named squareOf. Use this test driver.

```
int main()
{                                    // Expected output:
  cout << squareOf( 0)  << endl;  // 0
  cout << squareOf(-1)  << endl;  // 1
  cout << squareOf( 1)  << endl;  // 1
  cout << squareOf( 2)  << endl;  // 4
  cout << squareOf( 3)  << endl;  // 9
```

```
  cout << squareOf(-8)  << endl;  // 64
  cout << squareOf( 8)  << endl;  // 64
  return 0;
}
```

8D Compound Interest

Calculate the amount of money that will be in a savings account after one year when the interest is compounded on an annual, monthly, and daily basis. Input must consist of the annual interest rate and principal, which is the single amount deposited on the first day. The solution involves applying the appropriate interest rate to the principal the correct number of times. For example, to determine the `futureValue` of a principal amount that is to be compounded on a monthly basis, the monthly interest rate must be applied 12 times where the principal is updated (monthly interest added) for each month (period). Since you are to determine the future value over a one-year period, no `for` loop is required to determine the `futureValue` of an amount that is compounded annually. Format your output (with `ostream::width`) as follows:

```
Enter principal : 1000
Enter annual interest rate [0...25] : 6

               Annual      Monthly     Daily
FutureValue:   1060.00     1061.68     1061.83
```

8E Wind Speed Again: Indeterminate Loop

Write a program that determines the lowest, highest, and average of a set of wind speed readings, which are all positive or zero. Terminate the loop with any negative input. Be sure you notify the user how to terminate data entry.

DIALOGUE

```
Enter wind speed readings or a number < 0 to quit:
5.0
6.0
2.0
8.0
-999
   n: 4
High: 8
 Low: 2
 Ave: 5.25
```

8F Guessing Game

This program requires the use of random numbers. The file `stdlib.h` declares a function named `rand` that generates seemingly random numbers.

```
int rand()  // From stdlib.h
// post: Returns an integer in the range of 0 through RAND_MAX where
//       RAND_MAX is a large integer defined in stdlib.h
```

However, unless you initialize the random number generator `seed`, you always get the same list of random numbers. Therefore, first call the function `randomize` that has the following function heading:

```
void randomize()  // From "compfun"
// post: Initializes the random number generator
```

For example, the following program displays one random number:

```
#include <iostream>
using namespace std;
#include "compfun"  // For randomize()

int main()
{
  // Set a new seed for random number generator based on system clock
  randomize();

  // Set randNum to a random number (it will always be the same number
  // unless randomize is called)
  int randNum = rand();
  cout << "Random number: " << randNum << endl;
  return 0;
}
```

1. First, run the previous program several times to ensure that you get different daily numbers. Do not continue until you test the code that does this.

2. Change the program so `dailyNumber` is in the range of 1 through 100. (*Hint:* You will have to use the `%` operator to get integers under 100. To avoid zeros, you'll have to add 1.)

3. Once you understand how to use `rand` and `randomize`, begin to write the C++ program that implements a guessing game. Ask the user for a number in the range of 1 through 100 inclusive. If the guess is larger than the random number

you generated in the range of 1 through 100, inform the user that the guess was too high. If the guess is too low, say so, and when the guess matches the random number, say so. Also tell the user how many guesses were required. Here is a sample dialogue:

```
Pick a number from 1...100: 25
25 is too low
Pick a number from 1...100: 75
75 is too high
Pick a number from 1...100: 40
40 is too low
Pick a number from 1...100: 60
60 is too high
Pick a number from 1...100: 49
49 matches the random number
Number of guesses: 5
```

8G Surround the Grid

Write and test a function `surroundGrid` that instructs the mover to place things on every intersection that lies on an edge. Use the following test driver to get output like that shown below. Let the precondition assume the mover is in the bottom-left corner facing east. However, the number of rows and columns may differ.

```
int main()
{ // Test drive surroundWithCookies
  grid myGrid(4, 10, 3, 0, east);
  surroundGrid(myGrid);
  myGrid.display();
  return 0;
}
```

OUTPUT

```
The grid
O O O O O O O O O O
O . . . . . . . . O
O . . . . . . . . O
& O O O O O O O O O
```

The `&` icon means the intersection has a mover and a cookie.

8H The `elevator` Class (prerequisite: Chapter 6)

Write the class definition and implement the member functions for class `elevator` with a constructor that places an elevator at a selected floor. Include a `select` member function that allows floors to be selected. For every floor, the message `going up` or `going down` should be displayed before the current floor of the elevator. Here is one sample output to give you an idea of what a simulated elevator will look like on your screen.

```
// File name: test8h.cpp
#include "elevator"  // Includes elevator.h and elevator.cpp
int main()
{
  elevator aLift(1);
  aLift.select(5);
  aLift.select(3);
  return 0;
}
```

OUTPUT

```
start on floor 1
going up to 2
going up to 3
going up to 4
going up to 5
open at 5
going down to 4
going down to 3
open at 3
```

8.4 The do while Statement

The `do while` statement is similar to the `while` loop. It allows a collection of statements to be repeated while an expression is true. The primary difference is the time at which the loop test is evaluated. The `while` loop test is evaluated at the beginning of each iteration. The `do while` statement evaluates the loop test at the end of each iteration. This means that the `do while` loop always executes its repeated part at least once. Here is the general form of the `do while` loop.

GENERAL FORM 8.3. *do while loop*

do {
  repeated-part
} while (*loop-test* **) ;**

When a `do while` statement is encountered, all statements within the block (`{ }`) execute. The *loop-test* is evaluated at the *end* of the loop—not at the beginning. If true, the *repeated-part* executes again. If the test expression is false, the loop terminates. Although the block is not absolutely required with the `while` and `for` statements, braces must always exist between the `do` and the `while` in this statement.[3] Here is an example of the `do while` loop that displays the increasing value of `counter` to simulate its execution.

3. Most programmers put the opening curly brace to the right of `do` (on the same line) and the closing curly brace to the left of `while` (on the same line).

```
int counter = 1;
int n = 4;
cout << endl << "Before loop..." << endl;
do {
  cout << "Loop #" << counter << endl;
  counter++;
} while (counter <= n);
cout << "...After loop" << endl;
```

OUTPUT

```
Before loop...
Loop #1
Loop #2
Loop #3
Loop #4
...After loop
```

The `do while` loop is a good choice for repetition whenever a set of statements must be executed at least once to initialize objects used later in the loop test. For example, the `do while` loop is the preferred statement when asking the user to enter one of several options. For example, the `do while` loop in the `char` type function `nextOption` repeatedly requests the user to enter one of three choices. The loop does not terminate until the user enters a valid option. `main` also uses a `do while` loop to process as many deposits and withdrawals as the user wants.

```
// Use a do while loop that repeatedly asks for a valid option
#include <ctype.h>   // For toupper
#include <iostream>  // For cout, cin, and endl
using namespace std;

char nextOption()
{ // post: Return an uppercase W, D, or Q
  char option = '?';
  do {
    cout << "W)ithdraw, D)eposit, or Q)uit: ";
    cin >> option;
    option = toupper(option);
  } while((option != 'W') &&
          (option != 'D') &&
          (option != 'Q'));
  return option;
}

int main()
{
```

```
  char choice = 'Q';

  do {
    choice = nextOption();
    // assert: choice is either 'Q', 'W', or 'D'

    if('W' == choice)
      cout << "\nValid entry--process W\n" << endl;

    if('D' == choice)
      cout << "\nValid entry--process D\n" << endl;

    if('Q' == choice)
       cout << "\nHave a nice whatever :)" << endl;

  } while ( choice != 'Q' );

  return 0;
}
```

DIALOGUE (THE USER ENTERS ONE VALID ENTRY, THREE INVALID CHOICES, AND QUITS WITH Q)

```
W)ithdraw, D)eposit, or Q)uit: W

Valid entry--process W

W)ithdraw, D)eposit, or Q)uit: make
W)ithdraw, D)eposit, or Q)uit: 3
W)ithdraw, D)eposit, or Q)uit: invalid entries

W)ithdraw, D)eposit, or Q)uit: Q

Have a nice whatever :)
```

Because at least one character must be obtained from the keyboard before the test expression evaluates, the `do while` loop in `nextOption` is used instead of a `while` loop—the loop must iterate at least once. Also, a `do while` loop is used in `main` to get an option because it needs at least one user input to evaluate whether or not the user wants to quit.

Although `do while` is not necessary, it is a bit easier to implement than the following `while`, which requires the Prompt then Input pattern twice rather than once:

```
cout << "W)ithdraw, D)eposit, or Q)uit: ";  // Not necessary when
cin >> option;                              // do while is used
option = toupper(option);
```

```
while( (option != 'W') &&
       (option != 'D') &&
       (option != 'Q') )
 {
   cout << "W)ithdraw, D)eposit, or Q)uit: ";
   cin >> option;
   option = toupper(option);
 }
```

Of course you could use this trick to initialize `option` to any invalid value such as `'?'`:

```
option = ('?');
while( (option != 'W') &&
       (option != 'D') &&
       (option != 'Q') )
{
  cout << "W)ithdraw, D)eposit, or Q)uit: ";
  cin >> option;
  option = toupper(option);
}
```

Self-Check

8-27 Write the output produced by the following code:

-a
```
int j = 1;
do {
  cout << j << endl;
  j++;
} while(j <= 3);
```

-b
```
double x = -1.0;
do {
  cout << x << endl;
  x = x + 0.5;
} while(x <= 1.0);
```

8-28 Write a `do while` loop that prompts for and inputs numbers until the number is in the range of 1 through 10 inclusive.

8-29 Write a `do while` loop that prompts for and inputs characters until the user enters `w`, `W`, `d`, `D`, `q`, or `Q` at the prompt `Enter A)dd W)ithdraw Q)uit:`.

8.5 Loop Selection and Design

For some people, loops are easy to implement, even at first. For others, infinite loops and intent errors are more common. In either case, the following outline is offered to help you choose and design loops in a variety of situations:

1. Determine which type of loop to use.
2. Determine the loop test.
3. Write the statements to be repeated.
4. Bring the loop one step closer to termination.
5. Initialize objects if necessary.

8.5.1 Determine Which Type of Loop to Use

If the number of repetitions is known in advance or read as input, use the Determinate Loop pattern, which has a statement specifically designed for this—the `for` loop. Although you can use the `while` loop to implement the Determinate Loop pattern, consider using the `for` loop instead. The `while` implementation allows you to omit one of the key counting parts, making any intent errors more difficult to detect and correct. If you omit one of the counting parts of a `for` loop, you'll get an easy-to-detect-and-correct compiletime error.

If you need to wait until some event occurs during execution of the loop, the Indeterminate Loop pattern is more appropriate. If so, use the `while` loop. If the loop must always execute once, for example, when input data must be checked for validity (an integer value that must be in the range of 0 through 100), use the `do while` loop. A `do while` loop is also a good choice for menu-driven programs that repeatedly request options until the menu choice for *quit* is entered.

8.5.2 Determine the Loop Test

If the loop test is not obvious, try writing the conditions that must be true for the loop to terminate. For example, if you want the user to enter `QUIT` to stop entering input, the termination condition is

```
inputName == "QUIT"   // Termination condition
```

The logical negation `inputName != "STOP"` can be used directly as the loop test of a `while` or `do while` loop.

```
while(inputName != "STOP")
{
  // . . .
}

do {
  // . . .
} while(inputName != "STOP")
```

8.5.3 Write the Statements to Be Repeated

This is why the loop is being written in the first place. Some common tasks include keeping a running sum, keeping track of a high or low value, or counting the number of occurrences of some value. Other tasks that will be seen later include searching for a name in a list or repeatedly comparing all `string` elements of a list in order to alphabetize it.

8.5.4 Bring the Loop One Step Closer to Termination

To avoid an infinite loop, at least one action in the loop body must bring it closer to termination. In a determinate loop this might mean incrementing or decrementing a counter by some specific value. Inputting the next value is another way to bring loops closer to termination—for example, when the user inputs data until the sentinel is extracted from the input stream. In a `for` loop, the repeated statement should be designed to bring the loop closer to termination, usually by incrementing the counter. In general, the loop test should contain at least one object that is altered during each iteration of the loop.

8.5.5 Initialize Objects If Necessary

Check to see if any objects used in either the body of the loop or the loop test need to be initialized. Doing this usually ensures that the objects of the loop and the objects used in the iterative part have been initialized. For example, consider this loop:

```
double sum, x, average;
int n;

cout << "Enter numbers or -1 to quit: ";
while(x != -1)
{
  sum = sum + x;
  n++;
  cin >> x;
}
average = sum / n;
```

With this code, the value of `average` is garbage. What is the initial value of `sum`, perhaps -1,234.5 or 99,999.9? The first value of `x` is unknown, as is that of `n`. Consider each object in the loop test and the iterative part as potential candidates for initialization. This may require setting `n` to 0, but it may also require that some object becomes initialized through the input statement. Here is the corrected code.

```
double sum = 0.0;
int n = 0;
double x, average;  // x and average don't require initialization
cout << "Enter numbers or -1 to quit: ";
cin >> x;
while(x != -1)
{
  sum = sum + x;
  n++;
  cin >> x;
}
average = sum / n;
```

Self-Check

8-30 Which loop best accomplishes these tasks?

- -a Sum the first five integers (1 + 2 + 3 + 4 + 5).
- -b Find the average value for a set of numbers when the size of the set is known.
- -c Find the average value for a set of numbers when the size of the set cannot be determined by the program or the user until the data has been completely entered.
- -d Obtain a character from the user that must be an uppercase I, S, or Q.

8-31 For a loop to process inputs called `value` until `-1` is entered,

- -a write a termination condition.
- -b write the loop test for a `while` or `do while` loop.

8-32 For each loop, which objects are not initialized but should be?

-a
```
while(j <= n)
{
  // . . . ;
}
```

-b
```
for(j = 1; j <= n; j = j + inc)
{
  // . . . ;
}
```

Chapter Summary

- Repetition is an important method of control for all programming languages. Typically, the body of a loop has statements that may change the state of one or more objects during each loop iteration.
- The `for` loop is often used to implement the Determinate Loop pattern, which requires that the number of repetitions be determined *before* the loop is encountered.
- Determinate loops rely on this value (`n` perhaps) and a properly initialized and incremented loop counter (`j` perhaps) to track the number of repetitions. The counter is compared to the known number of iterations at the start of each loop. The counter is automatically updated at the end of each `for` loop iteration.
- There are a number of ways to determine the number of loop iterations before the loop executes. The number of iterations may be input from the user, passed as an argument to a function, initialized in advance, or `n` may be part of the state of some object. For example, every `grid` object knows its number of rows and number of columns. Every `string` object knows how many characters it has at any given moment.
- This Determinate Loop pattern is so common that a specific statement—the `for` loop—is built into almost all languages.
- Indeterminate loops rely on some external event for their termination. The terminating event may occur at any time.
- Indeterminate loops are used when the program is unable to determine, in advance, the number of times a loop must iterate. The terminating events include sentinels extracted from the input stream (-1 as a test or "Q" in a menu selection.) These types of loops allow any number of bank customers to make any number of transactions or repeatedly prompt a user for input until valid input is entered.
- Although the `while` loop is the only repetitive statement needed to solve any computer problem, the `for` loop is more convenient under certain circumstances. The `for` loop requires the program to take care of the initialization, loop test, and repeated statement all at once. The compiler protests if one of these important steps is missing. The `for` loop provides a more compact and less error-prone determinate loop.
- Remember these steps if you are having trouble designing loops:
  - Determine which type of loop to use.
  - Determine the loop test.

- Write the statements to be repeated.
- Bring the loop one step closer to termination.
- Initialize objects if necessary.

Exercises

14. How many times will the following loops execute `cout << "Hello ";`? "zero," "unknown," and "infinite" are perfectly legitimate answers.

a.
```
j = 1;
n = 10;
do {
  cout << "Hello ";
} while(j > n);
```

b.
```
n = 10;
j = 1;
do {
  cout << "Hello ";
  j = j - 2;
} while(j <= n);
```

c.
```
j = -1;
do {
   cout << "Hello ";
   j++;
} while(j != j)
```

d.
```
j = 1;
do {
   cout << "Hello ";
   j++;
} while(j <= 100)
```

15. Write a `do while` loop that generates this output.

```
10  9  8  7  6  5  4  3  2  1  0
```

16. Write the output generated by the following program:

```
#include <iostream>
using namespace std;

int main()
{
  int j = -2;
  do {
    cout << "    " << j;
    j--;
  } while(j > -6);
}
```

17. Convert the following code to its `do while` counterpart:

```
char option;
cout << "Enter option A, B, or Q: ";
cin >> option;
option = toupper(option);
while((option != 'A') && (option != 'B') && (option != 'Q'))
{
  cout << "Enter option A, B, or Q: ";
  cin >> option;
  option = toupper(option);
}
```

18. Write a function named `option` that prompts for and returns an uppercase S, A, M, or Q only. The return type of the `option` function must be `char`. Return S, A, M, or Q through the function name, not as a reference. The following code must assign one of the only four allowed letters to `choice`:

```
char choice(option());
cout << choice;  // Output must be either S, A, M, or Q only!
```

19. Rewrite the following `do while` loop as a pretest `while` loop (loop test first before the body):

```
int counter = 0;
do {
  cout << counter;
  counter = counter + 1;
} while(counter <= 100);
```

Programming Projects

8I Mini Teller

Write a C++ program that allows the user to create exactly one `bankAccount` object and then make as many withdrawals and deposits as desired. The final line of output should be the balance. Your code should not allow a withdrawal greater than the balance. Use the following dialogue as a guide to this problem's specification:

```
Enter customer name: Jackson
Enter initial balance: 0.00
W)ithdraw, D)eposit, or Q)uit: D
```

```
Enter deposit amount: 250.00
W)ithdraw, D)eposit, or Q)uit: W
Enter withdrawal amount: 300.00
**Amount requested exceeds account balance**
W)ithdraw, D)eposit, or Q)uit: w
Enter withdrawal amount: 200.00
W)ithdraw, D)eposit, or Q)uit: q
Ending balance: 50
```

8J Exponents

Write a program to display a table that shows exponents of 2. The exponent range must be 0...20. (*Note:* $2^0 = 1$). Input should include the first and last exponent of 2 to be displayed. Make sure that both high and low powers are in the range of 0...20 and that the low power is less than or equal to the high power. Ensure that both powers are in the correct ranges.

```
Enter low exponent from 0 to 20: -1
                       Try again
Enter low exponent from 0 to 20: 21
                       Try again
Enter low exponent from 0 to 20: 4
Enter high exponent from 4 to 20: 2
                        Try again
Enter high exponent from 4 to 20: 10

   X       2^X
  ==      ======
   4        16
   5        32
   6        64
   7       128
   8       256
   9       512
  10      1024
```

8K Find the Grid Exit

Write a C++ function named `findExit` that instructs the mover to find the lone exit in any grid. Make sure you initialize the `grid` object with only two arguments—number of rows and number of columns. This ensures that you will get a grid that has only one exit. Also, the mover will be at a random location facing a random direction every time you run the program. This will help you test your solution. Use the following test driver:

```
#include "grid"  // For the grid class

void findExit(grid & g)
```

```
{ // pre:  The grid has exactly one exit, but not at a corner
  // post: The mover is located at the lone exit

  // You complete the function here

}

int main()
{  // Test drive findExit
   grid tarpit(10, 16);
   // assert: The 10-by-16 grid has the mover in a random location

   tarpit.display();
   findExit(tarpit);
   tarpit.display();

   return 0;
}
```

Output

```
The grid:
# # # # # # # # # # # # # # # #
#                             #
#   . . . . . . . . . . . .   #
#   . . . . . . . . . . . .   #
#   . . . . . . . . .         #
#   . . . . . . . . . . . . . #
<   . . . . . . . . . . . . . #
# . . . . . . . . . . . . . . #
# . . . . . . . . . . . . . . #
# # # # # # # # # # # # # # # #
```

Chapter Nine

File Streams

Summing Up

The major control structures have now been presented—sequence, selection, and repetition. In the previous chapter, two major repetitive patterns emerged. The Determinate Loop pattern is used when the number of repetitions can be determined in advance. The Indeterminate Loop pattern occurs so frequently that the `while` loop is part of almost every programming language.

Coming Up

Chapter 9 presents two standard C++ classes—`ifstream` for obtaining input from an external file on a disk and `ofstream` for saving program output onto a disk file. Processing input from a disk file is a classic instance of the Indeterminate Loop pattern. After studying this chapter, you will be able to

- use `ifstream` objects for disk file input
- use `ofstream` objects for disk file output

Exercises and programming projects to reinforce file streams

9.1 `ifstream` Objects

Because keyboard input is fairly common, inclusion of `<iostream>` was designed to make `cin` immediately available. The `cin` object is automatically initialized and associated with the keyboard. However, input may also be obtained from many other sources, such as a mouse, a disk file, or a graphics tablet. An `ifstream` object is needed to read data from a disk file.

The `ifstream` (*i*nput *f*ile *stream*) class is declared in `fstream`. Therefore, this compiler directive must be added to programs intended to extract input from a disk file:

```
#include <fstream>  // For the ifstream class
```

The `ifstream` class is similar to the `istream` class. For example, the familiar extraction operator `>>` is also used to input data from a file stored on a disk. The same rules that apply to keyboard input for `int`s, `double`s, and `string`s also apply to input from a file.

An `ifstream` object is often constructed with the file name it will be associated with.

General Form 9.1. *Initializing `ifstream` objects for existing files*

```
ifstream object-name ("file-name");
```

The *file-name* is the name of an existing disk file. If the file is not found, the `ifstream` object initialization fails and an attempt to use the object name for input will fail. The state of the `ifstream` object can be tested immediately to determine if the file was found.

In the next example, `inFile` is the object name and `"input.dat"` is the associated operating system file name.

```
ifstream inFile("input.dat");  // Construct an ifstream object
```

Now this code will read input from the file `input.dat` rather than from the keyboard.

```
inFile >> intObject;
```

The following program uses an `ifstream` object to read three integers from a disk file. Notice that there are a few differences between programs that extract keyboard input and the one below.

- Before, programs used `cin`—an `istream` object—for keyboard input. Now `inFile` is used—an `ifstream` object—for file input.
- Whereas `cin` is automatically constructed, your program must construct an `ifstream` object with an existing disk file name associated with it.

- Prompts aren't needed anymore. The same >> operator reads an integer and stores it into the `int` object, but there is no need to prompt the file for the next input.

```
// Include fstream for I/O streams dealing with disk files

#include <fstream>   // For the ifstream class
#include <iostream>  // For cout
using namespace std;

int main()
{
  int n1, n2, n3;

  // Initialize an ifstream object so inFile is an input stream
  // associated with the operating system file named input.dat
  ifstream inFile("input.dat");

  // Extract three integers from the file input.dat
  inFile >> n1 >> n2 >> n3;
  cout << "n1: " << n1 << endl;
  cout << "n2: " << n2 << endl;
  cout << "n3: " << n3 << endl;

  return 0;
}
```

Assuming the file `input.dat` stores these three integers:

```
70
80
90
```

this output is generated:

OUTPUT

```
n1: 70
n2: 80
n3: 90
```

If the file `input.dat` stores these three integers:

```
-45    77    23
```

this output is generated:

OUTPUT

```
n1: -45
n2: 77
n3: 23
```

File input works just like keyboard input—spaces and new lines separate the input data. This applies to all data seen so far: `string`, `int`, and `double`. If an integer is encountered in the file during an attempt to read a `double`, the `int` is promoted to a `double`. The one input difference is this: With an `ifstream` object, keyboard input is not necessary for stream extraction. Once the program begins to run, data can be read from the disk file without user input.

Self-Check

9-1 Write a complete program that reads the first four `string`s from an input file named `9a.cpp` and displays them to the screen. Assume there will be at least four words in the file. The file starts like this:

```
// Programmer: Yazz Palmerton
// Due Date: October 28
```

9.1.1 Getting the Path Right

If your input file is not stored in the current working directory, you may need to use an operating system path to locate it. For the DOS and Windows operating systems, which use `\` to separate directory names, the escape sequence `\\` (two backslashes) must be used to specify full path names. So the file name may appear like this:

```
ifstream inFile( "c:\\mystuff\\input.dat" );
```

where `\\` represents only one backslash. Omitting one `\` from `\\` is virtually guaranteed to result in not finding the file:

```
ifstream inFile( "c:\mystuff\input.dat" );  // Need \\, not \
```

This problem doesn't exist in Unix because the `/` character is used to separate directories, and so `/` can be used "as is":

```
ifstream inFile("myC++Stuff/input.dat");
```

Also consider what happens if the file is not found. Input operations such as `inFile >>` will not execute. If you don't seem to be extracting input from the file or the values appear to be garbage, chances are the file does not exist as specified, it has a different name, it's in a different directory, you used \ rather than \\ in DOS or Windows, or your disk is bad, or . . . .

You can use the following alternate selection action to ensure that the user is notified that the file has not been found.

```
if( ! inFile )
{ // If true, the input file was not found.
  cout << "Failed to find the file numbers.dat" << endl;
}
else
{
  // Process file input data
  // . . .
}
```

9.2 The Indeterminate Loop Pattern Applied to Disk Files

The previous chapter on repetition showed how sentinel loops process an undetermined number of keyboard inputs. The same type of logic works with the *end-of-file* event, which requires some knowledge of the operating system you are using. The end-of-file event is entered from the keyboard using the key sequence Ctrl-Z (^Z) with DOS and Windows, Ctrl-D (^D) in Unix, or Command-Period in MacOS.

When the end-of-file event is encountered on an input stream, the input statement (`cin >>`, for example) returns false (`0`, actually). So once again, the `cin` statement can be used as a loop test for processing an undetermined number of inputs.

```
while(cin >> x)  // Input value at start of each iteration
{
  // Process value
}
```

Each time the `cin` statement returns true, the valid input is processed. When the user enters the end-of-file key sequence (Ctrl-C in DOS or Ctrl-D in Unix), the state of `cin` is altered to return false and the loop terminates.

The loop in the following program terminates when the user enters end of file. The loop test (`cin >> x`) returns false when end of file is detected.

```
// Use the end-of-file event to terminate a loop
#include <iostream>  // For cin, cout, and endl
using namespace std;

int main()
{
  double x = 0.0, sum = 0.0;
  int n = 0;

  cout << "Enter doubles, Ctrl-D, Ctrl-Z,"
       << " or Command-Period to quit" << endl;

  while(cin >> x)
  { // assert: cin is not at end of file, so process input
    sum = sum + x;
    n++;
  }

  if(n > 0)
  {
    cout << "Average: " << (sum / n) << endl;
  }
  else
  {
    cout << "Can't average 0 numbers" << endl;
  }

  return 0;
}
```

Dialogue

```
Enter doubles, Ctrl-D, Ctrl-Z, or Command-Period to quit
1  3  4 ^0
Average: 2.66667
```

A word of warning: End of file sets the state of the input stream such that subsequent keyboard input is ignored unless some extra work is performed.

Self-Check

9-2 What is the output of the preceding program if the user enters end of file first?

9.2.1 Processing Until End of File

You can use the end-of-file event to process all data in a file without determining the amount of data in that file beforehand. This is shown in the next program where an indeterminate loop breaks the loop when there is no more data in `inFile`—the end of the input file was detected.

```
// Count how many numbers are in a disk file. The ifstream object
// named is used as the input stream, not cin.

#include <fstream>  // For the ifstream class
#include <iostream>
using namespace std;

int main()
{
  ifstream inFile("numbers.dat");
  double x = 0.0;  // Store file inputs here temporarily
  int n = 0;

  if( ! inFile )
  { // If true, the input file was not found
    cout << "Failed to find the file numbers.dat" << endl;
  }
  else
  {
    cout << "The file was successfully constructed" << endl;
    while( inFile >> x )
    {
      n++;  // Track the number of loops
      cout << "iteration #" << n << ": " << x << endl;
    }
    cout << "End of file reached. " << n << " numbers found." << endl;
  }
  return 0;
}
```

To visualize this loop action, the repeated part simply displays each successfully extracted number. The output shown below appears when the file named `input.dat` contains the following four numbers:

```
0.001   9
    8.0

1.5
```

Output

```
The file was successfully constructed
iteration #1: 0.001
iteration #2: 9
iteration #3: 8
iteration #4: 1.5
End of file reached. 4 numbers found.
```

Self-Check

9-3 What is the output of the preceding program if:

-a the file `numbers.dat` does not exist?

-b the file `numbers.dat` contains one number?

-c the file `numbers.dat` contains zero numbers (the file is empty)?

9-4 Write the output of the following program with the various data stored in the file `input.dat`. (*Note:* `inFile >> intObject` will fail if an invalid number is encountered in the input file stream; input need not be on separate lines.)

-a `1 2 3`

-b `1 2 3 4 5.789`

-c `1 2 3 BAD`

-d `1.5 2.6 3.7`

```
#include <fstream>   // For the ifstream class
#include <iostream>  // For cout
using namespace std;
int main()
{
  ifstream inFile("input.dat");
  int sum = 0;
  int intObject;
  while(inFile >> intObject)
  {
    sum += intObject;
  }
  cout << sum << endl;
  return 0;
}
```

9.2.3 Letting the User Select the File Name

It is sometimes appropriate to allow the user to enter the file name while the program is running. In this situation, it is appropriate to read the file name as a `string`. However, the `string` object itself cannot be used to initialize an `ifstream` object.

```
string fileName;
cout << "Enter file name: ";
cin >> fileName;
ifstream inFile(fileName);
// ERROR: ifstream::ifstream(string) not found
```

The `ifstream` constructor needs the character portion of a `string`, which is returned with `string::c_str`. This message returns the characters of the `string` object.

```
ifstream inFile( fileName.c_str() );
```

9.3 Indeterminate Loop with More Complex Disk File Input

The Indeterminate Loop pattern is often used to process data stored in a file—and that data can be quite complex. To accomplish this, the programmer must know the format of that data or must be able to specify their format. This is possible even if there is a collection of input data of different types and those data are spread out over two or more lines.

The example of this section uses an input file where all data concerning one employee is stored on one line in the file. The algorithm works like this: Input one line of data and process it until there is no more data. The termination condition is end of file. So the loop test would be:

while (there is enough data)
  process the set of data

An indeterminate loop is capable of processing an unspecified number of inputs with data that need not be entered from the keyboard. Another advantage of disk file input with the end-of-file event as the termination condition is this: The number of iterations depends on the size of the file. The loop is easily written to effectively process all the employees in a file whether there are zero, one, two, or many employees. For example, if the file `employee.dat` contains the following data,

```
40   8.88  1 S Mary Demlow
42   7.77  2 M Harvey Barrister
 0  10.00  3 M Ho Manuala
38   9.99  0 S Sue Kline
```

a properly constructed loop should process exactly four employees. The same code should also work with files of different sizes (different numbers of employees). This is an advantage over determinate loops that require the number of iterations to be determined before the loop begins to execute.

The next program implements a loop that uses the end-of-file event as the termination condition. During the loop test, all items needed to construct one `weeklyEmp` object are read from `inFile`.

```
while(inFile >> hours >> rate >> exempts >> status >> fName >> lName)
```

If there are enough data (of the proper format), the `while` loop executes the repeated part. Once inside this block, the state of the `weeklyEmp` object is changed. The new file input data is used to initialize the state of `anEmp` by using a constructor call as the right-hand expression during assignment.

```
anEmp = weeklyEmp(lName + ," " + fName, hours, rate, exempts, status);
```

To illustrate a few `weeklyEmp` member functions show the gross pay and name of each employee in the input file.

```
// This program reads data from an input file to alter one weeklyEmp
// object just long enough to produce a simple payroll report of the
// gross pay and the name of each employee in the disk file

#include <fstream>   // For the ifstream class
#include <iostream>  // For the ostream class and cout
using namespace std;
#include "weekemp"   // For the weeklyEmp class
#include "compfun"   // For decimals(cout, 2)

int main()
{
  weeklyEmp anEmp;
  string fName, lName, name;
  double hours, rate;
  int exempts;
  string status;

  // Initialize an input stream with a disk file as the source
  ifstream inFile("payroll.dat");
```

```
  // Show error if the file "payroll.dat" is not found on the disk
  if(! inFile)
  {
    cout << "**Error opening file 'payroll.dat'" << endl;
  }
  else
  {
    cout.fill('*');
    decimals(cout, 2);
    cout << "Gross Pay   Name" << endl;

    // Process data until end of file
    while(inFile >> hours >> rate >> exempts >> status >> fName >> lName)
    {
      name = lName + ", " + fName;
      anEmp = weeklyEmp(name, hours, rate, exempts, status);
      // Then call some class member functions
      cout.width(9);
      cout << anEmp.grossPay() << "    " << anEmp.name() << endl;
    }
  }

  return 0;
}
```

OUTPUT

```
Gross Pay   Name
***355.20   Demlow, Mary
***334.11   Barrister, Harvey
*****0.00   Manuala, Ho
***379.62   Kline, Sue
```

Notice that the output shows exactly four employees were processed. Had the disk file contained a different number of employees, a different size report would have been generated without any change to the program or the need to determine the number of employees beforehand.

Self-Check

9-5 Describe what would happen if the S were omitted from the last line in the file used for input in the preceding program:

```
38   9.99   0 S Sue Kline
```

9-6 Describe what would happen if the 0 were omitted from the last line in the file used for input in the preceding program:

```
38   9.99   0 S Sue Kline
```

9.3.1 Mixing Numbers and `strings`

The preceding self-checks point to a problem that occurs when input contains numbers, characters, and `strings`. If one line of input is incorrect, the program will likely fail or produce incorrect output. Consider the following incorrect input when this line executes:

```
while(inFile >> hours >> rate >> exempts >> status >> fName >> lName)
                  ↑        ↑        ↑
                  38      9.99      S            Sue Kline
```

The first time through the loop, the `S` is encountered while attempting to read an integer for `exempts`. The input stream fails. The loop terminates. This results from a file with just one missing piece of data. So if you are having problems reading data from a file, make sure the input statement has the proper objects and that the input file has the correct data.

Now consider what happens when the programmer forgets to read `status`. `fName` becomes `S` and `lName` becomes `Kline`.

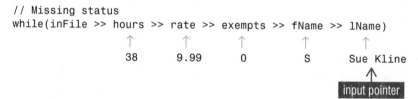

```
// Missing status
while(inFile >> hours >> rate >> exempts >> fName >> lName)
                  ↑        ↑        ↑          ↑        ↑
                  38      9.99      0          S     Sue Kline
                                                          ↑
                                                    input pointer
```

But now where does `Sue` go? During the next iteration of the loop, the input pointer is still pointing to the first piece of white space after `Kline`. The next attempt to read a number for `hours` results in an error because it finds a `string`. The loop will fail here also. Input is messy.

9.3.2 The `getline` Function

The previous example works because the program assumed there were two `strings` at the end of each line in the file. And just as importantly, the file had exactly two `strings` at the end of each line. But consider what would happen if the program could not assume there were going to be exactly two `strings`. For example, what if some employees had a middle initial, some had none, and others had two middle names for a total of four distinct `strings` in their names?

```
40   8.88  1 S Mary Louise Demlow
42   7.77  2 M Harvey Stephen Thorpe Barrister
 0  10.00  3 M Ho Manuala
38   9.99  0 S Sue I. L. Kline
```

The previous program read a file in which each line ended with a first name followed by a last name. An alternative approach would now be required to read the `string` input at the end of each line in the file above. This can be accomplished with a function named `getline` from the `string` library.

Here is a simplified function heading for the `getline` function. Notice that two parameters have `&` so they modify the arguments in the caller.

```
istream & getline(istream & is, string & str, char sentinel = '\n')
// post: Extracts string input from is (with blanks) until the end
//       of line has been encountered
```

This comes in handy for reading things like names and addresses. The nonmember `getline` function extracts all the characters from the input file stream until the end of file is encountered or the new-line character `'\n'` is found. This means that blank spaces normally used to separate `string`s become part of one larger `string` value.

The first argument to `getline` is any input file stream—`cin` or `inFile`, for example. The second argument is any `string` object that will be modified by `getline`. The `string` object will store all the characters from the current input stream until end of line. The third argument is optional. If omitted, the end-of-`string` marker is the new-line character `'\n'`.

This is the first example of a default argument. With the assignment of `'\n'` to sentinel in the parameter list, the `getline` function can be called with only two arguments. In this case, the third parameter is automatically assigned the value of the expression to the right of `=`. This is called a *default argument.* Therefore, the following two calls to `getline` are equivalent:

```
string fullName;
getline(inFile, fullName, '\n');
getline(inFile, fullName);
```

On the other hand, you can specify the third argument to be any sentinel character you wish. So to read an entire sentence from the keyboard, use this:

```
string sentence;
cout << "Enter a sentence ended with a period <'.'>: " << endl;
getline(cin, sentence, '.');
```

```
// assert: sentence has all characters up to, but not including
//         '.'. The '.' is pulled out of input stream (discarded).
```

The `getline` function also returns a reference to the input stream. The return value is true unless the end of file or the sentinel is found. This means `getline` can be used as a loop test. The following program demonstrates how `getLine` can be used to read all the lines in any input file. The input is the program itself, so the number of lines should be 19.

```
#include <iostream>    // 1  File name: getline.cpp
#include <fstream>     // 2
#include <string>      // 3
using namespace std;   // 4
                       // 5
int main()             // 6
{                      // 7
  string aLine;        // 8
  ifstream inFile("getline.cpp");
  int lineCount = 0;   // 10
                       // 11
  while( getline(inFile, aLine) )
  {                    // 13
    lineCount++;       // 14
  }                    // 15
                       // 16
  cout << "Lines in getline.cpp: " << lineCount << endl;
  return 0;            // 18
}                      // 19
```

OUTPUT

```
Lines in getline.cpp: 19
```

Self-Check

9-7 What is the value of `street` when the user enters each line at the prompt?

-a `1313 Mockingbird Lane.` -b `1214 West Walnut Tree Drive.`

```
#include <iostream>  // For cout
#include <string>    // For getline and string
using namespace std;
int main()
{
  string street;
```

```
  cout << "Enter street address, end with a period <.> " << endl;
  getline(cin, street, '.');
  cout << street;
  return 0;
}
```

Getting back to the problem of reading names that may have one, two, three, or any number of spaces, the `while` loop for the payroll problem could now be replaced by this to allow for any number of names.

```
string fullName;
// Process data until end of file
while(    ( inFile >> hours >> rate >> exempts >> status )
       && ( getline(inFile, fullName) )                   )
{
  // Extract first blank character in fullName
  fullName = fullName.substr(1, fullName.length() - 1);
  anEmp = weeklyEmp(fullName, hours, rate, exempts, status);
  cout.width(9);
  cout << anEmp.grossPay() << "    " << anEmp.name() << endl;
}
```

OUTPUT

```
Gross Pay    Name
***355.20    Mary Louise Demlow
***334.11    Harvey Stephen Thorpe Barrister
*****0.00    Ho Manuala
***379.62    Sue I. L. Kline
```

The loop indicates another detail of the difficulty in getting the correct input. The `getline` function starts where the input pointer left off at the previous input. So the input pointer is pointing to the blank character before the name.

```
40   8.88  1 S Mary Louise Demlow
              ↑
        input pointer
```

Unless you want this space first, remove the leading blank with this message:

```
fullName = fullName.substr(1, fullName.length() - 1);
```

9.4 ofstream Objects

Files storing large amounts of input data are typically created by other programs. This means there must be a way to write output data to a disk file. This section introduces the `ofstream` class for storing program output to more permanent disk files. The `ofstream` class is a specialization of the `ostream` class just as `ifstream` is a specialization of the `istream` class.[1] Therefore, the operations and messages that could be sent to `cout` can also be sent to `ofstream` objects.

```
#include <iostream>  // For cout
#include <fstream>   // For the ofstream class
using namespace std;
#include "compfun"   // For decimals(outFile, 3);

int main()
{
  ofstream outFile("c:\\temp\\out.dat");

  outFile << "This string goes to a disk file, not the screen" << endl;

  double x = 1.23456789;
  outFile << x << endl;   // Write x to a disk file in default format
  decimals(outFile, 3);   // Change the state of outFile
  outFile << x << endl;   // Write x to disk file with 3 decimal places
  outFile.width(30);      // Write a width message to outFile
  outFile << x << endl;   // Write x to a disk file in 30 columns

  cout << "This string goes to the screen" << endl;

  return 0;
}
```

OUTPUT (TO THE FILE ASSOCIATED WITH THE OBJECT NAMED `outFile`)

```
This string goes to a disk file, not the screen
1.23457
1.235
                         1.235
```

OUTPUT (TO THE SCREEN)

```
This string goes to the screen
```

1. `ofstream` is derived from `ostream`. This is an inheritance relationship. (See Chapter 16.)

Self-Check

9-8 What output goes to the disk file named "out.dat"?

```
ofstream out("out.dat");
for(int j = 1; j <= 5; j++)
  cout << j << " ";
```

Chapter Summary

* An `ifstream` object may be associated with a disk file so large that amounts of data may be input quickly—with no human intervention.
* The `!` operator is overloaded to determine if a file has not been properly opened for input. The extraction event is a useful loop test to use process data until the end of a file.
* You can use `ofstream` objects like `cout`. The only difference is that the output goes to a disk file rather than the computer screen.

Exercises

1. What does `ifstream` stand for?

2. Write the code that declares an input stream named `inFile` associated with the file called `student.dat` located in the current working folder (directory).

3. Which `#include` is needed to construct `ifstream` objects?

4. Write a loop that counts the number of words contained in a file. A word is any collection of characters separated by spaces, tabs, or new lines. For example, there are 14 words in the following sentence (recall that `string` constants are separated by blanks, tabs, and new lines):

```
Here's one
word, another,       and
 another.
      There is a total of 14 words here.
```

5. Write a sentinel event-controlled loop that counts the number of perfect test scores (the number 100) in a file named `"tests.dat"`.

Programming Tips

1. Use `getline` to read `strings` with blank spaces.

Sometimes several `strings` represent one `string` input. When asking for someone's name or address and you don't know how many values will be input, use the `getline` function.

```
string address;
cout << "Enter your address: ";
getline(cin, address);
cout << "Address: " << address << endl;
```

Dialogue

```
Enter your address: 1313 Mockingbird Lane, Washington D.C.
Address: 1313 Mockingbird Lane, Washington D.C.
```

2. A constructor call stands in for a constant of that class.

You can create a constant of any class you desire just by calling the constructor. This comes in handy during loops like this:

```
bankAccount anAcct;
while( inFile >> customerName >> currentBalance )
{
  anAcct = bankAccount(customerName, currentBalance);
  // . . .
}
```

3. Be careful when using `getline` and >> together.

Be careful when mixing `getline` with the >> operator on the same input stream. The >> operator skips whitespace; `getline` does not. Worse yet, `cin >>` will stop at the new line. A subsequent `getline` will go up to the new line, effectively reading nothing. You might need an extra `getline` to get beyond the end of the line.

4. Use test drivers for reading complex data.

Seemingly bizarre things can occur when you try to input complex data in an end-of-file loop. Consider first writing a test driver with code that inputs the first line from the file and then displays it.

5. Input is messy.

Using `istream >>` and `getline` on the same input stream can cause difficult-to-detect errors. Additionally, when there is a mix of integer, floating-point, character, and `string` input, it is not always easy to get the input statements correct. The number of objects in an input statement must always be correct. The input file must always be correct. Sometimes you might need a loop test that looks like this:

```
while(   ( inFile >> hours >> rate >> exempts >> status )
      && ( getline(inFile, fullName) )                  )
{
  // . . .
}
```

Programming Projects

9A Wind Speeds on File

Write a program that determines the lowest, highest, and average of a set of wind speed readings from a file. The number of readings is not known in advance. First create a file in your working (current) directory as `wind.dat` and use the `ifstream` constructor to open the file for input as follows:

```
ifstream inFile("wind.dat");
```

The program should work for all files containing only `int`s so any number of inputs should produce correct results. Run your program with the following file called `wind.dat`. Verify that the output is correct by producing results by hand and comparing your output.

```
 2  6  1  2  5
 5  4  3 12 16
10 11 12 13 14
```

Once you have verified the program with the test data started above, delete the third line and run the program again to verify that the hand-checked results match program output.

9B Words in a File

Write a C++ program that approximates the number of words in a file that has the file name input by the user. Remember to use `string::c_str` to initialize the `ifstream` object.

```
cin >> fileName;
ifstream inFile(fileName.c_str());
```

9C Payroll Report

In this project you are asked to use an existing class as the basis for a payroll program that processes many employees. The input data to be processed are stored in an external file with the following format:

```
Ross Greene          38.0 10.45  4 M
Mary Kristner        42.0 12.00  0 S
Melissa Nicholson    30.5  9.99  1 S
Samuel Woodley       40.0 11.57  1 S
```

Create a report that looks like the following (with ? replaced by the correct answers, of course). Also show all totals for every category except the pay rate.

```
   Pay    Hours    Gross    Income     FICA       Net    Employee
  Rate   Worked      Pay       Tax      Tax       Pay    Name
======    =====    =====   =======   ======     =====    =======
 10.45     38.0   397.10     26.16    30.38    340.56    Greene, Ross
 12.00     42.0        ?         ?        ?         ?    Kristner, Mary
  9.99     30.5        ?         ?        ?         ?    Nicholson, Melissa
 11.57     40.0        ?         ?        ?         ?    Woodley, Samuel
          -----    -----    ------   ------     -----
Totals    150.5   ???.??   ????.??  ????.??   ????.??
```

Either write all code from scratch or use the `weeklyEmp` class defined in `weekemp.h`. Recall that a `weeklyEmp` object is constructed as follows,

```
weeklyEmp emp1("Len Jupe," 40, 9.50, 4, "M");
```

where the arguments represent these values: name, hours worked, pay rate, exemptions, and filing status, respectively.

9D File the Report

After completing project 9C, change the program to send the payroll report to a disk file named `payroll.rpt`.

Chapter Ten
Vectors

Summing Up

Almost all objects studied so far either store one element of a specific value (e.g., `double` and `int`) or are heterogeneous objects made up of two or more possibly dissimilar elements (e.g., `weeklyEmp` and `bankAccount`).

Coming Up

This chapter introduces the C++ `vector` class for storing collections of similar objects where individual elements may be referenced with the subscript operator `[]`. The ability to store many elements under one object name is used to solve a wide variety of programming problems. After studying this chapter you will be able to

* construct and use `vector` objects that store collections of objects
* implement algorithms to process a collection of objects
* use the sequential search algorithm to locate a specific element in a `vector`
* pass `vector` objects to functions

  Exercises and programming projects to reinforce use of `vectors`
* sort `vector` elements into ascending or descending order
* understand the binary search algorithm

  Exercises and programming projects to reinforce sorting and searching algorithms

10.1 The Standard C++ `vector` Class

The `vector` class constructs objects that store *collections* of objects. All `vector` objects are considered *homogeneous* because the objects in the collection are of the same class—a collection of numbers or a collection of `string`s, for example. The objects in the collection may be any one of the standard classes such as `int`, `double`, or `string`. Additionally, any programmer-defined class that has a default constructor[1] can be contained in a `vector`. You can have a collection of any objects that you can dream up. Here are two general forms for initializing `vector`[2] objects.

GENERAL FORM 10.1. *`vector` initialization*

`vector` < *class-name* > *vector-name* **(***capacity***);**

- or -

`vector` < *class-name* > *vector-name* **(***capacity***,** *initial-value***);**

- *class-name* specifies the class of objects stored in the `vector`.
- *vector-name* is any valid C++ identifier.
- *capacity* is an integer expression representing the maximum number of elements that can be stored into the `vector` (unless the `vector` is resized).
- The optional *initial-value* is the value that will be assigned to every element in the `vector`. If there is only one argument (capacity), then the default constructor for that class sets the initial values (recall that with `double` and `int`, the default values will be garbage).

EXAMPLES OF `vector` INITIALIZATIONS

```
vector <double> x(100, 0.0);          // Store 100 numbers
vector <student> studentList(1500);   // Store 1500 students
vector <int> garbage (1000000);       // One million garbage integers
```

For example, all three `vector` objects shown next have the capacity to store a maximum of 20 objects:

1. A *default constructor* is one with zero arguments. These example calls to default constructors prove each class can be stored in a `vector`: `string s; bankAccount b; weeklyEmp e;`
2. If you do not have the `vector` class on your system, use the one that comes with this book stored in the file named `vector`. In this case, `#include "vector"` (use `" "` rather than < >).

```
#include <vector>   // For the vector<CLASS> class3
#include <string>   // For the string class
using namespace std;

int main()
{
  vector <string> myFriends(20);
  // assert: myFriends has capacity to store 20 null strings ""

  vector <double> x(20, 0.0);
  // assert: x has capacity to store 20 numbers. All are 0.0.

  vector <int> vectorOfInts(20, -1);
  // assert: vectorOfInts can hold 20 integers. All are -1.

  // . . . use any of the three vectors . . .

  return 0;
}
```

10.1.1 Accessing Individual Elements in the Collection

`vector` objects support random access. An individual `vector` element can be referenced directly through subscripts.

GENERAL FORM 10.2. *Accessing one vector element*

vector-name [*integer-expression*]

The subscript range of a C++ `vector` is an integer value in the range of 0 through its capacity - 1. Therefore, the individual objects of x declared as

```
vector <double> x(8, 0.0);
```

may be referenced using the integer subscripts 0, 1, 2, 3, . . ., 7—but not 8. So values are stored into the first two `vector` elements of x with these two assignments:

```
// Assign new values to the first two elements of vector named x
x[0] = 2.6;
x[1] = 5.7;
```

3. The comment `// For the vector<CLASS> class` lists the word `CLASS` between the angle brackets to indicate that `vector` requires a class name between < and >. For more on template classes such as `vector`, see Chapter 17, "Templates: Building Generic Classes."

Because C++ starts counting at zero, the first `vector` element is referenced with subscript 0 or `x[0]` and the fifth element with subscript 4 or `x[4]`. This subscript notation allows individual `vector` elements to be displayed, used in expressions, and modified with assignment and input operations. In fact, you can do anything to an individual `vector` element that can be done to an object of the same class.

The familiar assignment rules apply to `vector` elements. For example, a `string` constant cannot be assigned to a `double`, and a `string` constant cannot be stored in a `vector` element declared to store numbers.

```
x[2] = "Wrong type of constant";  // ERROR: x stores numbers
```

Since any two `doubles` can be added with `+`, subscripted `vector` elements can also be used in arithmetic expressions like this:

```
x[2] = x[0] + x[1];  // Store 8.3
```

Keyboard input can also be used to set the state of `vector` elements like this:

```
cout << "Enter two numbers: ";
cin >> x[3] >> x[4];
```

DIALOGUE

```
Enter two numbers: 9.9  5.1
```

After this user input of 9.9 and 5.1 into the fourth and fifth `vector` elements and the previous assignments to the first three `vector` elements, the state of `x` now looks like this:

The State of x	
`x[0]`	2.6
`x[1]`	5.7
`x[2]`	8.3
`x[3]`	9.9
`x[4]`	5.1
`x[5]`	0.0
`x[6]`	0.0
`x[7]`	0.0

10.1.2 `vector` Processing with Determinate `for` Loops

Programmers must frequently reference many consecutive `vector` elements. The simplest case might be to display all the meaningful elements of a `vector`. The C++ `for` loop provides a convenient way to do this.

```
int j = 0;
int n = 5;
```

```
// assert: n represents the number of meaningful elements

// Display the meaningful elements of x--the first n elements
cout << "The first " << n << " elements of x: " << endl;
for(j = 0; j < n; j++)
{
  cout << "x[" << j << "]: "
  cout << x[j] << endl;
}
```

OUTPUT

```
The first 5 elements of x:
x[0]: 2.6
x[1]: 5.7
x[2]: 8.3
x[3]: 9.9
x[4]: 5.1
```

The first `n` elements of `x` are easily referenced by altering the `int` object named `j` that acts both as the counter in the `for` loop and as the subscript inside the `for` loop (`x[j]`). With `j` serving both roles—as shown in the code above—the specific `vector` element referenced as `x[j]` will depend on the value of `j`. For example, when `j` is 0, `x[j]` is a reference to the first element in `x`; when `j` is 4, `x[j]` is a reference to the fifth element of `x`.

10.1.3 Processing the First n Elements of a vector

Here is another example of a `for` loop that compares the first `n` `vector` elements to find the largest floating-point value.

```
// First set the largest as the first element . . .
double largest = x[0];

// . . . then compare all other vector elements x[1] through x[n-1]
for(j = 1; j < n; j++)
{
  if(x[j] > largest)
    largest = x[j];
}

// Display the largest
cout << "The largest element in vector x = " << largest;
```

DIALOGUE

```
The largest element in vector x = 9.9
```

A `vector` often stores fewer meaningful elements than its capacity. Therefore, you usually need to have an object that stores the number of elements in the `vector` that are currently under consideration. In the previous code, n was used to limit the elements being referenced. Only the first five elements were searched to find the largest. Only the first five should have been searched. Although all eight elements could have been compared, imagine trying to find the smallest number in x. Without limiting the search to the elements under consideration, would the smallest be 2.6 or 0.0? Now imagine what the smallest would be if all elements in x were not initialized to 0.0—when they all hold garbage.

The Determinate Loop pattern with for loops conveniently performs vector processing, which is the inspection of, reference to, or modification of a selected number of vector elements. The number of elements (n here) is the predetermined number of vector elements that must be processed. Algorithms that include vector processing in this chapter include

- displaying some or all elements of a vector
- finding the sum, average, or highest of all vector elements
- searching for a particular object in the vector
- arranging elements in a certain order (ordering elements from largest to smallest or alphabetizing a vector of strings from smallest to largest)

10.1.4 Out-of-Range Subscript Checking

The standard vector class does not check subscripts to ensure that they are within the proper range of 0 through its capacity - 1. Therefore, the programmer must be careful to avoid subscripts that are not in the range specified at initialization.

This is difficult for those new to vector processing. It is far better to begin using a vector class that automatically checks the subscript range at runtime. It just so happens that the vector class on this textbook's disk does perform range checking. However, if you are using the standard vector class without subscript range checking, the following assignments may destroy some other portion of memory, such as another object's state.

```
x[-2] = 4.5;  // Careful! These out-of-range subscripts may not be
x[8]  = 7.8;  // guarded against and could crash your system.
```

The result could be seemingly unrelated errors or even a system crash. All subscripts should be in the range of 0 through the vector's capacity - 1.

With subscript range checking that is available on some—but not all—vector classes, the program may terminate early with an error message indicating the reason. However, this is preferable to fixing errors that are difficult to locate. Here is what will happen with the vector class implementation that comes with this textbook:

```
#include "vector"  // For a limited vector<CLASS> class
#include <iostream>
using namespace std;

int main()
{
  int j, n;

  cout << "Enter vector capacity: ";
  cin >> n;
  vector <int> x(n, -999);

  for(j = 0; j <= n; j++)  // WHOOPS: Used <= instead of <
  {
    x[j] = j;              // Eventually this is x[n]
  }
  // This program terminates before this cout
  cout << "After loop" << endl;

  return 0;
}
```

DIALOGUE (ASSUMING YOU USE THIS TEXTBOOK'S vector CLASS)

```
Enter vector capacity: 20
**Error** Subscript [20] is not in the range of 0..19
**Program terminated**
```

Without range checking, an out-of-range subscript destroys other areas of memory. This creates difficult-to-detect bugs. More dramatically, your computer may "hang" or "crash." Even worse, with a workstation that runs all the time, you may get a latency error that affects computer memory now, but won't crash the system perhaps for weeks.

You may also get difficult-to-track bugs. Consider what might happen with the following assignment:

```
result = x[n];
```

The value stored at x[n] is one beyond the vector's capacity. It is some random value. On one system, this statement produced the output shown in the comment.

```
// There is no warning or error with the statement
cout << "x[n]: " << x[n] << endl;  // x[n]: -33686019
```

The standard vector class provides the at member function to avoid out-of-range subscripts. The result may look different, but this message will gracefully terminate the program rather than store some random value into result:

```
result = x.at(n);  // Gracefully terminates the program. Good.
```

The temptation is there to always use vector::at in subsequent examples. However, programmers have been using subscripts for a very long time. You will see a lot of code with the square brackets ([ ]). So this textbook will rely on subscripts.

10.1.5 vector::capacity, vector::resize, =

Many messages can be sent to a standard C++ vector object. Two relate to the number of elements the vector can hold. Each vector object is responsible for knowing how many objects it can store—its capacity. A vector also knows how to increase or decrease that capacity—a vector can resize itself.

After a vector has been initialized, the vector::capacity message returns the maximum number of elements that the vector can hold. The vector::resize message tells the vector to change to the new size supplied as the single argument.

```
// Demonstrate capacity and resize
#include <vector>  // For the standard vector<CLASS> class
using namespace std;

int main()
{
  vector <int> v1;  // v1 cannot store any elements
  vector <int> v2(5);

  cout << "v1 can hold " << v1.capacity() << endl;
  cout << "v2 can hold " << v2.capacity() << endl;

  v1.resize(22);
  cout << "v1 can now hold " << v1.capacity() << endl;

  return 0;
}
```

OUTPUT

```
v1 can hold 0
v2 can hold 5
v1 can now hold 22
```

If you resize a `vector` to have more capacity, the original elements in the lower subscripts are still there. However, if you resize a `vector` to be smaller, the elements in the higher locations are lost. Truncation occurs.

One `vector` can be assigned to another. The `vector` to the left of the = operator becomes an exact copy of the `vector` to the right of =. The `vector` on the left, like any other object to the left of =, is destroyed.

```
// Demonstrate capacity and resize
#include <vector>  // For the vector<CLASS> class
using namespace std;

int main()
{
  vector <int> v1(3, -999);
  vector <int> v2(500, 1);
  // assert: v2 stores 500 elements == 1

  v2 = v1;
  // assert: v2 now stores 3 elements == -999

  for(int j = 0; j < v2.capacity(); j++)
  {
    cout.width(5);
    cout << v2[j];
  }

  return 0;
}
```

OUTPUT

```
 -999 -999 -999
```

Self-Check

Use this initialization to answer the questions that follow:

```
vector <int> x(100, 0);
```

10-1 How many integers can be stored in `x`?

10-2 Which integer subscript references the first element in `x`?

10-3 Which integer subscript references the last element in `x`?

10-4 What is the value of `x[23]`?

10-5 Write the code that stores 78 into the first element of `x`.

10-6 Write code that stores 1 into `x[99]`, 2 into `x[98]`, 3 into `x[97]`, . . ., 99 into `x[1]`, and 100 into `x[0]`. Use a `for` loop.

10-7 Write code that displays all elements of x on separate lines. Use a for loop.

10-8 What happens when this code executes: x[-1] = 100;

10-9 Name two vector member functions.

10-10 Write the output generated by the following program:

```
#include <vector>  // For the standard vector<CLASS> class
using namespace std;
int main()
{
  int j, n = 5;
  vector <int> x(n);
  for(j = 0; j < n; j++)
  {
    x[j] = j;
  }

  x.resize(2 * n);

  // Show the first five elements are still there
  for(j = 0; j < n; j++)
  {
    cout.width(5);
    cout << x[j];
  }
  cout << endl;

  x.resize(x.capacity() / 3);
  for(j = 0; j < x.capacity(); j++)
  {
    cout.width(5);
    cout << x[j];
  }
  cout << endl;
  return 0;
}
```

10.2 Sequential Search

One of the major reasons for using vectors is to have individual elements retained in the computer's fast memory, where they will be frequently accessed. This often means searching for the existence of some element in the collection. So another common vector-processing operation involves searching. Searching examples include, but are certainly not limited to, searching for a student name in the registrar's database, looking up the price of an item in an inventory, or obtaining information about a bank account. One such algorithm used to "look up" a `vector` element is called sequential search.

The *sequential search* algorithm attempts to locate a given element by comparing the item being sought with every object in the `vector`. The algorithm searches in a one-after-the-other (sequential) fashion. Sequential search continues as long as the search value has not been found or until there are no more elements left in the `vector` to compare.

This sequential search algorithm is presented first within the context of a `vector` of `string` objects. Although the search element here will be a person's name, the `vector` being searched could contain other kinds of objects—numbers, students, or employees, for example, as long as the object of the class can be compared with the `!=` operator.

```
// Initialize and show the first n elements of vector named name
#include <iostream>
#include <string>
#include <vector>  // For the vector<CLASS> class
using namespace std;

int main()
{
  int j, n;
  vector <string> myFriends(10);
  // assert: All of myFriends are the default null string ""

  n = 5;  // Set the number of meaningful elements to be searched
  myFriends[0] = "DEBBIE";
  myFriends[1] = "JOEY";
  myFriends[2] = "BOBBIE";
  myFriends[3] = "SUSIE";
  myFriends[4] = "MIKEY";

  // Just show the vector elements for now
  for(j = 0; j < n; j++)
  {
    cout << "myFriends[" << j << "]: " << myFriends[j] << endl;
  }

  // . . . TBA: Implement sequential search . . .

  return 0;
}
```

OUTPUT

```
myFriends[0] = DEBBIE
myFriends[1] = JOEY
myFriends[2] = BOBBIE
myFriends[3] = SUSIE
myFriends[4] = MIKEY
```

Self-Check

10-11 What is the value of each of the following expressions?

-a `myFriends[3]`

-b `myFriends[4]`

-c `myFriends[10]`

-d `myFriends[5]`

Before searching for something, you need to know what is being searched for. Here, the user will simply be asked for a name. Then there are at least these two possibilities:

1. `searchName` is in the `vector`.
2. `searchName` is *not* in the `vector`.

First let's assume `searchName` has an equivalent `string` in the `vector` `myFriends`. With a new integer object named `subscript` initialized to 0, the following code begins by comparing `searchName` to the first `vector` element, also known as `myFriends[0]`:

```
// Get a name to search for
string searchName;
cout << "Enter existing name to search for [UPPERCASE]: ";
cin >> searchName;

// assert: searchName is in myFriends--if it is not, watch out!

// Search for searchName starting at myFriends[0]
int subscript = 0;

while(searchName != myFriends[subscript])
{ // assert: searchName has not yet been found
  subscript++;  // Prepare to compare searchName to next element
}
```

The loop test, `(searchName != myFriends[subscript])`, is true as long as the object being searched for has not been found. In this case, the subscript is incremented with the statement `subscript++`. This prepares for a comparison of `searchName` to the next `vector` element. After `searchName` is compared to `myFriends[0]`, `searchName` is compared to `myFriends[1]`, then `myFriends[2]`, and so on. This continues until `searchName != myFriends[subscript]` becomes false. This works fine, assuming the name being searched for is actually in the `vector`.

Self-Check

10-12 What happens in the code above if `searchName` is not in the `vector`?

After the search loop terminates, the success of the search can be tested by examining the particular element at `myFriends[subscript]`:

```
// Report success or failure (see changes below)
if(subscript < n)
  cout << myFriends[subscript] << " found at subscript " << subscript << endl;
else
  cout << searchName << " not found" << endl;
```

DIALOGUE

```
Enter existing name to search for [UPPERCASE]: BOBBIE
BOBBIE found at subscript 2
```

EXAMPLE SEARCH WITH "BOBBIE"

Loop Iteration	searchName	n	Subscript	vector Element Being Compared
Before the loop	"BOBBIE"	5	0	N/A
1	"BOBBIE"	5	0	"DEBBIE"
2	"BOBBIE"	5	1	"JOEY"
3	"BOBBIE"	5	2	"BOBBIE"
After the loop	"BOBBIE"	5	2	N/A

Now, consider what would happen if `searchName` is not in the `vector`. Each iteration of the loop would increment subscript by + 1. However, what will stop the comparisons if `searchName` is not found in `myFriends`?

EXAMPLE SEARCH WITH "SOMEONE"

Loop Iteration	searchName	n	Subscript	vector Element Comparison
Before the loop	"SOMEONE"	5	0	N/A
1	"SOMEONE"	5	0	"DEBBIE"
2	"SOMEONE"	5	1	"JOEY"
3	"SOMEONE"	5	2	"BOBBIE"
4	"SOMEONE"	5	3	"SUSIE"
5	"SOMEONE"	5	4	"MIKEY"
6	"SOMEONE"	5	5	" "
7	"SOMEONE"	5	6	" "
8	"SOMEONE"	5	7	" "
9	"SOMEONE"	5	8	" "
10	"SOMEONE"	5	9	" "
11 perhaps	"SOMEONE"	5	10	*Ain't no more*
12 perhaps	"SOMEONE"	5	11	...

This attempt to implement the sequential search algorithm did not consider the possibility that the `searchName` might not be found. In fact, this may become an infinite loop, terminate the program early, or crash the system. If your `vector` class performs range checking, the program will likely terminate with a message indicating that subscript 10 is out of bounds.

To prevent the infinite loop, use `n` to store the number of meaningful elements. The loop test can be made to guard against referencing `myFriends[subscript]` when `subscript` becomes equal to `n`. This termination condition is recognized in the following correct implementation of sequential search:

```
int subscript = 0;
while( (subscript < n) && (searchName != myFriends[subscript]) )
{ // assert: searchName has not yet been found and there is at
  //         least one more meaningful element to compare
   subscript++;  // Prepare to compare searchName to the next
                 // vector element or terminate loop immediately
}
```

```
// assert: If subscript < n, searchName == myFriends[subscript]. If
//         == n, then searchName was not in the vector.
```

The logical expression (`subscript < n`) is placed first to avoid a particular case. Consider what happens when a `vector` is filled to capacity and the item is not in the `vector`. The integer `subscript` will go to the capacity in the final `while` loop evaluation.

```
n = 10;
myFriends.resize(n);
// assert: myFriends.capacity() == n, searchName not in myFriends
while( (subscript < n) && (searchName != myFriends[subscript]) )
            10    < 10 && ( "Not Here" != myFriends[10] )
```

Without short circuit evaluation, this would be an error. With guaranteed short circuit Boolean evaluation, `myFriends[10]` never evaluates. The first expression, `10 < 10`, was false. Since false and anything is always false, there will be no out-of-range subscript error in `myFriends[myFriends.capacity()]`. Reverse the operands around `&&` and you will get an error when the `vector` is filled and the search item is not there.

Self-Check

10-13 How many comparisons (iterations of the search loop) are necessary when `searchName` matches `myFriends[0]`?

10-14 How many comparisons are necessary when `searchName` matches `myFriends[3]`?

10-15 How many comparisons are necessary when `searchName` isn't in `myFriends`?

10-16 How many sequential search comparisons occur when the `vector` has no useful data in it, that is, when `n == 0`?

10.3 Messages to Individual Objects in a `vector`

The subscript notation must be used to send messages to individual elements. The `vector` name must be accompanied by a subscript to specify the particular `vector` element to which the message is sent.

GENERAL FORM 10.3. *Sending messages to individual vector elements*

vector-name [*subscript*] . *member-function-call*

The *subscript* distinguishes the specific object to which the operation is to be applied. For example, the length of `myFriends[0]` `"DEBBIE"` is referenced with this expression:

```
myFriends[0].length()  // The length of the first name in the vector
```

The expression `myFriends.length()` is not allowed because this would represent an attempt to find the length of the entire `vector`. The `length` function is not defined for the standard C++ `vector` class (although `vector::resize` and `vector::capacity` are).

Now consider determining the total assets of all `bankAccount` objects in a `vector` of `bankAccounts`. The following program first sets up a miniature database of four `bankAccount` objects. (*Note:* Although there is no `bankAccount` constant in C++, a constructor call—without the object name— generates a constant of any programmer-defined class.) Therefore, this assignment

```
account[0] = bankAccount("Hall," 0.00);
```

first constructs a `bankAccount` object with the name `"Hall"` and a balance of `0.00`. The `bankAccount` object is then assigned to the first `vector` element `account[0]`.

```
// Illustrates a vector of programmer-defined objects
#include <iostream>
#include <vector>    // For the vector<CLASS> class
using namespace std;
#include "baccount"  // For the bankAccount class
#include "compfun"   // For decimals(cout, 2);

int main()
{
  int j, n;
  vector <bankAccount> account(100);

  // Initialize the first n elements of account
  n = 4;
  account[0] = bankAccount("Hall," 0.00);
  account[1] = bankAccount("Small," 100.00);
  account[2] = bankAccount("Ewall," 200.00);
  account[3] = bankAccount("Westphall," 300.00);
  // assert: The first n elements of account are initialized
```

```
  double assets = 0.0;
  // Accumulate balance of n bankAccount objects stored in account
  for(j = 0; j < n; j++)
  {
    assets += account[j].balance();
  }

  decimals(cout, 2);
  cout << "Assets: " << assets << endl;

  return 0;
}
```

OUTPUT

```
Assets: 600
```

Self-Check

10-17 Write the output generated by the following program:

```
#include <iostream>
#include <vector>  // For the vector<CLASS> class
#include <string>  // For the string class
using namespace std;

int main()
{
  int j, n;
  vector <string> s(10);

  // Initialize the first n elements of account
  n = 4;
  s[0] = "First";
  s[1] = "Second";
  s[2] = "Third";
  s[3] = "Fourth";

  for(j = 0; j < n; j++)
     cout << s[j].substr(1, s[j].length() - 2) << "  ";

  return 0;
}
```

10.3.1 Initializing a `vector` of Objects with File Input

In some of the preceding programs, `vector`s of objects were initialized in several assignment statements. `vector`s are often initialized through disk file input. To demonstrate, imagine the following is part of the input data file named `bank.dat` with a total of 12 accounts on 12 lines:

```
Cust0          0.00
AnyName      111.11
Austen       222.22
Chelsea      333.33
Kieran       444.44
Cust5        555.55
```

. . . five lines are omitted . . .

```
Cust11      1111.11
```

If the `vector` is declared with a maximum capacity of 20 like this, then the first `bankAccount` object can be stored in `account[0]`:

```
vector <bankAccount> account(20);
// assert: account could store 20 default bankAccount objects
```

So an object named `numberOfAccounts` starts at 0 (rather than the usual `n`).

```
int numberOfAccounts = 0;
```

Then, the `vector` of `bankAccount` objects can be initialized one account at a time with these steps:

1. Input two items per line—a name and a balance.
2. Construct a `bankAccount` and store it into the next available `vector` location.
3. Increase the number of accounts by 1.

The `vector::capacity` function will also be used to safeguard against using subscripts beyond the account's boundaries of 0 through 19.

The following `while` loop test expression should be true before a `bankAccount` object can be added at the next available location in the `vector`. If there are no more data in the file, `(inFile >> name >> balance)` is false and the loop will terminate. Also, if there are more data in the file but no more room in the `vector`, `(numberOfAccounts < account.capacity())` is false and the loop terminates for a different reason—there is no room.

```
while( ( inFile >> name >> balance                ) &&
       ( numberOfAccounts < account.capacity() ) )
{
  account[numberOfAccounts] = bankAccount(name, balance);
```

```
    numberOfAccounts++;
  }
```

While there is room for another element and there are more data in the file, the repeated part executes. Inside the loop, the two objects (`name` and `balance`) are passed on to the `bankAccount` constructor to construct a `bankAccount`, which is then stored in the next consecutive `vector` element. This initialization and assignment must occur before `numberOfAccounts` is incremented from 0 to 1 during the first iteration of the loop.

Now `numberOfAccounts` accurately indicates the number of accounts processed so far and the first `bankAccount` object is stored into `account[0]`. During each loop iteration, `numberOfAccounts` represents not only the total number of meaningful accounts stored in the `vector`, but also the next available `vector` subscript into which the next `bankAccount` object can be stored. When the end of file is encountered, `numberOfAccounts` will have the correct value—it is one greater than the subscript storing the last account.

This processing is shown in the context of a complete program, which sets up a small database of bank customers.

```
// Initialize a vector of bankAccount objects through file input
#include <vector>     // For the vector<CLASS> class
#include <fstream>    // For the ifstream class
#include <iostream>   // For cout and endl
#include <string>     // For the string class
using namespace std;
#include "baccount"   // For the bankAccount class
#include "compfun"    // For decimals(cout, 2)

int main()
{
  string fileName("bank.dat");

  ifstream inFile(fileName.c_str());
  if(! inFile)
  {
    cout << "**Error** " << fileName << " was not found" << endl;
  }
  else
  {
    vector <bankAccount> account(20);
    string name;
    double balance = 0.0;
    int numberOfAccounts = 0;
    int j;
```

```
    while((inFile >> name >> balance) &&
          (numberOfAccounts < account.capacity()))
    { // assert: name and balance successfully input from inFile and
      //         vector can store one more bankAccount
      account[numberOfAccounts] = bankAccount(name, balance);
      numberOfAccounts++;
    }

  // Antibugging tip: Verify that a vector is properly initialized!
  // numberOfAccounts is very important as is data stored at each vector
  // element. First output numberOfAccounts and display each element in
  // vector before going on.

    cout << "Number of accounts on file: " << numberOfAccounts << endl;
    cout << endl;
    cout << "The accounts" << endl;
    cout << "===========================" << endl;
    decimals(cout, 2);
    for(j = 0; j < numberOfAccounts; j++)
    {
      cout.width(2);
      cout << j << ". ";
      cout << account[j].name();
      // Pad blanks so balances line up at the decimal point
      cout.width(12 - account[j].name().length());
      cout << " ";
      cout.width(10);
      cout << account[j].balance() << endl;
    }
  } // End else
  return 0;
}
```

OUTPUT

```
Number of accounts on file: 12

The accounts
============================
 0. Cust0             0.00
 1. AnyName         111.11
 2. Austen          222.22
 3. Chelsea         333.33
 4. Kieran          444.44
 5. Cust5           555.55
 6. Cust6           666.66
 7. Cust7           777.77
 8. Cust8           888.88
 9. Cust9           999.99
10. Cust10         1010.10
11. Cust11         1111.11
```

As suggested in the comments above, when working with `vector`s, it is recommended that you output the initialized `vector` elements and the number of initialized elements. This antibugging technique saves time and avoids frustration by preventing the bugs that arise when an incorrectly initialized `vector` is assumed to be set up properly. This antibugging effort requires only a few minutes and signals success up to that point in program development. Remember this adage:

Code a little, test a lot.

Self-Check

10-18 Write two assignment statements that initialize two additional `bankAccounts` with assignment statements in the next two `vector` locations. Use any data you desire.

10-19 What would happen if the input file `bank.dat` had contained 21 lines, each line representing one account? Remember, `account.capacity()` is 20.

10-20 Write code to initialize a `vector` of integers from a file named `int.dat`. Assume the file never has more than 1,000 integer values.

10-21 Which object in your code represents the number of initialized elements?

10-22 Write code that verifies proper initialization of the `vector` of the previous two self-checks.

10.4 `vector` Argument/Parameter Associations

Sometimes it may be necessary to pass a `vector` through argument/parameter association to either a member function or a nonmember function. This requires a different syntax in the parameter list. There are three ways to declare a `vector` parameter, but only these two should ever be used:

PASS BY REFERENCE (WHEN THE FUNCTION MUST MODIFY THE ASSOCIATED `vector` ARGUMENT)

return-type function-name **(vector** < *class* > **&** *vector-name***)**

PASS BY CONST REFERENCE (RUNTIME EFFICIENT WITH & AND SAFE WITH CONST)

return-type *function-name* **(const vector <** *class* **> &** *vector-name***)**

vectors should not be passed by value. This parameter passing mode is usually inefficient since vectors tend to consume a large amount of memory.

```
void foo( vector <bankAccount> acct, int n )
{ // VALUE parameter (should not be used with vectors)
  // All elements of acct are copied after allocating the
  // additional memory
}
```

Recall that passing by value causes the function to allocate memory for a copy of the object passed by value. This could be thousands or even millions of bytes. The program could terminate because of lack of memory. Additionally, every byte of the vector needs to be copied, which could noticeably slow down the program. Passing by const reference has the same meaning, but is more efficient.

Use pass by reference (with &) when a function is supposed to modify the associated argument.

```
void init( vector <bankAccount> & acct, int & n )
{ // REFERENCE parameter (allows changes to argument)
  // Only a pointer to acct is copied
  // A change to acct here changes the argument in the caller
}
```

And when a function requires a vector, but should not modify the associated argument, pass the vector by const reference.

```
void display( const vector <bankAccount> & acct, int n )
{ // CONST REFERENCE parameter (for efficiency and safety)
  // Only a reference to the acct is copied (4 bytes)
  // A change to acct does NOT change the argument
}
```

The next program passes a vector by providing an example of the first form. The main function passes by reference a vector of doubles to a void function named init. Because the vector parameter is declared as a reference parameter (with &), any change to x inside of init also changes the argument (test) in main.

```
#include <vector>  // For the vector<CLASS> class
#include <iostream>
```

```
using namespace std;

void init( vector <int> & x, int & n )  // Two reference parameters
{ // post: Initialize the first n elements of the argument
  n = 5;
  x.resize(n);
  x[0] = 75;
  x[1] = 88;
  x[2] = 67;
  x[3] = 92;
  x[4] = 51;
  // assert: The arguments associated with x and n (test and n)
  //         have been modified in main
}

void display(const vector <int> & x, int & n)  // Const reference
{
  int j;
  // Display the vector with n meaningful values
  cout << "The vector: ";
  for( j = 0; j < n; j++ )
  {
    cout.width(5);
    cout << x[j] << "  ";
  }
  cout << endl;
}

int main()
{
  vector <int> test(100, 0);
  int n;

  // Initialize test and n
  init( test, n );

  display( test, n );

  return 0;
}
```

OUTPUT

```
The vector:    75    88    67    92    51
```

10.4.1 Const Reference Parameters

The preceding program showed that the arguments—`test` and `n`—were passed to `init` by reference. This was done to allow the `init` function to modify these two arguments. However, sometimes a `vector` is passed as input to a function, where no changes should be made. In this case, the const reference form should be used. Part of the reason is efficiency—the program executes more quickly. The other consideration is better memory utilization—less memory is required to store the `vector` in the called function. A `vector` object passed by value requires as much memory as the associated argument.

```
void display(vector <double> x, int n)  // Value parameter
// This function must obtain the memory necessary to store x when x
// could have a large capacity of large objects
```

So if the `vector` argument had a capacity of 100,000 elements, `void display` would need to consume an additional 100,000 elements. Additionally, every single element would need to be copied from the client code (the caller) to the called function. This can be time consuming, especially when the `vector`'s capacity is large and/or the size of each element is large. The computer has to do a lot of unnecessary work. The program would run noticeably slower and might exhaust available memory.

Here are two alternatives to make any program more efficient in terms of space (saves memory) and time (runs faster).

1. Pass the `vector` by reference—efficient but dangerous.
2. Pass the `vector` by const reference—efficient and safe.

The second option is highly recommended—the computer program has much less work to do.

Using const is also an antibugging technique that will let the compiler catch attempts to modify the constant objects. Any const member function may still be called—`vector::capacity`, for example. However, the compiler will flag any attempt to send a nonconst message.

```
void display(const vector <int> & x, const int n)
{ // pre: x.capacity() > 0
  cout << "\nThe vector's capacity is " << x.capacity()  // <- OKAY
  cout << x[0];  // <- OKAY to reference vector element
  x[0] = 123;    // <- ERROR caught during compilation
}
```

Pass `vector`s or any large object (such as `grid`) by const reference.

Self-Check

10-23 Why should vectors and grids be passed by const reference when you have always seen ints and doubles passed by value?

10-24 If the average size of the bankAccount objects in a vector of capacity 100,000 is 57 bytes, how many bytes of additional memory would have to be reserved and then copied into each of the following functions? Remember, pass by reference typically requires four bytes of memory:

-a `void one( vector < bankAccount > v1 )`

-b `void two( vector < bankAccount > & v1 )`

-c `void one( const vector < bankAccount > & v1 )`

Exercises

1. Show the output generated by the following program:

```
#include <iostream>
int main()
{
  const int MAX = 10;
  vector<int> x(MAX);
  int j;
  for(j = 0; j < 3; j++)
    x[j] = j * 2;
  for(j = 3; j < MAX; j++)
    x[j] = x[j-1] + x[j-2];
  for(j = 0; j < MAX; j++)
    cout << j << ". " << x[j] << endl;
  return 0;
}
```

2. How many elements must be given meaningful values for a vector with 100 elements?

3. Declare a C++ vector called vectorOfInts that stores 10 integers with subscripts 0 through 9.

4. Write the code that determines the largest value of the following `vector`, assuming the first 52 values are meaningful:

```
vector<double> y(75, 12.3);
// Assume y[0] through y[51] are meaningful
int n = 52;
```

5. Write the code that determines the average element of the following `vector`, assuming only the first 43 elements are meaningful:

```
vector<double> z(100);
// Assume z[0] through z[42] have been initialized
int n = 43;
```

6. Write the output generated by the following program:

```
#include <vector>
#include <string>
using namespace std;

void init(vector<char> & data, int & n)
{ // post: Initialize data as a vector of chars.
  //       Initialize n as the number of meaningful elements.
  n = 5;
  data[0] = 'c';
  data[1] = 'b';
  data[2] = 'e';
  data[3] = 'd';
  data[4] = 'a';
}

void display(const vector<char> & data, int n)
{ // post: Show all meaningful elements of data
  int j;
  cout << endl;
  cout << "Vector of chars:  ";
  for(j = 0; j < n; j++)
    cout << data[j] << "  ";
  cout << endl;
}

void reverse(vector<char> & data, int n)
{ // post: Reverse the order of data
  int j, last;
  char temp;
```

```
  last = n - 1;
  for(j = 0; j < n / 2 + 1; j++)
  {
    temp = data[j];
    data[j] = data[last];
    data[last] = temp;
    last--;
  }
}
int main()
{
  vector<char> characters(10, ' ');
  int n;

  init(characters, n);
  display(characters, n);
  reverse(characters, n);
  display(characters, n);

  return 0;
}
```

7. Write a complete program that declares and initializes a `vector` of 10 `strings` with keyboard input. Your dialogue should look like this:

```
Enter string
#0 First
#1 Second
. . .
#9 Tenth
```

8. Write the code that sets `found` to `true` if a given `string` is found in the following `vector`. If a `string` is not in the `vector`, let `found` be `false`. Assume only the first `n` `vector` elements are initialized and are to be considered.

```
vector<string> s(200);
int n = 127;
bool found = false;
```

9. How many comparisons does a sequential search make when the search element is stored in the first `vector` element and there are 1,000 meaningful elements in the `vector`?

10. How many comparisons does a sequential search make when the search element does not match any `vector` element and there are 1,000 elements in the `vector`?

11. Assuming a large number of searches are made on a `vector`, and it is just as likely that an element is found in the first position as the last position, approximate the average number of comparisons after 1,000 searches when there are 1,000 elements in the `vector`.

12. Write the output generated by the following program (trick question):

```
#include <vector>  // For the vector<CLASS> class
#include <iostream>
using namespace std;

void init(vector<int> x, int n)
{ // post: Supposedly modify n and the first n elements of test in main
  x[0] = 0;
  x[1] = 11;
  x[2] = 22;
  x[3] = 33;
  x[4] = 44;
  n = 5;
}

int main()
{
  vector <int> test(100, 0);
  int j, n;

  // Initialize test and n
  init(test, n);
  // Display the vector with n meaningful values
  cout << "The vector: ";
  for(j = 0; j < n; j++)
    cout << test[j] << "  ";

  return 0;
}
```

13. How would you change the previous code such that the output is:

```
The vector: 0  11  22  33  44
```

14. Write the output generated by the following program:

```
#include <vector>  // For the vector<CLASS> class
#include <iostream>
using namespace std;
```

```
void f(const vector<int> & x)
{
  cout << x[0] << endl;
  cout << x.capacity() << endl;
}

int main()
{
  vector <int> test(10000, -1);
  f(test);
  return 0;
}
```

15. Which lines contain compiletime errors?

```
void f1(vector<int> x)
{
  cout << x[0] << endl;           // Line 1
  cout << x.capacity() << endl;   // Line 2
  x[0] = 999;                     // Line 3
}
```

16. Which lines contain compiletime errors?

```
void f2(const vector<int> & x)
{
  cout << x[0] << endl;           // Line 1
  cout << x.capacity() << endl;   // Line 2
  x[0] = 999;                     // Line 3
}
```

17. Which of the previous two functions is more efficient in terms of space and time, `f1` or `f2`?

Programming Tips

1. Remember, C++ begins to count at 0.

The first `vector` element is referenced with subscript 0, not 1 as is done in other programming languages. Imagine if the calendar had started with 0. Then the year 2000 would truly be the beginning of the new millennium.

2. A `vector` often has a capacity greater than its number of meaningful elements.

Sometimes `vector` objects are initialized to store more elements than are actually needed. In this case, only the first `n` elements are meaningful.

3. Use an object (named `n`, perhaps) to maintain the number of meaningful `vector` elements.

`vectors` will often be used as class data members along with another data members to store the number of meaningful elements (see Chapter 11, for example). However, when using `vectors` outside of a class, make sure you have an integer object that maintains the number of initialized elements. Consider the following code that counts the number of elements from a file as individual `vector` elements are initialized. The number of meaningful elements is maintained in `n` so it was necessary to initialize `n` to 0 and then increment `n` by 1 for each number on file.

```
vector <double> x(100, 0.0);
double aNumber;
int n = 0;

while( (inFile >> aNumber) && (n < x.capacity()) )
{
  x[n] = aNumber;
  n++;
}

// Antibugging tip: Verify that the vector is properly initialized
for(int j = 0; j < n; j++)
{
  cout.width(5);
  cout << x[j];
}
return 0;
```

4. Take the time to output a `vector` after initialization.

Although it may require writing a `for` loop you may not need, it really helps to ensure that your `vector` is properly initialized before continuing on with `vector`-processing algorithms. This tip is particularly helpful even in the relatively simple programming projects in this chapter. This test was done in the code above.

5. The last meaningful `vector` element is in `x[n-1]`, not `x[n]`.

Don't reference `x[n]`. This can be done in the code of the second programming tip by accidentally writing the `for` loop like this:

```
for(int j = 0; j <= n; j++)  // Used <= instead of <
{
  cout.width(5);
  cout << x[j];  // Will eventually reference garbage
}
```

6. Prevent assignments to a `vector` with out-of-range subscripts.

The code of the second programming tip has a loop test that terminates before assignment to `x[x.capacity()]`. When `n` equals the capacity, the loop terminates.

```
while( (inFile >> aNumber) && (n < x.capacity()) )
{ // The loop test prevents assignment to x[x.capacity()]
  x[n] = aNumber;
  n++;
}
```

It would also be useful to notify the user that something went wrong in this case. Terminating the program prematurely is an easy, but awkward way for doing this:

```
if(n == x.capacity() && inFile)
{
  cout << "**Error** Vector was too small. Terminating program" << endl;
  return 0;
}
```

7. Make your programs robust with `vector::resize` and `vector::capacity`.

The preceding code can be most irritating to users once they have purchased your software. A sounder way to handle the awkward situation of having too small a `vector` is to resize it when necessary.

```
while(inFile >> aNumber)
{
  if (n == x.capacity())
  {
    x.resize(n + 10);
  }
```

```
  x[n] = aNumber;
  n++;
}
```

With the preceding code, the vector's capacity will increase by 10 elements every time the vector fills up. The user will never know about it (unless all computer memory is exhausted, that is). The program will be more robust.

8. Never pass vectors by value.

Passing any big object by value slows down program execution and requires unnecessary memory runtime allocation. If a function needs the values of a vector but it is not supposed to modify the vector, pass the vector by const reference like this:

```
void MaGoo(const vector<double> & x, int n)  // Const reference
{
  // This function can reference any element in x, but cannot change x
}
```

As usual, if a function is meant to modify the argument (a vector in this case), pass it by reference like this:

```
void init(vector<double> & x, int & n)  // Reference parameter
{
  // This function can change any element in x
}
```

Even string objects should be passed by const reference rather than value because they are sometimes big.

9. The standard vector class does not check subscripts with [ ], but it does with vector::at(int).

Consider using x.at(subscript) instead of x[subscript]. They are equivalent expressions with one notable exception; when the subscript is out of range, vector::at reports it. You'll find out about the error right away during testing. This is preferable to using some random value accessed with an out-of-range subscript. Your code would look different than other C++ programs due to the historical use of [] and the newness of at.

```
#include <vector>  // For the vector<CLASS> class
#include <iostream>
using namespace std;
```

```
int main()
{
  int j, n;
  cout << "Enter vector capacity: ";
  cin >> n;
  vector <int> x(n);

  for(j = 0; j < n; j++)
  {
    x.at(j) = j;
  }

  cout << "First: " << x.at(0) << endl;

  cout << "Last: " << x.at(x.capacity() - 1) << endl;

  return 0;
}
```

DIALOGUE

```
Enter vector capacity: 100
First: 0
Last: 99
```

The previous code once again demonstrates that the first element in the `vector` is referenced with a subscript of 0, and the last with capacity - 1. So the following statement code would generate a runtime error and likely terminate the program:

```
cout << "Last: " << x.at(x.capacity()) << endl;  // Always an error
```

Programming Projects

10A Reverse

Write a complete C++ program that extracts an undetermined number of `ints` (maximum of 100) and displays them in reverse order. The user may not supply the number of elements, so a sentinel loop must be used. Here is one sample dialogue.

```
Enter up to 100 ints using -1 to quit:
70
75
90
60
80
-1
Reversed:  80  60  90  75  70
```

10B Show the Above-Average Ones

Write a complete program that inputs an undetermined number of positive numeric values, determines the average, and displays every value that is greater than or equal to the average. The user may not supply the number of elements, so use a sentinel loop. Here is one sample dialogue.

```
Enter numbers or -1 to quit
70
75
90
60
80
-1
Average: 75
Inputs >= average:  75  90  80
```

10C Sequential Search Function

Write a function named `search` that returns the subscript of the first found search element in a `vector` of `strings`. If the search element is not found, the search should return `-1`. Test your function with this test driver found on your disk.

```
// . . .
// File name: test10c.cpp
int main()
{
  vector <string> name(10);
  int n;
  // Initialize name and n
  init( name, n );
  display( name, n );
  // Search for every name in the vector
  // . . .
}
```

10D A Collection of `bankAccount` Objects

Write a complete C++ program that creates an undetermined number of `bankAccount` objects and stores them in a `vector`. The input should come from an exte.rnal file that looks like the following, but may contain 1, 2, 3, or up to exactly 20 lines (each line represents all data necessary to create one `bankAccount` object):

```
Hall      100.00
Solly      53.45
Kirstein  999.99
  . . .
Pantone  8790.56
Brendle     0.00
Kentish   234.45
```

After initializing the `vector` and determining the number of `bankAccount` objects, display every `bankAccount` that has a balance greater than or equal to $1,000.00. Then display every `bankAccount` that has a balance less than $100.00. Your output should look like this:

```
Balance >= 1000.00
Pantone:   8790.56
Kentish:    234.56

Balance < 100.00:
Solly:      53.45
Brendle:     0.00
```

10E Palindrome

A palindrome is a collection of characters that reads the same backward as forward. Write a program that extracts a `string` from the keyboard and determines whether or not the resulting `string` is a palindrome (recall that `string` objects reference individual characters with the subscript operator `[ ]`). Some examples of palindromes are YASISAY, racecar, 1234321, ABBA, level, and MADAMIMADAM. Here are two sample dialogues. (*Note:* Do not use any blank characters! If you want to, complete programming project 10F instead.)

```
Enter string: MADAMIMADAM
    Reversed: MADAMIMADAM
  Palindrome: Yes
```

```
Enter string: RACINGCAR
    Reversed: RACGNICAR
  Palindrome: No
```

10F Palindrome 2

A palindrome is a collection of characters that reads the same backward as forward. Write a program that extracts a line of characters from the keyboard using `getline(istream& is, string& aString)` and then determines whether or not the resulting `string` is a palindrome. The blank characters should be ignored. (*Hint:* First convert the individual characters to uppercase with the `toupper` function from `<cctype>`.)

```
Enter a line: A man a plan a canal Panama
AMANAPLANACANALPANAMA is a palindrome
```

10G Fibonacci Numbers

The Fibonacci numbers start as 1, 1, 2, 3, 5, 8, 13, 21. Notice that the first two are 1 and any successive Fibonacci number is the sum of the preceding two. Write an entire program that properly initializes a `vector` named `fib` to represent the first 20 Fibonacci numbers (`fib[1]` is the second Fibonacci number). Do not use 20 assignment statements to do this. Three should suffice.

10H Salaries

Write a program that inputs an undetermined number of annual salaries from an input file. After this, display all salaries that are above average. Also show the percentage of salaries that were above average. If the input file contains this data:

```
30000.00
24000.00
35000.00
32000.00
25000.00
```

then your output should look like this:

```
Average salary = 29200.00
Above average salaries:
30000.00
35000.00
32000.00
60% of reported salaries were above average
```

10.5 Sorting

The elements of a `vector` are often arranged into either ascending or descending order through a process known as *sorting*. For example, a `vector` of test scores is sorted into descending order by rearranging the numeric values in highest to lowest order. A `vector` of `string` objects sorted in ascending order establishes an alphabetized list ("A"s before "B"s, "B"s before "C"s). To sort a `vector`, the elements must be compared with a greater-than (>) relationship. If one object can be less than another object of the same class, then `vector`s of those objects are said to be *sortable*. For example, 85 > 79 and "B" > "A" are valid expressions. So `vector`s of `int` or `string` objects are sortable. (*Note:* C++ allows operators such as > for classes that do not already have this operator defined. For example, an employee class may be made sortable using a hire date data member or the employee's name (see Chapter 18, "Operator Overloading").)

The following code declares and gives meaningful values to a part of the `vector` named `test` to demonstrate sorting a `vector` of `int`s.

```
vector<int> test(10, 0);  // Store up to 10 integers
int n = 5;
test[0] = 76;
test[1] = 74;
test[2] = 100;
test[3] = 62;
test[4] = 89;
```

There are many sorting algorithms. Even though others are more efficient (run faster), the relatively simple selection sort will be used here. The goal is to arrange the following `vector` of five elements into descending order.

Object Name	Unsorted `vector`	Sorted `vector`
`test[0]`	76	100
`test[1]`	74	89
`test[2]`	100	76
`test[3]`	62	74
`test[4]`	89	62

With the selection sort algorithm, the largest test must end up in `test[0]` and the smallest in `test[n - 1]`. In general, a `vector` `x` of size `n` is sorted in descending order if `x[j] >= x[j + 1]` for `j = 0` to `n - 2`.

The selection sort begins by selecting the largest element in the `vector` from the first (`test[0]`) through the last (`test[4]`). The largest element, `test[2]` in this `vector`, will then be swapped with the top element, `test[0]`. Once this is done, the `vector` is sorted at least through the first element.

`top == 0`	Before	After	Sorted
`test[0]`	**76**	**100**	⇐
`test[1]`	74	74	
`test[2]`	**100**	**76**	
`test[3]`	62	62	
`test[4]`	89	89	

The subtask of finding the largest element is accomplished by examining all `vector` elements and keeping track of the subscript of the largest. After this, the largest element found is swapped with `test[0]`. Here is an algorithm that accomplishes these two subtasks:

// Find the largest in the vector and switch with the top-most element

(a) top = 0

// At first, assume that the first element is the largest

(b) subscriptOfLargest = top

// Check the rest of the list (test[top + 1] through test[n - 1])

(c) for j ranging from top+1 through n-1

(c1) if test[j] > test[subscriptOfLargest]

subscriptOfLargest = j

// Place largest element into the first position and also place the first element into the

// position where the largest was located

(d) swap test[subscriptOfLargest] with test[top]

The following algorithm walkthrough shows how the `vector` is sorted through the first element with the largest stored at `test[0]`. Notice that `subscriptOfLargest` changes only when a `vector` element is encountered (100) that is larger than the one stored in `test[subscriptOfLargest]` the second time step c1 executes.

Step	top	subscriptOf-Largest	j	$test_0$	$test_1$	$test_2$	$test_3$	$test_4$	n
?	?	?	?	76	74	100	62	89	5
(a)	0	?	?	76	74	100	62	89	5
(b)	0	0	?	76	74	100	62	89	5
(c)	0	0	1	76	74	100	62	89	5
(c1)	0	0	1	76	74	100	62	89	5
(c)	0	0	2	76	74	100	62	89	5
(c1)	0	**2**	2	76	74	100	62	89	5
(c)	0	2	3	76	74	100	62	89	5
(c1)	0	2	3	76	74	100	62	89	5
(c)	0	2	4	76	74	100	62	89	5
(c1)	0	2	4	76	74	100	62	89	5
(c)	0	2	5	76	74	100	62	89	5
(d)	0	2	5	**100**	74	**76**	62	89	5

This algorithm walkthrough shows `subscriptOfLargest` changing once to represent the subscript of the largest value in the `vector`. After traversing the entire `vector`, the largest element is swapped with the top `vector` element. In our example, the preceding algorithm swaps the values of the first and third `vector` elements, so 100 is stored in `test[0]` and 76 is stored in `test[2]`. The `vector` is now sorted through the first element!

The same algorithm can be used to place the second largest element into `test[1]`. But the second traversal must begin at a new top of the `vector`—subscript 1 rather than 0. This is accomplished by incrementing top from 0 to 1. Now a second traversal of the `vector` begins at the second element rather than the first. The largest element in the unsorted portion of the `vector` will be swapped with the second element. A second traversal of the `vector` ensures the first two elements are in order. In this example `vector`, `test[4]` is swapped with `test[1]` and the `vector` is sorted through the first two elements:

`top == 1`	Before	After	Sorted
`test[0]`	100	100	⇐
`test[1]`	**74**	**89**	⇐
`test[2]`	76	76	
`test[3]`	62	62	
`test[4]`	**89**	**74**	

This process repeats a total of `n - 1` times—all but the last. It is unnecessary to find the largest element in a subvector of size 1. This (`n - 1`)th element must be the smallest (or equal to the smallest) since all elements preceding the last element are already sorted. An outer loop changes `top` from 0 through `n - 2`.

SELECTION SORT ALGORITHM

```
for top ranging from 0 through n - 2
{
   subscriptOfLargest = top
   for j ranging from top + 1 through n - 1
   {
      if test[ j ] > test[ subscriptOfLargest ] then
            subscriptOfLargest = j
   }
   swap  test[subscriptOfLargest] with test[top]
}
```

The selection sort algorithm is shown as part of a program containing several nonmember functions. Notice that the test driver uses the `vector`'s default constructor. In this case, the capacity is set to the default 0. Therefore, it is necessary to resize the `vector` in the `init` function.

```
#include <iostream>
#include <vector>  // For the vector<CLASS> class
using namespace std;
```

```
typedef int vectorElementType;

void init(vector <vectorElementType> & x, int & n)
{ // post: x becomes a new vector precisely the size needed
  n = 5;
  x.resize(n);
  x[0] = 76;
  x[1] = 74;
  x[2] = 100;
  x[3] = 62;
  x[4] = 89;
}

void display(const vector <vectorElementType> & x, int & n)
{ // post: Show all elements
  int j;

  cout << "The vector: " << endl;
  for(j = 0; j < n; j++)
  {
    cout.width(2);
    cout << j << ". ";
    cout.width(5);
    cout << x[j] << endl;
  }
}

void swap(vectorElementType & a, vectorElementType & b)
{ // post: Exchange values of a and b
  vectorElementType temp = a;  // Hold on to a's value

  a = b;
  b = temp;
}

void sort(vector < vectorElementType > & data, int n)
{ // post: Data elements are in descending order
  int j, top, subscriptOfLargest;

  subscriptOfLargest = 0;
  for(top = 0; top < n - 1; top++)
  {
    subscriptOfLargest = top;
    for(j = top + 1; j < n; j++)
    {
      if(data[j] > data[subscriptOfLargest])
        subscriptOfLargest = j;
    }
    swap(data[subscriptOfLargest], data[top]);
  }
```

```
}

int main()
{
  vector<int> test;  // Default vector capacity is 0
  int n;

  init(test, n);
  sort(test, n);
  display(test, n);
  return 0;
}
```

OUTPUT

```
The vector:
 0.   100
 1.    89
 2.    76
 3.    74
 4.    62
```

The selection sort arranged a `vector` of integers into descending numeric order. However, the same sorting algorithm arranges any class of data that has > or < defined (such is the case with `double` or `string`, for example). Also, with just one change, data of any class may be arranged into ascending order. For example, a list of names could be arranged in ascending (alphabetical) order by switching > to < in the selection sort `if` statement.

```
if(data[j] > data[subscriptOfLargest])  // Descending order
```

becomes

```
if(data[j] < data[subscriptOfSmallest])  // Ascending order
```

Again, since operators may be overloaded, any class of object can be sortable by defining > and <. For example, `bankAccount` objects could be sorted by name, and students by grade point average.

Self-Check

10-25 Alphabetizing a `vector` of `strings` requires a sort in which order, ascending or descending?

10-26 If the largest element in a `vector` already exists as the first, what happens when the `swap` function is called for the first time (when `top` = 0)?

10-27 Write code that searches for and stores the largest element of `vector x` into `largest`. Assume that all elements from `x[0]` through `x[n-1]` have been given meaningful values, so all `vector` elements should be considered.

10.6 Binary Search

This chapter has shown the sequential search algorithm used to locate a `string` in a `vector` of `string` objects. This section examines the more efficient (runs faster) binary search algorithm. Binary search accomplishes the same search task more quickly. However, one of its preconditions is that the `vector` must be sorted.

The advantage of binary search is efficiency. It is faster than a sequential search, especially when the `vector` is large. By contrast, the slower sequential search does not require the `vector` to be sorted and the algorithm is simpler.

In general, binary search works like this. If a `vector` of objects is sorted, half of the `vector`'s elements are eliminated from the search each time a comparison is made. This is summarized in the following algorithm that searches for any element:

BINARY SEARCH ALGORITHM

```
while the element is not found and it still may be in the vector
{
  determine the position of the element in the middle of the vector
  if the element in the middle is not the one being searched for:
    eliminate the half of the vector that cannot contain the element
}
```

Each time the search element is compared to one `vector` element, the binary search effectively eliminates half the `vector` elements from the search field. In contrast, the sequential search only eliminates one element from the search field for each comparison. Assuming a `vector` of `strings` is sorted in alphabetic order, sequentially searching for `"Ableson"` does not take long since `"Ableson"` is likely to be located as one of the first `vector` elements. However, sequentially searching for `"Zevon"` would take much more time because the sequential search algorithm first searches through all names beginning with A through Y before arriving at the Zs. Binary search gets to `"Zevon"` much more quickly.

The binary search algorithm has these preconditions:

1. The `vector` must be sorted (in ascending order for now).
2. The subscripts that reference the first and last elements must represent the entire range of meaningful elements.

The element in the middle of the `vector` is accessed by computing the `vector` subscript that is halfway between the first and last positions of the meaningful elements. This is the average of the two subscripts that represent the first and last elements in the `vector`. These become subscripts in the search and will be referred to as `first`, `mid`, and `last`. Here is the `vector` to be searched.

```
vector <string> str(32);
int n = 7;

str[0] = "ABE"  // first == 0
str[1] = "CLAY"
str[2] = "KIM"
str[3] = "LAU"  // mid == 3
str[4] = "LISA"
str[5] = "PELE"
str[6] = "ROE"  // last == 6
```

The binary search algorithm is preceded with several assignments to get things going:

`searchString` = the `string` being searched for
`first` = subscript of the first meaningful `vector` element
`last` = subscript of the last meaningful `vector` element
`mid` = (`first` + `last`) / 2

At this point, one of three things can happen:

1. The element in the middle of the `vector` matches the search name—the search is complete.
2. The search element precedes the middle element. The second half of the `vector` can be eliminated from the search field.
3. The search element follows the middle element. The first half of the `vector` can be eliminated from the search field.

This is written algorithmically as:

BINARY SEARCH ALGORITHM (MORE REFINED WHILE ASSUMING ASCENDING SORT)

```
if searchString == str[mid] then
  searchString is found
else
  if searchString < str[mid]
    eliminate mid...last elements from the search
  else
    eliminate first...mid elements from the search
```

The binary search algorithm is implemented here assuming the `vector` named `str` has been constructed, initialized, and sorted. The C++ `break` statement terminates the loop when the `searchString` is found.

TRACE: *Binary search algorithm*

```
// pre: 1) The vector named str is sorted in ascending order.
//      2) str[0] through str[6] are defined vector elements.
//      3) The class defines < and ==.

int first = 0;
int last = n - 1;  // last = 6;
string searchString("LISA");

while( (first <= last) )
{
  mid = (first + last) / 2;  // (0 + 6) / 2 = 3
  if(searchString == str[mid])  // Check the three possibilities
   break[4];  // 1) searchString is found
   else
   if(searchString < str[mid])  // 2) It's in first half so
      last = mid - 1;           //    eliminate second half
    else   // 3) It's in second half so eliminate first half
      first = mid + 1;
  }
}
```

OBJECTS BEFORE COMPARING `searchString ("LISA")` TO `str[mid] ("LAU")`

`str[0]`	`"ABE"`	⇐ `first == 0`
`str[1]`	`"CLAY"`	
`str[2]`	`"KIM"`	
`str[3]`	`"LAU"`	⇐ `mid == 3`
`str[4]`	`"LISA"`	
`str[5]`	`"PELE"`	
`str[6]`	`"ROE"`	⇐ `last == 6`

After comparing `searchString` to `str[mid]`, `first` is increased and a new `mid` is computed:

```
str[0] "ABE"   // Because "LISA" is greater than str[mid], the
str[1] "CLAY"  // the objects str[0] through str[3] no longer need
str[2] "KIM"   // to be searched and can now be eliminated from
str[3] "LAU"   // subsequent search
```

4. When `break` executes inside a loop, the loop terminates. Control transfers to the statement immediately following the loop.

```
str[4] "LISA"    ⇐ first == 4
str[5] "PELE"    ⇐ mid == 5
str[6] "ROE"     ⇐ last == 6
```

Since `searchString < str[mid]` or `"LISA" < "PELE"` is true, `last` is decreased and a new `mid` is computed.

```
str[0] "ABE"
str[1] "CLAY"
str[2] "KIM"
str[3] "LAU"
str[4] "LISA"    ⇐ first == 5    ⇐ last == 5     ⇐ mid == 5
str[5] "PELE"  // Because "LISA" is less than str[mid], eliminate
str[6] "ROE"   // str[5] through str[6] from the search field
```

Now `str[mid]` does equal `searchString` so break out of the loop.

The binary search algorithm can be more efficient than the sequential search that only eliminates one element per comparison. Binary search eliminates half the elements for each comparison. For example, when n == 1,024, a binary search eliminates 512 elements from further search for each comparison.

Now consider the possibility that the element being searched for is not in the `vector`. For example, to search for `"CARLA"`, the values of `first`, `mid`, and `last` progress as follows:

Comparison	`first`	`mid`	`last`	Comment
1	0	3	6	Compare `"CARLA"` to `"LAU"`.
2	0	1	2	Compare `"CARLA"` to `"CLAY"`.
3	0	0	0	Compare `"CARLA"` to `"ABE"`.
4	1	0	0	`first <= last` is false—the loop is terminated.

The loop test (`first <= last`) evaluates to false when `searchString ("CARLA")` is not stored in the `vector`. Notice that `last` is less than `first`—the two subscripts have crossed each other.

```
str[0] "ABE" ⇐ last == 0   ⇐ mid == 0
str[1] "CLAY"⇐ first == 1
str[2] "KIM"
str[3] "LAU"
str[4] "LISA"
str[5] "PELE"
str[6] "ROE"
```

After searchString ("CARLA") is compared to str[1] ("ABE"), no further comparisons are necessary. This is the second of two conditions that terminate the loop. Since first is no longer less than or equal to last, searchString cannot be in the vector.

Self-Check

10-28 Write at least one precondition for a successful binary search.

10-29 What is the maximum number of comparisons (approximately) performed on a list of 1,024 elements during a binary search? (*Hint:* After one comparison, only 512 vector elements need be searched; after two searches, only 256 elements need be searched, and so on.)

10-30 During a binary search, what condition signals that the search element does not exist in a vector?

10-31 What changes must be made to the binary search when the elements are sorted in descending order?

Chapter Summary

- Whereas objects may store data of many different types at the same time (a string, an int, and even a vector, for example), a vector object stores collections of the same class (a vector of char, int, string, or bankAccount objects, for example).
- Individual vector elements are referenced with subscripts. With a C++ vector, the int expression of a subscript reference should be in the range of 0 through the capacity - 1. For example, the valid subscript range of vector <double> x(100) is 0 through 99 inclusive.
- Out-of-range subscripts may not be detected at compiletime and may cause system crashes, destruction of other objects, or some other system-specific problems. It depends on the vector class you are using. Programmers must guard against these potential hazards. One of the easiest ways to do this is to use vector::at.
- An integer named n or my_size is usually an important piece of data that must be maintained in addition to the vector elements themselves. The number of meaningful elements is important in any vector-processing algorithm.

- Any `vector` object can be resized to have a different maximum capacity. If it is resized to be bigger, the meaningful elements remain. However, if a `vector` is resized to be smaller, truncation of meaningful elements may occur.
- The capacity of a `vector` almost always differs from the number of meaningful elements. So a `vector` of capacity 1,000 may only be using the first 739 elements to store data—with room for more.
- The selection sort algorithm was used to arrange `vector` elements into descending order. Any object that can be compared with < or > may be sorted.
- Vectors may also be sorted in ascending order, which is more appropriate sometimes, especially with `string` elements where ascending order means alphabetical order.
- The binary search algorithm is more efficient than sequential search. However, the `vector` must first be sorted for binary search to work properly.

Exercises

18. Write the output generated by the program segment below using the initialized `vector` of `string` objects.

```
#include <iostream>
#include <string>
#include <vector>  // For the vector<CLASS> class
using namespace std;

int main()
{
  vector <string> x(10);
  int j;
  int top = 0;
  int n = 5;

  x[0] = "Aimee";
  x[1] = "Bob";
  x[2] = "Lauren";
  x[3] = "Alex";
  x[4] = "Morgan";
  for(top = 0; top < n - 1; top++)
  {
    int subscript = top;
    for(j = top + 1; j <= n - 1; j++)
    {
```

```
      if(x[j] < x[subscript])
        subscript = j;
    }
    string temp = x[subscript];
    x[subscript] = x[top];
    x[top] = temp;
  }
  for(j = 0; j <= n - 1; j++)
  {
    cout << x[j] << endl;
  }
  return 0;
}
```

19. Write the output of the program segment below using this initialized `vector` of `strings`:

```
vector <string> str(20);
str[0]  = "ABE"
str[1]  = "CLAY"
str[2]  = "KIM"
str[3]  = "LAU"
str[4]  = "LISA"
str[5]  = "PELE"
str[6]  = "ROE"
str[7]  = "SAM"
str[8]  = "TRUDY"

int first = 0;
int last = 8;
int mid;
bool found = false;
string searchString("CLAY");

cout << "First Mid Last" << endl;
while(first <= last)
{
   mid = (first + last) / 2;
   cout << first << "       " << mid << "     " << last << endl;
   if(searchString == str[mid])
     break;
   else
     if(searchString < str[mid])
       last = mid - 1;
     else
       first = mid + 1;
}
if(first <= last)
```

```
  cout << searchString << " found" << endl;
else
  cout << searchString << " was not" << endl;
```

20. Write the output generated by the preceding program segment when `searchString` is assigned each of the following values:

    a. `searchString = "LISA"`
    b. `searchString = "TRUDY"`
    c. `searchString = "ROE"`
    d. `searchString = "ABLE"`
    e. `searchString = "KIM"`
    f. `searchString = "ZEVON"`

21. List at least one condition that must be true before a successful binary search can be implemented.

22. Using a binary search, what is the maximum number of comparisons (approximately) that will be performed on a list of 256 sorted elements? (*Hint:* After one comparison, only 128 `vector` elements need be searched, after two searches, only 64 elements need be searched, and so on.)

Programming Tips

10. There are many sorting algorithms besides selection sort.

Selection sort is only one of the many known sorting algorithms. Several others have approximately the same runtime efficiencies. Some are much better. For example, C. A. Hoare's "Quick Sort" algorithm is usually much more efficient. This chapter was not written to cover sorting completely. It is only a very brief introduction to another category of `vector`-processing algorithms.

11. There are many searching algorithms besides sequential and binary search.

The two searching algorithms are only two of many known searching algorithms. However, for small amounts of data, sequential search works very nicely. For larger amounts of data stored in sorted `vector`s, binary search works well. Other ways to store very large amounts of data that can be searched rapidly include hash tables and binary trees, for example.

12. The searching and sorting algorithms presented here only work with data stored in `vectors`.

Programmers often need to sort and search data stored on a disk some place. The algorithms presented here only work on data stored in a `vector` in the computer's main memory. The `vector`-processing algorithms were intended only to present the notions of searching and sorting in a concrete way and to reinforce the use of `vectors`. Advanced sorting and searching algorithms along with different storage mechanisms are usually covered in a later course.

Programming Projects

10I A Nonmember Binary Search Function

Write a function named `search` that returns the subscript location of the first found search element in a `vector`. Use the binary search algorithm. If the search element is not found, `search` should return `-1`. Test your function, of course.

10J Frequency

Write a C++ program that reads integers from a file and reports the frequency of each integer. For example, if the input file contains the numbers, as shown to the left below, your program should generate the output shown to the right below, with the highest numbers first. Create the input file such that all numbers are in the range of 0 through 100 inclusive.

The File `test.dat`	The Program Dialogue

<pre>75 85   90 100
60 90 100   85
75 35   60   90
100 90   90   90
60 50   70   85
75 90   90   70</pre>
	<pre>Enter file name: test.dat
	100: 3
	 90: 8
	 85: 3
	 75: 3
	 70: 2
	 60: 3
	 50: 1
	 35: 1</pre>

10K The `stats` Class (prerequisite: Chapter 6)

Write the class definition and implement the member functions of the `stats` class to provide some descriptive statistics. These statistics include the largest, smallest, and other statistical measures such as the mean (average) and measures of dispersion around the mean such as the variance and the standard deviation.

a. $$\text{Mean} = \frac{1}{n}\sum_{j=0}^{n-1} x_j$$

b. $$\text{Variance} = \frac{1}{n}\sum_{j=0}^{n-1} x_j^2 - \frac{1}{n^2}\left(\sum_{j=0}^{n-1} x_j\right)^2$$

c. $$\text{Standard Deviation} = \sqrt{\text{Variance}}$$

Member Function	Description
`stats::stats()`	Construct empty `stat` objects with capacity 16
`stats::stats(int initCapacity)`	Construct empty `stat` objects of any capacity
`void stats::add(double newElement)`	Add a number to the collection
`void stats::sort()`	Arrange the numbers in ascending order
`int stats::size()`	The number of elements in the population
`double stats::mean()`	The average element
`double stats::max()`	The largest element in the set
`double stats::min()`	The smallest element in the set
`double stats::median()`	The value with as many above it as below it
`double stats::variance()`	The variance (see definition above)
`double stats::standardDeviation()`	The standard deviation (see definition above)
`void stats::display()`	Display all numbers

First, create the following input file called `tests.dat` in your working directory (folder):

```
76.0  65.0  93.0  95.5  84.5      ← The file tests.dat
85.0  91.0  76.5  65.0  70.6
86.0  82.5  68.0  79.5  83.0
```

Then create a new file named `stats.cpp` and implement all of the member functions of the class definition. Use the following test driver that is on your disk:

```
// File name: test10k.cpp
#include <fstream>
#include <iostream>
#include <string>
using namespace std;
#include "stats"  // Includes stats.h and stats.cpp. You must write both.

void show(const stats & tests)  // Be sure this is const reference with &
{
  cout << "Statistics for a set of tests"   << endl;
  cout << "     Size: " << tests.size()     << endl;
  cout << "     Mean: " << tests.mean()     << endl;
  cout << "     High: " << tests.max()      << endl;
  cout << "      Low: " << tests.min()      << endl;
  cout << "   Median: " << tests.median()   << endl;
  cout << " Variance: " << tests.variance() << endl;
  cout << "Stand Dev: " << tests.standardDeviation() << endl;
  tests.display();
}

int main()
{
  string fileName;
  cout << "Enter file name: ";  // Assume user will enter tests.dat
  cin >> fileName;
  ifstream inFile( fileName.c_str() );
  double x = 0.0;
  stats tests(24);

  while(inFile >> x)
  {
     tests.add(x);
  }

  show(tests);

  tests.add(100.00);
  tests.add(40.5);

  show(tests);

  return 0;
}
```

The file `stats`, which is on the accompanying disk and this textbook's Web site, will include your `stats.h` and `stats.cpp` files.

Chapter Eleven

A Container with Iterators

Summing Up

You have now experienced

- the control structures necessary to implement almost any algorithm:
  - Chapters 1–4, sequential control
  - Chapter 7, selection control
  - Chapter 8, repetition control
- ways to build programs: with nonmember functions or classes or a combination of the two
- the `vector` class, one of many container classes for storing and processing collections of items

Coming Up

This chapter introduces another container class named `bag`, which provides a review of vector processing, class definitions, and member function implementations. This chapter also presents the notion of *iterators,* which will help in future study of standard C++. After studying this chapter you will be able to

- declare and use `bag` objects that store collections of objects
- define classes with `vector` data members
- implement member functions that manipulate `vector`s
- implement and use iterator functions for traversing over all the items in a collection

  Exercises and programming projects

11.1 The bag Class

As you continue your study of computing, you will spend a fair amount of time exploring ways to manage collections of data. The `vector` class is only one of many classes designed for just this purpose. You will also use classes such as `list`, `stack`, and `queue` that manage collections of objects with higher-level messages such as `push_back`, `find`, and `sort`.

Containers have the following characteristics:

* The main responsibility of a container is to store a collection of objects.
* Objects may be added and removed from the collection.
* A container must allow clients to access the individual elements.
* A container may have search operations for locating a particular item and a sort operation for arranging items.

These characteristics are realized in a variety of ways. The `vector` class uses subscripts to access individual elements. However, the subscript notation is merely an artifact from the early days of computing. The nonstandard `bag` class shown next exemplifies a more modern, higher-level approach to containing objects. The relatively simple `bag` class also provides a review of class definitions and member function implementations. This time however, member functions employ vector-processing algorithms.

The main purpose of the `bag` class is to store a collection of items and to allow client code to access all elements in the `bag` from the first to the last. A `bag` object has the following characteristics:

* A `bag` may store any class of objects—kind of like `vector`.
* `bag` elements need not be unique. There may be duplicate entries.
* `bag` elements are not considered to be in any particular order.

A `bag` object can store any number of objects. A `bag` object understands messages such as `add`, `remove`, `display`, `capacity`, and `size`. Additional member functions allow iteration over all items in the collection. These are `first`, `next`, `currentItem`, and `isDone`. Data members include a `vector` named `my_item`, which stores added elements, and an integer named `my_size`, which stores the current number of elements that have been added to, and remain in, the `bag` object.

CLASS DEFINITION: *bag*

The bag Class

```
class bag {
public:
//--constructors
  bag();
  // post: Size of this bag is zero
  // initial capacity == DEFAULT_INITIAL_BAG_CAPACITY

  bag(int initCapacity);
  // pre:  initCapacity >= 1
  // post: Size of this bag is zero with capacity to
  //       store initCapacity BAG_ELEMENT_TYPE objects

//--modifiers
  void add(BAG_ELEMENT_TYPE newElement);
  // post: Add newElement to this bag and increase the
  //       size of this bag object by one

  bool remove(BAG_ELEMENT_TYPE removalCandidate);
  // pre:  removalCandidate must define !=
  // post: If found, removalCandidate is removed from this bag

//--accessors
  int capacity() const;
  // post: Return the maximum number of elements that could be stored

  int size() const;
  // post: Return the number of elements that are currently in this bag

  bool isEmpty() const;
  // post: Return true if there are zero items in the bag

//--iterator functions
  void first();
  // post: my_index points to the first item

  void next();
  // post: my_index points to the next item, or isDone now returns true

  bool isDone() const;
  // post: Returns true if the collection has been traversed

  BAG_ELEMENT_TYPE currentItem() const;
  // pre:  ! isDone && my_size > 0
  // post: Returns the item pointed to by my_index
```

Class Diagram

```
bag
---------------------------
add(item)
bool remove(item's id)
int capacity()
int size()
bool isEmpty()
first()
next()
item currentItem()
bool isDone()
---------------------------
vector <item> my_data
int my_size
```

Continued on next page

CLASS DEFINITION: *bag—Continued*

```
private:
vector <BAG_ELEMENT_TYPE> my_item;
  int my_size;
  int my_index;  // Internal pointer to traverse collection
};
```

This particular `bag` class depends on the client (the program with `int main()`) to supply the type of element to be stored in the `bag` object. The client code must supply a `typedef` such as the following:

```
typedef bankAccount BAG_ELEMENT_TYPE;
#include "bag"  // For a bag class that requires a typedef
```

The `typedef` specifies the class of elements that can be used as the arguments in `bag::add` and `bag::remove`, along with the type of elements stored in the private `vector` data member named `my_item`. The benefit is that client code can have `bags` that store collections of any class. For an improvement to this and to make a `bag` object initialization look like a `vector`, use `bag <string> aBag;` (see Chapter 17, "Templates: Building Generic Classes"). The following program shows example `bag` messages and the `typedef` necessary just before `#include "bag"`:

```
// This test driver creates a small bag of strings
#include <iostream>
#include <string>
using namespace std;

// Declare the type of item stored in the bag object. A typedef
// must precede #include "bag" (a better way is shown in Chapter 16).
// If you want a collection of strings, use the next line:
typedef string BAG_ELEMENT_TYPE;
#include "bag"  // For a bag class that requires the previous typedef

int main()
{ // Test drive bag
  bag bagOfStrings(10);
  cout << "Empty? " << bagOfStrings.isEmpty() << endl;

  // Add four items
  bagOfStrings.add("A string");
  bagOfStrings.add("Another string");
  bagOfStrings.add("and still another");
  bagOfStrings.add("and a fourth");
  // Take one away
```

```
  bagOfStrings.remove("and still another");

  // Send a remove message that doesn't find the argument
  if( bagOfStrings.remove("If I'm not in the bag, nothing happens") )
    cout << "remove successful" << endl;
  else
    cout << "string not found, bagOfStrings not changed" << endl;

  cout << "Empty? " << bagOfStrings.isEmpty() << endl;
  cout << "capacity is " << bagOfStrings.capacity() << endl;
  cout << "current size is " << bagOfStrings.size() << endl;

  return 0;
}
```

OUTPUT (1 MEANS TRUE, 0 FALSE)

```
Empty? 1
string not found, bagOfStrings not changed
Empty? 0
capacity is 10
current size is 3
```

11.1.1 The bag Constructors

The bag class definition (above) summarizes the messages that can be sent to any bag object. This is the interface available to any client code. The class definition also shows a vector data member (my_item) for storing the individual items. Each bag object also has an integer (my_size) to maintain the number of meaningful elements that are in the bag. The following member function implementations often reference these two data members.

11.1.1.1 bag::bag()

The default constructor function establishes an empty bag by setting my_size to 0. The capacity is specified to an arbitrary default capacity of 16.

```
const int DEFAULT_INITIAL_BAG_CAPACITY = 16;

bag::bag()
{
  my_size = 0;
  my_item.resize(DEFAULT_INITIAL_BAG_CAPACITY);
}
```

11.1.1.2 bag::bag(int initCapacity)

The constructor with one parameter establishes an empty bag—initializing my_size to 0. The initial capacity is set to whatever the programmer desires (as long as there is enough computer memory). The single argument initCapacity represents the maximum capacity desired.

```
bag::bag(int initCapacity)
{ // pre: initCapacity >= 1;
  my_size = 0;
  my_item.resize(initCapacity);
}
```

11.1.2 The bag-Modifying Member Functions

To add an element to the bag, the newElement will be placed at the "end"—or the first available location—of my_item. Both my_size and my_item must be referenced. However, this is not a problem since any bag member function has access to its private data. This two-step algorithm summarizes the processing:

Algorithm: *Add an Element*

myBagElement[my_size] = the arguments passed to bag::add
increment my_size by 1

First the new element is stored into the proper vector location using my_size as the subscript. Then my_size is incremented in response to this change. Incrementing my_size also conveniently sets up a situation such that the next added element will be inserted into the proper vector location. Incrementing my_size also maintains the number of elements in the bag.

The following implementation of bag::add shows that add occurs only after a check is made to ensure that the new item can be added. If my_size is greater than or equal to the capacity of the vector, the vector is resized to twice its current size.

```
void bag::add(BAG_ELEMENT_TYPE newElement)
{
  // First, increase the bag capacity if necessary
  if(my_size >= my_item.capacity())
  {
    my_item.resize(2 * my_item.capacity());
  }

  // Store the argument in the vector . . .
```

```
    my_item[my_size] = newElement;
    // . . . and make sure my_size is always increased by one
    my_size++;
  }
```

11.1.2.1 bool bag::remove(BAG_ELEMENT_TYPE removalCandidate)

To see another example of vector processing, consider a function that removes an element from a bag object. In order to concentrate on the remove algorithm, remember that my_item (a vector of BAG_ELEMENT_TYPE objects) and my_size (the number of elements in the bag) are always available.

removalCandidate, if found, is "removed" from the bag and my_size is reduced by one. For example, consider what happens when the parameter named removalCandidate becomes "Another string" with this message:

```
bagOfStrings.remove("Another string");
```

The remove operation will search through my_item for "Another string", which is the current value of removalCandidate. The bag::remove operation first attempts to locate the position of removalCandidate using the sequential search algorithm.

```
bool bag::remove(BAG_ELEMENT_TYPE removalCandidate)
{
  int subscript = 0;

  // Sequentially search for removalCandidate
  while((subscript < my_size) && (my_item[subscript] != removalCandidate))
  {
    subscript++;
  }
  // assert: my_item[subscript] == removalCandidate if found, otherwise
  //          subscript == my_size indicating it was not found

  if(subscript == my_size)
  { // The removalCandidate was not found
    return false;
  }
  else
  { // First, move the last element to where removalCandidate was found
    my_item[subscript] = my_item[my_size - 1];
    // And then decrease size by one
    my_size--;
    // Report success to the client code where the message was sent
    return true;
  }
}
```

If `removalCandidate` is not found, `bag::remove` simply returns false to notify the client that the attempt to remove the element was unsuccessful. When `removalCandidate` is found, the algorithm uses a little gimmick to not only remove `removalCandidate`, but also to free up one of the `vector` spaces for the next `bag::add` message. The following maneuver is possible because the elements in the `bag` need not be maintained in any particular order.[1]

First, examine the values of the data members `my_item` and `my_size` and of the local objects while trying to remove the `bag` elements `"Another string"`:

Data Member	State of `bagOfStrings`
`my_item[0]`	`"A string"`
`my_item[1]`	`"Another string"`
`my_item[2]`	`"and still another"`
`my_item[3]`	`"and a fourth"`
. . .	
`my_size`	`4`
Local Object	**State of Local Object**
`removalCandidate`	`"Another string"`
`subscript`	`1`

Now, `my_item[subscript]` must somehow be removed from the vector, which is currently `my_item[1]` or `"Another string"`. The simple way to do this is to move the last element into this spot. It is okay to overwrite `my_item[1]`. Since there is no ordering postcondition, it is also okay to move `my_item[my_size - 1]`, the last meaningful element in the `vector`. Then decrement `my_size` to reflect the removal. Here are the two statements that do it:

```
// assert: subscript is the index of the item to be removed
my_item[subscript] = my_item[my_size - 1];
my_size--;
```

The state of the bag would now look like this:

1. Rich Pattis suggested this solution.

Data Member	State of `bagOfStrings`
`my_item[0]`	`"A string"`
`my_item[1]`	`"and a fourth"   // Erase removalCandidate`
`my_item[2]`	`"and still another"`
`my_item[3]`	*`"and a fourth"`* `   // my_item[3] is no longer meaningful`
`. . .`	
`my_size`	`3                // my_size is 3 now`

Although the elements are not in the same order (this was not a precondition), the same elements still exist after the requested removal. Because the last element has been moved, `my_size` must be decreased by one. There are now only three, not four, elements in the `bag`.

The same code works even when removing the last element. With the code shown above, the assignment is still done even though it is not necessary. Merely decreasing `my_size` by one effectively eliminates the last element.

11.1.3 The bag Accessor Functions

11.1.3.1 `int bag::capacity() const`

The `capacity` function returns the maximum number of elements that the `bag` object can store. With a `vector` implementation, that piece of information is stored in the `vector my_item`.

```
int bag::capacity() const
{
  return my_item.capacity();  // The capacity of the vector
}
```

11.1.3.2 `int bag::size() const`

The `size` message returns the precise number of elements that have been added and not removed. The private data member `my_size` is incremented by one in `bag::add` and decremented by one in `bag::remove`. Of course, if either constructor fails to initialize `my_size` to zero, `my_size` will be garbage, causing unpredictable problems.

```
int bag::size() const
{
  return my_size;
}
```

11.1.3.3 `bool bag::isEmpty() const`

The `isEmpty` message returns true if there are zero items stored in the `bag`. It returns false if `my_size != 0`.

```
bool bag::isEmpty() const
{
  return my_size == 0;
}
```

Self-Check

11-1 What happens when an attempt is made to remove an element that is not in the `bag`?

11-2 Using the implementation of `bag::remove` just given, what happens when an attempt is made to remove an element from an empty `bag` (`my_size == 0`)?

11-3 Write a complete program, with the proper `#include`s, that adds and then removes your name from a `bag` object.

11-4 What would `bag::size` return at the end of the program in the previous question?

11-5 Must `bag::remove` always maintain the `bag` elements in the same order as that in which they were originally added?

11-6 What happens when an attempt is made to remove an element that exists more than once?

11-7 Write the output of the following program:

```
#include <iostream>
using namespace std;

typedef int BAG_ELEMENT_TYPE;
#include "bag"  // For the bag class

int main()
{
  bag aBagOfInts;
  int n = 35;
  for(int j = 1; j <= n; j++)
  {
    aBagOfInts.add(j);
  }
```

```
    cout << "size: " << aBagOfInts.size() << endl;
    cout << "capacity: " << aBagOfInts.capacity() << endl;
    return 0;
}
```

11.2 The Iterator Pattern

Because each `bag` object always knows how many elements it stores (`my_size`), a container object can be given functions designed to sequentially iterate over the entire collection of items. This can be made a part of any container object interface. The `vector` class provides subscripts.

This textbook's `bag` class uses iterator functions to visit the contained objects. The following `while` loop shows how the client code could iterate over the entire collection, without having to worry about going out of bounds:

```
#include <iostream>
using namespace std;
typedef int BAG_ELEMENT_TYPE;
#include "bag"  // For the bag class

int main()
{
  bag aBagOfInts;

  // Add 12 integers to aBagOfInts
  int n = 12;
  for(int j = 1; j <= n; j++)
  {
    aBagOfInts.add(j);
  }

  cout << "\nTraverse the entire collection:" << endl;
  cout << "\nThe bag: ";

  aBagOfInts.first();
  while ( ! aBagOfInts.isDone() )
  {
    cout << aBagOfInts.currentItem() << " ";
    aBagOfInts.next();  // Move to the next (or end)
  }

  return 0;
}
```

Output

```
Traverse the entire collection:
The bag: 1 2 3 4 5 6 7 8 9 10 11 12
```

The `for` loop provides a convenient way to iterate over all items in a container. The initial statement in the `for` loop—`aBagOfInts.first()`—sets the `bag`'s internal cursor to the first item in the collection. The `for` loop test `(! aBagOfInts.isDone())` is true as long as there is at least one more item to visit. And at the end of each `for` loop iteration, the repeated statement `aBagOfInts.next()` updates the internal cursor either to refer to the next item in the collection or to make sure `isDone` will return true.

```
double sum = 0.0;
for( aBagOfInts.first(); ! aBagOfInts.isDone(); aBagOfInts.next() )
{
  sum = sum + aBagOfInts.currentItem();
}
cout << "Average: " << ( sum / aBagOfInts.size() ) << endl;
```

Output

```
Average: 7.5
```

Self-Check

11-8 Write code that determines the maximum integer in `aBagOfInts`.

11.2.1 The Iterator Functions

The `bag` iterator member functions exist for the sole purpose of allowing client code to access any and all of the `bag` elements in a sequential fashion, from the first element to the last in the container. The `bag::first` function must be called first to set the private data member `my_index` to refer to the first element in the `bag`.

```
void bag::first()
{ // Make sure there is at least one item in the bag
  if(my_size >= 0)
    my_index = 0;
}
```

The `bag::isDone` member function returns true if there are no more elements to traverse. So it is typical to see this message used as the loop test:

```
while( ! aBag.isDone() )
```

The member function compares `my_index` to `my_size` and returns false unless `my_index` has gotten to be bigger than the `bag`'s current size.

```
bool bag::isDone() const
{
  return my_index >= my_size;
}
```

The `bag:next` member function simply increments the internal cursor named `my_index`.

```
void bag::next()
{
  my_index++;
}
```

And finally, the `bag::currentItem` function returns the element referred to by the internal cursor `my_index`. Notice that the return type is whatever the client code specified in the `typedef` before including `bag`.

```
BAG_ELEMENT_TYPE bag::currentItem() const
{
  return my_item[my_index];
}
```

If the programmer wrote

```
typedef bankAccount BAG_ELEMENT_TYPE;
#include "bag"
```

the `currentItem` function would return a `bankAccount` object. If the programmer wrote

```
typedef string BAG_ELEMENT_TYPE;
#include "bag"
```

the `currentItem` function would return a `string` object.

The `bag` class is given a different underlying data structure—with pointers and dynamic memory allocation—in Chapter 17, "Templates: Building Generic Classes." Also, that `bag` will be instantiated like `vectors`, as in the following:

```
bag <int> tests(100000);
bag <string> presidents;  // Chapter 17
bag <bankAccount> bBag;   // The bag class is turned into a
bag <book> bookBag(100);  // generic class with templates
```

Chapter Summary

- The `bag` class illustrates how a `vector` can be utilized as a storage mechanism in a class that provides higher-level messages such as `add` and `remove`—no subscripts required.
- Container classes such as `bag` and `vector` store collections of objects while providing suitable access to the elements.
- The `bag::remove` operation employs sequential search to locate `removalCandidate`. Binary search cannot be used here because there has been no attempt to maintain the order of the `bag` elements.
- The `bag` class introduced the notion of iterator member functions that allow client code to traverse the entire collection without revealing the underlying structure. The `for` loop provides a convenient way to do this.

Exercises

1. Write the output of the following program:

```
#include <iostream>
using namespace std;

#include "baccount"
typedef bankAccount BAG_ELEMENT_TYPE;  // Assume bankAccount's available
#include "bag"  // For a bag class that requires the previous typedef

int main()
{
  bag acct;
  acct.add( bankAccount("Jordy Gordon", 100.00) );
  acct.add( bankAccount("Hanna Helstrom", 200.00) );
  acct.add( bankAccount("Sammy Swanson", 300.00) );
  acct.add( bankAccount("Karly Kuprah", 400.00) );
  double assets = 0.0;

  for(acct.first(); ! acct.isDone(); acct.next())
  {
    assets = assets + acct.currentItem().balance();
  }

  cout << "Assets: " << assets << endl;
  acct.first();
```

```
    acct.next();
    cout << acct.currentItem().name() << endl;
    return 0;
}
```

2. Write code that displays the name of all bank accounts in the container object `acct` of the previous question.

3. What happens when a 17th element gets added to a `bag` object?

4. Write code that assigns the smallest item in any `bag` object to `smallest`. Assume < has meaning for the `bag` items.

5. Write code that assigns the largest item in any `bag` object to `largest`. Assume > has meaning for the `bag` items.

6. Write a program that creates a `bag` of messages where each message is one complete line of a file on disk.

7. What changes would have to be made to the `bag` class such that the iterator functions would traverse the `bag` in reverse order? You cannot change the names of any functions. Write out the complete member functions that would be changed.

Programming Tips

1. The requirement of `typedef` in `bag` objects is not a typical solution in standard C++ libraries. So don't expect to see it often in the future.

The little "trick" of using a `typedef` before including the container class allows for delayed coverage of the typical C++ method for managing collections of any class of object. By Chapter 17, "Templates: Building Generic Classes," you will see the `bag` class converted to allow it to be passed in the construction of an object, just like `vector` objects.

```
vector <int> x(100);
bag <int> b(100);
```

2. The iterator pattern used to traverse a bag has some drawbacks.

With the implementation shown, a bag cannot be traversed when passed by const reference. The following function highlights two errors when an attempt is made to modify a const object (bag::first sets my_index to 0).

```
void show(const bag & aBagOfInts)
{  // We should be able to pass bags by const reference
  cout << "\nThe bag: { ";
  aBagOfInts.first();  // ERROR: Cannot modify a const object
  while(! aBagOfInts.isDone())
  {
    cout << aBagOfInts.currentItem();
    aBagOfInts.next();  // ERROR: Cannot modify a const object
    if(! aBagOfInts.isDone())
      cout << ", ";
  }
  cout << " }" << endl;
}
```

The user should not care if bag::first and bag::next modify some private data member function. So to avoid these errors, both of these functions are actually implemented as const functions. A trick was then used to allow modification on a const object. If you are really interested, check out bag.cpp. You will see unfamiliar things unless you already know about pointers and the variable named this (see Chapters 14 and 15).

Another drawback to bag is that individual elements cannot be modified. If the bag class had a find function, you could search for an element and make changes, for example, deposit to a particular bankAccount. These drawbacks are addressed in Chapter 15.

3. There are many standard C++ container classes (vector, list, stack, queue) that are more versatile and robust than the bag class.

You do not need to use the bag class for any real work (nor should you). The bag class was presented here as a review of class definitions and vector processing. The bag class also introduced the notion of containers and iterators. And, by the way, other container libraries do have a bag class (Smalltalk, for example).

Programming Projects

11A A bag Object

Write a menu-driven program that allows the user to add as many elements as desired and to see the collection of elements at any time. Use the following dialogue to establish the prompts and choices:

```
Maintain a bag of 'strings':
Enter option: A)dd D)isplay Q)uit: d
The bag:
Enter option: A)dd D)isplay Q)uit: a
Enter string: First
Enter option: A)dd D)isplay Q)uit: A
Enter string: Second
Enter option: A)dd D)isplay Q)uit: d
The bag: First, Second
Enter option: A)dd D)isplay Q)uit: q
```

11B bag::occurrencesOf

Add a member function to the `bag` class that returns the number of occurrences of any element currently in the `bag`. The following code should produce the output shown:

```
bag bagOfInts;
bagOfInts.add(2);
bagOfInts.add(5);
bagOfInts.add(2);
bagOfInts.add(2);
cout << bagOfInts.occurrencesOf(2) << endl;   // Output: 3
cout << bagOfInts.occurrencesOf(9) << endl;   // Output: 0
```

11C bag::sort

Add a member function to the `bag` class that sorts the contained elements in ascending order. Write a precondition that `BAG_ELEMENT_TYPE` must define < (the less-than operator). Test your function with a collection of `int`, `string`, and `bankAccount` objects. Other classes (`libraryBook`, for example) cannot be sorted because < has no meaning (however, you could add the < operator to these classes after reading Chapter 18, "Operator Overloading"). Use this test driver:

```
// File name: test11c.cpp
#include <iostream>
using namespace std;
```

```
#include "compfun"  // For decimals

#include "baccount"  // Must include baccount before the typedef
typedef bankAccount BAG_ELEMENT_TYPE;
#include "bag"  // For the bag class

int main()
{
  bag account;
  account.add( bankAccount("Mellisa", 400) );
  account.add( bankAccount("Miguel", 200) );
  account.add( bankAccount("Bob", 300) );

  decimals(cout, 2);

  account.sort();

  bankAccount anAcct;
  for( account.first(); ! account.isDone(); account.next() )
  {
    anAcct = account.currentItem();        // Output:
    cout.width(8);                         // 300.00 Bob
    cout << anAcct.balance();              // 400.00 Mellisa
    cout << " " << anAcct.name() << endl;  // 200.00 Miguel
  }

  return 0;
}
```

11D bag::remove

Modify `bag::remove` so it removes an element while leaving all other elements in the same order. If the `bag` contains 3, 4, 5, 6, 7, a `remove(5)` message would change the `bag` to 3, 4, 6, 7.

```
bool bag::remove(BAG_ELEMENT_TYPE removalCandidate)
{
  int subscript = 0;

  // Sequentially search for removalCandidate
  while((subscript < my_size) && (my_item[subscript] != removalCandidate))
  {
    subscript++;
  }

  if(subscript == my_size)
  {  // The removalCandidate was not found
     return false;
```

```
  }
  else
  {  // Move all elements one vector location closer to 0

     // YOUR ANSWER

     return true;
  }
}
```

11E The `set` Class

Implement a `set` class that is similar to the `bag` class except that the collection may not have any duplicate elements. Write the `set.h` file to store the `set` class definition. Also, create a file named `set.cpp` to implement the member functions. The file on the disk named `set` will include both `set.h` and `set.cpp`. Make sure the `set::add` operation does not add duplicate elements. The class diagram to the right summarizes the list of operations that your `set` must have.

Test your `set` class with the following program, which should produce the output shown:

```
// File name: test11e.cpp
#include <iostream>
using namespace std;

typedef int SET_ELEMENT_TYPE;
#include "set"  // Includes set.h and set.cpp

display(const set & aSet)
{
 // YOU COMPLETE THIS FUNCTION
}

int main()
{ // Test drive the set class
  set aSet;
  aSet.remove(99);  // Try to remove an element
  cout << "size: " << aSet.size() << endl;
  cout << "capacity: " << aSet.capacity() << endl;

  cout << "The empty set: ";
  // ITERATE OVER THE SET TO SHOW IT
  // YOU WRITE THE CODE

  aSet.add(7);
  aSet.add(9);
```

set
add(item)
bool remove(item)
int capacity()
int size()
bool isEmpty()
first()
next()
itemType currentItem()
bool isDone()
vector <items>
int my_size

```
  aSet.add(10);
  aSet.add(10);
  aSet.add(8);
  aSet.add(9);
  aSet.remove(7);  // Remove an existing element
  aSet.remove(12);  // Try to remove a nonexistent element
  cout << "size: " << aSet.size() << endl;
  cout << "capacity: " << aSet.capacity() << endl;

  cout << "The set: ";
  // ITERATE OVER THE SET TO SHOW IT; YOU WRITE THE CODE

  return 0;
}
```

Output

```
size: 0
capacity: 16
The empty set:
size: 3
capacity: 16
The set: 9, 10, 8
```

Chapter Twelve

Object-Oriented Software Development

Analysis and Design

Summing Up

You have seen several class definitions, modified some classes, implemented class member functions (in programming projects for Chapters 6 through 11), and perhaps completely implemented a few classes (in programming project 8H, "The `elevator` Class"; 10K, "The `stats` Class"; or 11E, "The `set` Class"). All of these previous activities relate to the implementation of classes.

Coming Up

This chapter discusses another facet of the object-oriented paradigm—the analysis and design of a system with objects as the main building blocks.

You will study an object-oriented software development strategy in the context of a real-world problem—building a jukebox system for a campus student center. The analysis in this chapter will help the programming team design the class definitions and implement the member functions in Chapter 13. After studying this chapter, you will be able to

* identify classes that model a solution to a problem
* assign responsibilities to classes
* use Component/Responsibility/Helper cards to aid analysis and design
* understand the need for analysis and design before implementation

Analysis and design projects to reinforce object-oriented development

12.1 Object-Oriented Analysis

So far, we have only considered individual classes and some low-level design issues, such as where the data members should go in a C++ class, why constructors are needed, and member function implementations. However, before individual classes are designed and implemented, they are first recognized as part of some larger software system.

This section introduces an object-oriented design (OOD) methodology in the context of a real-world problem—the cashless jukebox. The strategy is based on the responsibility-driven design methodology of Wirfs-Brock, Wilkerson, and Wiener [Wirfs-Brock 90].

Another major component of object-oriented software development is the Component/Responsibility/Collaborator (CRC) card introduced by Kent Beck and Ward Cunningham [Beck/Cunningham 89]. This simple and effective tool consists of a set of 3-by-5-inch index cards. CRC cards were first used to help people understand object technology. Developers employ them to develop large-scale, object-oriented systems. Because the word *collaborator* has caused confusion, CRC cards will henceforth be referred to as Component/Responsibility/Helper (CRH) cards.

The first step in object-oriented analysis involves identification of the *key abstractions*—the major classes. The system is modeled as a set of classes, each with its own responsibilities. You will see how team members "become" an object through role playing. Playing the roles of the objects helps the team identify the responsibilities of each while determining the relationships between them. Role playing helps the team understand the problem, model a solution, and iron out the rough spots early in development, when it is relatively cheap and easy to do so.

Self-Check

To warm up to an object-oriented view of systems, first answer each of the following "Pre-Check" questions. Look at the answer for each before going on to the next. These "Pre-Check" questions are intended to get you to understand the essentials of planning the design of some larger systems.

12-1 On one piece of paper, sketch the design of a small one-branch bank such that someone unfamiliar with the system would understand the major components, the key purpose of each, and any interaction between those components.

12-2 On one piece of paper, sketch the design of a small one-branch library such that someone unfamiliar with the system would understand the major components, the key purpose of each, and any interaction between those components.

12.1.1 The Problem Specification

In the spring of 1997, the author suggested building a CD music jukebox using a 200-capacity compact-disc player. Sophomore Ed Slatt, a computer engineering major, guaranteed that he would figure some way to control that CD player from a computer. By the end of the semester, Ed had a prototype infrared remote (IR) unit working. He used a circuit design that Chris Dodge has made available on the Web.[1] His `IRDEV` class and some assembler code were wrapped up in a `cdPlayer` class. This allowed messages like these that play the fifth track on the CD in the third tray of a seven-disc CD player:

```
// Construct an object that can send signals to a real CD player
cdPlayer myCdPlayer;

// Play the fifth track in the third tray of the physical CD player
myCdPlayer.play(3, 5);
```

Ed then went on to pursue his computer engineering degree.

In the fall of 1997, several students asked the same author to provide an honors option for the first course in the computer science major. They decided to build the jukebox. The events you are about to read are based on this true story. The following problem statement begins the project:

1. At the time of this writing, Chris Dodge has the information located at this URL: **http://www.ee.washington.edu/eeca/circuits/PCIR/Welcome.html**

PROBLEM STATEMENT FOR THE CASHLESS JUKEBOX

The Student Affairs office has decided to put some new-found activity fee funds toward a music jukebox in the student center. The jukebox will allow a student to play individual songs. No money will be required. Instead, a student will swipe a magnetic student ID card through a card reader. Students will each be allowed to play up to 1,500 minutes worth of "free" jukebox music in their academic careers at the school, but never more than two selections on any given date. A student may select a CD from the available collection of CDs and then an individual song from that CD. Students may not play entire CDs.

This project is now assigned to a team that includes Blaine, Director of Student Affairs. Blaine is playing the role of the *domain expert*—the person who knows about student policies. His office is in the student center, not far from where the jukebox might be installed. Blaine also represents the *client*—the one with the money. The team will also have an *object expert*—Chelsea—to help guide the team though this, their first try at object-oriented software development. Chelsea's experience and knowledge of object-oriented design heuristics will likely help the team make better design decisions. The team has two chemical engineering majors—Jessica and Jason—who are taking an honors option in the middle of a first programming course. Also on the team are Matt, a computer engineering major, and Steve, an engineering science major, who are both taking the introductory course. The team also has Charlie, a second-year computer science major who promised to help Matt implement the jukebox (see Chapter 13). Charlie has more programming experience than any of the other team members. The team is completed by Misty, who is deciding between a math or a computer science career.

At the first meeting, the team decides to hammer out an idea of what this cashless jukebox should be able to do. During analysis, the team will be concerned with *what* the system must do. The team will not worry too much over the *how*. During analysis, the terminology and activities relate to those who requested the software. The analysts should be able to communicate their thoughts with those who requested the software. The analyst must also

- work with the clients to refine requirements
- challenge the requirements
- probe for missing information

12.1.2 The Goal of the Analysis Phase

The goal of the analysis phase is to create an abstract model in the vocabulary of the client (the Student Affairs office, in this case). This can be accomplished by way of the following three-step strategy:

1. Identify classes that model (shape) the system as a natural and sensible set of abstractions.
2. Determine the purpose, or main responsibility, of each class. The responsibilities of a class are what an instance of the class must be able to do (member functions) and what it must know about itself (data members).
3. Determine the helper classes for each. To help complete its responsibilities, a class typically delegates responsibility to one or more other objects. These are called *helpers.*

Before the team begins to analyze the problem, Chelsea tells them that software developers do not immediately find all classes. It is also unlikely that all responsibilities will be discovered in the first pass. Some of the helper classes may also be missed. It is perfectly acceptable to change the list and names of the classes that shape the solution as the problem is considered over time. Also, new classes may be required when moving into the design and implementation phases.

For now, don't worry about creating the perfect model. There are many false starts. And because analysis sometimes recognizes uncertainty in a problem statement, there may be some new concerns that need to be settled. The team will be trying to understand the requested software system at the level of those requesting the software.

Also realize that there is rarely one true correct best design. Relax. Tell yourself now that all designs are valid. So don't be afraid to make mistakes. It is much easier to change things during analysis and design than after the system has been deployed.

12.1.3 Identification of Classes that Model the Solution

The first goal, or deliverable, in object-oriented software development is a set of classes that potentially model the system. Each class will be assigned its major responsibility.

One simple tool for getting started is to write down all the reasonable nouns and noun phrases in the problem statement. Consider these as potential classes representing part of the solution. You may also record potential classes even if they were not written as nouns in the problem statement. For example, someone on the team with expertise in the problem area may suggest useful classes due to his or her understanding of the domain—in this case, students and music. Potential classes may come from words that are spoken while describing the system or questioning the problem statement. In summary, useful classes for modeling the system may come from sources such as these:

* the problem statement
* an understanding of the problem domain (knowledge of the system that the problem statement may have missed or taken for granted)
* the words floating around in the air during analysis of the problem

And while considering potential classes, consider the following object-oriented design heuristic:

OBJECT-ORIENTED DESIGN HEURISTIC 12.1 (RIEL'S 3.6)

Model the real world whenever possible.

This design heuristic leads to more understandable software. It not only helps during analysis, but also during maintenance when someone unfamiliar with the system must fix a bug, add an enhancement, or update the software to match real-world changes.

The team established the following list of noun phrases from the problem statement (redundant entries were not recorded).

NOUN PHRASES—ALL NOUNS IN THE PROBLEM STATEMENT

Student Affairs office	minutes	student ID card	student
activity fee funds	date	academic careers	money
music jukebox	card reader	student center	CD
collection of CDs	selection	jukebox music	song

The noun phrases of a problem statement fall into three categories that indicate their potential viability as classes to model a solution.

1. somewhat sure
2. not sure
3. should not be considered—irrelevant or has the propensity to muddle

There are many guidelines intended to help us discover useful classes. One guideline has already been used above—eliminate redundant entries. There was no useful purpose for writing down "student" three times, for example. Only consider the noun phrases that have meaning in the realm of the system. The activity fee funds provide the money to pay for the jukebox; however, that money will not be part of the design.

The following set of noun phrases represents a first attempt to identify the key abstractions in the problem statement (irrelevant nouns omitted).

POTENTIAL CLASSES—A FIRST PASS AT FINDING KEY ABSTRACTIONS

Somewhat Sure	Not Sure
jukebox	activity fee funds
student	money
song	jukebox music
card reader	date
student ID card	
CD	
collection of CDs	

Self-Check

12-3 Write a list of potential classes after reading the following problem statement: (*Note:* This problem specification will be used in later self-check questions.)

The college library has requested a system that supports a small set of library operations. Students may borrow books, return those borrowed books, and pay fees. The late fee and due date have been established as follows:

	Late Fee	Borrowing Period
Books:	$0.50 per day	14 days

The due date is set when a borrowed item is checked out. A student may borrow only seven books. Any student with seven books checked out may not borrow anything more.

The team considers each potential class in more detail for help in understanding the system.

12.1.3.1 Jukebox? YES, coordinates all activities

The programmers on the team feel that `jukeBox` seems an appropriate name for the class that will be responsible for coordinating activities such as handling requests from the users of this system. There might be one instance of `jukeBox` in the program that gets things going and keeps things going.

12.1.3.2 Student? YES, maintains student information

It is suggested that a class named `student` will prove itself a useful abstraction for modeling the users. After all, students will be involved in playing music. Chelsea advises the team to distinguish between the human version of the student that approaches the jukebox with a student ID card and the software model of that student stored inside the computer. A friendly argument ensues. Although no one seems to recognize it at first, the confusion is due to the name `student`. Steve suggests that the team employ the name "user" to indicate the physical student that uses the jukebox. The programmers agree to keep `student` as the name of the class that models that physical real-world user. `student` is the software equivalent of "user."

12.1.3.3 Song? NO; Track? YES, one of the tracks on a CD

Because students are allowed a certain amount of play time in minutes, it appears that `song` would be a useful class. Each `song` object should know its playing time in minutes and seconds along with its title. Jason and Jessica see this as an instance of the State Object pattern they learned about earlier in their first computer science course.

Matt changes the subject by claiming that there are some CDs that put two songs into one track. Other CDs have some blank air time at the end. Blaine observes, "Rock and roll has changed since I was young." He can't believe what he is hearing. Additionally, Charlie relates that he has a Beethoven CD where one "song" (symphony, actually) is distributed over several tracks. Each track is a movement—the first movement, the second movement, and so on.

Chelsea indicates that the team can better communicate the design if the name is changed to `track`. The user will select a `track` from a CD. That sounds better.

12.1.3.4 Card reader? YES, the object used to read the magnetic student ID cards

The card reader is one of several physical objects in the cashless jukebox. Should it be a class? No one is sure. Ed suggests that magnetic card readers are easy to come by. It may be a useful abstraction. After a quick check on the Web, Jessica produces this picture of a combination keyboard and magnetic card reader to solidify the concept of a card reader.

Figure 12.1. *Magnetic card reader keyboard*

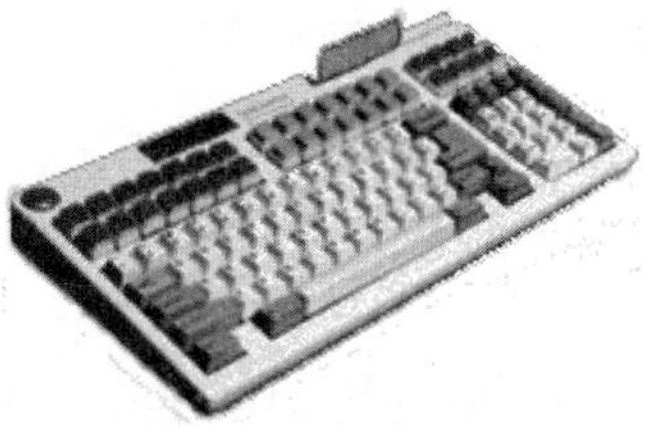

Picture courtesy of B & C Data Systems, Gorham, Maine

Although the physical card reader exists, it will still be useful to have a software abstraction for this physical entity—analogous to the user/`student` relationship. The team decides to use the class name `cardReader` for the object that gets input from magnetic ID cards.

12.1.3.5 Student ID card? NO, the object inserted into the magnetic card reader

The student ID card is one of several physical objects in the cashless jukebox. However, the team decides it is "outside" the system. Although it allows students to gain access to the jukebox, it need not be modeled. It is already done. Every student has a student ID card.

Chelsea congratulates the team as she tells them about a widely accepted object-oriented design heuristic:

Object-Oriented Design Heuristic 12.2

Eliminate classes that are outside the system.

According to Arthur Riel [Riel 95], the hallmark of such a class is one whose only importance to the system is the data contained in it. While the student identification number might be of great importance, the system should not care whether the ID number was read from a swiped magnetic ID card, typed in at the keyboard, or "if a squirrel arrived carrying it in his mouth."

12.1.3.6 CD? YES, each `CD` object stores a collection of `tracks`

Someone on the team doesn't agree that `CD` should be a key abstraction. Jason, one of the computer science majors, chimes in and suggests, "This is not a problem, I can visualize a `CD` object as a `vector` of `tracks`." Blaine asks, "What is a vector?" Chelsea tries to rectify unfamiliar and differing terminology with some anthropomorphic object-speak: "A `CD` is responsible for knowing what `tracks` it has." Blaine complains that Chelsea is trying to give human qualities to the CD. Jessica responds that this is precisely what anthropomorphism means. She also heard in her CmpSc class that giving human qualities to objects happens quite often during object-oriented software development. It really helps.

Steve still has a problem with the singularity of a CD and a song: "Certainly the system must maintain many `CD` objects, each of which may store many songs. How can we talk about just one class when there are many songs on so many CDs?" Jason retorts that one class is used to create many instances, or objects. And right now, the team should concentrate on identifying classes to model the real-world components that are part of a jukebox.

Steve agrees that there should be more than one CD for students to choose. Jason relates how they have just learned about two different container classes for storing collections of objects—`vectors` and `bags`. "Bags and vectors?" wonders Blaine. Jessica tells Blaine that he needn't worry about these implementation details and reminds Jason that the programming team can choose the appropriate container class later. Instead, Jessica introduces the notion of a class that is responsible for storing all the CDs. Steve asks if we could rename this `cdCollection`. The team unanimously approves.

12.1.3.7 Collection of CDs? YES, all CDs that could be listened to

Jason is thinking that behind the public interface of the `cdCollection` class, the data members may include a `vector` of `CD` objects and the number of CDs physically stored in the CD player. Matt suggests that someone will have to make sure the software version is always in sync with the physical CD collection. Chelsea encourages the team to postpone these implementation details for now.

12.1.4 Any Other Classes?

Steve and Matt launch into a discussion about who is allowed to play a track. Shouldn't a collection of students also be maintained? Jason agrees, but he complains it may be difficult to keep a collection of all valid students. Should the jukebox allow anyone in the world with a magnetic ID card to play a track? How might the system prevent unauthorized access? It appears certain that some part of the cashless jukebox will have to maintain a collection of students. Although the noun phrase "collection of students" does not exist in the problem statement, Jessica says that it helps her to think of a `studentCollection` class that is responsible for maintaining the time credit available for each student. Chelsea recommends the team go with their instincts and add a `studentCollection` class to the design.

12.1.4.1 `studentCollection` stores a list of students who could select songs

Of the original set of potential classes, all but one survived the first cut at modeling the system. Two new key abstractions (classes) were added. One is for storing the collection of CDs. The other maintains the list of students who are allowed to use the jukebox. However, an uneasy feeling pervades the team. Misty thinks there is something missing. The team reviews the classes. Ed suggests that there must be some object that actually plays the selected song.

Jessica suggests a solution. The team could purchase an old jukebox and modify it to allow card swipes. However, this would not prevent students from playing more than two songs on any given date. Ed says that a computer could be hooked up to the jukebox. Then the computer would be responsible for reading student ID cards and sending play messages to the physical jukebox. The physical jukebox has the responsibility of selecting the physical CD and playing the correct track. Commercially available jukeboxes do this. Ed states that another major advantage derives from the fact that jukeboxes also have built-in stereo systems. This could save money. Blaine reminds Steve that the student center already has a potent stereo system. Any money saved on this project could be funneled back into other student projects. So, as is done in the world of business, a decision must be made that relates to the bottom line.

Chelsea investigates on the Internet and finds a place to purchase a CD jukebox that holds 50 CDs. It looks very cool. However, it lists for $4,500. And this does not include the CDs. However, according to the Wurlitzer Jukebox Co. representative, they could probably modify their jukebox to allow magnetic ID card input.

FIGURE 12.2. *The Wurlitzer "One More Time" CD Jukebox*

Picture courtesy of Wurlitzer Jukebox Co., Pittsburgh, Pennsylvania

The team considers cost alternatives. Matt informs the team that the computer department has some personal computer components sitting around gathering dust. He suggests that for little or no money, he could put together a computer capable of implementing the appropriate classes. A card reader keyboard would have to be purchased no matter what.

Charlie suggests that a computer could be connected to a 200- or 300-disc CD player. The CD player in turn could easily be connected to the existing student center stereo system. Chelsea reminds the team, "Ed already did this." The team considers adding another object to model the system—a compact-disc player.

12.1.4.2 `cdPlayer` plays any track from any CD

The compact-disc player is yet another physical object in the cashless jukebox. But should it be a class? After all, several electronic stereo manufacturers already implement this physical device. Chelsea suggests the team try to understand the system using a common vocabulary. A CD player appears to be a very important part of the solution. The implementation would come later. The team decides to have a `cdPlayer` class to represent the responsibilities of this "real" object—analogous to the `student` and `cardReader` classes, which represent other real objects. The actual CD player has not been purchased yet. Jessica pulls a picture off the Web to help bring a more concrete feel to these abstractions.

Figure 12.3. *Sony CDP-CX200 CD player*

Picture courtesy of Sony Electronics Inc.

Now that the team has added a `cdPlayer` class, Misty suggests the team consider a stereo system class.

The stereo system certainly is part of the entire system. It is yet another one of those essential physical components. Chelsea asserts that we could consider the stereo system as part of the cashless jukebox. Its major responsibility is to take the output from the CD player and produce audible sounds at the right treble, bass, and volume settings. However, it is reasonable to set boundaries around the system under development. The team decides that sending a song selection message to `cdPlayer` represents such a boundary. The prebuilt electronic components will then take over and perform their well-defined responsibilities. Chelsea excitedly shouts out, "This is reuse!" The `cdPlayer` class is the interface to the music-generating part of this system. The team agrees that the stereo system is on the other side of the CD player, well outside the system being designed.

12.1.4.3 Stereo system? NO, amplifies the music

The team feels as though they have captured many key abstractions for this application. They have the beginning of a framework for analyzing the problem in more detail. There is a sense that the primary responsibility of each class has been recognized—or at least implied. Chelsea suggests that the class names be documented along with their major responsibilities.

Before splitting for pizza, the team documents the classes discovered during analysis with a sketch that includes

1. the class names
2. the primary responsibility of each class

3. arrows indicating possible message sends to helper classes
4. the boundaries of the software abstractions under development

FIGURE 12.4. *Analysis sketch of major classes that model a cashless jukebox (subject to change)*

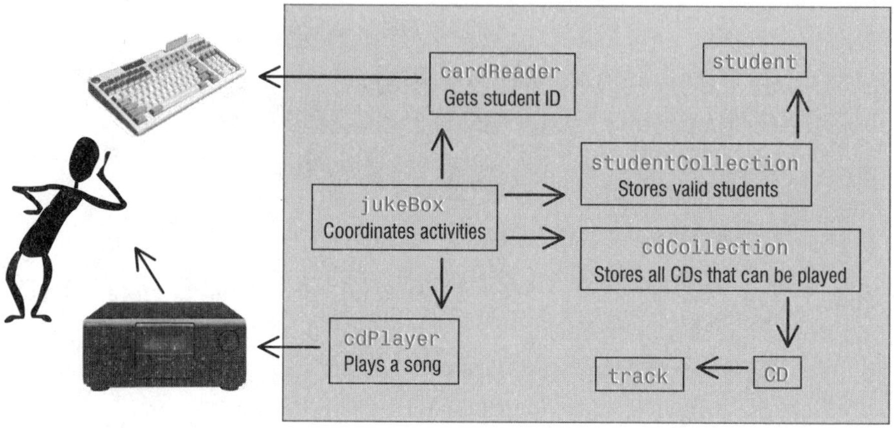

Chelsea congratulates the team again. The design looks good. Out of the original eight noun phrases, one was eliminated (student ID card). The `studentCollection` class was discovered as the result of someone knowing something about collections of data and the necessity for searching for a particular student. Chelsea reports that such changes are typical. Writing the noun phrases is a tool to help find classes that effectively model the solution. It doesn't mean all nouns must become classes. It doesn't pretend to find them all. Charlie suggests that some of these classes may never even get implemented. Chelsea says that other new classes may be discovered as the team proceeds with role playing.

Self-Check

12-4 Reconsider the key abstractions (classes) for representing the college library. (See Self-Check 12-3.) Draw a picture like Figure 12.4 above that does the following:

1. lists all the classes that reasonably model the system
2. lists the major responsibility of each class
3. marks the boundary of the system—it's okay to show entities that are outside the system

12.2 Role Playing and CRH Card Development

The primary responsibility of each class has now been identified. The team will now set about the task of identifying and recording other responsibilities. Responsibility-driven design emphasizes identifying responsibilities and assigning those responsibilities to the most appropriate class. Chelsea, the object expert, suggests that the team should often ask questions like this:

- What is this class responsible for?
- What class is responsible for a particular action (member function) or specific knowledge (data member)?

The team will also be identifying helpers. These are classes that one class needs to help carry out its responsibility. The object-oriented approach views the running solution as a collection of objects in which each object does its own thing for the good of the whole. There should not be any all-powerful class that does everything.

The team should try to answer questions such as: What are the other responsibilities needed to model the solution? Which class should take on this particular responsibility? and What classes help another class fulfill its responsibility? Responsibilities convey the purpose of a class and its role in the system. These questions are more easily addressed if the team remembers that each instance of a class will be responsible for

1. the knowledge that any object of the class must maintain, and
2. the actions that any object of the class can perform.

The team should always be prepared to ask these two questions:

1. What should any object of the class know (knowledge)?
2. What should any object of the class be able to do (action)?

"It's that anthropomorphism thing again," moans Blaine, the domain expert from the Student Affairs office.

Assigning a responsibility to a class means that every instance of that class will have the same responsibility. This is true when there are many instances of the class. There will be many `CD` and `student` objects for example. It is also true when there may be only one instance of the class—`jukeBox` and `cdCollection` for example. Later on, during design and implementation, the actions may become public member functions of a class. The knowledge may become data members.

The responsibilities may be identified from several sources such as:

- the problem statement (specification)

- the classes
- the ideas that float around the room, especially during role playing

These responsibilities must eventually be assigned to the appropriate class, either to the classes already identified or to new classes if necessary. For example, whose responsibility is it to play one particular song? This responsibility might be shared between several classes. `jukeBox` may send a message to `studentCollection` to find out whether or not a user may select a song. `jukeBox` cannot do this by itself—it needs help from `studentCollection` and `student`. In situations like this, when class A needs the help of class B, class B is said to be a helper of class A.

The object expert suggests that the team begin to assign responsibilities to classes using the simple tool of role playing. During role playing, each team member assumes the role of a class to see what happens when a certain situation arises; for example, what happens when a certain student wants to select a certain track. But before this is done, the object expert suggests that the team use another simple low-cost tool for capturing the decisions made during role playing.

12.2.1 CRH Cards

At this point, Chelsea writes the heading "Class:" at the top of a 3-by-5-inch index card. Under this, she also writes the column headings "Responsibilities:" and "Helpers:". Immediately, an inexpensive index card has metamorphosed into a Component/Responsibility/Helper (CRH) card. A CRH card records a class name, the responsibilities of the class, and the other classes required to help the class fulfill those responsibilities—the helpers. Here is an example CRH card with some possible responsibilities and helpers as it may appear much later in the software development phase.

FIGURE 12.5. *CRH card showing what `cdCollection` might develop into*

Class: `cdCollection`	
Responsibilities:	**Helpers:**
know all CDs	`vector` of CDs
retrieve a CD	
`addNewCD(CD aCD, int trayNumber)`	
`removeCD(int trayNumber)`	
`CD getCD(int trayNumber)`	

Although this CRH card for the `cdCollection` class contains return types and arguments, CRH cards typically list only the member function names (action responsibilities). Conversely, the CRH card might well indeed say "know all CDs" (knowledge responsibility). Knowledge responsibilities may later get turned into private data members such as `vector<CD> my_cds;`.

The responsibilities are what the object must be able to do and what the object must know. These responsibilities are written down on the front of the card under the heading "Responsibilities:". However, the previous CRH card represents design decisions yet to be made. It is only a preview of what it might look like.

Some CRH card practitioners use the backs of the CRH cards for recording different types of information. Chelsea suggests the team write down the class name along with its major responsibility on the back of the 3-by-5-inch index cards. Here is the result, using the design shown earlier.

FIGURE 12.6

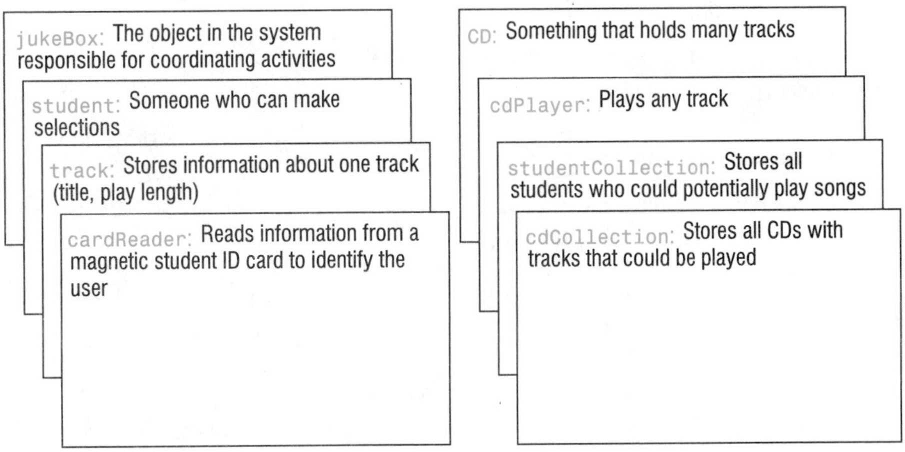

Each team member takes one or two of these CRH cards to "become" the class. The holder of each card will play the role of that class.

12.2.2 Role Playing

Each team member has now assumed the role of at least one class (one team member could role play several classes if necessary). Chelsea suggests that the team role play a scenario to see how one instance of a class could interact with instances of other classes. Jessica wants to know, "What is a scenario?" Chelsea responds, "A scenario is the answer to the question, What happens when . . . ?" Steve suggests the team role play the following scenario.

12.2.2.1 Scenario 1: "What happens when a student wants to select a track?"

The first thing to do is decide which object begins the scenario. Each team member looks on his or her CRH card to see who will start. The team member playing the role of `jukeBox` states, "I'm playing the role of the object responsible for coordinating activities, so I guess I'll start."

`jukeBox`: I'm playing the role of the jukebox so I'll start this scenario. Hey `cardReader`, has a user swiped a card?

`cardReader`: No.

`jukeBox`: Hmmm. Okay, `cardReader`, has a student swiped a card?

`cardReader`: No.

`jukeBox`: Hey, how often do I have to do this? I suppose I'll have to wait for a user.

The object expert suggests that Jason (`jukeBox`) add a `waitForUser` responsibility to his card.

`jukeBox`: Okay, I'm waiting for a user. Waiting, waiting, waiting . . .

`cardReader`: Okay, `jukeBox`, a user just swiped a card. Here is all the information on that magnetic strip ID card.

`jukeBox`: Thanks, `cardReader`, but I don't know what to do with all of this stuff. Which part of the input uniquely identifies the student?

The team wonders what information is recorded on a magnetic student identification card. Is there a name, a student ID number, the amount of money left in the student's food service balance, an address? Since no one knows for sure, perhaps `cardReader` could take on the responsibility for getting the unique student identification number of the user holding the magnetic card just swiped.

`cardReader`: Okay, I'll add `getStudentID` to my list of responsibilities.

`jukeBox`: Thanks, `cardReader`. By the way, although I first believed you weren't necessary as a class, I do believe so now. You not only communicate with the physical card reader, you also have access to the entire student ID card so you can return the information I seek—the student ID number. You just made my life simpler. I don't need to know what kind of physical card reader is out there, nor do I have to know details such as the format of the magnetic card being swiped. Now that I have the student ID number, I need to verify that the user can select a song.

`studentCollection`: Well, since it is my responsibility to store the collection of student objects, let me check to see if there is a student here with that ID. Yes, here is the `student` object associated with the student ID number you passed to me. I will add a responsibility to the front of my CRH card: `getStudent`.

`jukeBox`: Now that I know the user is valid, I suppose we should let the user select a song, I mean `track`. Okay, whose responsibility is it to maintain the list of all tracks on all CDs?

`cdCollection`: That's me! What do you want?

`jukeBox`: I'd like the collection of all CDs.

`cdCollection`: Well, all you have to do is ask. I've been here all along.

`jukeBox`: Okay, I now know I always have access to `cdCollection`. What do I do with you now?

There is a pause. No one knows. Should `jukeBox` display the CD choices to the user and then, based on the CD selection, show the tracks? This would mean that `jukeBox` will have much more to do (Jason and Jessica are thinking about all those loops). Chelsea suggests that it seems like some other object should be responsible for getting this information from the user. `jukeBox` coordinates activities; it can delegate authority to other classes. It does not have to do everything.

Chelsea points out that there are many object-oriented designers who use the following design heuristic when confronted with similar design decisions:

Object-Oriented Design Heuristic 12.3

Avoid all-powerful (omnipotent) classes.

It is undesirable to have a class that does everything, or even too much. The by-product of assigning too much responsibility is a complicated class that can be difficult to implement and maintain after deployment into the student center. Chelsea describes another related object-oriented design heuristic that helps software developers attain well-designed object-oriented systems:

OBJECT-ORIENTED DESIGN HEURISTIC 12.4 (RIEL'S 3.1)

Distribute system intelligence among the classes as evenly as possible. The top-level classes in a design should share the work uniformly.

Chelsea encourages the team to try to evenly distribute the work amongst the analysis classes that are currently being role played. The benefit is a more easily understood system. The design will be more easily communicated to the client and the programmers that will implement the design. It will be more easily understood when the inevitable bugs have to be fixed or enhancements are to be made.

`jukeBox`: Let me summarize: I won't try to get the user's track selection. I know that I will somehow have access to the CD collection, but what has to happen now? What should I do next to get the track?

Chelsea offers a suggestion: "A good object-oriented system has objects that delegate responsibilities to other objects. This is not about producing lazy objects. This is about understandable systems. Some other object could get the user selection." "But who?" asks Jason.

Chelsea proposes that to keep things simple, it might be appropriate to add a new class to interface with the user. The major responsibility would be `getTrack`. The team's computer engineer, Matt, and the computer science major Charlie, who are now quite familiar with interactive input and output, suggest that with a new `trackSelector` class, `jukeBox` need not worry about how to get output to and input from the user. It could come from the keyboard; from a touch screen; or through a graphical user interface for the Mac, a graphical user interface for a WinTel machine, a graphical user interface for a Unix or Linux system, or whatever. The `jukeBox` role player suggests backing up one step and finishing the current scenario with a new `trackSelector` class, which has the major responsibility of communicating with the user. `trackSelector` will get the user's selection.

12.2.2.2 `trackSelector`, a new class added to get student selections

`jukeBox`: Okay, I now have access to the collection of all CDs. I'll pass it to `trackSelector`. You tell me what track the user wants to hear.

`trackSelector`: Okay, I'll offer the options to the user and let him or her decide. Hey, what options are there? I'm in control here, but I still don't know how to get the user's selection.

`cdCollection`: I hold the collection of CDs, so it seems like I should have some mechanism to allow access to the CDs and all tracks on the CDs. Then you could look at every CD in my collection and show the artist and title, perhaps by artist name in alphabetic order. Once the CD is selected, you could iterate over all the tracks available on that CD.

`CD`: I think I can help. Those knowledge responsibilities are listed on my CRH card (know all tracks). However, I don't know how to reveal individual tracks. I will add that responsibility: "allow references to individual tracks."

"Yes, you could have a `vector` of `tracks` that are accessible with the subscript operator," asserts Jason. Chelsea warns Jason to avoid tying in implementation details at this point. He can decide later. For now it seems `cdCollection` must allow references to individual CDs and each CD must allow references to individual tracks. "Do you both have that responsibility on your individual CRH cards?" she asks.

`cdCollection`: No, I'll add the responsibility of allowing access to all CDs now. In fact, it seems like I will have to be able to add new CDs and delete others as the music in the physical CD jukebox changes. So I'll also add `addCD` and `removeCD`.

`CD`: I didn't list those responsibilities either, but I'll add them now. And in addition to knowing my play time, I could also be responsible for knowing my CD number and my track locations. This is all `cdPlayer` would need to know in order to play any track.

`trackSelector`: Look, you guys, if you are done for now, I'd like to just say that I can get the track selected by the user. Let's continue the scenario. Okay, `jukeBox`, here is the track selected by the user. I'll write the responsibility `getTrack` on my CRH card.

`jukeBox`: Thanks, `trackSelector`. Now I need to determine whether or not the current student can play the selected track. Who is responsible for knowing the play time of any track?

`track`: It seems like I should be responsible for knowing the duration of my track. For example, it might take 3 minutes and 34 seconds to be completely played. I'll add the operation "know play time" to my CRH card along with the responsibility to know the CD number and what track number I am.

"Whoooooaaaaa, this is confusing!" proclaims Blaine, the domain expert. "Why does `jukeBox` need to know the duration of the track?" Jessica suggests that some object must be made responsible for determining whether or not this particular student can play this particular song. Chelsea suggests that the team continue role playing until this scenario reaches some logical conclusion.

`jukeBox`: Okay, now I should check to make sure the student is able to select this track before telling `cdPlayer` to play it. I seem to remember I cannot simply play a track without checking on a few things. I know the current student and the selected track. What do I do now?

The team has stalled. They wonder what must be done next. Why did `jukeBox` need to know the student in the first place? Misty reminds the team that jukebox play time is reserved for this school's valid students only. Therefore `jukeBox` had to ask `studentCollection` to validate the user first. Well actually, `studentCollection` has that responsibility. The verification was done earlier in this scenario (even if it is not exactly clear yet how it was done). Additionally, as stated in the problem statement, a student must have enough time credit, and may not play more than two tracks on the same date. The role player of `track` has an idea. He suggests that the jukebox ask the track for its play time.

12.2.2.3 Alternative 1

`jukeBox`: So tell me, `track`, how many minutes and seconds do you require to be played?

`track`: 3 minutes and 34 seconds.

`jukeBox`: `student`, do you have at least 3 minutes and 34 seconds credit?

`student`: I'll be responsible for maintaining my remaining time credit (he adds this to his CRH card), so I can answer that. Yes, I have enough credit.

`jukeBox`: `student`, have you played fewer than two tracks on this date?

`student`: Yes, I have not played two tracks today.

`jukeBox`: Okay, now we can play the track. Here it is, `cdPlayer`.

`cdPlayer`: Okay, `jukeBox`, I would be willing to tell the physical CD player to play this track. Actually, I have no idea how I am going to do that, but I'll write a `playTrack` responsibility on my CRH card for now as long as you send me the track to be played during a `playTrack` message.

This scenario has now reached a logical conclusion. However, the team feels that `jukeBox` already has enough responsibilities. "Why should I have to figure out if the student can play the selected track?" asks the member role playing `jukeBox`.

Chelsea suggests that they follow their instincts and try to distribute system intelligence as evenly as possible—a principle of good object-oriented design. Another heuristic for good design is avoid all-powerful classes. This suggests that in a good design, `jukeBox` might not be the best class for determining whether or not a student can play a track. Perhaps some other class should have that responsibility. The person playing `student` thinks it is appropriate to let the `student` object be responsible for figuring out if its human equivalent is allowed to play the selected track.

12.2.2.4 Alternative 2

`jukeBox`: `student`, can you play this track?

`student`: I feel as though I should be responsible for maintaining my own time credit. It seems appropriate that I should also know how many tracks I've played today. So I should be able to do some simple calculations to give you the answer you seek. Yes, `jukeBox`, I can play the track you sent me. I'll add these responsibilities to my CRH card:

- know how much time credit I have left
- know how many tracks I've played on this date
- respond to a message like `student::canSelect(currentTrack)`

The team wonders which alternative is better. One way to assess the design is to ask what feels better. Alternative 2 feels better somehow. Wouldn't it be nice if there were some object-oriented design heuristics to make us feel better about feeling better?

Well, it turns out that the first alternative has a higher degree of *coupling,* which means more messages are sent from `jukeBox` to `student`. There were two different messages versus the single message of the second alternative (`canSelect`). Chelsea adds this heuristic to the repertoire:

Object-Oriented Design Heuristic 12.5

Minimize the number of messages between a class and its helper.

Additionally, the second alternative has better cohesion. This means that the two knowledge responsibilities necessary to answer a `canSelect` message are closely related.

The Responsibilities of Each `student`

1. know how much time credit I have
2. know how many tracks I've played on this date

Additionally, the first alternative requires `jukeBox` to know about the internal state of the track and the internal state of `student`. This is a violation of Object-Oriented Design Heuristic 6.1, "All data should be hidden within its class." In conclusion, the second alternative delegates responsibility to the more appropriate class.

Chelsea (the object expert) verifies that the team member holding the `student` card should add `canSelect` as a responsibility. The team feels this scenario has reached its logical conclusion.

Self-Check

12-5 Summarize the algorithm that lets one user make one selection. You may send any message that you desire to any object you desire. Use any of the objects shown next as if the classes were already implemented. Add any message you like.

You are currently designing. Pretend you will be passing off your CRH cards and the entire algorithm to another programmer who will have to make it all work according to your design.

```
student currentStudent;
track currentSelection;
cardReader myCardReader;
cdCollection myCdCollection;
studentCollection myStudentCollection;
trackSelector myTrackSelector;
cdPlayer myCdPlayer;
```

There are many other possible scenarios. For instance, what if the student does not exist in `studentCollection`? What should happen? Or what if a student does not have enough credit or has already selected two tracks?

12.2.2.5 Scenario 2: "What happens when a student who has already played two tracks on this date tries to select a third track?"

`jukeBox`: Let us skip up to the point where I send a `canSelect` message.

`student`: No, I can't select a track.

`jukeBox`: I could simply send an appropriate message to the user.

So far, so good. However, Steve, who is holding the `cdPlayer` card, wonders when and how a track ever actually gets played by the physical CD player so it can be enjoyed over the stereo system. It seems as if `cdPlayer` needs some stimulus. The team has questions. Which class is responsible for sending the message that plays a track? And what happens when another track is already playing? If there are many tracks to be played, when and how will more than one track be played? Will the CD player be able to tell anyone when a track has finished? Misty asks, "Who is role playing the play list?" The team members check the lists of classes and to their dismay, discover that there is no `playList` class.

Chelsea comforts the team. "This often happens. We are trying to discover classes that represent an abstract view of the system. It is not unusual to discover useful abstractions at any point of software development. So feel free to add a `playList` class now." `playList` should maintain the list of tracks selected by users.

12.2.2.6 `playList`, a new class to maintain track selections in order

Charlie wants to know if `playList` should be a data member of the `cdPlayer` class? Don't CD players maintain their own play lists? Yes they do. Steve, who is role playing `cdPlayer` suggests that he contain `playList` as a data member.

The object expert suggests that this decision could be made at a later meeting. However, the team wants to force the issue now, as it is difficult to arrange a meeting time that all members can attend.

Jessica and Jason then lead a conversation suggesting that the overall system would be easier to implement if the physical CD player maintained `playList`. First of all, there is reuse of existing software (play lists) and hardware (CD selection mechanism, a clock, and hardware to read digital songs and convert them to real sound). Modern CD players not only maintain their own play lists, they also know precisely when to play the next track! If the system under development has to send `playTrack` messages at the appropriate time, `jukeBox` or somebody else would also have to maintain the time remaining on the currently played track—independent of the physical CD player. And how long does it take to load up CD #199 after CD #3 has just been played—3 seconds, 10 seconds, 5 seconds, 1 minute? When should `jukeBox` ask `cdPlayer` to play the next track? Will a track be cut short? Will there be unnecessary delays?

Chelsea begins a discourse that addresses a recurring design decision with systems that have concurrent (simultaneous) processes. Since the primary responsibility of `jukeBox` is to coordinate activities, `jukeBox` could control when the next track will be played. This could happen by using what is known as a *polling design*. `jukeBox` would go out and frequently poll (ask) `cdPlayer` if it is playing a CD. If `cdPlayer` replies "Yes," `jukeBox` can go off and do other things. If `cdPlayer` replies "No, I am not playing a track," `jukeBox` could ask `playList` for the next track and then send a message to `cdPlayer` to play it. In this case `jukeBox` continuously polls `cdPlayer`. In fact, this sounds a lot like `waitForUser`, a responsibility accomplished by polling—continuously asking `cardReader` if a card has been swiped.

It is also possible to have an interrupt-driven design. Each time `cdPlayer` finishes playing a track, `cdPlayer` asks `jukeBox` for the next track to play. In this case, `cdPlayer` is said to interrupt `jukeBox`. The `jukeBox` accommodates by getting the next track as soon as possible.

Matt reminds the team they have two computers. One is the PC that interacts with users as it maintains `studentCollection` and `cdCollection`. The second is a processor inside the physical CD player. Why can't we reuse the existing software and hardware of the CD player? Matt goes on to tell the team that this is easily done by setting the CD player to its internal program mode. His CD player at home can queue up to 99 different tracks at any one time. Charlie says he could deal with either a polled design, an interrupt-driven design, or this third option of having concurrent processes perform their responsibilities simultaneously on two separate processors.

Chelsea repeats, "Now that would be reuse!" She suggests that the team role play a scenario assuming `playList` resides in the physical CD player and follow a concurrent process design. And even though `playList` is already implemented in the physical CD player with a separate microprocessor, it might be useful to keep `playList` as a class during role playing. "It really feels important," suggests Blaine.

Chelsea asks the team to simplify the analysis. "All we need to do is send a `playTrack` message to `cdPlayer`. The `cdPlayer` class will be responsible for communicating with the physical CD player." The CD player will continuously play songs in a first-to-last order all by itself while `jukeBox` is busy getting new track selections from users. In fact, if the computer fails, the physical CD player could play out the entire `playList`.

12.2.2.7 Scenario 3: "What happens when a student is willing and able to play a track, but several tracks are waiting to be played?"

Chelsea tells `trackSelector` to pick up a scenario that already has a valid student.

`jukeBox`: `trackSelector`, here is `cdCollection`. Please return the user's musical selection.

`trackSelector`: Okay, I now have the `cdCollection`, so user, please select a track. The user selects the "I'm the Cat" track from Jackson Browne's CD titled *Looking East*. `trackSelector` returns this selected track, which `jukeBox` knows as `currentSelection`—an instance of the `track` class.

`jukeBox`: `student`, can you play the `currentSelection`?

`student`: Yes.

`jukeBox`: `cdPlayer`, please `playTrack(currentSelection)`.

`cdPlayer`: Okay, I got it. However, a track is currently playing and there are other tracks to play before I can play your selection. What do I do now?

`playList`: Hey, that's my job. I'll add the `currentSelection` at the end of the queue (waiting line) of tracks to be played, if that's what everyone thinks is fair.

Chelsea asks Blaine, the customer and domain expert, if this is the proper policy—first come, first served. Blaine retorts, "Yes, absolutely." Charlie, who has a part-time job as a network administrator at Lucent Technologies, pronounces that such a fair policy is easily enforced as a first-in-first-out (FIFO) waiting line—what computer scientists call a queue. Blaine asks Charlie how one can set up a waiting line inside a computer. Charlie says a queue is like a `vector` except that new things can be added only at the end. Things can only be removed from the front. Blaine reminds Charlie that he knows a lot about student policies but very little about `vectors` and queues. Chelsea reminds Charlie to avoid discussing implementation details during analysis—even if he knows about an existing `queue` class that can easily "queue up" tracks.

`playList`: Okay, I'll write these responsibilities on my CRH card: `queueUpTrack` and `getNextTrackToPlay`, even if I already exist in the CD player.

12.2.2.8 Scenario 4: "What happens when a student ID card is not found in `studentCollection`?"

`jukeBox`: Okay, I'm waiting for a user. Waiting, waiting, waiting . . .

`cardReader`: Okay, `jukeBox`, a user just swiped a card. Here is the student ID.

`jukeBox`: Thanks, `cardReader`. Now that I have the student ID, I need to verify if the user is valid. Hey, you know what? I am going to give a name to what I am doing. It seems like I am performing an operation that gets the student ID, finds the student, asks `trackSelector` for the student's selection, and so on. I'm going to summarize this algorithm and write it on my card as `processOneUser`.

`studentCollection`: Well, since it is my responsibility to store the collection of `student` objects, let me check to see if there is a student here with that ID. No, we have no student with that ID. What do we do now?

`jukeBox`: I'll just tell the alleged user that it's a no-go.

"Whoooooaaa," groans Jason. "A student with a valid student ID is a valid student. Let 'em in." Jessica supports Jason's suggestion by suggesting that "valid student" means something different each semester. Some students drop out in the middle of a term. New students come in at the beginning of a term. Jessica expresses concern about maintaining an accurate list of valid students—would we have to access the registrar's database of students? Blaine suggests that the cashless jukebox isn't a mission-critical system. Nor could anyone profit from its abuse. So even if a few "invalid" students get in, so what? The team members unanimously agree that a nonexistent student with a valid ID card should have an account created automatically. "And how much time credit do we give that new student account?" questions Matt. "1,500 minutes, of course," replies Misty.

`jukeBox`: Let me change my previous action so the new student is added to the new collection. Who should have that responsibility?

`studentCollection`: Why, me of course. Give me the student ID number from the magnetic ID card, and I will add a new student. I'll write the action responsibility `addStudent` on my CRH card. So `jukeBox` will not have to worry about the student returned. It may be someone who had been in the system, or it may be someone who was just added.

Self-Check

12-6 Play out the following scenarios by writing the class name and narrative of each until it has reached its logical conclusion:

-a What happens when a student swipes her card for the first time on a given date and wants to play two different songs?

-b What happens when a student has no more time credit left, but wants to play a song?

-c What happens when the Student Affairs office wants to remove a CD from the jukebox?

-d What happens when the Student Affairs office wants to add a new CD to the jukebox?

-e What happens when `cdPlayer` receives a `playSong` message and the physical CD player is turned off or malfunctioning?

12-7 List several college-library scenarios that should be played out by a team.

12-8 Script a college-library scenario that describes what happens when a user wants to check out a book.

12-9 Script a college-library scenario that describes what happens when a user wants to return a book that is not late.

12.2.3 Why CRH Cards?

After role playing, discussion, arguments, laughter, and changed minds, the design is captured as a set of classes that model a solution. Class names and responsibilities have been recorded on CRH cards as the team role played the scenarios. CRH cards help the problem-solving and system-building processes in many ways. Rebecca Wirfs-Brock writes [Wirfs-Brock 90]:

> We have found that index cards work well because they are compact, easy to manipulate, and easy to modify or discard. Because you didn't make them, they don't feel valuable to you. If the class turns out to be spurious, you can toss the card aside with few regrets. . . . If you discover you have erroneously discarded a class card, it is simple to retrieve it, or make a new one.

This is but one example of the many dynamics of CRH card use in software that go beyond the scope of this textbook. The previous jukebox discourse was an attempt to represent real-world object-oriented analysis and design.

In actuality, during October and November 1997, six students role played these and other jukebox scenarios. Some of the issues that arose are left as analysis and design exercises. For example, the team members strongly felt that no track should be played within the same hour. The author (acting as the customer and domain expert Blaine) agreed this would be a good enhancement, but it would be a change dealt with as an enhancement later. It is an interesting design decision to make. There are several possibilities.

One of the benefits of having a team consisting of designers and customers is the opportunity for everyone to develop an understanding of the system in common terminology. Sometimes customers haven't asked for what they really want. Experienced teams familiar with customer needs can actually help customers sharpen their requirements. The team can also make suggestions like this: "Please don't let the same track play over and over again. I couldn't stand that. It happened too much in high school. We had to turn the jukebox off." Limits of two tracks a day could prevent a lot of complaints.

12.2.4 Responsibilities and Helpers

The following summary of responsibilities and helpers is the result of the preceding CRH card development with the team role playing individual classes. These will be used in the next chapter to document the class names, action responsibilities, knowledge responsibilities, and collaboration for creating the class definitions. Knowledge responsibilities could become data members. Action responsibilities could become member functions. A helper might become a message send, a data member (containment relationship), an argument in a message, or a return value from a message. You will see more about these relationships and class definition design in Chapter 13.

FIGURE 12.7. *Major classes with responsibilities and helpers*

Class: jukeBox	**Helpers:**
Responsibilities:	cdPlayer
know current track	trackSelector
know current student	student
waitForUser	cardReader
processOneUser	studentCollection
	cdCollection

Class: cardReader	
Responsibilities:	**Helpers:**
getStudentID	physical card reader, which
	in turn collaborates with
	the magnetic student ID card

Class: student	
Responsibilities:	**Helpers:**
know remaining credit	date
know how many songs played today	
canSelect	

Class: studentCollection	
Responsibilities:	**Helpers:**
know all students	student
getStudent	
addStudent	

Class: CD	
Responsibilities:	**Helpers:**
know tracks	
know CD title and artist name	
allow references to individual tracks	
know play time	

Class: `cdCollection`	
Responsibilities:	**Helpers:**
know all CDs	CD
allow references to individual CDs	
`addCD`	
`removeCD`	

Class: `trackSelector`	
Responsibilities:	**Helpers:**
`track getTrack(int)`	the user
	`track`
	CD
	`cdCollection`

Class: `track`	
Responsibilities:	**Helpers:**
know play time	
know physical location in the CD player (CD number, track number)	

Class: `cdPlayer`	
Responsibilities:	**Helpers:**
`playTrack`	the physical CD player
	`playList`
	CD

Class: `playList`	
Responsibilities:	**Helpers:**
maintain list of selected tracks	`track`
`getNextTrackToPlay`	`queue`
`queueUpTrack`	

12.3 An Uninterrupted Scenario

Chelsea congratulates the team. The responsibilities seem to be distributed over a reasonable number of classes. If you consider that `cdPlayer` and `playList` are already implemented, the team has to consider and implement only eight classes at once.

Steve complains that he is still a bit confused. Each time a scenario began, it was not completed without some interruption. Chelsea had a lot to say about object-oriented analysis and design. Blaine sometimes had to address policy issues such as the play policy. Charlie just seemed to say too much about implementation. Additionally, it seemed that while the team members were trying to understand the problem, they also had to stop and make design decisions; should it be a polled design, an interrupt-driven design, or a concurrent design?

Jessica and Jason admit to some confusion. Jessica proposes that the team role play a scenario without interruption. This may be a repeat of what has been done, but it might help us understand the system better—a summary of sorts. Chelsea believes this is a good idea. She suggests the team hold the same CRH cards and role play a scenario.

12.3.1 Summary Scenario: "What happens when a student without an account wants to select a track?"

`jukebox`: I'll start the scenario again. I'm `waitingForUser`, so `cardReader`, please `getStudentID`.

`cardReader`: No one has swiped their card.

`jukeBox`: Okay, `cardReader`, I'll ask again. Please `getStudentID`.

`cardReader`: No one has swiped their card.

`jukeBox`: Okay, I'm waiting for a user. Waiting, waiting, waiting . . .

`cardReader`: Okay, `jukeBox`, a user just swiped a card. Here is the student ID: 1234.

`jukeBox`: `studentCollection`, please `getStudent` with ID 1234.

`studentCollection`: Well, there is no such student, so I'll create a new student account and the student will have a time credit of 1,500 minutes and no songs played on this date. I suspect this would be a default `student` object.

`jukeBox`: Thanks, `studentCollection`, for the `currentStudent`. `trackSelector`, I'm giving you `cdCollection`. Would you please give me the user's `currentSelection`?

`trackSelector`: Okay, I'll use `cdCollection` to show all the CDs and tracks to the user. The user will have to select the track. Got it.

`jukeBox`: Okay, I have the `currentSelection`. `student`, can you select a song?

`student`: Yes, I can select a song.

`jukeBox`: Now, `cdPlayer`, please `playTrack(currentSelection)`.

`cdPlayer`: `playList`, please add this track to the music we'll eventually play.

`playList`: Okay, I can queue it up, but if you aren't currently playing anything, why don't you play it now?

`cdPlayer`: Well, I am playing some good stuff now, so please queue it up.

`playList`: Okay, I'll add it.

`jukeBox`: Actually, I don't need to worry about what you guys did, I'm already waiting for another user.

Chelsea suggests that this scenario has reached its logical conclusion. `jukeBox` is waiting for another user. The CD player is playing the selected tracks in an FIFO order from `playList`.

Jessica, who has been role playing `cdCollection`, observes that she played no role in the scenarios. "You sent me to `trackSelector`, but I was never asked for anything. Why did `trackSelector` need me?" Chelsea agrees that something is amiss. It appears that `cdCollection` must make individual CDs available to `trackSelector` in some reasonable order. "What about artist names alphabetically?" asks Jessica. Blaine replies, "Seems reasonable. It's probably easier for students to pick an artist first, then a CD by that artist, then a track from that CD."

Jessica recalls that `vectors` allow access to individual elements in the container of objects. So it seems reasonable that `cdCollection` must also allow access to individual CDs from first to last. Charlie says he can handle it. Don't worry about it. Chelsea thanks Charlie.

Now everything is wonderful, except . . . What happens if the same user wants to play a second and then a third track? A new account will not be created this time, but somehow `student` must know if it `canSelect`. This new account should not be able to select a third track. No student should have unlimited time credit. In other words, `student` must be modified to reflect the fact that it selected a track and the CD player played the music. When should student updates occur?

Chelsea, who was role playing `student`, suggests that she could have updated herself when asked the `canSelect` question. She had the `currentSelection`, so she could have deducted the time it takes to play that track during `canSelect`. She could also have recorded today's date. When a second track was selected, she could have modified herself again in the same way. When the third `canSelect` message was sent to `student`, `student` could simply reply, "No can do. And by the way, I won't deduct any time, nor will I record the fact that I selected a third song on today's date."

The team can live with this, except Matt wonders how `studentCollection` will know if one of its students has been modified. Charlie says `studentCollection` could remove the old student and add the modified student. Blaine doesn't like that suggestion. Charlie says, "Okay, simply return a reference to the student so any change to `student` by `jukeBox` will also update the `student` in the `studentCollection`." Blaine bemoans, "What's a reference?" Charlie stops before he says a word. Instead, he quietly contemplates how to change `students` and maintain them so they are the same later in the day and even later in the term or in a student's career. Charlie has completed two computer science courses and he knows that references and files will prove useful helper classes.

The team meeting is over after Chelsea sets up a meeting with Charlie and Matt. Stay tuned for the class definition design and member function implementations (see Chapter 13).

Chapter Summary

- Object-oriented software development begins by identifying the key abstractions—classes—that potentially model a solution. Software designers assign responsibilities to the appropriate classes.
- Analysis and design decisions can be documented as Component/Responsibility/Helper (CRH) cards. Each CRH card begins as a blank 3-by-5-inch index card (or it could be 4 by 6 inches) with a class name and major responsibilities written on the back.
- Collaborative design and role playing enhance the object-oriented development process. Possible analysis classes arise not only from the problem specification itself and domain expertise, but also from the words that are spoken as teams analyze problems.
- Team members assume the roles of these analysis classes, play out scenarios (what would happen when . . .), and establish relationships between classes. During role

playing, team members establish more detailed responsibilities—what an object should know and what it should be able to do—while recording them on the CRH cards.

Exercises

1. The students are complaining. The same song plays again and again. One person plays it twice and then has a friend play it twice. The Student Affairs office asks you to modify the jukebox so it will not play any song that has been played in the previous 60 minutes. The original team has graduated. You have to do it by yourself. List all classes that must be modified. What changes must be made to each?

2. What changes would need to be made to the jukebox design in order to maintain the CD collection in this way: The jukebox has been running for a while. The Student Affairs office wants to replace the 10 least frequently played CDs with a fresh 10. The original team has graduated. You have to do it by yourself. List all classes that must be modified. What changes must be made to each?

3. After the jukebox has been running for a while, students begin to complain because they can no longer select songs due to the fact that that they are out of time. The Student Affairs office asks you to modify the jukebox so users can play up to 3,000 minutes of music. The original team has graduated. You have to do it by yourself. List all classes that must be modified. What changes must be made to each?

4. After the jukebox has been running for a while more, students begin to complain because they can no longer select songs due to the fact that that they are running out of time again. The Student Affairs office asks you to modify the jukebox so there is no time restriction. The original team has graduated. You have to do it by yourself. List all classes that must be modified. What changes must be made to each?

5. Students want to be able to play entire CDs on the weekends. The Student Affairs office asks you to modify the jukebox so each student can play one entire CD on any given date. The original team has graduated. You have to do it by yourself. List all classes that must be modified. What changes must be made to each?

Analysis Tips

1. Model the real world when possible.

Meaningful well-named abstractions can make the system design easier to understand.

2. Anthropomorphize.

Don't be afraid to give human characteristics to your objects. Ask these questions often:

* What should an instance of this class be able to do?
* What should an instance of this class know?

3. On your CRH cards, write action responsibilities as if they were C++ identifiers (no spaces).

This will help as you move on to designing class definitions. Conversely, write knowledge responsibilities like this:

* know all CDs
* know all tracks
* know play time

4. Do not procrastinate.

Write down the responsibilities as soon as you realize them during role playing. Early bouts of laziness can end up in frustration later.

5. Distinguish objects that are outside of the system under development.

For example, the jukebox will communicate with the user. The jukebox will read the student ID card. However, both the user and the magnetic ID card are outside of the system.

6. The user is often confused as being a key abstraction to be modeled.

The user is important. However, there is usually some state object that models the real-world user. Remember that there is a physical user that selects songs, but there is also a software equivalent called `student` that knows how many songs the software equivalent has played today.

7. Definitely draw a picture of the major classes.

Make the classes rectangular boxes with the class name and the major responsibility (10 words or less). The picture should have arrows from the sender of a message to the receiver of that message (see the `jukeBox` picture).

8. Helpers usually represent a one-way relationship.

If class A asks class B for help, A is the sender, B is the helper. Write down that responsibility on B's card. `jukeBox` asked a helper named `studentCollection` to `getStudent`. `getStudent` should be on the `studentCollection` card.

9. It is not a good idea to ask the physical user if he or she can select.

However, it is perfectly okay to ask the software object. The physical student might say, "Sure I can play 100 songs today." Assume the programmer will not let the user's software equivalent lie. Besides, the user is not part of the system.

10. The first round of scenarios will often be interrupted by discussions.

Interruptions are okay. This is called brainstorming. Five heads are better than one. Genius is more easily accomplished with more than one person. At some point, have your team play out a familiar scenario without interruption. You will see the objects more clearly and understand their responsibilities.

11. The jukebox and the projects at the end of this chapter are relatively large systems.

They certainly do more than convert from Fahrenheit to Celsius. If you don't understand `jukeBox`, don't worry. The best way to understand it is to do an analysis with a team. This could take hours. On more complex systems, this could take months. The projects of this chapter are less complex. However, they are complex enough to benefit from an object-oriented approach to software development.

12. The jukebox has key abstractions that set a pattern for the analysis projects coming up at the end of this chapter.

As you perform your own analysis and CRH card development in a team project (12A, 12B, 12C, 12D) look for the following major classes (the analysis projects typically have five, six, or seven classes). Like the jukebox, they include

- a class that coordinates the major activities (`jukeBox` here)
- a collection of objects (`studentCollection` and `cdCollection` here)
- state objects (`student`, `track`, and `CD` here) stored in a container class
- one or more classes that model something in the real world (`student`, `cardReader`, and `cdPlayer`)

Object-Oriented Analysis/Design Projects

Each of the following analysis projects assumes you are using a team approach involving activities like those described in this chapter. Team size should be two, three, four, or five students.

1. Once you have a team, pick a project you want to do. Choose from this list:

   Bank Teller (12A)

   Voice Mail System (12B)

   Video Rental Store (12C)

   Checkbook (12D)

   make one up

2. Next, analyze the problem to establish a reasonable set of classes that model a solution. Draw the classes on a piece of paper. Make sure each class has a name and a major responsibility assigned to it.

3. For each useful class, write the name of the class and its major responsibility on the back of a 3-by-5-inch index card (or an 8½-by-11-inch piece of paper if you don't have index cards). On the front, list the class, the more finely detailed responsibilities, and any helpers the class uses to accomplish its task.

4. Run through scenarios that you invent. Using a pencil, write down responsibilities as they crop up. Remember, the class may have action responsibilities, knowledge responsibilities, or both. Also write down any helpers that exist. If you ask another object for help, that person (object) is a helper. You may erase, you may

cross off, or you may add responsibilities; in fact you may even tear up and recycle that CRH card.

5. Role play as many scenarios as you can think of. Do them until you really understand the system. The CRH cards should provide an accurate portrayal of the responsibilities of each class.

Save your CRH cards. They will be used to help you design class definitions (Chapter 13). Your project can be continued into the next chapter and on into complete implementation.

12A Bank Teller Application Adapted from *Problem Solving and Program Implementation* [Mercer 91]

First read the notes above. The bank teller application allows any bank customers access to their own bank accounts through their customer numbers. Once a customer swipes the bank card and enters the personal identification number (PIN), the user, with the help of a teller, may complete any of the following transactions: withdraw money, deposit money, and query account balance. Customers may also see their own transaction logs. The system must maintain the correct balances for all accounts and also log each and every successful transaction.

12B Voice Mail System Adapted from *Mastering Object-Oriented Design in C++* [Horstmann 96]

First read the notes above. Simulate a voice mail system. The system has a collection of mailboxes, each of which may be accessed by an extension number (3445, for instance). A user may put a message into any mailbox, so anyone on the computer may type in a mailbox number and then type in a message. Any user with a valid mailbox and the valid password may do any of the following:

- play back messages
- delete messages
- change the greeting
- change the password

An administrator is needed to activate new mailboxes and deactivate active mailboxes. The administrator is a user with a "super password."

12C Video Rental System from *Data Structures via C++* [Berman 97]

First read the notes above. Build a software system to support the operation of a video rental store. The system should automate the process of renting tapes and receiving returned tapes, including the calculation and printing of customer bills, which may or may not be done at the same time a tape is returned. The system must also give the clerk access to information about the tapes, such as the number of copies on the shelf of any given video owned by the store. The system must be able to add and remove customers and tapes to and from the database. Each customer and each copy of each tape are associated with a unique bar-coded label.

12D Checkbook Application Adapted from *Using CRC Cards* [Wilkinson 95]

First read the notes above. Simulate an electronic checkbook. The checkbook manages a limited set of entries: checks written and bank deposits. The checkbook must maintain the proper balance and a record of all entries. The checkbook will be able to print a statement of all activities. The user should be able to look up any check number individually and see the amount and who the check was written to.

Chapter Thirteen

Object-Oriented Software Development

Design and Implementation

Summing Up

The CRH cards of the previous chapter represent an analysis deliverable. Through role playing, the team discovered major classes while developing a deep understanding of the system. The team has established a common vocabulary amongst themselves. Even the client, Blaine, can continue to communicate with the programmers as long as they avoid implementation details concerning `vectors` and pointers.

Coming Up

These CRH cards will now be used to help design the class definitions. This roughly bounds the design phase. After this, the member functions will be implemented, roughly bounding the implementation phase. After studying this chapter, you will be able to

* use the analysis deliverable (CRH cards) to help design your class definitions
* implement action responsibilities as public member functions
* implement knowledge responsibilities as private data members
* add constructors to initialize the data members
* perform unit testing
* perform system testing

Exercises and programming projects

13.1 Designing Class Interfaces

The analysis phase helped the team understand *what* the system will do. It is now time to concentrate on the *how*. There is some haziness between analysis and design. In fact, during role-playing scenarios, some design decisions were made.

Chelsea comments that some software developers claim a separation between analysis and design. She is of the opinion that this is a holdover from the waterfall model of software development—before objects. This rigid waterfall model focused on well-defined deliverables. Practitioners want to complete the analysis phase before design, for example. The one-way waterfall model attempts to avoid revisiting previous steps (it is more difficult for water to travel uphill than downhill). The waterfall model was suggested in Chapter 1 to introduce analysis, design, and implementation as separate phases of software development. It was an attempt to suggest that there are things you can do before sitting at the computer and whacking out code. However, the problems were relatively simple. There was little need to revisit analysis and design.

Most of the problems up to this point haven't required much analysis or design. A small set of algorithmic patterns (IPO, Multiple Selection, Determinate Loop, and so forth) has solved most problems. And of course, it has been easy to guess that programming problems in the chapter where a certain algorithmic pattern or C++ structure (`if...else`, `for` loop) was introduced would need that construct to be completed. Software development usually isn't so easy.

Object-oriented software developers follow the iterative model of software development. This is a more flexible strategy that allows one to modify existing results in order to fix earlier mistakes or poor designs. Now, during design and implementation, the team must determine how things will get done. Now is the time to think about the computer system(s) that will be running the cashless jukebox and the programming language that will be used to implement it. The programmers have decided it will be easier to use text-based input and output. That's all they know. They have verified this decision with a quick call to the customer (Blaine). They will also use the language they know from their study of computing fundamentals: C++.

At this point, only three of the team members will continue the development. The other team members have agreed to help if the need arises. Chelsea will work with Matt, the computer engineer who was on the team during analysis. Charlie, the computer science major who has finished the first year of the computer science curriculum, has also promised to help. This is Matt's first experience with object-oriented software development. But Matt is also interested in how the computer communicates with the physical CD player.

The jukebox team derived 10 classes. Looking ahead to the design and implementation of these classes, Chelsea suggests that with Ed's hardware device, `cdPlayer` and `playList` need not be implemented. The `student` and `track` classes follow the State Object pattern. Charlie, Matt, and certainly Chelsea are quite familiar with classes that mostly exist to store state and provide suitable access to it. The `cdCollection` and `studentCollection` classes fit another pattern similar to that of the `bag` class that Charlie and Matt have studied. Both classes

* contain a collection of many objects
* provide a way to iterate over the collection—from the first to the last
* provide suitable access to any object in the collection

Both programmers see a relationship between the responsibilities on the CRH cards and the C++ class definitions. The things that each instance of a class must *do* might be implemented as public member functions or as statements in an algorithm. The things that each instance of a class must *know* might become private data members of that class. Chelsea warns Matt and Charlie that although CRH cards provide some input into class design, translation from CRH cards to C++ class definitions requires more design decisions. The translation is not direct. Some things may be added, others removed. For example, the CRH cards may not contain such things as return types or parameters.

CRH cards document analysis decisions. They fashion a solution. They also provide a glimpse of the class definitions that need to be designed. As mentioned earlier, each CRH card lists its set of action responsibilities, which might end up as class member functions or as statements in an algorithm. Each class's CRH card also lists its knowledge responsibilities, which might be implemented as data members, and its helper classes, which indicate relationships between objects.

Some CRH cards denote one or more helper classes that may be sent messages. The helpers listed on the CRH cards are potential receivers of these messages. Chelsea reminds the team of the differences between a sender and a receiver. For example, the `jukeBox` object may send a `getStudent` message to the `studentCollection` object. `jukeBox` is the sender, `studentCollection` is the receiver. `studentCollection` (the receiver, in this case) must implement the `getStudent` responsibility. Therefore, `getStudent` should be written as a class member function of `studentCollection`.

The next major activity in the development of the cashless jukebox begins with Chelsea, Matt, and Charlie designing the class definitions. The programming team will get the class definitions to compile. They will eventually choose the data members that most appropriately help each class fulfill its knowledge responsibilities. Later on, the constructors and other member functions will get implemented. Frequent compilation and testing will improve chances for a successful system.

The aforementioned design and implementation are iterative processes that include activities such as these:

- Design the class interfaces by specifying the member functions, including parameters and return types, for the class member function headings.
- Determine the knowledge responsibilities (data members) required to implement the action responsibilities.
- Add appropriate constructors (or other initialization routines).
- Implement the constructors that initialize the data members.
- Implement the member functions.

The iterative model of software development allows programmers to back up into analysis, delve into implementation, and return to class design. Not only will the programmers refine algorithms while implementing the member functions, they will also refine class definitions and data members. They may also change the CRH cards.

At Chelsea's suggestion, Ed and Matt first consider the `student` and `studentCollection` classes.

13.1.1 The `studentCollection` Class

The `studentCollection` CRH card lists two action responsibilities: `getStudent` and `addStudent`.

FIGURE 13.1. *CRH card for* `studentCollection`

Class: `studentCollection`	
Responsibilities:	**Helpers:**
know all students	`student`
`getStudent`	
`addStudent`	

These responsibilities could be written as member functions.

```
class studentCollection {  // First draft
public:
   ??? getStudent(???);
   ??? addStudent(???);
private:
   // TBA: Know all students
};
```

However, some things are missing. As the programming team designs class definitions, it must also make design decisions concerning parameters and return types of those functions.

Chelsea asks Matt and Charlie if the `getStudent` message requires any arguments. Yes, it appears that `studentCollection` will need the student ID number from the sender (`jukeBox`). Matt asks, "What return type should `getStudent` have?" Chelsea says that the return type should be `student`. If we assume the student ID will be represented as a `string`, the member function heading could look like this:

```
student getStudent(string ID);
// Return the student with the given ID
```

The `addStudent` signature might reasonably be

```
void addStudent(student newStudent);
// Add the given student to the collection
```

Matt wants to know what private data members are needed so `studentCollection` "knows all students." What data would the constructor(s) need to initialize a `studentCollection`? Chelsea answers, "Member function definitions first, data members later." Since we don't know how `studentCollection` is being stored yet, we will also postpone constructors. Charlie reminds Matt that accessing functions should be declared const. A `getStudent` message will return the `student` object associated with an ID number. It will not modify the `studentCollection` object. On the other hand, `addStudent` will. Here is a second refinement of the class definition that will allow an object to accept the preceding message. The class definition still omits data members and constructors.

```
class studentCollection {  // Second draft--no constructors yet
public:
  student getStudent(string ID) const;
  // Return the student with the given ID

  void addStudent(student newStudent);
```

```
    // Add the given student to the collection

  private:
    // TBA: Know all students
  };
```

Matt remembers from role playing that `jukeBox` also wanted to know if a student was valid. The current `getStudent` heading returns a `student`. However, what happens if the ID number from a student ID card does not match one of the students in `studentCollection`? Matt advises Charlie of an earlier design decision: "The team decided it was okay to simply create a new account." The new student would begin with 1,500 minutes credit and no songs played on the current date. Chelsea confirms that if `studentCollection` constructs a new student account automatically, `jukeBox` will have no knowledge nor concern over this detail. This is a cleaner design.

Matt wonders if `studentCollection` should be designed with `addStudent` as a public member function. Charlie says no. The `getStudent` operation will be the only one that sends an `addStudent` message. Chelsea remarks that `addStudent` has enough detail to justify implementing it as a separate function. However, thinking ahead to implementation, making `addStudent` public would make it easier to add students to the collection.

Of course, `studentCollection` requires a `student` class, so perhaps `student` should have been the first class implemented. Charlie tells Matt not to worry, "We'll work on `student` next."

13.1.2 The `student` Class

Charlie and Matt review the `student` CRH card next. The only action responsibility is `canSelect`. The knowledge responsibilities are closely related—know remaining time credit and how many songs played today. Matt remarks that each student should know its ID number. After all, `studentCollection` will be asked to look up students based on ID numbers. Charlie suggests the CRH card be changed by adding "know ID number."

FIGURE 13.2. *CRH card for* `student`

Class: student	
Responsibilities:	**Helpers:**
know remaining credit	date
know how many songs played today	
canSelect	
know ID number	

Charlie thinks it might also be necessary to search the Web for a date and time class to satisfy other knowledge responsibilities. However, the programmers decide to worry about that later—during implementation.

The team now considers the return type and parameters for the `canSelect` message. The `student` object needs to know if a certain track can be played. So a `track` object needs to be passed as an argument.

```
class student {  // First draft--no constructors yet
public:
  bool canSelect(track currentSelection);
  // Returns true if the student has enough time credit and has
  // played zero or one track(s) on today's date
  // Update the state to reflect a played track
private:
  string my_ID;
  // TBA: Other data members might be date and time objects
};
```

Matt and Charlie decide to define `cdCollection` and `CD` next. (*Note:* The process is similar to what was done for the `studentCollection` and `student` classes.)

Self-Check

13-1 This is a continuation of the college library system you began in Chapter 12. You should have found a `student` class in the college library. Design the class definition now as completely as possible.

13-2 This is a continuation of the college library system you began in Chapter 12. You should have found a `book` class in the college library. Design the class definition now as completely as possible.

13.1.3 The cdCollection Class

The cdCollection CRH card indicates that a cdCollection object must be able to add and remove CDs. It must also be able to store all CDs and let someone look at any or all CDs.

FIGURE 13.3. *CRH card for cdCollection*

Class: cdCollection	
Responsibilities:	**Helpers:**
know all CDs	vector of CDs
retrieve a CD	
addNewCD(CD aCD, int trayNumber)	
removeCD(int trayNumber)	
CD getCD(int trayNumber)	

Perhaps because Matt has just studied vectors, he wants to include one as a data member. Chelsea reluctantly agrees as she reminds Matt that this decision could wait. The underlying storage mechanism could change to a different container class.

Charlie says that since CD objects might be somewhat big, it makes sense to pass the CD object by const reference to addCD and removeCD. This leads to a first-draft definition for the cdCollection class:

```
class cdCollection {  // First draft--no constructors yet
public:
  void addCD(const CD & aCD);
  // Add a CD to the collection if possible

  bool removeCD(const CD & aCD);
  // Remove CD if possible. Return false if it doesn't exist.

private:
  vector <CD> my_data;
  int my_size;
};
```

Self-Check

13-3 This is a continuation of the college library system you began in Chapter 12. If you found a container class for books or students, write the C++ class definition as completely as possible.

Matt now recalls Jessica's complaint that as role player of `cdCollection`, she did not take part in the scenario of a user selecting a track. It reminds Matt that `cdCollection` must provide access to all `CD` objects. In fact, the CRH card states the `cdCollection` must "allow references to individual CDs." Chelsea suggests that the process of sequentially iterating over a collection of objects from first to last is done so often that it has now been documented as a *design pattern*. "This is a classic instance of the Iterator design pattern," claims Chelsea.

Charlie, who thinks he knows it all, admits that he is unaware of the Iterator design pattern. Chelsea reassures Charlie by informing him that the pattern is from a book written for an advanced audience, *Design Patterns: Elements of Reusable Object-Oriented Software* [Gamma/Helm/Johnson/Vlissides 95].[1] Charlie says he has studied other kinds of patterns—algorithmic and object patterns—but not any design patterns. Chelsea summarizes the Iterator pattern presented in the *Design Patterns* book:

DESIGN PATTERN 13.1

Pattern:	Iterator
Intent:	Provide a way to access the elements of a container object sequentially without exposing the underlying representation.
Motivation:	A container object, such as a `bag` of `book` objects, or a `cdCollection` of `CD` objects, should give access to its elements without exposing its internal structure. This allows the developer to specify an interface before the data members are chosen. It also allows the class designer to modify the internal structure of the container class without requiring changes in the code that uses the container. This pattern can be implemented with operations and a data member named `index` to index `currentItem`:

```
first()
next()
isDone()
currentItem()
```

Matt and Charlie have both seen the Iterator pattern used with the `bag` class. Individual objects in `bag` containers were visited using `first`, `next`, `isDone`, and `currentItem` messages. From his CS2 class (weeks 16–30), Charlie knows about

1. These four authors, inspired by Christopher Alexander's book *A Pattern Language* [Alexander 77], have been affectionately referred to as the Gang of Four (GOF).

changing underlying structure. Charlie's instructor asked him to modify underlying structures of container classes. The underlying data member used to store the items was first a `vector`, then a `list`. The data members and algorithms were dramatically different, yet the interface never changed! The programs using the containers did not have to be changed. Matt asks Charlie why his instructor asked him to change the underlying structure. Charlie tries to explain that there are different ways of doing the same thing, and that one way may be more appropriate than another when the collection gets really big: "Some containers are better when there is a small size, say in the hundreds. Other containers are more appropriate when there are millions of objects. Sometimes the objects need to be made persistent so they live beyond the program run—`vector` and `list` objects die off when the program ends." Matt is confused: "What has this got to do with iterators?"

Chelsea jumps in. She suggests that the design patterns were developed by professional software developers with a lot of combined experience and with contributions from many object-oriented software developers. Chelsea tells Matt to trust the pattern, even if it is not yet clear why the Iterator pattern leads to better design and a higher degree of usability.

The `bag` iterators were member functions. Although the *Design Patterns* book describes a more powerful and flexible design, its Iterator design pattern requires inheritance (see Chapter 16) and implementation of a separate iterator class. Charlie says he has an easier way to iterate over CDs in the `cdCollection`. The algorithm could look something like the following, where messages are sent to the appropriate public member functions of `cdCollection`.

```
// Iterate over cdCollection
for(theCdCollection.first() ! theCdCollection.isDone()
    theCdCollection.next());
{ // assert: theCdCollection has at least one more CD to visit
  aCD = theCdCollection.currentItem();
  // . . .
  // Do whatever you want with aCD
  // . . .
}
```

Charlie refines the class definition to include the iterator member functions. *Design Patterns* also recommends a private data member to refer to the items during traversals. It is named `my_index` here to match the conventions used in this textbook (precede all data members with `my_`).

```
class cdCollection {  // Third draft
public:
  void addCD(const CD & aCD);
  // Add a CD to the collection

  bool removeCD(const CD & aCD);
  // Remove CD if possible. Return false if it doesn't exist.

//--iterator functions
  void first();  // Let index point to the first item
  void next();   // Let index point to the next item (or end)
  bool isDone() const;     // Return true when traversal is done
  CD currentItem() const;  // Return the item referred to by next

private:
  vector <CD> my_data;    // Store the CDs
  int my_size;            // The number of CDs in the collection
  int my_index;           // The subscript of the current item
};
```

Now there are four additional members—the iterator functions—and a private data member named `my_index` to help. Chelsea states that CRH cards cannot, and do not pretend to, provide all operations during analysis. Some things become obvious only during design and implementation. Object-oriented software development is an iterative process. Chelsea reminds Matt and Charlie, "Things change during refinement."

13.1.4 The CD Class

The CRH card for CD indicates no action responsibilities.

FIGURE 13.4. *CRH card for CD*

Class: CD	
Responsibilities:	**Helpers:**
know tracks	
know CD title and artist name	
allow references to individual tracks	
know play time	

At first, it looks like CD will follow the State Object pattern. Each CD must know its artist, title, and tracks.

```
class CD {  // First draft--no constructors yet
public:
  string artist() const;
  string title() const;
private:
  string my_artist;
  string my_title;
  vector <track> my_data;  // Stores many tracks, typically 10
  int my_size;             // The total number of tracks
};
```

However, as with cdCollection, CD must allow someone to look over the individual tracks. The following algorithm uses an inner loop to iterate over all the tracks on one CD. The loop in int main() iterates over all CDs in the collection. Each of those CDs is passed to showOneCd that in turn iterates over all the tracks on the CD.

```
#include "cdcollec"  // For the CD, track, and cdCollection classes

void showOneCD(CD & aCD)
{ // post: Show titles of all the tracks on aCD
  track aTrack;
  for( aCD.first(); ! aCD.isDone(); aCD.next() )
  {
    aTrack = aCD.currentItem();
    cout << aTrack.title() << endl;
  }
}

int main()
{
  cdCollection theCDs;
  CD aCD;

  for( theCDs.first(); ! theCDs.isDone(); theCDs.next() );
  {
    aCD = theCDs.currentItem();
    cout << aCD.title() << " " << aCD.artist() << endl;
    showOneCD(aCD);
  }

  return 0;
}
```

CD is a collection. "That Iterator pattern again," observes Charlie. The following class CD refinement provides clients access to individual tracks:

```
class CD {  // Second draft
public:
  string artist() const;
  string title() const;

//--iterator functions
  void first();
  void next();
  bool isDone() const;
  track currentItem() const;

private:
  string my_artist;
  string my_title;
  vector <track> my_data;
  int my_size;
  int my_index;
};
```

Charlie wonders out loud how a CD should be initialized. If it didn't have a vector of tracks, it would be easy to simply have a constructor set the artist and title. It is not clear where and how CD data is or will be stored. Can the data be read from the CD? Charlie says he can easily look at the number of tracks and play time using Microsoft's "CD Player" program. But this doesn't list the track titles or the artist's name. As of this writing, many CDs do not yet contain that information.

Matt suggests the data could be obtained from the liner notes of each CD. The data could be maintained in a file. Chelsea suggests that the format of the CD data (and the student data) must be specified in a precise manner. Chelsea suggests the following format but warns that it might change as the CD and track classes are implemented and tested. This file provides at least some idea of how information will be stored:

```
#ARTIST Hashitani, Samantha
1 Samantha Hashitani
 1 3  4 Easy
 2 3 13 Step Aside
 3 0 26 Rokujo Interlude
 4 3  9 Rokujo
 5 4 46 Sweet
 6 3 11 Ain't that Lovin' You Baby
```

```
 7 4 30 Faith Never Leaves
 8 4 17 Falling in Love
 9 4  0 Boy
10 2 58 Taming
11 4 51 Until Then
12 6 10 Parts
13 2 44 Carousel Song
#ARTIST Browne, Jackson
2 Looking East
 1 4 56 Looking East
 2 5 42 Barricades of Heaven
 3 4 51 Some Bridges
 4 5 14 Information Wars
 5 3 55 I'm the Cat
 6 5 45 Culver Moon
 7 5  5 Baby How Long
 8 5 14 Nino
 9 4 51 Alive in the World
10 4 57 It Is One
#ARTIST Raitt, Bonnie
3 Luck of the Draw
 1 3 48 Something to Talk About
 2 3 33 Good Man, Good Woman
 // . . .
 // Much data deleted. Collection ends with R.E.M., Out of Time . . .
 // . . .
 10 4 9 Country Feedback
 11 5 6 Me in Honey
 #END
```

This file represents the data necessary to initialize `CD` objects. It could be created as part of a maintenance procedure. For now, the data will simply be typed into a plain text file.

Initializing one `CD` would involve reading the artist name, the tray where it is located in the physical CD player, and the title name. These are the first two lines beginning with `#ARTIST`. For example, the following two lines represent the artist's name (`Raitt, Bonnie`), the tray location in the physical jukebox (`3`), and the title of the CD (`Luck of the Draw`).

```
#ARTIST Raitt, Bonnie
3 Luck of the Draw
```

The `#ARTIST` label begins each and every new `CD`. `#END` is the end-of-file indicator—a sentinel. This data is followed by the tracks, listed on separate lines in a format easily generated from CD liner notes or perhaps a CD reader if the liner notes neglect to list the play time. For example, the following line means the track number 1 takes 3 minutes and 48 seconds to play, and it has the title "Something to Talk About":

```
1 3 48 Something to Talk About
```

Chelsea affirms that much progress has been made. At this point, the programmers could almost begin implementing the `student`, `studentCollection`, `CD`, and `cdCollection` classes. However, Matt remembers that `cdCollection` needs `CD` and `CD` needs `track`. So the programming team needs to define `track` before `CD` and `CD` before `cdCollection`.

13.1.5 The `track` Class

Each track must know its play time and where it is located in the physical CD player. Remember, the team decided that `cdPlayer` must be able to play a track. This means `track` has knowledge responsibilities for the CD number and the track number. The `track` class looks like another instance of the State Object pattern. It stores state and provides suitable access to it. Here is the CRH card.

FIGURE 13.5. *CRH card for `track`*

Class: `track`	
Responsibilities:	**Helpers:**
know play time	
know physical location in the CD player	
(CD number, track number)	

Charlie wonders about the return type of a `playTime` message. He has heard of a `time` class for manipulating time. Matt suggests that Charlie is going overboard. Play time could simply be stored as seconds. Chelsea argues that this may cause confusion since we think of play time in terms of minutes and seconds. Matt counters by stating that this is an implementation detail that the user will never see. Charlie argues that using an integer to store seconds will require conversions such as seconds into minutes and seconds. Client code would have to deal with the conversions.

Matt insists on using an `int` as the return type from `playTime`. Charlie argues that 500 minutes is 30,000 seconds. On some older compilers, the maximum `int` is only 32,767. What will happen if Blaine asks us to increase the maximum time credit to 777 minutes? Chelsea says overflow could occur as time credit goes negative. Charlie recommends `long`, which can store more than 2 billion seconds, more than enough. Chelsea recommends the following type definition. `seconds` provides a more meaningful name than `long`.

```
typedef long seconds;  // Seconds and long are interchangeable

class track {  // First draft--no constructors yet
public:
  seconds playTime() const;
  // Returns the number of seconds required to play this track

  int trackNumber() const;
  // This track's location in the CD

  int cdNumber() const;
  // The tray location of the CD in the physical CD player

private:
  seconds my_playTime;
  int my_trackNumber;
  int my_cdNumber;
};
```

Charlie makes a mental note to also use `seconds` for the `student` class. Instead of starting with 500 minutes, students can start with 500 * 60 = 30,000 seconds of play time. It will be an easy matter to deduct play time from a student's credit using integer subtraction.

13.1.6 The `cardReader` Class

The `cardReader` CRH card currently has only one action responsibility: `getStudentID`

FIGURE 13.6. *CRH card for* `cardReader`

Class: `cardReader`	
Responsibilities:	**Helpers:**
`getStudentID`	physical card reader, which
	in turn collaborates with
	the magnetic student ID card

Assuming the ID will be stored as a `string`, the class definition is easy.

```
class cardReader {  // First draft
public:
  string getStudentID() const;
  // Returns the user's ID number as a string
private:
  // TBA: Knows physical card reader
};
```

Until the money is there to buy the magnetic card reader, the `cdPlayer` class can simply read an ID number typed at the keyboard. The card reader is read as if it were the keyboard. Swiping a card through the card reader is equivalent to typing in the magnetically stored data. It will be easy to change the `cardReader` class later on after testing, as long as the class definition does not change.

13.1.7 The `trackSelector` Class

The `trackSelector` class has one major responsibility—`getTrack`. To accomplish this, `cdCollection` could be passed as an argument—by const reference because `cdCollection` will be fairly big and it should not be modified. The `trackSelector` object will show CDs and individual tracks on a selected CD in order to return the track desired by the user.

```
class trackSelector {  // First draft
public:
```

```
  track getTrack(const cdCollection & theCDCollection) const;
private:
  // TBA: May not have any private data
};
```

13.1.8 The `cdPlayer` Class

The innocent-looking `cdPlayer` CRH card only has one major responsibility: `playTrack`

FIGURE 13.7. *CRH card for `cdPlayer`*

Class: `cdPlayer`	
Responsibilities:	**Helpers:**
`playTrack`	the physical CD player
	`playList`
	`CD`

The `cdPlayer` object will "talk" to the physical CD player that Ed Slatt implemented from Chris Dodge's circuit design. The `cdPlayer` class also requires signal-capturing software to record the IR output to the CD player, use of the parallel port on the printer, some assembly language programming, and some complicated C++ code. However, `cdPlayer` proves to be the easiest class to deal with. Chris Dodge already completed most of it. It is already done. Here is the class definition for the `cdPlayer` class that acts as a wrapper around Chris's code:

```
#ifndef CDPLAYER_H
#define CDPLAYER_H
#include "track"  // For the track class
#include "irdev"  // For the IRDEV class and the assembler routine
                  // PlaySignal. The IRDEV class was implemented by
                  // Chris Dodge.
class cdPlayer {
public:
  void initKenwoodDP_M7740();
  // Because of the idiosyncrasies of my old CD player, for now I
  // want to have an initialization function named after my CD
  // player. This initialization may not work on other brands! This
  // cdPlayer class could eventually allow the same program to
  // initialize different brands of CD players.
```

```
  void playTrack (const track & currentSelection);
  // Plays a track using the CD number and track number on that CD

private:
  bool SIMULATING;  // If true allow testing; if false, music plays
  IRDEV my_cdPlayer;  // The IRDEV class was written by Chris Dodge
  string TrayCode(int cdNumber);  // Send codes to the CD player
  void delay(long n);  // Need this delay to send signals
};

#endif
```

13.1.9 The `jukeBox` Class

The `jukeBox` class coordinates most activities.

FIGURE 13.8. *CRH card for `jukeBox`*

Class: `jukeBox`	**Helpers:**
Responsibilities:	`cdPlayer`
know current track	`trackSelector`
know current student	`student`
`waitForUser`	`cardReader`
`processOneUser`	`studentCollection`
	`cdCollection`

Charlie suggests that `waitForUser` is only a small part of coordinating activities. `waitForUser` should not be part of the public interface. The `waitForUser` responsibility could be part of `jukeBox::processOneUser`. Matt wants to know, "Who will send the `processOneUser` message?" Chelsea advises the team to consider that "the answer might be found if you try to write the `main` function." Matt says, "That makes sense since `jukeBox` was always the object that got things going and because `int main()` is the first function executed." Charlie goes on, "And if `jukeBox` could be made to recognize when the system should be running and when it should be shut down, the `main` function might look like this":

```
#include "jukebox"  // For the jukeBox class

int main()  // First draft
{ // One possibility--still undecided
```

```
  jukeBox theJukeBox;

  while(theJukeBox.isRunning())
  {
     theJukeBox.processOneUser();
  }

  return 0;
}
```

This particular `main` function suggests two new public messages in the `jukeBox` interface: `processOneUser` and `isRunning`. The `waitForUser` member function moves to the private section. With the class definition suggested in `int main`, the single `jukeBox` object would contain most objects.

```
class jukeBox {  // Second draft
public:
  void processOneUser();
  // Do whatever is necessary to process one user request

  bool isRunning();
  // True until jukeBox somehow detects that it's time to shut down

private:
//--private operation
  void waitForUser();

//--data members
  cardReader my_cardReader;
  cdCollection my_cdCollection;
  studentCollection my_studentCollection;
  trackSelector my_trackSelector;
};
```

At this point, the class definitions have been started. Some have been refined. A different team might have established different classes, operations, names, data members, and algorithms.

Chelsea feels the team is now ready to implement individual classes. Because `cdCollection` needs `CD`, and `CD` needs `track`, Chelsea decides to complete `track`, `CD`, and `cdCollection`. Once these classes have been individually tested, they can be integrated and tested as part of the bigger system.

Chelsea reports the IR device built by Ed is no longer working. Apparently the power supply is inadequate. So Chelsea asks Matt, a computer engineering major, to either fix the existing piece of hardware or build a new one. Matt will also implement `cardReader` and `trackSelector`. Chelsea reminds Matt to have `cardReader` read from the keyboard until the physical card reader comes. Matt is also charged with the task of procuring the physical card reader and determining how to get the student ID number from the data during a card swipe.

This leaves Charlie to implement `student` and `studentCollection`. Chelsea also asks Charlie, who has built circuits before, to help Matt with the hardware. With that, the implementation has been divided somewhat evenly amongst the three-member team.

13.2 Implementing Member Functions and Refining Class Definitions

Charlie and Matt understand the process of reading class definitions and implementing the member functions based on those definitions. However, in their previous experiences they have always been given class definitions that already

* defined the constructors
* documented member functions with pre- and postconditions
* listed the data members

The class definitions had already been designed. They had to make few, if any, design decisions.

Chelsea encourages Matt and Charlie to proceed and make decisions on their own. "Select whatever data members you feel are appropriate. We have already made one design decision—use `vectors` in the container classes." Chelsea reviews the class definitions and writes a list of classes that, hopefully, will satisfy many knowledge responsibilities:

* `int`
* `string`
* `seconds` (`typedef seconds` as equivalent to `long`)
* `vector <track>`
* `vector <CD>`
* `vector <student>`

Charlie wonders if the standard C++ `list` class (see Chapter 14) would be better than `vector`. He can apply standard algorithms for finding students, adding students, removing students, and sorting the list of students. "Go for it, Charlie," says Chelsea. "The system will be insulated from actual implementation details—that's why we have public member functions and private data members."

The next step in divvying up the work involves getting the classes into the proper header files and making sure they compile. Here are the three header files Chelsea created from the class definitions under refinement:

```
// ----------------------------------------------------------------
// File name: track.h
// This file defines an early version of the track class
// ----------------------------------------------------------------
#ifndef TRACK_H
#define TRACK_H

typedef long seconds;

class track {  // Early draft
public:
  seconds playTime() const;
  // Returns the number of seconds required to play this track

  int trackNumber() const;
  // This track's location on the CD

  int cdNumber() const;
  // The tray location of the CD in the physical CD player

private:
  seconds my_playTime;
  int my_trackNumber;
  int my_cdNumber;
};

#endif

// ----------------------------------------------------------------
// File name: cd.h
// This file defines an early version of the CD class
// ----------------------------------------------------------------
#ifndef CD_H
#define CD_H

class CD {  // Early draft
public:
  string artist() const;
  string title() const;
//--iterator functions
  void first();
  void next();
  bool isDone() const;
  track currentItem() const;
```

```
private:
  string my_artist;
  string my_title;
  vector <track> my_data;
  int my_size;
  int my_index;
};

#endif

// ------------------------------------------------------------------
// File name: cdcollec.h
// This file defines an early version of the cdCollection class
// ------------------------------------------------------------------
#ifndef CDCOLLEC_H
#define CDCOLLEC_H

class cdCollection {  // Early draft
public:
  void addCD(const CD & aCD);
  // Add a CD to the collection if possible

  bool removeCD(const CD & aCD);
  // Remove CD if possible. Return false if it doesn't exist.

//--iterator functions
  void first();  // Let index point to the first item
  void next();   // Let index point to the next item (false at end)
  bool isDone() const;      // Return true when traversal is done
  CD currentItem() const;  // Return the item referred to by next

private:
  vector <CD> my_data;  // Store the CDs
  int my_size;          // The number of CDs in the collection
  int my_index;         // The subscript of the current item
};

#endif
```

These three class definitions can now be included from `int main()` with the file named `track`, which includes both files necessary to have `track` objects. This makes compilation and linking easy.

```
// File name: track
#ifndef _TRACK_
#define _TRACK_
#include "track.h"
#include "track.cpp"
#endif
```

Three other `.cpp` files (`track.cpp`, `cd.cpp`, and `cdcollec.cpp`) permit implementation and testing of these three classes. Even though the `.cpp` files are empty new files, they allow for the following start of a test driver, which compiles and creates an executable program that doesn't do much:

```
#include "track"  // Includes the .h file and an empty .cpp file
#include "cd"     // For class CD
#include "cdcollec"  // For the cdCollection class
int main()
{ // Invoke the compiler-supplied constructors
  CD aCD;
  track aTrack;
  cdCollection theCDs;
  return 0;
}
```

This program is executable due to a few facts about the C++ compiler:

- Member functions are not needed until link time. If a member of a class definition is never called, no error occurs.
- The C++ compiler automatically provides a default constructor for any class that has no constructor in the class definition.

So in actuality, these three constructors were automatically created by C++:

COMPILER-GENERATED DEFAULT CONSTRUCTORS

```
track::track()
{ // The C++ compiler creates this, unless the programmer does
}

CD::CD()
{ // The C++ compiler creates this, unless the programmer does
}

cdCollection::cdCollection()
{ // The C++ compiler creates this, unless the programmer does
}
```

Constructors have not been chosen yet for any of the jukebox classes. The team members will decide what to do about constructors and data member initialization while the data members are being selected. This happens next.

13.2.1 Testing Individual Classes

The framework has now been laid for Chelsea to get down to the task of implementing her three classes. The `main` function above can be used to test all three classes. Chelsea decides to take this approach:

1. Completely implement `track` and test it.
2. Completely implement `CD` and test it.
3. Completely implement `cdCollection` and test it.

13.2.2 Implementing `track`

The `track` class follows the State Object pattern. As usual, there is a default constructor necessary for storage in a `vector`. Chelsea also adds a constructor with four arguments. Chelsea notices that the team did not specify the track's title, so she adds `my_title` as a data member and an accessor member function named `title`. Here is the more refined class definition:

```
#ifndef TRACK_H
#define TRACK_H
#include <string>
using namespace std;

typedef long seconds;

class track {
public:
//--constructors
  track();

  track( string initTitle, seconds initPlayTime,
         int initCdNumber, int initTrackNumber );
  // Initialize the private data of a track

//--accessors
  string title() const;
  // Return this track's title

  seconds playTime() const;
  // Return the number of seconds required to play this track

  int cdNumber() const;
  // Where the CD is located in physical CD player (tray number)

  int trackNumber() const;
```

```
  // This track's location on the CD

private:
  string my_title;
  seconds my_playTime;
  int my_cdNumber;
  int my_trackNumber;
};

#endif
```

The `track` class took Chelsea about one hour to implement and test. Here is one test driver and the output it generated.

```
// This program test drives the simple track class. It should be
// run twice; once as is, and then with only the default object t1.
#include <iostream>
using namespace std;
#include "track"  // For the track class

int main()
{ // Test drive track
  track t1;
  track t2("I'm the Cat", 3*60+55, 2, 5);

  cout << "Title: " << t2.title() << endl;
  cout << t2.playTime() << " seconds, which is also "
       << t2.playTime() / 60 << " minutes and "
       << t2.playTime() % 60 << " seconds" << endl;
  cout << "CD# " << t2.cdNumber() << endl;
  cout << "Track# " << t2.trackNumber() << endl;

  return 0;
}
```

OUTPUT

```
Title: I'm the Cat
235 seconds, which is also 3 minutes and 55 seconds
CD# 2
Track# 5
```

Running the same test driver to test a default `track` object generated the following output:

```
Title: ?title?
0 seconds, which is also 0 minutes and 0 seconds
```

```
CD# 0
Track# 0
```

`track.cpp` and most of the other `.cpp` files are not shown in this chapter. The files with all their details can be found on the accompanying disk and at this textbook's Web site.

13.2.3 Implementing CD

During implementation, the programmers must decide on the data members that take care of the knowledge responsibilities. The programmers must also determine what, if any, constructors must be added to the class definition. Not until Chelsea considers adding constructors does it become obvious that an `addTrack` operation could prove useful. This will make it easier to get tracks added to a CD object. The algorithm might go like this:

```
while(there is another track to add to the CD)
{
   aCD.addTrack(aTrack)
}
```

Since this was an initialization issue that was purposely ignored during design, the `CD::addTrack` operation can be added during implementation. Chelsea logs her implementation efforts. One note states the following: "The test driver worked after some easy debugging. When I tried adding more than the default capacity tracks (10), it bombed. I forgot to resize the `vector` to be one bigger for each `track` over the default size of 10."

Here is the test driver for CD. It hints at what `trackSelector` might do to show a selected CD.

```
#include "cd"  // For the CD class

void show(const track & t2)
{
  cout.width(2);
  cout << t2.cdNumber();
  cout.width(3);
  cout << t2.trackNumber() << "  ";
  cout << t2.title() << " " << (t2.playTime() / 60)
                   << ":" << (t2.playTime() % 60) << endl;
}
```

```
int main()
{ // Test drive CD
  CD aCD("Browne, Jackson", "Looking East", 5);

  aCD.addTrack( track( "Looking East",          4*60+56, 5, 1 ) );
  aCD.addTrack( track( "Barricades of Heaven", 5*60+42, 5, 2 ) );
  aCD.addTrack( track( "Some Bridges",          4*60+51, 5, 3 ) );
  aCD.addTrack( track( "Information Wars",      5*60+14, 5, 4 ) );
  aCD.addTrack( track( "I'm the Cat",           3*60+55, 5, 5 ) );
  aCD.addTrack( track( "Culver Moon",           5*60+45, 5, 6 ) );
  aCD.addTrack( track( "Baby How Long",         5*60+05, 5, 7 ) );
  aCD.addTrack( track( "Nino",                  5*60+14, 5, 8 ) );
  aCD.addTrack( track( "Alive in the World",    4*60+51, 5, 9 ) );
  aCD.addTrack( track( "It Is One",             4*60+57, 5, 10) );
  // Add a couple more than the default CD capacity size of 10
  aCD.addTrack( track("Fake Eleventh", 0, 5, 11) );
  aCD.addTrack( track("Fake Twelfth",  0, 5, 12) );

  cout << aCD.artist() << "    " << aCD.title() << endl;

  // Iterate over all tracks in the CD
  track aTrack;

  aCD.first();
  while( ! aCD.isDone() )
  {
    aTrack = aCD.currentItem();
    show(aTrack);

    aCD.next();
  }

  return 0;
}
```

OUTPUT

```
Browne, Jackson   Looking East
 5  1  Looking East 4:56
 5  2  Barricades of Heaven 5:42
 5  3  Some Bridges 4:51
 5  4  Information Wars 5:14
 5  5  I'm the Cat 3:55
 5  6  Culver Moon 5:45
 5  7  Baby How Long 5:5
 5  8  Nino 5:14
 5  9  Alive in the World 4:51
 5 10  It Is One 4:57
 5 11  Fake Eleventh 0:0
 5 12  Fake Twelfth 0:0
```

The last two tracks cause the CD to expand beyond its capacity. Chelsea notes, "Later on, it may be appropriate to increase the default initial capacity (currently 10 tracks per CD) and the increase capacity by more than 1. That is because `vector::resize` is an expensive operation—it takes some time. On the other hand, if the program runs out of memory, the size of the increase capacity may need to be decreased." The member function includes some comments to this effect. However, Chelsea isn't worried as long as there are no more than 200, 400, or even 600 CDs.

```
void CD::addTrack(const track & nextTrack)
{ // This function tries to balance time/space tradeoffs. You could
  // increase DEFAULT_NUMBER_OF_TRACKS or resize by two.
  if(my_size + 1 >= my_data.capacity())
    my_data.resize( my_data.capacity() + 1 );
  my_data[my_size] = nextTrack;
  my_size++;
}
```

The `CD` class definition is refined to the following:

```
// ------------------------------------------------------------------
// File name: cd.h
// This file defines an early version of the CD class
// ------------------------------------------------------------------
#ifndef CD_H
#define CD_H
#include <vector>
#include <string>
using namespace std;
#include "track"  // For the track class

class CD {
public:
  CD();
  // Default constructor allows vector of tracks

  CD(string initArtist, string initTitle, int initCdNumber);
  // Initialize a CD with zero tracks

  void addTrack(const track & nextTrack);
  // Add a new track--missed this during design

//--accessors
  string artist() const;
  // Return this CD's artist

  string title() const;
  // Return the title of this CD

  int cdNumber() const;
  // Return physical location of this CD in CD player (tray number)
```

```
  track getTrack(int trackNum) const;

  int size() const;
  // Return the number of tracks in this CD

//--iterator functions
  void first();
  void next();
  bool isDone() const;
  track currentItem() const;

private:
  string my_artist;
  string my_title;
  vector <track> my_data;
  int my_size;
  int my_index;
  int my_cdNumber;
};
#endif
```

The `getTrack` and `size` member functions were added after Chelsea realized they might be useful and important for the algorithm in `trackSelector`. For example, the `CD::size` accessor could be used to get a valid track number with code like this:

```
do {
  cout << "Enter track number [1.." << aCD.size() << "]: ";
  cin >> trackNum;
} while (trackNum < 1 || trackNum > aCD.size());
cout << "You entered track " << trackNum << endl;
```

DIALOGUE

```
Enter track number [1..10]: 0
Enter track number [1..10]: -1
Enter track number [1..10]: 11
Enter track number [1..10]: 999
Enter track number [1..10]: 10
You entered track 10
```

This prevents users from entering track numbers that don't exist. `trackSelector` might also have trouble returning a track to `jukeBox` during the `getTrack` implementation. It is probably easy to get the CD number and a track number from the user. `trackSelector` can then use `CD::getTrack`.

```
track CD::getTrack(int trackNum) const
{
  return my_data[trackNum - 1];
}
```

Once `trackSelector` has a CD handy, it is easy to get the `track` object from the CD and return it to the client (`jukeBox`).

```
track aTrack( aCD.getTrack(trackNum) );
return aTrack;
```

The `cd.cpp` file containing the member function implementations is on the accompanying disk and at this textbook's Web site.

13.2.4 Implementing `cdCollection`

`cdCollection` is the most difficult of the first three classes to implement. Chelsea decides to have a default constructor do all the work. Here is the beginning of the default constructor that initializes the collection by reading from the file containing the CD data.

```
string CD_FILE_NAME = "cd.dat";

const int DEFAULT_NUMBER_OF_CDS = 200;

cdCollection::cdCollection()
{
  my_size = 0;
  my_index = -1;
  string fileName(CD_FILE_NAME) ;
  ifstream inFile(fileName.c_str());

  // Terminate right away if the file is not found
  if(! inFile)
  {
    cout << "**Error initializing CD collection from "
         << cdCollection::cdCollection() << endl;
    cout << "**Could not open '" << fileName
         << "'. Terminating program" << endl;
    exit(0);
  }
  // . . . Lots of initialization detail removed. See the file
  // cdcollec.cpp.
```

Here is the refined `cdCollection` class definition inside the file:

```
// ---------------------------------------------------------------
// File name: cdcollec.h
// This file defines an early version of the cdCollection class
// ---------------------------------------------------------------
#ifndef CDCOLLEC_H
#define CDCOLLEC_H
#include <vector>
#include <string>
using namespace std;
#include "cd"  // For the cd class

class cdCollection {
public:
  cdCollection();
  // pre:  The file with the CD data is in the right place
  // post: cdCollection represents all CDs in physical CD player

  void addCD(const CD & nextCD);
  // post: Add a CD to the collection if possible

  bool removeCD(const CD & aCD);
  // post: Remove CD if possible. Return false if it doesn't exist.

  int size() const;
  // post: Return the number of CDs in the collection

  CD getCD(int cdNumber) const;
  // pre:  cdNumber >= 1 and cdNumber <= cdCollection::size()
  // post: Return an entire CD based on the CD# argument

//--iterator functions
  void first();  // Let index point to the first item
  void next();   // Let index point to the next item (false at end)
  bool isDone() const;     // Return true when traversal is done
  CD currentItem() const;  // Return the item referred to by next

private:
  vector <CD> my_data;  // Store the CDs
  int my_size;            // The number of CDs in the collection
  int my_index;           // The subscript of the current item
};

#endif  // #ifndef CDCOLLEC_H
```

The `cdCollection` member function implementations are stored in the file `cdcollec.cpp` on the accompanying disk and at this textbook's Web site. The file `testcd.cpp` contains the `cdCollection` test driver, which you could run in simulation mode—just follow the prompts. `testcd.cpp` is omitted here for space reasons. Even the output from this test driver is extensive. Only two of many screens are shown here.

OUTPUT (FIRST SCREEN FROM TEST DRIVING `cdCollection` WITH `testcd.cpp`)

```
  1 Hashitani, Samantha      Samantha Hashitani
  2 Browne, Jackson          Looking East
  3 Raitt, Bonnie            Luck of the Draw
  4 Sting                    Ten Summoners' Tales
  5 Gabriel, Peter           Us
  6 R.E.M                    Out of Time
Enter CD number [1..6]: 2
```

OUTPUT (NEXT SCREEN)

```
 1  Looking East
 2  Barricades of Heaven
 3  Some Bridges
 4  Information Wars
 5  I'm the Cat
 6  Culver Moon
 7  Baby How Long
 8  Nino
 9  Alive in the World
10  It Is One
Enter track number [1..10]: 9
You picked:
==============
Looking East by Browne, Jackson
 title: Alive in the World
  time: 291
   cd#: 2
track#: 9

        Confirm <y/n>: y
```

At this point, a new team member, Jim Neumeyer, begins to work on the `student` and `studentCollection` classes. His development should be similar to `CD` and `cdCollection`. Therefore, to save space, these classes are not revealed in this chapter.

13.3 System Testing

At this point, most classes have been independently implemented and tested. The team is still waiting for student and studentCollection. Additionally, Matt admits he has not completed the cardReader class as suggested. "The money hasn't been made available to buy the hardware. However, I do have it working so it asks the student to type in their ID." Chelsea remarks, "Well at least that's okay. We could simulate the running jukebox system by having a fake ID typed in. And even though studentCollection is not complete, we can test the other major classes together." After a pause, Chelsea suggests the team could continue: "We'll allow anyone to select a song. We won't update the students in studentCollection. Let's just see if we can integrate what we have."

The team gets all their .h and .cpp files into the same directory on one computer. Chelsea makes a few changes with constant definitions and typedefs and stores the complete list in a file named cddefs.h, which is short for CD jukebox definitions.

```
// ----------------------------------------------------------------
// File name: cddefs.h
// Contains all typedefs and constant objects for jukebox classes
// ----------------------------------------------------------------
#ifndef CDDEFS_H
#define CDDEFS_H
typedef long seconds;
const int DEFAULT_NUMBER_OF_TRACKS = 10;
const string CD_FILE_NAME = "cd.dat";
const int DEFAULT_NUMBER_OF_CDS = 200;
#endif
```

Although some of the files had to be changed to include cddefs.h, the typedef and all global constants are now included in one file to make it easier to maintain the system. The final task now is to implement the jukeBox class.

From the analysis, it appears that jukeBox will be sending messages to most of the other major objects in the system. jukeBox will

* ask cardReader for the student ID
* ask studentCollection for a student
* ask trackSelector for the user's choice
* send a message to cdPlayer to play a track

Somehow, jukeBox must have access to these objects. Consider that trackSelector has a *uses relationship* with cdCollection. trackSelector needs cdCollection to fulfill its `getTrack` responsibility. To realize this relationship, the class was designed to have `cdCollection` passed as an argument to `getTrack`. But this is not the same as a `jukeBox` class that must send interesting messages to many objects. The jukebox could be designed to have these five objects passed as arguments to `jukeBox`: `cardReader`, `studentCollection`, `cdCollection`, `trackSelector`, and `cdPlayer`. Or referential attributes with pointers could be used. However, Matt doesn't know what pointers are and Charlie doesn't know what referential attributes are. Instead, Chelsea decides the jukebox should be designed with a *containment relationship*.

The containment relationship can be implemented by adding objects as data members. With a containment approach, `jukeBox` *contains* the objects as data members. "It does model a real-world jukebox," claims Matt.

```
#ifndef JUKEBOX_H
#define JUKEBOX_H
#include "cdcollec"   // For the cdCollection class
#include "selector"   // For the trackSelector class
#include "cdplayer"   // For the cdPlayer class
#include "cardread"   // For the cardReader class

class jukeBox {
public:
  jukeBox();
  // Initialize the cdPlayer and possibly do some other things

  void processOneUser();
  // Do whatever is necessary to process one user request

  bool isRunning();
  // True until jukeBox detects that it is time to shut down

private:
//--data members
  student my_currentStudent;
  track my_currentSelection;
  cardReader my_cardReader;
  cdCollection my_cdCollection;
  studentCollection my_studentCollection;
  trackSelector my_trackSelector;
  cdPlayer my_cdPlayer;
};
#endif  // #ifndef JUKEBOX_H
```

13.3.1 Assessing the Design

"Why is this a good design?" asks Matt. Chelsea defers to Riel's object-oriented design heuristics book to illustrate the design heuristics followed by the jukebox design.

OBJECT-ORIENTED DESIGN HEURISTIC 13.1 (RIEL'S 4.5)

> If a class contains objects of another class, then the containing class should be sending messages to the contained objects. The containment relationship should always imply a uses relationship.

"This is true for `jukeBox`," Charlie perceives. "`jukeBox` sends messages to all of its contained objects. The jukebox is *using* those objects to fulfill its responsibilities. This too is an example of the uses relationship. It is brought about through containment." Chelsea introduces a few other object-oriented design heuristics that apply in this situation:

OBJECT-ORIENTED DESIGN HEURISTIC 13.2 (RIEL'S 4.13)

> A class must know what it contains, but it should not know who contains it.

This allows the contained classes to be reused in other applications. The `cdCollection` class could be used in a system that records your personal CDs, for example. `cdCollection` could be used elsewhere. In fact, `cdCollection` was individually tested. This implies it can stand alone. It does not need `jukeBox`.

Chelsea highlights another guideline that indicates the design is good.

OBJECT-ORIENTED DESIGN HEURISTIC 13.3 (RIEL'S 4.14)

> Objects that share lexical scope—those contained in the same containing class—should not have a uses relationship between them.

Sharing lexical scope means the objects could potentially send messages to each other. The five major objects in the `jukeBox` class are:

```
cardReader my_cardReader;
cdCollection my_cdCollection;
studentCollection my_studentCollection;
trackSelector my_trackSelector;
cdPlayer my_cdPlayer;
```

During role playing, the team could have sent a message to anyone around the table. Now, with the current design of jukeBox, any of these five objects could send a message to any of the others also. During role playing, no message was sent from cardReader to cdCollection. No message went from cdPlayer to studentCollection. Additionally, the current design implements what the team felt was reasonable during role playing. The jukeBox class—containing the major abstractions—was designed well.

The algorithm for processOneUser is now actually quite simple. This simplicity is possible because the system intelligence has been distributed evenly amongst the key abstractions. Each class was implemented and thoroughly tested by different members of the programming team. Here is the algorithm before studentCollection was added. One of the programming projects asks you to add the studentCollection class and change this jukeBox::processOneUser.

```
void jukeBox::processOneUser()
{ // Do whatever is necessary to process one user request

  while ( ! my_cardReader.isCardSwiped() )
    ;  // Do nothing as the cardReader is continuously polled

  my_currentStudent = my_cardReader.getStudentID();

  // Need to get studentCollection before this is completed. For
  // now, just proceed as if every student were valid.

  my_currentSelection = my_trackSelector.getTrack(my_cdCollection);

  my_cdPlayer.playTrack(my_currentSelection);
}
```

All this makes it easy to create a very short system main function:

```
#include "jukebox"  // For the jukebox class

int main()
{
  jukeBox theJukeBox;

  while(theJukeBox.isRunning())
  {
     theJukeBox.processOneUser();
  }

  return 0;
}
```

All the necessary files were stored into one directory so the system can be tested. Along the way, modifications were made to get the running system. The current state of the project is a running program that allows anyone to enter a bogus ID and select as many songs as desired (see the programming projects to change this). Currently, the tester has a choice whether to actually play the music or to simulate selections so the software can be tested and enhanced without the IR device and an attached CD player. However, the disk files allow you to run and test in simulation mode only, since it is highly unlikely you have the same CDs and CD player and the IR device attached to your printer port.

Chapter Summary

- This chapter showed how to proceed from analysis to design of an object-oriented system. Along the way, several object-oriented design heuristics indicated that team decisions resulted in good design.
- Good design can be obtained and measured by such things as:
  - high cohesion—member functions and data members belong together
  - low coupling—allows easier partitioning of work amongst the team and easier unit testing
  - proper return types and arguments
  - proper messages
  - understandable set of major classes with descriptive names to model a solution that is understandable to one and all
  - actual application of object-oriented design heuristics—the jukebox contains objects that don't talk to each other, for example
- Designing class definitions roughly bounds the design phase of object-oriented software development. Programmers choose
  - member functions with appropriate return types, names, and arguments
  - the data members
- Implementing and testing the algorithms of the member functions roughly bound the implementation phase.
- Action responsibilities may be implemented as member functions.
- Knowledge responsibilities may be implemented as
  - data members
  - values returned from a message
  - data gotten as an argument in a message

Design / Implementation Tips

1. Refined CRH cards provide excellent input to the design of class definitions.

The better the CRH cards, the easier the class definitions are to design. Consider role playing your scenarios with class definitions in mind. The return types and arguments could be written directly on the CRH card. For example:

Class: `trackSelector`	
Responsibilities:	**Helpers:**
`track getTrack(int)`	the user
	`track`
	`CD`
	`cdCollection`

2. Look for divisions of labor.

Team members can divide some of the work up to completely implement and test individual classes. For example, one or two members of your team could be implementing `track`, `CD`, and `cdCollection` while other team members implement `student` and `studentCollection`. This can speed up a project.

3. If you say you're going to do it, do it!

A team is only as strong as its weakest member. If you don't show up for a meeting, you can hurt your team. If you commit to doing a specific task, don't let your team down. The whole project can fail if you don't do your part.

4. Learn to work as a team.

Industry wants students who know how to work with a team. The best way to learn this is to do it. Few people work by themselves. Analysis, design, and implementation benefit when people work together. Experience it. Be open to others' ideas. Learn to deal with diverse opinions. But don't be afraid to fight for what you believe in.

5. Take the time to write test drivers.

Each class you implement should be tested independently if possible. This may require writing a little program that does little more than call every member function of a class. However, this testing pays off in the long run.

6. If you need someone else's class, get it.

Pay attention to which class needs another class before it can be designed and implemented. For example, `jukeBox` needs just about every other class. So `jukeBox` might be defined last. In this case, your team members must make their classes available to you.

7. Sometimes a class declaration (not definition) will get you farther on down the line.

For example, consider that `trackSelector` needs `cdCollection` as a parameter. `jukeBox::getTrack` also needs `track` as a return type. The `trackSelector` class will compile with the following two class declarations standing in for the complete class definitions:

```
class cdCollection;  // C++ allows these declarations to stand in for
class track;         // the class definitions

class trackSelector {
public:
  track getTrack(cdCollection & theCDCollection);
private:
  // No data members when cout and cin are used
};
```

Now someone could go ahead and implement `trackSelector::message`.

8. Sometimes a class definition (not the implementation) will get you farther on down the line.

Now, if the `cdCollection` interface were available before the member functions were implemented, you could `#include` it and then go ahead and try to compile `getTrack`—even though it will not link until the `cdCollection` member functions are done.

```
// File name: ui.cpp
#include "cdcollec"  // Make cdCollection class definition available
class CD;  // Still need CD class definition to compile
class track;  // Still need track definition to compile
```

```
track trackSelector::getTrack(const cdCollection & theCdCollection)
{
  track aTrack;  // Will compile at least
  CD aCD;
  theCdCollection.first();
  int n = 0;

  while( ! theCdCollection.isDone() )
  {
    aCD = theCdCollection.currentItem();
   // . . .
  }

  return aTrack;
}
```

9. Don't be surprised to see yourself adding new stuff.

You might find new data members and member functions as you design the class definitions and implement the member functions. Don't be surprised if arguments and return types change.

Programming Projects—Complete the Jukebox

By completing the following programming projects, you will get the jukebox running in simulation mode. The major activity involves getting the student to become part of the system.

1. Run the program that simulates the running `jukeBox` and doesn't care what student ID you type in. You can select as many songs as you want. All files are in the `jukebox` directory on this textbook's disk. To run the program, you'll need many files. The file named `testjuke.cpp` looks like this:

```
#include "jukebox"  // For the jukebox class
int main()
{
  jukeBox theJukeBox;

  while(theJukeBox.isRunning())
  {
     theJukeBox.processOneUser();
  }

  return 0;
}
```

2. Implement the `student` class and test it independently. Consider using the `Date` class stored in `date.h` and `date.cpp` to deal with `student::canSelect`. Test the function.

3. Implement the `studentCollection` class and test it independently. Enter several IDs to ensure that no one ID can select more than two tracks on a given date.

4. Integrate `student` into the jukebox system.

Design/Implementation Projects

Each of the following design and implementation projects requires completion of the associated analysis and design project in the previous chapter.

13A Design and Implement 12A, Bank Teller Application

Make sure you complete 12A first. If you haven't already done so, read the "Analysis/Design Tips" section in Chapter 12 for help on how to do this. Then implement the bank teller system as a team. Also read the "Design/Implementation Tips" section of this chapter.

13B Design and Implement 12B, Voice Mail System

Make sure you complete 12B first. If you haven't already done so, read the "Analysis/Design Tips" section in Chapter 12 for help on how to do this. Then implement the voice mail system as a team. Also read the "Design/Implementation Tips" section of this chapter.

13C Design and Implement 12C, Video Rental System

Make sure you complete 12C first. If you haven't already done so, read the "Analysis/Design Tips" section in Chapter 12 for help on how to do this. Then implement the video rental system as a team. Also read the "Design/Implementation Tips" section of this chapter.

13D Design and Implement 12D, Checkbook Application

Make sure you complete 12D first. If you haven't already done so, read the "Analysis/Design Tips" section in Chapter 12 for help on how to do this. Then implement the checkbook system as a team. Also read the "Design/Implementation Tips" section of this chapter.

Chapter Fourteen

A Little Indirection

Pointers, Containers, and Iterators

Summing Up

If you have completed all previous chapters, you should now have a good feel for object-oriented software development. If you have skipped Chapters 6, 11, 12, and 13, you have at least used some objects, but you are probably more interested in problem solving and programming in C++ than in the object-oriented aspects of this textbook. This chapter can be studied any time after Chapter 10, "Vectors."

Coming Up

This chapter introduces the notion of *indirection*. Indirection occurs when there is a substitute for something. Consider a library catalog card that holds the Dewey decimal number of a book. The card itself is not the book. Rather, the card is a reference to the book. Because the card names the location of the book, in a sense, the card contains an "address." C++ has its own method for implementing indirection through a class of data known as *pointers*—objects that store addresses of other objects. This chapter also introduces iterator objects that refer to the elements in a collection during sequential traversal. After studying this chapter, you will be able to

- understand that pointer objects store addresses of other objects
- use several methods for initializing pointers
- use the standard `list` class
- use iterators to refer to all items in a container object in a sequential fashion

Exercises and programming projects to reinforce indirection for traversing items in a container

14.1 Memory Considerations

Every object has a name, state, and set of available operations. Objects also have scope—where they are known—and lifetime—the length of time from when they are constructed to when they go out of existence. From object initializations such as

```
int able = 123;
int baker = 987;
```

most of these characteristics of the objects can be ascertained. However, the location of the object in memory—its address—is not so obvious. Until now, we have relied on the system to manage addresses. C++ allows programmers to manipulate those addresses directly.

Each object resides in a specific memory location, which is one or more bytes of computer memory addressed as the first byte. For example, here is a machine-level view of objects showing `able` stored at address 6300 and `baker` at address 6304 (the addresses shown are arbitrary; do not infer that `int`s are always stored in four bytes of memory).

Address	Class	Name	State
6300	int	able	123
6304	int	baker	987

The object named `able` is shown to reside in the bytes 6300, 6301, 6302, and 6303. The address of `able` is the first of those four bytes of memory, or 6300. Although we do not always need to know the exact addresses of objects, the concept of objects that store addresses eventually becomes important in the study of computing fundamentals with C++.

The memory allocated for many objects is determined at compiletime. A `char` object might require one byte of memory, an `int` usually requires either two or four depending on the computer system, and a `double` object requires a specific and predictable (at least by machine) number of bytes. These types of objects are said to be *static* objects because the memory is allocated at compiletime. The amount of memory allocated for a static object is fixed and will not change while the program is running.

Pointer objects allow programmers to write code that allows for runtime allocation of memory. The space is made available while the program is running. These runtime-allocated objects are *dynamic* because they consume chunks of memory at runtime. The major benefit is this: memory is allocated on an as-needed basis. The memory is also deallocated, or returned, to the system when it is no longer needed.

Dynamic objects manage collections that may shrink and grow in size, where the size is limited only by available memory. Programmers can more effectively control computer resources. For example, `string` objects employ behind-the-scenes dynamic memory allocation that permits a runtime sizing of `string` objects. This implementation of the `string` class was chosen because there is no way to predict how many characters will be entered by the user at runtime.

```
string name;  // Memory allocated during input operation (cin >>)
cout << "Enter your name: "
cin >> name;
```

The `string` class also allows programmers to assign varying-length `strings`.

```
string a, b;  // The appropriate memory is allocated on assignment

a = "The string object a should have it's own space";  // 46 chars
b = "The string object b should also";                 // 31 chars
```

An alternative would be to allocate a `vector` of `chars` of arbitrary size for every `string` object during the call to the constructor. But what size should we use? We could pick a size large enough to accommodate most `strings`, but this would waste large amounts of memory. Imagine a `vector` of 1,000 `strings` in which each `string` is allocated 128 or 200 bytes of memory even if the average length of the `strings` ends up to be only 9 characters. Without the pointers discussed in this chapter, the programmer might be forced into this alternative of wasted computer memory. These memory management issues will be presented in Chapter 15, "Dynamic Memory Management." First, pointers must be understood. Pointers also will be used in Chapter 17 to implement a collection that has different classes of objects in it.

14.1.1 Pointer Objects

Pointer objects store the addresses of other objects—they point *to* other objects. A pointer object is declared with an asterisk (`*`) after the class name.

GENERAL FORM 14.1. *Declaring pointer objects*

*class-name** *identifier* ;

The asterisk indicates that *identifier* can store the address of an object of type *class-name*. For example, in the declaration

```
int* intPtr;
```

the pointer object named `intPtr` may store the address of one `int` object. The object named `intPtr` does not represent an `int`, it represents the address of an `int`.

A pointer object may have one of these states:

1. It may be undefined (garbage, as `intPtr` currently is).
2. It may contain the special pointer value `NULL` or `0`, signifying the pointer points to nothing.
3. It may point to an instance of the class it was declared to point to.

Currently any attempt to use the undefined value of `intPtr` will result in undefined system behavior. One way to set the state of `intPtr` is to assign it the special pointer constant `NULL` that means the pointer does not point to anything.

```
intPtr = NULL;  // intPtr points to nothing
intPtr = 0;     // 0 is another way to write NULL
```

Because pointer objects store addresses, their values become more meaningful when visibly written in a box with an arrow pointing to the object. So these statements:

```
int anInt = 123;  // Allocate memory for an int and initialize it
int* p;  // Allocate memory to store the address of an int object
```

can be graphically represented as follows:

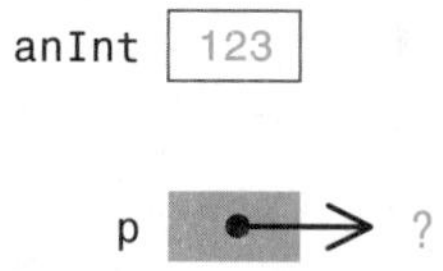

The ? signifies a pointer object that has not been assigned a value yet. The ? is the garbage value. When `NULL` is assigned to the pointer named `p` like this:

```
p = NULL;
```

the state of `p` could be pictured like this:

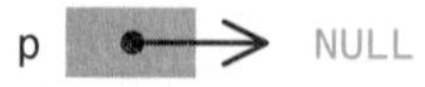

But how can a pointer be made to point to something?

Pointer objects may be assigned values through the address-of operator `&`. The `&` operator returns the address of the object that follows it.

GENERAL FORM 14.2. *Obtaining the address of an object*

&*object-name*

For example, the expression `&anInt` evaluates to the address of `anInt`. The following statement stores the address of `anInt` in the pointer object `p` (the expression `&anInt` is read as "address of `anInt`"):

```
p = &anInt;  // &anInt returns memory location (address) of anInt
```

This assignment is best presented pictorially by moving the arrow from ? to the object it holds the address of.

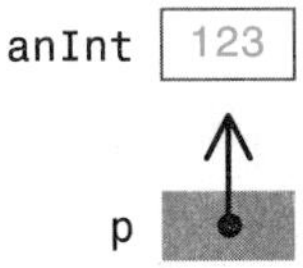

The arrow from `p` to `anInt` indicates that `p` is now pointing to the object `anInt`; however, the actual value stored in `p` is an address—the memory location of `anInt`.

The state of the object pointed to by a pointer object can be altered indirectly. For example, the state of `anInt` can be changed without even using the object name. This *indirect addressing* with the dereference, or indirection, operator `*` allows the program to inspect or change the memory pointed to by the pointer object. Here is an example of how the memory for the `int` pointed to by `p` may be altered.

```
*p = 456;  // Indirect addressing stores 654 in anInt
```

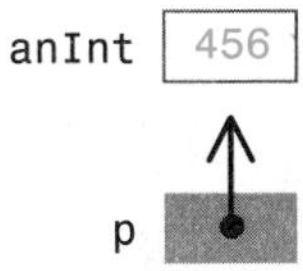

GENERAL FORM 14.3. *Indirect addressing*

**pointer-object*

Notice that the assignment to `*p` does not change `p`. Instead, it changes the state of the object pointed to by `p`. The `*` that precedes a pointer object indicates the object referenced, or pointed to, by the pointer object. So for example, if `anInt` were stored at address 6308, that address is stored in `p`.

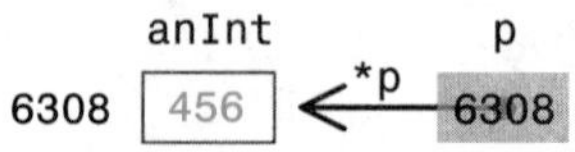

To illustrate the differences between `p`, `*p`, and `&anInt`, consider the indirect addressing method used in the following program that interchanges two pointers' values. By the end of the program, the two pointer objects `p1` and `p2` point to each other's original `int` object.

```
// Interchange two pointer values. The pointers are switched to
// point to the other's original int object.
#include <iostream>
using namespace std;

int main()
{
  double* p1;
  double* p2;
  double* temp;
  double n1 = 99.9
  double n2 = 88.8;

  // Let p1 point to n1 and p2 point to n2
  p1 = &n1;
  p2 = &n2;
  cout << "*p1 and *p2 before switch" << endl;
  cout << (*p1) << "    " << (*p2) << endl;

  // Swap the pointers by letting p1 point to where p2 is pointing
  // and letting p2 point to where p1 is pointing
  temp = p1;
  p1 = p2;
  p2 = temp;

  // Now the values of the pointers are switched to point to each
  // other's int object. The ints themselves do not move.
  cout << "*p1 and *p2 after switch" << endl;
  cout << (*p1) << "    " << (*p2) << endl;

  return 0;
}
```

OUTPUT

```
*p1 and *p2 before switch
99.9    88.8
*p1 and *p2 after switch
88.8    99.9
```

The values `99.9` and `88.8` were not moved in memory. Instead, the pointers to these `int` objects are interchanged. The following graphic representation traces this program execution. First, all five objects are initialized as follows (*Note:* All boxes represent memory storing the state of an object):

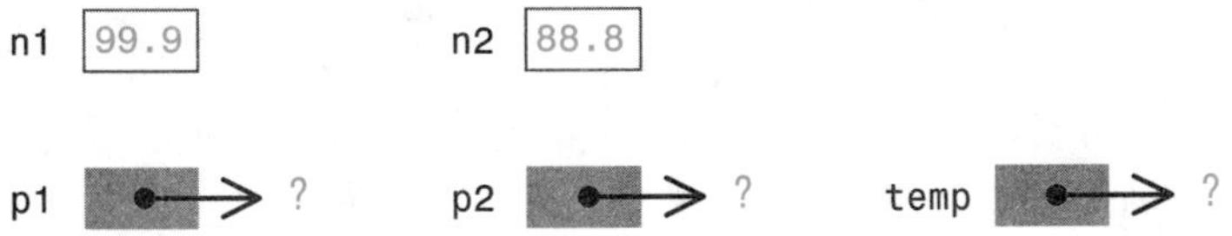

The next two statements (`p1 = &n1;` and `p2 = &n2;`) store the addresses of the integers in the pointers.

```
p1 = &n1;
p2 = &n2;
```

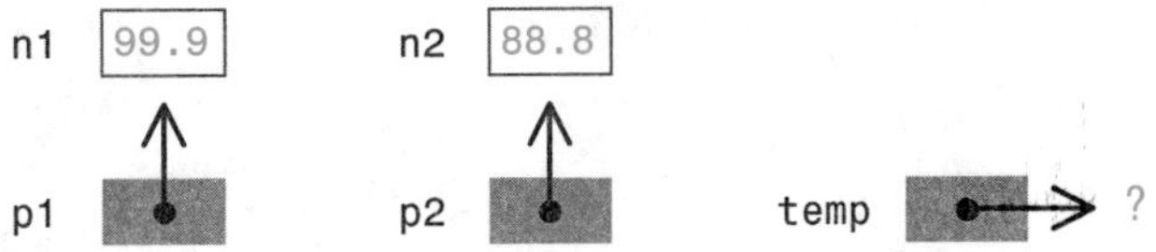

The statement `temp = p1;` means that the pointer object `temp` is set to point to the same memory location as `p1`. The address of `p1` was stored in `temp` (at this point the expression `temp == p1` would be true). This change (shown below) is indicated by the fact that arrows from both `p1` and `temp` point to the same location—the object named `n1`.

```
temp = p1;
```

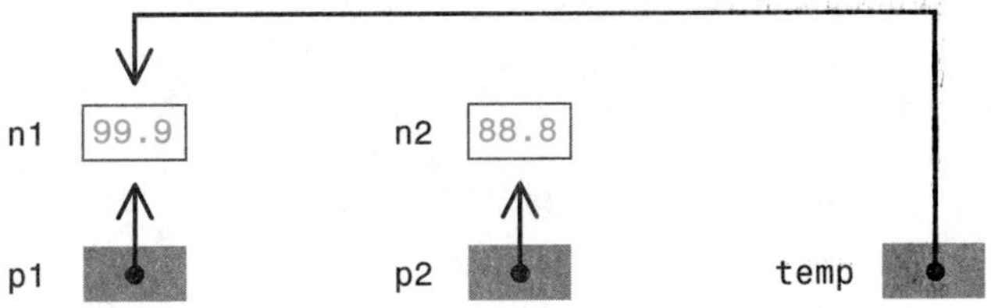

Next, the assignment `p1 = p2;` causes `p1` to point to the same place as `p2`. So `p1` and `p2` now store the same address. These two pointer values are equal.

```
p1 = p2;
```

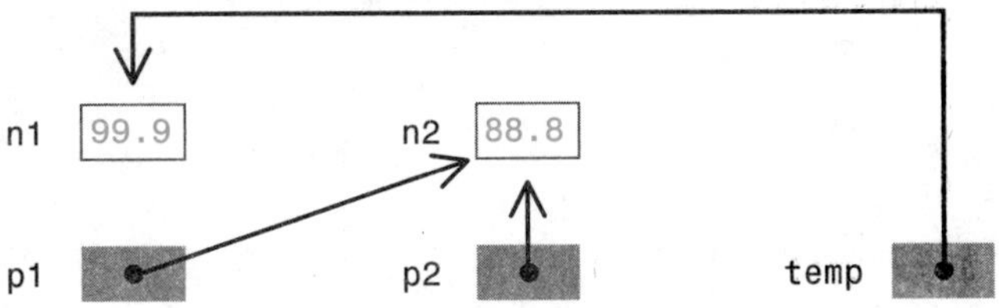

And finally, `p2 = temp;` causes `p2` to point to the same `int` to which `p1` was originally pointing.

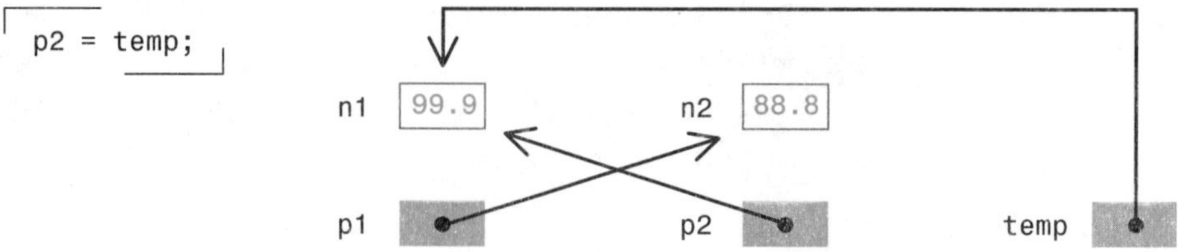

Now that p2 points to n1 and p1 points to n2, `cout << (*p1)` displays 88.8, rather than the original 99.9.

At first, working with pointers is not easy. It takes a shift from understanding objects that store values, to understanding objects that store addresses of other objects that in turn store values. Algorithm design and debugging are different. One low-cost tool that helps during debugging is the use of arrows to represent pointer values. Algorithms are traced by moving the arrow rather than writing the address.

Also when writing debugging code, the value being pointed to is usually more telling than the address of where that object is located. So debug with `*` as in `cout << (*aPointer);` rather than `cout << aPointer;`. With this, you see the more useful values of the objects, not their addresses.

14.1.2 Pointers to Objects

Pointers to `int`s and `double`s refer to one single value stored in those locations. There are no associated member functions. Now consider what happens with a pointer to an object during a message. Because the dereference operator has a lower priority than a function call, this code will not work:

```
bankAccount anAcct("Functions > Dereference", 123.45);
bankAccount* bp;
bp = &anAcct;
*bp.deposit(123.45);    // ERROR
```

One way to fix this is to override the priority scheme by wrapping the pointer dereference in parentheses. Now `*bp` returns the `bankAccount` object *before* the `deposit` function gets called.

```
(*bp).deposit(123.45);   // OKAY
```

Or you could use the C++ arrow operator `->` as a shortcut to denote that the pointer is pointing to an instance of a true class.

```
bp->deposit(123.45);   // SHORTCUT
```

Both techniques are used in the following program:

```
#include <iostream>
using namespace std;
#include "baccount"

int main()
{
  bankAccount anAcct("both (*bp) and bp-> work ", 100.00);
  bankAccount* bp;
  bp = &anAcct;

  // Wrap the dereference in parentheses because the dereference
  // operator * has lower precedence than function calls
  (*bp).deposit(123.45);
  cout << (*bp).name() << (*bp).balance() << endl;

  // Use -> for pointers to objects other than int or double
  bp->withdraw(111.11);
  cout <<  bp->name()  <<  bp->balance() << endl;

  return 0;
}
```

OUTPUT

```
both (*bp) and bp-> work 223.45
both (*bp) and bp-> work 112.34
```

Now consider one possible `studentCollection` class definition (see Chapter 13) that has a `getStudent` and a `putStudent` message:

```
class studentCollection {
public:
  student getStudent(string studentID);
  // Return the student from the collection with ID == studentID

  void putStudent(student updatedStudent);
  // Replace the current student with an updated version

  // . . .
};
```

A `processOneRequest` algorithm might go something like this:

```
student currentStudent = my_studentCollection.getStudent(currentID);
track currentSelection = my_trackSelector.getSelection(my_cdCollection);
// . . . Modify student to reflect that a selection has been played
```

```
if( currentStudent.canSelect() )
{  // assert: currentStudent has been updated
   my_cdPlayer.playTrack(currentSelection);
   my_studentCollection.putStudent(currentStudent);
}
```

At this point, the database of students would have been updated to reflect that `currentStudent` had played the song.

Another alternative is to indirectly reference the student while it is still in the database. `studentCollection` could have been designed to return a *reference* to the student to allow `jukeBox` to perform an update that is semantically equivalent.

```
class studentCollection {
public:
  student & getStudent(string studentID);
  // Return a reference (address) to student with ID == studentID
  // . . .
}
```

Now, `jukeBox` can send `student::canSelect` and `student::update` messages through the pointer like this:

```
// getStudent returns the address of a student
student* currentStudent = my_studentCollection.getStudent(currentID);
if( currentStudent->canSelect() )
{
   my_cdPlayer.playTrack(currentSelection);
}
```

The second design requires you to think of the student indirectly—through the pointer to the student—rather than talk to the student directly.

Self-Check

14-1 Write the value of each of the four attributes of `x`.

```
double x = 987.65;
```

-a	name	-c	state
-b	class	-d	address

14-2 What do pointer objects store?

14-3 Name two methods for initializing a pointer object.

14-4 What is the value of `doublePtr` after this declaration:

```
double* doublePtr;
```

14-5 Use these statements to answer the questions below:

```
double* doublePtr;
double aDouble = 1.23;
doublePtr = &aDouble;
```

-a What is the name of the pointer object?

-b What is the value of `*doublePtr`?

-c What is the value of `doublePtr`?

-d Write a statement that indirectly adds one byte to the memory storing 1.23.

14-6 Write the output generated by the following program:

```
#include <iostream>
using namespace std;
int main()
{
  int* p;
  int j = 12;

  p = &j;
  cout << ((*p) + (*p)) << "   " << ((*p) * (*p)) << endl;

  return 0;
}
```

14-7 Write statements that store the address of `ch`, a `char` object, into a `char` pointer object named `charPtr`.

14-8 Write the minimum declarations and statements that declare and initialize all the objects as shown in the diagram below:

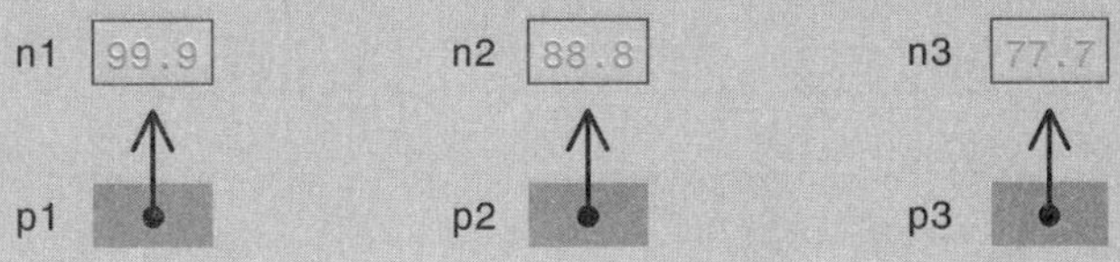

14-9 Using the code from your answer to the previous question, write a statement that indirectly displays the sum of all the objects using * (the dereference operator).

14.2 The Standard `list` Class

Recall from Chapter 11 that container classes have these two characteristics:

* The main responsibility of a container is to store a collection of objects.
* A container must allow clients to access individual elements.

These characteristics are realized in a variety of ways. The `vector` class has subscripts for access to individual elements. The nonstandard `bag` class uses member functions. The standard `list` class discussed in this section uses iterator objects.

As with `vector`, the standard C++ `list` class is a relatively new addition to the C++ standard. Like `vectors` and `bags`, `list` objects may contain zero to many objects of the same class. `lists`, like `vectors` and `bags`, also have the primary responsibility to store a collection of objects and allow programmers to traverse over that collection.

The following program constructs one `list` object and sends these standard `list` messages:

* `empty`—returns true if there are zero elements in the `list`
* `push_back`—adds one element at the end of the `list`
* `remove`—removes an object from the `list` if it's found
* `size`—returns the current number of objects in the container

```
// Demonstrate list, one of the standard container classes
#include <iostream>
#include <list>  // For the list class
using namespace std;

int main()
{
  list <int> intList;  // intList may store a collection of ints

  cout << "intList.size() == " << intList.size() << endl;

  // "Push" five new int objects onto the "back" of the list
  intList.push_back(111);
  intList.push_back(222);
  intList.push_back(333);
  intList.push_back(444);
  intList.push_back(555);
```

```
    // Remove an item that is in the list
    // and attempt to remove one that is not
    intList.remove(333);  // Remove 333
    intList.remove(999);  // Not found

    // assert: There are four (4) elements in the container intList
    // assert: The first in the sequence is 111 and the last is 555

    // Show the number of objects in the container
    cout << "intList.size() == " << intList.size() << endl;

    return 0;
  }
```

Output

```
intList.size() == 0
intList.size() == 4
```

Although some of the names are different (`list::push_back` instead of `bag::add`, for example), `list` has functionality similar to `bag`. However, there is an ordering to `list` elements. They are added to the end of the list in the above code (elements may be added at the beginning with `list::push_front`). The standard `list` class has many more operations.

14.2.1 Traversing a Standard `vector` Object

The C++ standard library has many classes for storing collections of objects in meaningful ways. Each container class must provide a way to traverse the objects in these collections. The most general method involves an indirect way to reference individual items.

The subscript operator `[ ]` provides random access to individual `vector` items. Individual `vector` elements can also be referenced with pointer syntax. Notice the `for` loop uses the object named `i`, which is first constructed as an iterator object—an object that can store the address of any element in `x`, a `vector` of integers.

```
// Demonstrate iteration with pointers
#include <vector>    // For the standard vector class
#include <iostream>  // For cout <<
using namespace std;

int main()
{
   vector<int> x(5);
```

```
    x[0] = 11;
    x[1] = 22;
    x[2] = 33;
    x[3] = 44;
    x[4] = 55;
    // Don't need a variable 'n' to store the number of elements

    // Construct an iterator object named i
    vector<int>::iterator i;
    // assert: i can indirectly reference any vector<int> element

    cout << "*i   x[j]" << endl;
    int j = 0;
    for(i = x.begin(); i != x.end(); i++)
    {
      cout << (*i) << "      " << x[j] << endl;
      // i stores an address, *i refers to the element
      j++;
    }
    return 0;
}
```

OUTPUT

```
*i   x[j]
11     11
22     22
33     33
44     44
55     55
```

The previous program suggests that there is a relationship between the `vector` operations `vector::begin` and `vector::end` because their return values can be stored in the iterator object named `i`. The standard `vector` class has these operations:

STANDARD `vector` OPERATIONS

`vector::begin`	Returns an iterator to reference the first object in the `vector` container
`vector::end`	Returns an iterator that is beyond the last object in the `vector` container

Additionally, the `++` operator, when applied to an iterator object, puts the address of the next element of the collection into the iterator object. So `i++` is similar in functionality to `bag::next`. Both messages do something behind the scenes to allow an indirect reference to the next element in the container.

By the same token, the expression `! aBag.isDone()` has something in common with the expression `i != v.end()`. Both expressions are true when all objects in the container have been traversed. Both loop tests allow programmers to iterate over the objects in the container.

Nonstandard bag	Standard Iterator	Effect of Both Expressions
`aBag.first()`	`i = x.begin()`	Set internal cursor to first element
`aBag.next()`	`i++`	Advance to the next element
`aBag.currentItem()`	`*i`	Reference the current element
`!aBag.isDone()`	`i != x.end()`	Is false when all elements have been visited

14.2.2 The Difference Between `i` and `*i`

In the previous program, `i` is an iterator object used to reference individual items in the `vector`. The notation `*i` is one of those elements. To accomplish the standard mode of iteration over the container object, the programmer must first construct an iterator object.

GENERAL FORM 14.4. *Construct an iterator object*

container-class **<** *class-of-elements* **> :: iterator** *object-name* **;**

The *container-class* is any one of the standard containers such as `list`, `stack`, `queue`, and `vector`. The *class-of-elements* is any class name that meets certain requirements such as having a default constructor. The *object-name* is the name of an object that can store a reference to an element in a similar container.

EXAMPLES OF ITERATOR CONSTRUCTIONS

```
vector<double>::iterator i;
list<string>::iterator namePtr;
queue<track>::iterator nextTrackToPlay;
```

Typically, both the container and the iterator objects are constructed next to each other as illustrated in these examples:

EXAMPLES OF CONTAINER/ITERATOR CONSTRUCTIONS

```
vector<double> x(10000, 0.0);
vector<double>::iterator i;

list<string> name(100);
list<string>::iterator namePtr;

queue<track> queuedTracks(99);
queue<track>::iterator nextTrackToPlay;
```

With preliminaries out of the way, here are some characteristics of the standard `list` class:

* manages a collection of objects
* is sequenced—there is a first, second, . . ., last
* can add objects at the beginning or at the end of the `list` with `push_front` and `push_back`
* always knows how big it is
* is generic because it may be declared to store collections of *any* class
* may grow as big as computer memory allows
* has many algorithms available such as `find`, `remove`, and `sort`

Let's look at an example first. The following code constructs a `list` object and an associated iterator, adds several objects, and then displays all elements with the help of the iterator object.

```
// Demonstrate list and list iterator objects
#include <list>  // For the standard list class
#include <iostream>
#include <string>
using namespace std;

int main()
{
   list<string> presidents;
   list<string>::iterator p;

   presidents.push_back("George Washington");
   presidents.push_back("John Adams");
   presidents.push_back("Thomas Jefferson");
   presidents.push_back("James Madison");
   presidents.push_back("James Monroe");

   cout << "The first " << presidents.size()
        << " presidents of the United States: " << endl;
```

```
    for(p = presidents.begin(); p != presidents.end(); p++)
    {
      cout << (*p) << endl;
    }

    return 0;
}
```

OUTPUT

```
The first 5 presidents of the United States:
George Washington
John Adams
Thomas Jefferson
James Madison
James Monroe
```

One of the benefits of using standard containers such as `list` is that you don't need to keep track of the size of the list. With iterators, you can always traverse the list from beginning to end.

14.2.3 Searching and Sorting `list` Objects with Standard Algorithms

The standard containers have many available operations. For example, a `list` object can be sorted with this message (it's a member function):

```
presidents.sort();
// assert: The list is in ascending order
```

A `list` can also be searched with the `find` algorithm, which is a nonmember available with `#include <algorithm>`.

```
presidents.push_back("Abraham Lincoln");
p = find(presidents.begin(), presidents.end(), "Abraham Lincoln");
```

The `find` function has two iterator arguments, followed by the item to be searched for. In the previous function call, the `list` is searched from beginning to end until the third argument is found or the end is reached. The `find` function returns an iterator object, which is stored in `p`. If the `string` `"Abraham Lincoln"` is in the `list`, the iterator value is the address of the found object. If not, `find` returns `iterator::end()`. This fact can be used to determine if the `find` function found the searched for item. `"Abraham Lincoln"` was in the `list`.

```
if(p != presidents.end())
  cout << "Found " << (*p)  << endl;
else
  cout << "Did not find Abe" << endl;
```

OUTPUT

```
Found Abraham Lincoln
```

The following function call searches for another `"Abraham Lincoln"`. Notice the search is restricted to the range of one past `p` to the end.

```
p++;  // Advance to the next president (or the end)

p = find(p, presidents.end(), "Abraham Lincoln");

if(p != presidents.end())
  cout << "We had two presidents of the same name" << endl;
else
  cout << "Abe is one in 41" << endl;
```

OUTPUT

```
Abe is one in 41
```

One catch to using the `find` operation is that the objects in the container must define the equality operator (==). To use the `sort` algorithm, the class must define the < operator. Whereas `string`, `int`, and `double` already define the relational operators, any new programmer-defined class must define all relational operators <, ==, <=, >=, !=, and >. This can be done through the process of operator overloading (see Chapter 18).

Here is a complete program that utilizes the handy `sort` and `find` operations (notice that you must `#include <algorithm>` for `find`).

```
#include <iostream>    // For cout <<
#include <string>      // For the standard string class
#include <algorithm>   // For find(iterator, iterator, object)
#include <list>        // For list<Type>
using namespace std;

int main ()
{ // list and iterator constructors
  list<string> stringList;
  list<string>::iterator si;

  stringList.push_back("One");
```

```
    stringList.push_back("Two");
    stringList.push_back("Three");
    stringList.push_back("Four");
    stringList.push_back("Five");

    si = find(stringList.begin(), stringList.end(), "Three");

    if(si != stringList.end())
    { // Found it before reaching the end of the list
      cout << "\nFound '" << (*si)
           << "'. Now modify it in the list." << endl;
      *si = *si + " 'modified with the iterator object'";
    }
    else
    { // Didn't find it
      cout << "\nThree not found" << endl ;
    }

    stringList.sort();  // Sort the list in ascending order

    cout << "\nThe strings after sorting: " << endl;

    for(si = stringList.begin();  si != stringList.end();  si++)
    {
      cout << (*si) << endl ;
    }

    return 0;
  }
```

OUTPUT

```
Found 'Three'. Now modify it in the list.

The strings after sorting:
Five
Four
One
Three 'modified with the iterator object'
Two
```

Chapter Summary

- Pointer objects store addresses of other objects. Objects are given meaningful values through assignment of one pointer to another, or with the & (address of) operator that returns the address of its operand.

* Pointer values are either undefined or `NULL` (`0`), or they contain the address of another object that can be indirectly referenced through the pointer.
* The `&` operator returns the address of the object. The `*` operator with a pointer returns the object being pointed to.

```
intPtr = &anInt;  // intPtr has the address of anInt
*intPtr = 123;    // Modify anInt
```

* The standard `list` class is one of several standard container classes. Like `vector`, one instance can store a collection of the same class of objects.
* The standard `list` class has many operations including `push_back`, `push_front`, `remove`, `sort`, and `size`.
* The `find` nonmember function requires `#include <algorithm>`.
* Iterator objects can refer to the items in a collection because the collection returns iterator values with functions like `begin`, `end`, `*`, and `++`.

```
list<int> intList;
list<int>::iterator i;
intList.push_back(12);
intList.push_front(15);
for(i = intList.begin(); i != intList.end(); i++)
{
   cout << (*i) << " ";
}
```

OUTPUT

```
15 12
```

Exercises

1. Write the values of these attributes supplied by this initialization:

   `double x = 987.65;`

   a. class
   b. name
   c. state
   d. address

2. Declare a pointer to an `int` and initialize the pointer somehow.

3. Use these statements to answer the questions that follow:

```
int* intPtr;
int anInt = 123;
intPtr = &anInt;
```

a. What is the name of the pointer object?

b. What is the value of `*intPtr`?

c. Without using `anInt`, write a statement that adds 100 to the memory storing `123`.

4. Write the minimum declarations and statements that declare and initialize all the objects as they are shown in the diagram below.

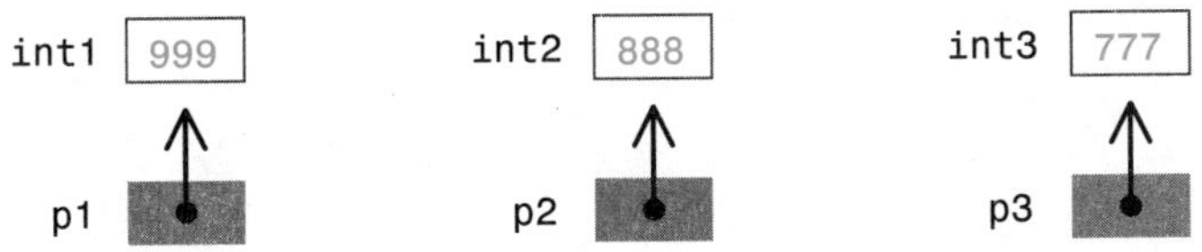

5. Using the code from the previous question, write the statements that will have a pointer object named `largestPtr` pointing to the largest integer no matter where it is stored among `int1`, `int2`, and `int3`.

6. Using the declarations shown, which of the following are valid assignments that do not generate an error:

```
int j = 456;
int* p;
```

a. `p = j;`

b. `p = &j;`

c. `p = 0;`

d. `j = p;`

e. `j = 123;`

f. `*p = j;`

g. `p = &p;`

h. `p = 123;`

i. `*p = "abc";`

j. `*j = 123;`

k. `j = &p;`

l. `*p = *p`

7. Write the output generated by the following program:

```
#include <iostream>
using namespace std;

int main()
{
  int * intPtr;
  int anInt = 987;
  intPtr = &anInt;
  *intPtr = *intPtr + 111;
```

```
    cout << *intPtr << "   " << anInt;
    return 0;
}
```

Note: Use these objects and the picture of memory to answer exercises 8, 9, and 10:

```
int n1, n2;
int* p1;
int* p2;
int* p3;
```

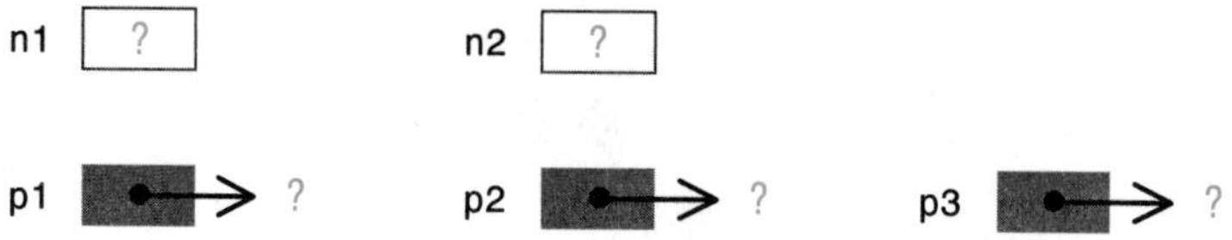

8. Trace the following program segment by drawing pictures of the modified objects:

```
n1 = 123;
p1 = &n1;
*p1 = *p1 + 111;
```

9. Trace the following program segment by drawing pictures of the modified objects:

```
n2 = 999;
p3 = &n2;
p2 = p3;
```

10. Trace the following program segment by drawing pictures of the modified objects:

```
int * intPtr;
intPtr = p3;
```

11. Write the output generated by the following program:

```
#include <iostream>
#include <list>  // For the list class
#include <string>
using namespace std;

int main()
```

```
{
  list <string> stringList;    // Store a collection of strings
  list <string>::iterator i;   // For traversing a list of strings
  stringList.push_back("one");
  stringList.push_back("two");
  stringList.push_back("three");
  stringList.push_front("four");
  stringList.push_front("five");
  stringList.remove("three");
  stringList.remove("six");
  for(i = stringList.begin(); i != stringList.end(); i++)
  {
    cout << i->length() << " " << (*i) << endl;
  }
  return 0;
}
```

12. Write the message that will sort the elements of `stringList` in ascending order.

13. Write code that displays a message indicating whether or not any given `string` is in `stringList`.

14. Write a message that removes `"four"` from `stringList`.

15. Write the output generated by the following program. (*Hint:* `i--;` places the pointer at the preceding element.)

```
// Demonstrate list, one of the standard container classes
#include <iostream>
#include <list>  // For the list class
using namespace std;
int main()
{
  list <int> stringList;
  list <int>::iterator i;
  stringList.push_back(1);
  stringList.push_back(2);
  stringList.push_back(3);
  stringList.push_back(4);
  stringList.push_back(5);
  i = stringList.end();
  do {
    i--;
    cout << (*i) << endl;
  } while( i != stringList.begin() );
  return 0;
}
```

Programming Tips

1. Remember that pointer objects store addresses of other objects.

A pointer object points to some object. In the following example, `ptr` is a pointer and `*ptr` is a reference to the `double` object that starts as `99.9`.

```
double * ptr;
double x = 99.9;
ptr = &x;
*ptr = 1.234;
```

2. When in doubt, use diagrams when debugging programs with pointer objects.

The value of a pointer object represents a location in the memory of the computer. These values are difficult to use in a program trace. A diagram with arrows and boxes makes execution simulation and pointer debugging much clearer.

3. Don't dereference the iterator object when it has an end value.

The state of iterator objects is often the end value. Consider this code:

```
for(i = stringList.begin(); i != stringList.end(); i++)
{
  cout << (*i) << endl;
}
// assert: i is not pointing to anything
if(i == stringList.end())
  cout << "Don't dereference i now!" << endl;
// Uh-oh
cout << (*i) << endl;  // <- Runtime error!!!!
```

The expression `(i == stringList.end())` is true. This is not only a legal expression, it can often be used to detect if an item was found in a list. However, the attempt to dereference the end result is an error that will likely shut down the program (or your computer).

4. You need the standard C++ library to use `list` and iterator objects.

If you are using an older compiler you may not be able to use `lists` and iterators (they are not included on the disk as are `vector` and `string`). The free Hewlett Packard implementation of the standard template library (STL) may be obtained by anonymous ftp from **butler.hpl.hp.com** in the directory **stl**. However, at the time of this writing there were some differences. For example, you'll need to `#include <algo.h>` rather than `<algorithm>` to get the `find` algorithm. Perhaps this will have been updated by the time you read this.

Programming Projects

14A A Little Indirection

Complete the following program that computes the average of any three numbers indirectly after they have been entered from the keyboard.

```
#include <iostream>
using namespace std;

int main()
{
  double n1, n2, n3;
  double* p1;
  double* p2;
  double* p3;
  // YOU COMPLETE THE KEYBOARD INPUT OPERATIONS
  cout << "Average: " << ( (*p1 + *p2 + *p3) / 3.0 ) << endl;
  return 0;
}
```

14B Practicing Pointer Syntax

Write a program that indirectly manipulates one `bankAccount` object by making one withdrawal and one deposit using the arrow operator `->`. Show the final balance, again with the arrow operator.

14C All the Presidents

Write a program that stores the names of all the presidents in a `list` object. The `list` must contain the presidents' names in chronological order. Use the file `pres.dat` to initialize your `list` object. Then remove any presidents you wish. Use an iterator object to display the entire list. Because you don't know if the file has two or three names for each president, use the following loop test to read the entire line of data:

```
// assert: inFile (pres.dat) has one president per line
while( getline (inFile, name) )
{ // assert: name stores an entire line of inFile (except end of line)
```

14D Random List

Write a program that generates a list of 1,000 random numbers (use `rand()` from `<cstdlib>` or `<stdlib.h>`). Display the list. Sort the list. Display it again.

14E Iterators with `find` (standard library required)

Write a program that removes all occurrences of a certain item in a list. To do this, first initialize a list that has more than one occurrence of the item (use an input file to read a file of words, for example). Although there are several ways to do this, use the standard `list` class, an iterator object, and the `find` algorithm. Show the list before and after the removal. Here is a sample dialogue.

```
This is the original list of the words found in the file words.dat.
Remove what word? the
The list after removing 'the'
This is original list of words found in file words.dat.
```

14F Reservations

Note: Try to solve the problem below with this object-oriented analysis and design approach:

1. Find potential classes.
2. Role play some scenarios—by yourself if necessary.
3. Use any existing class you can. (*Hint:* You should find `list` useful.)
4. Design any class definitions that aren't already implemented.

Write a program that maintains reservations for a bus trip to an upcoming away game. There is room for only 45 passengers. Seats will be assigned on a first-come, first-seated basis. Each reservation may be paid for any time as long as there is an initial deposit of $10.00. The total cost is $35.00. The system must be able to display the list of reservations, with each reservation having the name of the purchaser and how much has been paid. At any time before the trip, students can cancel their reservations and get their money back. This opens up seats for others. The reservation list should always be an accurate accounting of who has paid what.

Chapter Fifteen

Dynamic Memory Management

Summing Up

The previous chapter introduced the notion of indirection. A pointer object stores the address of another object. The address of an object is returned with `&`, the address-of operator. The object being pointed to is dereferenced with `*`, the dereference operator. To call a member function through a pointer to an object, use `->`, as in `bp->withdraw(100.00);`.

Coming Up

Pointer objects combine with memory management operations to allocate memory when it is needed at runtime and to release that memory when it is no longer needed, also at runtime. `string` and `vector` objects that grow and shrink while a program is executing use this dynamic memory management. This chapter will show how. To understand this, you first need to be introduced to the built-in C array and `char*` objects. After studying this chapter, you will be able to

- grow and shrink primitive C arrays
- manipulate pointers to a collection of `char`s
- use the `new` and `delete` operators for memory management
- recognize and use pointer objects within classes
- implement destructor member functions
- understand how the capacity of an object may grow and/or shrink at runtime
- implement copy constructor member functions
- implement a linked list class

Exercises and programming projects

15.1 The Primitive C Array

The `vector` class is a relatively new addition to C++. In the past, the built-in, primitive C array was frequently used to store collections of objects. Because an array actually stores the address of the first element, it is a useful example for illustrating pointer usage. The C array is used so frequently for implementing programs, you are likely to see it in existing code. But more importantly, the primitive C array illustrates the benefits of dynamic memory management. It provides a peek under the hood of `vector::resize` and `string` assignments. Both use pointers and dynamic allocation to better manage memory.

The primitive C array is a fixed-size collection of elements that are of the same class. Arrays are homogeneous because they store collections of like objects. The objects in the collection may be one of the built-in classes `char`, `int`, `long`, or `double`. The objects may also be declared as a programmer-defined class such as `bankAccount` as long as the class has a default constructor.

Here is the general form for declaring a primitive C array.

GENERAL FORM 15.1. *Array declaration*

class-name *array-name* [*capacity*] ;

The *class-name* specifies the type of objects stored under *array-name*. The *capacity* specifies the maximum number of elements that can be stored under the array name. The capacity must be an integer constant (such as 100) or a named integer constant. An array cannot be sized or resized at runtime as a `vector` object can, at least not as a standard operation.

The array shown next stores a maximum of seven numbers.

```
string name[100];
const int MAX = 7;
double x[MAX];  // Must use constant integers to build an array
```

Individual array elements are referenced through subscripts of this form (just like `vectors`):

GENERAL FORM 15.2. *Referencing individual array elements*

array-name [*int-expression*] ;

The subscript range of a primitive array is the same as vector: 0 through capacity - 1.

15.1.1 Differences between Primitive Arrays and C++ vector Objects

There are many similarities between arrays and vectors—especially in the referencing of individual elements. In fact, the same vector-processing algorithms of Chapter 10, "Vectors," could also be applied to primitive C arrays. The most noticeable difference is that primitive C arrays cannot be made to automatically check for out-of-bounds subscripts. This is one of the drawbacks of the C array. It is safer to have the subscript-range-checking feature available, especially when first learning about arrays and vectors.

Some very strange errors occur when the code lets the computer "walk off" the end of an array. The important state of other objects may be accidentally destroyed. With the subscript range checking of some vector classes, the program could notify the programmer if an attempt to reference out-of-bounds memory were made. This can be a preferable situation.

Here are the differences between C arrays and C++ vectors.

Difference	vector Example	C Array Example
vectors can initialize all elements at construction; arrays cannot	vector <int> x(100, 0); // All elements are 0	int x[100]; // Elements are garbage

vectors can be sized at runtime; arrays cannot	int n;
	cin >> n;
	// OKAY
	vector <int> x(n);
		int n;
		cin >> n;
		// Compiletime ERROR
		int s[n];

vectors can be made to prevent out-of-range subscripts	// You are told
	// something is wrong
	cin >> x.at(100);
		// Destroy memory.
		// Ugh!
		cin >> x[100];

vectors require an #include; primitive, built-in arrays do not	// #include and std // required #include <vector> using namespace std;	// No #include required. // Arrays are built-in.

15.1.2 The Array/Pointer Connection

It turns out that all primitive C array variables actually store the pointer to—or the address of—the first array element. Whenever the subscript operator is applied to an array object, an address is computed. For example, if `x` is an array of integers, each four bytes long, and `x` has the value of address 6000, the following formula computes `x[3]` as 6000 + (3 * 4):

FORMULA FOR COMPUTING THE ADDRESS OF INDIVIDUAL ARRAY ELEMENTS

address of first array element + (subscript * size of one element)

So `x[3]` is stored at address 6012.

Reference	Address	Value
x[0]	6000	?
x[1]	6004	?
x[2]	6008	?
x[3]	6012	?
x[4]	6016	?

15.1.3 Passing Primitive Array Arguments

When an array is passed to a function, the address of the first array element gets sent. Arrays are automatically passed by reference. An array parameter is declared with the class and the parameter name followed by `[ ]`. This is illustrated next where `int main()` passes an array to the function `init`. Notice that when the function `init` alters the array parameter `x`, the associated array argument `anArray` is also altered (the first three array elements are assigned value). This occurs even though `&` is not used for the parameter `anArray`. `anArray` is passed by value. However, that value just happens to be the address of—a reference to—the first array element. Subscripting parameter `x` results in the equivalent element of `anArray`.

```
// Pass the address of the array to three different functions.
// The & is not required; an array stores an address.
#include <iostream>
using namespace std;
```

```
void init(int x[ ], int & n)   // x and n are reference parameters;
{                              // however, x does not need &
  x[0] = 90;
  x[1] = 95;
  x[2] = 99;
  n = 3;
}

int main()
{
  int n;
  int anArray[5];

  init(anArray, n);  // When init changes x, also changes anArray
  for(int j = 0; j < n; j++)
  {
     cout << anArray[j] << "  ";
  }
  cout << endl;

  return 0;
}
```

OUTPUT

```
90  95  99
```

The following figure depicts that `anArray` was passed by reference, even though `&` was not used.

FIGURE 15.1

A change to x is a change to anArray

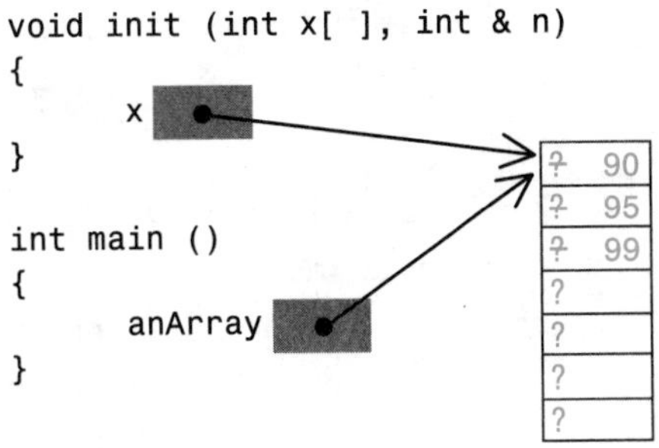

15.2 char* Objects

This section demonstrates the underlying structure of the string class on this textbook's disk. This implementation detail may or may not be used by your library's string class. A char* object is often used as the address of the beginning of a group of characters. Historically used in the absence of a string class, pointers to chars are declared as follows:

```
char* strPtr;  // strPtr is a pointer to a char
```

A char* pointer is used in conjunction with a *null-terminated string,* which is a group of characters in contiguous (next to each other) memory bytes that uses the null char value '\0' to mark the end of the string. On assignment, it is the address of the C++ string literal that gets stored in a pointer object with assignments like this:

```
strPtr = "Null-terminated string";
```

The pointer object strPtr now holds the address of the first char in the string literal—the byte that stores the char 'N' in this case. Consistently using char* (sometimes pronounced "char star") objects with null-terminating chars results in a quasi string class.

Although it may appear as if the entire string is assigned to strPtr, it is only the address of the string literal that is actually moved into strPtr. The 23 characters of this particular literal are located in some portion of the computer's memory. The pointer strPtr is merely the address used to locate those chars. This subtle distinction is represented graphically as follows:

For instance, if the character 'N' were stored at address 5000, the 'u' would be stored at address 5001, the 'l' at 5002, the other 'l' at 5003, and so on. The address stored in the pointer object strPtr would be 5000.

This type of string requires all programmers and implementers of functions managing char* objects to adhere to this implementation detail:

Null-terminated strings must always be terminated with the null character '\0'.

Sometimes the terminating null must be explicitly appended. But in most cases, the terminating null is appended automatically. For example, the terminating null automatically becomes part of all `string` literals.

To see that `'\0'` is indeed a part of `string` literals, first understand that all pointer objects, such as arrays and `char*` objects, may be subscripted to return the address of an object in the collection. In the case of a `char*` object, subscripts determine the addresses of individual `char`s. The first `char` pointed to by the `char*` object `strPtr` is referenced as `strPtr[0]`. Therefore, when `strPtr` assigns `"abcd"`, the fourth `char` is `strPtr[3]`, and the terminating null can be referenced as `strPtr[4]`. This is verified in the following program that tests both values and displays the message that a null `char` (`'\0'`) was indeed appended to the `string` literal `"abcd"`:

```
// Verify that a null character (\0) is at end of string constants
#include <iostream>
using namespace std;

int main()
{
  char* strPtr;

  strPtr = "abcd";
  if((strPtr[3] == 'd') && (strPtr[4] == '\0'))
    cout << "A null char was appended to 'abcd'"  << endl;

  return 0;
}
```

OUTPUT

```
A null char was appended to 'abcd'
```

A `char*` object can be assigned value with =, output with <<, and input with >>. Some of these operations are shown in the next program.

```
// Use char* pointer objects as a quasi string class
#include <iostream>
using namespace std;

int main()
{
  char* wife;      // These two pointer objects could store
  char* husband;   // addresses of null-terminated strings

  wife = "Joann";
  husband = "Charlie";
```

```
    cout << "   Characters pointed to by wife: " << wife    << endl;
    cout << "Characters pointed to by husband: " << husband << endl;

    return 0;
}
```

Output

```
   Characters pointed to by wife: Joann
Characters pointed to by husband: Charlie
```

It should be noted that C++ defines `cout <<` for `char*` objects. Output of the pointer object itself causes all `char`s up to the terminating null to be displayed. Output of the dereferenced pointer shows only the first `char`. Therefore, using the code above, the statement

```
cout << (*wife);
```

outputs `J`, while

```
cout << wife;
```

outputs `Joann`.

As with other pointer objects, the values stored in `wife` and `husband` are the addresses, not the entire null-terminated `string`s. This is depicted in the following representation of the two pointers and the memory in which the null-terminated `string`s are stored (subsequent discussion presumes the two `string`s are stored next to each other in computer memory):

Value	?	?	J	o	a	n	n	\0	C	h	a	r	l	i	e	\0	?	?
Address	...	49	50	51	52	53	54	55	56	57	58	59	60	61	62	63	64	...

To see that we are dealing with addresses, consider how this assignment of one pointer object to another:

```
husband = wife;
```

does not move characters from one memory location to another. Instead, the value of the pointer object `husband` is changed to point to the same byte of memory as `wife`.

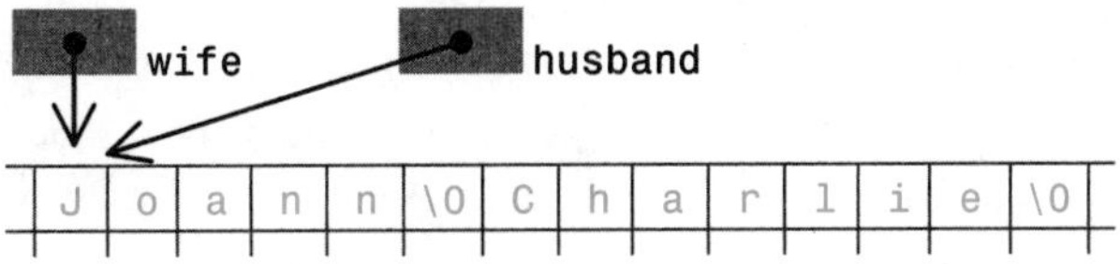

As you might expect, these two statements:

```
cout << "    The characters pointed to by wife: " << wife    << endl;
cout << "The characters pointed to by husband: " << husband << endl;
```

generate output indicating the `char*` objects `wife` and `husband` are equal—they both store the same address.

```
    The characters pointed to by wife: Joann
The characters pointed to by husband: Joann
```

But since these two quasi `strings` are pointing to the same memory, a change to one pointer object effectively alters the value pointed to by the other. This is one of several inherent dangers encountered when `char*` is used in place of the `string` class. It is also the major reason why this textbook uses the standard `string` class.

```
// This may cause a segmentation fault on some systems
husband[0] = 'X';  // Notice that wife is not being referenced;
husband[3] = 'Y';  // however, memory pointed to by wife is.
husband[5] = 'Z';  // The output may be surprising especially if
                   // one terminating null is destroyed.
```

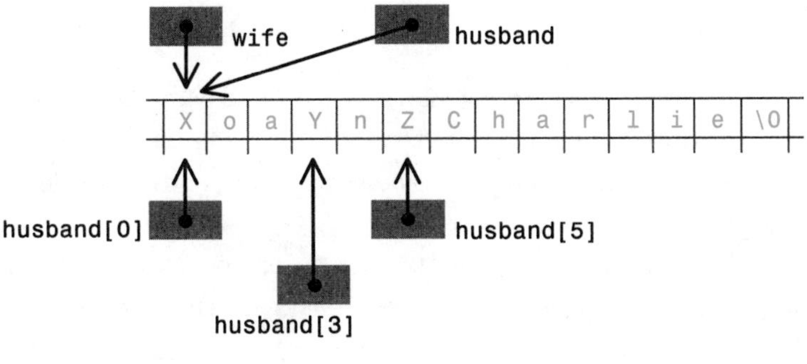

Self-Check

15-1 Using the state of memory illustrated above, evaluate the following expressions to true or false:

-a `wife[0] == husband[0]`

-b `wife[3] == husband[4]`

-c `husband == wife`

-d `wife == husband`

-e `wife[1] == wife[1]`

-f `wife[4] == husband[4]`

Even though `wife` does not appear to change, the memory near the byte pointed to by `wife` is altered. Here is the potentially surprising output:

```
cout << "   The characters pointed to by wife: " << wife << endl;
```

OUTPUT

```
   The characters pointed to by wife: XoaYnZCharlie
```

As you can see, changes to one subscript pointer object (`husband`) effectively alter the other (`wife`). The reason `Charlie` appears to be appended to `wife` is that the `<<` operator is overloaded for `char*` objects like this. All characters are displayed, beginning with the `char` pointed to by the pointer object and up to the null character `'\0'`. This is expressed in C++ as follows:

```
for(int j = 0; wife[j] != '\0'; j++)  // Display each char
{
  cout << wife[j];
}
```

The additional characters `Charlie` are printed because the assignment to `husband[5]` destroyed the null character `'\0'` that had earlier ended `wife`. Shortly we will see this as a major difference between quasi `strings` implemented as `char*` objects and "safe" `string` classes.

The following program presents one more example of how C++ passes addresses to functions. A `char*` object—an address—is passed to the `makeUpperCase` function. A change to the parameter (`p`) changes the argument (`arg`). Since the argument and the associated parameter are both pointers (`char*` objects), no reference (`&`) is required in the function heading—the same situation as just shown with the array parameters. Primitive C arrays and `char*` data automatically get passed by reference. The value stored in a `char*` object is an address.

```
// Illustrate a function call that passes a pointer as the argument
#include <iostream>
#include <cctype>[1]  // For char toupper(char)
using namespace std;

void makeUpperCase(char* p)
{ // post: The associated argument is changed to uppercase
  for(int j = 0; p[j] != '\0'; j++)
  {
     p[j] = toupper(p[j]);  // Convert each char to uppercase
  }
}

int main()
{
  char* arg;

  arg = "Teague";
  makeUpperCase(arg);
  cout << arg << endl;

  return 0;
}
```

OUTPUT

```
TEAGUE
```

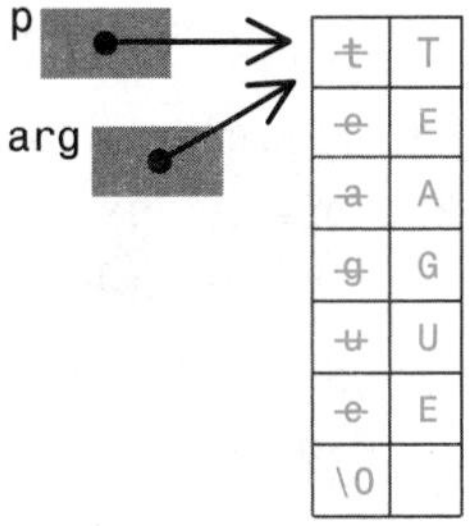

15.2.1 A Few <cstring> Functions

Including <cstring> provides many functions designed for use with `char*` objects terminated with the null character (`'\0'`).[2] When combined with `<<` and `=` operations, the `cstring` functions provide much of the functionality of the `string` class without the safety features. The code shown next demonstrates a few common `cstring` functions: `strlen`, `strcpy`, `strcmp`, and `strcat`.

`char* s;`	Declare a `char*` object named `s`.
`s = "string one!";`	Allocate memory at compiletime for 12 characters, append `'\0'`, and make `s` point to them: `s` → `"string one!\0"`
`cout << strlen(s) << endl;`	`strlen` returns the dynamic length of a `char*` object minus one for `'\0'`; output is `11`.

1. If your system cannot find the file named <cctype>, `#include <ctype.h>`.
2. If your system cannot find the file named <cstring>, `#include <string.h>`.

`strcpy(s, "new string");`	Write `"new string\0"` over memory pointed to by `s`: `s` → `"new string\0"`
`char* s2 = "another ";`	Initialize another `char*` object identified as `s2`: `s2` → `"another \0"`
`if(strcmp(s2, s) < 0)` `  cout << "s2 < s"`	The `strcmp` function returns `0` if `s2 == s`, a negative if `s2 < s`, and a positive if `s2 > s`; output is `s2 < s`.
`strcat(s2, s);`	Allocate more memory and concatenate `s` to `s2` with only one `'\0'`.
`cout << s2;`	Output the concatenated `chars` pointed to by `s2`; output is `another new string!`

To demonstrate the danger of `char*` objects, the code exactly as shown in the left column was tested as a C++ program. When first run, the program behaved as one would expect—there were no errors. When the `'!'` got removed from the end of the string literal `"string one"` and the program was run, the following results occurred on different systems:

- usual results
- abnormal program termination error
- message to save files, terminate applications, and reboot the computer
- segmentation fault error
- working results for a while, then a later attempt to load a different application was unsuccessful (this might have been a dreaded *latency error*—one that occurs minutes, hours, or even weeks later)

Suggestion: Use the standard C++ `string` class (or the one on this textbook's disk, declared in `ltstring.h` and implemented in `ltstring.cpp`).

Self-Check

15-2 Write the output generated by the following program:

```
#include <iostream>
using namespace std;
int main()
{
  char* p;
  char* q;
  p = " abc";
  q = "0123";
  p[0] = 'T';
  for(int j = 0; j < 4; j++)
```

```
  {
    cout << p[j] << q[j];
  }
  return 0;
}
```

15-3 Write the output generated by the following program:

```
#include <iostream>
using namespace std;

int main()
{
  char* p;
  char* q;
  p = "abcd";
  q = "1234";
  p = q;
  q = "A new string literal";  // A new string constant
  cout << "p = " << p << " and q = " << q << endl;
  return 0;
}
```

For the following self-checks, assume `#include <cstring>` is present and these initializations:

```
char* s1 = "abc";
char* s2 = "123";
```

15-4 What is the value of `strlen(s1)`?

15-5 What is the value of `strlen(s2)`?

15-6 What output is generated by the statement `cout << s1 << s2`?

15-7 What is the value of `s2` after the function call `strcpy(s2, s1);`?

15-8 What is the value of `s2` after the function call `strcpy(s2,"xyz");`?

15.3 Initializing Pointers with new

Pointer objects are frequently assigned values through the `new` operator. When the `new` operator precedes a class name, the resulting expression allocates a contiguous block of memory large enough to store one instance of that class. Additionally, the same expression returns the address, or a pointer to, this memory.

GENERAL FORM 15.3. *Dynamic memory allocation (for one object only)*

new *class-name* ;

The memory is allocated at runtime from the *free store*—a portion of computer memory reserved for this purpose (the free store is sometimes called the *heap*). For example, the following expression allocates enough memory to store one `int` value. The expression returns a pointer to that memory.

```
new int;  // Allocate memory, return a pointer value (an address)
```

Instead of ignoring the returned pointer value (the address where an integer could be stored), such pointer expressions are usually combined with pointer objects in initializations.

```
int* intPtr = new int;  // Allocate memory, store address in intPtr
```

The above is an abbreviated form of the following equivalent code:

```
int* intPtr;
intPtr = new int;  // Allocate memory, store address in intPtr
```

Now we have a situation where `intPtr` holds the address of an `int` object—where an `int` could be stored. This is shown in the next figure where the undefined `int` value is signified as ? and the pointer value is represented as an arrow indicating a value that points to that undefined `int`.

This statement initializes that new memory:

```
*intPtr = 123;
```

This resulting representation shows the state of the pointer and the `int`.

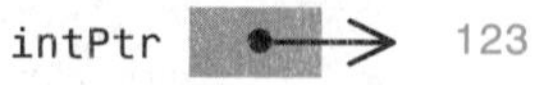

The following program shows dynamic allocation of one `int` object:

```
// Illustrate one pointer object and one int object
#include <iostream>
using namespace std;

int main()
```

```
{
  // Declare an intPtr as a pointer to an int
  int* intPtr;

  // Allocate memory for an int and store address in intPtr
  intPtr = new int;

  // Store 123 into memory referenced by intPtr
  *intPtr = 123;

  cout << "\n The address stored in the pointer object: " << intPtr;
  cout << "\nThe value of the int pointed to by intPtr: " << *intPtr;

  return 0;
}
```

OUTPUT (THE ADDRESS SHOWN IN HEXADECIMAL (BASE 16) AS 0x6310 IS 25,360 (BASE 10))

```
 The address stored in the pointer object: 0x6310
The value of the int pointed to by intPtr: 123
```

Notice that the pointer object, with value 25,360 (6310 hexadecimal), is referenced as `intPtr`. The actual `int` with value 123 is dereferenced as `*intPtr`.

15.3.1 Allocating More than One Object with new

There are many potential pitfalls with C arrays and `char*` pointer objects such as this one related to the `strcpy` function.

```
char* str;
strcpy(str, "A string");  // Watch out!
```

This results in a situation that could crash the system. It is an attempt to move characters into memory where none has been allocated—`str` does not have any new memory to point to! This can be surprising especially if you peruse the `strcpy` function heading in `cstring` (or in `string.h`, perhaps) and discover that `str`, a `char*` object, is in fact the proper type to use as the first argument to `strcpy`. Here is the heading:

```
char* strcpy(char* destination, char* source)
```

One way to avoid this problem is to first allocate the exact amount of memory to store the second `string` argument passed to `source`. Consider the case of the following `string` literal that appears to have nine `chars` between the double quotes:

```
"ten chars"  // Need 10 chars: 9 between " " plus '\0'
```

Enough memory must be allocated to store the nine characters plus one extra to store the terminating null. The C++ `new` operator accomplishes this by allocating memory for many objects with `[` *capacity* `]`, where *capacity* represents the number of objects to allocate.

General Form 15.4. *Dynamic memory allocation (capacity objects)*

new *class-name* **[** *capacity* **]** **;**

Example of Memory Allocation for 10 Characters

```
new char[10];  // Allocate memory for 10 char objects and return
               // a pointer to this newly allocated memory
```

Again, because `new` returns a pointer to the first byte of the 10 characters, it can be used for pointer object initialization with this shortcut initialization:

General Form 15.5. *Initializing pointer objects*

class-name ***** *identifier* **=** **new** *class-name* **[** *number-of-elements* **]** **;**

Example

```
char* my_chars = new char[10];
```

Now, the pointer object `my_chars` points to the first of 10 bytes of memory where each byte may store one `char` object.

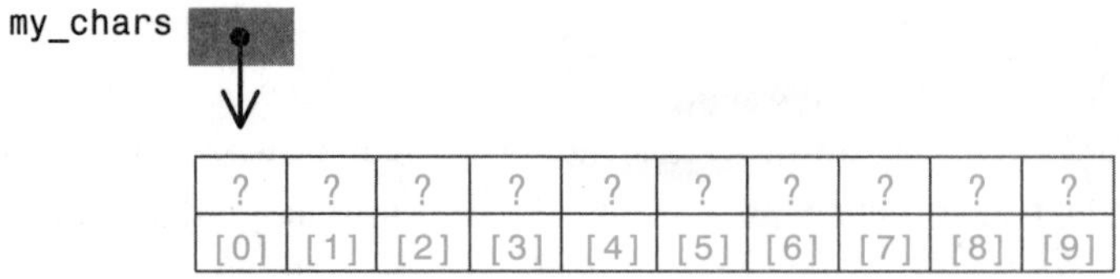

Since `strcpy` automatically appends a terminating null, a total of 10 `chars` will store the nine `chars` of the `string` literal `"ten chars"` plus the automatically appended terminating null.

```
strcpy(my_chars, "ten chars");
```

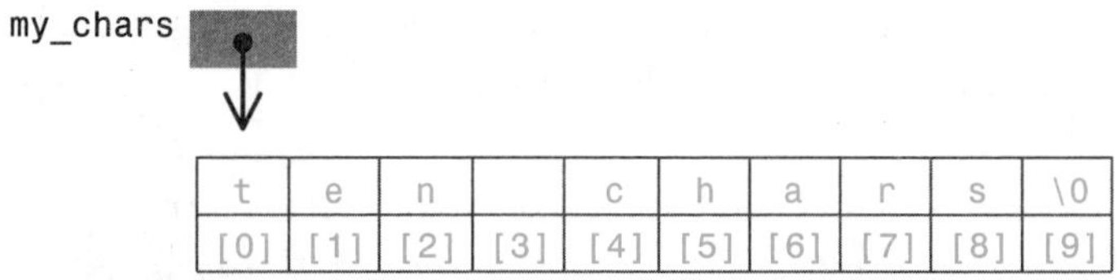

This memory management technique—allocating the exact amount of memory, no more, no less—is utilized in the constructors of the `string` class implementation on this textbook's disk. A portion of the `string` class definition is provided here to put in context the private data members `int my_len` and `chars* my_chars`.

```
class string {
public:
  string(const char* initText);
  // post: Construct a string object with a char* argument.
  //       Example constructor call: string aStr("A string");
  // . . .

private:
  int my_len;       // The dynamic length of any one string object
  char* my_chars;   // A pointer to characters of a string object
};
```

For example, this `string` constructor:

```
string str("Any length string");
```

calls the following constructor function. The `char*` pointer to the string literal `"Any length string"` gets passed to the constructor.

```
// From the file ltstring.cpp on this book's disk
// Your standard string class will be implemented quite differently

string::string(const char* initText)
{
   my_len = strlen(initText);          // Actual length without '\0'
   my_chars = new char[my_len + 1];    // Allocate memory + 1 for '\0'
   strcpy(my_chars, initText);         // my_chars points to initText
}
```

This `string` constructor performs several actions to store the `chars` and a length for any `char*` argument passed to it. First, the call to `strlen` returns the length of the `string` literal pointed to by `initText`. This length is assigned to the private data member `my_len` to store the current length of the `string`.

Next, the `new` operator allocates the exact amount of memory from the free store required to store `initText` along with a terminating null (`my_len` + 1). And finally, the characters are copied one-by-one into the newly allocated memory with the `strcpy` function. This generalized method guarantees that every `string` object stores the `char*` member of the `string` in its own space and places the terminating null in the correct position. These guarantees make the `string` class more user-friendly and much safer than primitive `char*` objects.

Self-Check

15-9 Write the output generated by the following program:

```
#include <iostream>
using namespace std;
int main()
{
  int* p = new int;
  *p = 678;
  *p = *p + 111;
  cout << (*p);
  return 0;
}
```

15-10 At the end of the next program, what can we say about the object named `p`?

```
#include <iostream>
using namespace std;
int main()
{
  double* p = new double;
  *p = 6.78;
  p = new double;
  cout << (*p)
  return 0;
}
```

15-11 Write the output generated by the following program:

```
#include <iostream>
using namespace std;
int main()
{
  double* p = new double;
  double* q = new double;
```

```
  *p = 1.23;
  *q = 4.56;
  p = q;
  cout << (*p) << "  " << (*q);
  return 0;
}
```

15-12 At the last statement of the preceding program, is it possible to retrieve the memory that stored 1.23?

15-13 Write the output generated by the following program:

```
#include <iostream>
#include "baccount"
using namespace std;
int main()
{
  char* name = "Hall";
  bankAccount* bp = new bankAccount;

  *bp = bankAccount(name, 100.00);
  bp->deposit(123.45);
  cout << bp->name() << "  " << bp->balance() << endl;
  return 0;
}
```

15-14 Write the output generated by the following program:

```
#include <iostream>
using namespace std;
int main()
{
  const int MAX = 6;
  int* x = new int[MAX];
  int j;

  for(j = 0; j < MAX; j++)
  {
    x[j] = 2 * j;
  }
  for(j = 0; j < MAX; j++)
  {
    cout << x[j] << "  ";
  }
  return 0;
}
```

15-15 Write one initialization using new to allocate memory for 1,000 numbers.

15-16 Write the code the initializes all 1,000 doubles of the previous question to 0.

15-17 Write the code that allocates new memory for any string literal pointed to by charPtr. Store that string along with a terminating null char into memory pointed to by my_chars. my_chars and charPtr must be pointing to separate memory.

15.4 The `delete` Operator and Destructor Functions

In the examples so far, the new operator has allocated only small amounts of memory. However, consider what happens when dynamic data grows to a large size. Using new without returning memory to the free store results in a *memory leak.* This limits the amount of memory available to a program. At some point, the program no longer needs the dynamically allocated memory. When this occurs, the unneeded memory should be allocated back to the free store. This makes it available for other objects that have yet to be dynamically allocated. This return of memory, or *deallocation,* is accomplished with the C++ built-in delete operator. The delete operator has two general forms.

GENERAL FORM 15.6. *Deallocating memory back to the system—a form of recycling*

delete *pointer-object* ;
delete [ ] *pointer-object* ;

The first line returns the memory allocated for one dynamic object back to the free store while leaving an undefined value in that pointer object. The second line returns memory allocated for a group of objects with new and [ ]. In the following program, the delete operator allocates enough memory for one double pointed to by p, 10 chars pointed to by my_chars, and 100 integers pointed to by x.

```
// Allocate and deallocate memory
#include <iostream>
#include <cstring>  // If cstring is not found, #include <string.h>
using namespace std;
```

```
int main()
{
  double* p = new double;
  *p = 123;

  char* my_chars = new char[10];
  strcpy(my_chars, "ten chars");

  int* x = new int[100];
  x[0] = 76;
  x[1] = 89;

  // Use p, my_chars, and x . . .
  // . . .
  // When no longer needed, deallocate p, my_chars, and x
  delete p;
  delete [ ] my_chars;
  delete [ ] x;

  // All the bytes of memory pointed to by p, my_chars, and x are
  // now returned to the free store
  return 0;
}
```

After the three `delete` statements return the allocated memory back to the free store, the pointer objects have undefined values that should not be used. Using them at this point results in unpredictable behavior.

15.4.1 Destructors

Any class that dynamically allocates objects should also have the means to return that memory allocated with `new` back to the free store. Failure to use `delete` results in a memory leak. Adding a C++ destructor function guarantees such memory deallocation. Whereas constructors are called at the point of object construction, the class destructors automatically execute when an object goes out of scope, such as local objects when a function is done, for example.

Within a class, a destructor has the same name as the class, no arguments, and no return type. A class destructor looks the same as a default constructor (no parameters), with the tilde character (~) preceding it.

GENERAL FORM 15.7. *The destructor member function*

```
class class-name {
public:
    class-name();    // Constructor
    ~class-name();   // Destructor
  // . . .
```

For example, a destructor for the class `myClass` would be written as `~myClass`.

```
class myClass {
public
  myClass();    // Constructor
  ~myClass();   // Destructor
  // . . .
```

The destructor member function is implemented like all other member functions with ~ written after the class name and the scope resolution operator (`::`).

```
myClass::~myClass()
{
   // . . . You will often see delete in the destructor
}
```

A destructor is called any time an object goes out of scope, the time at which a block is exited, for example. So the programmer need not call the destructor directly. In fact, the destructor cannot be called explicitly. Instead, the runtime system invokes the destructor at the proper time—when the object is no longer needed—at the end of its lifetime. The following program uses a `cout` statement to illustrate the time at which the destructor executes. This is when the object goes out of scope as the function terminates. The class definition and member function implementations are shown first.

CLASS DEFINITION

```
// File name: withdest.h
#ifndef WITHDEST_H
#define WITHDEST_H

class withDestructor {
public:
  withDestructor(char* initText);
  ~withDestructor();
```

```
private:
  char* my_chars;
};
#endif
```

MEMBER FUNCTION IMPLEMENTATIONS

```
// File name: withdest.cpp
#include "withdest.h"  // For class definition
#include <iostream>    // For cout
#include <cstring>     // For strlen and strcpy

withDestructor::withDestructor(char* initText)
{
  my_chars = new char[strlen(initText) + 1];
  strcpy(my_chars, initText);
  cout << "In constructor, my_chars: '" << my_chars << "'" << endl;
}

withDestructor::~withDestructor()
{
  cout << "'" << my_chars
       << "' will be deleted by this destructor" << endl;
  delete [ ] my_chars;
  // Memory has now been returned back to the free store
}
```

```
// Demonstrate constructor and destructor calls
#include <iostream>  // For cout
using namespace std;
#include "withdest"  // #include withdest.h and withdest.cpp

void f()
{
  cout << "just entered f()****************" << endl;
  withDestructor source("A string of any length");
  cout << "****************about to exit f()" << endl;
}

int main()
{
  f();
  return 0;
}
```

OUTPUT

```
just entered f()****************
In constructor, my_chars: 'A string of any length'
****************about to exit f()
'A string of any length' will be deleted by this destructor
```

Whereas the constructor allocates memory, the destructor returns that memory so it can be allocated at some later point. The output indicates that `source`'s data member `my_chars` was still valid at the time the destructor was called.

```
'A string of any length' will be deleted by this destructor
```

However, immediately after this `cout`, the following statement executes and `my_chars` becomes undefined:

```
delete [ ] my_chars;
```

With `delete` or `delete[]` in the destructor, memory allocated by the constructor automatically returns to the free store. This guarantee applies to each and every object as it goes out of scope.

The `string` class that comes with this textbook[3] employs a similar approach to effective memory management. The constructor allocates memory with `new` and the destructor deallocates that memory with `delete`. The memory allocated for the private data member (`my_chars`) automatically becomes available again. The `string` class destructor deletes it each time a `string` object goes out of scope. So the programmer need not worry about returning memory when using a `string` class. The destructor takes care of this. This prevents one form of memory leak.

```
string::string(char* initText)
{ // Constructor called with one argument: string s("Initial text")
  my_len = strlen(initText);        // Actual length without '\0'
  my_chars = new char[my_len + 1];  // Memory for initText plus one
                                    // for '\0'
  strcpy(my_chars, initText);  // Let my_chars point to initText
}

// The string destructor
string::~string()
```

3. Other `string` classes are implemented differently, even though they may have the same interface (collection of operations).

```
{ // The string destructor is called automatically to deallocate
  // memory as the object goes out of scope
  delete [ ] my_chars;
}
```

15.5 Copy Constructors

One object of any class may be copied to another object of the same class. This is guaranteed by the C++ system for all classes in that one object can be copied to another of the same class, either through assignment or argument/parameter association. The default copying process, called *memberwise copy,* copies each data member of one object to another object. This works fine for classes with no pointer data members. However, the default behavior must be modified for classes with pointer data members and dynamic memory allocation. Consider this program.

```
#include <iostream>
using namespace std;
#include "withdest" // From the previous section

void f(withDestructor destination)
{
}

int main()
{
   withDestructor source("The source's memory");
   f(source);
   cout << "Does this statement execute?" << endl;
   return 0;
}
```

With memberwise copy in effect, the pointer data member `my_chars` is copied from `main` to `f` like this:

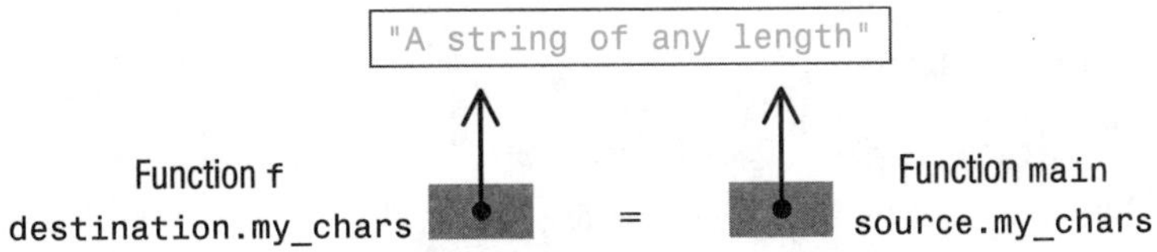

Since the lone data member s is a pointer object, an address is copied. The pointer data member `my_chars` of both object instances (`source` and `destination`) are now both pointing to the same memory!

Problems occur when destructors delete pointer data members and two different pointers are pointing to the same memory. When `destination.my_chars` is deleted as function `f` finishes (during the destructor), `source.my_chars` points to deallocated memory! Now when the destructor is called for `source`, the attempt is made to delete memory that is already deleted. The resulting behavior is undefined.

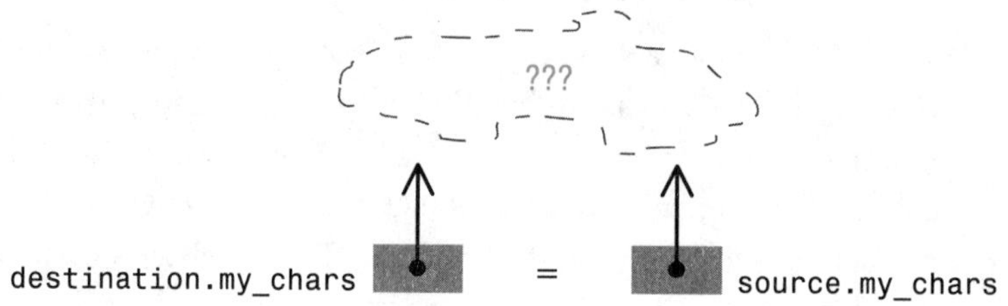

This subtle detail of class implementation is summarized in the following program in which the function `doSomething()` uses a few `withDestructor` objects:

```
#include "withdest"  // For the withDestructor class

void processSome()
{
  withDestructor source("Any length string, well this is longer");
  withDestructor destination(source);
  withDestructor aThirdObject(destination);
  // assert: There are three pointers pointing to the same string

  // Do something with the objects

  // When this function is done, the three objects will go out of
  // scope and the class destructor will be called to delete the
  // same memory three times (Note: Errors may not always be
  // noticeable)
}

int main()
{
  processSome();

  return 0;
}
```

If one pointer is deleted, the memory is deallocated. The pointer is undefined. Then an attempt to delete the other memory is an attempt to delete memory that has already been deleted. You may see errors such as:

- `'Null pointer assignment'`,
- `'Segmentation fault'`,
- `'General Protection Fault'`, or
- some other system-dependent behavior, which may be intermittent.

When pointers and dynamic memory allocation are involved in a class, some scheme must be used to maintain separate memory for each dynamic object. The default memberwise copy only copies addresses. Therefore, the same memory may have several references to it. The `withDestructor` class allocates no new memory when an instance gets passed by value to another function. The class implementers must override this situation.

For classes with no pointer data members, the default copy mechanism is acceptable for successful assignments, initializations, and the passing of arguments by value. But in the case of classes with pointer data members, a *copy constructor* must be added to the class.

Copy constructors are fairly easy to add to any class. A copy constructor takes exactly one argument. Here is the general form of a copy constructor prototype for any class.

General Form 15.8. *Copy constructor*

class-name **(const** *class-name* **&** *parameter-name* **) ;**

The copy constructor gets called when an object is being passed by value to a function. It also gets called to return a value back from a function. Therefore, the parameter must be the same class as the argument. For the sake of efficiency, the parameter is passed by reference with `&`. And finally, because we never want to alter the object being copied, the keyword `const` is added for safety. For example, the `string` copy constructor in `ltstring.h` is declared like this:

```
// Copy constructor
string(const string & source);
// post: Object is copied after argument/parameter associations
//       and during function returns
```

The problem with the `withDestructor` class disappears when the following copy constructor is added to the class definition:

```
withDestructor(const withDestructor & source);
```

The action of the copy constructor guarantees that the destructor does not delete two pointers to the same memory. This is accomplished for the `withDestructor` class by the allocation of new memory for the pointer data member `s`.

```
withDestructor::withDestructor(const withDestructor & source)
{ // This copy constructor allocates new memory for s . . .
  s = new char[strlen(source.s) + 1];
  // . . . and then copies all characters into the new memory
  strcpy(s, source.s);
  // This is different from s = source.s; which only copies an
  // address and leaves two pointer data members pointing to the
  // same memory
}
```

The same memory management is used with the `string` class copy constructor where `my_len` is copied directly, but new memory is allocated to copy all characters from `source` to `destination`.

```
string::string(const char * source)
{
  my_len = strlen(source);  // Actual length without '\0'
  my_chars = new char[my_len + 1];  // Allocate memory + 1 for '\0'
  strcpy(my_chars, source);  // Let my_chars point to initText
}
```

Virtually every class with pointers and dynamic memory allocation will have a copy constructor.

OBJECT-ORIENTED DESIGN HEURISTIC 15.1

C++ classes with pointer objects and dynamic memory allocation must add a copy constructor, a destructor, and an overloaded assignment operator (see Chapter 18, "Operator Overloading").

Copy constructors emphasize some of the difficulties with working with pointer objects. Pointers carry their own set of unique problems to accompany their benefits of efficient memory management. In the next chapter, you will see pointers and dynamic memory allocation used as the new underlying structure of the `bag` class.

Self-Check

15-18 What does the `delete` operator do?

15-19 Why is the `delete` operator needed?

15-20 Describe the difference between these two uses of `delete`:

```
delete s;
delete [ ] x;
```

15-21 Write the code that allocates memory to store 100 integers pointed to by `quiz` and then deallocate that memory.

15-22 What should a destructor do?

15-23 What should a copy constructor do?

15.6 Linked Lists (and the C `struct`)

A linked list is a popular data structure for storing a collection of elements in a sequential fashion. In fact, it is probable that your standard `list` class has been implemented using a linked structure and some of the concepts presented in this section. To accomplish this, a pointer data member is added to a class or a `struct`. A `struct` is the same thing as a class except that by default, members of a class are private and members of a `struct` are public. However, if you use public and private explicitly, there is no difference other than the name. The `struct` is used here for historical reasons and because `struct`s typically have constructors and data members only. Because `struct` data members are public by default, adding `public:` is not necessary.

AN EXAMPLE `struct` WITH TWO PUBLIC DATA MEMBERS

```
typedef string Type;  // Define type of data stored in each node

struct node {
//--constructors
  node();
  node(Type data);

// Two public data members
  Type my_data;
  node* next;
};

// Both constructors set next to NULL

node::node()
{
```

```
  next = NULL;
}

node::node(Type data)
{
  my_data = data;
  next = NULL;
}
```

The following code constructs a new `node` object pointed to by `nodePointer` and displays the value using the `->` operator, which is necessary for dereferencing the public data members of `node`.

```
// Let nodePointer reference a dynamically allocated node object
node* nodePointer = new node("Dream Walkin'");
// assert: nodePointer->next == NULL

// Display the state of the public data member my_data
cout << "  The value: " << nodePointer->my_data << endl;
cout << "#characters: " << nodePointer->my_data.length() << endl;
```

OUTPUT

```
  The value: Dream Walkin'
#characters: 13
```

A PICTURE OF MEMORY

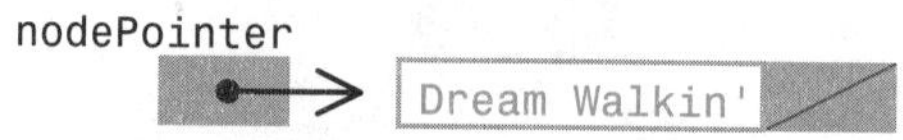

A linked structure has the characteristic that one element can be referenced from another element. With a data member to store a pointer to another object of the same class, objects can be linked together in such a way that the pointer in the first `node` object can be used to find the second `node`. The following code constructs three `node` objects that are linked together. Notice that a reference to the data of the second `node` is made using the pointer `p->next`.

```
// Build the first node
node* p = new node("First");

// Construct a second node pointed to by the first node's next
p->next = new node("Second");
```

```
// Build a third node pointed to by p->next->next
p->next->next = new node("Third");
```

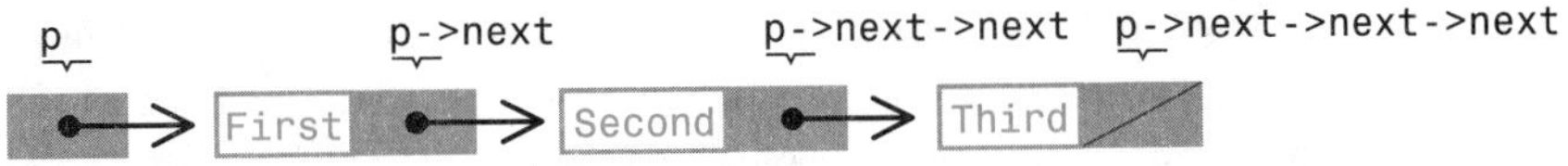

Three Linked nodes

These three nodes can be traversed by allowing a pointer, named `temp` here, to refer to all three nodes. It begins by having `temp` point to the first node. If `temp` is not `NULL`, the node's data is displayed (inside the loop).

```
// Traverse the nodes until a next field is NULL
node* temp = p;
while(temp != NULL)
{
  cout << temp->my_data << endl;
  temp = temp->next;
  // assert: Either temp points to the next node or temp == NULL
}
```

Output

```
First
Second
Third
```

`temp` is updated to point to the next node or it is set to `NULL` with the statement `temp = temp->next`.

15.6.1 A Simple Linked List Class

This section demonstrates a linked list class that stores a collection of objects. Using the Iterator pattern, this particular list can be traversed in a sequential fashion much like a `bag` object. However, the `currentItem` member function now returns the address of the element.

```
listElementType& currentItem()  // & to return address of value
// Returns address of the node data value so it can be modified
```

This allows individual contained list elements to be modified while they are still in the list. `LinkedList::currentItem` now has `&` in the return type. A `bag` element (see

Chapter 11) could not be modified from outside the container because it simply returned the value of the `currentItem`.

The following program shows two sequential traversals over the elements contained in the `LinkedList` object named `myFriends`. The first traversal pads all the elements in the container with blank spaces while they are still in the list. This is done by assigning the address of each `node`'s value—returned by `currentItem`—to a pointer of type `listElementType*`.

```
// Demonstrate LinkedList messages before examining the
// implementation
#include <iostream>
#include <string>
using namespace std;

typedef string listElementType;
#include "llist"  // For the LinkedList class

void show(const LinkedList& list);  // Implemented after int main()
// post: Show all elements in list

int main()
{
  LinkedList myFriends;
  myFriends.append("Tommy");
  myFriends.append("Didi Fickle");
  myFriends.append("Chuckie");
  myFriends.append("Zirconium Lil");

  show(myFriends);

  // Modify each element
  listElementType* p;
  for(myFriends.first(); ! myFriends.isDone(); myFriends.next())
  {
    p = &myFriends.currentItem();
    // Pad with blanks to make length at least 15
    int len = (*p).length();
    for(int j = len; j < 15; j++)
    {
      *p = *p + " ";
    }

    // Indirectly modify the currentItem again
    *p = *p + " --these should line up" ;
  }

  // Now show the modified elements
```

```
  cout << "\nThe list elements after modification: " << endl;
  show(myFriends);

  return 0;
}

void show(const LinkedList& list)
{
  listElementType current;
  for(list.first(); ! list.isDone(); list.next())
  {
    current = list.currentItem();
    cout << current << endl;
  }
}
```

OUTPUT

```
Tommy
Didi Fickle
Chuckie
Zirconium Lil

The list elements after modification:
Tommy           --these should line up
Didi Fickle     --these should line up
Chuckie         --these should line up
Zirconium Lil   --these should line up
```

These `LinkedList` objects can now be searched for a particular object that needs modification—when, for example, updating a student's jukebox play time, depositing to a `bankAccount`, or as shown in the example above, padding a list of names with blank spaces at the ends. Here are the class definitions for the `LinkedList` class and a `struct` used to hold the value of each `node` and the link to the next one in the list.

```
// File name: llist.h
// Define the struct needed by the LinkedList class
struct node {
public:
//--constructors
   node();
   node(listElementType data);

// Public data
   listElementType my_data;
```

```
    node* structs_next;
};

class LinkedList {
public:
//--constructor
  LinkedList();
  // Construct an empty list

//--modifiers
  void append(const listElementType& newElement);
  // List == List with newElement added at the end

  bool remove(const listElementType& removalElement);
  // pre:  The listElementType defines ==
  // post: List == List with removalElement removed if found

//--accessor
  int size() const;
  // Return the number of elements currently stored in the list

//--iterator functions
  void first() const;
  // post: my_index points to the first item, or if this
  //       LinkedList is empty, isDone would now return true

  void next() const;
  // post: my_index points to next item, or isDone now returns true

  bool isDone() const;
  // post: Returns true if the collection has been traversed

  listElementType& currentItem();
  // pre:  ! isDone && my_size > 0
  // post: Returns address of the item pointed to by my_index

  const listElementType& currentItem() const;
  // pre:  ! isDone && my_size > 0
  //       Allows const reference lists to be traversed

private:
  node* my_first;
  node* my_last;
  node* my_index;
  int my_size;
};
```

LinkedList CLASS DIAGRAM

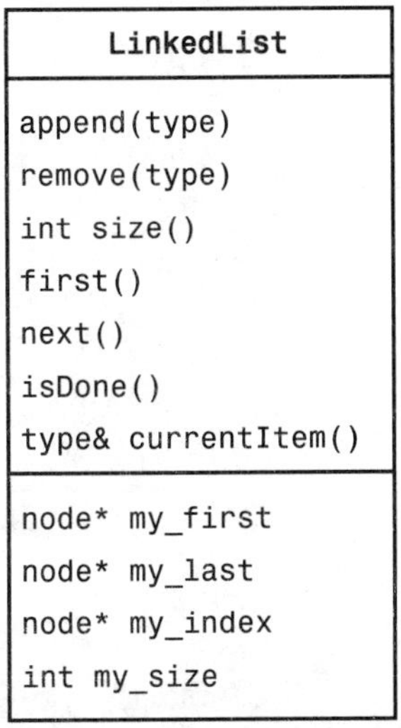

15.6.2 The LinkedList Operations

This section describes some LinkedList member functions that use these node constructors. Both set the link data member (structs_next) to NULL automatically. Otherwise, client code such as the LinkedList class would have to do this.

```
node::node()
{
  structs_next = NULL;
}

node::node(listElementType data)
{
  my_data = data;
  structs_next = NULL;
}
```

15.6.2.1 LinkedList::LinkedList

The LinkedList constructor establishes an empty list using a dummy node. This makes the coding easier during append and remove.

```
LinkedList::LinkedList()
{
  // Create a dummy node to make things easier
```

```
  my_first = new node;  // Call node's default constructor
  my_last = my_first;
  my_index = NULL;
  my_size = 0;
}
```

Here is a picture of memory that results from `LinkedList aList;`.

An Empty List with a Dummy First node

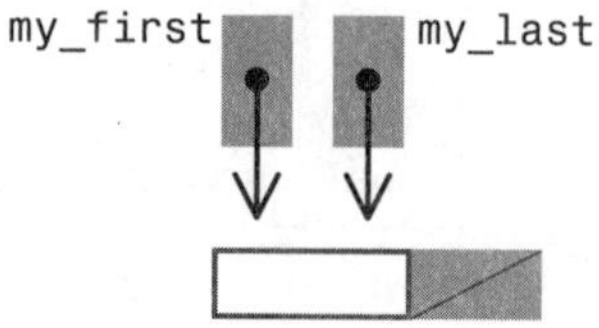

Self-Check

15-24 Write `LinkedList::isEmpty`, which returns true only when the list has zero nodes in it. (*Note:* There are several ways to accomplish this.)

15-25 Write the output generated by the following program:

```
#include <iostream>
#include "track"
using namespace std;

typedef track listElementType;
#include "llist"

int totalPlaytime(const LinkedList& list);

int main()
{
  LinkedList aCD;
  aCD.append( track("doctor my eyes",      3*60+20, 1, 1) );
  aCD.append( track("these days",          4*60+40, 1, 2) );
  aCD.append( track("fountain of sorrow", 6*60+53, 1, 3) );
  aCD.append( track("late for the sky",    5*60+38, 1, 4) );
  aCD.append( track("the pretender",       5*60+53, 1, 5) );
  aCD.append( track("running on empty",    4*60+48, 1, 6) );

  int average = totalPlaytime(aCD) / aCD.size();
  cout << "Average play time per track is "
       << (average / 60) << ":" << (average % 60) << " m:s"
       << endl;
```

```
    return 0;
  }

  int totalPlaytime(const LinkedList& list)
  {
    int result = 0;
    for(list.first(); ! list.isDone(); list.next())
    {
      result += list.currentItem().playTime();
      cout << result << endl;
    }
    return result;
  }
```

15.6.2.2 LinkedList::append

Adding an element at the end of a list (appending) has different meanings for ordered and unordered lists. An ordered linked list would store objects in ascending or descending order based on the meaning of < or >. The linked list developed here is not ordered. So the elements will not be in alphabetic or numeric order (like the standard `list` class). Since this linked list is unordered, all new elements can be appended at the very end of the list. This is easy when the dummy `node` is employed to avoid the special case of appending to an empty list.

Simply create a new object pointed to by `last->structs_next`, update the pointer to the last `node` and increment the current size by 1.

```
void LinkedList::append(const listElementType& newElement)
{
  // Allocate and initialize a new node
  my_last->structs_next = new node(newElement);

  // Update the last pointer
  my_last = my_last->structs_next;

  // Maintain current size
  my_size++;
}
```

These `append` messages result in the pictures of memory shown below.

```
#include <iostream>
#include <string>
using namespace std;
```

```
typedef string listElementType;  // Maintain a list of tracks on CD
#include "llist"

int main()
{
  LinkedList stringList;             // mysize == 0
  stringList.append("First");        // mysize == 1
```

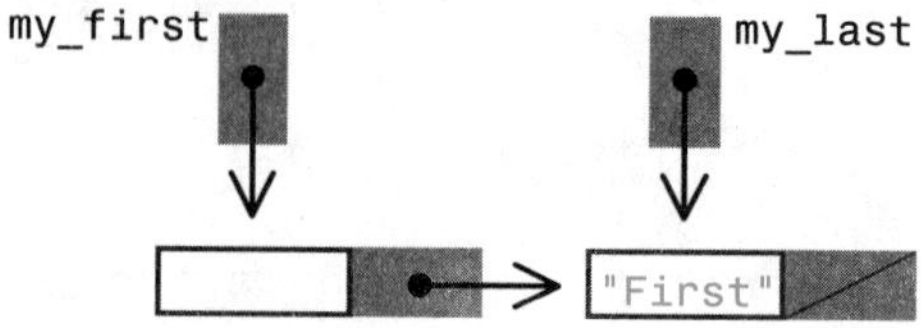


```
  stringList.append("Second");       // mysize == 2
  stringList.append("Third");        // mysize == 3
```

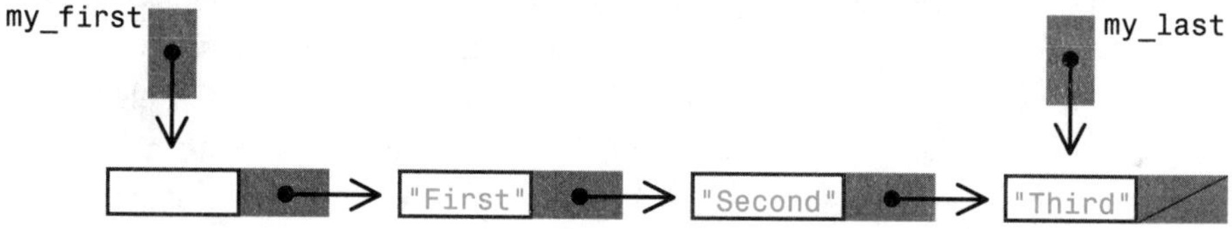


```
  return 0;
}
```

15.6.2.3 LinkedList::remove

These two possibilities must be considered when removing an element from a linked list:

1. the == operation does not match an element in the list
2. the == operation does match an element in the list

The search for a particular element in a linked list is similar to a sequential search through a `vector`. The difference is that now, instead of a subscript, a pointer value will be used to access the elements.

If the element is not in the list, `LinkedList::remove` returns false. If the removal `node` is found, careful adjustment of the pointer fields must occur before the element is deleted. The `remove` operation assumes the `listElementType` has defined the == operator.

The search begins by pointing a variable named `current` to the first element in the list. The `prev` pointer will be used to keep track of the `node` immediately before the `node` being compared. The initialization of `prev` and `current` are shown before the `while` loop of `LinkedList::remove` below.

```
myCD.remove("Second");   // Initializes prev and current
```

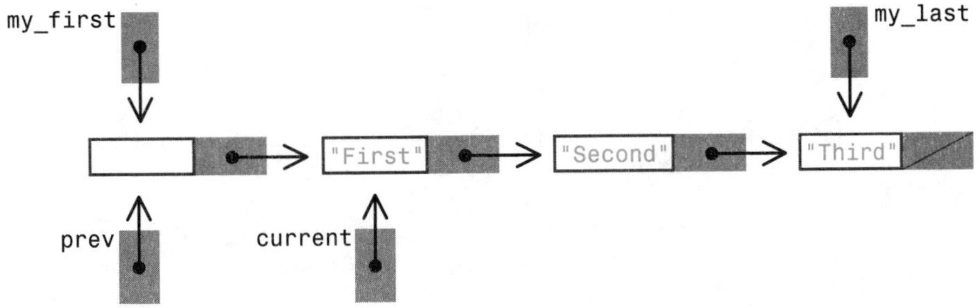

Since `current->my_data == removalElement ("First" == "Second")` is false, the loop advances `prev` and `current` by one `node` in the list. At this point, `current` points to the `node` with the value to be removed.

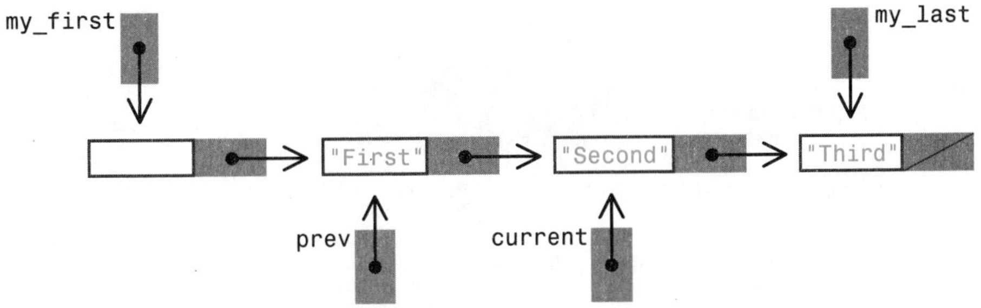

The next diagram shows that the `node` pointed to by `prev` is adjusted to point to the `node` after the `node` to be removed. This allows the current `node`, the one with the unwanted value, to be deleted. At this point, the first `node` points to the third. The second `node`, the one with the unwanted value, can now be safely returned to the free store with `delete`. This algorithm is shown in `LinkedList::remove`.

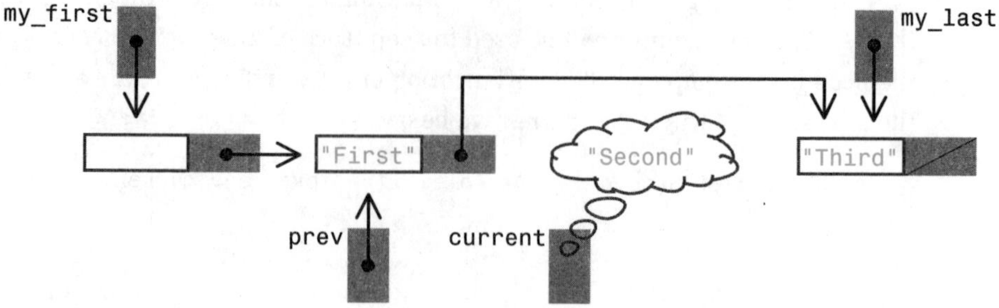


```
bool LinkedList::remove(const listElementType& removalElement)
{ // pre: The listElementType defines ==

  // Let current point to the first (there is a dummy node)
  node* current = my_first->structs_next;
  node* prev = my_first;

  // Check the remaining list elements until found or no more
  while(current != NULL)
  {
    if(current->my_data == removalElement)
    {
      break;
    }
    else
    {
      prev = current;
      current = current->structs_next;
    }
  }

  // Don't delete a nonexistent node
  if(current == NULL)
  { // removalElement was not found
    return false;
  }
  else
  { // Take out the element
    prev->structs_next = current->structs_next; // Move link around
    delete current;  // Deallocate memory
    my_size--;       // Maintain current size
    return true;     // Report successful removal
  }
}
```

Self-Check

15-26 Draw a picture of a linked list with two `nodes` before and after removing the first `node`.

15-27 Draw a picture of a linked list with one `node` before and after removing the first `node`.

15-28 What happens if `removalValue` is not found in the list?

15-29 *True or False:* The size of a dynamically linked list must be determined before the program begins to execute.

15-30 *True or False:* Elements in a linked list are referenced through subscripts.

15-31 *True or False:* Elements may be inserted into or deleted from a linked list at the beginning, end, or even the middle.

15-32 *True or False:* When an element is to be inserted into or deleted from a linked list, the list should be checked to see if it is empty.

15-33 *True or False:* When an element has been removed from a dynamically linked list, the memory it used should be returned to the free store.

Chapter Summary

- Pointers, used with the `new` and `delete` operations, allow programmers to better utilize computer memory. For example, the `string` class is designed to allocate the minimum amount of memory at the instant needed. When an object is no longer needed, the memory is deallocated back to the free store for use by other objects. Implementations of the `string` class vary.
- The primitive C array—similar to the C++ `vector` class—is available on all compilers and will often be seen in existing C and C++ code.
- Using pointers to `chars` (`char*` objects) and functions of `cstring` provides a quasi `string` class that must be used very carefully. The safer standard `string` class defines operators that make `strings` look more like built-in data types such as `int` and `double`.
- Working with pointers and dynamic memory allocation can prove tricky. One helpful tool is the use of arrows to represent address values. Pointer objects can be in-

serted for output, but it is their use with the dereference operator `*` that helps the debugging process.

- The `new` operator allocates memory from the free store. The `delete` operator deallocates memory. If more than one object is allocated as in

  ```
  char* name = new char[10];
  ```

  it must be deallocated with `[ ]` as in

  ```
  delete [ ] name;
  ```

- Classes with dynamic memory allocation, such as `vector` and `string`, should have a destructor, a copy constructor, and an overloaded assignment operator (see Chapter 18).

Exercises

1. Write the output generated by the following program:

```
#include <iostream>
using namespace std;
int main()
{
  double* x;
  x = new double[5];
  int j;
  for(j = 0; j < 5; j++)
  {
    x[j] = (j + 0.1) + (j * 0.1);
  }
  for(j = 0; j < 5; j++)
  {
    cout << x[j] << "  ";
  }
  return 0;
}
```

2. Write the output generated by the following program:

```
#include <iostream>
#include <cstring>  // Or #include <string.h> on older compilers
using namespace std;
int main()
```

```
{
  char* c;
  int j;
  c = new char[5];
  c = "Four";
  for(j = 0; j < strlen(c); j++)
  {
    cout << j << ". " << char(toupper(c[j])) << endl;
  }
  return 0;
}
```

3. Write the output generated by the following program:

```
#include <iostream>
using namespace std;
#include "baccount"
int main()
{
  bankAccount* p1;
  bankAccount* p2;
  bankAccount* temp;
  bankAccount p1, p2;

  p1 = new bankAccount("Hall", 111.11);
  p2 = new bankAccount("Westphall", 999.99);

  cout << "p1 points to " << (*p1).name() << endl;
  temp = p1;
  p1 = p2;
  p2 = temp;
  cout << "p1 now points to " << (*p1).name() << endl;
  cout << "p2 now points to " << (*p2).name() << endl;
  return 0;
}
```

4. Write a loop that changes any letter in a given `string` to another letter.

```
char oldLetter = 'a';
char newLetter = 'x';
// "all a's should be made to x" becomes "xll x's should be mxde to x"
```

5. Write code to display all elements of `char*` variables up to, but not including, any given character named `sentinel`.

6. Write code to copy all elements from `x` into a new array named `y`.

```
const int n = 100;
double x[n];
```

Use the following `struct` to answer exercises 7 through 15:

```
struct LittleRecord {
//--constructors
  LittleRecord();
  LittleRecord(int anInt, string aString);
// public:
  int my_int;
  string my_string;
  LittleRecord* next;
};
```

7. Implement both constructors. Make sure `next` is always `NULL`.

8. Write the code necessary to create the following linked list:

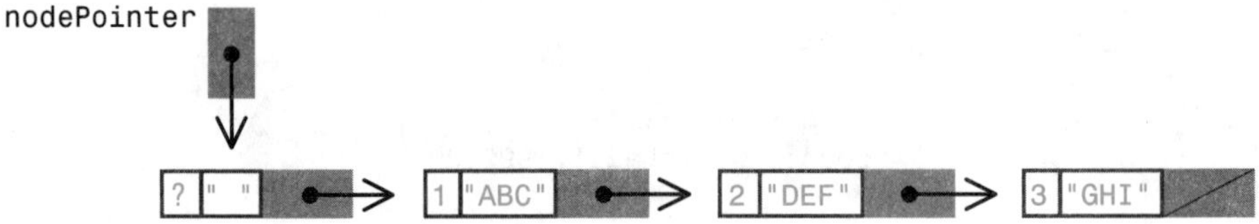

9. What is the value of `nodePointer->next->next->next`?

10. What is the value of `nodePointer->next->my_int`?

11. What is the value of `nodePointer->next->my_string`?

12. What is the value of `nodePointer->next->next->my_string`?

13. Write one assignment statement that will increment `3` by +17 thereby storing `20` where `3` was.

14. Write the code that effectively eliminates the first `node` and returns the memory back to the free store, keeping the remaining portion of the linked `node`s intact.

15. Write code that would sum all integers in this linked structure even if there were thousands. Use a loop.

Programming Tips

1. Memory for dynamic objects must be allocated before values can be stored in them.

The `new` operator allocates memory from the free store as it returns the location of that memory—the address. An assignment to an object pointed to by an uninitialized pointer allows that value to be stored anywhere in the free store. This could cause the program to crash or hang the computer.

```
double* ptr;  // No one knows where 123.4 will go
*ptr = 123.4;
```

2. Even after a pointer object is deleted, its value can still be pointing to the same dynamic object; but don't count on it.

Don't trust these values. Consider the following code and output:

```
int* ptr = new int;
cout << *ptr << endl;    // Should display garbage
*ptr = 123456;
cout << * ptr << endl;   // Should display 123456
delete ptr;              // ptr is undefined, but may still point to the
cout << * ptr << endl;   // same place; output may be 123456
```

OUTPUT (VARIES)

```
-842150451
123456
-572662307
```

The first line of output is garbage since neither `ptr` nor `*ptr` have been assigned a value yet. Both the pointer object and the dynamic object have meaningless values. After both objects have been assigned a value, the proper value of 123456 is displayed. The same value may be displayed even after `ptr` is deleted. It didn't on the system that ran the previous code.

3. Don't use `char*`. Use `string` instead.

Using `char*` variables requires careful use of memory allocation and deallocation. The `string` class takes cares of things behind the scenes. So why is `char*` in this chapter? You'll see it in other existing C and C++ programs. It also demonstrates how memory can be allocated at runtime with `new` and deallocated at runtime with `delete`. There are times when `char*` must be used.

4. Primitive arrays require an integer constant at compiletime.

The following code is illegal because `n` is not a constant integer:

```
int n = 100;   // Precede with const to declare a primitive array
double x[n];
```

Use either a named `int` constant `n` or an integer constant in the array `double x[100];`.

5. Remember to dispose of all pointer variables when the dynamic variables they point to are no longer needed.

One of the reasons for using pointers is so that the amount of memory taken can expand and contract. Failure to deallocate memory may result in an out-of-memory error later on. If you forget to dispose of the unwanted `node`, you may have a memory leak. This means you should add a destructor to any new class with dynamic memory allocation.

Programming Projects

15A `char* lowerCase(char*)`

Using pointer syntax (and not a `string` class), write a function called `lowerCase` that converts any `char*` argument into its lowercase equivalent. First find the difference between `'A'` and `'a'` on your system (32 on most), and recall that - and + can be applied to `char` operands like this:

```
int main()
{
  cout << ('a' - 'A') << endl;
  cout << char('A' + 32) << endl;  // char(int) converts int to char
  return 0;
}
```

OUTPUT

```
32
a
```

Use this exact function heading to return a char* value. Because of const, any change to s will not affect the argument str.

```
char* toLower(const char* s)
```

Then test your function with the following main function:

```
int main()
{ // Test drive toLower
  cout << toLower("AbCdEfG") << endl;
  cout << toLower("ABC!@#$XYZ") << endl;
  char* str = "<def123GHI-+'?>";
  cout << toLower(str) << endl;
  return 0;
}
```

OUTPUT

```
abcdefg
abc!@#$xyz
<def123ghi-+'?>
```

15B toUpper

Using pointer syntax (and not a string class), write a function toUpper that returns the uppercase equivalent of the char* object passed to it. Use the following function heading:

```
char* toUpper(const char* s)
```

Hint: Read 15A first to realize that #include <cctype> provides the function named toupper that makes things easier.

```
int toupper(int ch);
// Return the uppercase value (A to Z) if ch is lowercase a to z. Otherwise
// return ch.
```

The toupper function returns an int, so if you want to see the char equivalent, typecast the return value.

```
cout << toupper('a') << endl;         // Output: 65
cout << char(toupper('a')) << endl;   // Output: A
```

15C string Reversal

Using pointer syntax (and not a string class), write a function reverse that reverses the order of the characters pointed to by a char* object. Use this test driver program that generates the dialogue that follows:

```
#include <iostream>
using namespace std;
```

```
// Implement reverse function here

int main()
{ // Test drive reverse
  char* s = new char[100];

  cout << "Enter a string: ";
  cin >> s;
  reverse(s);
  cout << "reversed: " << s << endl;

  return 0;
}
```

DIALOGUE

```
Enter a string: Madam
reversed: madaM
```

15D subString

Using pointer syntax (and not a `string` class), write a free function named `subString` that returns the portion of a `string` specified by the two integer arguments. Use the following test driver to produce the output shown:

```
#include <iostream>
using namespace std;

// Implement subString function here

int main()
{ // Test drive subString
  char* charPtr = new char[26];

  strcpy(charPtr, "abcdefghijklmnopqrstuvwxyz");
  cout << subString(charPtr, 0, 5) << endl;
  cout << subString(charPtr, 5, 5) << endl;
  cout << subString(charPtr, 10, 5) << endl;
  cout << subString(charPtr, 15, 5) << endl;
  cout << subString(charPtr, 20, 6) << endl;
  return 0;
}
```

OUTPUT

```
abcde
fghij
klmno
pqrst
uvwxyz
```

15E A Class with a Destructor

Write a complete class named `mystery` that has one constructor, one destructor, and one `char*` data member named `my_message` (do not use the `string` class which has its own destructor). Implement the constructor to allocate memory for the data member with the message `"Constructor message goes here"`. Implement the destructor so it displays the message `"Destructor called as the mystery object goes out of scope"`. Test your class to see if you have properly managed memory using the following program:

```
// assumption: The mystery class has been defined and implemented
void f()
{
  mystery source;
}

int main()
{
  f();
  return 0;
}
```

OUTPUT

```
Constructor message goes here
Destructor called as the mystery object goes out of scope
```

Your output should be the same as that shown above. If it is not, make it so. If you get a runtime error, make sure you are properly allocating and deallocating memory with `new` and `delete`, respectively.

15F The `myArray` Class

Implement the `myArray` class that stores a collection of objects of type `ARRAY_ELEMENT_TYPE`. Individual elements may be indexed through the member functions `myArray::set` and `myArray::sub`. If the subscript is outside of this range, the member function must display an error message (shown in the output below).

- Create a new file named `myarray.h`, and retype the following class definition. Notice that this class has a copy constructor and a destructor.

```
#ifndef MYARRAY_H
#define MYARRAY_H

class myArray {
```

```
public:
//--constructors
  myArray();
  // Memory for 10 ARRAY_ELEMENT_TYPE objects

  myArray(int initMax);
  // post: Memory for 10 ints, pointed to by x, is allocated

  myArray(const myArray & source);
  // post: Dynamically allocate memory during pass by value

//--destructor
  ~myArray();
  // post: Memory allocated for my_data is deallocated

//--modifier
  void set(int subscript, ARRAY_ELEMENT_TYPE value);
  // post: x[subscript] = value when subscript is in range.
  //       If not, an error message is displayed.

//--accessor
  ARRAY_ELEMENT_TYPE sub(int subscript) const;
  // post: x[subscript] is returned when subscript is in range.
  //       If not, display an error message and return [0].

private:
  ARRAY_ELEMENT_TYPE* my_data;
  int my_capacity;
};
#endif
```

- Implement all six member functions of the `myArray` class. Remember to
  - allocate with `new [ ]` in the default, initializing, and copy constructors
  - set `my_data = new ARRAY_ELEMENT_TYPE[my_capacity];`
  - deallocate with `delete [ ] my_data` in the destructor
  - check to ensure the subscripts are in the range of `myArray::set` and `myArray::sub` and generate error messages if they are not
- The copy constructor for the `myArray` class must perform these steps:
  - Allocate memory for `my_capacity new ARRAY_ELEMENT_TYPE`.
  - Copy each and every element from the parameter to the new subscripted pointer data member `my_data`. Use a `for` loop to do this.

Retype the following test program (or load up `test15f.cpp`). Use the output shown below as you test drive `myArray`.

```
// File name: test15f.cpp
#include <iostream>
using namespace std;

typedef double ARRAY_ELEMENT_TYPE;
#include "myarray"  // For the myArray class

void show(myArray arrayCopy, int n)
{
  for(int j = 0; j < n; j++)
  {
    cout << arrayCopy.sub(j) << endl;
  }
}

int main()
{
  int n = 6;
  myArray a(6);
  a.set(0, 1.1);
  a.set(1, 2.2);
  a.set(2, 3.3);
  a.set(3, 4.4);
  a.set(4, 5.5);
  a.set(5, 6.6);
  show(a, n);
  cout << a.sub(6) << endl;         // Out-of-range error
  cout << a.set(-1, -1.1) << endl;  // Out-of-range error
  return 0;
}
```

OUTPUT

```
1.1
2.2
3.3
4.4
5.5
6.6
**Error: subscript 6 not in range 0..5. Returning first element.
1.1
**Error: subscript -1 not in range 0..5. The array is unchanged.
```

15G LinkedList::prepend

Add `LinkedList::prepend` that inserts new elements at the beginning of a `linkedList` object.

15H LinkedList::sort

Add `LinkedList::sort` to sort the elements of the linked list in ascending order. Assume the contained elements define the < operator. Consider using the selection sort described in Chapter 10, "Vectors." When the elements being sorted are `node`s in a linked list, the selection sort requires pointers to advance through the linked list. These pointers replace a `vector`. A pointer to the smallest key is also useful. This means that three local pointer variables should be declared within the sort operation, such as:

```
node* outer;
node* inner;
node* smallestPtr;
```

15I OrderedList::sort

Implement an `OrderedList` class that stores elements in order. Instead of `append` and `prepend`, this list class will have only one operation to place objects in the container:

```
OrderedList::insert(orderedListElementType newElement)
// post: Place newElement into the list, maintaining ascending order
```

Chapter Sixteen

Object-Oriented Software Development

Inheritance and Polymorphism

Summing Up

The previous chapter introduced dynamic memory allocation and a linked list. The notions of indirection and dynamic memory allocation, introduced in the preceding two chapters, will be used in this chapter to store a collection of dissimilar elements.

Coming Up

This chapter uses a team-based approach to introduce the two other major features of the object-oriented paradigm:

* inheritance: the ability to derive a new class from an existing class
* polymorphism: the ability of different types of objects to respond to the same message in different ways

A case study presents another object-oriented approach to software development. Along the way, the team discovers a class hierarchy that provides experience with inheritance, polymorphism, and heterogeneous collections. After studying this chapter, you will be able to

* recognize generalization that may be implemented with inheritance
* derive new classes from old ones
* override member functions and add new features to derived classes
* apply object-oriented design heuristics for inheritance
* understand and use polymorphism

16.1 Discovery of Inheritance through Generalization

This section provides another case study in object-oriented software development. This time the problem is from the domain of a college library system. It follows the same methodology presented with the Chapter 12 cashless jukebox case study. This problem is very similar to a problem described in Nancy Wilkinson's book *Using CRC Cards* [Wilkinson 95]. Related items such as a library class hierarchy, inheritance, polymorphism, a date class, and a data structure capable of storing different classes of objects are described in *Problem Solving and Program Implementation* [Mercer 91].

THE PROBLEM STATEMENT: *College library application*

The college library has requested a system that supports a small set of library operations: students borrowing items, returning borrowed items, and paying fees. Late fees and due dates have been established at the following rates:

	Late Fee	Borrowing Period
Book:	$0.50 per day	14 days
Videotape:	$5.00 one day late plus $1.50 for each additional day late	2 days
CD-ROM:	$2.50 per day	7 days

A student with more than seven borrowed items, any one late item, or late fees greater than $25.00 may not borrow anything new.

Object-oriented software development attempts to model a real-world system as a collection of interacting objects—each with its own set of responsibilities. This helps organize the system into workable pieces. The three-step object-oriented software development strategy introduced in Chapter 12 is repeated here for your convenience:

1. Identify classes that model (shape) the system as a natural and sensible set of abstractions.
2. Determine the purpose, or main responsibility, of each class. The responsibilities of a class are what an instance of the class must be able to do

(member functions) and what each object must know about itself (data members).

3. Determine the helper classes for each. To help complete its responsibility, a class typically delegates responsibility to one or more other objects. These are called helper classes.

The team consists of the library domain expert, Deena, and five students who are analyzing the college library system as part of a computer science honors option: Jessica, Jason, Steve, Matt, and Misty. Austen is the object expert this time.

16.1.1 Identify the Classes

The team now has some experience with object-oriented software development. They plan to use their experience. The first goal, or deliverable, is a set of potential classes that model the problem statement. Each class will describe its major responsibility. The team starts by writing down all the nouns and noun phrases in the problem statement, redundant entries not recorded.

NOUNS (FROM THE PROBLEM STATEMENT)

college library	system	library operations	CD-ROM
librarian	student	item	seven borrowed books
fee	book	videotape	
late fee	day	due date	

The following list represents the set of potential classes for modeling a solution:

POTENTIAL CLASSES: *A first pass at finding key abstractions*

Somewhat Sure	Not Sure
librarian	system
student	operations
book	late fees
video	due date
CD-ROM	day
seven borrowed books	fine
college library	

Matt recommends keeping `librarian` as the name for a class responsible for coordinating the activities of checking books in and out.

A `student` class will be a useful key abstraction. After all, students will be checking books out, checking them in, and paying fines. The domain expert, Deena, mentions that `librarian` should also be allowed to lend books to faculty, staff, and other members of the community. After all, it's a state university paid for in part by state taxes. So the team decides to change the class name to `borrower` to reflect the general notion of someone who can borrow a book from the library.

Misty doesn't believe "seven borrowed books" should be a key abstraction. One of the programmers on the team chimes in and suggests, "This is not a problem. I can see this as a `bag` of `book` objects." The domain expert Deena remarks, "A book bag?—cool." Since the team is currently looking for classes that help observers understand what the system does rather then how the system will eventually do it, the team decides that "seven borrowed books" is not a class. Instead, this is a knowledge responsibility.

Austen uses some object-speak: "A `borrower` should know its own collection of borrowed books." Matt jumps in and asks Austen, "Aren't CD-ROMs and videotapes in the same category? They can be borrowed too!" Deena agrees. Austen states that Matt has implicitly discovered a basic concept of object-oriented analysis. Some classes have things in common. In this case, there are several categories of things that can be borrowed: books, CD-ROMs, and videotapes. The team considers the responsibilities these classes have in common. After some discussion, Jason and Jessica produce the following list of responsibilities that all three classes of objects have in common. Each `book`, `cdRom`, and `video` should:

- know its due date
- compute its due date
- determine its late fee
- know its borrower
- check itself out
- check itself in

Self-Check

16-1 Which responsibilities are the same for these three classes?

16-2 Which responsibilities should be carried out differently?

Jason notices that the term "borrowable item" has been floating around. Austen suggests there could be an abstraction named `borrowableItem` that supplies the attributes and behavior common to all items that could be borrowed from the library. Although differences exist in the computation of late fees and the setting of due dates, each `borrowableItem` has several common responsibilities. Steve complains that `borrowableItem` is a bit of a tongue-twister. Matt suggests `lendable`: "`lendable` represents things that are, well, lendable." Deena likes this new name. `lendable` it is.

Austen points out that the team has intuitively discovered the inheritance relationship between classes. *Inheritance* is another name for generalization. Matt instinctively saw several seemingly different objects and found some common things. He generalized. Since no one has seen or heard of the inheritance relationship, Austen draws the following diagram on the chalkboard:

FIGURE 16.1. *The inheritance relationship in UML notation (`lendable` is the abstract class)*

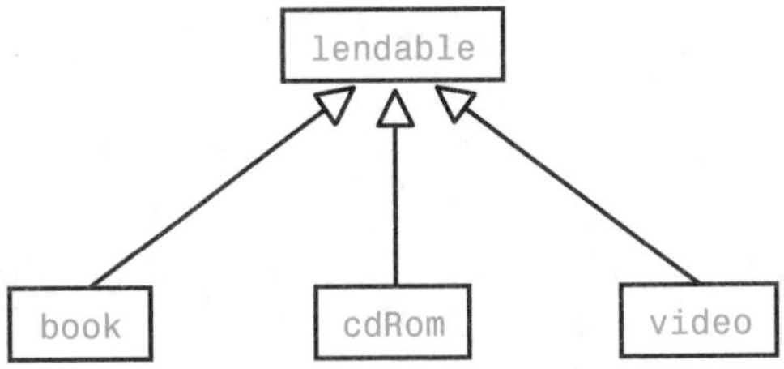

Austen explains that the C++ culture would refer to `lendable` as the *base class.* The other three classes—`book`, `cdRom`, and `video`—are known as *derived classes.* The member functions and data members common to all lendables should be listed in the base class (`lendable`). Through inheritance, each derived class (`book`, `cdRom`, and `video`) inherits member functions from the base class (`lendable`). Austen then displays a design heuristic in order to explicitly encourage the team to accept the inheritance relationship between classes as good design.

OBJECT-ORIENTED DESIGN HEURISTIC 16.1 (RIEL'S 5.10)

If two or more classes have common data and behavior, then those classes should inherit from a common base class that captures those data and methods.

The common data and operations include:

- a date for knowing the borrower and the due date
- operations such as check self out and check self in

However, without some difference amongst the derived classes, there is no reason to use the inheritance relationship. Instead, there should be just one class. So, in addition to commonalities as mentioned above, there must be enough differences to justify having more than one class. There are two, possibly three, major differences between the three classes:

1. computation of the due dates
2. computation of late fees
3. different attributes (`video` has a movie-studio attribute, for example)

Jason is confused and questions Austen. Jason doesn't understand why there is a `lendable` class in the library system. Austen decides it might prove useful if he explained the difference between an abstract class and a concrete class. An *abstract class* describes the data and operations meant to be common to all derived classes. An abstract class cannot be instantiated. Therefore, this code should be rendered illegal:

```
lendable aLendable;  // ERROR--attempt to construct abstract class
```

Abstract classes exist to capture common operations and data. They are not to be constructed.

A *concrete class* is one that can be instantiated. Therefore, these constructions must be legal:

```
book aBook;  // To be implemented later
cdRom aCDROM;
video aVideo;
```

Self-Check

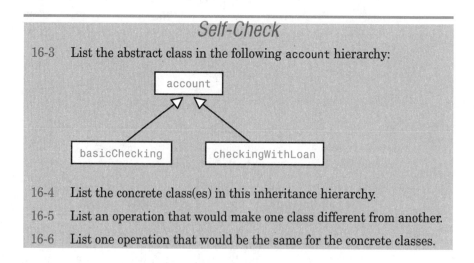

16-3 List the abstract class in the following `account` hierarchy:

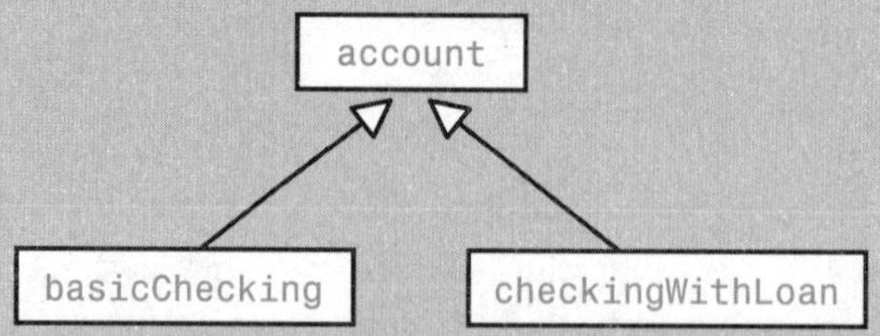

16-4 List the concrete class(es) in this inheritance hierarchy.

16-5 List an operation that would make one class different from another.

16-6 List one operation that would be the same for the concrete classes.

16-7 List one data member that both derived classes would likely have.

16-8 List one data member that would exist in one class, but not in the other.

Jessica claims to understand the notion of the inheritance relationship, although the implementation is not in her head yet. Austen remarks, "I could show you how all this works, but don't worry about it for now. I'll show the implementation details in a bit." Matt articulates that the team should get back on task with analyzing the college library system.

Jason reminds the group that the following classes have been identified so far:

* `librarian`
* `borrower`
* `lendable` (and the derived classes: `book`, `cdRom`, and `video`)

With some consensus realized, Steve wants to know what the user interface will look like. Will there be text-based input and output communication between the user and the system? Is a graphical user interface desired? What about a card reader or touchscreen for input? Steve enjoyed the touchscreen ordering system recently tested at the local Taco Bell™. Misty points out that it has since been removed. Deena, the domain expert, isn't sure what the interface should look like. She believes the library will be okay with a text-based interface to the system. Text-based input and output are acceptable. Matt draws a picture so everyone can understand the relationship between a user and `librarian`:

FIGURE 16.2

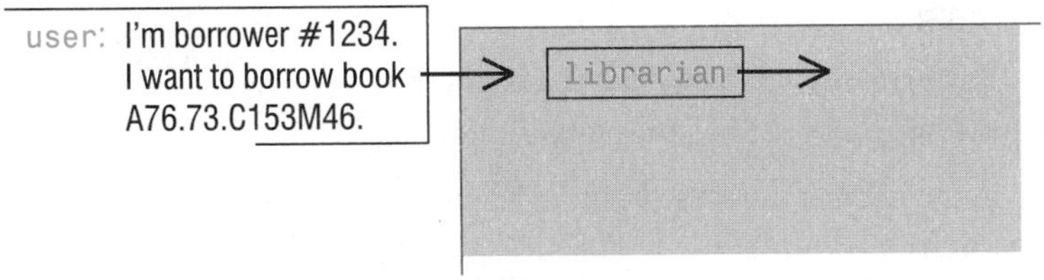

Steve wonders whether `user` should be included as one of the classes to model the problem. Misty reminds Steve that the user is a person who approaches `librarian`, shows identification, and makes a request. `borrower` represents an object inside the system that knows everything about that user that the system will need to know. For example, `borrower` could also be responsible for knowing if its human counterpart (the user) owes any late fees. User is not going to be a class. However, it could play a part in the scenarios. Austen confirms that this is a good decision. Matt lets Austen in on a little secret: "We went through this once before with the cashless jukebox that's jammin' in the student center."

Deena has a problem with the concept of a `book` class and a `borrower` class. Certainly the system must maintain many borrowers and many books. Matt relates, "One class can create many instances, or objects. Since there will be many lendables and many borrowers, we should probably add two new classes named `borrowerList` and `lendableList` to store, retrieve, and delete `borrowers` and `lendables`, respectively." The team agrees. It worked for the jukebox.

The team feels as though they have captured several key abstractions (classes) for this application. They now have a framework for analyzing the problem in more detail. There is a sense that the primary responsibility of each class has been recognized. The team documents their progress with a table that lists class names along with their primary responsibilities.

Class Name	Primary Responsibility
`librarian`	Represent object responsible for coordinating activities of checking books in and out.
`borrower`	Represent one instance of someone who can borrow a `lendable`. There may be thousands of `borrowers`.
`lendable`	Represent an abstract class from which many "borrowable" items can be derived. This abstract class captures the common member functions and data members of any item that can be borrowed from the college library.
`book`	Represent one book that can be checked in and checked out. There may be thousands of `books`.
`cdRom`	Represent one CD-ROM that can be checked in and checked out. There may be thousands of `cdRoms` stored in the database.
`video`	Represent one videotape that can be checked in and checked out. There may be thousands of `videos`.
`borrowerList`	Retrieve, delete, add, or update any `borrower` from the thousands of `borrowers` in the database of valid `borrowers`.
`lendableList`	Retrieve, delete, add, or update any `lendable` from thousands of "borrowable" items.

This following picture provides an abstract view of the system so far. It also marks the boundaries of the system. Everything in gray is in the system under development. The users and physical items that can be borrowed are outside the system.

Figure 16.3

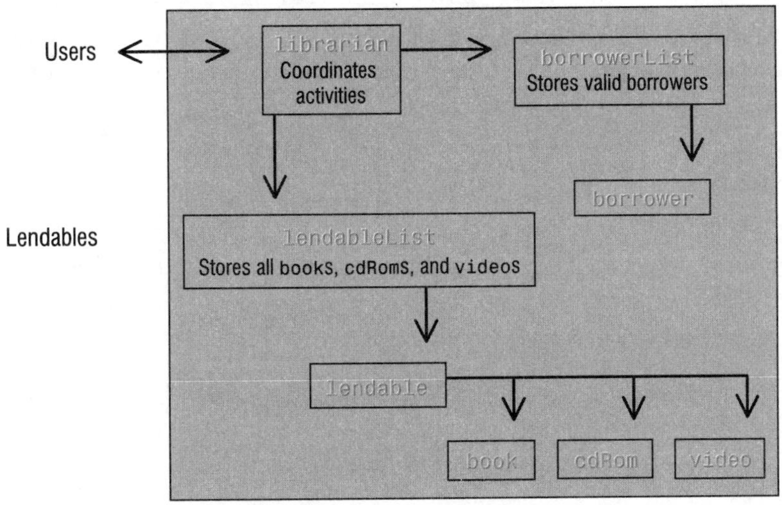

16.2 Refinement of Responsibilities

With primary responsibilities identified, the team now sets about the task of identifying and refining other responsibilities. The team will also identify helpers—the other classes needed to carry out a specific responsibility. The team will try to answer questions such as: What are the responsibilities? Which class should take on each of the responsibilities? and What class(es) help accomplish another class's responsibility? Responsibilities convey the purpose of a class and its role in the system. Analysis is enhanced when the team thinks that each instance of a class will be responsible for two things:

1. the knowledge each object of the class must maintain
2. the actions each object of the class can perform

Austen recommends that the team to be prepared to ask the following two questions:

1. What should an object of the class know about itself (knowledge)?
2. What should an object of the class be able to do (actions)?

Assigning a responsibility to a class means that every instance of that class will have that responsibility. This is true when there are many instances of the class—as in `lendables` and `borrowers`. It is also true when there is only one instance of the class—such as `librarian` and `lendableList`.

The next team activity involves assigning more specific responsibilities to the classes already identified. One technique involves role playing. Each team member assumes the role of one of the classes. The team members play out scenarios while adding responsibilities and helpers to CRH cards.

16.2.1 A "User Cannot Borrow" Scenario

At this point, team members assume the roles of the classes. They plan to try scenarios to see how one instance of a class interacts with other objects. A scenario is the answer to the question What happens when . . . ? The team decides the first scenario will be the response to this question:

16.2.1.1 Scenario 1: "What happens when user #1234 wants to check out a book and currently has seven borrowed `lendables`?"

`librarian`: Well, I'm the librarian so I guess I'll start. I just got a user ID. It's #1234. Now User, what do you want to do?

User: I want to check out a book.

`librarian`: Now I need to know the call number of the book.

User: The book's call number is QA76.1.

`librarian`: Okay, now let me verify that this user can borrow. I'll ask `borrowerList` to look up the `borrower` with ID #1234.

`borrowerList`: I found the `borrower` you asked for. I'm sending it back to you. I'll add `getBorrower` to my responsibility list. I must know all borrowers.

`librarian`: Thanks, `borrowerList`. Now I have the software object that represents the human user. I believe my job will be easier if I can send `borrower` a `canBorrow` message. I am now helping `borrower`. What about it, current `borrower`, can you borrow a new book?

`borrower`: Since I am responsible for knowing my borrowed `lendables`, I should be able to tell you if I have seven or more things checked out. Hey wait a minute, you didn't ask me if I had seven borrowed items. You asked me if I could borrow. So I am going to add a `canBorrow` responsibility to my list. I will return a code indicating that I can borrow. Will false or true do? To borrow, my late fine must be $25.00 or less and I must have fewer than seven borrowed items, none of which can be overdue. It seems like I'll need to know my own borrowed `lendables`. I have seven borrowed items. No, I cannot borrow.

`librarian`: Thanks, `borrower`. Things are made easier for me because I can delegate the `canBorrow` responsibility to you. Also, remember when we were working on the jukebox. Chelsea told us that we should try to distribute system intelligence as evenly as possible. We had a `canSelect` message to simplify the jukebox. Now, I can just send a `canBorrow` message to you. I think I now must send an appropriate message to the user that borrowing a book is not an option.

The team decides they have run this particular scenario to its logical conclusion. They also feel that there are obviously many possible scenarios to role play such as successfully checking out a book and returning a lendable. The team also wonders if users should be able to look up a book by call number to see if it is in or out. Perhaps a user might want to know when a book is due back in the library. This suggests that a `lendable` should know when it is due and it should be able to tell someone the actual due date.

Deena confirms that this is certainly desirable behavior. However, the problem specification does not list these requirements. The team agrees to plan for the possibility of adding such enhancements later.

16.2.2 A Check-Out Scenario

16.2.2.1 Scenario 2: "What happens when user #1234 wants to borrow a `lendable` with call number QA76.2, has three books out, none of which are late, and has late fines of only $5.00?"

`librarian`: I'll start again; I'll get the user ID.

User: My ID is #1234.

`librarian`: Let me ask `borrowerList` for the proper borrower. Please `getBorrower` with ID #1234.

`borrowerList`: I found the `borrower` you asked for. I'm sending it back to you.

`librarian`: User, what do you want to do?

User: I want to borrow something with call number QA76.2.

`librarian`: Now I have the current `borrower` and the current `lendable` in my possession. I think I'll check with `borrower`: can you borrow?

`borrower`: Let me see if I have fewer than seven borrowed items. Yes, I currently am borrowing three `lendables`. Now, are any `lendables` overdue? Let me ask the first `lendable` in my list of borrowed items: $\texttt{lendable}_0$, are you overdue?

$\texttt{lendable}_0$: I am responsible for knowing if I am overdue. I'll have to ask `date` to compare my due date with today's date. I will add the responsibilities "know due date" and `isOverdue`. I asked `date` for help.

"Who's `date`?" asks Deena. She wants to know what a `date` class would be responsible for. The team decides to add `date` as a key abstraction and see what its responsibilities are. One of the programmers writes down `date` as a helper on a CRH card and agrees to play the role of `date`.

`date`: To compare the due date with today's date, I must be able to get today's date and to compare two dates. Yes $\texttt{lendable}_0$, today's date is less than or equal to the due date. I'll add <= and `todaysDate` to my responsibilities.

$\texttt{lendable}_0$: Thanks, `date`. I am not overdue.

`borrower`: I'll check my other `lendables`. $\texttt{lendable}_1$, $\texttt{lendable}_2$? None are overdue. Since I also have no late fees, I can tell `librarian`, "Yes, I can borrow something new."

`librarian`: `lendableList`, please get me the `lendable` QA76.2.

`lendableList`: Okay, here is the `lendable`.

`librarian`: What should I do now?

The team pauses and considers a couple of possibilities. It seems as if the current `borrower` and the current `lendable` both need to be updated somehow to record that the `lendable` has been checked out. It seems logical to update the `lendable` first and then send it to the `borrower` to add to its list of `lendables`. It also seems appropriate to update `lendableList` and `borrowerList`. That ensures that all `borrowers` and `lendables` are accurately updated.

Austen recommends that the team first ask the question, What should be done to update `lendable`? The team decides that the `book`'s status should become "not available." Also, `lendable`'s `dueDate` should be set to the appropriate day in the future so later on the `borrower` can ask the `book` if it is overdue. The team also believes that it is important to know who has borrowed the `lendable`—in case someone wants to find out who has it. The team comes up with two alternatives.

The first alternative places the responsibility of updating a `lendable` upon `librarian`. The second alternative delegates this responsibility to the `lendable` itself. The team decides to role play both alternatives. Here is the first.

16.2.2.2 Alternative 1 (updating the `lendable`)

`librarian`: `lendable`, compute and set your due date.

`lendable`: Okay, I'll `setDueDate` to either 2, 7, or 14 days from today—depending on what class of `lendable` is currently being checked out.

Austen breaks in saying, "That's polymorphism!" The class can be determined while the program is running. The particular version of `setDueDate` will depend on the class of the object. And the class of object cannot be determined until the moment the `lendable` is being checked out—at runtime.

`lendable`: I'll set the due date. I'll add a `computeDueDate` responsibility to my CRH card.

`librarian`: `lendable`, now please record #1234 as your borrower.

`lendable`: Okay, I'll set my borrower ID as user #1234.

`librarian`: Okay, now mark yourself as not available.

`lendable`: Done.

16.2.2.3 Alternative 2 (updating the `lendable`)

`librarian`: `lendable`, you could be responsible for checking yourself out. If I tell you who the `borrower` is, could you check yourself out?

`lendable`: Sure. I add these new responsibilities to my CRH card: `computeDueDate` and `checkSelfOut`.

Which alternative is better? One way to assess the design is to ask yourself what feels better. Alternative 2 feels better somehow. But wouldn't it be nice to have some design heuristics to make us feel better about feeling better? Well, it turns out that the first alternative has a higher degree of coupling. There were three different message sends versus the single message send of the second alternative. Additionally, the second alternative has better cohesion—the three responsibilities of `lendable` accomplished by a `lendable::checkSelfOut` message are closely related.

1. Know my `borrower`.
2. Compute my due date and set my due date.
3. Update my availability status.

Additionally, the first alternative requires `librarian` to know more than is necessary about the internal state of the `lendable`. Alternative 2 delegates responsibility to the more appropriate class. So the team member holding the `lendable` card adds `lendable::checkSelfOut(borrower)` to the set of responsibilities on the CRH card.

Now, has this scenario reached its logical conclusion? No. The `borrower` does not know about its new borrowed `book`. Remember that it is the responsibility of each `borrower` to know its borrowed `books`. The `borrower` must be updated. Here is one conclusion to this scenario.

`librarian`: `borrower`, let's follow the design heuristic we just talked about. I'll just send this message: `borrower.checkOut(lendable)`

`borrower`: It seems as though I should be able to add a `lendable` to my list of borrowed `lendables`. I'll add `borrower::checkOut(lendable)` as a responsibility on my CRH card.

`librarian`: Please inform the user that everything is okay—the user may take the `lendable` along. Whoops, I almost forgot. I better update `borrowerList` and `lendableList`. `borrowerList`, please put this `borrower` away.

`borrowerList`: Okay, I'll add `putBorrower(borrower)` to my CRH card.

`librarian`: `lendableList`, please but this `lendable` away.

`lendableList`: Okay, I'll add `lendableList::putLendable(lendable)` to my CRH card.

`librarian`: So User, anything else?

User: No, I'm outta here.

`librarian`: Okay, I'm ready to process another user.

The check-out scenario has reached a logical conclusion.

Self-Check

16-9 Write a check-out algorithm that sends any message you desire to any object you desire. Use any of the objects shown next as if the classes were already implemented. Add any message you like.

Remember you are designing now. You will be passing off your CRH cards and the check-out algorithm to another programmer who will have to make it all work according to your design.

```
borrowerList theBorrowerList;
lendableList theLendableList;
borrower currentBorrower;
lendable currentLendable;
```

16.2.3 A Check-In Scenario

The team knows that there are many scenarios that should be played out. Deena wants to know:

16.2.3.1 Scenario 3: "What happens when a user returns a book that is not overdue?"

`librarian`: I'll start again; I'll get the user ID.

User: My ID is #1234.

`librarian`: Let me ask `borrowerList` for the proper `borrower`. Please `getBorrower` with ID #1234.

`borrowerList`: I found the `borrower` you asked for. I'm sending it back to you.

`librarian`: User, what do you want to do?

User: I want to return something with call number QA76.2.

`librarian`: User #1234 wants to return a `lendable` with call number QA76.2. Seems like I need `checkIn` on my CRH card. Before I just thought I had to check things out. Now I know I must do both. I'll make sure I have both `checkIn` and `checkOut` on my CRH card. Let me get the current state of this `borrower` and `lendable` from their respective lists. First, get me the `borrower` with ID #1234.

`borrowerList`: Okay, here is the `borrower`.

`librarian`: `lendableList.getLendable(QA76.2)`. Wait, maybe I'll just get it from the `borrower`. No, in fact, I want my life to be easy. `borrower`, please `checkIn(QA76.2)`.

`borrower`: Okay, let's see if I can do that. I am currently borrowing that `lendable`. So `lendable`, are you overdue?

`lendable`: No.

`borrower`: Okay, I'll just remove you from my borrowed list. If you were overdue, I'd probably have to adjust my late fees. I've been updated. Back to you, `librarian`.

`librarian`: I still need to update `lendable` and `lendableList`, but first, let me put you (the `borrower`) back where you belong so the next time you try to borrow something, I will get back your current state.

`borrowerList`: Okay, I think I can handle that, but I will need to know the `borrower` you are putting back. My major responsibilities are to know all borrowers and to allow `librarian` to get `borrowers` and put updated `borrowers` back. I'll just replace the current state of the `borrower` with the updated `borrower` you send me. I need this written down so I can see it better and remember it.

Matt designs a first draft of a `borrowerList` class definition:

CRH Card

Class: `borrowerList`	**Helpers:**
Responsibilities:	`borrower`
know all borrowers	`vector`
`getBorrower(borrower)`	
`putBorrower(borrower)`	

Class Definition, First Draft

```
class borrowerList {
public:
  void getBorrower(borrower);
  void putBorrower(borrower);
private:
  vector <borrower> my_data;
  int my_size;
};
```

`librarian`: Now that the `borrower` is taken care of, I have to update `lendable` and `lendableList` to reflect the fact that the physical equivalent (a book) has been returned. So `lendable`, check yourself out.

`lendable`: I should be able to do that. Okay, I'll mark myself as available. I wonder, is there anything else I should do? Perhaps I could set my due date to today or perhaps sometime way in the past. What about 1-1-1900? No, that would make me a century overdue. What about a day in the future, say 9-9-9999. Or I could set my `borrower` to something like "?no borrower?" Let me think about it; perhaps being available is enough. No one should care about `borrower` or due date if I am available. Anyway, consider me updated.

`librarian`: Now I just need to put the book away. I send this message: `lendableList.putLendable(currentLendable);`

lendableList: Okay, I think I can handle that. I do need to know the lendable. My major responsibilities are to know all lendables and to allow librarian to get lendables and put them back. I'll just replace the current lendable state with the updated lendable you send me. I need this written down also.

Matt designs a first draft for the lendableList class definition:

CRH Card — Class Definition, First Draft

Class: lendableList	**Helpers:**
Responsibilities:	lendable
know all lendables	vector
getLendable(lendableID)	
putLendable(lendable)	

```
class lendableList {
public:
  void getLendable(string lendID);
  void putLendable(lendable);
private:
  vector<lendable> my_data;
  int my_size;
};
```

librarian: Everything is cool.

This scenario has reached its logical conclusion. Along the way, librarian also added a few major responsibilities: checkIn and checkOut. Austen claims these two scenarios might be implemented as private member functions. The team member role playing librarian feels it is time to review her CRH card. Once again, Matt designs a first draft of a librarian class definition to better visualize the class.

CRH Card — Class Definition, First Draft

Class: librarian	**Helpers:**
Responsibilities:	lendable
coordinate activities	borrower
know current borrower and	lendableList
lendable	borrowerList
checkIn	
checkOut	

```
class librarian {
public:
  void processOneUser();
private:
  borrower currentBorrower;
  lendable currentLendable;
  void checkOut(lendable);
  void checkIn(lendable);
};
```

Jessica and Jason are anxious to see what happens when a user returns an overdue `lendable`.

16.2.4 A "Return of an Overdue Book" Scenario

16.2.4.1 Scenario 4: "What happens when a user returns a book that is five days overdue?"

`librarian`: User #1234 wants to return a `lendable` with call number QA76.2. So I'll execute my `checkIn` algorithm. The first thing I want to know is if the `lendable` is overdue. Who can answer that?

The team debates whether `librarian` should get the software version of the borrowed item from the `borrower` or from `lendableList`. The `lendable` should be in the same state in either location—the `lendableList` or the `borrower`'s set of borrowed `lendables`. Jessica, who is role playing `borrower`, says, "I know what I have borrowed and since I may need to register a late fee, why not just ask me?" `librarian` would rather do what she did before: "I don't want to get confused. I'll get `currentLendable` from `lendableList` and `currentBorrower` from `borrowerList`. Then I can do whatever I need to. When I'm done, I'll put them both away."

`librarian`: `lendableList.getLendable(QA76.2).`

`lendableList`: Here is that `lendable` you seek.

`librarian`: `borrowerList.getBorrower(#1234).`

`borrowerList`: Here is that `borrower` along with all known borrowed items.

`librarian`: `borrower, checkIn (QA76.2).`

`borrower`: Okay, I do have a record that I am borrowing the `lendable` with ID QA76.2. So `lendable`, are you overdue?

`lendable`: I'll ask `date`. Is `dueDate` < today's date?

`date`: Yes. The `dueDate` was some time ago. I guess there will be money to owe.

`lendable`: That's real clever rhyming, `date`. Yes `borrower`, I am overdue.

`borrower`: I'll ask `lendable` to `computeLateFee`.

`lendable`: `date`, how many days overdue? Tell me `todaysDate - dueDate`.

`date`: There is a difference of five days. I'll add "compute number of days between two dates" to my CRH card.

`lendable`: The late fee is 5 * (`per_day_late_fee`), which as a `book` is $2.50.

`borrower`: Okay, I'm supposed to know my total late fee, so I'll add that $2.50 to my late fee. Remember, I'll be implemented as software to ensure my late fees are always honest. I'll write `recordLateFee` on my CRH card.

"That was an awful lot of action going on to return a book," moans Steve. "I think we could simplify things by sending messages like this":

```
currentBorrower.checkIn(currentLendable);
```

Austen explains that this can and actually did happen. It's just that we observed the details from the perspective of `borrower`, `lendable`, and `date`. All of these details could be encapsulated into the `checkIn` algorithm. `librarian` simply sends a `checkIn` message to the `borrower`. The `borrower` gets help from `lendable` and `lendable` gets help from `date`. The `borrower` can do everything it needs to do to update itself. This design means less coupling (fewer message sends from `librarian` to `borrower`). "A better design," remarks Austen.

`borrower`: So in summary, when I receive a `checkOut` message, I'll adjust my late fees if necessary; I'll also remove the `lendable` from my list of borrowed items. So I will add `checkIn` to my CRH card. Might as well add `checkOut` also. And in case you ever want to know what my late fees are, I'll make them accessible with a `lateFee` accessor member function. I'm going to follow the trend and write all this down before I forget. Matt, please design a class definition for me while you're at it.

CRH Card

Class: borrower	**Helpers:**
Responsibilities:	lendable
know borrowed lendables	bag or vector?
recordLateFee	librarian
canBorrow	
checkIn(lendable)	
checkOut(lendable)	
double lateFee()	

Class Definition, First Draft

```
class borrower {
public:
  checkOut(lendable aLendable);
  checkIn(lendable aLendable);
  double lateFee() const;
  bool canBorrow() const;
private:
  double my_fines;
  vector <lendable> my_borrowedItems;
  int my_numberOfBorrowedItems;
};
```

`librarian`: Okay, now that the `borrower` is updated, put it away:
 `borrowerList.putBorrower(currentBorrower)`

`borrowerList`: Done. I replaced the old state of the `borrower` with the updated version you just sent me.

`librarian`: Now I have to deal with the `lendable`. Say `lendable`, could you do a `checkOut` also?

`lendable`: Let me see, I'll mark myself as available, set my due date to a special date way in the future, and then set my `borrower` to some special value also. I'll call this algorithm `lendable::checkSelfOut` to distinguish it from `borrower::checkOut`. I have a lot to remember. Let me review my CRH card too.

Matt says, "Sure, I'll sketch a design of the class definition."

CRH Card

Class: `lendable`		**Helpers:**
Responsibilities:		`date`
know due date		
know borrower		
`computeDueDate`	`isOverdue`	
`computeLateFee`	`isAvailable`	
`checkSelfIn`	`setDueDate`	
`checkSelfOut(borrower)`		

Class Definition, First Draft

```
class lendable {
public:
  void checkSelfIn();
  void checkSelfOut(borrower);
  bool isOverdue() const;
  bool isAvailable() const;

private:
  date my_dueDate;
  string my_borrowersID;
};
```

`librarian`: `lendableList`, please put away this updated `lendable`.

`lendableList`: I'll replace my current but outdated version of `lendable` with the updated version you just sent me.

`librarian`: We're done. I can now get another user request or get the next user.

Austen congratulates the team. So far, there is a reasonable set of classes with clearly defined responsibilities. Austen remarks, "The design feels right. Whether you knew it or not, you were actually using many of the object-oriented design heuristics. Even if you weren't thinking of them. Also notice that the first selection of classes held up."

Figure 16.4

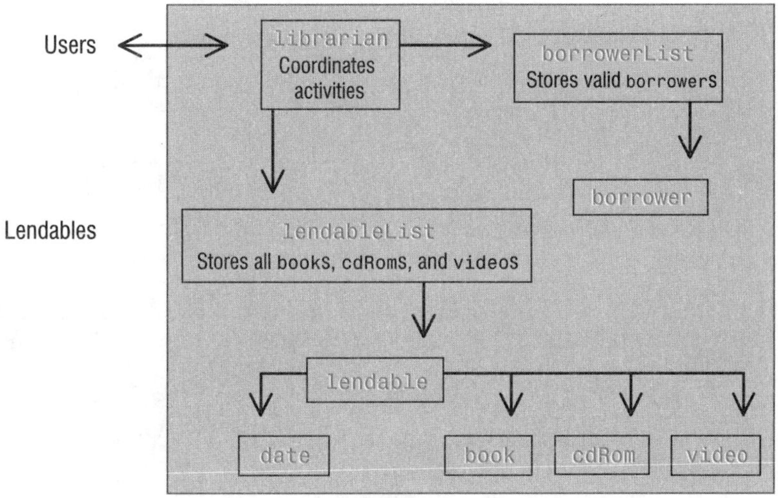

There are a few new lines of helpers. `librarian` gets help not only from two lists but now also from individual instances of `borrower` and `lendable`—`borrower::checkIn` and `lendable::checkSelfIn`, for example.

The new class is `date`. In some ways, `date` is like classes such as `string` and `vector`. It could be considered a utility like `string`, `double`, `bool`, `int`, and `vector`—ready to serve. The picture above shows only domain-specific classes such as `lendable`, `librarian`, and `lendableList`. So why is `date` there? First, the `date` class played a role in helping `lendable`. `date` is present because the team will certainly have to do something about a `date` class during design and implementation. Here is the current state of `date`'s CRH card to remind the team of some of the things a `date` object should be able to do. Matt says he will not design a class definition for `date` until he checks with his teacher who told him he knew about a `Date` class on the Internet that is available for free from a gracious computer science professor.

Class: `date`	**Helpers:**
Responsibilities:	
compute number of days between two dates	
less than or equal <=	
`todaysDate`	

Self-Check

With a team, run the following additional scenarios:

16-10 What happens when a user enters an ID number that is not found in `borrowerList`?

16-11 What happens when a user wants to pay a late fee?

16-12 What happens when a user want to check on the availability of a `lendable`?

16-13 Write a `checkIn` algorithm that sends any message you desire to any object you desire. Use any of the objects shown next as if the classes were already implemented. Add any message you like.

Remember you are designing now. You will be passing off your CRH cards and the `checkIn` algorithm to another programmer who will have to make it all work according to your design.

```
borrowerList theBorrowerList;
lendableList theLendableList;
borrower currentBorrower;
lendable currentLendable;
```

16.3 Design

Now that there is some understanding of the system, the programming team—Charlie and Matt—turns its focus to designing the class definitions. This programming team already knows there is a relationship between the responsibilities on the CRH cards and C++ class definitions. The things that each instance of a class must do could be listed as the public member functions. The things that each instance of the class must know can become the private data members.

Austen suggests that the team first cope with the new class relationship of inheritance. The first thing to do is ensure that the `lendable` class captures all the knowledge and action responsibilities that will be common to the derived classes. The CRH card ends up looking like this with an additional mention of the derived classes that make up the current inheritance hierarchy:

Class abstract: `lendable`		
Derived classes: `book, video, cdRom`		
Responsibilities:		**Helpers:**
know due date		`date`
know borrower	`setDueDate`	
`computeDueDate`	`isOverdue`	
`computeLateFee`	`isAvailable`	
`checkSelfIn`	`checkSelfOut(borrower)`	

Austen tells the team, "In a short time, you will see action responsibilities inherited by the derived classes (`book`, `video`, and `cdRom`) that have the same name, but execute differently." For example, each class will `computeDueDate`, but each class will do it differently. A book can be borrowed for 14 days but a video for only 2. At the same time, the base class can define and implement member functions that all derived classes will usefully inherit—`checkSelfIn`, for example. That behavior is the same for all derived classes.

16.3.1 The `lendable` Action Responsibilities (member functions)

The `lendable` card currently lists the names of seven possible messages. `isOverdue` and `isAvailable` seem to be the easiest to consider. Neither requires arguments. Both return either true or false indicating the state of the `lendable`. The check-out operation needs to know the `borrower`, so `checkSelfOut` requires the borrower's ID, which could be a `string`.

The team next considers the `checkSelfIn` responsibility. Matt believes the function needs no arguments. It is a `void` function. `librarian` simply sends a `checkSelfIn` message and `book` or `video` will update itself. This leads to a refined design of the base `lendable`.

```
class lendable {  // Second draft
public:
  // . . .
  bool isOverdue() const;
  bool isAvailable() const;
  void checkSelfIn();
  void checkSelfOut(string borrowersID);

private:
  // TBA
};
```

The first four member functions are common to all derived classes and do not vary between those derived classes. However, the two other responsibilities—`computeDueDate` and `computeLateFee`—have different meanings to the derived classes. They will be implemented differently for each of the three classes. For example, `book` will compute due date differently than `video`. The late fees also vary amongst all three classes to be derived from `lendable`.

Misty wonders if these two operations should be part of the interface. Austen proposes that it can be decided by answering the question, Who will send the `computeLateFee` and `computeDueDate` messages? Charlie claims the `computeLateFee` message might be sent from within the `checkSelfIn` message. To do that, the object must also `getDueDate`. Neither function is part of the public interface. Instead they are part of the hidden details. And the actual code to do each of these differs amongst the derived classes.

Austen points out that the public interface should be kept as simple as possible. There is even a design heuristic for this.

Object-Oriented Design Heuristic 16.2 (Riel's 2.5)

Do not put implementation details into the public interface of a class.

No one outside of the `lendable` hierarchy has to send a `computeLateFee` or `computeDueDate` message. And it seems safe to assume that no one will send a `computeDueDate` or `computeLateFee` message. One of the objects might want to ask a `lendable` for its due date or late fee, but probably no one will directly ask `lendable` to compute them. These are implementation details. Therefore these two operations should not be made public.

"Make them private," proclaims Matt. "Better to make them protected," claims Austen. He goes on to explain that derived classes inherit both public and protected members. However, protected members are invisible to users. The protected-access mode allows access only to member functions of the base class and to any class derived from the base class. These protected members will not be accessible to `librarian` or anyone else outside the `lendable` hierarchy. Also, because they do not change anything (`checkSelfOut` changes the state, not `computeDueDate`), they are declared const. The team now recognizes that two other accessors should have the `const` tag.

```
class lendable {  // Third draft
public:
  // . . .
  void checkSelfIn();
  void checkSelfOut(string borrowersID);
  bool isOverdue() const;
  bool isAvailable() const;

protected:
  date computeDueDate() const;
  double computeLateFee() const;

private:
  // TBA
};
```

Austen points out that these messages will be called from the base class's `checkSelfIn` and `checkSelfOut` messages. `checkSelfOut` will send a `computeDueDate` message. `checkSelfIn` will send a `computeLateFee` message. Jessica wonders, "But how will `lendable::checkSelfIn` know which of the three `computeDueDate` messages to send?" Matt recommends that the team consider applying multiple selection.

EXPLICIT CASE ANALYSIS

```
if (lendableIsBook())
    book::computeDueDate()
else if (lendableIsVideo())
     video::computeDueDate()
else
     cdRom::computeDueDate()
```

Austen explains that the inheritance relationship is an attempt to avoid such explicit multiple selection. Otherwise at some later point, when more `lendables` are added, the `checkSelfOut` and `checkSelfIn` member functions will have to be changed. Additionally, each derived class would have to carry around some data member value indicating the class.

Object-Oriented Design Heuristic 16.3

Don't add a data member that indicates a class's type. If you have to make a decision based on different classes of objects, implement an inheritance hierarchy.

This redundancy is not necessary. Each class knows what type it is. It will be easier to add a few `lendables` later by planning for them now. "How is this possible?" asks Matt. "Through polymorphism," replies Austen.

16.3.2 Polymorphism

Polymorphism makes it possible to have a collection of heterogeneous objects (e.g., `video`, `book`, and `cdRom`) that appears to be a container of homogenous objects (e.g., a lists of `lendables`). This works because the program can distinguish the class of objects at runtime. This means a `vector` could store `books`, `videos`, `cdRoms`, and, as it turns out, any other class of object derived from the same base class—`lendable`.

Polymorphism allows the same message to be sent to every object in a container, even though those objects are instances of different classes. However, the same message will activate different member functions. For example, if the current object is a book, `book::computeLateFee` will be called. However, if the current object is a CD-ROM, `cdRom::computeLateFee` will be called. So imagine a container (`vector` or `list`) that has two `books`, followed by a `video`, followed by a `cdRom`, followed by another `book`.

Message	Class	Days Overdue	Message Returns
`item[0].computeLateFee()`	`book`	2	2 * 0.50
`item[1].computeLateFee()`	`book`	2	2 * 0.50
`item[2].computeLateFee()`	`video`	2	5.00 + 1 * 1.50
`item[3].computeLateFee()`	`cdRom`	2	2 * 2.50
`item[4].computeLateFee()`	`book`	2	2 * 0.50

These five messages call three distinct functions. When the container item is a `book`, `book::computeLateFee` applies the $0.50 per day fine. When the `lendable` is a `video`, `video::computeLateFee` applies the $5.00 first late day fee plus 1 * the $1.50 additional late day fee. When the container item is a `cdRom`, `cdRom::computeLateFee` applies the $2.50 per day fine.

Matt remarks to Austen, "This is what you meant when you said earlier one name can have different meanings." "Yes," says Austen. "Now how do you get this to work?" questions Charlie.

First, place the common action responsibilities in the base class. That has already been done. Then identify the responsibilities that have different meanings for each of the derived classes. In this inheritance hierarchy, they are the following two:

1. `computeLateFee`
2. `computeDueDate`

These member functions should be made into *pure virtual functions*. That means that every derived class must implement that function in a manner appropriate to the particular `lendable`. It also means no programmer can ever instantiate `lendable` because it has a pure virtual function. Here is what pure virtual functions look like in the `lendable` class.

```
class lendable {  // Fourth draft
public:
  // . . .
  void checkSelfIn();
  void checkSelfOut(string borrowersID);
  bool isOverdue() const;
  bool isAvailable() const;

protected:
  virtual Date computeDueDate() const = 0;    // Implement in
  virtual double computeLateFee() const = 0;  // derived classes

private:
  // TBA
};
```

Virtual functions are necessary for implementing polymorphism. Once declared as virtual in the base class, the runtime system will search for the appropriate function of that name. Because the runtime system knows the class of object that sent the message, it can call the proper implementation.

A virtual function implies the implementation will vary amongst the derived classes. You specify a function as polymorphic by preceding it with the C++ keyword `virtual`:

```
virtual Date computeDueDate() const = 0;
virtual double computeLateFee() const = 0;
```

The strange ending `= 0` specifies the functions as pure virtual.

```
virtual Date computeDueDate() const = 0;
virtual double computeLateFee() const = 0;
```

Every derived class must implement every pure virtual function in its ancestor. Errors result when a programmer forgets to implement the function in any one of the derived classes. So declaring a function pure virtual is an antibugging technique.

Additionally, it is impossible to instantiate a class that has one or more pure virtual functions with `= 0`. This ensures that the class is abstract, rather than concrete. The keyword `virtual` signifies that the implementation will depend on whether the object is a `book`, `video`, or `cdRom`. And finally, `const` is added because these two functions are accessors.

Since `Date` just showed up again, Matt begins to explain where the `Date` class came from. It is the current return type for `computeDueDate`.

```
virtual Date computeDueDate() const = 0;
```

Austen replies that a `date` class is referred to even though it isn't implemented yet. But now we have a `Date` class as seen in Owen Astrachan's book *A Computer Science Tapestry* [Astrachan 97]. He says, "When I asked Owen if we could use his `Date` class to save ourselves a lot of time, he graciously offered to give it to us or to anyone else who wanted it. We'll come back to that class definition later. For now I can assure you that it does everything we need it to do such as compare dates, get the current date, add days to a date, subtract days from a date, and find the difference between two dates. I should also tell you that Owen, like many other computer scientists, likes to capitalize the first letter of his classes—so he named it `Date` rather than `date`."

Now let us consider the data members we'll need for all `lendables`.

16.3.3 The Knowledge Responsibilities (data members)

The team examines the `lendable` CRH card and notices `date` is often written as a helper. `computeDueDate` returns a `Date` object, but does `lendable` need a `Date` data member?

Consider that every derived class must maintain its due date. Therefore, this common knowledge responsibility should be declared in the base class. Austen informs Matt and Charlie that private data members are not inherited by derived classes. The common solution is to place a due date object in the `lendable` private section and then provide an accessor to that data member in the `protected:` access mode (this has been done). The fifth draft of the `lendable` class definition declares these newest considerations.

```
class lendable {  // Fifth draft
public:
//-- modifiers
  void checkSelfIn();
  void checkSelfOut(string borrowersID);

//--accessors
  bool isOverdue() const;
  bool isAvailable() const;
  string lendableID() const;
  Date dueDate() const;

protected:
  virtual Date computeDueDate() const = 0;     // Implement in
  virtual double computeLateFee() const = 0;  // derived classes

private:
  Date my_dueDate;
  string my_ID;
};
```

The data member `my_ID` and an accessor were added because there is a need to search for `lendables`. `my_ID` should make each `lendable` unique. And now, it appears that other information about a book's author or a CD-ROM's artist or software vendor name should be added later in the derived classes.

So now that the data members are established, the constructors can be considered. One constructor parameter can be used to initialize `my_ID`. An accessor to `my_ID` should also be added. By reviewing the `lendable` CRH card, Charlie also noticed the borrower's responsibility was still not part of the class definition. Instead of storing the entire `borrower` however, it seems as though the borrower's ID number will suffice. The availability knowledge responsibility was missing too. And finally, Matt recalled that someone asked the `lendable` for its late fee. So that too should be added as an accessor. The final version of the `lendable` class summarizes all of the above considerations.

```
class lendable {
public:
//--constructors
  lendable(string initID);

//--accessors
  bool isOverdue() const;
  bool isAvailable() const;
  string lendableID() const;
```

```
    string borrowersID() const;
    double lateFee() const;
    Date dueDate() const;

  //--modifiers
    void checkSelfIn();
    void checkSelfOut(string borrowersID);

  // Pure virtual functions to be implemented
  protected:
    virtual Date computeDueDate() const = 0;
    virtual double computeLateFee() const = 0;

  private:
    Date my_dueDate;
    string my_ID;
    bool my_availability;
    string my_borrowersID;
  };
```

Now the `lendable` member functions must be implemented, all but the pure virtual functions that is. First, a detail is added that has nothing to do with inheritance.

While testing the classes derived from `lendable`, it was found that a `book` and a `video` had a `dueDate` in the future, even after they were returned. Matt and Charlie decide to establish an "empty" value for a due date. When a `lendable` gets checked back in, the due date is set to something in the future, 9-September-9999, to be precise. Any `lendable` with this `emptyDueDate` value cannot be considered overdue. It also helps to set the `borrower` to someone other than the user who had already checked it in—an "empty" `borrower`. Here are the two global constants:

```
// Use two special values to indicate irrelevant dueDate and
// borrowersID
const Date emptyDate = Date(9,9,9999);
const string emptyID = "?";
```

16.3.3.1 The `lendable` Constructor Has an Initializer List

The following familiar pattern for constructors could be followed to implement the constructor `lendable::lendable`.

```
lendable::lendable(string initID)
{ // Less efficient, and inadequate when this is a derived class
  my_ID = initID;
  my_dueDate = emptyDate;
  my_availability = true;
```

```
    my_borrowersID = emptyID;
  }
```

However, a different method of initialization must now be employed. Initialization lists, like the one you are about to see, have been avoided as unnecessary syntax details. They are introduced now because they are absolutely, positively needed to implement the derived class's constructors. Additionally, using initialization lists makes the program run faster. Here is the initialization list for `lendable` (not really necessary in a base class):

Example of Initialization List

```
lendable::lendable(string initID)
         : my_ID(initID),
           my_dueDate(emptyDate),
           my_availability(true),
           my_borrowersID(emptyID)
{
  // More efficient initialization already occurred
}
```

An *initialization list* begins immediately after the function heading with a colon (`:`) followed by each data member (initial value) pair separated by commas. The effect of both implementations of `lendable::lendable`—with four assignments or one long initialization list—is the same. Both adequately initialize all data members of `lendable`.

Although an initialization list isn't necessary to implement the base class constructor, the initialization list must be used by all derived classes. For only in an initialization list can the base class constructor be called. Observe the call to `lendable`'s constructor here in the `book` constructor:

```
book::book(string initID, string initAuthor, string initTitle)
     : lendable (initID),       // Call base class constructor
       my_author(initAuthor),   // Could have used less efficient
       my_title(initTitle)      // assignment
{
  // The initialization list took care of everything. Remember, the
  // lendable constructor was also called to initialize the data
  // members that are common to all derived classes.
}
```

The highlighted part of the initialization list calls the `lendable` constructor with one argument, which in turn, initializes all the other common data members (see `lendable::lendable` above).

16.3.3.2 The Accessors

The `lendable` accessors require no additional explanation other than perhaps the `Date` member functions that were used. Astrachan's `Date::Absolute` function returns a number that can be compared with <= and == as in the first guarded action that checks to see if the `dueDate` is equal to the `emptyDate`.

```
bool lendable::isOverdue() const
{
  if(my_dueDate.Absolute() == emptyDate.Absolute())
     return false;

  Date today;
  // assert: today stores today's date
  return my_dueDate.Absolute() <= today.Absolute();
}

bool lendable::isAvailable() const
{
  return my_availability;
}

string lendable::lendableID() const
{
  return my_ID;
}

string lendable::borrowersID() const
{
  return my_borrowersID;
}

Date lendable::dueDate() const
{
  return my_dueDate;
}

double lendable::lateFee() const
{
  return computeLateFee();
}
```

16.3.3.3 The Modifiers

The `lendable` modifiers show polymorphism in action. A `checkSelfOut` message sends a `computeDueDate` message.

```
void lendable::checkSelfOut(string borrowersID)
{
  my_dueDate = computeDueDate();
  // Polymorphism in action. At runtime, the system will know
  // which computeDueDate implementation to use.
  my_availability = false;
  my_borrowersID = borrowersID;
}
```

Since there were three `computeDueDate` functions, which one will get called?

The small `lendable` hierarchy presents three possibilities: If the `lendable` is a book, the system will send a `book::computeDueDate` message. If the `lendable` is a video, the system will send a `video::computeDueDate` message. And if the `lendable` is a CD-ROM, the system will send a `cdRom::computeDueDate` message. Each of these three classes implements its own `computeDueDate` function. Because the `lendable` class definition was designed with inheritance in mind, `computeDueDate` was declared as a pure virtual function. This forces all derived classes to implement their own `computeDueDate` member function.

A `checkSelfIn` message performs three actions. They are summarized first as discovered during the scenario and then as the algorithm for `lendable::checkSelfIn`.

16.3.3.4 From an Earlier Scenario

`lendable`: Okay, I'll mark myself as available, set my due date to a special date that is not a valid due date, and then set my borrower to some special value also.

```
void lendable::checkSelfIn()
{
  my_availability = true;
  my_borrowersID = emptyID;
  my_dueDate = emptyDate;
}
```

The algorithms for the `checkSelfIn` and `checkSelfOut` messages are the same for any derived class with one exception. During `checkSelfOut`, the `computeDueDate` message will call one of three different operations; it all depends on the sender's class.

```
my_dueDate = this->computeDueDate();
// Call either 1. book::computeDueDate
//          or 2. video::computeDueDate
//          or 3. cdRom::computeDueDate
```

If a fourth class gets added to the `lendable` hierarchy (`artWork`, for example) by inheriting from `lendable`, it too will have to implement a `computeDueDate` member function (`artWork::computeDueDate`, for example). Let's now look at how inheritance gets done in C++.

16.4 The Derived Classes

The general form for deriving one class from another is a class definition with the base class listed after the derived class name and a colon (`:`) to indicate inheritance.

General Form 16.1. *Defining a derived class*

```
class derived-class-name : public ancestor-class-name {
public:
   new-function-heading-1 ;
   overridden-function-heading -1 ;
   new-function-heading-2 ;
   overridden-function-heading -2 ;
private:
   additional-data-members
};
```

The colon (`:`) followed by `public` could be read as "inherits public and protected things from." The ancestor's public and protected member functions are passed on to derived classes (the descendants). The *derived-class* inherits the operations of the ancestor. Member functions and data members can be added to the derived class. Finally, the *ancestor-class* member functions can be overridden (given new meaning).

For example, the `book` class adds a constructor, `book`, and it overrides the `computeDueDate` and `computeLateFee` member functions. `book` also adds two private data members, `my_author` and `my_title`, and accessors to this data.

```
class book : public lendable {
public:
// A new constructor
   book(string initID, string initAuthor, string initTitle);

// The two virtual functions that must be implemented by all
// derived classes
   Date computeDueDate() const;
   double computeLateFee() const;
```

```
// Additional accessors
   string author();
   string title();

private:
// Additional data members
   string my_author;
   string my_title;
};
```

The `video` class also adds a constructor, overrides `computeDueDate` and `computeLateFee`, and adds one private data member.

```
class video : public lendable {
public:
// A new constructor
  video(string initID, string initTitle);

// The virtual functions to be implemented by all derived classes
  Date computeDueDate() const;
  double computeLateFee() const;

// Additional accessors
  string title();

private:
  string my_title;
};
```

16.4.1 Implementing the Derived Classes

First, the data relating to overdue `lendables` are summarized as a collection of global constant objects at the top of the `lendable.h` file.

```
const int BOOK_BORROW_DAYS = 14;
const int VIDEO_BORROW_DAYS = 2;
const int CDROM_BORROW_DAYS = 7;
const double BOOK_LATE_FEE = 0.50;
const double VIDEO_LATE_FEE = 1.50;
const double FLAT_VIDEO_LATE_FEE = 5.00;
const double CDROM_LATE_FEE = 2.50;
```

The `book` constructor also uses an initialization list.

```
book::book(string initID, string initAuthor, string initTitle)
     : lendable (initID),
       my_author(initAuthor),
```

```
        my_title(initTitle)
{
  // Initialization list took care of everything
}
```

The book constructor could initialize its newly added private data members. However, the initialization list is necessary because it allows the base class constructor to be called from the derived class. Calling the base class constructor guarantees that the same thing will be done for every single derived class. Besides, this is the only way to call the lendable constructor—in an initialization list. This call to the base class constructor:

```
: lendable (initID),
```

passes initID along to initialize the private data member declared in lendable. However, a set_ID member function could have avoided this. So why bother with the base class constructor and initialization list?

The real purpose for calling the base class constructor is to guarantee that whatever initialization is important to all derived classes will in fact occur. The programmer adheres to this by ensuring that all derived classes use initialization lists. The base class constructor is called via an initialization list. This guarantees that anything the base class does will be done for any and all derived classes.

In this next example, lendable::lendable(string initID) initializes all lendable objects as available (my_availability(true)) and sets my_dueDate and my_borrowersID to a global named constant recognized as being meaningless.

```
lendable::lendable(string initID)
        : my_ID(initID),
          my_dueDate(emptyDate),
          my_availability(true),
          my_borrowersID(emptyID)
{
  // More efficient initialization already occurred
}
```

The remaining book member function implementations have a few new items. First, while testing, it was discovered that nothing was ever overdue. Rather than running the program over a several week period, a conditional compilation was put in place to allow testing of due dates and late fines. The computeDueDate function gets called from lendable::checkSelfOut.

```
Date book::computeDueDate() const
{
  Date today;
#ifdef DebuggingLateFee
  return today - BOOK_BORROW_DAYS;  // Compile only when defined
#else
  return today + BOOK_BORROW_DAYS;  // Otherwise only compile this

#endif
}
```

If the test driver has this compiler directive:

```
#defines DebuggingLateFee
```

then the due date gets set to 14 days in the past. An immediate call to `lendable::dueDate` finds the `book` was due two weeks ago. A `lendable::lateFee` message returns 0.50 * 14 or $7.00 (see the test driver below).

16.4.2 Astrachan's `Date` Class

The following `Date` operations were used from Astrachan's `Date` class:

```
// a class for manipulating dates
// written 2/2/94, Owen Astrachan
// Date()                      --- construct default date (today)
// Date(int m, int d, int y) --- constructor requires three
//                                 parameters:
//                                 month, day, year, e.g.,
//                                 Date d(4,8,1956); initializes d to
//                                 represent the date April 8, 1956.
//                                 Full year is required
//
// long int Absolute() --- returns absolute # of date assuming that
//                         Jan 1, 1 AD is day 1.  Has property that
//                         Absolute() % 7 = k, where k = 0 is sunday
//                         k = 1 is monday, ... k = 6 is saturday
//
// string ToString()    -- returns string version of date, e.g.,
//                      -- d.SetDate(11,23,1963); then d.ToString()
//                         returns string "November 23 1963"
// ************************************************
//         arithmetic operators for dates
// ************************************************
// dates support some addition and subtraction operations
// Date d(1,1,1960);         // 1960 is a leap year
// Date d2 = d + 1;          // d2 is January 2, 1960
// Date d4 = d - 1;          // d4 is December 31, 1959
```

The `Date::Absolute` function returns the number of days since 1-1-1 AD. This allows dates to be compared with <, >, <=, and so on. The following function used == to return 0.00 as the late fee when the book gets checked in:

```
double book::computeLateFee() const
{
  Date today;
  int daysLate;
  daysLate = today - dueDate();  // Call protected base member
  // daysLate will be negative unless the book is overdue
  if(daysLate > 0)
    return daysLate * BOOK_LATE_FEE;
  else
    return 0.00;
}
```

The other member functions are typical accessors.

```
string book::author()
{
 return my_author;
}

string book::title()
{
  return my_title;
}
```

The `video` class looks almost exactly the same, except a `video` adds a `my_title` data member only. If you want to see the code, visit the class definitions for `lendable`, `book`, and `video` stored in `lendable.h`. You can also see the member function implementations in `lendable.cpp`. Both are on this textbook's disk and at this textbook's Web site.

16.4.3 Testing the Derived Classes

The following program test drives `video` and `book` in a `DebuggingLateFee` mode. Notice that the `void show` function takes a reference to a `lendable` object as an argument. There is no `lendable` object passed! Remember that an abstract class cannot be constructed. So without the little `&`, this function heading would be an error:

```
void show(lendable aLendable)  // Error, can't instantiate lendable
```

This test driver passes two different classes of arguments: `aBook` and `aVideo`.

```
// File name: testlend.cpp
//
#include <iostream>
using namespace std;

#define DebuggingLateFee  // lendable.h now sets dueDate in the past
#include "lendable"  // For the lendable, book, and video classes
#include "compfun"   // For decimals(cout, 2)

void show(const lendable & aLendable)
{
  cout << "The lendable " << aLendable.lendableID();
  if(aLendable.isOverdue())
    cout << " is overdue. ";
  else
    cout << " is not overdue. ";

  cout << "Late fee = $" << aLendable.lateFee() << endl;

  cout << "Due date: " << aLendable.dueDate().ToString() << endl;

  if(aLendable.isAvailable())
    cout << "It is available. " << endl;
  else
    cout << "It is not available. " << aLendable.borrowersID()
         << " has it." << endl;

   cout << "--------------------------------------------" << endl;
}

int main()
{ // Test drive video and book

  decimals(cout, 2);  // To show late fees nicely

  cout << "TEST BOOK: " << endl;
  book aBook("QA76.1M46", "Rick Mercer", "Computing Fun.");
  show(aBook);

  aBook.checkSelfOut("555-55-5555");
  show(aBook);

  aBook.checkSelfIn();
  show(aBook);

  cout << "\nTEST VIDEO: " << endl;
  video aVideo("MGM10023", "Spartacus");
  show(aVideo);
```

```
  aVideo.checkSelfOut("555-55-5555");
  show(aVideo);

  aVideo.checkSelfIn();
  show(aVideo);

  return 0;
}
```

OUTPUT (WITH `DebuggingLateFee` DEFINED; WITHOUT IT, NOTHING IS OVERDUE, FINES ARE 0)

```
TEST BOOK:
The lendable QA76.1M46 is not overdue. Late fee = $0.00
Due date: September 09 9999
It is available.
---------------------------------------------
The lendable QA76.1M46 is overdue. Late fee = $7.00
Due date: April 27 1998
It is not available. 555-55-5555 has it.
---------------------------------------------
The lendable QA76.1M46 is not overdue. Late fee = $0.00
Due date: September 09 9999
It is available.
---------------------------------------------

TEST VIDEO:
The lendable MGM10023 is not overdue. Late fee = $0.00
Due date: September 09 9999
It is available.
---------------------------------------------
The lendable MGM10023 is overdue. Late fee = $6.50
Due date: May 09 1998
It is not available. 555-55-5555 has it.
---------------------------------------------
The lendable MGM10023 is not overdue. Late fee = $0.00
Due date: September 09 9999
It is available.
---------------------------------------------
```

16.5 `lendableList`: A Heterogeneous Container

The power of inheritance and polymorphism comes in very handy when you need to store a collection of objects that are not of the same type. Consider the `lendableList` class. Its knowledge responsibility is to know all `lendables`. This implies that there could be `books`, `videos`, `cdRoms`, or any other new class of objects added to the `lendable` hierarchy. Actually, `lendableList` will hold all three types of objects. When a container holds a collection of dissimilar objects, it is said to be a heterogeneous container.

The `lendable` class name represents any class of `lendable`. For this collection, the trick is to have a collection of *pointers* to `lendable`. The following `vector` can store 10 instances of any class derived from `lendable`:

```
vector <lendable*> item(5);
```

The elements in `item` are not `lendables`; instead the elements are pointers to any class derived from `lendable`. A snapshot of memory could look like this:

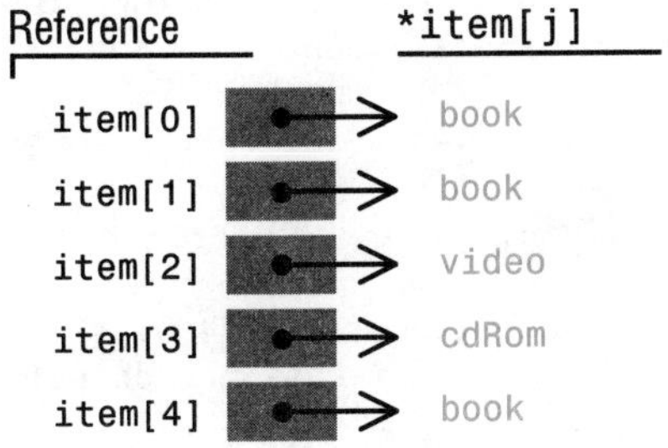

Here is a program that constructs a `vector` of pointers to `lendables`. Notice that the assignment statements assign different classes of objects to the same `vector`.

```
// File name: testleli.cpp
#include <vector>
using namespace std;

#define DebuggingLateFee  // Sets due dates 2, 7, or 14 days ago
#include "lendable"       // For the lendable class
#include "compfun"

void show(const lendable & aLendable)
{
  cout << "The lendable " << aLendable.lendableID();
  if(aLendable.isOverdue())
    cout << " is overdue. ";
  else
    cout << " is not overdue. ";

  cout << "Late fee = $" << aLendable.lateFee() << endl;

  cout << "Due date: " << aLendable.dueDate().ToString() << endl;
```

```
  if(aLendable.isAvailable())
    cout << "It is available. " << endl;
  else
    cout << "It is not available. " << aLendable.borrowersID()
         << " has it." << endl;

   cout << "----------------------------------------------" << endl;
}

int main()
{
  decimals(cout, 2);  // To show late fees nicely

  vector<lendable*> item(10);
  item[0] = new book("BOOK 1", "Author One", "Title One");
  item[1] = new video("VIDEO 1", "Video Title One");
  item[2] = new book("BOOK 2", "Author Two", "Title Two");
  item[3] = new video("VIDEO 2", "Video Title Two");

  // Check out four lendables for borrower 444-44-4444; show them
  int j;
  for(j = 0; j < 4; j++)
  {
    item[j]->checkSelfOut("444-44-4444");
    show( *item[j] );  // Pass the object pointed to by item[j]
  }
  return 0;
}
```

OUTPUT

```
The lendable BOOK 1 is overdue. Late fee = $7.00
Due date: April 27 1998
It is not available. 444-44-4444 has it.
---------------------------------------------
The lendable VIDEO 1 is overdue. Late fee = $6.50
Due date: May 09 1998
It is not available. 444-44-4444 has it.
---------------------------------------------
The lendable BOOK 2 is overdue. Late fee = $7.00
Due date: April 27 1998
It is not available. 444-44-4444 has it.
---------------------------------------------
The lendable VIDEO 2 is overdue. Late fee = $6.50
Due date: May 09 1998
It is not available. 444-44-4444 has it.
---------------------------------------------
```

The new operator allocates memory for the object and returns the address to that object. Later on, because item is a vector of pointers, operations are performed on the items in the vector by dereferencing them with ->, the arrow operator. For example, during testing, all lendables can be checked back in with this loop:

```
// Check 'em all back in, no matter what class they are
for(j = 0; j < 4; j++)
{
  item[j]->checkSelfIn();   // Polymorphic message
}
```

16.5.1 The lendableList Class

The vector of pointers to lendables can be written as a data member.

CRH Card	Class Definition, First Draft

Class: lendableList	**Helpers:**
Responsibilities:	lendable
know all lendables	vector
getLendable(lendableID)	
putLendable(lendable)	

```
class lendableList {
public:
  void getLendable(string lendID);
  void putLendable(lendable);
private:
  vector<lendable*> my_data;
  int my_size;
};
```

Here is the final version of lendableList after it has undergone further design, testing, and a few changes—especially related to the need for indirection (pointers) in the parameter lists. Also, three member functions were added, and another removed (putLendable was not necessary).

```
class lendableList {
public:
// Default constructor initializes the list of lendables
  lendableList();

//--destructor
  ~lendableList();

//--modifiers
  void addLendable(lendable* lendPtr);
```

```
    // Add the lendable to the lendable list

    void removeLendable(string lendableID);
    // Add the lendable to the lendable list

  //--accessors
    bool getLendable(string searchID, lendable* & lendPtr) const;
    // If found return true, set second argument to point to lendable
    // inside this lendableList. The client can update me indirectly.

  private:
    int my_size;
    int my_index;
    vector <lendable* > my_data;  // vector of pointers to any class
  };                              // derived from the lendable class
```

Because the `lendableList` now returns a pointer to an element, `librarian` can update the `lendable` indirectly like this:

```
lendableList lendList;
lendable* lendPtr;
if( lendList.getLendable("QA76.2", lendPtr) )
{ // assert: lendPtr is a pointer to lendable with ID "QA76.2"
  //         inside the lendable list
  lendPtr->checkSelfOut("Robert Evans");
  // assert: The lendable list has been updated
}
```

The `addLendable` and `removeLendable` member functions were added because it seems that eventually some maintenance program will have to be able to add and remove `lendable`s. Besides, you'll see that `addLendable` proves useful in the constructor. A destructor was added because there are many pointers in any `lendableList` (this one starts with 2,000 chunks of allocated memory). When the program terminates, the destructor returns memory. More importantly, however, the destructor also updates the files that store the `lendable`s. This makes `lendableList` somewhat *persistent.* The objects will remain intact until the next time the program gets called (assuming the power stays on, that is). To be truly persistent, each object should be stored to a disk as soon as a change is made. This could be done with any number of database management systems, but since we haven't discussed this, the `lendableList` class will instead will get help from the `ifstream` class to maintain the data.

16.5.2 A Heterogeneous Collection

The `lendableList` class is heterogeneous. The elements stored in a `lendableList` object can be of any class derived from `lendable`. This has several implications. First, the container that stores the elements is a `vector` of pointers to the base class. So you see this data member:

```
vector <lendable*> my_data;
```

The next thing you might notice is parameters with `*`. Now that the underlying data structure is a `vector` of pointers, there will be a lot of argument/parameter association where the value being passed is a *pointer* to a `lendable`:

```
void addLendable(lendable* lendPtr); // Can't pass lendable, need *
bool getLendable(string searchID, lendable* & lendPtr) const;
```

The `getLendable` function heading was changed during testing because it suddenly seemed important to indicate whether or not a `lendable`'s ID was actually found. The return type is now `bool`. This also means that the pointer has to be passed back to `librarian` as a reference parameter `lendPtr`.

```
bool getLendable(string searchID, lendable* & lendPtr) const;
```

The `&` was needed because `getLendable` now returns two values: either true or false and a pointer to the object if found. A `getLendable` message now looks like this (shown earlier):

```
if( lendList.getLendable("QA76.2", lendPtr) )
{
  lendPtr->checkSelfOut(currentBorrower->borrowersID());
}
```

This guarded action also protects against dereferencing a pointer that points to nothing when `lendList` is empty, for example, when the input files are not found.

The constructor initializes the `lendableList` by reading from two different input files: `books.dat` and `video.dat`. Maintaining the `cdRoms` is left as a programming project.

`lendableList::addLendable` should look familiar to those of you who studied the `bag` and `set` classes.

```
void lendableList::addLendable(lendable* lendPtr)
{
```

```
    if(my_size >= my_data.capacity())
     { // Avoid running out of room and out-of-range subscripts
      my_size = my_size + sizeIncrement;
      my_data.resize(my_size);
    }
    my_data[my_size] = lendPtr;
    my_size++;
  }
```

Once again, sequential search is employed to find a `lendable`.

```
bool lendableList::getLendable(string searchID,
                               lendable* & lendPtr) const
{
  int subscript;
  string nextID;

  // Perform a sequential search
  for(subscript = 0; subscript < my_size; subscript++)
  { // Search all items or break out of the loop when found
    nextID = my_data[subscript]->lendableID();
    if(nextID == searchID)
    { // Found it
      break;
    }
  }

  if (subscript < my_size)
  { // Found it
    lendPtr = my_data[subscript];  // Assign a pointer
    return true;
  }
  else
  { // Have to return something, so let it be the first
    lendPtr = my_data[0];  // Return a pointer that hopefully
    return false;          // will never be used by the client!
  }
}
```

Here is a test driver that traverses the entire `lendableList` and then searches for a particular `lendable`. The `librarian` object would often send `getLendable` messages.

```
#include <iostream>
using namespace std;
#include "lendlist"  // For lendableList, lendable, book, video, cdRom
#include "date"      // For Date::ToString
```

```
int main()
{
  lendableList lendList;
  lendable* lendPtr;  // Store a reference to any lendable object

  string searchID = "QA76.2";
  if( lendList.getLendable(searchID, lendPtr) )
  {
    if( lendPtr->isAvailable() )
    { // Don't check out something that is unavailable
      cout << "Check out " << lendPtr->lendableID() << endl;
      lendPtr->checkSelfOut("Robert Evans");
    }
    else
    {
      cout << lendPtr->lendableID() << " unavailable" << endl;
    }
  }
  else
  {
    cout << searchID << " not found." << endl;
    cout << "Please recheck the lendable ID" << endl;
  }

  // Show updated status to indicate lendable list was in fact updated
  if(lendList.getLendable(searchID, lendPtr))
  {
    cout << "Borrower: " << lendPtr->borrowersID() << endl;
    cout << "Due: " << lendPtr->dueDate().ToString() << endl;
  }

  return 0;
}
```

OUTPUT (PROGRAM EXECUTED ON 11-MAY-1998)

```
Check out QA76.2
Borrower: Robert Evans
Due: May 25 1998
```

Chapter Summary

- This chapter presented another case study for object-oriented software development to reinforce the object-oriented design strategy introduced in Chapters 12 and 13.
- The notion of inheritance was discovered when several classes were found that had common behavior, common data, and at least one difference, such as different behavior for the same message.

- An abstract class captures common operations and data amongst the classes derived from that base class. The derived classes capture the differences.
- Role playing produced design decisions.
- `lendable` was the major class definition discussed in this chapter. It was designed slowly to indicate the new consideration in designing an abstract class intended to have derived classes.
- Initialization lists were introduced as a way to allow derived classes to call the base class constructor.
- A heterogeneous container was implemented as a `vector` of pointers to the base class. This allows for a collection of objects, where the elements may be constructed from different classes.

Exercises

1. Provide a first-draft design of the base class for an `account` hierarchy. You should be familiar enough with bank accounts to know what might be common. If you are not, consult a domain expert—someone at a bank for example. The difference between `basicChecking` and `checkingWithLoan` is this: `basicChecking` does not allow withdrawals more than the balance but `checkingWithLoan` does. A `checkingWithLoan` object also maintains the amount of money that has been "loaned" to the account. A savings account earns interest; the other two do not.

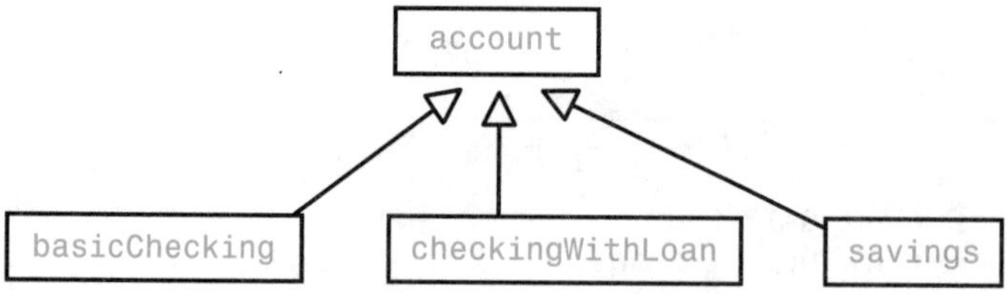

2. Provide a first-draft design of the three derived classes in the `account` hierarchy. Do not worry about the constructors yet.
3. Write the constructors for one of the derived classes above.
4. Rewrite the `track` class constructor using an initialization list (see `track.cpp`).
5. What action requires an initialization list?

6. Provide a first-draft design of the base class for a United States `employee` hierarchy to capture the operations common to all employees that are paid on an hourly basis with hours over 40 paid at 1.5 times the hourly rate. Then, the only difference amongst the derived classes is in the way the U.S. federal income tax is computed for withholding from the paycheck. For a start, see `weekemp.h` and programming project 7N, "Maintain `weeklyEmp`." Also check out **http://www.irs.ustreas.gov/prod/forms_pubs/pubs.html** for the different tax tables for the current year or use the tax tables given below for 1998. (*Note:* A complete design for all classes of employees would look quite different.)

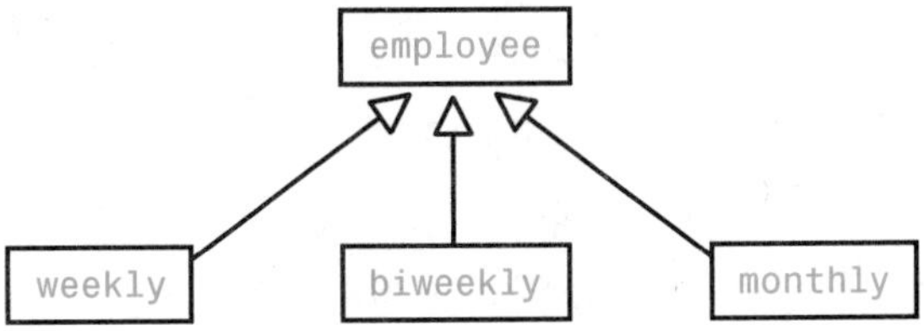

TABLE 16.1. *Weekly payroll period (1998)*
One withholding allowance = $51.92

(a) SINGLE person (including head of household)			(b) MARRIED person		
If the amount of wages (after subtracting withholding allowances) is:	The amount of income tax to withhold is:		If the amount of wages (after subtracting withholding allowances) is:	The amount of income tax to withhold is:	
Not over $51 . . .	$0		Not over $124 . . .	$0	
Over–	**But not over–**	**Of excess over–**	**Over–**	**But not over–**	**Of excess over–**
$51	$517 . . 15%	$51	$124	$899 . . 15%	$124
$517	$1,105 . . $69.90 plus 28%	$517	$899	$1,855 . . $116.25 plus 28%	$899
$1,105	$2,493 . . $234.54 plus 31%	$1,105	$1,855	$3,084 . . $383.93 plus 31%	$1,855
$2,493	$5,385 . . $664.82 plus 36%	$2,493	$3,084	$5,439 . . $764.92 plus 36%	$3,084
$5,385	. . . .$1,705.94 plus 39.6%	$5,385	$5,439	. . . .$1,612.72 plus 39.6%	$5,439

TABLE 16.2. *Biweekly payroll period (1998)*
One withholding allowance = $103.85

(a) **SINGLE person** (including head of household)			(b) **MARRIED person**		
If the amount of wages (after subtracting withholding allowances) is:	The amount of income tax to withhold is:		If the amount of wages (after subtracting withholding allowances) is:	The amount of income tax to withhold is:	
Not over $51 . . .	$0		Not over $51 . . .	$0	
Over–	**But not over–**	**Of excess over–**	**Over–**	**But not over–**	**Of excess over–**
$102	$1,035 . . 15%	$102	$248	$1,798 . . 15%	$248
$1,035	$2,210 . . $139.95 plus 28%	$1,035	$1,798	$3,710 . . $232.50 plus 28%	$1,798
$2,210	$4,987 . . $468.95 plus 31%	$2,210	$3,710	$6,167 . . $767.86 plus 31%	$3,710
$4,987	$10,769 . . $1,329.82 plus 36%	$4,987	$6,167	$10,879 . . $1,529.53 plus 36%	$6,167
$10,769	. . . .$3,411.34 plus 39.6%	$10,769	$10,879	. . . .$3,225.85 plus 39.6%	$10,879

TABLE 16.3. *Monthly payroll period (1998)*
One withholding allowance = $225.00

(a) **SINGLE person** (including head of household)			(b) **MARRIED person**		
If the amount of wages (after subtracting withholding allowances) is:	The amount of income tax to withhold is:		If the amount of wages (after subtracting withholding allowances) is:	The amount of income tax to withhold is:	
Not over $51 . . .	$0		Not over $51 . . .	$0	
Over–	**But not over–**	**Of excess over–**	**Over–**	**But not over–**	**Of excess over–**
$221	$2,242 . . 15%	$221	$538	$3,896 . . 15%	$538
$2,242	$4,788 . . $303.15 plus 28%	$2,242	$3,896	$8,038 . . $503.70 plus 28%	$3,896
$4,788	$10,804 . . $1,016.03 plus 31%	$4,788	$8,038	$13,363 . . $1,663.46 plus 31%	$8,038
$10,804	$23,333 . . $2,880.99 plus 36%	$10,804	$13,363	$23,571 . . $3,314.21 plus 36%	$13,363
$23,333	. . . .$7,391.43 plus 39.6%	$23,333	$23,571	. . . .$6,989.09 plus 39.6%	$23,571

7. Design the class definitions for the derived classes `weekly`, `biWeekly`, and `monthly`.

Analysis/Design/Programming Tips

1. Inheritance and polymorphism are part of object-oriented analysis, design, and programming. But they are not the only things.

Object-oriented (OO) thinking also involves encapsulation—a public interface to private data. Additionally, OO software development involves making analysis and design decisions with the object as the major architectural structure. If there is inheritance, so be it. If there is not, you are still doing things in an object-oriented fashion.

2. Use the delegation model to help with your design.

Object-oriented software often has one object delegating responsibility to another object that may in turn delegate responsibility to another object. Try to think that way. Users of the class can then have a clearer understanding of the system. For example, `librarian` may send a `checkSelfIn` message that in turn fires off messages to other objects. This is analogous to making a call to a free function, that may in turn call another function behind the scenes. For example, the `find` function from `<algorithm>` most likely makes several function calls and/or message sends behind the scenes.

3. Role playing helps because three or four minds are better than one.

Any project can benefit from many people. Most software is developed in a team setting. Anyone can have ideas. Someone with no knowledge of programming can help simply by asking questions that others may be too shy to ask, feeling they are supposed to know it already. The team approach also helps set up a common vocabulary among the stakeholders. Besides, it can be more fun working in groups, even though it can also be challenging to deal with a diversity of opinions.

4. Use inheritance when you can generalize about two or more objects.

If you recognize that several classes have some common behaviors and attributes but there is some distinguishing behavior, there is a chance that inheritance might prove useful. However, with all the special considerations necessary to plan for adding new derived classes, it might not seem worth it. Sometimes inheritance is the best way to go. For example, consider a window on your computer screen. It has a collection of other windows, buttons, menus, selector lists, icons, and so on. Think of that window as a heterogeneous list of graphic objects (kind of like `lendableList`). All graphic objects can be "drawn" in a screen, but they are drawn in different ways. When the window draws itself, the polymorphic draw operation is applied to all the graphics in the window collection. There are some commonalities between the graphic objects; however, there are enough differences to justify many derived classes. This has proven to be an effective use of inheritance.

5. Put only public messages in the public section.

Don't clutter the public interface with member functions best kept private. If you have an inheritance hierarchy, place the utility functions (those not called by any client) in the `protected:` access sections. With public inheritance, all derived classes inherit the ancestor's `public:` and `protected:` members.

6. This has been only a brief introduction to inheritance.

This chapter did not attempt to demonstrate all concepts related to inheritance. It was only an introduction. Proper use of inheritance is still being debated and opinions vary widely.

7. There is a heavy use of indirection in `lendableList`. Here is a summary.

First, the container that stores the elements is a `vector` of pointers to the base class. So `lendableList` has this data member:

```
vector<lendable*> my_data;  // Elements can point to derived objects
```

Another new thing was pointer parameters (with `*` after them). These parameters are used to communicate addresses of objects rather than objects themselves. This is part of the syntax required for implementing polymorphism in C++.

```
void addLendable(lendable* lendPtr);  // Need *; cannot pass a lendable
```

A new kind of parameter was shown in `lendableList::getLendable`.

```
bool getLendable(string searchID, lendable* & lendPtr) const;
```

The second parameter is a reference to a pointer. The `&` is added so a change to `lendPtr` in the function also changes the pointer argument in the message, which in the following call is `lendPtr`.

```
lendList.getLendable("QA76.2", aPointerToALendable)
```

Programming Projects

16A Implement `cdRom`

Completely implement and test the `cdRom` class as a class derived from `lendable`. You will need these files: `lendable.h` and `lendable.cpp`.

16B Implement the `account` Hierarchy

Completely implement and test the `account` hierarchy described in exercise 1.

16C Implement the `employee` Hierarchy

Completely implement and test the `employee` hierarchy described in exercise 6.

16D Complete the College Library System

Find two or three others and

- walk through some scenarios with the college library system
- develop your own CRH cards or modify the ones that exist in this chapter

When you have a full understanding of the system (have practiced those scenarios)

- design all class interfaces (the `lendable` hierarchy has mostly been completed in `lendable.h` and `lendable.cpp`)
- separately test all classes
- integrate the classes and test the entire system

Chapter Seventeen

Templates

Building Generic Classes

Summing Up

The previous chapter introduced inheritance as a way to generalize classes. A base class captures the operations and data common to several classes. Each derived class can add operations, override operations, and add data members. Collections of heterogeneous objects are made possible by constructing a container of pointers to the base class. The operation that gets called depends on the derived class the pointer is pointing to—polymorphism.

Coming Up

With the help of the C++ template mechanism—the focus of this chapter—`vector` and other containers can store collections of *any* class of objects. This chapter demonstrates implementation of template classes such as `vector` and `bag`. In future study, you will find templates a useful tool for implementing other container classes. The `bag` class will be converted into a generic (pass-the-class) `bag` with a different underlying structure (no `vector`). This new `bag` class uses the template mechanism so classes can be passed as arguments. This new `bag` class also provides a review of destructors, copy constructors, and dynamic memory allocation. After studying this chapter, you will be able to

- implement a function that can search and sort `vector`s of any class
- pass class names to container classes just like the C++ standard:

```
bag <book> myBookBag;  // A bag that holds book objects
bag <CD> myCDs;        // A bag that holds CD objects
```

- implement generic container classes that store collections of any class of elements

17.1 Templates

In somewhat the same manner as expressions such as `x` or `1.5` are passed as arguments to functions, class names such as `int`, `double`, `string`, and `bankAccount` can be passed as "arguments" to a class. The C++ template mechanism allows programmers to use the same container class to hold any class of objects. Classes such as `vector` and `list` are considered *generic* because they are general enough to contain different classes of objects.

The standard template library uses the template mechanism to implement the standard container classes: `vectors`, `lists`, `stacks`, and `queues`. Rather than implementing a `vector`, `list`, `stack`, and `queue` for each new class a programmer might think of, the compiler instead uses the single class template to create them automatically.

With templates, only one class needs to be implemented for each type of container. For each class name passed as an argument, a new class is automatically created to manage collections of that class. For example, Chapter 10 presented the user side of templates.

```
vector <string> address(100);  // Store many addresses
vector <double> x(10000);      // Store many numbers
```

Here are some other possibilities using the standard classes `vector`, `list`, `stack`, and `queue`.

Some Generic Container Classes

```
vector <int> x(100, 0);
list <bankAccount> acct;
list <string> str;
stack <double> operand;
stack <char> operator;
queue <automobile> car
queue <track> playList;
```

The implementation side of such classes requires an understanding of C++ function template and class template definitions.

17.1.1 Function Templates

Any class for which the less-than operator (<) has meaning can have one object considered to be less than another. Imagine that a programmer is required to implement a function to return the lesser of any two objects. There are several choices. One is to have a different function name for every class:

```
int lesserInt(int a, int b)
double lesserDouble(double a, double b)
string lesserString(string a, string b)
char * lesserCharStar(char * a, char * b)
```

Or the programmer could use the same function overloading technique that allows for multiple constructors in a class. *Function overloading* permits one program to have many functions with the same name. The trick is to have a distinguishable number and/or class of parameters.

```
int    lesser(   int a, int b   );
double lesser(double a, double b);
string lesser(string a, string b);
char * lesser(char * a, char * b);
// And so on . . .
```

Although function overloading allows for many functions of the same name and for multiple constructors in the same class, a simpler solution exists. *Function templates* make the compiler do the work by creating many overloaded functions automatically.

GENERAL FORM 17.1. *Function templates*

template < class *template-parameter* **>**
function-definition

For each function call with a distinguishably different class that is encountered, the compiler uses the function template declaration to construct a different function. The programmer needs to write only one function. The following program output indicates that one template function can return the lesser of any two objects when < has meaning.

```
#include <iostream>
using namespace std;

template<class TheClass>
TheClass lesser(TheClass a, TheClass b)
{ // pre:  The class must have a default constructor
  // post: Return the lesser of the two arguments
  TheClass result;
```

```
  if(a < b)
    result = a;
  else
    result = b;
  return result;
}

int main()
{ // Test drive a function template
  cout << lesser(-12, 23) << endl;
  cout << lesser(0.01, 0.009) << endl;
  cout << lesser('a', 'A') << endl;
  cout << lesser("Baker", "Able") << endl;

  return 0;
}
```

OUTPUT

```
-12
0.009
A
Able
```

The template parameter named `TheClass` has scope that extends throughout the entire function definition that follows. This includes the parameter list and the function body, or `{` through `}`. At this point, `lesser` may be called with any `TheClass` argument that defines <. Each unique argument class encountered in a call to `lesser` creates a new function. In this particular test driver, the compiler generated the following overloaded functions—same name, different class of parameters.

```
int lesser(int a, int b)
{
  int result;
  if(a < b)
    result = a;
  else
    result = b;
  return result;
}

double lesser(double a, double b)
{
  double result;
  if(a < b)
    result = a;
  else
```

```
    result = b;
  return result;
}

char lesser(char a, char b)
{
  char result;
  if(a < b)
    result = a;
  else
    result = b;
  return result;
}

char * lesser(char * a, char * b)
{
  char * result;
  if(a < b)
    result = a;
  else
    result = b;
  return result;
}
```

The following code would cause the compiler to generate a fifth `lesser` function returning a `string`:

```
string s1("need a 5th function");
string s2("that accepts string, not char* arguments");

cout << lesser(s1, s2) << endl;
```

Here is a generic sort routine that returns the index of the found item (or `-1` otherwise).

```
// This program uses a generic search routine to search for objects stored
// in different classes of vectors
#include <vector>
#include <string>
#include <iostream>
using namespace std;

template<class VectorType>
int locationOf(const vector<VectorType> & v, int n, VectorType searchItem)
{ // pre:  The type must have the != operator available
  // post: Return the index of searchItem in the vector or -1 if not found
  int result = -1;
  int subscript = 0;
```

```
    while( (subscript < n)  &&  (searchItem != v[subscript]) )
    {
      subscript++;
    }
    if(subscript < n)   // searchItem was found
      result = subscript;

    return result;
  }

  int main()
  {
     const int n = 3;

     vector <int> x(n);
     x[0] = 1111;
     x[1] = 2222;
     x[n-1] = 3333;
     cout << locationOf(x, n, 3333) << endl;
     cout << locationOf(x, n, 9999) << endl;

     vector <string> s(n);
     s[0] = "first";
     s[1] = "second";
     s[n-1] = "third";

     cout << locationOf(s, n, string("first")) << endl;
     cout << locationOf(s, n, string("not there")) << endl;

    return 0;
  }
```

OUTPUT

```
2
-1
0
-1
```

In summary, a function template acts as a model for constructing many distinct functions. This is accomplished by the replacement of the parameter—named `VectorType` here—with the class argument such as `int`, `double`, `string`, or `bankAccount`. Every occurrence of `VectorType` from the return type down to the enclosing `}` is replaced with the class argument. A function template causes the compiler to automatically build a function for each new type of argument. The next section shows how the template mechanism builds any number of classes.

17.2 Class Templates

Class templates have the same general form[1] as function templates. In this case, however, `template < class` *identifier* > is followed by a class definition rather than a function definition.

General Form 17.2. *Class templates*

template < class *template-parameter* **>**
class-definition

Template declarations written before a class give the template parameter scope that extends throughout the entire class definition. For example, the `vector` template class (on the enclosed disk[2]) looks a bit like this:

```
template<class VectorElementType>
class vector {
public:
  vector();
  vector(int initCapacity);
  vector(int initCapacity, VectorElementType initialValue);
  vector(const vector<VectorElementType> & source);
  ~vector();

  // . . .

private:
   VectorElementType * x;   // Pointer to the first of many items
   // . . .
};
```

The `vector` class makes frequent use of the template parameter `VectorElementType`. For example, when a `vector` is constructed like this:

```
vector <string> s( 100, "???" );
```

1. Actually, there may be more than one class parameter. For example, one could legally write `template <class QueueType, class Priority>`. The general form here has just one class parameter because that is all this textbook uses.
2. Your system may have a `vector` class that is implemented in a dramatically different way but still supplies familiar operations such as `[ ]`, capacity, and resize.

the parameter `VectorElementType` is replaced by the class name that was passed as the argument. That argument is between angle brackets—`string` in this case. Therefore the second parameter in this constructor:

```
vector(int initCapacity, VectorElementType initialValue);
```

would become

```
vector(int initCapacity, string initialValue);
```

However, if a constructor were invoked to initialize a `vector` of `int`s,

```
vector <int> s(100, 0);
```

the second parameter in the constructor

```
vector(int initCapacity, VectorElementType initialValue);
```

would see `VectorElementType` replaced with `int`:

```
vector(int initCapacity, int initialValue);
```

Because `vector` is defined as a template class, the compiler can use it as a model to build any number of other classes.

The class parameter named `VectorElementType` has scope that extends to the end of the class definition. This means that `VectorElementType` may be used anywhere in the class definition, such as in the public section for the copy constructor or in the private data member section. For example, writing the `VectorElementType` parameter before the pointer data member `x` in the array class definition is critically important to the `vector` class:

```
template <class VectorElementType>
class vector {
public:
  // . . .
private:
  VectorElementType * x;
  // assert: x can point to any class
  int my_capacity;
};
```

The parameter named `VectorElementType` in the private data section becomes the class of objects that `x` will store. At declaration, the `VectorElementType` identifier is replaced with the argument specified at declaration. For example, these object initializations cause `x` to point to `int`, `string`, and `bankAccount` objects, respectively.

```
vector<int> a1(5);        vector<string> a2(6);     vector<bankAccount> a3(7);
      ↓                           ↓                            ↓
VectorElementType * x;    VectorElementType * x;    VectorElementType * x;
      ↓                           ↓                            ↓
    int * x;                  string * x;               bankAccount * x;
```

Once the `VectorElementType` pointed to by `x` is known, the `new` operator allocates the proper amount of memory. Because a `VectorElementType` argument must be passed during the call to the `vector` constructor, the class of data allocated by `new` is known. The `VectorElementType` parameter specifies not only the class of data pointed to by `x` but also the amount of memory needed to allocate each object of that class (each object requires a specific number of bytes for each data object). For example, this construction:

```
vector <int> intVector(6);
```

allocates enough memory to store six elements of class `int`—not `double`, `string`, or `bankAccount`. The private data member `x` will point to `int`s, not `string`s or `bankAccount`s.

17.2.1 Member Function Templates

When a class has been defined with a template parameter, all member functions automatically become template functions.

```
template<class VectorElementType>  // Template parameter
class vector {
public:
  vector();
  vector(int initCapacity);
  vector(int initCapacity, VectorElementType initialValue);
  vector(const vector<VectorElementType> & source);
  ~vector();
  void resize(int newCapacity);

  // . . .

private:
  VectorElementType * x;
  int my_capacity;
};
```

This means that member function implementations must be preceded by the same template declaration that precedes the class definition.

General Form 17.3. *Member function templates syntax*

```
template < class parameter >
class-name < parameter > :: member-function-name ( parameters )
{
  // ... member function implementation
}
```

The class parameter name—`VectorElementType`—will repeat often in the `vector` class example. Every member function implementation requires this line of code:

```
template<class VectorElementType>
```

Additionally, the parameter name must be added to the qualifier between < and >. The following attempt at a member function has an error:

```
template<class VectorElementType>
vector::vector(int initCapacity) // ERROR: need <VectorElementType>
{
  my_capacity = initCapacity;
  x = new VectorElementType[my_capacity];
  // . . .
}
```

To correct this syntax error, the parameter name must be added in between < and >.

```
template<class VectorElementType>
vector<VectorElementType>::vector(int initCapacity)
{
  my_capacity = initCapacity;
  x = new VectorElementType[my_capacity];
  // . . .
}
```

The template syntax is required for all member functions, even if the member function does not reference the parameter name `VectorElementType`. For example, the simple `vector::capacity` function carries the extra template syntax baggage.

```
template<class VectorElementType>
int vector<VectorElementType>::capacity() const
{
```

```
  return my_capacity;
}
```

17.2.2 A Simple Class with a Template

Unfortunately, the class template mechanism does add a lot of additional syntax. So a shortcut will be used in this section. The member functions can be implemented inside the class definition. This means only one file is necessary. A second reason for implementing member functions in the header file has to do with compiler idiosyncrasies. Some compilers require that the member functions of template classes be implemented in the same file.

A simple class is presented here to summarize template classes. It has a template parameter `Type`. Instances of this class store precisely one object of the `Type` class. The data member value is initialized when the constructor is called and `one<Type>::display` simply displays the single data member.

```
// ------------------------------------------------------------------
// File name: one
// Define and implement a simple generic class named one
// ------------------------------------------------------------------

template<class Type>
class one
{ // pre: Type must define ostream <<
public:
  one(Type initValue)
  {
    value = initValue;
  }

  void display()
  { // pre: Type can be output with cout <<
    cout << "The value: " << value << endl;
  }

private:
  Type value;
};
```

The following `main` function creates objects of three different classes. Each object asks the compiler for a unique class—one each of types `int`, `double`, and `string`. All three classes are created from the template class named `one`.

```
#include <iostream>
#include <string>
```

```
using namespace std;
#include "one"  // For the one class

// This main function will cause three classes to be generated by
// the compiler with Type replaced by int, double, and string
int main()
{
  one<int> anInt(-999);
  one<double> aDouble(1.23e-02);
  one<string> aString("abcdefg");

  anInt.display();
  aDouble.display();
  aString.display();

  return 0;
}
```

OUTPUT

```
The value: -999
The value: 0.0123
The value: abcdefg
```

A class template acts as a model for constructing many distinct classes. This is analogous to a class that constructs many distinct objects. Specifically, the `one` class acted as a template for the three different classes specified in the function `main` with the three different template arguments: `int`, `double`, and `string`.

17.3 A Generic `bag` Class

Recall the `bag` class of Chapter 11 that has operations such as `bag::add` and `bag::remove`. This section shows the conversion of that `bag` class to a generic class. The template mechanism makes the `bag` class general enough to store collections of any class. A generic `bag` object will be constructed with this general form:

GENERAL FORM 17.4. *A generic `bag` object*

bag < *class-name* > *identifier* ;

Here is a sample program to summarize the capabilities of the generic `bag` class.

```
#include <iostream>
#include <string>
using namespace std;
#include "genbag"  // For a generic (with templates) bag class

int main()
{
  bag <int> aBag;
  int sum = 0;
```

```
  // Add 35 integers to aBag
  int n = 35;
  for(int j = 1; j <= n; j++)
  {
    aBag.add(j);
  }

  // Then remove all the odd bag elements
  for(int k = 1; k <= n; k = k + 2)
  {
    aBag.remove(k);  // Remove the ints 1, 3, 5, 7, . . ., n - 2, n
  }

  cout << "Traverse the entire collection" << endl;
  for(aBag.first(); ! aBag.isDone(); aBag.next())
  {
    cout.width(4);
    cout << aBag.currentItem();       // Reference the "current" bag
                                      // element
    sum = sum + aBag.currentItem();   // Reference it again
  }

  cout << "\n\nSum of all bag elements: " << sum << endl;

  return 0;
}
```

OUTPUT (RECALL THAT ORDERING OF bag ELEMENTS IS NOT REQUIRED)

```
Traverse the entire collection
  18   2  34   4  26   6  32   8  20  10  30  12  24  14  28  16  22

Sum of all bag elements: 306
```

One of the advantages of this bag class, and an issue that becomes important in many applications, is the number of elements that may be stored with one bag object. The capacity cannot always be determined. The number of objects that may be contained in one bag object depends on the size of the objects and the amount of available memory in the free store. The best answer is this: A bag object will store as many objects as memory allows; there is no fixed maximum size, as previously seen in primitive C arrays (see Chapter 15).

To remove an object from a bag, the equality operator (==) must be defined for the class.[3] Also, since there is a collection, the type of bag element must have a default constructor.

3. This is also true for standard C++ containers such as list and vector.

Self-Check

Use this object declaration to answer the following questions:

```
bag <int> intBag;
```

17-1 How many `ints` can be stored in `intBag`?

17-2 Write the code that displays the first two elements in `intBag`.

17-3 Write the message that adds 89 to the collection of integers in `intBag`.

17-4 Write the message that will remove 89 from `intBag`.

This section shows how pointers and genericity are combined to implement this new version of the `bag` class. This generic `bag` object

1. is generic because it manages data of most classes (some restrictions do apply)
2. does not have a fixed maximum size—it allocates memory as long there is some in the free store

The intentionally limited set of operations is summarized by the class definition as it exists in the file `genbag`.

CLASS DEFINITION: *A bag class with a class parameter*

```
template <class BagElementType>
class bag {
public:
//--constructors/destructor
  bag();
  bag(const bag & source);
  ~bag();

//--modifiers
  void add(BagElementType newElement);
  // post: Add newElement to this bag, increase size

  bool remove(BagElementType removalCandidate);
  // post: If found, removalCandidate is removed from this bag

//--accessors
  int capacity() const;
  int size() const;
  bool isEmpty() const;
```

```
//--iterator functions
  void first();
  void next();
  bool isDone() const;
  BagElementType currentItem() const;

private:
  BagElementType * my_data;   // Pointer to the first of many
  int my_size;
  int my_capacity;
  int my_index;
};
```

The class parameter named BagElementType is used where a specific class would be, so the extra overhead involves the addition of a class template.

```
template <class BagElementType>
```

This template extends the scope of BagElementType throughout the entire class. So the class parameter named BagElementType is used rather than a specific class such as string. This applies to the use of BagElementType as a parameter or as the class of elements pointed to by my_data of the private section.

This represents a slight improvement over the earlier bag class that required a typedef before #include "bag".

```
typedef int BagElementType;  Not necessary with the generic bag
#include "genbag"  // For a generic bag class (with templates)
```

Now the programmer may construct bag objects in a fashion similar to standard containers such as vector and list.

```
bag <double> tests;
bag <string> names;
```

17.3.1 bag::bag()

As with the original bag constructor, this bag constructor guarantees that a bag starts empty—my_size = 0. Now my_data points to my_capacity number of BagElementType objects.

```
template <class BagElementType>
bag<BagElementType>::bag()
{ // post: Size of this bag is 0
  //       Initial capacity == DEFAULT_INITIAL_BAG_CAPACITY
```

```
    my_size = 0;
    my_capacity = DEFAULT_INITIAL_BAG_CAPACITY;
    my_data = new BagElementType[my_capacity];
  }
```

Now with subscripts, `my_data` points to `DEFAULT_INITIAL_BAG_CAPACITY` elements, currently defined in `bag.h` as 16.

```
const int DEFAULT_INITIAL_BAG_CAPACITY = 16;
```

The following representation shows the private data of a `bag` object and how that data can be referenced through subscripts.

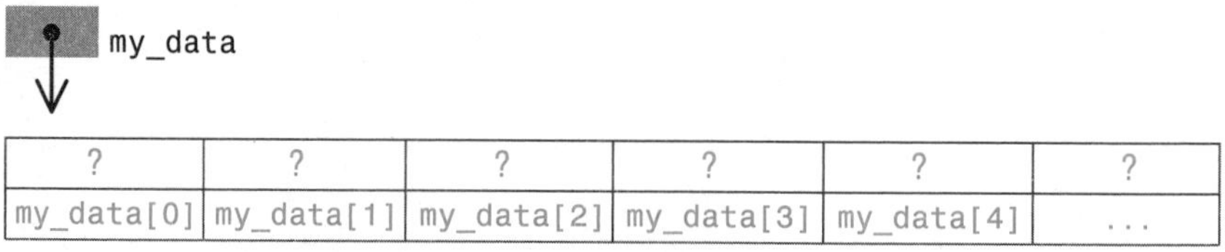

17.3.2 bag::add()

With `DEFAULT_INITIAL_BAG_CAPACITY` initialized to 16, each `bag` is initially capable of storing up to 16 objects. However, when a 17th object gets added, nothing bad should happen. Something different must happen. The `new` operator allocates additional memory to store twice as many objects. In general, each newly added object appends to the end of the subscripted pointer object named `my_data`. When the value of `my_size` is less than `my_capacity`, new objects are added with little fuss. If this portion of code from `bag::add`'s implementation looks familiar, it's because this is what happened during the earlier `bag` `add` operation class (see Chapter 11).

```
// Store the argument in the block of memory pointed to by my_size
my_data[my_size] = newElement;
// And make sure the size is always increased by one
my_size++;
```

If there is no more room to add an object, several steps are taken to increase the amount of memory so the `bag` container can hold more. The `bag` class will not add a new element at the risk of destroying other objects. The `bag` capacity automatically increases instead. The original `bag` class used a `vector` resize operation. This is the obvious thing to do when there is a `vector` data member. However, this `bag` example intentionally uses a pointer to demonstrate dynamic memory allocation. Here is the algorithm:

ALGORITHM: *Growing the bag bigger*

```
// Check to see if we need to grow the list
if( my_size >= my_capacity )
{
  Increase the amount of memory to hold more elements
  Increase my_capacity
  Copy old elements into the newly allocated space
  Deallocate the old memory that is no longer needed
  Let my_data point to the new larger space
}
```

Whenever an attempt is made to add a new `bag` element and there is not enough room, the `bag` first increases its storage capacity two-fold before adding the new element.

The code of `list::add` below shows that an attempt to add a 17th object will make room for 16 * 2 = 32 objects with `my_capacity` doubled to 32. Next a temporary pointer (named `extraData`) and a `new` operation allocate additional storage space for all objects currently in the `bag` plus that many again.

```
my_capacity = 2 * my_capacity;
BagElementType * extraData = new BagElementType[my_capacity];
```

With all the existing objects copied into the newly allocated memory, there is an additional copy of `bag` elements.

```
for(int j = 0; j < my_size; j++)
{
  extraData[j] = my_data[j];
}
```

However, `extraData` points to memory that can now store twice as many elements. With `extraData` available, the memory pointed to by `my_data` can be deleted to return the old list memory to the free store.

```
// Looks dangerous; but extraData also points to the elements
delete [ ] my_data;
```

The next statement sets `my_data` to point to the same memory location as the newly created `bag` elements (with space for twice as many).

```
my_data = extraData;
```

The bag is now back to its original state, except my_data is now pointing to memory for twice as many elements. Here is the complete member function that accomplishes these tasks.

```
template<class BagElementType>
void bag<BagElementType>::add(BagElementType newElement)
{
  // First check to see if we need to grow the bag
  if(my_size >= my_capacity)
  { // Inadequate capacity so double the capacity
    my_capacity = 2 * my_capacity;

    // Allocate memory to store more objects
    BagElementType * extraData = new BagElementType[my_capacity];

    // Copy elements into the newly allocated memory
    for(int j = 0; j < my_size; j++)
    {
      extraData[j] = my_data[j];
    }

    // Deallocate old memory that is no longer needed
    delete [ ] my_data;

    // Now let my_data point to the new larger memory
    my_data = extraData;
  }

  // Add newElement to the bag
  my_data[my_size] = newElement;
  // And make sure the size is always increased by one
  my_size++;
}
```

As a simpler example, suppose DEFAULT_INITIAL_BAG_CAPACITY had been initialized as 3 instead of 16. Then these three bag::add messages are sent:

```
aBag.add(90);
aBag.add(80);
aBag.add(70);
```

The portion of memory storing the state would look something like this where my_size == 3 and my_capacity == 3:

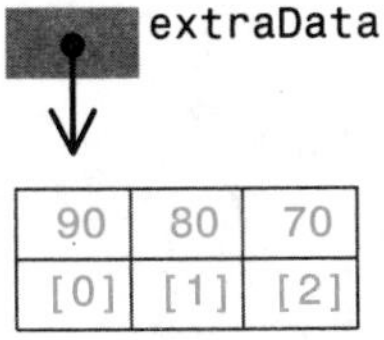

Then an attempt to add a fourth would result in this expression being true:

```
if(my_size >= my_capacity)
```

The fourth `add` would first grow the list by three elements (double its size) and then place the fourth—the newly added element—at `my_data[3]`.

```
aBag.add(60);
```

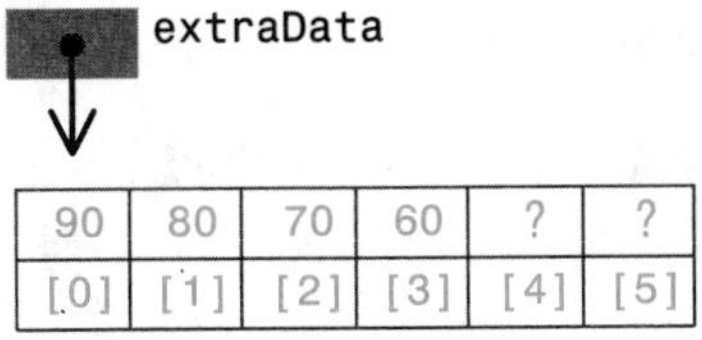

With these two `add`s:

```
aBag.add(50);
aBag.add(40);
```

there would be no need to grow the `bag`. Memory would look something like this when `my_size == 6` and `my_capacity == 6`:

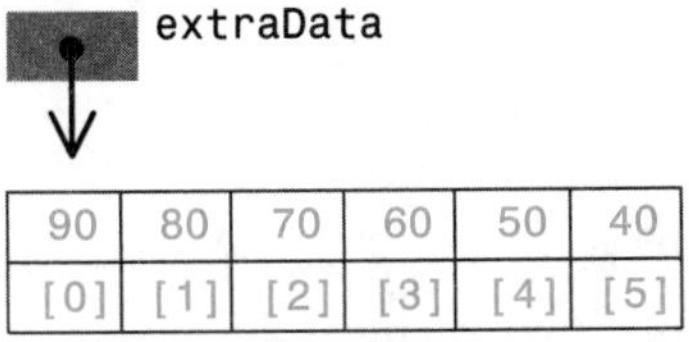

Now, to add another, the `bag` would once again double its size. The picture representation of this code:

```
// Allocate memory to store more objects
BagElementType * extraData = new BagElementType[my_capacity];

// Copy elements into the temporary array
for(int j = 0; j < my_size; j++)
{
  extraData[j] = my_data[j];
}
```

results in memory that looks like this:

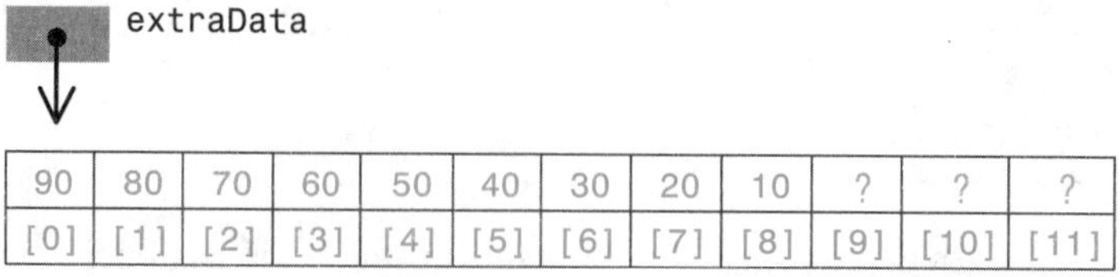

With this exact copy of data pointed to by `extraData`, `my_data` can now be deleted to return the unneeded memory to the free store. With `extraData` pointing to a `bag` containing the same elements, `my_data` is made to point to the same memory as `extraData`.

```
my_data = extraData
```

The `bag` is now back to its original state except that it has room for twice as many elements. So if this call is made with `my_size == 9`:

```
intList.add(99);
```

we end up with this collection (`extraData` is no longer necessary):

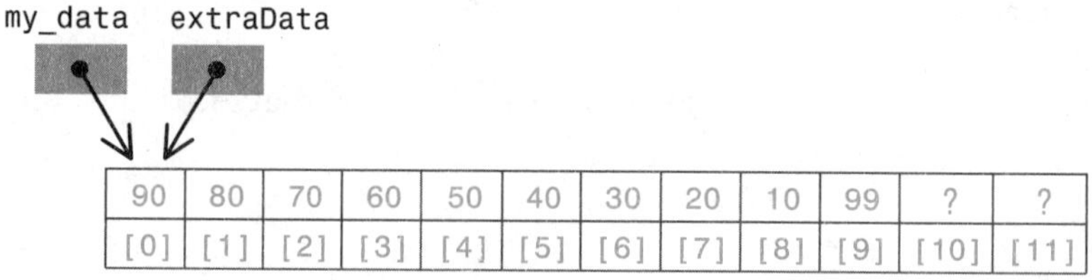

17.3.3 The Copy Constructor

The copy constructor for `bag` allows for *deep copying.* This is a necessity because the class contains a pointer object with dynamic memory allocation. The copy constructor's algorithm is much like that of the `vector` class on this textbook's disk.

```
template<class BagElementType>
bag<BagElementType>::bag(const bag<BagElementType> & source)
{
  // Copy the data members (memberwise copy)
  my_size = source.my_size;
  my_index = source.my_index;
  my_capacity = source.my_capacity;
```

```
  // Allocate the memory for the new bag
  my_data = new BagElementType[my_capacity];

  // Copy all values from source to destination
  for(int j = 0; j < my_capacity; j++)
  { // Deep copy all elements, not just the address of the first
    my_data[j] = source.my_data[j];
  }
}
```

Now, bags can be passed by value to functions without any danger of deleting a pointer to memory that has already been deleted (see Chapter 16).

```
void show( bag<int> b )
{
  cout << "==================" << endl;
  cout << b.currentItem()      << endl;
  cout << "==================" << endl;
}
```

The copy constructor overrides the default memberwise copy constructor given to each class. So when show is called, the entire bag is copied— element by element— after new memory is allocated. Without this deep copy, only the address of the first bag element would get copied and errors would occur. When passed by reference (with &), the copy constructor does not get called.

17.3.4 bag::~bag()

A destructor needs to be added because this generic bag dynamically allocates memory to store the elements. The default constructor allocates space for 16 objects. The bag::add operation carefully copied all bag elements into memory pointed to by my_data. bag::add also carefully deleted all memory in the temporary memory pointed to by extraData. However, when the bag object would be about to go out of scope through function or program termination, my_data would be pointing to all the data elements allocated. A destructor guarantees that all of that memory will be returned back to the system. The memory allocated in the constructor, and possibly later by new, will not be regained unless bag implements a destructor function like this:

```
template <class BagElementType>
bag<BagElementType>::~bag()
{  // Restore all allocated memory back to the free store
   delete [ ] my_data;
}
```

17.3.5 The Other Member Functions

The other member functions of the generic bag are not much different than the original bag class. To save space, they are not included here. Most differ only because they would now have template syntax like this:

```
template <class BagElementType>
int bag<BagElementType>::capacity() const
{
  return my_capacity;  // The capacity of the bag
}
```

Again, this is a lot of code for simply returning one of the data members. An alternative is to complete all or some of the member functions in the class definition—some accessors can actually be written on only one line.

```
template <class BagElementType>
class bag {
public:
  // . . .

// These accessors are implemented in the class definition
int capacity() const { return my_capacity; }
int size() const { return my_size; }
bool isEmpty() const { return my_size == 0; }

private:
  BagElementType * my_data;
  // . . .
};
```

This is inconsistent with the convention of this textbook to separate interface from implementation. However, a lot of programmers do it. Additionally, on some systems you must put the template member functions in the same file as the class definition anyway.

Self-Check

17-5 How many classes are constructed when this code is compiled?

```
vector<int> tests;
vector<int> quizzes;
vector<string> name;
```

17-6 Assuming `DEFAULT_INITIAL_BAG_CAPACITY == 16`, what is the value of `my_capacity` after each of these situations? Assume the capacity doubles each time a `bag::add` message is sent to a "full" bag.

-a 10 adds then 5 removals

-b 40 adds then 5 removals

-c 40 adds then 40 removals

-d 64 adds

-e 65 adds

-f 1,025 adds followed by 1,024 removals

Chapter Summary

- Function templates act as models for the compiler to use when creating other functions. A class template also permits the compiler to create many different classes. The compiler does the work. The programmer need not implement separate `stringVector`, `intVector`, and `bankVector` classes, for example.
- Classes with parameters allow the user to pass a class name as an argument to a class. This allows container classes such as `vector`, `list`, and `bag` to manage any class of objects.
- The `bag` class demonstrates that pointers and dynamic memory management can be hidden from users of a class.
- Even though some `bag` member functions were changed from those shown in Chapter 11, the same public member functions exist. The programs using a `bag` class need not be changed even though the underlying data structure changed.
- The single statement in the `bag` destructor returns all dynamically allocated memory back to the free store as any `bag` object goes out of scope—at the end of the function, for example.
- These `bag` implementation details illustrate class templates and how pointers, along with `new` and `delete` operations, hold promise for effective memory management.
- Templates provide the means to implement reusable container classes in addition to standard C++ generic containers such as `vector` and `list`.

- Member functions may be implemented in class definitions. This makes sense for template classes that otherwise would require a large amount of repeated syntax. Some compilers require it.

Exercises

1. Implement a template function named `greaterThan` that returns true each time the first argument is greater than the second. All of these function calls should return true even though only one template function exists.

```
cout << greaterThan(2, 3) << endl;
cout << greaterThan(0.001, 0.001) << endl;
cout << greaterThan("Abe", "Bill") << endl;
```

2. Implement a template class named `plus` that shows what happens to two values when + is applied. The following code should generate the output shown in the comments:

```
// You only need one template class
plus a(2, 3);
plus b(2.2, 3.3);
plus c("Abe", "Lincoln");
a.show();  // 5
b.show();  // 5.5
c.show();  // AbeLincoln
```

3. Use this code to answer each of the questions below:

```
#include "bag"
int main()
{
   bag<double> db;
   // . . .
```

   a. How many `double`s can `db` store?
   b. Write the code that adds at least five elements to `db`.
   c. Write the code that displays all elements in `db`.
   d. Write the code that determines the smallest value in `db`.

Programming Tips

1. Templates provide genericity.

The value of templates can be appreciated if you realize that many of the standard classes are generic. We have used `vector` and `list` and now `bag` classes with templates that were constructed like this:

```
list<lendable*> lendablePtr;
vector<CD> cdCollection;
queue<track> playList;
```

As you continue your study of C++, you will see other template classes.

2. Templates provide a lot of extra syntax.

Consider this very simple function and all the syntax wrapped around it.

```
template<class VectorElementType>
int vector<VectorElementType>::capacity() const
{
  return my_capacity;
}
```

This member function does not even use `VectorElementType`. If this `vector` were not generic, you could simply write this:

```
int vector::capacity() const
{
  return my_capacity;
}
```

A way to avoid this is to write the function inside the class definition.

```
template<class VectorElementType>
class vector {
public:
  // . . .
  // This accessor is implemented in the class definition
  int vector::capacity() const { return my_capacity; }

};  // End definition of the vector<VectorElementType> class
```

Many programmers use this technique, even though they may have different reasons for doing so.

Programming Projects

17A Implementing Function Templates

Implement a generic function that returns the largest of any three of these objects: `char`, `int`, `double`, and `string`. If the objects are equal, return any one.

17B Modifying `bag::remove` to Conserve Memory

Modify the remove member function of the `bag` class (stored in the file named `genbag`) such that it checks to see if some memory can be returned to the free store. When the current number of elements falls 30 elements below one of the cut-offs (64, 128, 256, 512, 1,024, and so on), return half the current memory back to the free store. The reason to wait for 30 elements below the cut-off is to avoid excessive doubling and halving when adding and removing around one of the cut-off capacities.

17C `bool bag::howMany (Type matchingElement)`

Add a member function to the `bag` class that returns the number of `bag` elements that equal the argument in calls like this:

```
aBagOfInts.howMany(5);  // Return the number of 5s in the bag
```

The class must be comparable with ==; so when testing, only instantiate `bag` objects that hold `int`s, `double`s, or `string`s.

17D Implementing a Class

Implement a generic (with templates) stack. A stack allows elements to be added and removed in a last-in, first-out (LIFO) manner. Stacks have an operation called `push` to place elements at the "top" of the stack and another operation called `pop` to remove elements from the top of the stack. The only element on the stack that may be referenced is the one on the top. This means that if two elements are pushed onto the stack, the topmost element must be popped (removed) from the stack before the first pushed element can be referenced. Here is a stack for storing up to 10 `char` objects:

```
// Declare s as a stack object that can store up to 10 elements
stack<char> s(10);
// Push one element onto the empty stack
s.push('a');
```

The stack started as empty, but now has one `char` element on it. The current state of the stack is represented as follows:

```
'a'        <= Top of the stack
```

After two more push operations, charStack would contain three elements with the top one having the value of 'c'.

```
charStack.push('b');
charStack.push('c');

'c'        <= Top of the stack
'b'
'a'
```

Use the following template class definition to completely implement a generic stack class:

```
template <class StackElementType>
class stack {
public:
  stack(int InitMax);
  ~stack
  void push(StackElementType element);
  // pre:  There is room to add an element on top
  // post: Insert element onto the top of the stack

  // You design stack::pop and stack::isEmpty . . .

private:
  StackElementType * bottom;   // Pointer to the bottom-most element
  int my_size;                 // The number of elements on the stack
  int my_capacity;             // The maximum number of elements
};
```

Implement the member functions in the same file (some systems don't allow separate definition and implementation files).

```
template <class StackElementType>
stack<StackElementType>::stack(int initMax)
{
  my_size = 0;
  my_capacity = initMax;
  bottom = newType[max];
}

template <class StackElementType>
void stack<StackElementType>::push(StackElementType element)
{
  bottom[my_size] = element;
  my_size++;
}
```

```
// You implement stack::pop and stack::isEmpty
```

Then use the following program to test your `stack` class:

```
#include <iostream>
using namespace std;
#include "stack"  // For a generic stack class

int main()
{
  char element;
  stack<char> charStack(10);
  cout << "After initialization, stack::isEmpty() returns: "
       << charStack.isEmpty() << endl;

  charStack.push('a');
  charStack.push('b');
  charStack.pop(element);
  // 'b' is on top of the stack
  cout << element << " popped from stack" << endl;
  charStack.push('c');
  charStack.push('d');
  charStack.push('e');
  charStack.push('f');
  // 'f' is on top of the stack
  charStack.pop(element);
  cout << element << " popped from stack" << endl;

  cout << "Before popping, charStack::isEmpty() returns: "
       << charStack.isEmpty() << endl;
  // Pop and display all remaining elements
  while(! charStack.isEmpty())
  {
    charStack.pop(element);
    cout << element << endl;
  }
  cout << "First in, last out!" << endl;
}
```

OUTPUT

```
After initialization, stack::isEmpty() returns: 1
b popped from stack
f popped from stack
Before popping, charStack::isEmpty() returns: 0
e
d
c
a
First in, last out!
```

Chapter Eighteen

Operator Overloading

Summing Up

The container classes under study require that objects define the == operator. To remove an object from a `bag`, the algorithm compares the removal candidate to the elements in the container. More importantly, the STL algorithms also expect that the class of objects stored in a container define == for searching and < for sorting. Other algorithms require the other relational operators.

Coming Up

In this chapter you will learn how to overload relational operators such as == and <. Then any class you build can be stored in a standard container. You will also learn how to overload the assignment operator (=) for `strings`, `vectors`, and any class that uses dynamic memory allocation. The end of this chapter presents a complete case study of a complex number class. Most of the work involves overloading arithmetic operators and the input and output operators >> and <<. After studying this chapter, you will be able to

- overload the relational operators for any state object you want contained in a standard container
- perform complex arithmetic
- overload << and >> so you can output or input any new class you build
  Exercises and programming projects to reinforce operator overloading

18.1 Operator Overloading

Built-in types (like `int` and `double`) define operators such as <, ==, !=, >, <=, >=, +, -, and /. The process of *operator overloading* allows these same operator symbols to have different meanings depending on the operands in the expression. Consider the differences between the two expressions `int + int` and `string + string` and between the two expressions `int / int` and `double / double`.

Expression	Value
`2 + 5`	`7`
`"2" + "5"`	`"25"`
`2 / 5`	`0`
`2.0 / 5.0`	`0.4`

The different expressions are possible because the different operands give different meanings to the operators.

To many C++ programmers, operator overloading also makes it easier to read code. Consider the difference between a named member function `weeklyEmp::lessThan` and an operator function that defines <. Which operation do you prefer?

```
weeklyEmp e1, e2;

if(e1.lessThan(e2))  // Could be a named member function
  // . . .

if(e1 < e2)  // Could be an operator function (see below)
  // . . .   // Which one is easier for you to read and use?
```

Overloaded operators allow classes to look like built-in types. In fact, some standard C++ classes overload operators—`string` and `complex`, for example. Consider the `string` class.

```
// This code calls operator functions for <<, >>, <, +=, and +
string s1, s2;
cin >> s1 >> s2;
if(s1 < s2)
   s1 += s2;
else
   s2 = s1 + s2;  // Perform s2 += s1;
cout << s2;
```

The `Date` class, shown in Chapter 16, also overloads several operators to make `Date` arithmetic appear like built-in operations.

```
// Demonstrate overloaded operators ++, --, and +=
#include <iostream>
using namespace std;
#include "date"  // For Astrachan's Date class

const double dayInOneYear = 365.25;

int main()
{
  Date d(4, 3, 1982);        // April 3, 1982
  d++;                       // April 4, 1982
  d = d - 2;                 // April 2, 1982
  d += 18 * dayInOneYear;    // Add 18 years
  cout << d.ToString();

  return 0;
}
```

OUTPUT

```
April 01, 2000
```

18.1.1 Overloading for the Standard Containers and Algorithms

As further motivation to learn operator overloading, recall the standard function `list::sort` (see Chapter 14).

```
presidents.sort();
```

This message will sort any class of elements in ascending order. And it does it very efficiently. The `find` function locates an object in a standard container like this:

```
presPtr = find(presidents.begin(), presidents.end(), "Abraham Lincoln");
```

However, there are some preconditions for performing standard searches and sorts.

1. To sort, the class must define <.
2. To find, the class must define == (or perhaps `!=`).

The standard `vector` and `list` sort methods compare objects to see if one is more or less than another. That's why < is required. To search for an object, the algorithm compares objects in the collection to the searched-for object until it finds one that is equal (==). So to make collections of new objects searchable and sortable, you must define < and == operators for each state object. Additional algorithms in the C++ standard library may also use `!=` and the other relational operators <=, >, and >=. Without defining these operators, you cannot use the standard containers and algorithms.

For example, the `bankAccount` files declare and define ==. Two `bankAccount` objects are defined to be equal when both names are equal. One `bankAccount` object is less than another if its name alphabetically precedes the other. You may have noticed some free function headings at the bottom of the `baccount.h` file; they are *operator functions.*

```
class bankAccount {
public:
  // . . .
private:
  // . . .
};
// . . .

//--auxiliary functions
bool operator == (bankAccount left, bankAccount right);
bool operator <  (bankAccount left, bankAccount right);
bool operator != (bankAccount left, bankAccount right);
// . . .
```

The first two operator functions declare == and < to provide each with a new meaning when both operands are `bankAccounts`. This allows a list of `bankAccount` objects to be sorted and searched with standard member functions and algorithms. The process of giving new meaning to existing operators such as == is called operator overloading.

The major difference between operator functions and the other functions you have seen is this:

- There is no function name. Instead, you see the reserved word `operator` followed by an operator such as ==, `!=`, or <.

In the case of binary operators, such as < and ==, the two parameters represent the two expressions that are to the left and to the right of the operator when the operator function is called. So for example, in the following program, the logical expression `one < two` calls this function in `baccount.cpp`:

```
// From the file baccount.cpp
bool operator < (const bankAccount& left, const bankAccount& right)
{
  return left.name() < right.name();
}
```

Here is the < operator function call used in context:

```
#include <iostream>
using namespace std;
#include "baccount"

int main()
{
  bankAccount one("Bob", 222.00);
  bankAccount two("Carla", 111.00);

  if(one < two)
    cout << one.name() << " < " << two.name() << endl;
  else
    cout << one.name() << " >= " << two.name() << endl;

  return 0;
}
```

OUTPUT

```
Bob < Carla
```

Most operators can be overloaded for any class. This is especially useful for classes that follow the State Object pattern, which are likely to eventually end up inside a standard container. Here is the general form for declaring the function heading for an operator function (add a semicolon to the end and these can become a part of the `.h` file without an implementation).

GENERAL FORM 18.1. *Binary operator functions*

return-type **operator** *an-operator* **(** **const** *class***&** *left* **,** **const** *class***&** *right* **)**

The *return-type* is any known class. The *an-operator* is one of the operators that can be overloaded, which is almost all of the operators. The *class* specifies the left and right operands of *an-operator* that will call the particular operator function. *left* and *right* are the parameter names used by the operator function to complete its task. Traditionally, these are typically declared as const reference parameters because the class of objects might be big and you don't want to accidentally change the objects. Here is the other `bankAccount` operator function:

```
bool operator != (const bankAccount& left, const bankAccount& right)
{
  return left.name() != right.name();
}
```

This operator function returns true when two `bankAccount` objects are compared with the `!=` operator and the names are not equal. The same function returns false when the names are equal.

```
if( bankAccount("Jodie", 100.00) != bankAccount("Judy", 100.00) )
   cout << "These two bankAccounts are NOT equal" << endl;
```

Of course in a more real-world `bankAccount` class, the `!=` operator would most likely compare account numbers, not names.

Classes that overload `!=` can be compared in sequential search like this:

```
while( (subscript < n) && (searchItem != account[subscript]) )
```

Classes that overload == can be compared in sequential search like this:

```
while( (subscript < n) && ! (searchItem == account[subscript]) )
```

Classes that overload < can be sorted in the sort operations:

```
if(account[j] < account[smallestIndex])
  smallestIndex = j;
```

For you to use the standard C++ libraries, your state objects should define all of the relational operators: `!=`, ==, <, <=, >, and >=. The `bankAccount` class files do this, as illustrated by this code in `baccount.cpp`:

```
// . . . from baccount.cpp . . .

// These nonmember functions may be required by standard C++
// container classes such as list. Without all six defined, you will
// likely get many cryptic compiletime error messages.

bool operator < (const bankAccount& left, const bankAccount& right)
{
  return left.name() < right.name();
}

bool operator == (const bankAccount& left, const bankAccount& right)
{
  return left.name() == right.name();
}
```

```
bool operator != (const bankAccount& left, const bankAccount& right)
{
  return left.name() != right.name();
}

bool operator > (const bankAccount& left, const bankAccount& right)
{
  return left.name() > right.name();
}

bool operator >= (const bankAccount& left, const bankAccount& right)
{
  return left.name() >= right.name();
}

bool operator <= (const bankAccount& left, const bankAccount& right)
{
  return left.name() <= right.name();
}
```

Self-Check

18-1 Write a function that makes one `bankAccount` less than another if its balance is less than the other `bankAccount` balance.

18.2 Using Friend Functions

Each call to operator functions such as == during a search, and each of the many calls (millions perhaps) to < during a sort, requires the calling of member functions. These function calls have some runtime overhead that, when eliminated, makes standard searches and sorts run much faster. To accomplish this, C++ has added the `friend` function. To speed up programs, operator functions may be placed in the class definition following the reserved word `friend`.

```
class bankAccount {
public:

// . . .

//--accessors
  double balance() const;
  string name() const;
```

```
//--friend operator functions
  friend bool operator == (const bankAccount& left, const bankAccount& right);
  friend bool operator < (const bankAccount& left, const bankAccount& right);

private:
  string my_name;      // Uniquely identify an object
  double my_balance;  // Store the current balance (nonpersistent)
};
```

A `friend` function has access to the private data members. When you declare == and < as `friends`, the overhead of calling the same member function twice disappears. This allows the program to run faster, especially when the operator function is called millions of times (during a sort, for example). The proper implementations show the private data members directly compared.

```
bool operator == (const bankAccount& left, const bankAccount& right)
{
  return left.my_name == right.my_name;  // Reference members directly
}

bool operator < (const bankAccount& left, const bankAccount& right)
{
  return left.my_name < right.my_name;  // Avoid function-call overhead
}
```

Calling the accessor member function is no longer necessary because `friend` functions can access private data members. The scope of private data members extends to `friend` functions.

However, defining == and < for each of your state objects is not enough for the C++ standard containers and algorithms such as `sort` and `find`. The libraries may often use other operators such as `!=`. In order to prepare state objects such as `bankAccounts` for future use, all six equality and relational operators are overloaded to compare two `bankAccount` objects in a variety of expressions (see `baccount.cpp`).

Self-Check

18-2 Overload < to return true when one `weeklyEmp` object has an hourly rate less than the object to the right of <. (*Note:* You will need a `friend` function—because there is no accessor for hours.)

18.3 Overloading = for Classes with Pointer Data Members

Consider the following program. Does b2 really equal b1?

```
// Demonstrate that one bag can be assigned to another
#include <iostream>
using namespace std;

typedef int BAG_ELEMENT_TYPE;
#include "bag"  // Does not have a pointer data member; vector
                // defines =

void show(const bag& b)
{
  for(b.first(); ! b.isDone(); b.next())
  {
     cout << b.currentItem() << " ";
  }
  cout << endl;
}

int main()
{
  bag b1;
  bag b2;
  for(int j = 0; j < 6; j++)
  {
    b1.add(j);
  }

  b2 = b1;
  // b2 is exactly like b1, because vector overloads = (assignment)

  cout << "b1: ";
  show(b1);
  cout << "b2: ";
  show(b2);

  cout << "This program runs fine.";

  return 0;
}
```

OUTPUT

```
b1: 0 1 2 3 4 5
b2: 0 1 2 3 4 5
This program runs fine.
```

The answer is yes. On the other hand, the following program will fail using the current implementation of the generic `bag` class from `"genbag"`:

```
// Demonstrate that one generic bag cannot be assigned to another
#include <iostream>
using namespace std;
#include "genbag"  // Has a pointer private data member

void show(bag<int> b)
{
  for(b.first(); ! b.isDone(); b.next())
  {
    cout << b.currentItem() << " ";
  }
  cout << endl;
}

int main()
{
  bag <int> b1;
  bag <int> b2;

  // Initialize with silly data
  for(int j = 0; j < 6; j++)
  {
    b1.add(j);
  }

  b2 = b1;
  // b2 won't be b1 until = is overloaded

  cout << "b1: ";
  show(b1);
  cout << "b2: ";
  show(b2);

  cout << "Program bombs!";

  return 0;
}
```

OUTPUT

```
b1: 0 1 2 3 4 5
b2: 0 1 2 3 4 5
<ERROR>
```

This second program with the generic `bag` generated the same output, but then it bombed while displaying `b2`!

The difference relates to the underlying structure that stores the items in the collection. Recall that the `bag` class from `#include "bag"` uses a `vector` to store the items. But the generic `bag` class from `#include "genbag"` uses a pointer to address the first memory location.

When this assignment statement executes with the generic `bag`:

```
b2 = b1;
```

the default memberwise assignment operation takes over. The generic `bag` fails because only the address of the first `bag` element gets copied. And that data member is a pointer. The `bag` class with the `vector` data member works fine because the `vector` overloads the assignment operator. The `vector` = operator function copies all elements after separate memory is allocated for the left operand. Here is the overloaded assignment operator for the `vector` class that comes with this textbook (the C++ standard `vector` implements = quite differently).

```
// This operator function is defined inside the vector class
// definition. It is a vector member function.

vector& operator = (const vector<VectorElementType>& right)
{
   if( this != &right )  // Skip deleting when aVec == aVec
   {
     // Deallocate unneeded memory (x is a pointer to a collection)
     delete [] x;

     // Copy the capacity data member
     this->my_capacity = right.my_capacity;

     // Allocate precisely correct amount of memory to make copy
     this->x = new VectorElementType [this->my_capacity];

     // Copy the individual items from the right to the left
     for(int j = 0; j < this->my_capacity; j++)
     {
       this->x[j] = right.x[j];
     }
   }
   return *this;
}
```

The assignment operator differs from other binary operators such as `!=` and `<` in that there is only one parameter in the heading (`right`). The other parameter is the object to the left of =, which is also known as `this`. The = operator function is implemented as a `vector` member function.

The binary = operator works because the left operand always has access to the hidden pointer named `this`. In fact, every object has access to `this`. `this` contains the address of the object. So in the assignment statement

```
vector <int> aVec(20, 0);
vector <int> anotherVec(50, -1);
aVec = anotherVec;
```

`this` is the address of `aVec`. The `vector` itself is dereferenced as `*this`.

The logical expression in the `if` statement compares `this` with the address of the right operand as follows:

```
if( this != &right )  // Don't do anything when aVec = anotherVec;
```

This guarded action prevents destruction of the object on the left just in case it is the same as the object on the right. `this` contains the address of the object to the left of =, and `&right` returns the address of the operand to the right. If they are equal, as shown in the next picture, the function will not destroy the object to the right of =.

Figure 18.1. *When one object is assigned to the same object*

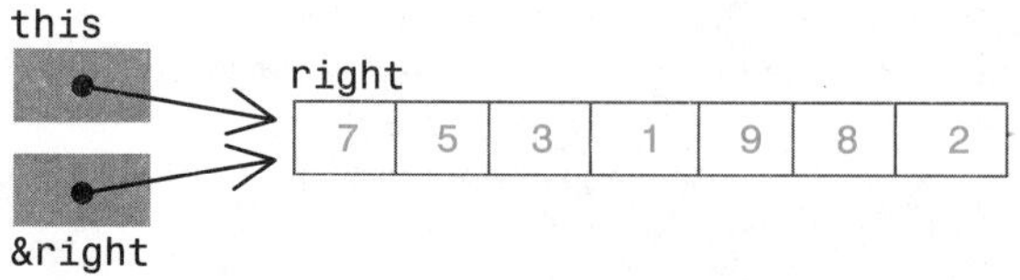

This situation would probably not be done intentionally, but the guarded action is necessary just in case a programmer assigns an object to itself. It is more likely that the object to the right of = is a different object, but you can't count on it. Let's look at what happens when a `vector` is assigned to a different `vector`. In this case, the object to the left is released back to the free store with this statement in `vector::operator =`:

```
delete [ ] x;
```

The same expression could have been written like this (`this->x` is equivalent to `x`):

```
delete [ ] this->x;
```

Next, the capacity of the right operand is copied into the object on the left; a statement that could also have been written like this:

```
this->my_capacity = right.my_capacity;
```

Then the precise amount of memory gets allocated for the left operand with the statement that could have been written like this:

```
this->x = new VectorElementType [this->my_capacity];
```

Next, every element in the right operand is copied into the left operand with code that could have been written like this:

```
for(int j = 0; j < this->my_capacity; j++)
{
  this->x[j] = right.x[j];
}
```

And finally, in all cases, `vector::operator =` returns a reference to the operand on the left of = and allows for chained assignments like this:

```
aVec = anotherVec = aVec = anotherVec;
```

Recall that the dereference operator (`*`) returns the object stored at the address in the pointer object that follows. Therefore, this statement:

```
return *this;
```

returns the object to the left of =. Although you may not use chained `vector` assignments very often, returning the assigned object makes `vector` assignments consistent with all other assignments (recall that `x = 1.5;` returns 1.5). Assignment operations return the value assigned to the object to the left of =.

The function heading for `vector` assignments is shown once again. It has a return type that is a reference to an object, rather than a return to the object itself.

```
vector& vector::operator = (const vector<VectorElementType>& right)
```

This function could return the entire vector. However, since vector objects are usually big, the function returns a reference to the vector. This saves the time of copying all vector elements. It is more efficient. This is the same reason the vector to the right of = is passed by reference. Making the parameter const prevents accidental modification of the object on the right of =.

18.3.1 The string Assignment Operation

The string class that comes with this textbook also overloads =. The string class has a char* data member and uses dynamic memory allocation to ensure safe, efficient use of memory. Therefore, during assignment, the data pointed to by that pointer must be carefully copied from the string expression to the right of = into newly allocated memory for the operand on the left of =. Whereas the vector = operator copies items with a for loop, the string class employs the standard strcpy function from <cstring>.

```
string& string::operator = (const string& right)
{
  if(this != (&right))
  {
    delete [] my_chars;  // Deallocate memory of old string object
    my_len = right.my_len;
    my_chars = new char[my_len + 1];
    strcpy(my_chars, right.my_chars);
  }
  return *this;
}
```

As with vector, the comparison (this != &right) avoids the damage that could occur when assigning one object to the same object; the object to the right would be destroyed before being copied to the object on the left of =. Otherwise, the string to the left is destroyed with delete. Then there is enough memory to hold the characters of the right operand. The characters are copied. In either case, the string::operator = function returns a reference to the string to allow chained assignments like this:

```
string a, b, c, d;
a = b = c = d = "equal";
```

18.4 Developing the complex Class

This section presents the development of a complex number class. As a prelude to the implementation of this class, the complex number system is reviewed. As you read through this introduction, think of a complex number as one point on the Cartesian (complex) plane. The point is usually written as (1, 2) where 1 is the number on the real axis and 2 is a value on the imaginary axis.

The `complex` class will be used to provide simple ways to find the center of a line and the center of a triangle. Before embarking upon this discussion of complex numbers, examine the following program and discover that the center of a line represented by two points, `a` and `b`, is the average of those two complex numbers: ((0, 0) + (1, 1)) / 2 = (0.5, 0.5). The center of a triangle represented by points `a`, `b`, and `c` is the average of those three complex numbers.

```
// This program assumes that "ltcomplex" has complex class and
// division and addition operators (/ and +) have been overloaded
#include <iostream>
using namespace std;

#include "ltcomplex"  // For an author-supplied complex class

int main()
{
  complex a(0, 0);
  complex b(1, 1);
  complex lineCenter, triangleCenter;

  lineCenter = (a + b) / 2.0;
  cout << "\nCenter of the line (" << a << " + " << b << ") / 2 "
       << endl;
  cout << lineCenter << endl;

  complex c(0.75, 2.15);
  triangleCenter = (a + b + c) / 3.0;
  cout << "\nCenter of triangle ("
       << a << " + " << b << " + " << c << ") / 3" << endl;
  cout << triangleCenter << endl;

  return 0;
}
```

Output

```
Center of the line ((0, 0) + (1, 1)) / 2
(0.5, 0.5)
Center of triangle ((0, 0) + (1, 1) + (0.75, 2.15)) / 3
(0.583333, 1.05)
```

Notice that all complex numbers are displayed here as two numbers separated by `,` and enclosed in `(` and `)`. This is made possible by overloading the `<<` operator for output.

18.4.1 Analysis

The following specification of a complex number class is well short of a full complex class which would define subtraction, multiplication, and many other functions such as absolute value, complex conjugate, square root, and so on. (The `lt` in `ltcomplex` stands for "lite.") This keeps the discussion shorter and simpler. And the additional operations could be completed as programming projects.

Problem: Implement a complex number class that computes the average of a set of complex numbers as easily as if they were of a primitive numeric class like `int` or double. Users should be able to construct complex numbers and perform complex addition and division on those complex objects. Users should also have I/O operations available.

The set of real numbers contains solutions to many, but not all, equations. For example, the real solution of the equation $x^3 = -1$ is -1. On the other hand, there is no real solution to the equation $x^2 = -1$ since the square of any real number is always positive. To work around this, mathematicians invented the complex number system. The workaround involves using the symbol i as the solution of the equation $x^2 = -1$ such that i = sqrt(-1) or $i^2 = -1$. A complex number is expressed in the form $a + bi$ where a and b are floating-point numbers. For the complex number

$c1 = a + bi$

a is the real part and b is the imaginary part. But a number such as $a + bi$ where $b = 0.0$ has a real number equivalent since there is no imaginary part. Stated another way, the coefficient of i in this case is zero.

The complex numbers $3 + 2i$, $-2 + i$, $3.5 + 0i$, $1.5 - 2i$, and $-3 - 3i$ are written here as points on the complex plane:

FIGURE 18.2

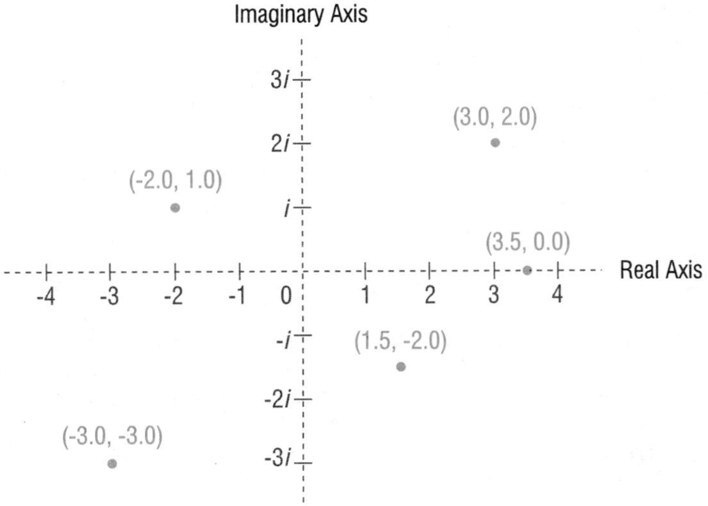

Complex arithmetic defines many of the familiar arithmetic operators. For example, addition and division operations have different meanings. Complex addition and division follow these rules (the subtraction and multiplication operations discussed later are left as a programming project).

COMPLEX ADDITION

$(a + bi) + (c + di) = (a + c) + (b + d)i$

$(3 + 4i) + (5 + 6i) = (3 + 5) + (4 + 6)i = 8 + 10i$

$= (8, 10)$

COMPLEX DIVISION (ASSUMING $c^2 + d^2 \mathrel{!}= 0$)

$$(a + bi) / (c + di) = \frac{a * c + b * d}{c^2 + d^2} + \frac{b * c - a * d}{c^2 + d^2} i \quad \text{when } c^2 + d^2 \mathrel{!}= 0$$

Example: $(3 + 4i) / (5 + 6i) =$

$$\frac{3 * 5 + 4 * 6}{5^2 + 6^2} + \frac{4 * 5 - 3 * 6}{5^2 + 6^2} i = \frac{15 + 24}{25 + 36} + \frac{20 - 18}{25 + 36} i = \frac{39}{61} + \frac{2}{61} i =$$

$0.63934 + 0.03279i =$

$(0.63934, 0.03279)$

18.4.2 Design

To perform tasks requiring complex arithmetic, design complex objects that handle addition and division as easily as if the operands were `int`s or `double`s. A less desirable design is to keep track of the four components involved—those four objects indicated by `a`, `b`, `c`, and `d`. With this design, the user is always responsible for making sure that the arithmetic is done properly. This weaker design does not take advantage of the abstraction made possible by implementing a complex class as a natural part of the language. For example, without a complex class the programmer must remember the complex arithmetic rules. The programmer must code the operations, as shown in a program that is more complex than it needs to be:

```
// This is the difficult way of doing things. Without a complex
// class, programmers must remember many details (especially with
// /). Also, this approach increases the probability of errors.
#include <iostream>
#include <cmath>
using namespace std;

int main()
{ // Find the center of a line given two points
  double a, b, c, d;
  a = 0.0;
  b = 0.0;
  c = 1.0;
  d = 1.0;
  // First, add two complex numbers
  double realSum = a + c;
  double imaginarySum = b + d;
  // The sum is now  (realSum + imaginarySum * i),
  // so to divide by (   2    +       0      * i)
  // four numbers are needed:
  a = realSum;
  b = imaginarySum;
  c = 2.0;  // c and d represent the real and imaginary
  d = 0.0;  // parts of the divisor

  // Determine the common denominator as c squared plus d squared
  double denominator = pow (c, 2) + pow (d, 2);

  // Now create a new complex number
  double numerator1 = (a * c + b * d);
  double numerator2 = (b * c - a * d);
  double real = numerator1 / denominator;
  double imag = numerator2 / denominator;
```

```
  // Output
  cout << "Center of line: " << "(" << real << ", " << imag << ")";
  return 0;
}
```

OUTPUT

```
Center of line: (0.5, 0.5)
```

With a well-designed `complex` class, the much simpler abstract view of complex numbers could look like this:

```
#include <iostream>
using namespace std;
#include "ltcomplex"   // For a lite complex class
// Note: C++ provides a complete complex class with #include
// <complex>. Construct those complex objects like this:
// complex<double> c(4.5, -19);

int main()
{
  complex c1(0.0, 0.0);
  complex c2(1.0, 1.0);

  cout << "Center of line: " << (c1 + c2) / 2.0 << endl;

  return 0;
}
```

OUTPUT

```
Center of line: (0.5, 0.5)
```

This second, more elegant solution uses operator overloading to hide many of the details from the user and to provide appropriate operations such as `+` and `/`. This makes complex objects as easy to use as `int` and `double` objects. The second solution is the preferred method, at least from the user's perspective, but it requires a class definition and member function implementations. This time however, some of the member functions will be overloaded operator functions. Once a `complex` class is completed, it exists for continued use. The goal here is to implement a complex number class that will be reused. This example also places operator overloading into context while illustrating the importance of abstraction in computer science.

Although there are many other complex operations required for a full `complex` class, the complex number specification restricts the operations to two basic arithmetic operations (addition and division). The constructor functions provide easy initialization. There will also be a member function for displaying a complex number as shown in the preceding output and a member function for reading complex numbers.

18.4.3 Implementation

A complex number has a real part and an imaginary part. The real part could be represented as a float, but to obtain maximum precision a `double` data member is preferred. The imaginary part is also best represented by a `double` that acts as the coefficient of *i*. For example, the complex number `a + b`*i* is represented by `a` and `b` as `doubles`. Two private data members, identified as `my_real` and `my_imag`, successfully represent a complex number.

The `complex` class will also return the real and imaginary parts—`my_real` and `my_imag`. There are applications for which it is necessary to reference only the real part or only the imaginary part of a `complex` object.

As for the constructor(s), a design decision is made to allow objects that cannot be assigned a value until later. This is accomplished by adding a default constructor for instantiations such as `complex c1;`. Another constructor is required for complete initialization, such as `complex c2(1.5, 2.5)`. Another constructor will be added to allow for a second default argument of 0.0 and constructions such as `c3(2.0)`. This construction is a complex number with the real equivalent of 2.0 + 0.0*i*. This leads to a class definition with five public member functions and two private data members.

```
class complex {
public:
//--constructors
  complex();                  // complex a;
  complex(double initReal);   // complex b(1.0);
  complex(double initReal,    // complex c(1.0. 2.0);
          double initImag);

//--accessors
  double real();
  double imag();

//--operator functions
  friend complex  operator +  (complex left, complex right);
```

```
    friend complex  operator /  (complex left, complex right);
    friend ostream& operator << (ostream& os, complex right);
    friend istream& operator >> (istream& is, complex& right);

  private:
    double my_real;
    double my_imag;
  };
```

With arguments supplied, the default constructor `complex::complex()` initializes the real and imaginary parts of the class, arbitrarily making the complex value (0.0, 0.0). This constructor is called when no arguments are supplied. It uses the initialization list introduced in Chapter 16.

```
complex::complex() : my_real(0.0), my_imag(0.0)
{
}
```

The constructor with one parameter initializes complex numbers with 0.0 as the imaginary part. When there is no imaginary part (`my_imag == 0.0`), the complex number resides on the real number line—the x-axis of the complex plane.

```
complex::complex(double initReal)
: my_real(initReal), my_imag(0.0);
{
}
```

When two arguments are supplied at instantiation, the real and imaginary parts are initialized with the values of the first and second arguments, respectively.

```
complex::complex(double initReal, double initImag)
: my_real(initReal), my_imag(initImag)
{
}
```

In summary, complex objects are constructed in these three ways:

```
complex a;             // my_real = 0.0, my_imag = 0.0
complex b(1.0);        // my_real = 1.0, my_imag = 0.0
complex c(2.5, 3.5);   // my_real = 2.5, my_imag = 3.5
```

The other two accessor functions simply return the private data.

```
double complex::real() const
{
  return my_real;
}

double complex::imag() const
{
  return my_imag;
}
```

18.4.4 Overloading the + Operator for Complex Addition

The `complex` class should be intuitive and easy to use. Overloading operators such as +, /, <<, and = for `complex` objects will help. For example, instead of requiring the users of our class to remember to make two assignments (one to the real part, another to the imaginary part), the following assignment is preferable:

```
complex a;
a = complex(1, 4);
```

This assignment is allowed because the C++ compiler automatically provides a memberwise = operator. We don't need to overload = because there is no pointer data member.

Other operators such as + and / require programmer-defined operator functions. This relieves the user of the `complex` class of having to remember all the rules of complex division. The following overloads / and + while allowing expressions that are much more intuitive:

```
complex center, a(0, 0), b(1, 1);
center = (a + b) / 2;
```

Users of the class can immediately recognize the meanings of these three operations (=, +, and /). Remember that binary operators are treated as functions with two arguments. For example, the declaration to implement the + function to add two complex numbers could look like this:

```
complex operator + (complex leftOperand, complex rightOperand);
```

This function prototype is called for expressions such as the following (assuming `a` and `b` are `complex` objects):

```
a + b        b + a        a + complex(1, 2)        complex(1, 2) + b
```

In general, overloading operators requires a function prototype containing the reserved word `operator`. The reserved word `operator` must be preceded by a return type such as `int`, `double`, `string`, or `complex` and followed by one of the "overloadable" C++ operators such as `+`, `/`, `=`, or `<<`. After the operator, the left and right operands are declared as parameters. Here is the general form again:

return-type `operator` *an-operator* `( const` *class*`&` *left* `, const` *class*`&` *right* `);`

The parameter list for binary operators declared outside a class must contain exactly two parameters. The first parameter represents the operand to the left of the operator and the second parameter represents the operand to the right of the operator. For example, when given an implementation such as this:

```
complex operator + (complex left, complex right)
{ // Complex addition
  // (a + bi) + (c + di)  =  (a + c) + (b + d)i
  double tempReal = left.my_real + right.my_real; // Real part
  double tempImag = left.my_imag + right.my_imag; // Imaginary part
  complex temp(tempReal, tempImag);
  return temp;
}
```

and the following expression is encountered:

```
complex(1, 2) + complex(3, 4)
```

The parameter named `left` is given a copy of `complex(1, 2)` and the parameter identified as `right` becomes `complex(3, 4)`. The rules of complex addition are applied and a temporary `complex` value (`temp`) is created using the `complex` constructor. This temporary `complex` value becomes the value that is returned to the point of the complex addition.

Notice that the code inside the `+` operator function refers directly to the data members and avoids making several calls of the `real()` and `imag()` accessor functions. Declaring `operator +` as a `friend` function made this more-efficient implementation possible.

C++ also allows for implicit conversions (number promotions). For example, when the following expression is encountered, the left operand (`2`) is implicitly converted into a complex (with 0.0 as the coefficient of the imaginary part) by calling the constructor function with one parameter:

```
2 + a    // 2 is replaced by complex(2.0, 0.0);
b / 3.0  // 3.0 is replaced by complex(3.0, 0.0);
```

18.4.5 Overloading the / Operator for Complex Division

Because / is a binary operator, a function designed to overload / for complex division also requires two parameters. So the function heading is very similar to binary +. In both functions, the return type is `complex` since both addition and division of complex numbers result in complex numbers. The algebra used to do division is more involved than addition, so it is simplified by calculating the denominator and numerators separately before creating and returning the temporary complex number `temp`. The resulting complex value is again created via the constructor function.

```
complex operator / (complex left, complex right)
{ // Complex division:
  //                                 a * c + b * d     b * c - a * d
  // (a + b * i) / (c + d * i) = ------------- + ------------- * i
  //                                 c * c + d * d     c * c + d * d

  double den;        // c squared + d squared (denominator)
  double nuR, nuI;   // The numerators: R for Real, I for Imaginary

  den = pow(right.my_real, 2) + pow(right.my_imag, 2);
  nuR = (left.my_real * right.my_real) + (left.my_imag * right.my_imag);
  nuI = (left.my_imag * right.my_real) - (left.my_real * right.my_imag);

  // Create and return a new complex number
  complex temp(nuR / den, nuI / den);
  return temp;
}
```

The following program shows complex division with two `complex` operands and two divisions in which implicit conversion is applied to the operand `2`.

```
#include <iostream>
using namespace std;
#include "ltcomplex"

int main()
{
  complex a(1.0, 1.0);
  complex b(2.0, 2.0);

  cout << b / a << endl;
  cout << a / b << endl;
  cout << a / 2 << endl;  // Implicit conversion from int to
                          // complex

  return 0;
}
```

OUTPUT

```
(2, 0)
(0.5, 0)
(0.5, 0.5)
(0.5, -0.5)
```

18.4.6 Overloading the << Operator for Complex Output

To make the `complex` class even easier to use, overload the output operator (<<). The programmer could show a complex number as 1 + 5i, 1.000 + 5.000i, or, as was previously shown, (2, 0)—any way desired. As with the + and / operators, the `stream` insertion operator << is also a binary operator—one that requires two operands. While it may be obvious that the right operand should be a complex number, what may not be so obvious is that the left operator must be a reference to output streams—an `ostream` object.

```
cout << c1;  // Left operand is an ostream object
```

The identifier `cout` is just one example of an `ostream` object. With `#include <iostream>`, `cout` is automatically initialized and associated with the computer screen. Whenever `ostream` objects occur as a parameter or a return type, it is essential that they be passed by reference, rather than by value. Since there are updates that occur behind the scenes during input and output operations, it is necessary to make sure the object is allowed to change. You should pass `ostream` by reference for every << operator overload. Here is the function heading as declared in `ltcomplex.h`:

```
//--operator function
friend ostream& operator << (ostream& os, complex right);
```

Now in the << operator function shown next, `os` is a parameter declared as an `ostream` object. When `cout` is passed by reference in a statement like this:

```
cout << complex(1.0, 2.0);
```

any change to `left` alters the associated argument, which in this case is `cout`.

```
ostream& operator << (ostream& os, complex right)
{
  left << "(" << right.my_real << ", " << right.my_imag << ")";
  return os;
}
```

After the first statement of this overloading function executes with a statement like this:

```
complex c1(2.0, 3.0);
cout << c1;  // Call ostream& operator << (ostream&, complex)
```

the function call `cout << c1;` displays these expressions:

1. An opening paren—`(`
2. The real part—`2`
3. A comma and a space
4. The imaginary part—`3`
5. The closing paren—`)`

So the statement `cout << c1` generates this output:

```
(2, 3)
```

Any change to the output stream associated with the left operand (`cout`, in this case) makes the proper change to the correct stream. Any change to `left` in the function is a change to `cout` where the function was called because the parameter (`os`) is associated with the argument (`cout`) by reference (`&`). This is necessary to allow for multiple insertions of `complex` objects. Chain insertions are made possible by returning a reference to the `ostream` object involved in the original function call. Upon close examination of this operator function, you will notice a reference (`&`) in the return type:

```
ostream& operator << (...
```

The value that is returned to the point of the function call (`cout << c1`) is the modified output `stream` object passed as the first parameter `cout`. The return value is used as the next parameter for another insertion operation (<<). Whenever there is more than one << operator in an output statement, the expressions are inserted into the output stream in a left-to-right order. The reference in the return type is necessary to allow the chaining of outputs as in the following expression (`c1`, `c2`, and `c3` are `complex` objects):

```
cout << c1 << c2 << c3;
```

The first function call is `cout << c1`. In order for subsequent << operations, the value that replaces (`cout << c1`) must be a reference to the same output stream.

This allows for a second function call (`ostream& << c2`) which in turn allows for a third function call (`ostream& << c3`). The entire expression can also be written with parentheses indicating that there are three function calls to the `ostream& operator <<` function.

```
( ( (cout << c1) << c2)  << c3 );  // Insert c1 and return cout
       ↓
( (   cout     << c2)  << c3 );    // Insert c2 and return cout
           ↓
(          cout        << c3 );    // Insert c3 and return cout
           ↓
           cout                    // Return value ignored
```

18.4.7 Overloading the >> Operator for Complex Input

Overloading >> allows input of complex values. To do this, overload >> such that the real and imaginary components of a complex number are entered as two consecutive numbers. This code:

```
complex c1;
cout << "\nEnter a complex number: ";
cin >> c1;
```

requires a dialogue such as this:

```
Enter a complex number: 3.75  -1.5
```

One difference between overloading << and >> is consideration of the class from which `cin` and `cout` are constructed. The following function heading uses `istream` in place of `ostream`:

```
//--operator function
friend istream& operator >> (istream& is, complex& right);
```

One other difference is the fact that the right operand, a `complex` object, must be passed by reference. This makes sense because the state of the right operand is supposed to change. Without the reference before `left`, the expression `cin >> c1` would call this function but not alter the state of `c1`.

```
istream& operator >> (istream& left, complex& right)
{
  double x, y;

  // Get two numbers
  is >> x >> y;
```

```
  // Now modify the right argument (c1) in the call cin >> c1;
  right = complex(x, y);

  return is;
};
```

As was the case for overloading <<, the return type for the function that overloads >> must be a reference to the input stream. The reference in the return type (`istream&`) allows the chaining of extraction operations as in this expression:

```
cin >> c1 >> c2 >> c3;
```

The return type of the >> operator is a reference to the same input stream passed as the first parameter (`istream& is`). The first function call (`cin >> c1`) returns a reference to `cin`—the left operand for `istream& >> c2`. This is the second function call which again returns `istream&` to allow output of the third complex number `c3`. The entire expression can also be written with parentheses indicating the evaluation.

```
(((cin >> c1) >> c2) >> c3);
```

Self-Check

18-3 Determine the complex numbers that result from each of the following arithmetic operations.

-a (1.0, 3.0) + (2.0, 4.0)

-b (4.0, 3.0) + (-1, -1)

-c (-1.0, -1.0) + (-2.0, -2.0)

-d (4.0, 4.0) / (1.0, 1.0)

18-4 What error would you expect with the operation (2.0, 3.0) / (0.0, 0.0)?

18-5 Write the output of the following program:

```
#include <iostream>
using namespace std;
#include "ltcomplex"
int main()
{
  complex c1(3.5, 6.25);
  cout << c1.real() << "   " << c1.imag();
  return 0;
}
```

18-6 Write the output of the following program:

```
#include <iostream>
using namespace std;
#include "ltcomplx"
int main()
{
  complex c2(-1.0, -2.0);
  c2 = c2 + 6.0;
  cout << c2;
  return 0;
}
```

Chapter Summary

- This chapter began with the overloaded `bankAccount` operators `!=`, `==`, and `<`. When a class overloads `<`, it can have the `sort` member function applied to it. When a class overloads `!=` or `==`, it can be used in the `find` function from `<algorithm>`.
- The C++ standard may require that your state objects define many or all of the relational operators.
- A binary operator function differs from other function definitions in the following ways:
  - It uses the keyword `operator`.
  - The operator being overloaded is part of the function heading.
  - The operand to the left of the operator is sent to the function as parameter number 1.
  - The operand to the right of the operator is sent to the function as parameter number 2.

  Here is an example:

  ```
  bool operator < (const bankAccount& left, const bankAccount& right)
  ```

- The preceding function gets called whenever `bankAccount` objects are found both to the left and the right of the `<` operator. Here are some examples:

  ```
  bankAccount b1("bob", 120.00);
  bankAccount b2("charlie", 220.00);
  if( b1 < b2 )
    cout << "true\n";
  if( b1 < bankAccount("alice", 200) )
  ```

```
  cout << "false\n";
if( bankAccount("alice", 200) < b1 )
  cout << "true\n";
```

- This chapter also introduced complex numbers along with some overloaded complex operators. By no means complete, the `complex` class shows how much simpler complex arithmetic can be.

Exercises

1. Write the overloaded free function < so that one `libraryBook` object is less than another if the title of the left operand is less than the title of the right `libraryBook` operand. Use your current versions of `libbook.h` and `libbook.cpp`.

2. When implemented, which functions will have access to the private data members a and b? Which functions will not?

```
class X {
public:
  void one();
  friend void two();
private:
  int a, b;
};

void three();
void four();
```

3. Define expressions equivalent to the following using only the > operator.

```
a > b   // Already defined
a < b   // Redefine without using <
a >= b  // Redefine without using >=
```

4. Define expressions equivalent to the following using only the == operator.

```
a == b   // Already defined
a != b   // Redefine without using !=
```

5. Overload = for the generic `bag` such that all elements are copied and no errors occur.

6. Rewrite the function that overloads `<<` for `complex` objects such that output appears without parentheses and with the symbol *i*. The `+` or `-` operator should always be between the real and imaginary parts. These statements:

```
complex c1(1.1, 3.5);
cout << c1;
```

should generate this output:

```
1.1+3.5i
```

Programming Tips

1. Implement a minimal public interface that will allow your classes to be reused.

If you want to design your classes for reuse, there are several things that should be done to prepare them for general use. These considerations allow client code to pass your objects by value, have `vector`s of your classes, let your objects be sorted with `list::sort` and `vector::sort`, and so on. In summary, every class without a pointer should have these things:

* a default constructor to allow for collections of that class and guaranteed initialization of key data members
* other constructors with one or more parameters for easy initialization
* overloaded relational operators to allow the collection to be searched and sorted by standard containers (`vector` and `list` for example)

Additionally, every class with a pointer must also add

* a copy constructor to allow passing by value
* a destructor
* an overloaded assignment operator to prevent shallow copying

2. Many of the class examples in this book do not follow the preceding heuristic.

Even though many classes of this book do not implement the minimal public interface, they could be made to in order to be useful. Some of the essentials for allowing reuse of these classes were omitted simply because the topic had not yet been covered.

3. When writing operator functions, both parameters might as well be const reference parameters.

That is if you want efficiency and you don't want to accidentally change the arguments (the operands). The `&` is for efficiency. The `const` is for safety because the `&` is there. For example, all `string` comparisons pass the `string` object by const reference.

```
// From the file ltstring.h
bool operator  < (const string& left, const string& right);
bool operator <= (const string& left, const string& right);
bool operator  > (const string& left, const string& right);
bool operator >= (const string& left, const string& right);
bool operator == (const string& left, const string& right);
bool operator != (const string& left, const string& right);
```

4. Use the standard C++ `complex` class if you have it.

The standard library includes a `complex` class that has numerous functions. There are many more functions. Here are the functions made available with `#include <complex>`.

```
abs arg  conjg cos cosh exp imag log log10 norm
operator!= operator* operator+ operator- operator/
operator<<  operator== operator>> polar pow
```

5. If you use the standard `complex` class, realize it is a generic class. Use `double` to store the real part and the imaginary part.

Here is a program that simply outputs a standard `complex` object.

```
#include <complex>
#include <iostream>
using namespace std;
int main()
{
  complex<double> a(2, 3);
  cout << a << endl;
  return 0;
}
```

OUTPUT

```
(2, 3)
```

Programming Projects

18A Overload < and == for `track` Objects

Add `friend` functions so `track` objects can be sorted and searched within `list` containers. Define == to mean that the `track` titles are equal. Define < to return true if the left operand's track number (9) is less than the right's (10). The following program should generate the output shown:

```
// File name: test18a.cpp
#include "track"
int main()
{
  track a("Shape of my Heart" , 4*60+38, 4, 9);
  track b("Something the Boy Said" , 5*60+28, 4, 10);

  if(a < b)
     cout << "a < b" << endl;
  if(! (a == b));
    cout << "a != b" << endl;

  return 0;
}
```

OUTPUT

```
a < b
a != b
```

18B Make `track` Containable

Define all six relational operators for `track` and verify that they can work with the standard `list` class. The following program should generate the output shown:

```
// File name: test18b.cpp
// Unless you overload < <= > >= != and ==, you will get many errors
#include <list>
#include <iostream>
using namespace std;
#include "track"

int main()
{
  list <track> aCD;
  list <track>::iterator i;

  aCD.push_back( track("Something the Boy Said" , 5*60+28, 4, 10) );
  aCD.push_back( track("Shape of my Heart" , 4*60+38, 4, 9) );
  aCD.sort();  // Sorted by track numbers, the fourth argument 10 and 9
  for(i = aCD.begin(); i != aCD.end(); i++)
  {
```

```
    cout << (*i).title() << " " << (*i).trackNumber() <<  endl ;
  }

  return 0;
}
```

OUTPUT

```
Shape of my Heart 9
Something the Boy Said 10
```

18C Make libraryBook Containable

Add all six relational operators to `libraryBook` and verify that they work. Write a program that allows `libraryBook` objects to be sorted with `vector::sort` and searched with `find`.

18D bag::operator =

Make it possible to assign one generic `bag` to another. The following program should generate the output shown:

```
// File name: test18d.cpp
#include <iostream>
using namespace std;
#include "track"
#include "genbag"

int main()
{
  track a("Shape of my Heart", 4*60+38, 4, 9);
  track b("Something the Boy Said", 5*60+28, 4, 10);
  bag <track> aBag;

  aBag.add(a);
  aBag.add(b);

  bag <track> anotherBag;

  // Assign one bag to another
  anotherBag = aBag;

  track current;
  for( anotherBag.first(); ! anotherBag.isDone(); anotherBag.next() )
  {
    current = anotherBag.currentItem();
    cout << current.title() << endl;
  }

  return 0;
}
```

OUTPUT

```
Shape of my Heart
Something the Boy Said
```

18E Overload Complex - and *

Modify the `complex` class by overloading the - operator for complex subtraction and * for complex multiplication. Test your program by hand-calculating some complex expressions and comparing them with C++ program output.

Complex Subtraction:

$(a + bi) - (c + di) = (a - c) + (b - d)i$

$(3 + 4i) - (5 + 6i) = (3 - 5) + (4 - 6)i = -2 + -2i$

$= (-2, -2)$

Complex Multiplication:

$(a + bi) * (c + di) = (ac - bd) + (ad + bc)i$

Example: $(2 + i) * (3 - 2i) =$

$2 * 3 + 2 * (-2i)i + i * 3 + i * (-2i)$

$6 - 4i + 3i - 2i^2$ (replace i^2 with -1)

$6 - i - 2 * (-1)$

$6 - (-2) - i$

$= (8, -1)$

18F Complex Roots

Write a function that returns the complex roots of a quadratic equation using the quadratic formula

$$\frac{-b \pm \sqrt{b^2 - 4ac}}{2a}$$

where a, b, and c represent the coefficients of a quadratic equation in the form $ax^2 + bx + c$. If the discriminant $(b * b - 4 * a * c)$ is positive, two distinct real roots exist. If the discriminant equals 0.0, then two nondistinct real roots exist. In both of these cases, the imaginary part is 0.0, indicating that the roots are real. If the discriminant is negative, two distinct complex roots exist. In this third case, factor out i (sqrt(-1)) by taking the absolute value of the discriminant before applying the square root function. In all cases, the roots should be returned as complex numbers. Real roots have 0.0 as the imaginary part; imaginary roots have nonzero coefficients of i. Use the quadratic equation for real roots with 0.0 as the imaginary part. Call the one argument constructor with

```
r1 = complex( (-b + sqrt(disc)) / (2 * a) );
r2 = complex( (-b - sqrt(disc)) / (2 * a) );
```

For the nonreal roots, return these two complex numbers as the roots:

```
r1 = complex( -b / (2 * a), +sqrt(abs(disc)) / (2 * a) );
r2 = complex( -b / (2 * a), -sqrt(abs(disc)) / (2 * a) );
```

Use the following program and output as a test driver:

```
#include <iostream>
#include <cmath>
using namespace std;
#include "ltcomplex"  // For a "lite" complex class

// Include function roots here. Remember to use references
// for both complex parameters representing the roots.

int main()
{ // Test drive roots
  complex r1, r2;
  roots(1.0, 2.0, 3.0, r1, r2);
  cout << r1 << " and " << r2 << endl;
  roots(1.0, 0.0, -1.0, r1, r2);
  cout << r1 << " and " << r2 << endl;
  roots(1.0, 1.0, -6.0, r1, r2);
  cout << r1 << " and " << r2 << endl;
  roots(1.0, 1.0, 2.0, r1, r2);
  cout << r1 << " and " << r2 << endl;
  return 0;
}
```

OUTPUT

```
(1, 1.414214) and (-1, 1.414214)
(1, 0) and (-1, 0)
(2, 0) and (-3, 0)
(-0.5, 1.322876) and (-0.5, -1.322876)
```

18G Walking Drunkard Simulation

A walking drunkard is at the end of a dock. When this drunkard takes a step, there is only a 50% chance that he or she will step forward. At any given moment, the drunkard may step to the left, to the right, or even backward with these probabilities:

- 50% chance the drunkard steps forward
- 5% chance the drunkard steps backward
- 25% chance the drunkard steps to the left

* 20% chance (the remaining possibility) the drunkard steps to the right

By the end of this project, you will have written a program that simulates the drunkard's walk 20 times. The program must display the drunkard doing one of the following four things:

1. makes it to dry land
2. falls off the left edge of the dock
3. falls off the right edge of the dock
4. falls backward into the water

One way to solve this problem is to use the complex plane from (0, 0*i*) through (10, 0*i*) to represent the right edge of the dock. Also let (0, 10*i*) through (10, 10*i*) represent the left edge, (0, 0*i*) through (0, 10*i*) to represent the water edge, and (10, 0) though (10, 10) as the edge of the dock on the land side.

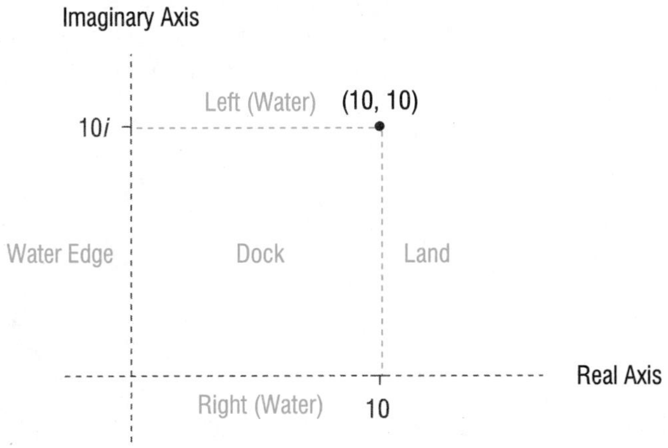

Begin by implementing one simulation. Begin a program that includes the files `<iostream>`, `<stdlib.h>` for `RAND_MAX` (or its equivalent), `"ltcomplex"`, and `"myfuns"`. Also begin the function `main` as shown next. The `int` objects `cutoffOne`, `cutoffTwo`, and `cutoffThree` are portions of the maximum pseudorandom `int` (`RAND_MAX`) used later to determine the direction in which the drunkard steps. For example, if the maximum random `int` is 32,767, the cut-offs can be determined as follows:

```
int cutoffOne = 0.5 * RAND_MAX;                    // 50% of all possible ints
int cutoffTwo = cutoffOne + 0.05 * RAND_MAX;       // 5% of all possible ints
int cutoffThree = cutoffTwo + 0.25 * RAND_MAX;     // 25% of all possible ints
// Any other pseudorandom number represents the 20% possibility that the
// step is right
```

Before going on, write a program that displays only the cut-offs. Verify that the `int` ranges represent the correct percentages of all `int`s from 0 to `RAND_MAX`. This can be done with these statements:

```
#include <iostream>
using namespace std;
#include <stdlib>  // For RAND_MAX
#include "compfun"  // For decimals(cout, 2)

int main()
{
  int cutoffOne = RAND_MAX * 0.50;
  int cutoffTwo = cutoffOne + 0.05 * RAND_MAX;
  int cutoffThree = cutoffTwo + 0.25 * RAND_MAX;

  decimals(cout, 2);
  cout <<  cutoffOne                 / double(RAND_MAX) << endl;
  cout << (cutoffTwo - cutoffOne)    / double(RAND_MAX) << endl;
  cout << (cutoffThree - cutoffTwo) / double(RAND_MAX) << endl;
  cout << (RAND_MAX - cutoffThree)   / double(RAND_MAX) << endl;

  return 0;
}
```

OUTPUT

```
0.50
0.05
0.25
0.20
```

- Do not proceed until you have identified the cut-offs. Do this by adding code to display the `int`s representing the cut-offs. Run the program and verify that the cut-offs are correct.
- Change the `main` function to simulate one drunkard's walk. If the random `int` is in the range of 0 through `cutoffOne`, simulate the drunkard walking forward by adding `complex(1, 0)` to the drunkard's position. Make similar adjustments to the position until the drunkard falls in the water or makes it to dry land. Make sure the proper message is displayed.
- Run this simulation 20 times, displaying the result.
- Does your output indicate a reasonable number of falls into the water and successful walks to land?

Chapter Nineteen

Doubly Subscripted Objects

`matrix` Objects

Summing Up

This chapter can be studied any time after Chapter 10, "Vectors," which introduced singly subscripted `vectors` for storing collections of objects. You should also now be familiar with class definitions and member function implementations (see Chapter 6); however, this is not absolutely necessary, as you should be able to understand the example that uses member functions. You are also expected to know how to read and implement nested `for` loops.

Coming Up

This chapter discusses a class that uses two subscripts to manage data logically stored in a tablelike format—in rows and columns. This proves useful for storing and managing data in applications such as electronic spreadsheets, games, topographical maps, and student record books and many other data best viewed as collections of rows and columns. After studying this chapter, you will be able to

- process tabular data
- perform row-by-row and column-by-column processing of tabular data
- declare primitive arrays with two or three subscripts
- manipulate the data of a visibility research study using a doubly subscripted (one for rows, one for columns) object

  Exercises and programming projects to reinforce doubly subscripted processing

19.1 `matrix` Data

Consider this table of data that represents a lab attendance sheet for 10 students over a 15-week semester.

FIGURE 19.1. *An attendance sheet*

Student	Week Number														
Number	0	1	2	3	4	5	6	7	8	9	10	11	12	13	14
0	1	1	1	1	1	0	1	1	1	1	1	1	1	0	1
1	1	1	1	0	1	1	1	1	1	1	1	1	1	1	1
2	1	1	1	1	1	1	1	0	1	1	1	1	1	1	1
3	1	1	1	1	1	1	1	1	1	1	1	1	1	1	1
4	1	1	1	1	1	1	1	1	0	1	1	0	1	1	1
5	1	0	1	0	1	1	1	0	1	1	1	1	1	0	0
6	1	1	1	1	1	1	1	1	1	1	1	1	1	1	1
7	0	1	1	0	1	1	1	1	1	1	0	1	1	1	1
8	1	1	1	1	1	1	1	1	1	1	1	1	1	1	1
9	1	1	1	1	1	1	1	1	1	1	1	1	1	1	1

1 represents attendance, 0 indicates absence.

This data could be processed in a variety of ways:

- Use column 5 as the attendance record for the sixth week.
- Use row 9 to determine the number of absences for the tenth student.
- Use the entire table to determine the ratio of class attendances to absences.
- Use the table to determine whether or not any student was present or absent for any recorded week.

19.1.1 Constructing `matrix` Objects as a `vector` of `vectors`

Data that conveniently present themselves in this tabular format are represented well with a `vector` of `vectors`, henceforth called a *matrix*. `matrix` objects can be constructed out of the standard `vector` class.

General Form 19.1. *A* `matrix` *object as a* `vector` *of* `vectors`

```
vector <vector<class> > identifier(rows, vector<class> (cols, initialValue));
```

Examples of `matrix` Constructions

```
vector <vector<int> > student(10, vector<int> (15, -1));
vector <vector<double> > table(4, vector<double> (8, 0.001));
vector <vector<string> > name(5, vector<string> (100, "Dunno"));
```

These constructions are perhaps the most complicated you'll see in this textbook. So if you find these constructions too daunting (or if you do not have a standard compiler), consider using the built-in array declared with two subscripts:

Equivalent Primitive Array Declarations (acceptable on all compilers, but unsafe)

```
int student[10][15]; // Write code to initialize all to -1
double table[4][8];  // Write code to initialize all to 0.0001
string name[5][100]; // Write code to initialize all to "Dunno"
```

Or better yet, consider an author-supplied class named `matrix` that has automatic subscript range checking and optional element initialization.

Equivalent Author-Supplied `matrix` Objects (safe with range checking and easy)

```
matrix <int> student(10, 15, -1);      // 150 integers set to -1
matrix <double> table(4, 8, 0.1);      // 32 floating-point numbers
matrix <string> name(5, 10, "Dunno"); // 50 strings == "Dunno"
```

This chapter will continue using the safer and easier-to-construct nonstandard `matrix` class. All other `matrix`-processing code is acceptable on any compiler with any of the three different constructions shown on this page.

General Form 19.2. `matrix` *construction (for safe, easy-to-construct* `matrix` *objects)*

```
matrix <class> identifier(rows, columns, initialValue);
```

The *class* must be a class with a default constructor. The *identifier* is the name of the `matrix` object. *rows* specifies the number of rows stored in the `matrix` and *columns* is the number of columns that can be subscripted. *initialValue* is optional, but when supplied, will be the value of every element in the `matrix`. For example, the following `matrix` construction builds `student` as an object that stores `10` rows, where each row stores up to `15` integers. All elements are initialized to `-1`.

```
matrix <int> student(10, 15, -1);  // Store up to 150 -1s
```

The `matrix` class diagram below shows the operations available and lists the constructor to indicate it is indeed a template class, capable of storing any class of object. This `matrix` class is made available with `#include "matrix"`.

```
matrix
-----------------------------------
matrix<T> (rows, columns)
matrix<T> (rows, columns, value)
[] []
resize (rows, columns)
int rowCapacity()
int columnCapacity()
-----------------------------------
vector<vector<T>> my_matrix
int my_rowCapacity
int my_columnCapacity
```

19.1.2 Referencing Individual Items with Two Subscripts

A reference to an individual element of a `matrix` requires two subscripts (row and column).

GENERAL FORM 19.3. *Accessing individual `matrix` elements*

matrix-object [*row*] [*column*]

Each subscript must be bracketed individually. For example, assuming `student` stores the attendance data shown earlier, the value of `student[7][0]` is 0 and `student[7][2]` is 1. Student 7 was absent in week 0, week 3, and week 10. The sum of these three elements is 0:

```
// Because columns 0, 3, and 10 of row 7 are 0, output is 0
cout << (student[7][0] + student[7][3] + student[7][10]) << endl;
```

The first subscript of a doubly subscripted object specifies the row, and the second subscript specifies the column. For example, the attendance percentage of student 0 can be found with the loop where row 0 refers to the data for one student (assuming `student` is initialized as shown in Figure 19.1).

```
double present = 0.0;
for(int column = 0; column < nWeeks; column++)
{
  if(student[0][column] == 1)
     present++;
}
double attendanceRate = (present / 15.0);
cout << "Student #0 attended " << (attendanceRate * 100)
     << " percent of the time";
```

OUTPUT

```
Student #0 attended 86.6667 percent of the time
```

19.1.3 Nested Looping with Doubly Subscripted `vectors`

Nested looping is commonly used to process the data of doubly subscripted objects. If we start with this construction:

```
matrix<int> table(5, 8, 0);
```

enough memory is allocated to store 40 integers—a `matrix` with five rows and eight columns. All 40 entries have been initialized to 0. After some assignments, the following program uses nested loops to display each row on a separate line:

```
#include <iostream>
using namespace std;
#include "matrix"  // For the matrix class
int main()
{
  matrix<int> table(5, 8, 0);
  table[0][0] = 53;
  table[1][1] = 64;
  table[2][2] = 75;
  table[3][3] = 86;
  table[4][4] = 97;
  table[4][5] = 106;
  table[4][6] = 117;
  table[4][7] = 128;
  table[0][7] = -1;

for(int row = 0; row < 5; row++)
{ // Display one row
  for(int col = 0; col < 8; col++)
  { // Display each column of the row
    cout.width(6);
```

```
      cout << table[row][col];
    }
    cout << endl;
  }
  return 0;
  }
```

OUTPUT

53	0	0	0	0	0	0	-1
0	64	0	0	0	0	0	0
0	0	75	0	0	0	0	0
0	0	0	86	0	0	0	0
0	0	0	0	97	106	117	128

Self-Check

19-1 Which class more appropriately manages lists of data, `vector` or `matrix`?

19-2 Which class more appropriately manages data viewed in a row/column format, `vector` or `matrix`?

19-3 Construct a `matrix` object named `sales` such that 120 numbers are stored in 10 rows.

19-4 Construct a `matrix` object named `sales2` such that 120 numbers are stored in 10 columns.

19.2 Row and Column Processing

A doubly subscripted object manages tabular data that is typically processed by row, by column, or in totality. These forms of processing are examined in an example class that manages a contrived grade book. The data consists of six quizzes for each of 11 students. The 66 quizzes shown next are used throughout this section to demonstrate several forms of processing the data of doubly subscripted objects.

FIGURE 19.2. *Quiz data for a semester*

Student	Quiz Number					
Number	0	1	2	3	4	5
0	67.8	76.4	88.4	79.1	90.0	66.0
1	76.4	81.1	72.2	76.0	85.6	85.0
2	87.8	76.4	88.7	83.0	76.3	87.0
3	86.4	54.0	82.6	82.5	95.6	98.4
4	76.8	79.0	58.0	77.0	80.0	87.7
5	94.4	63.0	92.9	45.0	75.6	99.5
6	85.8	75.0	78.1	100.0	60.0	65.8
7	76.4	84.4	100.0	94.3	75.6	74.0
8	67.9	79.5	98.8	76.4	80.0	96.0
9	86.1	76.0	72.0	88.1	55.6	71.3
10	87.2	95.5	68.1	67.0	89.0	76.8

The quiz average is computed for each student by processing this tabular data one row at a time—row-by-row processing. The average, highest, and lowest scores of each quiz are found by processing one column at a time—column-by-column processing. The overall quiz average is found by referencing all `matrix` elements. But before any processing occurs, the `matrix` object must be constructed and given a defined state.

Each of these `matrix`-processing algorithms will be represented as the implementation of a `quizData` member function:

```
class quizData {
public:
  quizData(string filename);
  // post: Initialize matrix using file name

  void display();
  // post: Display the entire matrix

  void studentStats();
  // post: Display row-by-row report

  void quizStats();
```

quizData
quizData(filename)
display()
studentStats()
quizStats()
double average()
int my_lastStudent
int my_lastQuiz
matrix<double> my_data

```
    // post: Display column-by-column report

    double average();
    // post: Returns overall quiz average

  private:
    int my_lastStudent, my_lastQuiz;
    matrix <double> my_data;
  };
```

19.2.1 Initializing Doubly Subscripted Objects with File Input

In programs with little data required, interactive input suffices. Initialization of `vector` and `matrix` objects quite often involves large amounts of data. The input would have to be typed in from the keyboard many times during implementation and testing. Because so much interactive input is tedious and error prone, the data will come from an external file.

The first line in `"quiz.dat"` specifies the number of rows and columns of the input file. Each remaining line represents the quiz scores of one student.

```
11    6
67.8  76.4  88.4   79.1   90.0  66.0
76.4  81.1  72.2   76.0   85.6  85.0
87.8  76.4  88.7   83.0   76.3  87.0
86.4  54.0  82.6   82.5   95.6  98.4
76.8  79.0  58.0   77.0   80.0  87.7
94.4  63.0  92.9   45.0   75.6  99.5
85.8  75.0  78.1  100.0   60.0  65.8
76.4  84.4 100.0   94.3   75.6  74.0
67.9  79.5  98.8   76.4   80.0  96.0
86.1  76.0  72.0   88.1   55.6  71.3
87.2  95.5  68.1   67.0   89.0  76.8
```

The `ifstream` object `inFile` will be associated with this external file in the constructor, and the number of rows and columns will be extracted from the first line in the file (`11` and `6`) with this statement:

```
inFile >> my_lastStudent >> my_lastQuiz;
```

Because these private data members are known throughout the `quizData` class, the doubly subscripted object named `my_data` can from this point forward communicate its subscript ranges for both row and column at any time and in any function.

The next step is to resize the matrix using a matrix::resize message.

```
my_data.resize(my_lastStudent, my_lastQuiz);
```

Now with a matrix precisely large enough to store 11 (my_lastStudent) rows of data with six (my_lastQuiz) doubles in each row, the matrix gets initialized with the file data using nested for loops. These steps are encapsulated in the quizData constructor.

```
quizData::quizData(string filename)
{
  // Initialize my_data
  ifstream inFile(filename.c_str());
  if(!inFile)
  {
    cout << "**Error** opening file '" << filename << "'" << endl;
    cout << "**Program terminated**";
    exit(0);
  }
  else
  {
    int row, col;
    inFile >> my_lastStudent >> my_lastQuiz;

    // The matrix data member must be initialized in the constructor
    my_data.resize(my_lastStudent, my_lastQuiz);

    // Initialize a my_lastStudent by my_lastQuiz two-dimensional
    // vector
    for(row = 0; row < my_lastStudent; row++)
    {
      for(col = 0; col < my_lastQuiz; col++)
      {
         inFile >> my_data[row][col];
      }
    }
  }
}
```

As with vectors, the antibugging technique of displaying all initialized elements of a matrix can help prevent errors. This echo of the input data is accomplished again with the help of nested loops in quizData::display. The output is meant to look just like the input file.

```
void quizData::display()
{
```

```
    int row(0), col(0);
    int row, col;
    decimals(cout, 1);
    cout << "\nQuiz data:" << endl;

    for(row = 0; row < my_lastStudent; row++)
    {
       for(col = 0; col < my_lastQuiz; col++)
       {
          cout.width(6);
          cout << my_data[row][col];
       }
       cout << endl;
    }
  }
```

The following program initializes and displays the data stored in a `matrix` after using file input to initialize the individual `matrix` elements:

```
#include "quizdata"

int main()
{
  quizData CmpSc("quiz.dat");
  CmpSc.display();

  return 0;
}
```

OUTPUT

```
Quiz data:
67.8   76.4   88.4   79.1   90.0   66.0
76.4   81.1   72.2   76.0   85.6   85.0
87.8   76.4   88.7   83.0   76.3   87.0
86.4   54.0   82.6   82.5   95.6   98.4
76.8   79.0   58.0   77.0   80.0   87.7
94.4   63.0   92.9   45.0   75.6   99.5
85.8   75.0   78.1  100.0   60.0   65.8
76.4   84.4  100.0   94.3   75.6   74.0
67.9   79.5   98.8   76.4   80.0   96.0
86.1   76.0   72.0   88.1   55.6   71.3
87.2   95.5   68.1   67.0   89.0   76.8
```

The output looks like the input file (`quiz.dat`) shown earlier (minus the line with `11` and `6`). This `matrix` is now correctly initialized and stores 66 quiz scores, with each row representing the records of one student and each column representing the records of one quiz.

When working with `matrix` objects, take a little extra time to output all elements and the number of assigned elements. Do this immediately after the code that initializes the objects. Do not continue until you are satisfied the `matrix` has been properly initialized. The same advice goes for `vector` objects. Otherwise, a lot of debugging effort could be wasted on the wrong portion of a program. It may appear that there is a bug later on in the program, when in fact, the `vector` or `matrix` object was never initialized correctly to begin with.

19.2.2 Finding a Student Average (row-by-row processing)

The average for one student is found by adding all the elements of one row and dividing by six (the number of quizzes taken by each student). Dropping the lowest quiz score provides an interesting twist. To drop the lowest, find the column with the lowest score and subtract it from the total of all six quizzes. Then divide by five instead of six. Since the data for each student is stored in one row of the `matrix`, it is processed in a row-by-row manner.

Row-by-row processing is characterized by nested loops with the row subscript changing in the outer loop and the column subscript changing more quickly in the inner loop. The column subscript increments faster than the row subscript to process one complete row of data before proceeding to the next row. The following code is an example of row-by-row processing with each row of data used to sum every column of data to find the average quiz score.

```
void quizData::studentStats()
{ // pre: my_lastQuiz > 1
  // An example of row-by-row processing
  double sum, lowest, average;
  int row, col;
  cout << endl;
  cout << "   Student        Average" << endl;
  cout << "   =======        =======" << endl;
  decimals(cout, 1);

  for(row = 0; row < my_lastStudent; row++)  // Outer loop
  {
    // Assume the first quiz is the lowest
    lowest = my_data[row][0];
    // Assign sum the value of the first quiz
    sum = lowest;
    // Process remaining quizzes (start with second quiz in row)
```

```
        for(col = 1; col < my_lastQuiz; col++)  // Inner loop
        {
          sum = sum + my_data[row][col];
          if(my_data[row][col] < lowest)
          lowest = my_data[row][col];
        } // End inner loop
        // Drop the lowest quiz
        sum = sum - lowest;

        // Average is based on dropping lowest, so divide by n - 1
        average = sum / (my_lastQuiz - 1);
        cout.width(10);
        cout << row;
        cout.width(15);
        cout << average << endl;
      } // End outer loop
    }
```

OUTPUT

```
   Student         Average
   =======         =======
         0            80.3
         1            80.8
         2            84.6
         3            89.1
         4            80.1
         5            85.1
         6            80.9
         7            86.1
         8            86.1
         9            78.7
        10            83.3
```

19.2.3 Finding an Overall Quiz Average (processing all elements)

Finding the overall average without dropping any quiz scores is a simple matter of summing every single element in the `matrix` and dividing by the total number of quizzes.

OUTPUT

```
Average of all quizzes (no quizzes dropped)  79.9
```

Most students will appreciate the fact that they appear to have done better than the class average. This is because the reports by student dropped the lowest quiz scores, but the overall average included the lowest scores. The implementation of `quizData::average` is left as programming project 19A.

19.2.4 Finding a Quiz Average (column-by-column processing)

Column-by-column processing occurs when data of a doubly subscripted object are processed such that all the rows of one column are referenced before the program proceeds to the next column. The row subscript changes faster than the column subscript. Since each element in a quiz is represented as one column, processing the data column by column generates quiz statistics such as the lowest, highest, and average scores for each quiz.

OUTPUT

```
 Quiz       High       Low    Average
 =====     =====     =====    =======
     1      94.4      67.8       81.2
     2      95.5      54.0       76.4
     3     100.0      58.0       81.8
     4     100.0      45.0       78.9
     5      95.6      55.6       78.5
     6      99.5      65.8       82.5
```

Implementation of `quizData::quizStats` is left as programming project 19B.

Self-Check

19-5 In row-by-row processing, which subscript increments more slowly, row or column?

19-6 In column-by-column processing, which subscript increments more slowly, row or column?

19-7 Using this beginning of a program, construct an `ifstream` object to initialize the `matrix` object `t`.

```
#include <fstream>
using namespace std;
#include "matrix"   // For the matrix class

int main()
{
  int r, c, rows = 10, cols = 5;
  matrix <int> t(rows, cols);
```

Assume the file has the number of rows and columns written as the first two pieces of data (as shown in the file "quiz.dat").

19-8 Write code that determines the sum of all elements in t.

19-9 Write code that displays the largest element in each column of t.

19.3 C++ Primitive Arrays with Two Subscripts

The concepts of row-by-row and column-by-column processing also apply to primitive C arrays declared with two subscripts. A primitive C array declared with two subscripts has int expressions that specify the number of rows and columns. For example, x is declared here to store 10 rows and five columns of data for a total of 50 numbers:

```
double x[10][5];  // Row subscripts 0...9, column subscripts 0...4
```

The other important difference is that the primitive C array has no range checking of the subscripts. The following table compares the matrix class to the primitive C array declared with two subscripts:

	matrix	Primitive C Array
General Form:	matrix <class> identifier (rows, columns, initialValue);	class identifier [rows] [columns];
Example:	matrix <int> unitsSold(9, 12, 0); // Each element is 0	int unitsSold[9][12]; // Each element is garbage
Subscript Checking?	Yes	No
Resize?	Yes	No
Runtime Sizing?	Yes	No
First Row:	0	0
Last Row:	Row capacity - 1	Row capacity - 1
First Column:	0	0
Last Column:	Column capacity - 1	Column capacity - 1
#include:	#include "matrix"	No #include required

The matrix named unitsSold manages nine rows and 12 columns of integers (108 elements altogether). The equivalent primitive C array of the same name (declared in the right column previously) manages the same number of integers with the same subscript range; however, it does not range check subscripts. Individual array elements are referenced in the same manner, whether you are using a primitive C array, a vector of vectors, or the author-supplied matrix class. Subscripts always start at 0 in any case. This means that the following code may be used with either a matrix object, a vector of vectors, or a primitive doubly subscripted C array:

```
int r, c;
for(r = 0; r < 8; r++)
{
  for(c = 0; c < 12; c++)
    unitsSold[r][c] = r + c;
}
```

19.3.1 Arrays with More than Two Subscripts

Singly and doubly subscripted vectors occur more frequently than vectors with more than two subscripts. However, vectors with three and even more subscripts are sometimes useful. Triply subscripted arrays are possible because C++ does not limit the number of subscripts. For example, the declaration

```
double q[3][11][6]
```

could represent the quiz grades for three courses, since 198 (3 * 11 * 6) grades can be stored under the same name (q). This triply subscripted object:

```
q[1][9][3]
```

is a reference to quiz index 3 of student index 9 in course index 1. In the following program, an array with three subscripts is initialized (with meaningless data). The first subscript—representing a course—changes the slowest. So the vector object q is initialized and then displayed in a course-by-course manner.

```
// Declare, initialize, and display a triply subscripted vector
// object. The primitive C subscripted object is used here, but we
// could also use a vector of matrix objects to do the same thing.

#include <iostream>
using namespace std;
```

```
int main()
{
  const int courses = 3;
  const int students = 11;
  const int quizzes = 6;
  int q[courses][students][quizzes];
  int c, row, col;

  for(c = 0; c < courses; c++)
  {
    for(row = 0; row < students; row++)
    {
      for(col = 0; col < quizzes; col++)
      { // Give each quiz a value using a meaningless formula
        q[c][col][row] = (col + 1) * (row + 2) + c + 25;
      }
    }
  }

  for(c = 0; c < courses; c++)
  {
    cout << endl;
    cout << "Course #" << c << endl;
    for(row = 0; row < students; row++)
    {
      for(col = 0; col < quizzes; col++)
      {
        cout.width(5);
        cout << q[c][col][row];
      }
      cout << endl;
    }
  }
  return 0;
}
```

OUTPUT

```
Course #0
   27   33   41   49   57   65
   28   34   43   52   61   70
   29   35   45   55   65   75
   30   36   47   58   69   80
   31   37   49   61   73   85
   32   39   46   53   60   67
   33   41   49   57   65   73
   34   43   52   61   70   79
   35   45   55   65   75   85
   36   47   58   69   80   91
   37   49   61   73   85   97

Course #1
   28   34   42   50   58   66
   29   35   44   53   62   71
   30   36   46   56   66   76
   31   37   48   59   70   81
   32   38   50   62   74   86
   33   40   47   54   61   68
   34   42   50   58   66   74
   35   44   53   62   71   80
   36   46   56   66   76   86
   37   48   59   70   81   92
   38   50   62   74   86   98


Course #2
   29   35   43   51   59   67
   30   36   45   54   63   72
   31   37   47   57   67   77
   32   38   49   60   71   82
   33   39   51   63   75   87
   34   41   48   55   62   69
   35   43   51   59   67   75
   36   45   54   63   72   81
   37   47   57   67   77   87
   38   49   60   71   82   93
   39   51   63   75   87   99
```

The following table provides another view of the object declaration. The first subscript is the same for each course. For example, every quiz for course 0 has 0 as the first subscript. The second and third subscripts represent the student (row) and quiz (column), respectively.

AN ARRAY WITH THREE SUBSCRIPTS

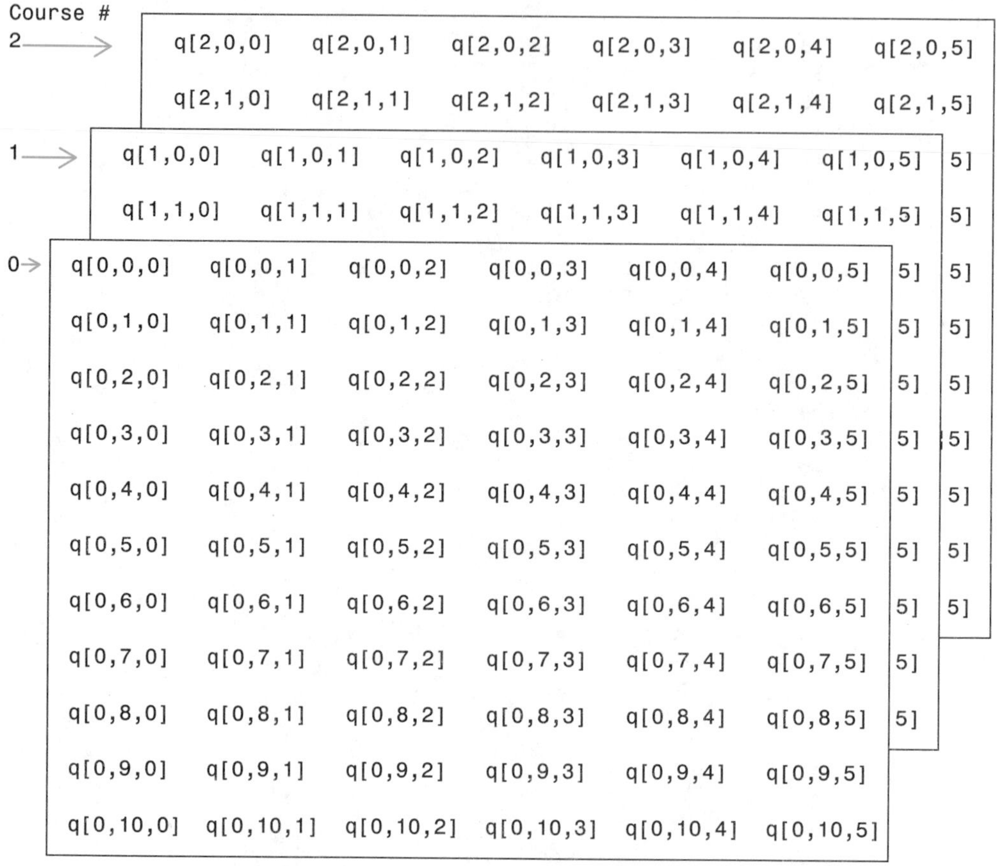

Self-Check

Use this declaration to answer the questions that follow:

```
int a[3][4];
```

19-10 Does a get its subscripts checked?

19-11 How many `int` elements are properly managed by a?

19-12 What is the row (first) subscript range for a?

19-13 What is the column (second) subscript range for a?

19-14 Write code to initialize all elements of a to 999.

19-15 Write code to display all rows of a on separate lines with eight spaces for each element.

Use this declaration to answer the questions that follow:

```
int t[3][4][5];
```

19-16 How many elements are properly stored by t?

19-17 Which of the following references to t can be properly used as the object to the left of an assignment operator?

-a `t[0][0][0]`

-b `t[1][1][1]`

-c `t[3][4][5]`

-d `t[0, 0, 0]`

-e `t[2][3]`

-f `t[1]`

19.4 Case Study: Visibility Study Report

A research study by the Electric Power Research Institute (EPRI) was conducted to investigate factors contributing to decreasing visibility in pristine and near-pristine areas. A large amount of data was collected for many reasons, including these:

- to help determine why we can't see as far as we once could
- to establish measurement techniques for visibility environmental impact studies
- to establish baseline data for future comparisons of visibility

The data included human-observed estimates of visibility that were compared to nephelometer (an instrument that measures light refraction in a closed unit) and teleradiometer (an instrument that measures radiance generated by far-off targets) electronic estimates of visibility collected at the same time. Here are human-observed visibility measurements for one day:

ONE-DAY HUMAN ESTIMATES OF VISIBILITY IN THREE DIRECTIONS (MILES)

```
         8:00    9:00   10:00   11:00   12:00   13:00   14:00   15:00
Path +-----------------------------------------------------------------
   1 |   40.0    35.0    38.0    40.0    40.0    40.0    35.0    35.0
   2 |    2.5    15.0    23.0    50.0    50.0    65.0    65.0    50.0
   3 |   52.0    60.0    35.0    35.0    20.0    60.0    60.0    60.0
```

Every hour on the hour, from 8:00 a.m. to 3:00 p.m., a site technician used known targets such as ridges and mountains in the distance to estimate visibility. There were three paths numbered 1, 2, and 3. The estimates of visibility by the site technician were recorded to the nearest tenth of a mile for distances less than four miles and were rounded to the nearest mile for distances greater than four miles. A report is now described that will produce statistics for one day's worth of human-observed estimates of visibility.

19.4.1 Analysis

Problem: Using data such as that shown above, produce a report of human-observed visibility. The visibility report should display the input in a similar manner. Additionally, show the following four statistics for each path and for the day:

1. farthest estimate of visibility
2. shortest estimate of visibility
3. range of visibility (range = farthest - shortest)
4. average of the visibility estimates

The visibility report should look like the following (with question marks replaced by the correct output):

```
17-JUNE-81
SITE 2
ESTIMATES OF HUMAN-OBSERVED VISIBILITY

           8:00  9:00 10:00 11:00 12:00 13:00 14:00 15:00
         +-----------------------------------------------
Path 1 | 40.0  35.0  38.0  40.0  40.0  40.0  35.0  35.0
     2 |  2.5  15.0  23.0  50.0  50.0  65.0  65.0  50.0
     3 | 52.0  60.0  35.0  35.0  20.0  60.0  60.0  60.0

         Farthest   Shortest     Range   Average
         ========   ========     =====   =======
Path 1       40.0       35.0       5.0      37.9
Path 2       ??.?       ??.?      ??.?      ??.?
Path 3       ??.?       ??.?      ??.?      ??.?
   Day       60.0        2.5      57.5      ??.?
```

The input comes from a file named *site#* + `h` (for *h*uman-observed) + *day* + *month* + *year* + `.` + `dat`. For example, the data for site 2's human-observed estimates of visibility for the 17th of June, 1981, are stored in the file `"2h170681.dat"`.

```
 2 17-JUNE-81
 40.0   35.0   38.0   40.0   40.0   40.0   35.0   35.0
  2.5   15.0   23.0   50.0   50.0   65.0   65.0   50.0
 52.0   60.0   35.0   35.0   20.0   60.0   60.0   60.0
```

The data in this file are shown differently from the actual raw data. This is done to keep input simple and avoid more details in the study. In reality, there was much more data for each day such as electronic measurements, hourly anemometer (wind speed and direction) readings, and the potential for a large number of codes to describe anomalous conditions such as snow on the mountain or dark clouds behind.

19.4.2 Design

Nine sites were involved in this study, each site collecting hundreds of data items per day over a two-year period. But the problem statement reduces this huge database to a report on one day's human-observed visibility captured in a file with a meaningful name. Performing a complete analysis of all data at all nine sites requires a much larger view of this narrow case study. To accomplish a larger scale problem we might need the ability to

- find the range of visibility in the western United States on any given day by comparing all nine sites
- compute average visibility at any site when the humidity was less than 20% (or greater than 80%)
- compare human-observed estimates to teleradiometer estimates at any particular time of day, or on any path, or at all sites

Other views of the data are needed including some operations that have not been anticipated. This is quite complex, but reusing other software such as a database management system would reduce the complexity of the system while saving money. Also, we would be starting with a fairly well-tested and debugged system—another advantage of software reuse.

A scaled-down version of software will help implement this scaled-down problem. A programmer could reuse any objects identified in the vocabulary of the problem statement. Data is stored in a file. So reusing the `ifstream` class saves a lot of work that would otherwise be necessary to implement input and output operations.

Visualize a `site` object with a `reportHOV` member function that takes a file name as an argument. This external file contains the site number and date on the first line followed by three rows of the human-observed estimates of visibility (eight valid numeric data per line). These data are read from the file stream and stored in a `matrix`. You then have the ability to manage the data in a variety of ways. You can produce a report and determine statistics for each path, each hour, and/or the entire day, for example. To do this, we must also maintain the number of paths (rows) and observations (columns) as data members of each object. The member functions and data members of the `site` class can now be summarized in the following class diagram:

site
reportHOV (filename)
matrix<double> my_humanData

19.4.3 Implementation

Each site object has a `matrix` object named `my_humanData`.

```
//---------------------------------------------------------------------
// File name: site.h
//---------------------------------------------------------------------
#ifndef SITE_H
#define SITE_H

#include <string>
using namespace std;
#include "matrix"  // For the matrix class

class site {
public:
  void reportHOV(string fileName);

private:
  matrix <double> my_humanData;
};

#endif  // SITE_H
```

Notice that the `matrix` data member of the `site` class is constructed without arguments. C++ simply does not allow arguments in class definitions. This is a major reason why `matrix` (and `vector` for that matter) has a resize function. Initially, a default `vector`, or `matrix`, has size 0. A class constructor will typically resize the `vector` automatically to the appropriate capacity.

Although implementing and testing this class are left as a programming project, the single member function is partially implemented for you (see `site.cpp`). If you ran the following program, you would currently get the output shown.

```
#include "site"  // For the site class

int main()
{
  site site2;
  site2.reportHOV("2h170681.dat");

  return 0;
}
```

OUTPUT

```
Site #2
17-JUNE-81
ESTIMATES OF HUMAN-OBSERVED VISIBILITY

        8:00  9:00 10:00 11:00 12:00 13:00 14:00 15:00
Path +--------------------------------------------------+
```

Some of the code has been implemented for you, but you will be asked to complete the `matrix`-processing-specific code.

Self-Check

19-18 The farthest, shortest, range, and average statistics for paths 1, 2, and 3 are examples of row-by-row or column-by-column processing?

Chapter Summary

- The new concept introduced in this chapter was an object replete with row- and column-processing algorithms written in C++ code.
- Some of the new ideas presented with storing data in a `matrix` format include:
  - A doubly subscripted `vector` manages data that is logically organized in a tabular format—that is, in rows and columns.
  - The first subscript of a doubly subscripted `vector` specifies the row of data in a table; the second represents the column.
  - The elements stored in a `matrix` object can be processed row by row, column by column, or by rows and columns.
  - `for` loops are commonly used to process `matrix` objects. In the case of a doubly subscripted `vector` being processed row by row, the outer loop usually increments the row index and the inner loop usually increments the column index.

Exercises

1. Write the output generated by the following program:

```
#include <iostream>
using namespace std;
#include "matrix"  // For the matrix class

class huh {
public:
  huh(int initLastRow, int initLastColumn);
  void add(int increment);
  void show() const;
  int rowSum(int currentRow) const;
private:
  int lastRow, lastCol;
  matrix<int> m;
};

huh::huh(int initLastRow, int initLastColumn)
{
  lastRow = initLastRow;
  lastCol = initLastColumn;
  // The vector of vectors must be initialized in the constructor
  m.resize(lastRow, lastCol);

  for(row = 0; row < lastRow; row++)
  {
    for(col = 0; col < lastCol; col++)
    { // Give each item a meaningless formula
      m[row][col] = (row + 1) + (col + 1);
    }
  }
}

void huh::show() const
{
  int row, col;
  for(row = 0; row < lastRow; row++)
  {
     for(col = 0; col < lastCol; col++)
     {
       cout.width(4);
       cout << m[row][col];
    }
  cout << endl;
  }
```

```
}

int main()
{
  huh h(4, 4);
  h.show();
  return 0;
}
```

2. Complete the member function `huh::add` that adds the value of the parameter named `increment` to every element in the `matrix`.

```
cout << h.add(5);  // Adds 5 to every element in h

void huh::add(int increment)
{
   // You complete this code
}
```

3. Complete the member function `huh::rowSum` that returns the sum of all the elements in a given row. A valid call to `huh::rowSum` is shown in this `cout` statement:

```
cout << h.rowSum(2);

int huh::rowSum(int currentRow) const
{
   // You complete this code
}
```

4. For each doubly subscripted object declaration below, determine
   a. the total number of elements
   b. the value of all elements (*Note:* "garbage" is an acceptable answer)

```
matrix<double> x(6, 11);
vector<vector<string>  > teacher(41, vector<string> (7));
double budget[6][1000];
int y[12][20];
vector<<int> > test(1, vector<int> (1));
matrix <string> s;
matrix <bankAccount> b(15, 1000, bankAccount("?", 0.00));
```

5. Detect the error(s) in the following attempts to declare a doubly subscripted `vector`:

   a. `int x(5,6);`

   b. `double x[5,6];`

   c. `matrix <int> x[1, 5, 1, 6];`

   d. `matrix x(5, 10, -1);`

   e. `vector<vector<int> > x(5, 6);`

6. Declare a doubly subscripted object identified with three rows and four columns of floating-point numbers.

7. Write C++ code to accomplish the following tasks:

   a. Declare a doubly subscripted object called `aTable` that stores 10 rows and 14 columns of numbers.

   b. Set every element in `aTable` to 0.0.

   c. Write a `for` loop that sets all elements in row 4 to -1.0.

8. Show the output from the following program when the dialogue is:

   a. `# rows? 2`
      `# cols? 3`

   b. `# rows? 3`
      `# cols? 2`

   c. `# rows? 4`
      `# cols? 4`

   d. `# rows? 1`
      `# cols? 1`

   e. `# rows? 1`
      `# cols? 2`

   f. `# rows? 2`
      `# cols? 1`

```
#include <iostream>
using namespace std;
#include "matrix"  // For the matrix class

int main()
{
  int maxRow, maxCol;
  cout << "# rows? ";
  cin >> maxRow;
  cout << "# cols? ";
  cin >> maxCol;

  matrix<int> aTable(maxRow, maxCol);

  int row, col;
```

```
  // Initialize matrix elements
  for(row = 0; row < maxRow; row++)
  {
    for(col = 0; col < maxCol; col++)
    {
      aTable[row][col] = row * col;
    }
  }

  // Display table elements
  for(row = 0; row < maxRow; row++)
  {
    for(col = 0; col < maxCol; col++)
    {
      cout.width(5);
      cout << aTable[row][col];
    }
    cout << endl;
  }
  return 0;
}
```

9. Using this doubly subscripted object named `t`:

```
int nRows = 12;
int nCols = 15;
matrix<int> >  t(nRows, nCols);
// Assume all 12 * 15 elements of t are initialized
```

and assuming all elements of `t` have been properly initialized, write code that displays the range of elements (highest to lowest) in each row on its separate line.

Programming Tips

1. Consider using the author-supplied `matrix` class.

The `matrix` class, on this textbook's disk and Web site, has two major advantages over the standard `vector` of `vectors` approach.

1. `matrix` objects are much easier to construct: `matrix<double> m(10, 15);`
2. Both subscripts of a `matrix` object are range checked to avoid otherwise difficult-to-detect errors.

However, using a `vector` of `vectors` is standard and does not require a class defined by someone else.

2. When constructing `vectors` of `vectors`, be careful not to write >> in your constructions.

```
vector<vector<int>> error(10, vector<int> (10, -1));
                 ↑
// Error: Need space between > and >
```

3. When using `vectors` of `vectors`, consider using the range-checking member function `vector::at`, especially when first using two subscripts.

The standard `vector` class does not automatically check the subscripts, but it can be made to with the `vector::at` member function.

```
vector<vector<int> > aTable(3, vector<int> (3, -1));
aTable.at(2).at(3) = 23;     // Column 3 out of bounds
aTable.at(3).at(2) = 32;     // Row 3 out of bounds
cout << aTable.at(0).at(0)   // Output: -1
```

It is common to get a subscript variable out of bounds. The sooner you know about it, the better. With range checking on, you'll know immediately.

4. When initializing a `matrix`, display the values before continuing.

After initializing a `matrix` (or a `vector` for that matter), write it back to the screen immediately before continuing with the program implementation. This allows you to visualize the contents of the `matrix` and to verify that it has been initialized correctly. Otherwise, a lot of debugging effort could potentially be wasted on the wrong portion of a program. It may appear that there is a bug later on in the program, when, in fact, the `vector` had never been correctly initialized to begin with.

5. Many of the programming tips for `vectors` with one subscript can be applied to doubly and triply subscripted objects.

- Subscripts must be an enumerated type: `int`, `char`, or `enum`.
- The elements of any `vector` must be of the same class. For example, a `matrix` cannot store both `string` and integer values.
- Any object that uses a large amount of memory may be passed as a const reference parameter. As with singly subscripted `vectors`, memory is saved and only one value (the address of the `matrix`) needs to be copied. However, when a `matrix` is passed as a value parameter, every single element gets copied, making the program less efficient.

```
void foo(const matrix<double> & m)  // Pass by const reference
```

  is more efficient than

```
void foo(matrix<double> m)
```

- Range checking should be employed while you are learning to manipulate doubly subscripted objects.

Programming Projects

19A `quizData::average`

Implement and test `quizData::average` in `quizdata.cpp` as described on pages 728–729.

19B `quizData::quizStats`

Implement and test `quizData::quizStats` in `quizdata.cpp` as described on page 729.

19C Initialize a `matrix` Object with File Input

Write a program that reads data from an external file to initialize a `matrix`. The first line of the file contains the number of rows and columns for the table data that follows.

```
2  3
 -7.5    8.1   12.3
 22.19  16.7   -9.99
```

This file store represents a doubly subscripted `vector` that is `2` rows by `3` columns where `12.3` is the third element in row 1. Your program should be able to store doubly subscripted `vector`s of any size. The elements may be `int`s or `double`s. The output should show the elements of the `matrix`. Using the file shown above, your output should look exactly like this:

```
Initialized Table
    -7.50     8.10    12.30
    22.19    16.70    -9.99
```

Now create a data file named `table.dat` with five rows of data where each row has three columns of any numeric data. To indicate a 5-by-3 `matrix`, the first line of data must look like this:

```
5  3
```

19D Add Matrices

An m-by-n `matrix` is a collection of numeric values stored in m rows and n columns. The sum of two matrices a and b stored into `matrix` c is defined as follows:

$c[j][k] = a[j][k] + b[j][k]$ for j ranging from 0 to m - 1 and k ranging from 0 to n - 1

Write a program that initializes two `matrix` objects named `a` and `b` using data stored in a file. Since `a` and `b` must have the same number of rows and columns, the first line of the input file will be used to specify the number of rows followed by the number of columns. First create the following input file:

```
 3 4
 1   2   3   4
 5   6   7   8
 9  10  11  12

-1   2   0   0
 3   0  -1   3
 3   2   1   0
```

Store the sum of the two matrices in a `matrix` object named `c`. Display all three `matrix` objects. Your output should look exactly like this:

```
matrix a:
  1   2   3   4
  5   6   7   8
  9  10  11  12

matrix b:
 -1   2   0   0
  3   0  -1   3
  3   2   1   0

matrix c: (a + b)
  0   4   3   4
  8   6   6  11
 12  12  12  12
```

19E Initialize `matrix`

Write a complete program that initializes a `matrix` through file input. The row and column size are located as the first two integers in the file. The size of the `matrix` cannot exceed 20 rows by 20 columns. The output should include the entire `matrix` with the highest and lowest number in each row displayed to the right of each row. A sample input file is shown with the output that should be generated. First create the following input file:

```
3 5
11  53  6  -1  5
21  34  6  12  0
31  91  3 -12 55
```

Then complete the code to generate output that appears as close to the following as possible (assuming you use the previous input file):

```
     Col# 1    2    3    4    5       Hi     Lo
Row#    ----------------------       --     --
    1|   11   53    6   -1    5       53     -1
    2|   21   34    6   12    0       34      0
    3|   31   91    3  -12   55       91    -12
```

19F Implement a Magic Square

A magic square is an n-by-n `vector` where the integers 1 to $n2$ appear exactly once and the sum of the integers in every row, column, and on both diagonals is the same. For example, the following magic square results when n = 7. Notice that each row, column, and both diagonals total 175.

	1	2	3	4	5	6	7
1	30	39	48	1	10	19	28
2	38	47	7	9	18	27	29
3	46	6	8	17	26	35	37
4	5	14	16	25	34	36	45
5	13	15	24	33	42	44	4
6	21	23	32	41	43	3	12
7	22	31	40	49	2	11	20

Implement the `square` class with two member functions: a constructor and display. The following code should generate output like that shown above:

```
square magic(7);
magic.display();
```

You should be able to construct an n-by-n magic square for any odd value n from 1 to 15. When j is 1, place the value of j in the middle of the first row. Then, for a counter value ranging from 1 to $n2$, move up one row and to the right one column and store the counter value unless one of the following events occurs:

1. When the next row becomes 0, make the next row equal to n (this assumes you used 1 for the first row).
2. When the next column becomes n + 1, make the next column equal to 1 (this assumes you used 1 for the first column).
3. If a position is already filled, or the upper-right corner element has just obtained a value, place the next counter value in the position that is one row below the position where the last counter value has been placed.

19G Test Drive Magic Square

After implementing the `magicSquare` class, add a test member function to verify the sums of all the rows, columns, and both diagonals to ensure that each sum is the same. When n = 7, the output generated by `square.test()` should look like this (assuming 1 refers to the first row and column):

```
Sum of row 1 = 175
Sum of row 2 = 175
Sum of row 3 = 175
Sum of row 4 = 175
Sum of row 5 = 175
Sum of row 6 = 175
Sum of row 7 = 175

Sum of col 1 = 175
Sum of col 2 = 175
Sum of col 3 = 175
Sum of col 4 = 175
Sum of col 5 = 175
Sum of col 6 = 175
Sum of col 7 = 175

Sum of diagonal one = 175

Sum of diagonal two = 175
```

19H Visibility I

Complete the `site` class that was begun in the case study earlier in this chapter. Make the report appear as shown there. First create a test driver to test the `site` class independently with a calculator or by hand. The high, low, and range for each path and for the day are easily determined by inspecting the input file. You can create these files from the case study or use the following files on the disk that accompanies this textbook:

```
mysite.h
2h170681.dat
```

Test your changes with the following `main` function:

```
#include "mysite"  // For the site class

int main()
{
  site two;

  two.reportHOV("2h170681.dat");  // File must be in working directory

  return 0;
}
```

19I Visibility II

During the visibility study described in the case study, radiance measurements were made by an electronic instrument called a teleradiometer. Two measurements were taken, the radiance emitted by a mountain target and the radiance emitted from the sky directly above the mountain target. The electronic estimate of visibility (`visEst`) is computed using this formula:

$$\texttt{visEst} = \texttt{distance} * \frac{\texttt{skyRad - tarRad}}{1 + \texttt{log(skyRad - tarRad)}}$$

where

- `tarRad` is the teleradiometer reading of the mountain target
- `skyRad` is the radiance measurement of the sky above
- `log` is a function from `cmath` (or `math.h`)
- `distance` is the distance to the mountain target:
  1. distance for target 1 on path 1 = 16 miles
  2. distance for target 2 on path 2 = 23 miles
  3. distance for target 3 on path 3 = 15 miles

For example, the electronic visibility estimate for path 1 at 10:00 a.m. when `tarRad` = 203 and `skyRad` = 211 is evaluated as:

```
visEst = 16 * ( 211 - 203 ) / ( 1 + log( 211 - 203 ) )
         16 * 8 / ( 1 + log ( 8 ) )
         16 * 8 / ( 1 + 2.079441542 )
         16 * 8 / 3.079441542
         16 * 2.597873637
visEst = 41.565978190
```

The data for one day's radiance measurements are stored in a file shown next. Two consecutive integers determine the value of one `matrix` element.

```
File name: 2r170681.dat
2 17-6-1981
  654 671 483 501 203 211 604 615 406 416 203 212 359 372 505 513
   45  43 107 108 230 230  44  49 105 114 127 140  43  49 101 109
  400 411 200 212 225 234 400 403 200 212 235 254 401 418 200 215
```

Two integers in a row represent one mountain-target and sky-reading pair. The first line of the file above represents target one; line 2 is the data collected for target 2; line 3 is the data for target 3. For example, the fifth and sixth values of row 1 represent the target (203) and sky-radiance measurements (211) for path 1 recorded at 10:00 (this produced an electronic estimate of 41.6 miles).

To the `site` class add `site::reportRAD("file-name.dat")` such that it also reports the electronic estimates of visibility using the data file shown above. Given this program:

```
#include "site"  // For the site class

int main()
{
  site two;

  two.reportRAD("2r170681.dat");  // File must be in working directory

  return 0;
}
```

the output format should be similar to this (the question marks should be replaced with the correct visibility estimates):

```
17-06-81
SITE 2
ESTIMATES OF ELECTRONICALLY MEASURED VISIBILITY

            8:00  9:00 10:00 11:00 12:00 13:00 14:00 15:00
    Path ------------------------------------------------
       1 |  ??.?  ??.?  41.6  ??.?  ??.?  ??.?  ??.?  ??.?
       2 |  ??.?  ??.?  ??.?  ??.?  ??.?  ??.?  ??.?  ??.?
       3 |  ??.?  ??.?  ??.?  ??.?  ??.?  ??.?  ??.?  ??.?
```

Make sure you avoid function calls to `log(x)` when `x` <= 0.0. The `log` function is only defined for values greater than 0.0. If the sky radiance measurement is less than or equal to the target, set the visibility estimate to be the distance to the target. This should occur for path 2 with the 8:00 and 10:00 data.

19J Grade Book

Implement a `gradeBook` class. Design the file and the C++ class yourself. Responsibilities must include at least these:

1. Initialize the grade book from an external file.
2. Determine the high, low, and average of any one student.
3. Determine the high, low, and average of any one quiz.
4. Compute the overall high, low, and average.

19K Game of Life

"The Game of Life" was invented by John H. Conway to simulate the birth and death of cells in a society. The following rules govern the birth and/or death of cells between two consecutive time periods in the society. At time *T*,

1. a cell is born if there was none at time *T* - 1 and exactly three of its neighbors are alive
2. an existing cell remains alive if at time *T* - 1 there were either two or three neighbors
3. a cell will die from isolation if at time *T* - 1 there were fewer than two neighbors
4. a cell will die from overcrowding if at time *T* - 1 there were more than three neighbors

A neighborhood consists of the eight elements around any element:

```
0 0 0
0   0
0 0 0
```

The following patterns would occur for *T* = 1 . . . 5, if the first society was that shown for *T* = 1. `0` represents a live cell; a blank indicates that no cell exists at that particular location in the society.

```
T=0    T=1    T=2    T=3    T=4

0 0    0 0
000    0 0    0 0     0             // Society dies off at T = 4
        0      0      0
```

Other societies stabilize like this:

```
T=0    T=1    T=2    T=3    T=4

        0             0
000     0     000     0     000  // This pattern repeats
        0             0
```

Implement a class named `gameOfLife` that works with the following driver:

```
#include "gamelife"  // For the gameOfLife class

int main()
{
```

```
  gameOfLife society("society1.dat");
  while( ! society.isDone() )
  {
    society.display();
    society.update();
  }
  return 0;
}
```

Here are some suggestions:

1. Use a triply subscripted C++ `vector` to represent two consecutive societies. Let the first subscript be either 0 or 1 to represent changing societies. This `vector` is given next in the context of a class declaration:

```
const int LASTROW = 22;
const int LASTCOL = 72;

class gameOfLife {
public:
  gameOfLife::gameOfLife(string fileName);
  // post: 3D array is initialized ignoring row 0 and 23 and column 0
  //       and 71. Cells exist only in rows 1...22 and columns 1...72.
  //       First set all cells = ' ', then set other cells to '0' based
  //       on input file specified as filename.c_str(). Here is an
  //       example file:
  //
  //                                0
  //          0                    000
  //         0 0                   000
  //                                0          000
  //

  void gameOfLife::display();
  // post: The current society is displayed

  void gameOfLife::update();
  // post: Change to the next society (the most difficult task)

  int gameOfLife::isDone();
  // post: Asks the user if he or she wants to quit and returns true
  //       when the user responds positively or false otherwise

private:
  char society[2][LASTROW + 2][LASTCOL + 2];  // Triply sub. array
  // . . . You may need some other data members or member functions
};
```

2. Allow the user to view a society for as long as he or she wishes, but clear the screen between successive societies so the patterns can be observed. (*Hint:* Use `clearScreen` and `causeApause` from `compfun`.)

3. The input should consist of an initial society contained in an external file with no more than 72 columns and 22 lines (rows) where a live cell is represented by `'0'`.

4. Allow the outer rows and columns to be used as a border in which no cell may be placed. The rules no longer apply once the border is in a neighborhood. When this occurs, display a meaningful message and terminate the program with `exit(0)` (from `stdlib.h`).

5. The input file(s) used to represent an initial society should include organisms around the middle of the available space.

   Use an input file like the one below to more easily initialize your triply subscripted `vector` (extracting blanks from input streams can be a bit tricky without `istream::getline`). The periods represent empty cells and the `0`s represent live cells. Use several lines above and below the live cells in your input file to avoid "running off the edge of the world." You may convert the periods to blanks for nicer output.

```
....................................................
....................................................
....................................................
....................................................
....................................................
....................................................
.........................................0..........
......0.0........0..............0........00.........
......000........0.....000.....000.......000........
.................0..............0........00.........
.........................................0..........
....................................................
....................................................
....................................................
....................................................
....................................................
....................................................
```

6. *Suggestion:* Implement the constructor first, the `gameOfLife::display` member function second, `gameOfLife::update` as a do-nothing function third, and finally implement `gameOfLife::isDone`. Your program should display the same society

until the user desires to quit. Once you get the bugs out of the nonchanging society, concentrate on the update operation.

19L Heat Index

Write a function `heatIndex` that takes as arguments, the temperature (F) and the relative humidity, to compute and return the heat index. For example, this function call should return a heat index of 114:

```
cout << heatIndex(95, 60) << endl;  // 114
```

Use the following table. Report an error if there is no result.

		Relative Humidity															
		15	20	25	30	35	40	45	50	55	60	65	70	75	80	85	90
T	110	108	112	117	123	130	137	143	150								
e	105	102	105	109	113	118	123	129	135	142	149						
m	100	97	99	101	104	107	110	115	120	126	132	138	144				
p	95	91	93	94	96	98	101	104	107	110	114	119	124	130	136		
	90	86	87	88	90	91	93	95	96	98	100	102	106	109	113	117	122
F	85	81	82	83	84	85	86	87	88	89	90	91	93	95	97	99	102
	80	76	77	77	78	79	79	80	81	81	82	83	85	86	86	87	88
	75	71	72	72	73	73	74	74	75	75	76	76	77	77	78	78	79

If there is no exact match, return the closest heat index.

Chapter Twenty

Recursion

Summing Up

This chapter may be studied at any time after Chapter 5, "Functions and Parameters."

Coming Up

A recursive function call occurs whenever a function calls itself. Making unrestricted recursive calls usually will cause errors if care is not taken to allow for the time when that function no longer needs to call itself. This chapter examines how it is possible to use recursive calls as a valid programming technique to solve certain problems. It begins with a comparison of several iterative and recursive solutions to the same problem as a brief introduction to recursive algorithms. After studying this chapter you will be able to

- compare iterative and recursive solutions to the same problem
- identify the recursive case and the base (or simple) case in a recursive algorithm
- implement simple recursive functions

20.1 Understanding Recursion

Recursion involves decomposing a problem into simpler subproblems. Recursion requires that each subproblem be identical in structure to the original problem. Let's look at a noncomputer example first. Imagine you are the instructor in a night class with 62 students and for some reason you need to cancel one night's class. Maybe your school just won the national championship, maybe you're sick, or maybe the class is cancelled because of drifting snow. You now need to call every student in the class. One iterative solution could look something like this:

```
for (int j = 1; j < 62; j++)
{
   Call student [j]
   Give the message
}
```

Another solution is possible if we assume that a phone tree has been set up in advance and everybody is home. A phone tree works something like this: the instructor calls two students and gives them the cancellation message. Those two students do the same thing that the instructor did—call two more students and give them the cancellation message. In this manner, each phone call simplifies the original problem until the base case occurs. The *base case* (or simple case) of a recursive algorithm occurs when no recursive call is involved. This recursive-like solution is more elegant than its iterative solution for two reasons: 1) The instructor needs to make only two phone calls instead of 62. 2) The entire class is notified in a much shorter time.

Each phone call results in a problem that is closer to the final solution. There are fewer and fewer phone calls to be made. Eventually, an occurrence of the base case is obtained when a student does not have to call anyone else. Here are two characteristics of recursive algorithms that can be applied to this noncomputer example.

1. It must be possible to decompose the problem into subproblems that have the same structure as the original problem.
2. A base case must eventually be reached so no more recursive calls are made.

The recursive phone tree solution can be illustrated as follows, where each ○ represents a phone call that has been made.

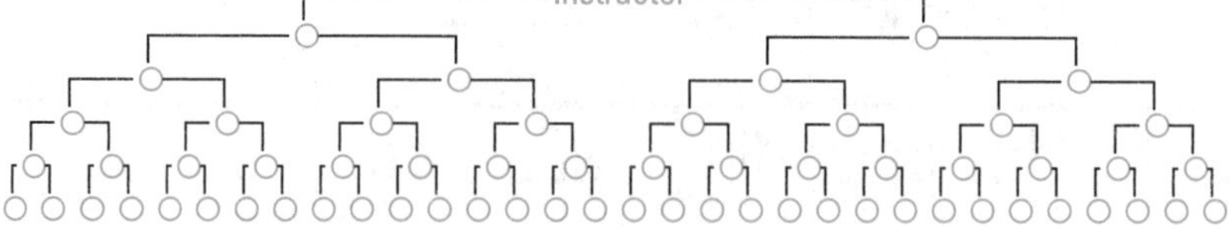

What should two students do who each receive a phone call? Either they will do what their caller did, or in the case of the last 32 students, they will do nothing at all. This means that each time a phone call is made, the solution to the subproblem is either another similar occurrence of the original solution, or it is nothing at all. It is important to note that the solution of the subproblem has the same structure as the original problem, only the data (phone numbers) are different. Each time a person is called he or she could use the following pseudocode for part of the solution:

If I need to make two phone calls
  Simplify the problem by making two phone calls
Otherwise
  Do nothing

20.1.1 Characteristics of Recursion

A recursive definition is one in which some part of the definition includes a simpler version of itself. One example of a recursive definition is given next as the power function that raises an integer (x) to an integer power (n).

$$x^n \begin{cases} 1 \text{ if } n = 0 \\ x * x^{n-1} \text{ if } x > 1 \end{cases}$$

This definition is recursive because x^{n-1} is defined as part of the definition itself. For example,

$4^3 = 4 * 4^{(n-1)}$

But what is $4^{(n-1)}$? Using the recursive definition above, 4^3 is determined as follows:

$$\begin{aligned} &4^3 \\ &= 4 * 4^2 && (4^3 = 4 * 4^2) \\ &= 4 * 4 * 4^1 && (4^2 = 4 * 4^1) \\ &= 4 * 4 * 4 * 4^0 && (4^1 = 4 * 4^0) \\ &= 4 * 4 * 4 * 1 && (4^0 = 1) \\ &= 64 \end{aligned}$$

The recursive definition of 4^3 includes three other recursive definitions such as $4 * 4^2$ and $4 * 4 * 4^1$. The base, or simple case, in this recursive definition occurs when n = 0:

$x^n = 1$ if n is 0

When 1 replaces 4^0, $4 * 1$ replaces 4^1, $4 * 4^1$ replaces 4^2, $4 * 4^2$ replaces 4^3, and 4^3 is defined as 64. To be called recursive, an algorithm or function requires at least one potential recursive case and at least one potential base case. At times the base case may be that no statements are executed. It is also possible to define the power function with two base (or simple) cases. In the following recursive definition, one base case occurs when x^n is defined as x when $n == 1$. The other base case is $x^n = 1$ if $n == 0$.

$$x^n \begin{cases} 1 \text{ if } n = 0 \\ x \text{ if } n = 1 \\ x * x^{n-1} \text{ if } x > 1 \end{cases}$$

The power function has been shown here to illustrate the three characteristics of a recursive solution to a problem:

1. The problem can be decomposed, using recursion, into a simpler version of itself in order to bring the problem closer to a base case.
2. There is at least one base case that does not make a recursive call.
3. The partial solutions are managed in such a way that all occurrences of the recursive and base cases can communicate their partial solutions to the proper locations (discussed later).

20.1.2 Comparison of Iterative and Recursive Solutions

For many problems involving repetition, both recursive and iterative solutions exist. For example, an iterative solution to the power function is shown to the left with a recursive solution to the right.

Iterative Solution

```
// Iterative version

#include <iostream>
using namespace std;

long int power(int x, int n)
{ // pre: x and n are positive.
  long int result;
  if(n == 0)
    result = 1;
  else
    result = x;
  for(int j = 2; j <= n; j++)
  {
    result = result * x;
  }
  return result;
}

int main()
{
  cout << power(2, 3) << endl;
  cout << power(3, 2) << endl;
  cout << power(2, 0) << endl;
```

Recursive Solution

```
// Recursive version

#include <iostream>
using namespace std;

long int recursivePower(int x, int n)
{ // pre: x and n are positive. x!=0.
  if(n == 0)
    return 1;
  else
    return x * recursivePower(x, n-1);
}

int main()
{
  cout << recursivePower(2, 3) << endl;
  cout << recursivePower(3, 2) << endl;
  cout << recursivePower(2, 0) << endl;
```

Iterative Solution *continued*	Recursive Solution *continued*

`cout << power(2, 1) << endl;`
`cout << power(5, 2) << endl;`
`cout << power(5, 3) << endl;`
`cout << power(2, 10) << endl;`
`return 0;`
`}`
	`cout << recursivePower(2, 1) << endl;`
	`cout << recursivePower(5, 2) << endl;`
	`cout << recursivePower(5, 3) << endl;`
	`cout << recursivePower(2, 10) << endl;`
	`return 0;`
	`}`

OUTPUT 8 9 1 2 25 125 1024	OUTPUT 8 9 1 2 25 125 1024

In both versions, the simple case is the same. If `n` is 0, return 1. When `n` > 0, the recursive solution calls the same function again with a simpler version—an argument reduced in value by one. For example, `recursivePower(4, 1)` calls `recursivePower(4, 1-1)`, which immediately returns 1. For another example, `recursivePower(2, 4)` calls `recursivePower(2, 3)`, which calls `recursivePower(2, 2)`, which calls `recursivePower(2, 1)`, which calls `recursivePower(2, 0)`, which finally returns 1. Then 2 * `recursivePower(2, 0)` evaluates to 2 * 1 or 2, so 2 * `recursivePower(2, 1)` can evaluate to 4, so 2 * `recursivePower(2, 2)` can evaluate to 8, so 2 * `recursivePower(2, 3)` can evaluate to 16, so 2 * `recursivePower(2, 4)` can evaluate to 32.

20.1.3 How Recursion Works

How does a function that calls itself so many times know when to quit calling itself? Consider the analogy of a stack of boxes that can be stacked one on top of another (without ever falling down). Each box contains certain vital information that allows a function to execute correctly. At the beginning of a program, there are no boxes on the stack. When a function is called, the vital information needed by that function is put into a box. This box is then placed on the stack.

Next, the computer begins to execute the statements in the function. As the function executes its statements, the information is available from the box on top of the stack. For example, if a change is made to a local object, that object can be found in the top box.

When a function has finished executing its own statements, the return point must be available in order to continue from the point of the function call. A return point is the place the program returns to when a function has finished executing. More specifically, the return point is the address of the next machine instruction to be executed.

So where is the value of the return point stored? It is in the box on top of the stack. It was placed there along with the other vital information when the function was originally called. But before the program begins to execute from the return point found in the box, the top box is removed from the stack.

A recursive function is handled in the same manner. When a function calls itself, the vital information is put into a new box (actually called an *activation frame*) and this box is placed on top of the stack. The only thing that may appear to be different is that the return point just happens to be in another instance of the same function that has just been called. The computer will then begin executing the statements of the function associated with the vital information in the top box. Every instance of the function is associated with a box on the stack so the stack of boxes "remembers" the vital information for every function that has been called but has not yet finished executing.

When one instance of a function is finished, the top box is removed from the stack and the program continues from the correct return point. The vital information for the current function is now in the box at the top of the stack. This allows a function to remember its own set of vital information even though there may have been many other boxes piled on top of it.

This stacking of boxes provides a useful tool for tracing recursive functions. At the same time the stack provides insights into how recursion works. Let's illustrate this stack analogy with a simple recursive function that displays the integers 1 through `n`, where `n` is an argument. The recursive function `forward` contains a comment to show the return point put into the box before the recursive call was made.

```
#include <iostream>
using namespace std;

void forward(int n)
{
  if(n > 1)
  {
    forward(n - 1);
    // RP# FORWARD
  }
```

```
  cout << n << endl;
}

int main()
{
  int arg = 3;
  forward(arg);
  // RP# MAIN
  cout << "In main: " << arg << endl;
  return 0;
}
```

Before the program begins executing, the stack is empty. When the function call in `main` is encountered, the return point, `RP# MAIN`, and the value of `n` (3) are put into a new box and placed on the stack. The stack is now represented as one box containing the return point (in the `main` program) and the value of the argument.

Since `n` > 1 is true, the recursive call is made which causes the return point and the value of `n` to be placed into another new box and placed on the stack.

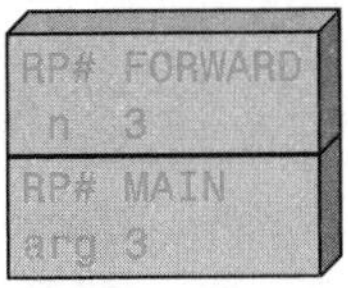

During the second call to `forward`, the recursive call of the `if` statement executes once again, causing the stack to look like this:

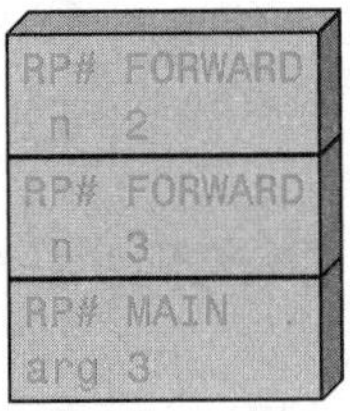

During the third call to `forward`, the recursive call of the `if` statement executes once again causing the stack to look like this:

The code in `forward` begins to execute again, but now the recursive call of the `if` statement is skipped because `n` > 1 is false. The last statement in the third instance of this function is executed: `cout << n`. But since there are three values of `n` stored on the stack, which value is referenced? It is the value found in the box on the top of the stack. Therefore, the integer 1 is displayed and the third execution to `forward` is complete. Once the program is about to continue from the return point contained in the box on the top of the stack, that top box can be removed. So now the stack would contain only three boxes and the program continues executing from `RP# FORWARD` in the previous instance of `forward`.

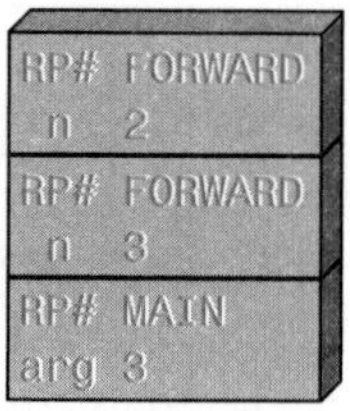

`RP# FORWARD` is located immediately after the `if`, so the `cout` statement of the previous instance executes causing the value of `n` to be output. The value of this variable is stored along with other vital information in the box at the top of the stack. Here `n` has the value of 2 so the output is 2. Now that the second instance of forward has finished executing, the program returns to `RP# FORWARD` in the first instance of `forward`. The stack now looks like this:

The value of `n` (3) is then output and control returns to `main` at `RP# MAIN`. The output statement in `main` executes. When `main` terminates, the stack now becomes empty and the program finishes. Here is the complete output from the program above.

OUTPUT

```
1
2
3
In main: 3
```

Notice that this recursive function has the characteristic that the last value of `n` was the first one displayed. This last-in/first-out (LIFO) characteristic of the stack is useful for keeping track of function calls. Also notice that `n` had the value of 3 during the first call to `forward`. This value 3 was the first parameter on the stack and was saved as the last value displayed. Another way to view the LIFO characteristic of a stack as discussed here (and earlier in Chapter 17), is to view a stack as first-in/last-out (FILO).

The stack analogy is similar to the stack that is implemented in a computer system. The main difference is that the computer uses memory to store the vital information. Each time a function is called, more memory is used up because each function must have its own set of vital information stored in order to remember such things as the values of parameters and the return point. The space reserved for this stack has a limit. When an attempt is made to store another set of vital information when there is no more memory, a runtime error occurs.

Self-Check

20-1 Implement a function named `backward` that recursively displays the integers from `n` down to -10 without using a loop. Do it recursively.

20.2 Defining the Base and Recursive Cases

Being able to determine the base case and the recursive case is a requirement of recursive programming. In `forward`, the base case was `n <= 1`, the logical negation of the `bool` expression `n > 1`. When this base case was reached, no statements were executed. Even if nothing happens when the base case is reached, it is critical that a base case is available. Without an appropriate base case, a function may call itself endlessly.

Returning to the first recursive definition used to define the function of raising an integer to an integer power (x^n), you should recognize that the base case occurs when $n == 0$. At this point x^0 is defined as 1. The recursive case occurs whenever $n > 0$. At that point, x^n is defined as $x * x^{(n-1)}$.

20.2.1 Recursive Functions

Recursion can be implemented with a function. Recursive functions can also be traced using the stack concept just described. Consider the function `mystery` that contains two parameters (`mystery` serves no useful purpose other than illustrating a recursive function). The recursive definition of `mystery` is

$$\text{mystery}(j, k) \begin{cases} 1 \text{ if } j <= k \\ j + k + \text{mystery}(j - 1, k + 2) \text{ if } j > k \end{cases}$$

From this definition the recursive and base cases can be easily determined:

BASE CASE

```
if(j <= k)
  mystery = 1;
```

RECURSIVE CASE

```
if(j > k)
  mystery = j + k + mystery(j - 1, k + 2);
```

When the base case is encountered, `mystery` is simply assigned the value of 1. Otherwise the function is called recursively with the first argument decreased by one and the second argument increased by two. Note that the return point after a recursive function call is in an expression. Only after `mystery(j - 1, k + 2)` is evaluated can the entire expression be evaluated.

```
#include <iostream>
using namespace std;

int mystery(int j, int k)
{
  if(j <= k)
    return 1;
  else
    return j + k + /* RP# MYST */ mystery(j - 1, k + 2);
```

```
}

int main()
{
  cout << "mystery(4, 2) = " << mystery(4, 2) << endl;   // 7
  cout << "mystery(2, 4) = " << mystery(2, 4) << endl;   // 1
  cout << "mystery(8, 1) = " << mystery(8, 1) << endl;   // 31

  return 0;
}
```

Let's trace the last function call `mystery(8, 1)`, observing how the stack grows and shrinks.

TRACING THE RECURSIVE FUNCTION `mystery`

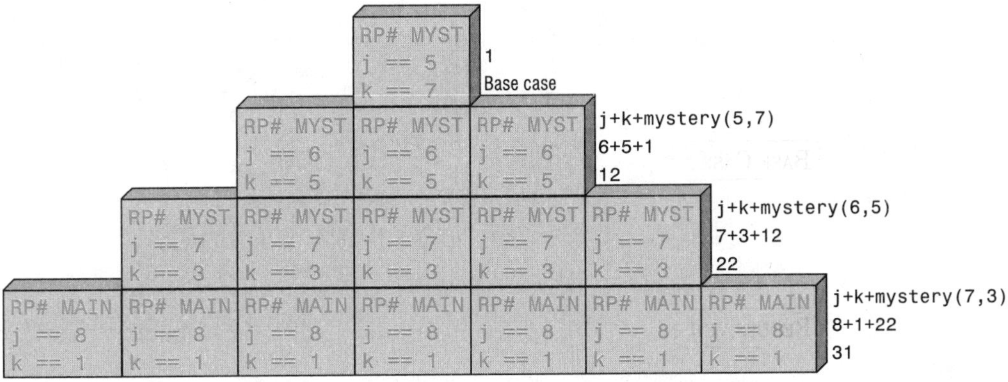

When each instance of `mystery` finishes, the box on the stack is replaced with the value of the function using the arguments shown in the box to the left. This value is then used to replace the recursive part of the expression in the previous (lower) function call.

20.2.2 A Factorial Function Using Iteration

Consider the `factorial` function (designated by !, an exclamation mark). $n!$ has the following nonrecursive definition:

ITERATIVE DEFINITION FOR `factorial`

$$n! \begin{cases} 1 \text{ if } n = 0 \text{ or } n = 1 \\ n * (n - 1) * (n - 2) * (n - 3), \ldots, * 3 * 2 * 1 \text{ if } n > 1 \end{cases}$$

EXAMPLES

$0! = 1$

$1! = 1$

$5! = 5 * 4 * 3 * 2 * 1 = 120$

The following version of the `factorial` function is written to return $n!$ using iteration. It is assumed that the only values for n are fairly small (13! would be too large to be represented even as a `long int`). The `factorial` function is undefined for $n < 0$.

```
#include <iostream>
using namespace std;
#include "compfun"

double factorial (int n)
{ // pre: n >= 0 and n is not too large
  double result = 1;
  for(int j = 2; j <= n; j++)
  {
    result = j * result;
  }
  return result;
}

int main()
{
  cout << factorial(0) << endl;  // 1
  cout << factorial(1) << endl;  // 1
  cout << factorial(2) << endl;  // 2
  cout << factorial(3) << endl;  // 6
  cout << factorial(4) << endl;  // 24

  decimals(cout, 1);
  cout << factorial(12) << endl;  // 479001600

  return 0;
}
```

The `factorial` function also has a recursive definition.

$$n! \begin{cases} 1 \text{ if } n = 0 \\ n * (n - 1)! \text{ if } n \geq 1 \end{cases}$$

This definition of the `factorial` function uses the function itself as part of the definition when $n > 0$. Here are some examples:

0! = 1

5! = 5 * (5 - 1)! = 120

Now, 5! can be calculated by repeatedly bringing the solution one step closer to the base case (n == 0):

5! = 5 * (4)! = 5 * 4 * (3)! = 5 * 4 * 3 * (2)! = 5 * 4 * 3 * 2 * (1)! = 5 * 4 * 3 * 2 * 1 * (0)!

At this time 0! is assigned the value of 1 and we can start backtracking by replacing previous calls with the partial solution.

```
                  0!              1!              2!         3!      4!   5!
                  |               |               |          |       |    |
5 * 4 * 3 * 2 * 1 * 1 = 5 * 4 * 3 * 2 * 1 = 5 * 4 * 3 * 2 = 5 * 4 * 6 = 5 * 24 = 120
```

When `main` calls `factorial(12)`, the first occurrence of `factorial` sees `n == 12`. The function will call itself 12 more times for `n` = 11, 10, 9, . . ., 0, where each recursive call uses the argument `n - 1`. The base case is finally reached when the function is called with `n == 0` and 1 is assigned to the function.

```
#include <iostream>
using namespace std;

double factorial(int n)
{ // pre: n >= 0 and n is not too large
  if( n == 0 )  // Base case
    return 1;
  else
    return n * /* RP# FACT */ factorial(n - 1);   // Recursive case
}

int main()
{
  cout << /* RP# MAIN */ factorial(3) << endl;  // 24

  return 0;
}
```

TRACING `factorial(3)`

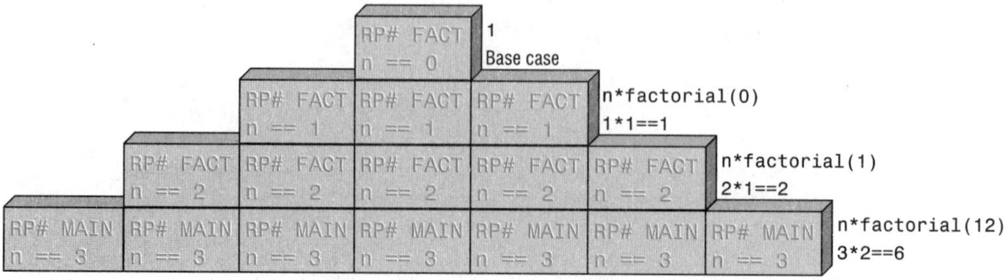

20.3 Converting Decimal Numbers to Other Bases

The problem introduced in this section contains an example of a recursive solution that converts a decimal number to a variety of different number bases. Most of us grew up with the familiar base 10 (decimal) number system that uses the digits from 0 to 9. Other number systems can be understood better by reviewing this more familiar decimal system. A decimal number such as 9,507 can also be written in an expanded form in this way:

$$9{,}507 = 9 * 10^3 + 5 * 10^2 + 0 * 10^1 + 7 * 10^0$$
$$9{,}000 \quad + \quad 500 \quad + \quad 0 \quad + \quad 7$$

Each digit in the decimal number system represents a coefficient of a power of 10. The right-most coefficient is multiplied by 10^0, the second right-most coefficient is multiplied by 10^1, and so on.

The base 8 (octal) number system contains the eight digits in the range of 0 to 7. Each digit is a coefficient of a power of the base, which in this case is 8. Therefore, the octal number 1567 can be written in an expanded form in this way:

$$1{,}567_8 = 1 * 8^3 + 5 * 8^2 + 6 * 8^1 + 7 * 8^0$$

or in decimal notation as

$$512 + 320 + 48 + 7 \quad (887_{10} = 1{,}567_8)$$

So 1,567 octal is equivalent to 887 base 10. The problem now is to write a recursive function that will convert a decimal number to other number systems with bases in the range of 2 through 9. The function must be tested with calls like this:

Function Call	Output
`Convert(99, 2)`	1100011
`Convert(99, 3)`	10200
`Convert(99, 4)`	1203
`Convert(99, 5)`	344
`Convert(99, 6)`	243
`Convert(99, 7)`	201
`Convert(99, 8)`	143
`Convert(99, 9)`	120

A decimal number can be converted to another number system by dividing the decimal number by the new base and writing the remainders in a right-to-left order. Each time the decimal number is divided, the quotient will become the next dividend. This process continues as long as the decimal number is greater than 0. The divisor is always the base of the number to be converted. For example, converting 5_{10} to its binary equivalent (base 2) goes like this:

Example: Convert 5_{10} to Its Base 2 (Binary) Equivalent

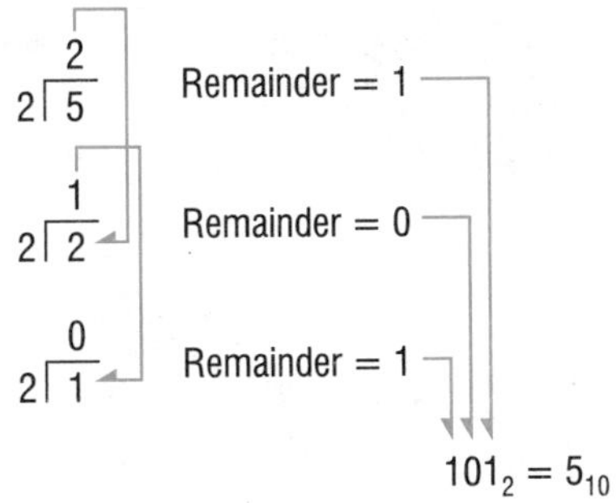

Another Example: Convert 99_{10} to Its Base 8 (Octal) Equivalent

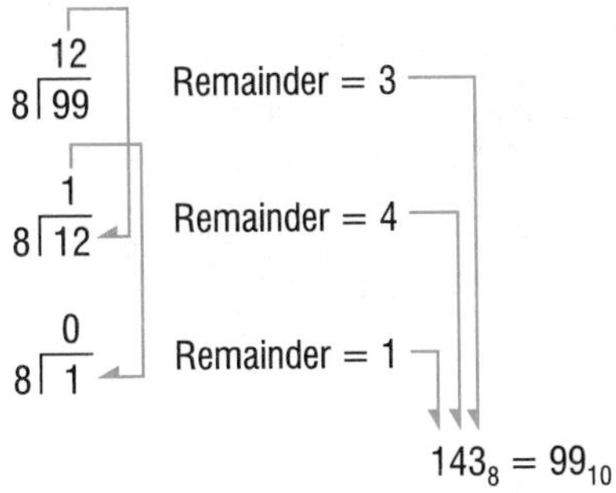

An iterative algorithm is given as follows:

```
While the decimal number > 0
{
   Divide the decimal number by the new base
   Set the decimal number to the decimal number divided by the base
   Write the remainder to the left of any preceding remainders
}
```

One of the problems with this algorithm is that C++ does not include a function for displaying digits in a right-to-left order. C++ output with `cout` goes in a left-to-right order. Since recursion has a last-in/first-out characteristic to it, we can overcome this problem with a recursive solution. In either an iterative or recursive solution, a function that converts a decimal number to a specified base requires two arguments:

1. `decimalNumber`: the decimal number to be converted
2. `base`: the base of the number system that the decimal number is to be converted to

Recall that the division of `decimalNumber` by `base` should occur until the quotient is 0. This leads to the base case:

BASE CASE

```
if decimalNumber <= 0
   Stop--Do nothing
```

Therefore the recursive call should be invoked whenever this is true:

RECURSIVE CASE

```
decimalNumber > 0
```

We now have to determine what should happen when the recursive case is encountered. Recursion is being used to postpone the display of the remainder until the base case is reached. Therefore, the first thing to do is to convert the quotient, `decimalNumber / base`, using the same base. By stacking the value of each quotient, each remainder can then be displayed in a last-in/first-out (or first-in/last-out) fashion. This leads to the recursive case:

RECURSIVE CASE

```
if decimalNumber > 0
{
    convert (decimalNumber / base, base)
    display decimalNumber % base   // Output postponed until decimalNumber is 0
}
```

All of the remainders will be stored on the stack until the quotient becomes 0. As the stack shrinks, the last remainder, `decimalNumber % base`, is output followed by the second to last and so on. In other words, the statement `cout << decimalNumber % base;` does not execute until the quotient of `decimalNumber / base` becomes zero.

The following program tests the input described earlier in this demonstration. The decimal number 99 is converted to base 2 through base 10 number systems.

```
#include <iostream>
using namespace std;

void convert(int decimalNumber, int base)
{
  if(decimalNumber > 0)
  {
    convert(decimalNumber / base, base);
    cout << decimalNumber % base;
  }
}

int main()
{
  for(int base = 2; base <= 10; base++)
  {
    cout << "99 base " << base << " = ";
    convert(99, base);
    cout << endl;
  }
  return 0;
}
```

OUTPUT

```
99 base 2 = 1100011
99 base 3 = 10200
99 base 4 = 1203
99 base 5 = 344
99 base 6 = 243
99 base 7 = 201
99 base 8 = 143
99 base 9 = 120
99 base 10 = 99
```

Self-Check

20-2 *True or False:* The base case sometimes includes a recursive call.

20-3 *True or False:* Recursive calls can go on indefinitely.

20-4 *True or False:* A function that includes its name in an expression will result in a recursive call.

20-5 *True or False:* The decimal number 5 is represented by 101 in the binary number system.

20-6 *True or False:* The decimal number 10 is represented as 25 in the base 8 number system.

20-7 Write the output generated by the following program:

```
#include <iostream>
using namespace std;

typedef int Type;  // Define type of data in each node
struct node {
  node(): next(0) {}
  node(Type data) : next(0), my_data(data) {};
  Type my_data;
  node* next;
};

void showReverse(node* temp)
{
  if(temp != 0)
  {
    showReverse(temp->next);
    cout << temp->my_data << endl;
  }
}

int main()
{
  node* p = new node(111);
  p->next = new node(222);
  p->next->next = new node(333);
  showReverse(p);
  return 0;
}
```

Chapter Summary

- A recursive call occurs when a function has a statement within it that invokes another occurrence of itself.
- For many problems, both recursive and iterative solutions exist.
- The base case of a recursive algorithm refers to the time when a recursive call is not needed. The base case is sometimes called the simple case.
- A recursive definition has some part that includes a simpler definition of itself. Some examples are the `power` and `factorial` functions.
- The characteristics of recursion are:
    1. The problem can be decomposed, using recursion, into a simpler version of itself in order to bring the problem closer to a base case.
    2. There are one or more base cases that can be solved without recursion.

Exercises

1. Write the output from the following program or write "stack overflow" if the base case does not occur:

```
#include <iostream>
using namespace std;

void go(int n)
{
 if(n > 0)
   go(n - 3);
 else
   cout << "Base Case " << n << endl;
}

int main()
{
  go(9);
  return 0;
}
```

2. Write the output from the following program or write "stack overflow" if the base case does not occur:

```
#include <iostream>
using namespace std;

void go(int n)
{
 if(n > 0)
   go(n + 3);
 else
   cout << "Base Case " << n << endl;
}

int main()
{
  go(9);
  return 0;
}
```

3. Write the output of the following program:

```
#include <iostream>
using namespace std;

int recurse(int n)
{
  if(n < 1)
    return 0;
  else if (n == 1)
    return 1;
  else
    return 2 * recurse(n - 1);
}

int main()
{
  cout << recurse(-5) << endl;
  cout << recurse(1)  << endl;
  cout << recurse(2)  << endl;
  cout << recurse(3)  << endl;
  cout << recurse(4)  << endl;

  return 0;
}
```

4. Let the `strange` numbers be defined as

```
strange(0) = 5
strange(1) = 3
```

```
strange(n) = 2 * strange(n - 2) for n > 1 only
```

Write a recursive function that returns `strange(n)` for values of `n` in the range of 0 through 12 and a `main` function containing the function call `strange(3)`.

5. What is the value of `strange(4)`?

6. List one actual parameter to `strange` that would cause a stack overflow.

7. Write a function `backward` that displays the integers 10, 9, 8, . . ., 1 on separate lines with the function call `backward(10)`. Use recursion to implement the iteration.

8. The Fibonacci sequence is

   1 1 2 3 5 8 13 21 34

   where each Fibonacci number is the sum of the preceding two except for the first two. Write a recursive definition for `fibonacci`.

9. List the base and recursive cases for the following function definition. For each case, list the action taken.

$$\text{binomial}(n, k) \begin{cases} 1 \text{ if } k = 0 \\ 1 \text{ if } n = k \\ \text{binomial}(n - 1, k - 1) + \text{binomial}(n - 1, k) \text{ if } 0 < k < n \end{cases}$$

10. Write a recursive function `binomial` as defined in exercise 9.

11. Evaluate `binomial(n, k)` for the following values of `n` and `k` or write "undefined" if `binomial` is not assigned a value:

n	k	binomial(n, k)
1	0	
0	1	
8	8	
2	1	

Programming Tips

1. Before developing a recursive algorithm, identify the recursive and base cases.

There may be one or more recursive and base cases. Once these are identified, the algorithm is more easily developed. Don't forget that when a base case is encountered, it is possible that nothing will occur. In other words, no recursive call is made.

2. Make sure each recursive call brings you closer to the simple case.

When you write recursive functions, you must have a step that brings the problem closer to the base case. This could involve incrementing or decrementing a parameter as an argument to the next call or advancing a pointer while traversing a linked list.

```
// Decrement n
return 2 * recursiveFunction(n - 1);

// Advance a pointer
showReverse(temp->next);
```

3. Use the stack analogy to debug recursive functions.

Using recursion can lead to stack overflows or incorrect results. The stack analogy is one tool that can be used to help detect logic errors in recursive algorithms.

4. Recursion can be elegant, but it can also be costly.

In future studies you will find very nice recursive solutions to difficult problems. Examples you should soon see include the recursive quicksort algorithm and binary tree traversal. While such elegant uses of recursion provide runtime efficiency, some recursive functions are tremendously slow. An iterative solution is much better. You can verify this by completing programming problem 20A and counting how many seconds it takes to compute `fibonacci(40)` recursively.

Programming Projects

20A Fibonacci

Implement the recursive function `fibonacci` described in exercise 8. Determine the largest Fibonacci number than can be represented as a `long int`.

20B Number Conversions

Modify the `convert` function to allow for a conversion of decimal numbers up to base 16 (hexadecimal). Use the following conversion table to allow symbols that represent the decimal numbers 10 through 15:

Decimal Value	Symbol to Display
10	A
11	B
12	C
13	D
14	E
15	F

A function call that would convert 142 base 10 to its base-16 equivalent should be `convert(142, 16)`. Test your program by converting the decimal numbers 1 through 17 to their hexadecimal equivalents (1, 2, 3, 4, 5, 6, 7, 8, 9, A, B, C, D, E, F, 10, 11).

20C `reversePrint`

Write a recursive operation `reversePrint` that will print out a `vector` of integers where the first element printed has the largest subscript (the last meaningful element) and the last element has the smallest. Use a `vector` of integers with five elements to test your program.

Appendix
Answers to Self-Check Questions

Chapter 1 Analysis and Design

1-1 Study, examination

1-2 Plan and outline

1-3 Execution and fulfilling

1-4 A college degree perhaps (other answers are possible)

1-5 Input: `pounds` and perhaps `todaysConversionRate`; output: `USDollars`

1-6 `cdCollection` `selectedCD`

1-7

Problem	Object Name	Input/Output	Sample Problem
Compute distance traveled	`meterPerSecond`	Input	28.0
	`secondsInFlight`	Input	3.1
	`distance`	Output	86.8

1-8

Problem	Object Name	Input/Output	Sample Problem
Compute the future value of an investment	`presentValue`	Input	1000.00
	`periods`	Input	360
	`rate`	Input	0.0075
	`futureValue`	Output	14730.58

1-9 Turn the oven off (or you might recognize some other activity has been omitted)

1-10 No (at least the author thinks it's okay)

1-11 No (at least the author thinks it's okay)

1-12 No. The `courseGrade` would be computed using undefined values for `test1`, `test2`, and `finalExam`.

1-13 No. The details of the process step are not present. The formula is missing.

1-14 // Input

Retrieve values from the user for the three inputs:

```
test1:      0
test2:      50
finalExam:  100
```

// Process
Retrieve object state and compute `courseGrade` as follows:

```
courseGrade = (0.25 * test1) + (0.25 * test2) + (0.50 * finalExam)
              (0.25 * 0.0) + (0.25 * 50.0) + (0.50 * 100.0)
              (0.0 + 12.5 + 50.0)
courseGrade = 62.5
```

// Output
Show `courseGrade` (62.5) to the user

1-15 -a I, II, II, and VI -b IV and V

1-16 No

1-17 No

1-18 The program is wrong

1-19 The prediction is wrong

1-20 The program is wrong

1-21 Numbers with a fractional part—floating-point numbers such as -1.2 or 1.023

1-22 A collection of characters such as "A collection of characters"

1-23 Integers—numbers without a decimal point such as -32,768 and 32,767. *Caution:* the range of numbers on any computer is limited. However, the range just mentioned is available on all systems. The actual range of integers is system dependent (unfortunately). Most systems implement `int` to store integers in the range of -2,147,483,648 to 2,147,483,647.

1-24 + - * (also = output with `cout` << and input with `cin` >>)

1-25 `double`, `int`, `bool`, and `char`. (*Note:* It isn't clear from the information provided if `ostream` and `istream` objects store more than one value as their state.)

1-26 `vector` and `string`

Chapter 2 Implementation

2-1 22 plus or minus two. Actually, it is easy to miscount, so let the compiler worry about it.

2-2
-a VALID
-b 1 can't start identifier
-c VALID
-d # not allowed
-e Space not allowed
-f # not allowed
-g ! not allowed
-h VALID
-i ( ) not allowed
-j VALID (`double` is not)
-k VALID
-l Periods (`.`) not allowed
-m `double` is a reserved word
-n Can't start identifiers with `5`
-o Space not allowed
-p VALID
-q VALID
-r VALID (but weird)
-s VALID (but weird)
-t / not allowed
-u VALID

2-3 + - (also , : ; ! () = {})

2-4 << >> (also != == <= >=)

2-5 `cin` and `cout` (also `string` `vector` `width` `sqrt`)

2-6 `thisIsOne` and `this Is_YET_Another_1`

2-7 -a `string` constants: `"H"` and `"integer"`

-b Integer constants: `234` and `-123`

-c Floating-point constants: `1.0` and `1.0e+03`

2-8 -a and -d only

2-9
```
double aNumber = -1.0;
double anotherNumber = -1.0;
```

2-10
```
string address;
```

2-11

Standard Compiler	Almost Any Compiler

`#include <iostream>`
`using namespace std;`
`int main()`
`{`
` cout << "Your name" << endl;`
` return 0;`
`}`
	`#include <iostream.h>`
	`int main()`
	`{`
	` cout << "Your name" << endl;`
	` return 0;`
	`}`

2-12 -b and -c only

2-13 -a 10.5 -b 1.75 -c 3.5

-d -0.75 -e -0.5 -f 1.0

2-14 -a 3.2 16.0/5.0 -b 1.9 9.5/5.0 -c 2.8 14.0/5.0

2-15 -a 99.0 -b "Canada" -c 1.5

-d "Two" -e 1.5 -f "2.6"

Chapter 3 Function Calls and Headings

3-1 `pow(4.0, 3.0)` is 4.0 * 4.0 * 4.0 or 64

3-2 `pow(3.0, 4.0)` is 3.0 * 3.0 * 3.0 * 3.0 or 81

3-3 `floor(1.6 + 0.5)` is 2.0

3-4 `ceil(1.6 - 0.5)` is also 2.0

3-5

Problem	Object Name	Input/Output	Sample Problem
Round x to n decimals	x	Input	6.789
	n	Input	1
	x	Output	6.8

3-6 Obtain x and n from the user
Round x to n decimal places
Display x

3-7 Trace 9.99 rounded to one decimal place

x	n
99.9	1
100.4	1
100.0	1
10.0	1

3-8 Three sample problems

x	n	Changed x
0.567	1	0.6
1234.56789	2	1234.57
-1.5	1	-1.0

3-9 `3.2`

3-10
```
x = x * pow(10, n)
x = x - 0.5   // Subtract 0.5
x = ceil(x)   // Take the ceiling of x
x = x / pow(10, n)
```

3-11 -a `16.0` or `16` -b `4.0` or `4` -c `-1.0` or `-1`

-d `1.0` -e `23.4` -f `16.0`

3-12 -a Valid -b Wrong function name -c Too many arguments

-d Incorrect class of argument -e Missing (and)

-f Valid—the `int` is promoted to a `double`

3-13 -a Missing class in parameter -b Missing , -c No return type

-d Okay if `myClass` exists, but it doesn't -e Extra , before)

-f Attempt at parameter is a `string` constant

3-14 1. `floor(1.9999)` 2. `floor(0.99999)` 3. `floor(1.0)` 4. `floor(-1.5)`

3-15 1. 1.0 2. 0.0 3. 1.0 4. -2.0

3-16 `"1st"` 3-17 `3.4`

3-18 -a `double` -b `pow` -c 2

-d `double` -e `double` -f There is no third argument

3-19 `pow(-81.0, 2)`

3-20 No, the preconditions are not met. The return value is undefined.

3-21 Yes, `10.0` 3-22 Yes, `32.0`

3-23 Yes, `2.0` // You might have needed a scientific calculator. $x^{0.5}$ is the square root of x.

3-24 No, missing second argument. Return value cannot be determined.

3-25
```
double fractmod(double dividend, double divisor)
// pre:  Divisor is not zero
// post: Return the floating-point remainder of dividend/divisor
```

3-26 `0`

3-27 -a `0` -b `1` -c `0` -d `1` -e `0` -f `0`

3-28 -a 0 -b 0.555556 -c 0.555556 -d 10 -e 12 -f 2

3-29 Don't know—it depends on the garbage value of `x`.

3-30 Average should be `25.0` instead of `0.04`. This is an intent error.

3-31 Change `cin >> n` to `cin >> sum` and `cin >> sum` to `cin >> n`.

3-32 -a Intent—you'll see the `string sum / n` and not the average.

-b Runtime on older compiler but this is not error; division by 0 returns infinity.

-c Compiletime—the , should be <<

-d Compiletime—missing ;

Chapter 4 Messages and Member Functions

4-1 -a Missing second argument

-b Missing first argument

-c `BankAccount` is an undefined symbol. Change `B` to `b`.

-d Missing a numeric argument between `(` and `)`

-e Missing `(`, the argument, and `)`

-f Wrong class of argument. Pass a number, not a `string`.

-g `B1` is undefined

-h. `Deposit` is not a member of `bankAccount`. Change `D` to `d`.

-i Need an object and a dot before `withdraw`

-j `b4` is not a `bankAccount` object; it was never declared to be anything

-k Missing `()` after `name`

-l `name` takes zero arguments, not one

4-2
```
B. Kreible: 202.22
N. Li: 545.55
```

4-3 `6`

4-4 `"efg"`

4-5 `8`

4-6 `"Wheatley, Kay"`

4-7
```
string mid;
string aString = "abcdefghi";
int midChar = aString.length() / 2;
mid = aString.substr(midChar-1, 3);
```

4-8 -a error -b error -c error -d `3` -e `y str` -f error

4-9
```
123456789012345
  1  2.3   who
```

4-10
```
9.88
1
1.2
```

4-11 -a
```
Enter an integer: 123
Good? 1
```
-b
```
Enter an integer: XYZ
Good? 0
```

4-12 -a `istream` -b `grid` -c `ostream`

-d `string` -e `bankAccount` -f `istream`

4-13 `changeMe.replace(4, 5, "12345");`

The `string` is changed from `abcdefghijklmnopqrstuvwxyz` to `abcd12345jklmnopqrstuvwxyz`

4-14
```
. . . . . .
. . <     .
. . . .   .
. . . .   .
. .       .
. . . . . .
row: 1
col: 2
```

4-15
1. Moving off the edge of the grid.
2. Moving through a block.
3. Attempting to pick up something that isn't there.

4-16 1

4-17 35

4-18
```
#include "grid"
#include <iostream>
using namespace std;
int main()
{
grid g(5, 5, 2, 3, east);
g.move(1);
g.face(north);
g.move(1);
g.face(west);
g.move(1);
g.face(south);
g.move();
g.display();
```

```
return 0;
}
```

4-19 35 + 112 + 15 + 112 + 15 + 112 + 15 + 112 + 15 + 6 = 209

4-20 Less code to write. Abstraction allows us to think of what the function does, not the details of the implementation.

4-21 Use the phone without worrying about how sound travels.
Walk around without worrying about how to walk and breathe.

Chapter 5 Functions and Parameters

5-1 -a `double` -b `double` -c `int` -d `string`

5-2 -a `-1.0` -b `7.0` -c `17.0`
-d One too many arguments -e One too few arguments -f `66.28`

5-3 `1.5`

5-4 No. The argument is supposed to be positive. The result depends on the system you are using. You could get `Infinity`, `NaN` for not a number, or a square root of a negative number error.

5-5 `0.1`

5-6 -a Remove `;` after `)` -b `j` is unkown in `f2` -c `j` is unkown in `f3`
-d Return missing—you cannot assign a number to a function name.
-e Must return a number, not the `double` class name.
-f Must return an `int`; `f6` tries to return a `string` instead.

5-7
```
double times3(double x)
{
return 3 * x;
}
```

5-8

`cout:`	`f1`, `f2`, and `main`		
`b`	`f1` only	`cin`	`f1`, `f2`, and `main`
`MAX`	`f1`, `f2`, and `main`	`c`	`f2` only
`f1`	`f1`, `f2`, and `main`	`a`	`f1` only
`d`	`f2` only	`f2`	`f2` and `main`
`main`	`main` cannot be called or referenced	`e`	`main` only

5-9 Parameters and objects declared within the function's block.

5-10 Anywhere to the end of the file unless it is redeclared within a block; then the global is hidden from that particular function.

5-11 `string`, `cout`, `endl`, `cin`, `good`, `width`, and many others not previously discussed in this textbook.

5-12 -a `arg1` is `0` -b `arg1` is `77`

5-13 -a `arg1 is 5` `arg2 is 5` -b `arg1 is 11` `arg2 is 123`

5-14 -a `4`

-b `0.00000` `1.23457`

-c `0`

-d If you answered `0.00000` and `1.23457`, you understand the missing &. However, this is an atypical compiletime error. `ostream` cannot be passed by value.

Chapter 6 Class Definitions and Member Functions

6-1
```
Name: Moss
Balance: 440
Default Name:
Default Balance: 0
```

6-2 `withdraw  deposit  balance  name`

6-3 `my_name` and `my_balance`

6-4 -a The balance increases by 20.00 during this withdraw message.

-b The balance goes to -50.00.

-c The balance is changed from 300.00 to 200.00. Everything is normal here.

-d The deposit of -20.00 decreases the balance by 0.00.

-e The balance increases by 20.00. Everything is normal here.

6-5 `libraryBook`

6-6 `borrowBook  returnBook  borrower`

6-7 `string`

6-8 None (or void)

6-9 a `string` (the borrower's name)

6-10 Two: the author and book title

6-11 `libraryBook aBook("Computing Fundamentals with C++", "Rick Mercer");`

6-12 `aBook.borrowBook("My Name");`

6-13 `cout << aBook.borrower() << endl;`

6-14
```
not currently borrowed
Chris Miller
not currently borrowed
```

6-15 The member function is an accessor—it does not change the state of the object.

6-16 The constructors

6-17 Allow access to the state of any object so humans or other objects can either inspect or use that state. An accessor may return a data member, or some sort of processing may occur to return some information about the state of the object.

6-18 Modify the state of the object. At least one data member gets changed for each modifying message—otherwise it is an accessor.

6-19 Allow clients to initialize objects with either the default state or their own initial values.

6-20 To store the state of any object. Each instance of the class has its own copy of the data members.

6-21 By adding the class name and `::` before the function name (after the return type). Of course the rest of the function heading must *exactly* match the function heading in the class definition.

6-22 Yes

6-23 No

6-24 Lines 2 and 3 are attempts to send a modifying message to a `const` object (the parameter `b`)

6-25 Its member functions

6-26 No

6-27 Yes

6-28 The scope of public members extends to all member functions of the class and on to wherever an object of that class is declared.

6-29 Private members can only be accessed by the member functions of that class.

6-30 It prevents accidental modification of an object's state.
The client code relies on the interface, not the internal implementation details.
There is a design heuristic for this.

6-31 No. The client code does not access private data—another benefit of private data members.

6-32 Yes. This is why it is a good idea to design the class interface so carefully that it rarely (if ever) needs to be changed.

6-33 The `libraryBook` object

6-34 No. That would not be tight cohesion. The message is obviously not related to `bankAccounts`.

6-35 Sounds reasonable.

6-36 Both. However, a modifying message will *not* modify the associated argument.

6-37 Both. With the `&` parameter, modifying messages *do* modify the associated argument.

6-38 Accessors only (unless you have Borland, which reduces the compiletime error to a warning).

6-39 No.

Chapter 7 Selection

7-1 -a true -b false -c false -d true -e true -f true
-g false // = is assignment, not equality (which is ==) -h true // 165 is nonzero

7-2 -a `addRecord` -b `deleteRecord` -c (no output) `option` is a lowercase "a"
-d `failing` -e `dubious` -f

```
g: 45
at cutoff
g: 70
you get one
g: 1
```

7-3 `Tune-up due in 0 miles`

7-4 -a 38.0 -b 40.0 -c 43.0 -d 45.25

7-5 -a

```
true
after if...else
```

-b `zero or pos` -c `x is low` -d `neg`

7-6
```
if(option == 1)
  cout << "Your name" << endl;
else
  cout << "Your school" << endl;
```

7-7 -a true -b false -c true -d false

-e true -f false -g true -h true

7-8 `(score >= 1) && (score <= 10)` 7-9 `(test > 100) || (score < 0)`

7-10 `President's list` // Always true because = was used instead of ==

7-11

Row	Column	Output
3	4	`Not`
4	3	`Not`
2	2	`Not`
0	2	`On edge`
2	0	`On edge`

7-12 -a true -b false -c false -d false

7-13 All four. The right-most expression had to be evaluated because the first three are false (as is the fourth).

7-14 The last three `cout`s were not evaluated. This is weird code meant to vividly demonstrate short circuit Boolean evaluation.

7-15 -a
```
Enter four integers: 1 2 3 4
Success!
The four ints: 1 2 3 4
```

-b
```
Enter four integers: 1 2 3 Bad
Failure!
The four ints: 1 2 3 0
```
The 0 is garbage, it may be any other number

-c
```
Enter four integers: Bad 2 3 4
Failure!
The four ints: 0  4216728  6618612  4261405
```
All four could be any garbage number

7-16 -a `okay` -b `failed` -c `okay` -d `failed`

7-17 70

7-18 This unfortunate student gets a D instead of the deserved C.

7-19 I know I wouldn't be happy; I doubt you would be either.

7-20 `-40: extremely frigid` `20: warm` `-1: below freezing`

`42: toast` `15: freezing to mild` `31: very hot`

7-21 20 through 29 inclusive 7-22 0 through 19 inclusive

7-23 -41 -40 0 20 30 40 41 7-24 -a `AAA` -b `one`

7-25 `BBB` 7-26 `Invalid`

7-27 `Invalid`

7-28
```
switch(choice)
{
  case 1:
    cout << "Favorite music is Jazz" << endl;
    break;
  case 2:
    cout << "Favorite food is Tacos" << endl;
    break;
  case 3:
    cout << "Favorite teacher is John Cleese" << endl;
    break;
  default
    cout << "Error" << endl;
}
```

Chapter 8 Repetition

8-1 No, the `init` statement happens first (and only once).

8-2 No, you can use increments of any amount, including negative increments (or decrements).

8-3 No; for example: `for(j = 1; j < n; j++)` when n == 0.

8-4 If the update step does not increment `j`. Or inside the loop `j` is decremented as much as it is incremented: `for(j = 1; j < n; j){ }` - or - `for(j = 1; j < n; j++){j--;}`

8-5 -a `1 2 3 4` -b `1 2 3 4 5` -c `-3 -1 1 3`

-d `0 1 2 3 4` -e `5 4 3 2 1` -f
```
before
after
```

8-6
```
for(j = 1; j <= 100; j++)
{
  cout << j << endl;
}
```

8-7
```
for(j = 10; j >= 1; j--)
{
  cout << j << " ";
}
```

8-8 An attempt is made to block an intersection at a nonexistent row. The program terminates.

8-9 No big deal, the right corners would be blocked twice.

8-10 The function would alter a copy of the `grid`, not the `grid` in `main`. The border would be set locally in `setBorder`, but it would not modify the argument `myGrid` in `main`.

8-11 Range = 3

8-12 `range = 29` (this is correct)

`highest`	-9999	-5	8	22	22	22
`lowest`	9999	-5	-5	-5	-7	-7

8-13 `range = 4` (this is correct)

`highest`	-9999	5	5	5	5	5
`lowest`	9999	9999	4	3	2	1

8-14 `range = -9998` (this is obviously incorrect)

highest	-9999	5	4	3	2	1
lowest	9999	9999	9999	9999	9999	9999

8-15 -b When the input is entered in ascending order.

8-16 Get rid of the `else`.

8-17 The client code will never know in advance how many moves must be made. It cannot be determined in advance.

8-18 -a 56.33333—the first test (70.0) is destroyed before it's added to the accumulator. Additionally, the sentinel -1 is incorrectly added to the accumulator.

-b 80.0

8-19 Observe the location of the second `cin >> testScore`. Redo till you arrive at the preceding answers of 56.3333 for -a and 80.0 for -b.

8-20 -b The input statement comes immediately before it is compared to the sentinel (-1).

8-21 Zero

8-22 Input another `cin >> testScore` at the bottom of the loop.

8-23 A tricky question. Remove the `;` after `)`. This loop does nothing infinitely because `;` represents the null statement. It is legal code, but it was not what was likely intended.

8-24 -a `1 2 3` -b `2 4 6 8 10`

8-25 -a unknown -b zero -c 5

-d infinite -e infinite -f infinite, notice the `;` after `)`

8-26
```
int sum = 0;
int x = 0;
while( (cin >> x) && (x != 999) )
{
  sum += x;
}
```

8-27 -a
```
1
2
3
```
-b
```
-1
-0.5
0
0.5
1
```

8-28
```
int x;
do {
  cout << "Enter a number in the range of 1 through 10: ";
  cin >> x;
} while( x < 1 || x > 10);
```

8-29
```
do {
  cout << "Enter A)dd W)ithdraw Q)uit: ";
  cin >> option;
  option = toupper(option);
} while( option != 'A' && option != 'W' && option != 'Q');
```

8-30 -a Determinate `for` loop -b Determinate `for` loop

-c Indeterminate `while` loop -d Indeterminate `do while` loop

Chapter 9 File Streams

9-1
```
// Programmer: Yazz Palmerton
// Due date: October 28
// file name: THISPROG.CPP
#include <fstream>  // For the ifstream class
#include <iostream> // For cout
#include <string>
using namespace std;

int main()
{
  string aString;
  ifstream inFile("THISPROG.CPP");
  for(int j = 1; j <= 4; j++)
  {
    inFile >> aString;
    cout << aString << " ";
  }
  cout << endl;
  return 0;
}
```

9-2 Can't average zero numbers.

9-3 -a Failed to find the file `numbers.dat`

-b
```
iteration # 1: 0.001
End of file reached. 1 numbers found.
```

-c
```
End of file reached. 0 numbers found.
```

9-4 -a `6` -b `15` -c `6`

-d `1` (The period `.` sets `inFile` to a bad state and the loop terminates.)

9-5 The loop would terminate since there would be no last name for `Kline`. The status would be `Kline`, the last name `Sue`. The employee `Kline` would never be constructed.

9-6 The loop would terminate when `S` was encountered for `exempts`. The employee `Kline` would never be constructed.

9-7 -a `1313 Mockingbird Lane` -b `1214 West Walnut Tree Drive`

Chapter 10 Vectors

10-1 100

10-2 0

10-3 99

10-4 0

10-5 `x[0] = 78;`

10-6
```
int n = 100;
for(int j = 0; j < n; j++)
{
  x[j] = n - j;
}
```

10-7
```
for(j = 0; j < n; j++)
{
  cout << x[j] << endl;
}
```

10-8 That depends. The computer may "crash"; you may destroy the state of another object; or with subscript range checking, you may get a runtime error before the program terminates.

10-9 `vector::resize` and `vector::capacity`

10-10
```
0   1   2   3   4

0   1   2
```

10-11 -a `"SUSIE"` -b `"MIKEY"`

-c Cannot say—the subscript is out of bounds. -d `""` (the null string)

10-12 The behavior is undefined. Either the program terminates gracefully with a protection error, a message appears stating that the subscript is out of bounds, or there could be a system crash, segmentation fault, hang, ... The loop is an infinite loop; however, eventually your program will access memory that no longer belongs to your program or to the computer.

10-13 1

10-14 4

10-15 `n`

10-16 0 (because of short circuit Boolean evaluation)

10-17 `irst econ hir ourt`

10-18
```
account[12] = bankAccount("A12thCustomer", 1212.12);

account[13] = bankAccount("Cust13", 1313.13);
```

10-19 The 21st account on the 21st line of the file would not become part of the account database. The `vector` size would not be big enough and the loop would terminate because `numberOfAccounts < account.capacity()` would be false.

10-20
```
#include <iostream>
#include <fstream>
using namespace std;
int main()
{
  vector <int> vectorOfInts(1000);
  // File name will do if it is in the working directory
  ifstream inFile("int.dat");
  int n = 0;
  int el;

  while( (inFile >> el) && (n < vectorOfInts.capacity()) )
  {
    vectorOfInts[n] = el;
    n++;
  }
  return 0;
}
```

10-21 `n`

10-22
```
cout << "Number of meaningful ints in vectorOfInts is " << n << endl;
cout << "Here they are" << endl;
for(int j = 0; j < n; j++)
{
  cout << j << ". " << vectorOfInts[j] << endl;
}
```

10-23 `grid` and `vector` objects are much bigger than `int`s and `double`s—that is, it takes more memory to store a `grid` than an `int` (appoximately 800 bytes versus 4 bytes). A `vector` of 1,000 `double`s is 1,000 times larger than 1 `double`.

10-24 -a 100,000 * 57 or 5.7 million bytes -b 4 -c 4

10-25 Ascending

10-26 The first element in the `vector` is swapped with itself. That means three extra assignments, but it is not worth worrying about this special case.

10-27
```
double largest = x[0];
for(int j = 1; j < n; j++)
{
  if( x[j] > largest )
    largest = x[j];
}
```

10-28 The `vector` is sorted and the binary search knows whether it is ascending or descending order.

10-29 1. 1024 2. 512 3. 256 4. 128 5. 64 6. 32 7. 16 8. 8 9. 4
10. 2 11. 1 The highest number of comparisons is 11.

10-30 When `first` exceeds `last`, the beginning and end of the `vector` no longer make any sense. For example, when `first` == 1028 and `last` == 1026.

10-31 1. Swap the location of the two statements `last = mid - 1;` and `first = mid + 1;`
- or -
2. Change the expression `if(searchString < str[mid])` to
`if(str[mid] < searchString)`

DO NOT make both changes.

Chapter 11 A Container with Iterators

11-1 `bag::remove` returns false; the `bag` object is not modified.

11-2 Nothing noticeable to the user, the sequential search loop test `(subscript < my_size)` is false immediately so subscript remains 0. Then the expression `if(subscript == my_size)` is true and false is returned.

11-3
```
#include <iostream>
#include <string>
using namespace std;
typedef string BAG_ELEMENT_TYPE;
```

```
#include "bag"

int main()
{
bag names;
  names.add("Your Name");
  names.remove("Your Name");
  cout << "0? " << names.size() << endl;  // Verify size is zero
  return 0;
}
```

11-4 Zero

11-5 No. The last element may be moved to the first `vector` position, or the second, or anywhere else. There are other containers used to store elements in order.

11-6 `bag::remove` will remove the first occurrence. All other occurrences of the same value remain in the `bag`.

11-7
```
size: 35
capacity: 64
```

11-8
```
#include <iostream>
using namespace std;

typedef int BAG_ELEMENT_TYPE;
#include "bag" // For the bag class

int main()
{
  bag aBagOfInts;
  // Add a few integers
  aBagOfInts.add(1);
  aBagOfInts.add(4);
  aBagOfInts.add(0);
  aBagOfInts.add(8);
  aBagOfInts.add(9);
  aBagOfInts.add(7);
  aBagOfInts.add(6);

  // Initial the largest as the first
  int current;
  aBagOfInts.first();
  int largest = aBagOfInts.currentItem();
  aBagOfInts.next();

  // Check the second through last bag elements
  while(! aBagOfInts.isDone())
  {
    current = aBagOfInts.currentItem();
    if(current > largest)
      largest = current;
    aBagOfInts.next();
  }
```

```
    cout << "Largest: " << largest << endl;

    return 0;
}
```

Chapter 12 Object-Oriented Software Development: Analysis and Design

12-1 Illustration by Robert W. Becker III

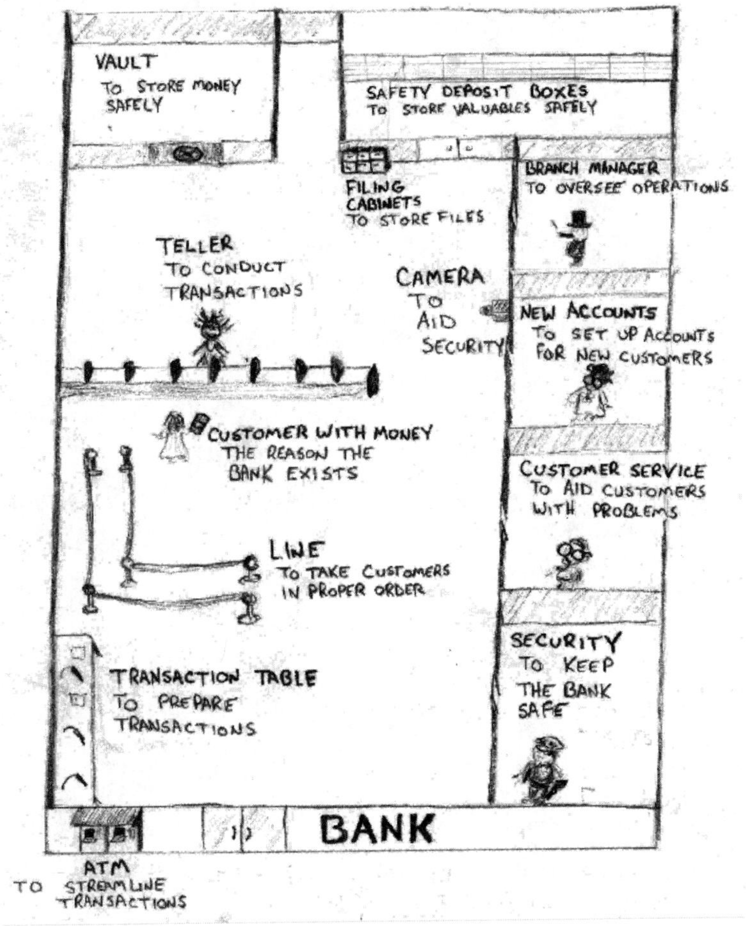

12-2 Illustration by Robert W. Becker III

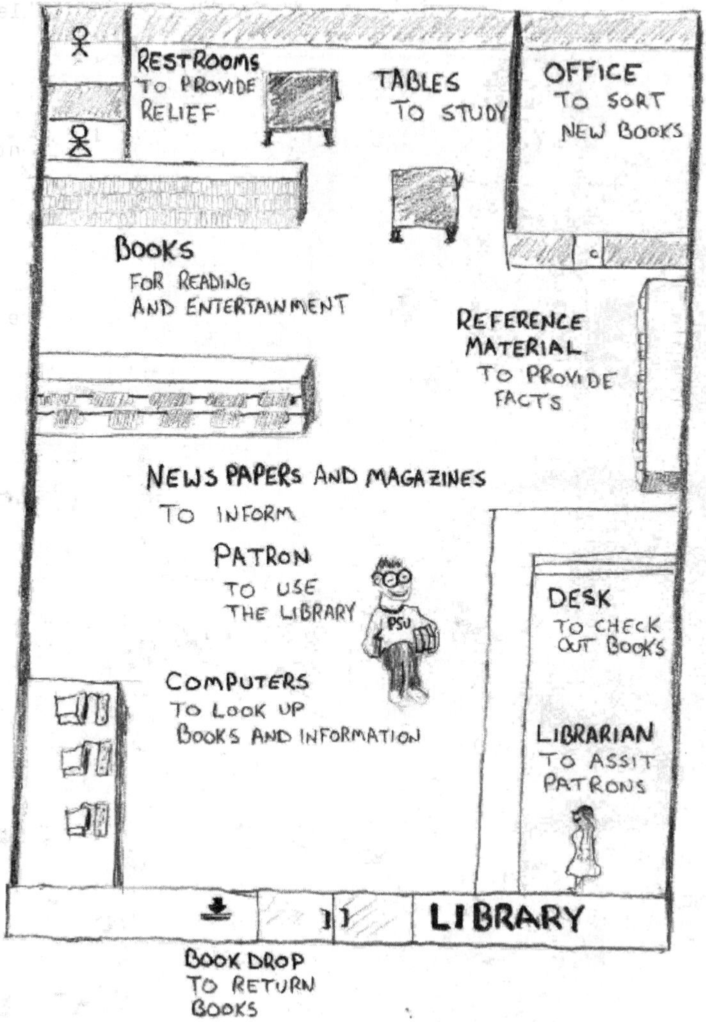

12-3 College library: librarian, student, book, fees, date

12-4

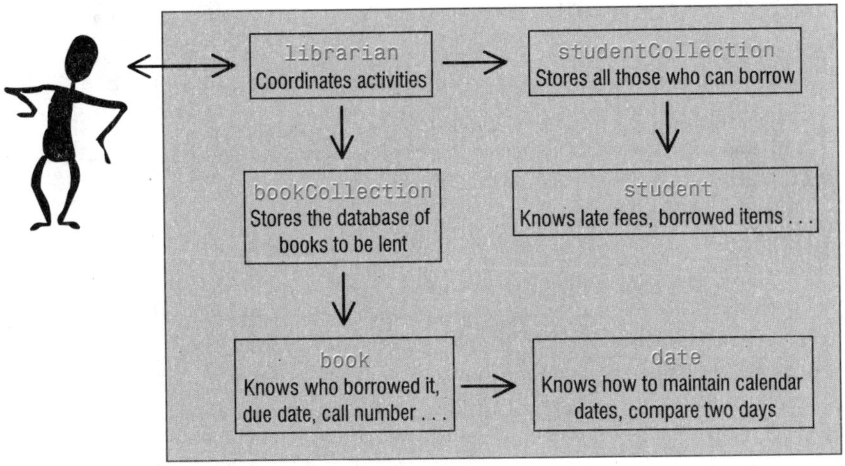

12-5
```
string ID = myCardreader.getStudentID();
currentStudent = myStudentCollection.getStudent(ID);
currentSelection = myTrackSelector.getSelection(myCdCollection));
if(student.canSelect)
  myCdPlayer.playTrack(currentSelection)
```

12-6 -a New account is created; she plays two songs; time credit is deducted for those two songs.

-b Tell the student she has no more time credit.

-c The database of CDs in the CD collection must be updated to reflect any physical changes to the CDs in the physical CD player.

-d Same as 12-6-c.

-e Probably, the student will get time credit deducted, even though the track does not play.

12-7 Return a book with no late fee.
Return a book with a late fee.
Have a student pay a fine.

12-8 `librarian`: Well, I'm the librarian so I guess I'll start. I just got a user ID. It's #1234. Someone give me the student with ID 1234.
`borrowerList`: I found the borrower you asked for. I'm sending it back to you.
`librarian`: User, what do you want to do?
User: I want to check out a book.
`librarian`: Now I need to know the call number of the book.
User: The book's call number is QA76.1.
`librarian`: Okay, now let me verify if that user can borrow. I'll ask `bookList` to look up the borrower with ID #1234.
`bookList`: Here is the book.
`librarian`: Okay now, what about it current `borrower`, can you borrow a new book?
`borrower`: Yes I can. I'll update myself to be holding the borrowed `book`.

`librarian`: `book`, check yourself out.

`book`: Okay, you give me the `borrower`, and I'll update myself so I'm not available and I'll set my due date.

12-9 `librarian`: Well, I'm the librarian so I guess I'll start. I just got a user ID. It's #1234.

`borrowerList`: Get me the borrower with ID #1234.

`borrowerList`: I found the borrower you asked for. I'm sending it back to you.

`librarian`: Now User, what do you want to do?

User: I want to return a book.

`librarian`: Now I need to know the call number of the book.

User: The book's call number is QA76.1.

`librarian`: Okay `bookList`, get me the book with call number QA76.1.

`bookList`: Here it is.

`librarian`: `book`, check yourself out.

Chapter 13 Object-Oriented Software Development: Design and Implementation

13-1
```
class student {
public:
  // Not sure about the constructor yet, is input from a file?
  // Should there be a readFromFile and a writeToFile operation?
  void checkOut(book aBook);
  void checkIn(book aBook);
  bool canBorrow() const;
  double lateFee() const;
private:
  vector <book> my_borrowedBooks;
  int my_numberOfBorrowedBooks;
  string my_name, my_ID;
  double my_lateFees;
};
```

13-2
```
class book {
public:
  book(string author, string title, string callNumber);
  void checkOut(const student & borrower);
  // Record borrower's ID
  void checkIn();
  // Indicate the book is available
  date dueDate() const;
  bool isAvailable() const;
private:
  string my_author, my_title, my_borrower;
  date my_dueDate;
  bool my_availability;
};
```

13-3
```
class bookCollection {
public
  addBook(const book & aBook);
  removeBook(const book & aBook);
private:
  vector <book> my_data;
  int my_size;
};
```

Chapter 14 A Little Indirection: Pointers, Containers, and Iterators

14-1 -a `x` -b `double` -c 987.65 -d Unknown, address cannot be determined without `&x`

14-2 Addresses (the memory locations) of other objects

14-3 1. Assign it 0 2. Assign an address with `&`

3. Assign it the value of another pointer object: `p1 = p2;`

14-4 Undefined (garbage)

14-5 -a `doublePtr` -b 1.23 -c It stores the address of `aDouble`

-d `*doublePtr = *doubleptr + 1.0;`, `(*doublePtr)++;`, or `++*doublePtr`

14-6 `24 144`

14-7
```
char* charPtr;
char ch;
charPtr = &ch;
```

14-7
```
double n1 = 99.9, n2 = 88.8, n3 = 77.7;
double *p1, *p2, *p3;
p1 = &n1;
p2 = &n2;
p3 = &n3;
```

14-9 `cout << (*p1 + *p2 + *p3) << endl;`

Chapter 15 Dynamic Memory Management

15-1 -a true -b false -c true

-d true (The same address is stored in both `wife` and `husband`) -e true -f true

15-2 `T0a1b2c3`

15-3 `p = 1234 and q = A new string literal`

15-4 3

15-5 3

15-6 `abc123abc`

15-7 `"abc"`

15-8 `"xyz"`

15-9 `789`

15-10 `p` is undefined. The output is based on the value in some portion of memory, but it's not clear where or what the output is.

15-11 `4.56  4.56`

15-12 No, unless you store its address before resetting the pointer object `p` to point to the same `double` pointed to by `q` before the assignment `p = q;`.

15-13 `Hall 223.45`

15-14 `0  2  4  6  8 10 12`

15-15 `double* x = new double[1000];`

15-16
```
for(int j = 0; j < 1000; j++)
  x[j] = 0;
```

15-17
```
char* charPtr = new char[100];
strcpy(charPtr, "Any old string");
int len = strlen(charPtr);
char* theChars = new char[len + 1];
strcpy(theChars, charPtr);
```

15-18 Deallocates memory previously allocated with `new` and makes the pointer object undefined.

15-19 The operator returns memory allocated with `new`. Without `delete`, you loose the advantages of allocating memory on an as-needed basis and you will get memory leaks—a problem that is proportional to the size of the application.

15-20 `delete s` deallocates memory for one pointer object, `delete [ ] x` is used if `x` is pointing to memory allocated with *class* `x` = *new-class* `[` *number-of-elements* `]`

15-21
```
int* quiz(new int[100]);
delete [ ] quiz;
```

15-22 Roughly the opposite of the constructor in terms of memory allocation. Destructors should delete any memory allocated by `new` in the constructor and/or other member functions.

15-23 Override memberwise copy and allocate memory for all pointer members with the `new` operator.

15-24
```
bool linkedList::isEmpty()
{
   return my_first == my_last;  // Or my_first->structs_next == NULL;
}
```

15-25
```
200
480
893
1231
1584
```

```
1872
Average play time per track is 5:12 m:s
```

15-26

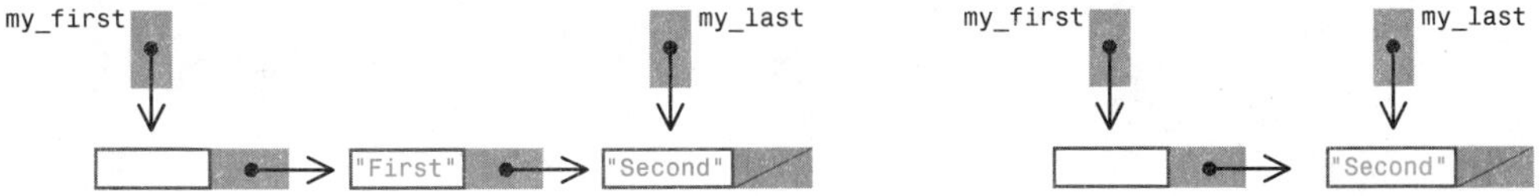

15-27

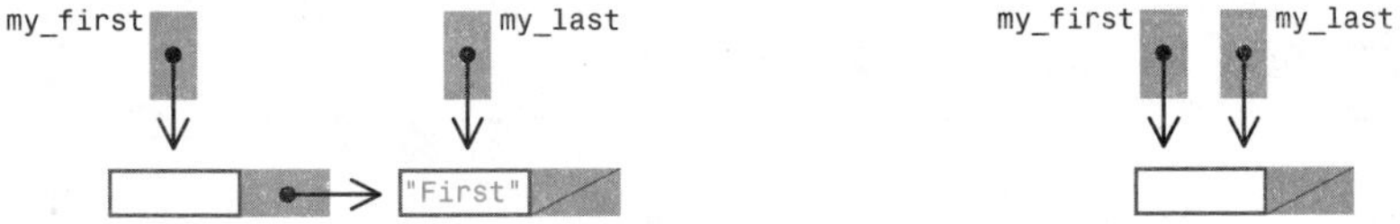

15-28 Nothing except `linkedList::remove` returns false to indicate an unsuccessful search.

15-29 False—it is determined at runtime

15-30 False—at least not the one just described. You could overload `[]` (see operator overloading).

15-31 True—an `orderedInsert` might just do that

15-32 False—not necessary with a dummy head node; without this extra node, the special cases might need to be considered.

15-33 True—absolutely, otherwise use a `vector`

Chapter 16 Object-Oriented Software Development: Inheritance and Polymorphism

16-1 Know its due date
Know its borrower
Check itself out
Check itself in

16-2 Compute its due date
Determine its late fee

16-3 `account`

16-4 `basicChecking` and `checkingWithLoan`

16-5 `withdraw` would behave differently for the two derived classes

16-6 `deposit`, `construct`, `getBalance`, `getID`

16-7 `my_balance`

16-8 `my_loanAmount` could be in `checkingWithLoan` only

16- 9 Get borrower's ID
Get call number
currentBorrower = theBorrowerList.getBorrower(borrowers ID)
currentLendable = theLendableList(call number)
if(!currentBorrower.canBorrow(currentLendable))

Tell student he or she cannot borrower
else
currentLendable.checkout(currentBorrower)
currentBorrower.checkout(currentLendable)

16-10 *Scenario:* Whatever your team does

16-11 *Scenario:* Whatever your team does

16-12 *Scenario:* Whatever your team does

16-13 Get borrower's ID
Get call number
currentBorrower = theBorrowerList.getBorrower(borrowers ID)
currentLendable = theLendableList(call number)
display currentLendable.lateFee();
currentLendable.checkin(currentBorrower)
currentBorrower.checkin(currentLendable)

Chapter 17 Templates: Building Generic Classes

17-1 As many as memory will allow. Other possible answers: "I don't know," "That depends."

17-2
```
intBag.first();
cout << intBag.currentItem() << endl;
intBag.next();
cout << intBag.currentItem() << endl;
```

17-3 `intBag.add(89);`

17-4 `intBag.remove(89);`

17-5 The compiler generates two different classes.

17-6 -a 16 -b 64 -c 64 -d 64 -e 128 -f 2,048

Chapter 18 Operator Overloading

18-1 You would have to "comment out" the existing < operator function in `baccount.cpp`.
```
#include <iostream>
#include "baccount"
bool operator < (const bankAccount& left, const bankAccount& right)
{
   return left.balance() < right.balance();
}
int main()
{ // Test drive < assuming baccount.cpp removes operator <
  b1("harry",  100);
  bankAccount b2("harry",  200);
  if(b1 < b2)
    cout << " < compares balances here " << endl;
  return 0;
}
```

18-2 You would have to "comment out" the existing < operator function in `weekemp.cpp`. You would also need to declare the operator function inside the class definition of `weekemp.h`.

```
class weeklyEmp {
public:
// . . .
  friend bool operator < (const weeklyEmp& left, const weeklyEmp& right);
private:
// . . .
};
// Then, the function can access the private data member my_hours
bool operator < (const weeklyEmp& left, const weeklyEmp& right)
{
   return left.my_hours < right.my_hours;
}
```

18-3 -a (3, 7) -b (3, 2) -c (-3, -3) -d (4, 0)

18-4 Division by zero

18-5 `3.5 6.25`

18-6 `(5, -2)`

Chapter 19 Doubly Subscripted Objects: `matrix` Objects

19-1 `vector`

19-2 `matrix` (or a `vector` of `vectors`)

19-3 `matrix<double> sales(10, 12);`

19-4 `matrix<double> sales2(12, 10);`

19-5 Row

19-6 Column

19-7

```
#include <fstream>
#include "matrix" // For the matrix class
int main()
{
  int r, c, rows = 10, cols = 5;
  matrix <int> t(rows, cols);
  ifstream in("quiz.dat");
  if(! in)
  {
    cout << "ERROR** File not found" << endl;
    return 0;
  }
  int nRows, nCols;
  in >> nRows >> nCols;
  for(r = 0; r < nRows; r++)
  {
    for(c = 0; c < nCols; c++)
    {
      in >> t[r][c];
    }
  }
  // Use t
```

```
  return 0;
}
```

19-8
```
double sum = 0.0;
for(r = 0; r < nRows; r++)
{
  for(c = 0; c < nCols; c++)
  {
    sum = sum + t[r][c];
  }
}
cout <<  "sum: " << sum << endl;
```

19-9
```
int large;
for(c = 0;  c < cols; c++)
{
  large = t[0][c];
  for(r = 1; r <= cols; r++)
  {
    if(t[r][c] > large)
      large = t[r][c];
  }
  cout << "Largest in column "
       << c << " is " << large;
}
```

19-10 No, this is a primitive array.

19-11 12

19-12 0 through 2

19-13 0 through 3

19-14
```
for(row = 1; row <=3; row++)
{
  for(col = 1; col <= 4; col++)
  {
    b[row][col] = 999;
  }
}
```

19-15
```
for(row = 1; row <=3; row++)
{
  for(col = 1; col <= 4; col++)
  {
    cout.width(8);
    cout << b[row][col];
  }
}
```

19-16 60

19-17 -a and -b only

Chapter 20 Recursion

20-1
```
void backward(int n)
{
  cout << n << endl;
  if(n > -10)
    backward(n - 1);
}
```

20-2 False

20-3 False: Eventually you will encounter a stack overflow; however, answering true would be okay.

20-5 True: 1 * 22 + 0 * 21+ 1 * 20 = 4 + 0 + 1 = 5

20-6 False: 12 base eight = 10 base 10. 1 * 81 + 2 * 80 = 8 + 2 = 10 base 10

20-7.
```
333
222
111
10
```

Bibliography

Alexander, Christopher. *A Pattern Language: Towns, Buildings, Construction.* Oxford: Oxford University Press, 1977.

Astrachan, Owen. *A Computer Science Tapestry: Exploring Programming and Computer Science with C++.* New York: McGraw Hill, 1997.

Beck, Kent, and Ward Cunningham. "A Laboratory for Teaching Object-Oriented Thinking." *SIGPLAN Notices* 24, no. 10 (October 1989): 1–6.

Booch, Grady. *Object-Oriented Design.* Menlo Park, CA: Benjamin Cummings, 1991.

Davis, Alan. *201 Principles of Software Development.* New York: McGraw Hill, 1995.

Dodge, Chris. "PC IR Remote Control." April 9, 1996. **http://www.ee.washington.edu/eeca/circuits/PCIR/Welcome.html**. July 2, 1998.

Gamma, Erich, Richard Helm, Ralph Johnson, and John Vlissides. *Design Patterns: Elements of Reusable Object-Oriented Software.* Menlo Park, CA: Addison Wesley, 1995.

Horstmann, Cay S. *Mastering Object-Oriented Design in C++.* New York: John Wiley and Sons, 1995.

Clancy, Michael J., and Marcia C. Linn. *Designing Pascal Solutions: Case Studies Using Data Structures.* New York: W. H. Freeman and Company, 1996.

Mercer, Rick. *Problem Solving and Program Implementation Using Turbo Pascal.* Wilsonville, OR: Franklin, Beedle and Associates, 1991.

Pattis, Richard. *Karel the Robot: A Gentle Introduction to the Art of Programming.* New York: John Wiley and Sons, 1981.

Riel, Arthur J. *Object-Oriented Design Heuristics.* Menlo Park, CA: Addison Wesley, 1996.

Roberts, Eric S. "Loop Exits and Structured Programs: Reopening the Debate." *SIGSCE Bulletin* 27, no. 1 (1995): 268–72.

Soloway, Elliot. "Learning to Program = Learning to Construct Mechanisms and Explanations." *Communication of the ACM* 29, no. 9 (1986): 850–58.

Wallingford, Eugene. "Toward a First Course Based on Object-Oriented Patterns." *SIGSCE Bulletin* 28, no. 1 (1996): 27–31.

Wilkinson, Nancy M. *Using CRC Cards: An Informal Approach to Object-Oriented Development.* Upper Saddle River, NJ: Prentice Hall, 1995.

Wirfs-Brock, Rebecca, Brian Wilkerson, and Lauren Wiener. *Designing Object-Oriented Software.* Upper Saddle River, NJ: Prentice Hall, 1990.

Index

E

F

G–H

P

Q–R

S

T